Disputation Literature in the Near East and Beyond

Studies in Ancient Near Eastern Records

General Editor:
Gonzalo Rubio

Editors:
Nicole Brisch, Eva Cancik-Kirschbaum, Petra Goedegebuure,
Amélie Kuhrt, Peter Machinist, Piotr Michalowski, Cécile Michel,
Beate Pongratz-Leisten, D. T. Potts, and Kim Ryholt

Volume 25

Disputation Literature in the Near East and Beyond

Edited by
Enrique Jiménez and Catherine Mittermayer

DE GRUYTER

ISBN 978-1-5015-2725-8
e-ISBN (PDF) 978-1-5015-1027-4
e-ISBN (EPUB) 978-1-5015-1021-2
ISSN 2161-4415

Library of Congress Control Number: 2020935600

Bibliographic information published by the Deutsche Nationalbibliothek
The Deutsche Nationalbibliothek lists this publication in the Deutsche Nationalbibliografie; Detailed bibliographic data are available in the Internet at http://dnb.dnb.de.

This volume is text- and page-identical with the hardback published in 2020.
Printing and binding: CPI books GmbH, Leck

www.degruyter.com

Table of Contents

Enrique Jiménez and Catherine Mittermayer
1 **Introduction — 1**

Section I **Disputations from the Ancient Near East**

Catherine Mittermayer
2 **The Sumerian Precedence Debates**
The World's Oldest Rhetorical Exercises? — **11**

Manuel Ceccarelli
3 **An Introduction to the Sumerian School Disputes**
Subject, Structure, Function and Context — **33**

Jana Matuszak
4 **"She was dumbstruck and took it to heart"**
Form and Function of Insults in Sumerian Literary Disputations between Women — **57**

A. R. George
5 **The Tamarisk, the Date-Palm and the King**
A Study of the Prologues of the Oldest Akkadian Disputation — **75**

Enrique Jiménez
6 **Antiques in the King's Libraries**
Akkadian Disputation Poems at Nineveh — **91**

Bernard Mathieu
7 **La «fable» égyptienne du Corps et de la Tête (tablette Turin CG 58004)**
Un *procès* littéraire au temps des Ramsès — **105**

Andréas Stauder
8 **Opposing Voices in Ancient Egyptian Literature — 121**

Andrés Piquer Otero
9 **Those Who Cannot Do, Reign?**
The Sources of the Fable of Jotham — **143**

Section II **Eastern Disputations during the Middle Ages**

Sebastian Brock
10 **Disputations in Syriac Literature — 159**

Geert Jan van Gelder
11 **The Debate of Spring and Autumn in Arabic Literature — 175**

David Larsen
12 **Night and Day in Islamicate Literary Disputation — 191**

Amparo Alba Cecilia
13 **Disputation Poems in Medieval Hebrew Literature in Spain — 215**

Firuza Abdullaeva-Melville
14 **Debate in Iranian Literary Culture — 237**

Asghar Seyed-Gohrab
15 **The Rhetoric of Persian Verbal Contests**
Innovation and Creativity in Debates between the Persians and the Arabs — **261**

Hatice Aynur
16 **A Survey of Disputation Texts in Ottoman Literature — 283**

Sergio La Porta
17 **Dispute Poems in Armenian — 309**

Section III **Western Disputations during the Middle Ages**

Vicente Cristóbal and Juan Luis Arcaz Pozo
18 **Tradition and Innovation in the Early Medieval Latin Debates**
Alcuin's Conflictus veris et Hiemis, Scottus' Rosae liliique certamen, and the Eclogue of Theodulus — **335**

Thomas Honegger
19 **Owls, Nightingales, Cuckoos and Other Feathered Disputants**
The Genre of the Bird Debate in Middle English, with Special Focus on *The Owl and the Nightingale* — **353**

Laëtitia Tabard
20 **De la dispute des clercs au dialogue des *acteurs***
L'expansion du débat poétique en France à la fin du Moyen Âge — **369**

Section IV **Contemporary Disputation Texts**

Alessandro Mengozzi
21 **Neo-Aramaic Dialogue and Dispute Poems**
The Various Types — **391**

Clive Holes
22 **Modern Vernacular Disputation Poems from Bahrain and the Wider Gulf**
Speculations on Their Origin — **415**

Section V **Other Traditions of Disputations**

John A. Chaney
23 **Ludic Disputations in the East-Asian Cultural Sphere**
An Overview — **435**

Index of Contestants — 457

Enrique Jiménez and Catherine Mittermayer

1 Introduction

Said tea to coffee: "Oh you burnt one,
All blackened and crushed, your good looks gone, (...)
How come you're so proud and so haughty?
Loquacity's truly your forte!
Yellow one, shall I list your disasters,
One by one to your Bedouin masters?
You dullard! Your real name is coffee,
To all who imbibe, catastrophe!
A fruit you are not, nor a savour,
Nor relief for the tired from their labour.
But me, I give all relaxation,
I'm a balm, soothing wounds and vexation."

(Holes 1996: 312 ll. 16 – 20)

The passage above belongs to a poem written by a Bahraini named ʿAbdallāh Ḥusayn al-Qārī in 1955. The poem recounts how, on a Thursday evening – traditionally a time for relaxation and leisure – the poet is lying on his bed watching the coffee-pot and the tea-kettle bubbling away in front of him. Suddenly, the two come to life, greet him, and ask him to adjudicate a dispute between them. A bitter discussion follows, during which each of the contenders pleads its case in order to establish its own superiority over its rival. After a series of extravagant and colorful pleas, the poet rules that both beverages are to marry each other, thus reflecting the Gulf tradition of alternately drinking small cups of bitter coffee and sweet tea.

The poem is part of a locally published *dīwān*, which contains poems composed in Bahrain between the 1930's and 1950's. The poems deal, half in earnest half in jest, with contemporary, vibrant topics, such as 'Pearl-Diving versus Oil Wells'. However, poems of the same type had been composed in roughly the same area for over four thousand years. The striking similarity between these 20th century CE debates and their ancient Mesopotamian forerunners is clear from reading, for instance, a passage from the Sumerian debate between Bird and Fish, composed some four thousand years earlier, during the reign of King Šulgi of Ur (21st century BCE). In that text, both contenders assert their precedence over the other litigant by means of no less colorful arguments and vocabulary:

https://doi.org/10.1515/9781501510274-001

> Bird replied to Fish: (...)
> "Your mouth is a mound of ruins, surrounded by teeth, you cannot look behind you!
> Cripple, your limbs are clipped, your fins are to the right and left of your neck!
> Your foul smell make people vomit and wrinkle their nose. (...)
> But I am the beautiful, wise bird!
> Fair artistry was put into (the finishing of) my inlays,
> While no equal effort has been applied to your pale body.
> Strutting around in the king's palace, I am an adornment."
> (Mittermayer 2019: 71 ll. 56–71)

Certain features of debate literature remain stable from its earliest inception to its most recent avatars. First and foremost, debates normally present two litigants (such as trees, animals, drinks, seasons or human beings) and basically have a tripartite structure:

1. Introduction describing the contestants and the occasion of the disputation
2. Disputation proper
3. Judgement scene

The main part, the verbal disputation, is formally structured as a dialogue and contains highly sophisticated speeches. No transcendent question is at stake in these light-hearted texts: the litigants simply try to argue their superiority over their rivals. As stated in one of the Akkadian poems, two animals came to quarrel because "their hearts rejoiced in disputation."

In scholarly literature, texts consisting mainly of dialogue are frequently divided between disputations/debates and dialogues. Such labels can be misleading, as they result in an artificial segregation of a coherent group of texts, as was the case of the Sumerian dialogues and disputations (Mittermayer 2019: 2–7). As Carmen Cardelle de Hartmann (2007: 265–66) shows, the dialogue form is a basic component of several text categories, among them instructive or philosophic dialogues as well as disputations. The present volume, therefore, includes papers on texts traditionally classified as "dialogues" and on texts labelled in the secondary literature as "disputations," in an attempt to regroup traditions that have earlier been studied separately, but which should be considered together. The difference between "disputations" and "dialogues," if there is any, should be considered in each of the cultures in which they appear: whereas in Egyptian literature there is a difference between disputations and "scientific" dialogues (see the paper by Andréas Stauder), in Syriac literature texts traditionally classified as belonging to both categories were transmitted side by side (Sebastian Brock).

Texts usually classified as "disputations" differ substantially in the many traditions in which they are attested. They can be independent compositions or part of larger literary works, and vary in length, style and purpose (e.g. humoristic vs instructive). These differences reflect the strong embeddedness of the disputations in their own literary tradition and justify the integration of seemingly different kind of texts in this volume. However, as stated in Jiménez 2017: 11–12), it is possible to postulate the existence of a set of universals, features that are common to the texts in most literary traditions in which they appear. These universals are:

1. Disputations are poetic texts, usually written in verse or in literary prose.
2. The structure of disputations is usually tripartite: introduction, disputation proper, and adjudication
3. The second section ("disputation proper") normally contains only dialogue. Their dialectical character sets disputations apart from fables, which are usually narrative texts.
4. The litigants, generally two, tend to be entities that are otherwise non-articulate, such as trees, animals, and human types.
5. The only goal of the discussion is to establish the pre-eminence of one of the speakers. Since no serious matter is at hand, disputations tend to be humorous.

Texts fulfilling all or most of these universals represent a relatively rare category in world literature. However, they have a remarkably long history: we can trace a history of this text type that spans almost four thousand years, from the 21st century BCE to the 21st century CE. The oldest known disputations were written in the Sumerian language, the earliest recorded language in history. Most of them were composed at the end of the third millennium BCE, but their manuscripts date to the first part of the second millennium BCE. Three different categories of Sumerian debates can be established: precedence debates (see the contribution by Catherine Mittermayer), debates between students (Manuel Ceccarelli) and those between two women (Jana Matuszak). In all three categories, the debates are carefully constructed pieces of rhetoric, which make use of a plethora of devices to make their arguments convincing: it is often clear from the arguments who the winning and who the losing party would be.

The oldest manuscript of an Akkadian disputation dates to around the same time as the manuscripts of the Sumerian ones, viz. the first quarter of the second millennium BCE. Its prologue, clearly inspired by Sumerian models, tells how the first king of the city of Kish planted a tamarisk and a palm in his courtyard, thus provoking their unremitting enmity (Andrew R. George). Whereas the Sumerian disputations appear to have died out after the first quarter of the second millennium BCE, their Akkadian counterparts continued to be transmitted and adapted for almost two millennia. The latest manuscripts of Akkadian debates date to the second century BCE, but by then the genre was a literary fossil (Enrique Jiménez).

Perhaps influenced by Mesopotamian models, disputes of quarrelling pairs first appear in Egypt during the 14th century BCE, with the *Trial of Body and Head* (Bernard Mathieu). Egyptian disputations are related, and probably derived from, the so-called "discourses," dialogues or monologues with performative features that flourished during the Middle Kingdom (2000–1700 BCE), and whose *Sitz im Leben* was – as in the case of the Mesopotamian debates – the royal court (Andréas Stauder).

The Fable of Jotham (*Judges* 9: 7–21) is almost the sole witness to a Northwest Semitic tradition of disputation poems in Antiquity. Clearly an adaptation of a once independent composition, it opens a small window onto a now lost ancient tradition of disputations in Hebrew, and represents one of the earliest examples of the adaptation of a disputation for a new literary context (Andrés Piquer Otero).

A famous Parthian disputation was composed in late Antiquity: the "Assyrian Tree" (*Draxt ī āsūrīg*), which displays clear influences of the Babylonian tradition (Firuza Abdullaeva). The genre resurfaces in Syriac in the 4th century CE in the works of Ephrem of Nisibis. Influenced by the Jewish Aramaic literary tradition, they often feature biblical characters as protagonists (Sebastian Brock). From the beginning of its written tradition, Armenian literature was in close contact with the Western and Southern neighboring cultures. Armenian debates are first attested in the 5th century, in the form of translations of poems by Ephrem. Independent Armenian debates, however, are only attested from the beginning of the 17th century CE onwards, coinciding with the rising popularity of itinerant bards (Sergio La Porta).

The first Arabic disputations (*munāẓara* and *muḥāwara*) appear around the 9th century CE, and the genre survives in Arabic literature until the present day. Some of the topics, such as Spring/Summer and Autumn/Winter, are attested since the time of al-Jāḥiẓ (9th century CE) until the 20th century CE (Geer Jan van Gelder). A relatively late comer to the Arabic tradition, Night and Day, is attested in Arabic, Persian, and Turkish literature (David Larsen). Arabic disputations were highly influential, and were skillfully emulated by Hebrew poets in Spain, who adapted them to the Hebrew literary tradition and inserted frequent references to Biblical and Rabbinical literature (Amparo Alba). Turkish debates, first attested in the 11th century CE, bloomed during the Ottoman period: Turkish poets showed a weakness for disputes between mind-altering substances, the first of which ('Hashish and Wine') was written by the famous poet Fuzûlî (Hatice Aynur). The Persian tradition of literary disputations, whose roots plunge deep into the Parthian period, flourished during the Iranian Renaissance and found its most famous cultivator in Asadī Ṭūsī, who added a socio-political and religious dimension to the Persian disputations. He is the first to write a debate poem on the contest between the Arabs and the Persians, a topic that will remain popular for hundreds of years (Asghar Seyed-Gohrab).

In Medieval Europe, the genre of the debate emerges during the Early Middle Ages. The oldest examples are written in Latin and date to the 8th and 9th century CE. They are heavily dependent on bucolic poetry, in particular on Vergil's *Eclogues* (Vicente Cristóbal and Juan Luis Arcaz Pozo). In the following centuries, debate poetry flourishes in vernacular European languages. The debate of *The Owl and the Nightingale* was written in Middle English around 1200 CE, at a time when Latin and French were the literary languages (Thomas Honegger). The genre in England was influenced by the Occitan *tensos*, which have a similar structure and are attested throughout the Middle Ages. They also constitute the "point de passage" for the French *dêbat*, a genre that develops in the 15th century and falls at the confluence between lyric poetry and the Latin *conflictus* (Laëtitia Tabard).

Two literatures whose traditions of disputations began in the early Middle Ages, Syriac and Arabic, still cultivated the millennia-sanctioned genre in the 19th and 20th centuries. Disputation poems composed in an elevated vernacular Arabic are attested in the Gulf well into the 20th century: they use the old form to discuss topics as current as "Pearl Diving vs Oil Wells." The astounding survival of the genre in popular poetry can perhaps be linked with the no less astonishing existence of certain Akkadian loanwords in the local dialects (Clive Holes). Neo-Aramaic dialogue and dispute poems, in contrast, do not represent a living genre: the handful of known Neo-Aramaic dialogues are translations of Classical Syriac debates, only one of which, "The Cherub and the Thief," is used in liturgy still today (Alessandro Mengozzi).

Chinese ludic disputations attest to the existence of a parallel tradition in the Far East, whose origin goes back to the rhetorical tradition of the Warring States period (453–221 BCE). Beginning in the Tang dynasty (618–907 CE), Vietnamese, Korean and Japanese literature started imitating and adapting the Chinese models (John Chaney).

A double paradox surrounds the transmission of disputations. First, there is a tension between the *vertical*, transcultural aspects of the transmission and their *horizontal* role in the individual literary traditions in which they are attested (Reinink and Vanstiphout 1991: 2, Jiménez 2017: 148–49). Indeed, although disputations represent a wandering literary type, they are remarkably well integrated in the different traditions in which they appear. Thus, while undoubtedly related to their Sumerian counterparts, Akkadian disputations allude to and quote from other works of Akkadian literature, and not from Sumerian literary works. It would be absurd to postulate that the embeddedness of disputations in Sumerian and Akkadian means that they emerged independently in both of them, since the two literatures remained in close contact for the greater part of their existence. However, the more removed in time and space two literary traditions are from each other, the more difficult it becomes to postulate a borrowing.

The second paradox in the history of disputations involves the channels of transmission. Not a single case of direct transmission, i.e., of translation of one disputation into another language, is known (Jiménez 2017: 125–27). This fact is perhaps best explained by the deep cultural embeddedness of the texts, which made them unpalatable products for any culture other than the one in which they originated. Moreover, as mentioned earlier, disputations are literary texts, and indeed frequently highly sophisticated literary texts: their bookish character would seem to militate against the oral transmission of literary disputations. If a written transmission is not attested, and an oral tradition seems impossible, how were disputations transmitted? One has to follow Clive Holes in assuming that two parallel transmission channels existed, a "high," literate channel, and a "low," popular level (Holes 1995: 103 and *id.* in this volume).

Both sets of axes –vertical and horizontal, high and low– should, therefore, be studied simultaneously to gain a holistic understanding of the transmission of the genre and of its various incarnations. The diversity of languages and literary traditions in which disputations are attested makes it impossible for a single scholar to study the genre diachronically, or to decide whether or not the genre was transmitted throughout all these cultures and periods, or rather originated independently in different places as different times. Because of the complexity of the topic, it is a highly suitable theme for a group of scholars to treat within the framework of a multidisciplinary volume.

The present volume has one illustrious predecessor: the pioneering, much-cited volume by Gerrit J. Reinink and Herman Vanstiphout *Dispute Poems and Dialogues in the Ancient and Mediaeval Near East* (1991) with articles on Sumerian, Akkadian, Hebrew, Byzantine, Syriac, and Medieval Arabic and Latin disputations. That volume represents the proceedings of the symposium "The Literary Debate in Semitic and Related Literatures," held in 1989 at the University of Groningen. Over the course of the past thirty years a wealth of new information has become available, which has substantially altered our picture of disputations in many of the literary traditions in which they are attested. The Groningen volume remains, however, a model of interdisciplinary work and a must-have manual for diverse fields. The present editors can only hope that this book will be a fitting tribute to Reinink and Vanstiphout and a worthy continuation of their labor.

* * *

The volume contains the proceedings of two consecutive international conferences, in Madrid (2017) and Geneva (2018). The first, entitled *Disputation Poems in the Near East and Beyond. Ancient and Modern*, was organized by Enrique Jiménez at Universidad Complutense (Madrid) on 12–13 July 2017. The main concern of the Madrid conference was the study of the transmission of the genre of disputation in the Near East throughout the ages. The conference was generously funded by the Department of Hebrew and Aramaic Studies, The Institute of Sciences of Religions (both Universidad Complutense de Madrid), The Spanish Center of Near Eastern Studies, the Anneliese Maier Research Award of the Alexander von Humboldt Foundation (courtesy of Maribel Fierro), and the Spanish Association of Hebrew and Judaic Studies. A special debt of gratitude is owned to Andrés Piquer Otero, without whose generous assistance the conference would not have been possible.

The second conference, entitled *4000 mille ans de disputes: de l'Orient à l'Occident*, was organized by Catherine Mittermayer at Université de Genève on 15–16 February 2018. The participants of the Geneva conference focused on formal and generic features of disputations in a wide range of cultures, which included traditions from medieval Europe and the Far East. Particular attention was paid to the question of the dialogues on the one hand as a formal designation of disputations and on the other hand as a distinct taxonomy of texts. The Geneva conference was financed by the Swiss National Science Foundation within the scope of the four year project "Disputation Literature in the Ancient Near East: A text editing project." Warmest thanks are expressed to Prof. Carmen Cardelle de Hartmann for her presence and insightful remarks during the conference.

The group of scholars that participated at both conferences was both international and multidisciplinary – reflecting the tradition of disputations itself. The editors would like to express their gratitude to the speakers for their outstanding lectures and papers, and to the audiences on both occasions for some enriching and lively discussions.

Thanks are also expressed to the two anonymous peer-review readers of the volume and to the editor of the series for their valuable remarks.

Bibliography

Cardelle de Hartmann, Carmen. 2007. *Lateinische Dialoge 1200–1400: Literaturhistorische Studie und Repertorium.* Mittellateinische Studien und Texte 37. Leiden: Brill.

Holes, Clive. 1995. The Rat and the Ship's Captain: A Dialogue Poem from the Gulf, with Some Comments on the Social and Literary-Historical Background of the Genre. Pp. 101–120 in *Dialectologia Arabica. A Collection of Articles in Honour of the Sixtieth Birthday of Professor Heikki Paiva*, Studia Orientalia 75. Helsinki: Finnish Oriental Society.

Holes, Clive. 1996. The Dispute of Coffee and Tea: A Debate-Poem from the Gulf. Pp. 302–315 in *Tradition and Modernity in Arabic Language and Literature*, ed. J. R. Smart. Padstow: Curzon.

Jiménez, Enrique. 2017. *The Babylonian Disputation Poems. With Editions of the Series of the Poplar, Palm and Vine, the Series of the Spider, and the Story of the Poor, Forlorn Wren.* Culture and History of the Ancient Near East 87. Leiden: Brill.

Mittermayer, Catherine. 2019. *‚Was sprach der eine zum anderen?' Argumentationsformen in den sumerischen Rangstreitgesprächen.* Untersuchungen zur Assyriologie und Vorderasiatischen Archäologie 15. Berlin/Boston: De Gruyter.

Reinink, Gerrit J., and Vanstiphout, Vanstiphout, Herman L.J. 1991. *Dispute Poems and Dialogues in the Ancient and Mediaeval Near East. Forms and Types of Literary Debates in Semitic and Related Literatures.* Orientalia Lovaniensia Analecta 42. Leuven: Peeters.

Section I Disputations from the Ancient Near East

Catherine Mittermayer*

2 The Sumerian Precedence Debates

The World's Oldest Rhetorical Exercises?

In Sumerian literature, there exist a number of texts that are referred to by modern scholars as "precedence poems," "disputation (poems)" or "debate (poems)." The exact number of these texts is highly controversial, as can best be seen in the most recent volume that was published on the "Dispute Poems and Dialogues in the Ancient and Mediaeval Near East."[1] Whereas Jean Bottéro (1991: 11) listed seven "tensons," some pages later Herman Vanstiphout (1991: 25 – 26) studied ten Sumerian "disputations/debate poems."

The discussion on the number of precedence debates is still ongoing (see Tab. 1). Recently, Enrique Jiménez (2017: 13 – 14) established a number of six Sumerian "disputation poems," which is comparable to the rather short lists given by van Dijk (1953: 41), Gordon (1960: 145 – 46), Cunningham (2007: 386)[2] and Herrmann (2010: 41 – 47). Some years earlier, Konrad Volk (2012) had based his article on the term "Streitgespräch" in the "Reallexikon für Assyriologie und Vorderasiatische Archäologie" on nine disputations "im engeren Sinne (...) zwischen Werkzeugen, Abstraktionen, Gegenständen, Pflanzen und/oder Tieren" and three disputations "historischen (epischen) und mythologischen Charakters" which makes a total of twelve compositions. With the creation of subcategories for the disputations he follows a line opened by Dietz Otto Edzard (1987 – 90) who differentiated between "(epische) Streitgespräche" and "Schulstreitgespräche" (Edzard 1987 – 90: 43 – 44). Only a few years later, Claus Wilcke (1992) suggested three subcategories, namly "Streitgedichte historischen Charakters," "Streitgedichte mythologischen Charakters" and "Streitgedichte über naturkundliche Themen."[3]

Six texts have been present in every proposition since the nineteen-fifties: *Tree and Reed, Copper and Silver, Hoe and Plough, Ezinam and Ewe,*[4] *Winter and Summer, Bird and Fish.* They all feature the term **a-da-min$_3$** in the last

---

* University of Geneva. The present article was written within the research project "Streitliteratur im Alten Orient: Ein Editionsprojekt" at the University of Geneva financed by the Swiss National Science Foundation.

1 Edited by Reinink and Vanstiphout 1991.

2 His list is based on Miguel Civil's catalogue of Sumerian literature.

3 The classification of the precedence debates is extremely complex. For a new proposition see Mittermayer 2019a: 3 – 13.

4 Formerly *Grain and Sheep* or *Ewe and Wheat*; see also n. 12.

https://doi.org/10.1515/9781501510274-002

Table 1: The corpus of Sumerian precedence debates

	van Dijk (1953)	Gordon (1960)	Edzard (1987–90)	Vanstiphout (1990)	Wilcke (1992)	Cunningham (2007)	Rubio (2009)	Herrmann (2010)	Volk (2012)	Jiménez (2017)
Tree Reed	✓	✓	✓	✓	✓	✓	✓	✓	✓	✓
Copper Silver	✓	✓	✓	✓	✓	✓	✓	✓	✓	✓
Hoe Plough	✓	✓	✓	✓	✓	✓	✓	✓	✓	✓
Ezinam Ewe	✓	✓	✓	✓	✓	✓	✓	✓	✓	✓
Winter Summer	✓	✓	✓	✓	✓	✓	✓	✓	✓	✓
Bird Fish	✓	✓	✓	✓	✓	✓	✓	✓	✓	✓
Dumuzi Enkimdu	✓	–	✓	✓	✓	–	(✓)	✓	✓	(✓)
Song Millstone	–	✓	–	✓	?	–	–	–	–	–
Enmerkara Ensukukeš.	–	–	✓	–	✓	–	–	–	✓	–
Heron Turtle	–	–	✓	✓	✓	–	–	–	✓	–
Goose Raven	–	–	–	✓	?	–	–	–	–	–
Datepalm Tamarisk						✓	✓	✓	✓	–
Enmerk. Lord of Arata	–	–	–	–	(✓)	–	–	–	✓	(✓)
Enki Ninmaḫ	–	–	–	–	✓	–	–	–	✓	(✓)

lines which gives us the emic designation of the verbal contest carried out in the main part and which can be translated as "contest (between) two" (**ada** "contest," **min** "two"). The doxology is a stereotypical formula stating the winner and praising a god(ess) for the fact that one has surpassed the other.[5] This is normally done with the following words:

> A B-**e a-da-min$_3$ du$_{11}$-ga** / A B-**(r)a diri-ga-ba** / god(ess) (+ epithet) **za$_3$ mim**
> "(Divinity) is praised for (the fact) that A has surpassed B in the disputation held between A and B."

The same doxology is also present in *Dumuzi and Enkimdu* as well as in *Enmerkara and Ensukukešdana*, two disputations normally excluded from the discussion because of their human protagonists and/or their differing structure.[6]

Vanstiphout (1990: 272) argued against a grouping of the **a-da-min$_3$** based on their doxologies. He emphasizes that "it does not indicate, or at least was not intended to indicate, a generic category. Therefore the occurrence of the term is not decisive for the adscription of a given poem to the genre, and should certainly not be used to group together compositions which are obviously different in nature, as is sometimes done on this slippery ground."[7] If in the present paper all eight texts mentioning the term **a-da-min$_3$** in the last lines are grouped together, this is not based on the assumption that **a-da-min$_3$** designates an emic genre. Vanstiphout (1990: 272) is right by saying "this is merely a name for the main or the only *action* described in the text, *viz.* a verbal contest." But if we want to study the **a-da-min$_3$** contest in Sumerian literature we have to study all the texts which show this designation in their doxology and not only those that correspond to our perception of what a debate should be.

The basic structure of the eight precedence debates mentioned above encompasses five parts:[8]

(1) Prologue
(2) Transition 1 (giving the *occasio litigandi*)

---

5 The deity is not necessarily identical with the judge (see Tab. 2).

6 For a detailed analysis of the structure of these two texts see Mittermayer 2019a: 10–11; see also Wilcke 1975: 251. Both texts are integrated in the lists of Edzard (1987–90), Wilcke (1992) and Volk (2012).

7 See also Jiménez 2017: 13–14. Contra Wilcke (1975: 250–51) who understands the term **a-da-min$_3$** as a genre designation.

8 This is an extension of the classical structure given by van Dijk (1975: 39–40). See already Mittermayer 2009: 45. Vanstiphout (1990: 287–288) also reconstructed a five-partite structure for the **a-da-min$_3$**, differing from my reconstruction only in point 4 (Transition 2 vs. Vanstiphout's "D: Narrated actions" as we have them e.g. in *Bird and Fish*).

(3) Main part
(4) Transition 2 (giving the decision of at least one party to see a judge)
(5) Verdict (with reconciliation)

The main part reports the **a-da-min$_3$** contest held between the two protagonists. An **a-da-min$_3$** is limited to a verbal exchange[9] and it consists of alternate speeches, which can vary in length, form, and number (see Tab. 2).

Table 2: The number of speeches in the /adamin/-contest

Debate	**Speeches**	**1st Speaker**	**Winner**	**Judge**	**Praise**
Ezinam Ewe	3 : 2	Ezinam	Ezinam	Enki	Enki
Winter Summer	2 : 2	Winter	Winter	Enlil	Enlil
Tree Reed	2 : 2	Tree	Tree	Šulgi?	Enlil
Bird Fish	2 : 2	Fish	Bird	Enki?	Enki
Hoe Plough	2 : 1	Hoe	Hoe	Enlil	Nisaba
Enmerkara Ensukukešdana	1 : 1	Ensukukešdana	Enmerkara	(Nisaba)	Nisaba
Copper Silver	?	?	Copper	Enlil?	Enlil
Dumuzi Enkimdu	1 : 0	Dumuzi	(Dumuzi)	(Innana)	Innana

In three cases (*Ezinam and Ewe*, *Hoe and Plough*, *Dumuzi and Enkimdu*) the winner, who is at the same time the first speaker in the contest, has more speeches than the loser. In four cases the number of speeches is even, and in two of these four cases the loser is (in an exception to the general rule) the first speaker.

If we compare the length of the speeches in these four debates it becomes obvious that the winner always benefits in total from more speaking time than his opponent (see Tab. 3).[10] It seems a prerogative for the winner to speak longer.

9 Even though more concrete or physical confrontations can mirror these verbal contests. In *Bird and Fish*, the latter attacks Bird's nest physically and kills the fledglings. In return, Bird destroys Fish's spawn. The physical fight is not part of the **a-da-min$_3$**, but it contributes to the characterization of the protagonists (see Mittermayer 2019a: 81–83 and ead. 2019b). Alster (1990: 4) suggests, on the basis of the Enmerkara texts (*Enmerkara and the Lord of Aratta*, *Enmerkara and Ensukukešdana*), that an **a-da-min$_3$** "could also be a duel performed by two persons."

10 The line numbers in Table 3 are based on score texts that I prepared for my habilitation. *Tree and Reed* is omitted, as this debate cannot yet be fully reconstructed. The numbers given for *Bird and Fish* correspond to the long version; in the short version Fish's first speech is even shorter. For the different versions of *Bird and Fish* see Hermann 2010: 97–98 and Mittermayer 2014: 201–202.

Table 3: The distribution of speaking time in the debates with an equal number of speeches

Debate	Speeches	1st Speech	2nd Speech	Total	Winner
Winter Summer	2 : 2	29 : 27	69 : 18	98 : 45	Winter
Bird Fish	2 : 2	23 : 20	15 : 16	38 : 36	Bird
Enmerkara Ensukukešd.	1 : 1	36 : 15	–	36 : 15	Enmerkara

When the winner has more speeches and/or more speaking time, he receives a strong advantage on the structural level of the debate, as, thanks to these longer speeches, he can bring forth more arguments either in his own favor or against his opponent.

In the following, I would like to show that this advantage on the winner's side is not limited to the structure of the contest. It can also be observed in the quality of the speeches, viz. on the level of argument. Vanstiphout (1990: 280) has already suggested that "in most cases the victor wins on *rhetorical* points: he is the cleverest debater. This has to do with the nature of the contenders, insofar as one of the means used by the clever victor consists in building up a cogent presentation of the superiority of the *values* he represents over those of his antagonist." If we accept that the "cleverest debater" is the winner, this has to be seen in the organization and presentation of his speeches. Alster and Vanstiphout (1987: 9) have already postulated, that "one should start from the result, and see whether the means used by the contestants are effective towards the goal desired (in the case of the winner) or not (in the case of the loser) and why this is so." But this idea has never been taken up.

In my research on the Sumerian precedence debates I was able to detect a number of argument techniques that can be found in most of the **a-da-min$_3$**:[11]

- self-praise
- disparagement
- self-presentation
- comparison
- expression of relationship
- refutation
- outperformance
- anticipation
- demand
- reproach
- threat

11 For a thorough discussion of these techniques see Mittermayer 2019a: chapter 6.

Self-praising and disparagement are the basic techniques employed in every speech. They can be labeled as unidimensional, as they focus either on the speaker or on the winner:

> self-praise "I am good" vs. disparagement "you are bad"

In the course of self-praising more complex techniques can be used. They are all two-dimensional in the sense that they construct an argument in favor of the speaker or against the opponent by involving the other party. See for example the following comparison:

> "I am strong (in a certain situation), you are weak (in the same situation)"

As the precedence debate between *Ezinam and Ewe*[12] is normally described by scholars as being very balanced,[13] it provides a good starting point for the study of the quality of speeches.[14]

At the beginning of the debate, a long tripartite prologue takes us back to a remote past where – in the first scene – people do not yet know sheep and grain (ll. 1–24). In the second scene (by which time, people have been created), Ezinam and Ewe live among the gods but they cannot sate them (ll. 25–35). That is why – in the third scene – Enki and Enlil, two major gods, decide to send them down to the human beings where they introduce animal husbandry and agriculture (ll. 36–63).[15]

---

12 Viz. *Sheep and Grain* or *Ewe and Wheat*. As the names of the protagonists are Ezinam (deified grain) and Ewe, the debate should be referred to as *Ezinam and Ewe*. The name of the protagonists shows another preference for the winner: whereas Ezinam is a goddess, Ewe is a simple animal. Both protagonists are female as they address each other with "my sister."

13 See Vanstiphout 1984: 248 n. 36 "the dispute is very evenly constructed, and there seem to be no bias as in our [= *Hoe and Plough*; C.M.] dispute." Alster and Vanstiphout (1987: 9–10) were the first to show in general lines Ezinam's superiority and the rhetorical mistakes made by Ewe. But this idea has not been explored further. Bottéro (1991: 18) formulated in a more general way "(...) les combats, dont l'issue est incertaine et dont les spectateurs se demandent toujours qui va gagner"; he suggested that this "élément de hazard" explains the long survival of the precedence debate.

14 An edition of the text is presented in Mittermayer 2019a: chapter 8.1 (with score text) and Alster and Vanstiphout 1987. A reconstructed text with translation can be found on ETCSL (etcsl.orinst.ox.ac.uk); for further translations see Vanstiphout 1997: 575–578; 2004: 186–194.

15 For the prologue see also Vanstiphout 1990: 292 and Alster and Vanstiphout 1987: 2–3.

The first transition explains why the two of them start an **a-da-min$_3$** contest. It is not for a very sophisticated reason, they simply get drunk during a banquet (ll. 64–69):[16]

> They were drinking sweet wine, they enjoyed sweet beer. After they had been drinking sweet wine, after they had enjoyed sweet beer, they started a quarrel on the cultivated fields. At the place of the banquet they started the contest.

In the main part (ll. 70–178) Ezinam opens the contest. She (as the grain goddess) will speak three times, whereas Ewe will only have to speeches. In the end Ezinam will be selected as winner.[17]

In the first two speeches (Ezinam 1 and Ewe 1), the two contestants present themselves by listing their positive aspects. They both use self-praise as basic technique.[18] Ezinam opens her first speech by praising her beauty (l. 72 "from all the lights in the land I am the most magnificent"). She continues by talking about her force which she confers to the warrior. This "force" is probably an allusion to her being a food product. Ewe's list of positive qualities is much longer. She provides everybody with wool, leather and oil, and she is the sustenance of the gods (ll. 110–112):[19]

> "The *gudu*-priest, the 'anointed-one' and all those who bathed themselves, after each of them got dressed thanks to me (= my clothes) for my holy purification rites, I will step with them to my holy food allocation."

The first round thus seems to favor Ewe because she presents more positive qualities than her opponent (4:2). But in the second (Ezinam 2 and Ewe 2) and the third rounds (Ezinam 3), Ezinam adds two positive qualities per speech: she opens her second speech by referring to the beer she produces, and she ends by praising her own strength. The beginning of her third speech remains difficult to understand, but she seems to present herself as being humble. At the end, she

---

16 *Ezinam and Ewe* 64–69: **ĝeštin niĝ$_2$ du$_{10}$ i-im-na$_8$-na$_8$-ne / kaš niĝ$_2$ du$_{10}$ i-im-du$_{10}$-du$_{10}$-ge-ne / ĝeštin niĝ$_2$ du$_{10}$ u$_3$-mu-un-naĝ-eš-a-ta / kaš niĝ$_2$ du$_{10}$ u$_3$-mu-un-du$_{10}$-ge-eš-a-ta / a-gar$_3$-a-gar$_3$-ra du$_{14}$ mi-ni-ib-mu$_2$-mu$_2$-ne / ki ĝešbun-na-ka a-da-min$_3$ mu-un-**AK**-ne.**

17 Cf. the analysis of Alster and Vanstiphout 1987: 3–9.

18 They both end their first and second speeches with a one-line anticipation and a one-line demand. For simplicity's sake, this pair of arguments is omitted in the figures (and the discussion). As it is present in both parties' speeches it has no impact on the evaluation of their quality. For a complete evaluation of their speeches see Mittermayer 2019a: chapter 3.4.

19 *Ezinam and Ewe* 110–112: **gudu$_4$ pa$_4$-ses lu$_2$ a tu$_5$-a / šu-luh ku$_3$-ĝa$_2$ um-ma-da-an-mu$_4$-re / šuku ku$_3$-ĝa$_2$ ĝiri$_3$ mu-da-an-gub-be$_2$.**

shows that she has a value as a currency, in the sense that the one who has barley can buy an ewe with it (ll. 176 – 178):[20]

> "If someone brings your innards to the market place and puts your very own strap around your neck, one will say to the other 'fill barley into the measuring cup for my ewe'."

Enki, the divine judge of the contest, will take up this argument in his judgment where he declares Ezinam the winner.

Fig. 1 recapitulates the use of the self-praise in Ezinam's three and Ewe's two speeches, respectively. Ezinam utilizes self-praise in all three speeches, listing two positive aspects for herself in each of them. On the other hand, Ewe limits her self-praise to the first speech. In the second she takes over a technique that has been introduced by Ezinam in her second speech: the disparagement, a counterpart to self-praising. Ezinam therefore finally surpasses her opponent by listing more positive aspects (6:4). As a whole, Ezinam gives the impression that she is following an elaborate system by structuring her argument well, whereas Ewe fires all her powder right in the beginning, failing to employ any self-praise in her second speech.

If we add self-presentation as third technique to the overview given in Fig. 1, another difference shows up between the two speakers (see Fig. 2 on p. 20). Self-presentation is a technique that can be found in all the winner's speeches; it is less typical in the loser's speeches. The same is true for the present debate. Ezinam opens, and ends, her first speech presenting herself as superior to her rival (ll. 71 – 72 and l. 88):[21]

> "Sister, I have precedence over you (lit. I am your superior), I stand before you. From all the lights in the land I am the most magnificent."[22]
>
> "I am Ezinam-Kusu, I am Enlil's daughter."[23]

Ezinam seems to place this self-presentation consciously at the beginning and at the end, thus creating a framing device for her first speech. In the second speech, the framing device is repeated through the use of self-praise to frame her dispar-

---

20 *Ezinam and Ewe* 176 – 178: **ša$_3$-tur-zu** KI.LAM**-ka lu$_2$ u$_3$-bi$_2$-in-**DU / ^{tu9}**niĝ$_2$-dara$_2$ ni$_2$-zu gu$_2$-za u$_3$-bi$_2$-in-la$_2$** / **u$_8$-ĝa$_2$ še ^{ĝeš}ba-an-e si-ma-ab lu$_2$ lu$_2$ in-na-ab-be$_2$.**

21 A self-presentation always ends in a copula of the 1st person singular "I am" (Sumerian **-me-en**).

22 *Ezinam and Ewe* 71 – 72: **nin$_9$ dub-saĝ-zu-me-en igi-še$_3$ ma-ra-gub-be$_2$-en** / **sud-ra$_2$-aĝ$_2$ kalam-ma-ka ĝe$_{26}$-e giri$_{17}$-zal-bi-me-en.**

23 *Ezinam and Ewe* 88: ^{d}**ezinam$_2$** ^{d}**ku$_3$-su$_3$-me-en dumu** ^{d}**en-lil$_2$-la$_2$-me-en.** Kusu is an epithet of Ezinam.

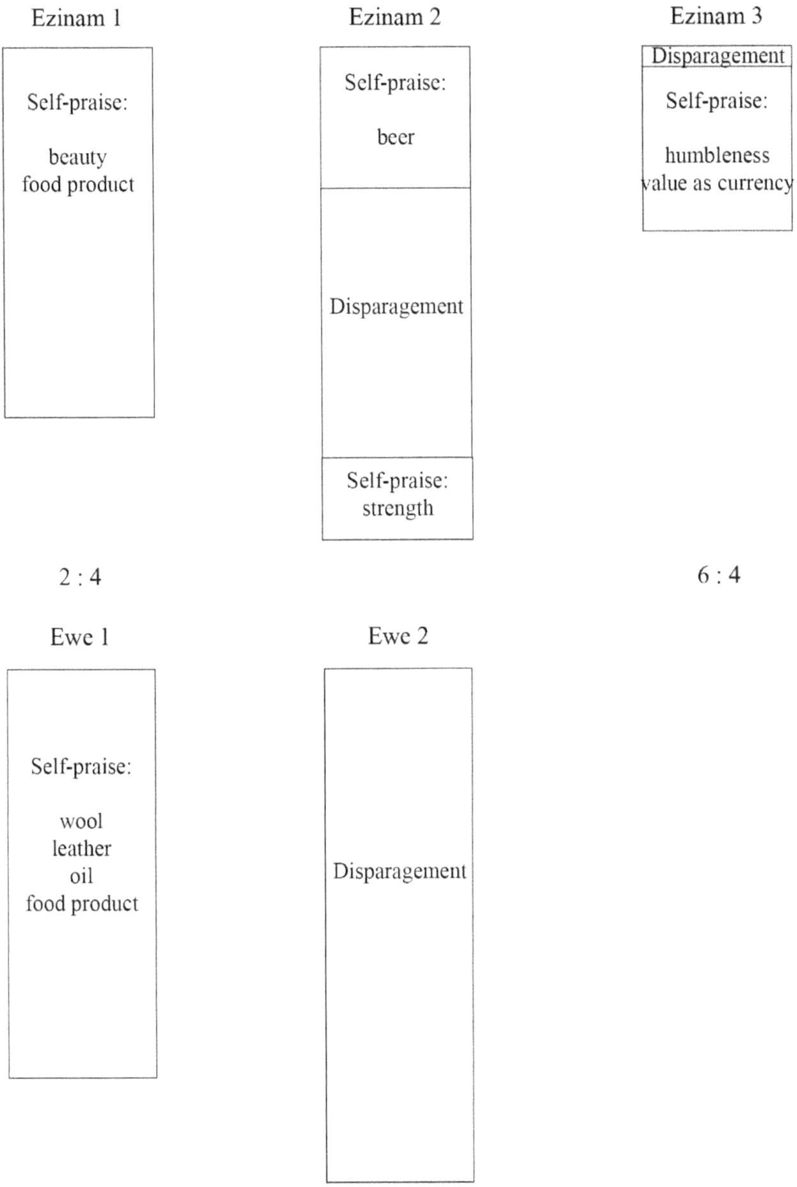

Fig. 1: The use of self-praise and disparagement by Ezinam and Ewe

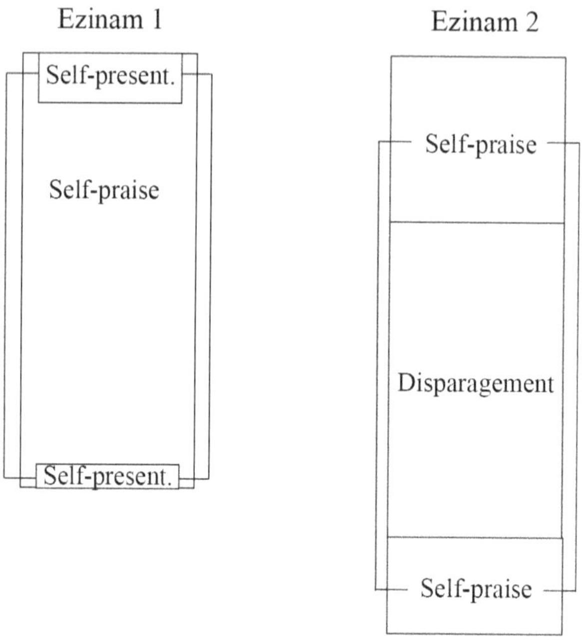

Fig. 2: The framing device in Ezinam 1 and 2

agement of Ewe. On Ewe's side, no equivalent structure can be detected. Again, Ezinam's speech gives the impression of being well-prepared and thought-through.

As mentioned earlier, more complex techniques, such as comparison, expression of relationship, refutation, and outperformance, can be used in synchrony with the two basic techniques. As the beginning of Ezinam's first speech shows, up to three techniques can be applied at the same time (l. 71; see n. 22):

> Sister, I have precedence over you, I stand before you.

The phrase includes a self-praise because it is a positive statement about the speaker. As it is constructed with the copula at the end (**dub-saĝ-zu-me-en** literally "I am your superior"), it is at the same time a self-presentation. In contrast to the self-presentation in l. 88 at the end of the first speech ("I am Ezinam-Kusu, I am Enlil's daughter") which only refers to the speaker, the self-presentation in l. 71 sets Ezinam in relation to her opponent. We therefore have, in the self-praise and in the self-presentation, an expression of relationship – another technique that is mostly found in the winner's speeches.

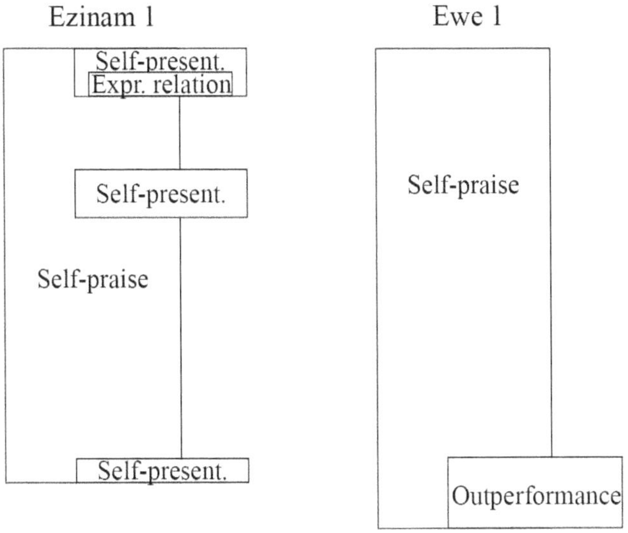

Fig. 3: The use of the complex techniques in the first speeches

In her first speech, Ezinam uses the complex techniques of self-presentation and the expression of relationship. None of these techniques were appropriated by Ewe. At the end of her speech Ewe introduces the technique of outperformance. The latter is a very strong technique as it turns the opponent's argument into an argument for the speaker. To simplify, it could be said that the speaker steals an argument from his adversary.

In order to outperform her opponent, Ewe focuses on a positive aspect presented by Ezinam in her first speech. She had praised herself for giving force to the warrior, which alludes to her nutritive aspect. Ewe now argues that different priests allocate her food product (see citation of ll. 110 – 112 above). This elevates her into the religious sphere, as she embodies food that is suitable for gods to eat, whereas Ezinam is food only for warriors. Ewe takes over the argument "I am food for X" and she outperforms Ezinam by adding a higher-ranking consumer.

In her second speech, Ezinam reacts to this immediately. She explains that she is preparing beer with Ninkasi, the goddess of beer, and that Ewe's food products are delivered to her (= Ezinam's) banquet (ll. 117 – 122):[24]

24 *Ezinam and Ewe* 117 – 122: **babir$_2$ udun-na mim u$_3$ ba-ni-du$_{11}$ / titab$_2$ udun-na u$_4$ a-ba-ni-ib-zal / ^{d}nin-ka-si-ke$_4$ ma-ab-šar$_2$-šar$_2$-re / maš$_2$ gal-gal-zu udu-ua$_4$ gal-gal-zu / ki ĝešbun-ĝu$_{10}$ mu-un-til-le-eš / niĝ$_2$-ĝu$_{10}$-ta a$_2$ gur-ra im-da-su$_8$-su$_8$-ge-eš.**

> After the sourdough has been carefully prepared in the oven and the draff has spent the day in the oven, Ninkasi is mixing it for me. (Your) big goats and your big breeding rams all end up at my banquet. On bowed legs they all stand far away from my products.

As her opponent, Ezinam uses the technique of outperformance. She takes up Ewe's argument that she is doing something with priests (she steps with them to her food allocation) and she tops it by referring to an action she performs with the help of a goddess (preparation of beer). Furthermore, she picks up the word "food allocation/ration" (**šuku**) used by Ewe and turns it into "banquet" (**ĝešbun**) which has, of course, a higher status. She concludes by outperforming Ewe's reference to the products that are delivered to her (= Ezinam's) banquet, by which she makes clear that she is the protagonist on this banquet. She becomes even more explicit in l. 121, putting her into a relationship with her opponent at the moment of the banquet where Ewe's products stand far away from Ezinam's products, which of course indicates that they are less important.

She then goes on to attack her opponent. Her disparagement is not a simple accumulation of invectives; rather, she uses this technique to prepare an argument in her favor. The main theme of the disparagement is Ewe's vulnerability (ll. 128 – 136):[25]

> Snake and scorpion, bandits and creatures of the steppe want your life in the high plain. Day after day you are counted and your tally-stick is put in the ground, so everybody can tell your herdsman how many ewes and young lambs there are and how many goats and young kids there are. When gentle winds call a storm, when gentle winds scatter (everything) they build a milking pen for you.

In the following self-praise she takes up the last lines of the disparagement and creates the same scene for herself, only with a contrasting outcome (ll. 137–139):[26]

> When gentle winds call a storm, when gentle winds scatter (everything) I will stand up confronting Iškur (the weather god).

The repetition of the wind theme allows Ezinam to make a comparison between the two. Whereas Ewe needs shelter, she can confront wind and rain. At the same

---

25 *Ezinam and Ewe* 128 – 136: **muš ĝiri$_2$ lu$_2$ la-ga niĝ$_2$ edin-na-ke$_4$ / zi-zu an-edin-na ku-kur ba-ni-ib-be$_2$ / u$_4$ šu$_2$-uš-e niĝ$_2$-ka$_9$-zu i$_3$-**AK**-e / ĝeš šudum-ma-zu ki i$_3$-ta$_3$-ge / na-gada-za u$_8$ me-a sila$_4$** TUR.TUR **me-a / ud$_5$ me-a maš$_2$** TUR.TUR **me-a lu$_2$ mu-un-na-ab-be$_2$ / tumu tur-tur-e uru$_2$ di-da-bi / tumu tur-tur-e ^{sag3}saga$_7$ di-da-bi / ze$_4$-e e$_2$-ubur-ra ma-ra-an-du$_3$-u$_3$-ne.**

26 *Ezinam and Ewe* 137 – 139: **tumu tur-tur-e uru$_2$ di-da-bi / tumu tur-tur-e ^{sag3}saga$_7$ di-da-bi / ^{d}iškur-ra gaba-ri-a mu-da-an-gub-be$_2$-en.**

time, she surpasses Ewe's vulnerability with her own strength. This example shows how Ezinam is connecting her own positive qualities to the disparagement of her opponent. The first positive aspect in the second speech ('beer at the banquet') surpasses Ewe's positive aspect ('food allocation') and the second outperforms a negative one that Ezinam has attributed to Ewe.

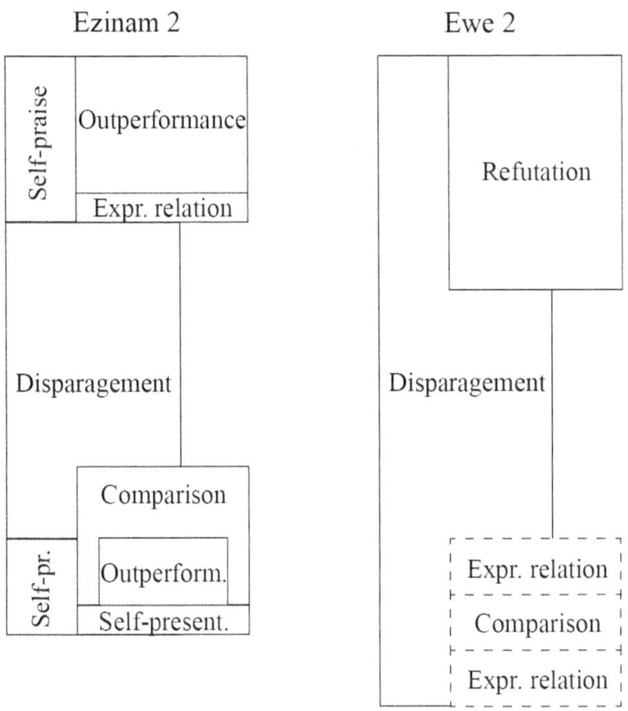

Fig. 4: The use of complex techniques in the second speeches

Ewe's second speech is completely based on disparagement. She takes over this newly introduced technique and uses it as a counterpart to the self-praise in her first speech. On the structural level, she seems to follow a very simple system which allows only one basic technique per speech (without any framing device). Limiting herself to disparagement has significant consequences. She cannot employ all of the more complex techniques, and she can only argue against her opponent but not in favor of herself, as Ewe does right in the beginning of her second speech. Ewe introduces a refutation to attack Ezinam's argument that she (Ezinam) is strong and resistant, whereas Ewe is vulnerable (ll. 146 – 152):[27]

> After the evildoer, the expelled, the foreign slave, the young man, the one with the young spouse and the young children, after he tied up everything with his rope of one cubit, after he brought you up to the threshing-floor, after his cudgel pounded your eyes and your mouth and after he [...] the block of the barley flour on you, [he makes you be carried] away by the south wind and the north wind.

As she is employing a disparagement, she can neither refute her own vulnerability nor outperform Ezinam's strength. She must limit herself to refuting a positive aspect of her adversary's. Ewe's vulnerability is uncontested and remains a negative point on her side.

Another consequence of the disparagement is that complex techniques can miss their point, as is the case at the end of Ewe's second speech. She takes up the food/banquet theme developed by Ezinam in her second speech and tries to turn it back into her argument (ll. 160 – 165):[28]

> When you lie on the table, am I above you or beneath you? Ezinam, turn the attention to yourself! Like me you are (just) something to eat. Am I second, (just) because one has looked at your *essence/force* (**me**)?

Ewe tries to challenge Ezinam's argument that her goats and rams stand far away from Ezinam's products. She compares her opponent to herself by saying that both of them are just something to eat. But this comparison is not well chosen, as she ends up downgrading herself. As *tertium comparationis* she chooses a common ground (both are eatable), but such a comparison only works if the adversary is opposed to a positive aspect of oneself. If the argument is based on a common attribute, every accolade as well as every criticism will be valid for both of them.

In the same passage she tries to describe the relationship between the two with two rhetorical questions. In the first she asks whether she is (hierarchically) above or beneath Ezinam. Later she becomes even more explicit with the ques-

27 *Ezinam and Ewe* 146 – 152: **lu$_2$** NE.RU **bar tab-ba saĝ kur-ra / [ĝu]ruš-e lu$_2$ dam tur-ra-ke$_4$ dumu tur-tur-ra-ke$_4$ / eše$_2$-da diš kuš$_3$-na um-ma-an-la$_2$ / ki-su$_7$-še$_3$ um-ma-an-e$_3$-de$_3$ / ^{ĝeš}tukul-a-ni igi-zu um-ra-ra ka-zu um-ra-ra / lagab zi$_3$-gu-ka um-ma-ri-in-**[...] / **tumu u$_{18}$-lu tumu mer-ra bala-še$_3$ mu-**⸢x⸣-[...-AK].

28 *Ezinam and Ewe* 160 – 165: **ze$_4$-e ^{ĝeš}banšur-ra ĝal$_2$-la-zu-ne / an-ta ma-ra-ĝal$_2$-en ki-ta ma-ĝal$_2$-en / ^{d}ezinam$_2$ ni$_2$-za $^{\text{ĝeš-tu9}}$ĝeštu** AK-**ni / u$_3$ ze$_4$-e ĝe$_{26}$-e-gen$_7$ niĝ$_2$-gu$_7$-u$_3$-me-en / me-za igi mi-ni-ib-il$_2$-la-ke$_4$-eš / u$_3$ ĝe$_{26}$-e egir-bi im-us$_2$-en.**

tion “Am I second?” This is a question that should never be asked in a precedence debate. The opponent simply has to confirm her second place and the discussion is over.

The abortive statement of relationship towards the end of Ewe’s second speech stands in sharp contrast to Ezinam’s first line:

“I have precedence over you” (l. 71)	vs.	“Am I second?” (l. 165)
dub-saĝ-zu-me-en		**u_3 ĝe$_{26}$-e egir-bi im-us$_2$-en**

In fact, these two statements summarize the whole debate. They reflect the eloquence of the speakers and anticipate the judgment. Ezinam never doubted her superiority.

It is obvious that Ezinam, as the winner, uses a wider variety of argumentation techniques than Ewe (see Tab. 4). Furthermore, she employs self-praise in all her speeches, whereas Ewe makes use of self-praise only once. Some techniques are not utilized at all in the loser’s speeches, as, for example, the self-presentation. In addition, Ewe fails by misapplying complex techniques. For example, she attempts a comparison and an expression of relationship but she uses them in the course the disparagement instead of the self-praise (as it is done by Ezinam).

Table 4: The use of the argumentation techniques by the two contestants[29]

	Ezinam 1	Ewe 1	Ezinam 2	Ewe 2	Ezinam 3
Self-praise	✓	✓	✓	–	✓
Disparagement	–	–	✓	✓	✓
Self-presentation	✓	–	✓	–	–
Refutation	–	–	–	✓	✓
Outperformance	–	✓	✓	–	–
Comparison	–	–	✓	(✓)	–
Expression of relationship	✓	–	✓	(✓)	✓

A last point that seems to be a rule in an **a-da-min$_3$** but can mainly be observed in the winner’s speeches, is the taking over of a newly introduced technique. Ewe, for example, introduces outperformance in her first speech and Ezinam usurps this technique to show that she is able to surpass her opponent in her line of argument as well. A second example is the refutation introduced by Ewe in her second speech and usurped by Ezinam in her third speech. The

29 (✓) marks failed techniques; for the reproach in Fish’s first speech see n. 30.

loser, on the other hand, often neglects this rule. Ewe only appropriates the self-praise from Ezinam's first speech but not the self-presentation and expression of relationship. She will come back to the latter in her second speech, but she will fail by using it. After Ezinam's second speech, Ewe adopts the disparagement, and she attempts to integrate a comparison, but there as well she fails.

A comparison with the use of argumentation techniques in the disputation between *Bird and Fish* (Fig. 5) shows that the observations made above seem to be effective in all the **a-da-min$_3$.**

Again, the winner (Bird) focuses more on self-praise and uses a larger variety of argumentation techniques. Fish limits himself, in his first speech, to the disparagement and the demand,[30] which gives him a bad starting position compared to Bird's powerful first speech. The total number of instances of disparagement in Fish's speeches surpasses by far the use of this technique in Bird's speeches. The latter uses disparagement more reasonably and with more control, and he is always combines it with a self-praise. On the other hand, Fish is extremely limited in his self-praise.

It is interesting to see that Bird basically takes over the structure of Fish's speeches, but he always changes or adds a technique to improve it:

Fish 1: (Reproach) – Disparagement – Demand
Bird 1: Reproach – Disparagement – *Self-praise* – Demand

Fish 2: Disparagement – Reproach – Self-praise – Threat
Bird 2: Disparagement – Reproach – Self-praise – *Demand*

In his first speech, Bird adds self-praise to the basic structure used by Fish, which is an essential technique in a precedence debate. In his second speech he replaces the threat[31] with the more convenient demand.

Fish, on the other hand, starts with a rather poor speech. In his second speech, he tries to adopt as many techniques as possible from Bird's first speech (see Fig. 5). He obviously respects the rule that the speaker has to take over the newly introduced techniques of the opponent. Even though he fails (as Ewe did) in his attempt to use outperformance and expression of relationship, he nevertheless considerably improves his second speech.

---

30 The reproach marked before Fish's first speech is actually part of the *occasion litigandi* in transition 1. Bird integrates this technique into his first speech as if it had been used in the preceding speech.

31 Fish threatens Bird "I will pay back your false words" (l. 99 **sun$_7$-na enim lul-la bala-zu šu-za ga-ba-ni-ib-si**).

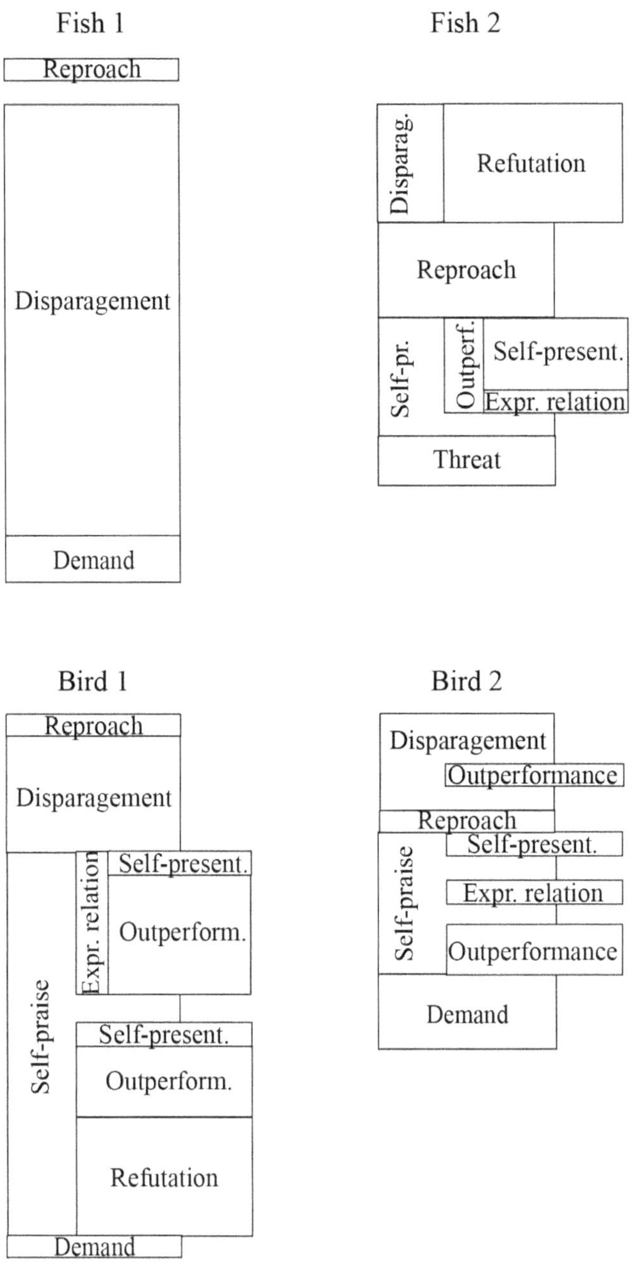

Fig. 5: The use of argumentation techniques in *Bird and Fish*

The analysis of *Ezinam and Ewe* and the comparison with *Bird and Fish* shows clear discrepancies between the eloquence of the two contestants.[32] The winner is a highly skilled orator, whereas the loser seems rather to act on impulse. In *Ezinam and Ewe* the quality of the loser's speeches decreases from the first to the second speech, as it is in the second speech that disparagement is introduced, and this technique is often the undoing of the loser. In *Bird and Fish* the loser opens the verbal contest. He seems to be completely unaware of argumentation techniques, as he only uses the basic techniques of disparagement and demand in his first speech. His second speech improves remarkably, as he can base it on the good example given by Bird. But his inferiority is made clear by his repeated failure to use complex techniques.

The dialogue structure of the precedence debates, combined with their aim to surpass the rival by verbal means and to convince the arbiter and the public of one's merit, make it highly plausible that these texts had a rhetorical background. Even though we do not have a term for "rhetoric" either in Akkadian or in Sumerian, and there is no theoretical evidence for the existence of a *rhetorike techne / ars bene dicendi* for Ancient Mesopotamia,[33] we do know, especially from a royal hymn of King Šulgi of Ur (21st century BC), that speaking skills were considered praiseworthy.[34] In a very interesting passage of this hymn, the king praises himself for having instructed his generals in eloquence (Šulgi B ll. 225–227):[35]

> so that the assembly may take decisions by discussing and debating, therefore I taught my generals to discuss and to debate

---

32 See already Alster and Vanstiphout (1987: 10) for *Ezinam and Ewe* and Vanstiphout (1984) for *Hoe and Plough.*

33 Sallaberger (2007: 69–70) points to the omen series *Šumma kataduggû* which deal with the "Art und Wirkung von Rede und Verhalten" (edition by Böck 2000: 130–147). For rhetoric in Mesopotamia see also Hallo 1996: 170–171 and id. 2004: 25–26.

34 Šulgi B; for an edition see Castellino 1972 und ETCSL (etcsl.orinst.ox.ac.uk). See especially l. 230 **enim-ta ^{ĝeš}tukul-gen$_7$ iri** DU.DU**-me-en** "I am the one who captures cities with words as (if they were) weapons" and l. 235 **ša$_3$ izi-gen$_7$ bar$_7$-a se$_{25}$-bi mu-zu** "I know how to cool down hearts which are burning like fire."

35 Šulgi B ll. 225–227: **ad ge$_4$-ge$_4$-da enim šar$_2$-šar$_2$-da / pu-uḫ$_2$-ru-um^{ki} nam tar-tar-re-de$_3$ / šagina-ĝu$_{10}$-ne-er ad ge$_4$-ge$_4$ mu(-un)-zu enim šar$_2$-šar$_2$ mu(-un)-zu.**

Furthermore, the myth of *Innana and Enki* mentions the capacity of "discussing" (**ad** $\mathbf{ge_4}$-$\mathbf{ge_4}$), "deliberating" ($\mathbf{ša_3}$ $\mathbf{kuš_2}$) and "arguing" ($\mathbf{du_{14}}$ $\mathbf{mu_2}$-$\mathbf{mu_2}$) in a judicial context in a long list enumerating cultural achievements and moral values.[36]

Šulgi's self-praise suggests that eloquence was trained in the scribal schools, at least towards the end of the third millennium BC when Sumerian was still the dominant language in southern Mesopotamia. In absence of a theoretical basis for these studies, eloquence seems to have been learned by imitation.[37] The precedence debates[38] might have served as examples[39] for teaching the apprentice scribe, at an advanced stage of his education, the different argumentation techniques.[40] Thanks to the opposition of a good speaker to a bad speaker in the precedence debates, the student can not only learn how to apply these techniques, but he can also recognize the risks in using more complex techniques. The winner's speeches serve him as a good example, whereas the loser's speeches warn him of possible mistakes.

In the following Old-Babylonian period (2003–1595 BC) Sumerian was no longer an everyday language, but it survived as an official and cultic language. As the large number of manuscripts dating to the Old-Babylonian period show the precedence debates were studied at school in the first part of the second millennium. But did they still form the basis for rhetorical training? Unlike Latin in the Middle Ages, which was the language of the *disputationes* at the universities, Sumerian did not have a comparable function. It is therefore possible that the Sumerian precedence debates (as well as the debates between students or be-

---

36 *Innana und Enki* I iii 22 $\mathbf{du_{14}}$ **[**$\mathbf{mu_2}$**-**$\mathbf{mu_2}$ $\mathbf{u_3}$**-ma] ad** $\mathbf{ge_4}$**-**$\mathbf{ge_4}$ $\mathbf{ša_3}$ $\mathbf{kuš_2}$**-**$\mathbf{u_3}$ **di [**$\mathbf{ku_5}$ **ka-aš bar]** "argu[ing, triumphing] discussing, deliberating, judg[ing, decision-making]"; line counting of Farber-Flügge 1973.

37 The principle of *imitatio* is well attested for classical antiquity; see Ueding and Steinbrink 2011: 35 and 47.

38 The manuscripts of the precedence debates all date to the Old-Babylonian Period (2003–1595 BC). But as some of them mention Urnamma, Šulgi and Ibbisîn they probably go back to the earlier Ur III Period. This is supported by the attestation of the term **a-da-**$\mathbf{min_3}$ in the administrative texts of the Ur-III Period (see Attinger 1993: 419 with n. 1129 and Herrmann 2010: 65 n. 276). For the discussion of the dating of the **a-da-**$\mathbf{min_3}$ see most recently Jiménez (2017: 24) with related literature and Vacín (2018).

39 For classical antiquity, the term "Musterrede" is in use; see Ueding and Steinbrink 2011: 15. We should not apply this term to the Sumerian precedence debates as, in contrast to a "Musterrede," Sumerian precedence debates do not provide any explanatory comments, and they always oppose a good speaker to a bad speaker.

40 Schäfer (2001: 62–63) compares the Sumerian precedence debates with the "Synkrisis, die Technik des Vergleichs" who was part of the so-called "Progymnasmata – Übungen, mit Hilfe derer ausgehend von thematischen Vorgaben Ausdrucksfähigkeit und Gliederungsvermögen geschult wurden (p. 63). See also Wagner 2004: 196 and Jiménez 2017: 131.

tween women) rather served as an instrument to improve the speaking skills of the students. A similar situation can be found in the humanistic education system of the 15th and 16th century AD.[41] After initial exercises in Latin vocabulary and grammar, concentration was then put on oral communication skills. The student first learned single sentences by heart before turning to the *dialogi* (dialogues between students) (see Bömer 1897: 3 – 5).

In Sumerian, single sentences could correspond to the proverbs, by which the scribe could slowly get in touch with the spoken language.[42] As a second step, he would turn to the precedence debates (and the debates between students and women), perhaps with the diatribe as an intermediate stage.[43] The dialogue structure, and the humorous touch of the precedence debates, would be a pleasant tool to integrate and apply the Sumerian vocabulary painstakingly learned from the rather tedious lexical lists.[44]

Bibliography

Alster, Bendt. 1990. Sumerian Literary Dialogues and Debates and Their Place in Ancient Near Eastern Literature. Pp. 1 – 16 in *Living Waters: Scandinavian Orientalistic Studies Presented to Professor Dr. Frede Løkkegaard on his Seventy-fifth Birthday, January 27th 1990*, ed. Egon Keck et al. Kopenhagen: Museum Tusculanum Press.

Alster, Bendt and Herman L. J. Vanstiphout. 1987. Lahar and Ashnan: Presentation and Analysis of a Sumerian Disputation. *Acta Sumerologica* 9: 1 – 43.

Attinger, Pascal. 1993. *Eléments de linguistique sumérienne: la construction de du11/e/di "dire"*. Orbis Biblicus et Orientalis Sonderband. Fribourg/Göttingen: Editions universitaires Fribourg and Vandenhoeck & Ruprecht.

Böck, Barbara. 2000. *Die babylonisch-assyrische Morphoskopie*. Archiv für Orientforschung Beiheft 27. Wien: Institut für Orientalistik der Universität Wien.

Bömer, Aloys. 1897. *Die lateinischen Schülergespräche der Humanisten. Auszüge mit Einleitungen, Anmerkungen und Namen- und Sachregister*. Berlin: J. Harrwitz Nachfolger.

Bottéro, Jean. 1991. La "tenson" et la réflexion sur les choses en Mésopotamie. Pp. 7 – 22 in *Dispute poems and dialogues in the Ancient and Mediaeval Near East: Forms and Types of Literary Debates in Semitic and Related Literatures*, ed. Gerrit J. Reinink and Herman L. J. Vanstiphout. Orientalia Lovaniensia Analecta 42. Leuven: Peeters Press.

Castellino, Giorgio R. 1972. *Two Šulgi Hymns (BC)*. Studi Semitici 42. Rome: Istituto di studi del Vicino Oriente – Università di Roma.

41 See Civil 1985: 67, Volk 2000: 15 and id. 2012: 221.

42 For the Sumerian proverbs as rhetoric collections see Gordon 1959: 19 – 20 and Falkowitz 1980: 30 – 48.

43 Similarly Volk (2000: 13 – 15) without the diatribe as an intermediate stage.

44 See Jiménez 2017: 121 – 122 with related literature n. 328 f. Cf. already Walther 1920: 19: "die Dialogform sollte den Unterricht lebendiger und den Lehrstoff verständlicher machen."

Civil, Miguel. 1985. Sur les "livres d'écolier" à l'époque paléo-babylonienne. Pp. 67–78 in *Miscellanea Babylonica: mélanges offerts à Maurice Birot*, ed. Jean-Marie Durand and Jean-Robert Kupper. Paris: Editions Recherche sur les Civilisations.

Cunningham, Graham. 2007. A Catalogue of Sumerian Literature (based on Miguel Civil's Catalogue of Sumerian Literature). Pp. 351–412 in *Analysing Literary Sumerian: Corpus-based Approaches*, ed. Jarle Ebeling and Graham Cunningham. London/Oakville: Equinox Publishing Ltd.

van Dijk, Johannes J. A. 1953. *La sagesse suméro-accadienne: recherches sur les genres littéraires des textes sapientiaux.* Leiden: Brill.

Edzard, Dietz Otto. 1987–90. Literatur – § 3 Überblick über die sumerische Literatur. Pp. 36–48 in *Reallexikon der Assyriologie und Vorderasiatischen Archäologie* 7, ed. Dietz Otto Edzard. Berlin: De Gruyter.

Falkowitz, Robert S. 1980. *The Sumerian rhetoric collections* (Ph. D., University of Pennsylvania). Ann Arbor: UMI.

Farber-Flügge, Gertrud. 1973. *Der Mythos "Inanna und Enki" unter besonderer Berücksichtigung der Liste der me.* Studia Pohl 10. Rome: Biblical Institute Press.

Gordon, Edmund I. 1959. *Sumerian Proverbs: Glimpses of Every Day Life in Ancient Mesopotamia.* Philadelphia: The University Museum. University of Pennsylvania.

Gordon, Edmund I. 1960. A New Look at the Wisdom of Sumer and Akkad. *Bibliotheca Orientalis* 17: 122–52.

Hallo, William W. 1996. *Origins: The Ancient Near Eastern Background of Some Modern Western Institutions.* Leiden [et al.]: Brill.

Hallo, William W. 2004. The Birth of Rhetoric. Pp. 25–46 in *Rhetoric Before and Beyond the Greeks*, ed. Carol S. Lipson and Roberta A. Binkley. Albany: State University of New York Press.

Herrmann, Sabine. 2010. *Vogel und Fisch – Ein sumerisches Rangstreitgespräch: Textedition und Kommentar.* Hamburg: Verlag Dr. Kovač.

Jiménez, Enrique. 2017. *The Babylonian Disputation Poems: with Editions of the Series of the Poplar, Palm and Vine, the Series of the Spider, and the Story of the Poor, Forlorn Wren.* Culture and History of the Ancient Near East 87. Leiden/Boston: Brill.

Mittermayer, Catherine. 2009. *Enmerkara und der Herr von Arata: Ein ungleicher Wettstreit.* Orbis Biblicus et Orientalis 239. Fribourg/Göttingen: Academic Press and Vandenhoeck & Ruprecht.

Mittermayer, Catherine. 2014. mušen ku6: Viel Vogel und wenig Fisch in MS 2110/1. *Altorientalische Forschungen* 41/2: 201–222.

Mittermayer, Catherine. 2019a. ‚*Was sprach der eine zum anderen?' Argumentationsformen in den sumerischen Rangstreitgesprächen.* Untersuchungen zur Assyriologie und Vorderasiatischen Archäologie 15. Berlin/Boston: De Gruyter.

Mittermayer, Catherine. 2019b. Animals in the Sumerian Disputation poems. Pp. 175–186 in *Animals and Their Relation to Gods, Humans and Things in the Ancient World*, ed. Sebastian Fink et al. Wiesbaden: Springer VS.

Reinink, Gerrit J. and Herman L. J. Vanstiphout (eds.). 1991. *Dispute Poems and Dialogues in the Ancient and Mediaeval Near East: Forms and Types of Literary Debates in Semitic and Related Literatures.* Orientalia Lovaniensia Analecta 42. Leuven: Peeters Press.

Rubio, Gonzalo. 2009. Sumerian Literature. Pp. 11–75 in *From an Antique Land. An Introduction to Ancient Near Eastern Literature*, ed. Carl S. Ehrlich. Lanham [et al.]: Rowman & Littlefield.

Sallaberger, Walther. 2007. Alter Orient. 1. Mesopotamien. Pp. 67–74 in *Historisches Wörterbuch der Rhetorik* 8, ed. Gert Ueding. Tübingen: Max Niemeyer.

Schäfer, Antje. 2001. *Vergils Eklogen 3 und 7 in der Tradition der lateinischen Streitdichtung. Eine Darstellung anhand ausgewählter Texte der Antike und des Mittelalters.* Frankfurt: Peter Lang.

Ueding, Gert and Bernd Steinbrink. 2011. *Grundriß der Rhetorik. Geschichte – Technik – Methode.* 5th ed. Stuttgart/Weimar: J. B. Metzler.

Vacín, Luděk. 2018. All the King's Adamindugas: Textual Images of Ur III sovereigns as managers of the Universe. Pp. 447–457 in *Text and Image. Proceedings of the 61e Rencontre Assyriologique Internationale, Geneva and Bern, 22–26 June 2015*, ed. P. Attinger et al. Orbis Biblicus et Orientalis Series Archaeologica 40. Leuven/Paris/Bristol: Peeters.

Vanstiphout, Herman L. J. 1984. On the Sumerian Disputation Between the Hoe and the Plough. *Aula Orientalis* 2: 239–251.

Vanstiphout, Herman L. J. 1990. The Mesopotamian Debate Poems: A General Presentation (Part I). *Acta Sumerologica* 12: 271–318.

Vanstiphout, Herman L. J. 1992. 5. Disputations. Pp. 575–588 in *The Context of Scripture*, vol. 1: *Canonical Compositions from the Biblical World*, ed. William W. Hallo. Leiden [et al.]: Brill.

Vanstiphout, Herman L. J. 2004. Eduba: Schrijven en lezen in Sumer. Amsterdam: SUN.

Volk, Konrad. 2000. Edubba'a und Edubba'a-Literatur: Rätsel und Lösungen. *Zeitschrift für Assyriologie* 90: 1–30.

Volk, Konrad. 2012. Streitgespräch. Pp. 214–22 in *Reallexikon der Assyriologie und Vorderasiatischen Archäologie* 13, ed. Michael P. Streck. Berlin: De Gruyter.

Wagner, Ewald. 2004. Rangstreit. Pp. 194–199 in Enzyklopädie des Märchens Bd. 11, ed. Kurt Ranke. Berlin: De Gruyter.

Walther, Hans. 1920. Das Streitgedicht in der lateinischen Literatur des Mittelalters. Hildesheim [et al.]: Georg Olms.

Wilcke, Claus. 1975. Formale Gesichtspunkte in der sumerischen Literatur. Pp. 205–316 in *Sumerological Studies in Honor of Thorkild Jacobsen on his Seventieth Birthday June 7, 1974*, ed. Stephen J. Lieberman. Assyriological Studies 20. Chicago: University of Chicago Press.

Wilcke, Claus. 1992. Sumerische Streitgedichte. Pp. 603–606 in *Kindlers Neues Literaturlexikon* Bd. 19, ed. Walter Jens. München: Kindler.

Manuel Ceccarelli*

3 An Introduction to the Sumerian School Disputes

Subject, Structure, Function and Context

1 Introduction

1.1 The School

The school that is portrayed in the school disputes is the so-called e_2-dub-ba-a, a Sumerian term which seems to mean "House in which tablets are assigned."[1] This institution was apparently established by Urnamma, the third dynasty Sumerian king of Ur (ca. 2112–2095) and it played a central role in the formation of scribes. As George (2005) has pointed out, we have little evidence about the Edubba'a of the Ur III Period, not even knowing which buildings may have been used as schools, but we do know that the Edubba'a was charged with the production and transmission of literary texts in praise of the king. This is what King Sulgi, Urnamma's son, says in a hymn where he praises himself and his cleverness in the scribal art (*Sulgi B* 311–315):[2]

311. **šudu$_3$ e$_2$ kur-ra ki he$_2$-us$_2$-sa-ĝu$_{10}$-uš**
312. **dub-sar he$_2$-DU šu-ni he$_2$-eb-dab$_5$-be$_2$**
313. **nar he$_2$-DU gu$_3$ hu-mu-un-ni-ri-de$_2$**
314. **e$_2$-dub-ba-a da-ri$_2$ hur nu-kur$_2$-ru-dam**
315. **ki-umum da-ri$_2$ hur nu-silig-ge-dam**

311. For my prayers, which I place in the Ekur-Temple,
312. Should be a scribe responsible and he should hold them in his hand;

* University of Geneva. I would like to thank Catherine Mittermayer for her remarks and suggestions. The present paper was written within the research project "Streitliteratur im Alten Orient: Ein Editionsprojekt" at the University of Geneva financed by the Swiss National Science Foundation.

1 Volk (2000: 1–3) discusses various interpretations of this term. For various approaches to the Edubba'a see Sjöberg 1976; Civil 1992; Vanstiphout 2004; George 2005; Waetzoldt and Cavigneaux 2009; Michalowski 2010: 199–205; Peterson 2015; Rubio 2009: 39–42; id. 2016: 246–252. Note the Akkadian translation of **e$_2$-dub-ba-a:** *bīt ṭuppi*. See also the references in note 4.

2 Reconstructed text after ETCSL. For this passage see also Klein and Sefati 2014: 86–88; for the bilingual manuscript see Peterson 2011: 153–156.

https://doi.org/10.1515/9781501510274-003

313. A singer should be responsible for them too and he should read them from (the tablets).
314. The Edubba'a is not to be changed!
315. The place of Wisdom (**ki umum**) is not to be given up!

We have some more information about the Edubba'a from texts of the Old Babylonian Period. By this time, Sumerian was no longer spoken and the students were native Akkadian or Amorite speakers who were required to learn the Sumerian language, which had retained its status and importance as the language of culture and of official cultic practice.

According to the texts, the people active in the Edubba'a included masters, overseers, supervisors in matters of discipline, advanced students (the so-called 'Big Brothers') and students. Discipline in the school was quite severe. Common reasons for corporal punishment included talking in class, standing up, leaving the classroom, not being able to read the homework aloud, speaking Akkadian, or slurring Sumerian.[3] Almost all the manuscripts of literary texts we have from this period are the products of students who learned and wrote them during the final stage of their scribal training.[4]

1.2 Definition of the Text Corpus

The literary production of Ancient Mesopotamia is particularly rich. As in the Middle Ages,[5] we find compositions which can be labeled 'school disputes' because they are concerned with school life.[6] But the matter of definition and terminology is not easy. Mittermayer (2019: chap. 1.2) has established a list of four

3 See *Schooldays* (= *Edubba'a A*) especially ll. 35–40 (latest translations by Volk 2015a; Attinger 2017); and *Rules of the School* (*Edubba'a R*) sec. 3 ll. 26–27 (edition by Gadotti and Kleinerman 2017).

4 The scribal curriculum was thoroughly studied by Veldhuis 1997 (see especially pp. 40–67); Tinney 1999; Veldhuis 2000; Robson 2001; Delnero 2010a; Delnero 2010b; Tinney 2011; see as well Waetzoldt 1989; Civil 1992; Wilson 2008; Ohgama and Robson 2010; Volk 2011.

5 For an overview, see Cardelle de Hartmann 2007: 58–77; for the Late Middle Ages see, for example, the school dialogues and school disputes of Paulus Niavis in Kramarczyk and Humberg (eds.) 2013.

6 Miguel Civil introduced the designations 'Dialogue (1, 2, ...)' and 'Edubba'a (A, B, ...)' in his unpublished *A Catalogue of Sumerian Literature*; these designations have been adopted by most sumerologists, see Cunningham 2007: 351, 385 (sub school stories), 386 (sub scribal dialogues).

'school disputes' ('Schulstreitgespräche');[7] these same texts had previously been designated as either dialogues or satire.[8]

Mittermayer: 'school disputes'

Enkiheĝal and Enkitalu	→ *dialogue*
Enkimanšum and Ĝirinisa	→ *dialogue*
Two Scribes	→ *dialogue*
Edubba'a D	→ *satire*

According to Cardelle de Hartmann (2007: 265) a dialogue is:

> "nicht als Textsorte sondern als Form zu definieren: Die Dialogform stellt eine konkrete Ausprägung der Personensprache und somit eine Möglichkeit der literarischen Gestaltung dar, die in verschiedenen Textsorten Anwendung finden kann. Sie ist durch formale Merkmale charakterisiert."

Some of the formal characteristics that Cardelle de Hartmann (2007: 261–63) refers to include:

1. The compositions are centred on a conversation, which have either no narrative sequences at all or only an introduction that explains why the conversation or dispute arose.
2. They involve at least two speakers who are either not, or only scarcely, characterized.
3. They can fulfil different functions. They provide an articulation of the content, which is distributed between the speakers in the form of a variety of arguments.

Following Cardelle de Hartmann, we can establish a list of eight to nine 'school dialogues' (see below). They are entirely structured in dialogue form without any narrative parts.[9] Within these 'school dialogues', four compositions can be speci-

---

7 Mittermayer (2019: § 1.2.) understands *Schooldays* (*Edubba'a A*) and *The Wayward Child and his Father* (*Edubba'a B*) as 'Schulsatiren'. For *Dispute between two Women A & B* (*Dialogue 4 & 5*) she adopts the term 'Frauenstreitgespräch'.

8 See most recently Mittermayer (2019: § 1.2.) with previous literature and Volk (2011–13: 214–15, 220–21) who defines *Two Scribes* (*Dialogue 1*), *Enkiheĝal and Enkitalu* (*Dialogue 2*), *Enkimanšum and Ĝirinisa* (*Dialogue 3*), *Dispute between two Women A & B* (*Dialogue 4 & 5*) as 'Dialoge' and uses the term 'Schulsatire' for *Schooldays* (*Edubba'a A*), *The Wayward Child and his Father* (*Edubba'a B*), *Graduate Student and Supervisor* (*Edubba'a C*), *Edubba'a D* and *Rules of the School* (*Edubba'a R*).

9 Since *Edubba'a A* contains long narrative sequences (ll. 51–58; 66–69), it does not meet the first condition. Single lines introducing a direct speech occur in *Graduate Student and Supervisor* (l. 29) and *Enkimanšum and Ĝirinisa* (ll. d 17 – d 18a).

fied as 'school disputes'.[10] In these texts, each speaker attempts to present himself as the more outstanding one of the two.

School dialogues (i.e. texts in dialogue form concerning school life) are:

- *Graduate Student and Supervisor (Edubba'a C)*[11]
- *The Wayward Child and his Father (Edubba'a B)*[12]
- *Examination Text A & B*[13]
- *(Rules of the School (Edubba'a R))*[14]
- *(Edubba'a E)*[15]
- *Enkiheĝal and Enkitalu (Dialogue 2)* → *school dispute*
- *Enkimanšum and Ĝirinisa (Dialogue 3)* → *school dispute*
- *Two Scribes (Dialogue 1)* → *school dispute*
- *Edubba'a D* → *school dispute*

1.3 School Disputes

We know of four compositions in which each speaker tries to outclass his rival in matters of skill, knowledge, and social status. Only in two disputes are the speakers mentioned by name: *Enkiheĝal and Enkitalu* and *Enkimanšum and Ĝirinisa.*

1.3.1 *Enkiheĝal and Enkitalu*

Enkiheĝal and Enkitalu are not depicted as junior scribes or students of the scribal art but as music students in training to become singers.[16] Michalowski (2010: 199–203) has proposed that this dispute was located in a conservatory, an institution which –according to his proposal– is considered to be separate from the

10 They correspond to Mittermayer's list (see above).
11 Translations by Vanstiphout 1997b, Volk 2015b and ETCSL 5.1.3.
12 Edition in Sjöberg 1973.
13 Edition of *Examination Text A* in Sjöberg 1975.
14 *Rules of the School* (= *Edubba'a R*) begins with a dialogue between a teacher and a student but, as Gadotti and Kleinerman (2017: 90) state, "there is no evidence that the dialogue continued beyond the introduction"; for this reason *Rules of the School* is not certainly classifiable as a dialogue. The Disputes between two women (A & B) have been excluded as they do not concern school life.
15 *Edubba'a E* includes various extracts from other compositions (*Schooldays*, *Enkimanšum and Ĝirinisa*; *Graduate Student and Supervisor; Abaindasa to Sulgi 1* [CKU 4 = ETCSL 3.1.21]), see Volk 2011–2013: 221. Since *Edubba'a E* is not entirely preserved, his nature is not easy to define.
16 An edition of this text is in preparation by the author.

Edubba'a. However, it is equally possible that Enkiheĝal and Enkitalu might just follow a specialised track within the Edubba'a to become singers (Ceccarelli 2018: 136–37). This possibility is supported by the fact that, according to the school dialogue *Examination Text A*, a scribe was expected to know different kinds of songs and how to perform them.

It is quite difficult to determine the *casus litigandi* between Enkiheĝal and Enkitalu, because it is not always clear who is speaking. It seems that Enkiheĝal accuses Enkitalu of having insulted a third person. Enkitalu denies it, and then the dispute begins and continues with many insults coming from both sides. It is noticeable that positive arguments in favor of a speaker are found only at the very beginning and at the end of the dispute. In the central part of the dispute, each speaker attempts to denigrate his rival. In order to settle the dispute, the two students appeal to a 'Big Brother', an advanced student, who in turn eventually appeals to an overseer. It seems that the latter exculpates Enkitalu and sets the ground rule that nobody should quarrel in the Place of Wisdom again.

1.3.2 *Enkimanšum and Ĝirinisa*

Enkimanšum and Ĝirinisa consists of a dispute between two students in training to become scribes.[17] The dispute begins because Enkimanšum wants Enkitalu to recognize him as a 'Big Brother'. There are some gaps in the text, which prevents a detailed understanding. It seems that Ĝirinisa and Enkimanšum appeal to an overseer to settle their dispute, and this overseer in turn appeals to a teacher. The latter blames Enkimanšum for his insolence and sets the rule that students, here called brothers, should not offend each other.

1.3.3 *Two Scribes*

Johnson and Geller (2015: 1–2)[18] suggest that the two interlocutors are a 'professor' of the Edubba'a and a 'bureaucrat,' and that "these two old school buddies have met up again many years after leaving the Edubba." Since this claim is difficult to prove, I prefer the traditional designation 'scribes'. A particular feature of this dispute is that each of the scribes only insults his opponent, in an effort to

17 An edition of this text is in preparation by Klaus Wagensonner and the author. See the partial translation in Römer 1990, Vanstiphout 2004: 210–224 and Ceccarelli 2018.

18 For *Two Scribes* (= *Dialogue 1* = *The Class Reunion*) see the new edition in Matuszak 2019 and the translations in Vanstiphout 1997a and Vanstiphout 2004: 229–35.

demonstrate his inferiority. Neither one praises himself, or says anything positive about himself. The dispute ends quite abruptly when one scribe, who according to the editors was the initiator of the dispute, tells his opponent that he should not fight. Obviously, he means that his opponent is not able to debate at his level.

1.3.4 *Edubba'a D*

This is the only school dispute, which contains the term *adamin.*[19] Moreover, it is the only known *adamin* that ends in a tie (see below § 2.3). The text has only been partially edited. It begins with two scribes testing their skills and scribal knowledge against each other. The dispute degenerates quickly into a tirade of insults.

2 The Structure of the School Disputes

2.1 The Onset

In the first twenty lines of *Enkitalu and Enkiheĝal* and *Enkimanšum and Ĝirinisa* the speeches are quite short; they can even be reduced to a single line. A common difficulty with these disputes is the identification of the speaker because the direct speeches lack introductions. This problem is particularly evident at both the beginning and towards the end of the disputes, because here we find no double ruled lines that graphically mark the speeches. As an example, we can consider ll. a 1–14 of *Enkimanšum and Ĝirinisa:*[20]

a 1. **dumu e_2-dub-ba-a u_4-da egir dub-me-ka a-na-am_3 ga-$ab^!$-sar-en-de_3-en**
a 2. **u_4-da u-ta** KA**-enim-ma** AŠ.AŠ**-me nu-sar-en-de_3-en**
a 3. **na-an-ga-ma um-mi-a ba-zu-zu-ma mu-e-da-sis-en-de_3-en**
a 4. **a-na an-na-an-ni-ib-ge_4-ge_4-en-de_3-en**
a 5. DU **$ĝe_{26}$-e $niĝ_2$-$ša_3$-$ĝa_2$ ga-ab-sar a_2 mu-da-$aĝ_2$-en**

19 A partial edition of this text was provided by Civil 1985. The term **a-da-$min_{(3)}$** can be rendered as "dispute between two." For compositions referred to by this term, see the contribution of C. Mittermayer in the present volume and Rubio 2009: 58, 64.
20 Reconstructed text from: UET 6/1: 150 (Foto CDLI: P346235) obv. 1–14 = a 1–14; TMH NF 3: 42 (HS 1606) obv. iv 5′-18′ = a 1–$14^?$; SLFN 60 (3N-T 904, 170) = a 2–9; CBS 13984 + N 2419 (Foto CDLI: P268978) obv. i 1′-11′ = a 5–14; SLFN 60 (3N-T 904, 165) vs i 1′-5′ = a 8–12; *AulOr.* 15, p. 35: 18 obv. 1–14 = a 1–14.

a 6. **tukum-bi a$_2$ ba-e-da-an-aĝ$_2$ ses-gal-zu nu-me-en**
a 7. **a-na-ta-am$_3$ nam-ses-gal-ĝa$_2$ i(-ni)-in-ku$_4$-re(-en)**
a 8. **nam-dub-sar(-ra)-ta mu-diri-ge-en(/ma) nam-ses-gal(-ĜA$_2$) mu-ub-du$_7$-du$_7$(-un)**
a 9. **di-ib-ba(/umuš) $^{\text{ĝeš-tu9}}$ĝeštu dugud a-ga-aš ge$_4$ e$_2$-dub-ba-a**
a 10. **u$_2$-hub$_2$ nam-dub-sar-ra u$_2$-**UG **eme-gi$_7$-ra**
a 11. **šu zu-hu-ul šu ge-dub-ba-a nu-du$_7$**
a 12. **im-ma nu-tum$_2$-ma šu ka-ta nu-sa$_2$**
a 13. **ĝe$_{26}$-e-gen$_7$-nam dub-sar-me-en**

---

a 14. **a-na-aš ze$_4$-e-gen$_7$ dub-sar nu-me-en**

a 1. Enkimanšum: "Schoolboy, what should we write today on the reverse of our tablets?"
a 2. Today we will not write (ten =) several times each (word) of our curricular material."[21]
a 3. Ĝirinisa: "All the more so as our teacher will find it out, we will (feel uncomfortable =) have problems because of you.
a 4. What will we answer him?"
a 5. E.:"Wait! I will write down what I want and I will give you instructions!"
a 6. Ĝ.:"If someone gives me instructions, then I am not your 'Big Brother'!"
a 7. E.:"Why did someone appoint you to the post of 'Big Brother' over me?[22]
a 8. Are you regarding the scribal art more outstanding then me?[23] I am qualified for the post of 'Big Brother'."[24]
a 9. Ĝ.:"(You are) *in every respect*[?] slow of understanding,[25] backward in the school,

---

21 For this meaning of KA-**enim-ma** see Peterson 2015: 87 and Matuszak 2019: 27 ad l. 7.
22 The proposed interpretation is based on the verbal form, which is transitive ({i+ni+n+$B_{ḫ}$+en}) at least in two duplicates. This means that the speaker is wondering why someone appointed his rival as a 'Big Brother'; I understand **nam-ses-gal-ĝu$_{10}$** as corresponding to an objective genitive: "post of 'Big Brother' (of mine =) over me." The simplest solution is that the speaker who wants to challenge the established hierarchy is Enkimanšum, who wants to know why his rival, not him, was appointed as 'Big Brother'. If Ĝirinisa were to ask why someone had appointed his rival to his own post of 'Big Brother,' it would mean that someone had actually decided to promote Enkimanšum. However, this was not the case, as we know from the rest of the composition (a translation like "why should someone appoint you..." would implicate an epistemic modality, which is unexpected for the prefix {i}). Moreover, the proposed interpretation best matches the structure of the dispute and the break in l. a 9, where a tirade of insults begins: Enkimanšum pretends to give instructions (l. a 5); Ĝirinisa defends his own status as 'Big Brother' (l. a 6); Enkimanšum challenges Ĝirinisa's status (l. a 7–8); Ĝirinisa answers Enkimanšum, insulting him (l. a 9–12). Römer (1990a: 92) and Vanstiphout (1997a: 589) understand the line as part of the speech of Enkimanšum, but their translations ("aus welchem (Grunde) trittst du in meine Eigenschaft (als die) eines >großen Bruders< ein!?"; "why do you encroach on my status of 'big brother'!") do not take into account the transitivity of the verbal form.
23 Interpreting **mu-diri-ge-en** as {mu+'+e+R+en}.
24 Variant: "are you qualified for the post of 'Big Brother' over me?"
25 The translation of **di-ib-ba** is speculative. **di-ib-ba** could be a syllabic writing for **dib**+**{a}**; for **dib** akk. *rabbumma* "by all means[(?)]," see CAD R, 17 s.v. *rabbumma*. A second possibility is

a 10. deaf to the scribal art and dumb for the Sumerian language,
a 11. with clumsy hands, which are unfit for the stylus
a 12. and for the clay-tablet, with hands, which cannot keep up with the mouth,[26]
a 13. are you a scribe like me?"

---

a 14. E.: Why should I not be a scribe like you?

The attribution of the speeches to Ĝirinisa or Enkimanšum is based on secondary evidence that comes at the end of the dispute where the master criticizes Enkimanšum for his arrogance in insulting and bragging to his 'Big Brother'. It is thus quite certain, that Ĝirinisa is the speaker in l. 6, where he defends his position as 'Big Brother'. Using this assumption, it is possible to determine who speaks the other lines.

An example of a different kind of onset is the dispute *Two Scribes* (*Two Scribes* 1–10):[27]

1. **dumu e$_2$-dub-ba-a u$_4$-ul-la-am$_3$ ĝa$_2$-nu ga-na ga-ab-sa$_2$-sa$_2$-en-de$_3$-en**
2. **tukum-bi nam-dub-sar-ra i$_3$-zu a-na-am$_3$ i$_3$-šid**
3. **mu** AŠ.AŠ **zi-ga nam-dub-sar-ra**
4. **niĝ$_2$-zi-ĝal$_2$ edin-na za$_3$ lu$_2$** *šu*-**ka-še$_3$**
5. **i$_3$-sar egir-bi gu$_2$ mu-e-du$_3$**
6. **a-ra$_2$ igi diri niĝ$_2$-ka$_9$ sahar ĝar-ra za$_3$-bi-še$_3$ i$_3$-zu**
7. KA-**enim-ma nam-dumu-e$_2$-dub-ba-a-ke$_4$-ne**
8. **ga-ab-šid-en-de$_3$-en diri-zu-še$_3$ i$_3$-zu**
9. **ĝa$_2$-nu gaba-ri-ĝu$_{10}$-še$_3$ gub-ba in-zu ga-mu-ra-ab-til**

---

10. **lu$_2$-tumu u$_2$-hub$_2$ $^{\text{ĝeš-tu9}}$ĝeštu la$_2$-a**

1. Scribe A: "Schoolboy, it is late, come here! Come on! Let us debate!
2. If you are trained in the scribal arts, what did you perform?
3. Each excerpted line in of scribal art,
4. from the *ṣâtu*-list up to the **lu$_2$** = *šū* list:
5. You wrote them out but afterwards you neglected them.
6. Do you know the calculation of multiplication, reciprocals, accounts and volumes up to its hilt?
7–8. Let us recite the curricular material (pertaining to) the status of students! I know it better than you!

---

dib akk. *halālu* "to creep; slink; steal," see CAD H, 33–34 s.v. *halālu* A, but this option does not really fit the context. The variant has "slow of thought and understanding."

26 "Hands which cannot keep up with the mouth" can allude to the fact that a person cannot write quickly enough to follow the dictation of the teacher or that he is not able to write down his own words according to the right orthography, in which case it would be a euphemism for 'illiterate'.

27 Reconstructed text after Matuszak 2019: 13–14.

9. Come on! Just try to oppose me! I will put an end to your insults!”[28]

---

10. Scribe B: “You windbag,[29] deaf and dumb!”

Dumu e$_2$-dub-ba-a u$_4$-ul-la-am$_3$ in the first line is a standard incipit found in other texts, and it is used here as an invitation to debate:[30] Scribe A calls to Scribe B because he wishes to start a debate with him.

Also *Edubba’a D* begins *in media res*, with a student challenging his classmate on his scribal skills and knowledge (*Edubba’a D* 1–7):[31]

1. **lu$_2$-tur [dumu e$_2$-dub-ba-(a)-me-en dumu] ⸢e$_2$⸣-[dub-ba-me-en]**
2. **⸢tukum⸣-bi ⸢dumu e$_2$-dub-ba⸣-[(a-)me-en]**
3. **[eme]-gi$_7$ e-zu-⸢u$_3$⸣-a[m$_3$]**
4. **[eme-g]i$_7$-ta ⸢enim⸣ e-da-bala-e-en**
5. **[ze$_4$-e] ⸢al-tur-re⸣-en a-na-gen$_7$-nam / ⸢KA⸣-za enim ab-bala-e-en**
6. **niĝ$_2$ ka [u]m-mi-a-ĝa$_2$-ka 1 2 ĝeš ba-ni-tuku-am$_3$**
7. **⸢enim⸣-bi ga-mu-ra-ab-ge$_4$**

1. Student A: “Young boy, [are you a student?”] – (Student B:) [“I am a] stu[dent]”
2. A:”If you are a student,
3. do you know Sumerian?”
4. B:”I can speak Sumerian“
5. A:”You are young, how can you talk (properly) with your mouth?”
6. B:”I have repeatedly listened to the comments of my teacher.
7. With these words I will answer to you“

It is evident that in *Two Scribes* as well as in *Edubba’a D* that there is no concrete *casus litigandi* between the two opponents, but rather the wish to debate. I will come back on this point in § 4.

---

28 Johnson and Geller (2015: 102–103) understand l. 9 to be a single-line speech by Scribe B. This is questionable because five manuscripts present a double ruled line after this line but not after l. 8; see also Matuszak 2019: 5, 13.

29 **lu$_2$-tumu** is a recurring insult in the disputes, see Johnson and Geller 2015: 104–106.

30 These texts are *Graduate Student and Supervisor*, *Enkiheĝal and Enkitalu*, *Edubba’a E* and *Schooldays*. I understand **u$_4$ ul-la-am$_3$** as an expression indicating “the day is late = late in the day.” For the grammatical and semantic interpretation of this line see the discussion in Attinger (2002/2019 n. 1 ad l. 1): “Ecolier, dépêche-toi;” Volk (2015a: 110, 420): “zukünftiger Schulabsolvent;” Matuszak (2019: 12) “(He,) Schüler, es ist schon spät.” See also Koslova (2014: 317) “—Schüler! – immer (bereit)!” and Cavigneaux (2019) “—”Schüler!”, – “immer (zu Diensten)!”.”

31 Reconstructed text after Civil 1985: 69.

2.2 Some Features of the Disputes

As an example of the structure of disputes, I will discuss some passages from *Enkiheĝal und Enkitalu*. The core of the dispute consists of short tirades of insults, often ending with a rhetorical question that employs standard formulations, for example “and you would be a human being?,” “and you would be my opponent?,” or “do you really want to quarrel with me?”

Most of the speeches in *Enkiheĝal and Enkitalu* are only weakly related to each other: a speaker does not reply directly to all the insults directed at him by his opponent. Mostly he replies only to a portion of the insults, introduces some new arguments, and occasionally he comes back to the preceding offense in a successive speech. Consider the following example (*Enkiheĝal and Enkitalu* 82–99):[32]

81. **gu$_3$ de$_2$-de$_2$ zi$_2$-za nar-e-ne**
82. **bun$_2$ du$_{11}$-du$_{11}$ im šu-a nu-guru$_6$**
83. **mah-bi gu$_7$-gu$_7$ ša$_3$-gal-bi i$_3$-hul-lu**
84. **dim$_2$-ma sah$_4$ ĝalga hulu-dim$_2$-ma ma-ni-ib$_2$-gi$_4$-gi$_4$-in**

---

85. **uĝ$_3$-e ba-an-la$_2$ uĝ$_3$-e ba-an-la$_2$**
86. **šu dag-dag-ge e-sir$_2$-ra ni$_{10}$-ni$_{10}$**
87. **e$_2$ lu$_2$-ne-ka gu$_2$ gid$_2$-gid$_2$ e$_2$ a-ra$_2$-bi zu$^{!}$**
88. **lu$_2$ si-ga dumu lum-ma buluĝ$_3$-ĝa$_2$**
89. **enim gaba-ri-ka mu-da(-an)-gub-be$_2$-en**

---

90. **lu$_2$-tumu lu$_2$ lul-ta** DU.DU
91. **in tub$_2$-tub$_2$-bu niĝ$_2$ ni$_2$-ba nu-un-zu**
92. **lu$_2$ saĝ šal-la na-ĝa$_2$-ah lu$_2$ kara$_2$-ga**
93. **ĝe$_{26}$-e-gen$_7$ nam al-dim$_2$-me-en**

---

94. **^{ĝeš}za$_3$-mim an-da-ĝal$_2$ nam-nar nu-un-zu**
95. **a-ga-aš ge$_4$ ge$_4$-me-a-aš-e-ne**
96. **ad ša$_4$ za-pa-aĝ$_2$ nu-sa$_6$**
97. **eme-gi$_7$-še$_3$ al-dugud eme-ni si nu-ub-sa$_2$**
98. **en$_3$-du nu-un-da-di(silim?) ka ĝal$_2$ nu-un-taka$_4$**
99. **u$_3$ ze$_4$-e lu$_2$ til$_3$-le-me-en**

32 Reconstructed text from: ISET 1, 123 (Ni 9497) + TMH NF 3: 42 (HS 1606) obv. ii 25–26 + obv. ii 1′-15′ = 81–82; 85–99; UET 6/2: 152 rev. 6–14 = 81–89; SLTN 132 obv. 8′-11′ = 81–84; rev. 1–9 = 85–92; ISET 1, 148 (Ni 4384) obv i 16′-17′ = 81–82; UM 55–21–307 (Foto CDLI P257246) rev. i 12′-21′ = 81–89; N 4104+4115 (Foto CDLI P 278992) obv. i′ 7′-10′ = 81–84; ISET 2, 108 (Ni 4114+4139) rev. 1′-5′ = 95–99; ISET 1, 146 (Ni 4352) obv. 1′-2′ = 98–99; UET 6/3: 632 2′-15′ = 81–93; A 24192 obv. ii 34 – iii 5 = 81–99.

81. Student A: “Shouter, one with the scratchy voice among the singers![33] → **arg. 1**[34]
82. Blaring, who cannot hold a tablet in the hand!
83. Glutton, but the *available*[35] fodder is bad.
84. You reply to me with confused concepts and bad determinations.” → **arg. 2**

---

85. Student B: “He depends$^?$ on the people (around him), he depends$^?$ on the people (around him)![36]
86. Who potters about, sauntering in the street.
87. Who sticks his nose[37] into the House of the people and knows the occurrences of the house.
88. Weak one. Boy, who grew up in pains and labor.
89. Can you really keep up with me?”

---

90. A: “Windbag, who comes along deceptively.
91. Who always insults and does not understand things in their context- → **arg. 2**
92. Despised person, dolt and scorned man[38]
93. Are you created like me?”[39]

---

94. B: “A lyre is with him, but he does not know the musical art.
95. Backward one among the colleagues, → **arg. 2**
96. with a bad tremolo and a bad voice. → **arg. 1**
97. He is thick for the Sumerian language; his tongue is not adequate for it.[40] → **arg. 1**
98. He could not *successfully execute a complete* hymn;[41] he could not even open the mouth.
99. And you would be one who can cheer the people up?”

---

33 **zi$_2$-za nar-e-ne** is also attested in *Engardu the fool* a 3. For **nar zi$_2$-za** see Shehata 2009: 16–17 with n. 52 “krächzender/seufzender Sänger;” Matuszak 2019: 38–39 ad l. 125.

34 Here, and in the following examples, I highlight only related arguments (= arg.).

35 Literally “its fodder,” i.e. “the fodder for the meal.” Another possibility is that Student A uses {bi} to dehumanize his rival, suggesting that he eat fodder like an animal.

36 For **la$_2$** with the meaning “to depend (on something$_{\text{directive}}$)” see Attinger 2010/2015: n. 378 ad l. 176. Maybe also: “he is inferior$^?$ to the people (around him),” but compare *Edubba’a D* f 46 **a-da-min du$_{11}$-ga lu$_2$ lu$_2$-u$_3$ la-ba-ta-la$_2$-la$_2$-a** “a carried-out dispute where no one is inferior to the other,” where the verbal form contains the ablative prefix (see below note 55 for the manuscripts).

37 Literally: “the neck.”

38 For **saĝ šal** akk. *qullulu* “to despise; disdain” see Gadotti 2014: 299–300; Lämmerhirt 2010: 664 n. 117. For **na-ga-ah** akk. *nû’u* “dolt” see Johnson and Geller 2015: 264 “rude; uncivilized.” For **lu$_2$ kara$_2$-ga** akk. *ṭaplu* see Johnson and Geller 2015: 268, 278–279.

39 For the expression **x-gen$_7$ dim$_2$** “to be created like x” see Wilcke 2014: 546–547 n. 208.

40 **si nu-ub-sa$_2$** is also attested in *Two scribes* l. 53; I understand the verbal form as an intransitive form {eme+ani+e$_{\text{Dir.}}$ si+Ø nu+b+i+sa$_2$+Ø}, compare BIN 8: 173 rev. 2 **di$_2$-be$_6$ si ab-sa$_2$** “This trial has been straightened out,” see Jagersma 2010: 418 ex. 11b.

41 For **en$_3$-du** DI and for the possible reading **silim**, see Ludwig 1990: 220–21.

The speeches are only faintly related. For example, in the first tirade of insults (ll. 81–84), student A insinuates, among other things, that his rival has a bad voice (arg. 1), and he insults his intelligence (arg. 2). Student B replies to these arguments, not directly, but only in ll. 94–99, where he even tops Student A's insult: not only does he have a bad voice, he cannot even speak properly.

Sometimes the speaker repeats his rival's last sentence, as we can see in this passage from *Enkiheĝal and Enkitalu* (32–35):[42]

32. **a$_2$ [munus-ta-am$_3$] a$_2$ ninta$_2$-ta-am$_3$**
33. **ĝe$_{26}$-e-gen$_7$-nam dumu lu$_2$ nu-me-en**
34. **gub-ba diri-še$_3$ ni$_2$-zu na-ab-gur$_4$-re-en egir-zu nu-ĝal$_2$-la**
35. **a-na-am$_3$ egir-ĝu$_{10}$ nu-ĝal$_2$-la am$_3$-ma-ab-šid-de$_3$-en**

32. Scribe A: "Neither on the (female =) mother's side nor on the (male =) father's side
33. you are the son of a distinguished citizen like me!"
34. Scribe B: "Wait! You really should not overstate yourself. Your importance[43] does not exist! → **arg. 1**
35. A: "Why do you tell me, my importance does not exist?" → **arg. 1**

This feature can also be found in the dispute *Ĝirinisa und Enkimanšum*. In this composition, the speeches are more articulate than in *Enkiheĝal und Enkitalu*, and each speaker replies to his rival's insults. Consider, for example, *Ĝirinisa und Enkimanšum* a 21–33:[44]

a 21. **e$_2$ ba-e-de$_3$ ĝen-na e$_2$ nu-mu-e-da-ba-e-en**
a 22. **a-ša$_3$ si-ge$_4$-de$_3$ ĝen-na eše$_2$ gana ge 1 nindan nu-e-da-ha-za**
a 23. **^{ĝeš}gag-a ki nu-mu-e-da-du$_3$-e dim$_2$-ma nu-mu-e-da-an-ku$_4$**
a 24. **lu$_2$ du$_{14}$ mu$_2$-a-ba zi li-bi$_2$-ib$_2$-gi$_4$-gi$_4$-in**
a 25. **ses ses-da teš$_2$-bi bi$_2$-ib$_2$-dab$_5$-be$_2$-en**
a 26. **lu$_2$-tumu nu-ub-**DU[45] **dub-sar-e-ne**
a 27. **a-na-še$_3$-am$_3$ la-ba-ab-du$_7$ me-še$_3$ lu$_2$ he$_2$-en-tum$_2$-mu**

---

a 28. **a-na-aš niĝ$_2$ na-me-še$_3$ la-ba-ab-du$_7$-un**
a 29. **e$_2$ ba-e-de$_3$ ga-ĝen e$_2$ mu-da-ba-e-e[n]**

---

42 Reconstructed text from: TMH NF 3: 42 (HS 1606) obv. i 11′-15′ = 32–35; CBS 8126 (Foto CDLI P263032) obv. i′ 6′ – rev. i 3 = 32–35; A 24192 obv. i 31–33 = 33–35.
43 For **egir** "importance," see Attinger 2013/2019: n. 15 ad l. 16 and Volk 2000: 22 n. 110.
44 Reconstructed text from: UET 6/1: 150 obv. 21 – rev. 1 = a 21–33; CBS 13984 + N 2419 (Foto CDLI P268978) obv i 17′-22 = a 21–26; SLFN 60 (3N-T 916, 341) 1′-5′ = a 29–33; *AulOr.* 15, p. 35: 18 rev. 1′-8′ = a 21–28; YBC 4614 obv. 21 – rev. 1 = a 21–33; YBC 7198 obv. 1 – rev. 1 = a 22–33; 3N-T 312 obv. 20 – rev. 10 = a 21–33.
45 2×: DU; 1×: **du$_7$**; 1×: **du-un.**

a 30. **a-ša$_3$ si-ge-de$_3$ ga-ĝen ki eg$_2$ si-ge-bi mu-zu**
a 31. **lu$_2$ du$_{14}$ mu$_2$-a-ba ša$_3$-bi ab-huĝ$_2$-e zi [b]i$_2$-ib$_2$-gi$_4$-gi$_4$-in**
a 32. **ses ses-da teš$_2$-bi bi$_2$-ib$_2$-du$_{10}$-ge ša$_3$ m[u-d]a-sed$_4$-de$_3$-en**
a 33. **ze$_4$-e gu$_2$-zal du[b]-sar-[e-n]e ki-še$_3$ dumu lu$_2$-u$_3$-ne**

a 21. Enkimanšum: "Having gone to divide a house, you are not able to divide the house. → **arg. 1**
a 22. Having gone to *mark* a field,[46] you are not able to hold the measuring rope and the 1-nindan-rod in the hand → **arg. 2**
a 23. You cannot determine a spot with the peg; you have no idea of this. → **arg. 2**
a 24. You cannot pacify the people who started a quarrel, → **arg. 3**
a 25. (but) you let brothers fight each other. → **arg. 4**
a 26. Windbag, never-do-well among the scribes! → **arg. 5**
a 27. You are not skilled at anything (→ **arg. 6**), where should you lead the people?"

---

a 28. Ĝirinisa: Why should I not be skilled at anything? → **arg. 6**
a 29. Do I want to go to divide a house? I can divide the house. → **arg. 1**
a 30. Do I want to go to *mark* a field? I know how to *mark* the ground → **arg. 2**
and the canals. → **arg. 2a**
a 31. I can appease the heart of quarrelling people, I can pacify them. → **arg. 3**
a 32. I let the brothers reconcile each other → **arg. 4**
and I can soothe the Hearts → **arg. 4a**
a 33. You, paltry one among the scribes (→ **arg. 5**), lowermost of the people.[47] → **arg. 5a**

Ĝirinisa replies to almost every insult leveled at him by Enkimanšum. He emphasizes that he can do anything (arg. 6): he can divide a house (arg. 1), mark a field (arg. 2), pacify quarreling people (arg. 3), and reconcile brothers (arg. 4). He even adds a new argument, pointing out that he has skills over and above those that his rival tried to deny him: he can mark canals (arg. 2a). In the same way that Enkimanšum did, Ĝirinisa in turn denigrates his rival, comparing him unfavorably to other scribes (arg. 5). Moreover, Ĝirinisa exceeds Enkimanšum's accusation with a new one, by saying that Enkimanšum is the lowermost not only of the scribes, but of all people (arg. 5a).

---

46 For **a-ša$_3$ si$_3$.g** "to mark out a field" see Friberg 2000: 152–52; Volk 1996: 190 n. 74 "ein Feld eintiefen; ein Feld abteilen"; Johnson and Geller 2015: 99 "to delimit shares of fields; to measure a field."
47 Literally: "son of the men."

2.3 The Outcome

Each of the four school disputes has a different outcome. The only one in which the teacher confirms the superiority of a speaker is *Enkimanšum and Ĝirinisa*. We read the master's words to Enkimanšum (*Enkimanšum and Ĝirinisa* d 13 – 16):[48]

d 13. **a-na-aš-am$_3$ lu$_2$ ses-gal-zu al-me-a**
d 14. **u$_3$ nam-dub-sar-ra-ka diri-zu-uš an-zu-a**
d 15. **a-na-aš-am$_3$ ka-tar-re-a-bi in-ne-du$_{11}$**
d 16. **saĝ im-ta-DU aš$_2$ in-ne-sar in in-ne-tub$_2$**

d 13 – 16 Why did you brag to the one who is your 'Big Brother' and knows the scribal art better than you? Why did you revile, slander and insult him?

In *Enkiheĝal und Enkitalu* nothing is said about the superiority or inferiority of any of the students. In these compositions, the teachers and the overseers intervene to pacify the quarreling students because their disputes had escalated to an intolerable level. We read in *Enkiheĝal und Enkitalu* 218 – 220:[49]

218. **a-na-gen$_7$-nam ki umum-ma du$_{14}$**[50] **i-ni-in-ĝar-re-ze$_2$-en**
219. **al-zil$_2$-zil$_2$-le du$_{14}$ ba-e-AK-ze$_2$-en**
220. **min-am$_3$ enim ia$_2$-am$_3$ u$_3$-na-du$_{11}$ zi gi$_4$-ba-an-ze$_2$-en**

218. How could you$^!$ begin a quarrel in the 'Place of Wisdom'?[51]
219. It's good, you had a quarrel,[52]
220. (but) after I have told to each of you two some words, then calm down!

In *Enkimanšum and Ĝirinisa*, as well as in *Enkiheĝal and Enkitalu*, the dispute has unpleasant consequences: the master and overseer prohibit the students

48 Reconstructed text from: TMH NF 3: 42 (HS 1606) rev. vii 7 – 9 = d 13 – 16; CBS 13984 + N 2419 (Foto CDLI P268978) rev. ii 7′-10′ = d 13 – 16; UET 6/1: 151 obv. 9 – 13 = d 13 – 16; PBS 1/2: 96 (CBS 14045) obv. 10 – 13 = d 13 – 16; ISET 2, 94 (Ni 4160) rev. 4′-6′ = d 13 – 16.

49 Reconstructed text from: SEM 73 obv. 13 = 218; SEM 72 rev.$^!$ 7 – 12 = 218 – 220; N 1771+ N 7399 (Foto CDLI P276891) rev. ii′ 9′ = 218; UM 55 – 21 – 377 (Foto CDLI P257268) rev. 11 = 218; UET 6/2: 154 obv. 12 – rev. 14 = 218 – 219.

50 UET 6/2: 154 obv. 12: **du$_{14}$**; UM 55 – 21 – 377 rev. 11: ⌜**du$_{14}$**⌝; SEM 72 rev.$^!$ 7: LU$_2$.

51 According to UET 6/2: 154 and UM 55 – 21 – 377 but note the /n/ before the base in both manuscripts, which I cannot explain (the 2. pl. of the prefix-conjugation is {e+B+enzen}).

52 That is to say, "ok, you had a dispute, but now stop it."

from carrying out such disputes in the future. We read in *Enkimanšum and Ĝiri-nisa* (d 25–27):[53]

d 25. **u$_4$-da-ta ĝeš igi-ne bi$_2$-hur**
d 26. **lu$_2$-lu$_2$ sikil-du$_3$-a-bi na-an-AK-e**
d 27. **ses ses-da nam-mu-da-ne$_2$-e ka-silim nam-mu-e**

d 25. For the future I have made rules (for the eyes =) to observe.
d 26. Nobody should offend someone else.
d 27. A brother should not speak to a brother in that way, he should not boast himself!

In the dispute *Two Scribes*, there is nobody who judges the quarreling students. At the end of his speech, one of the scribes tells his rival he should not fight. (*Two Scribes* 142):[54]

142. **gub-ba lu$_2$-tumu ga-ba-al he$_2$-mu-e-du$_3$ nam-du$_3$-du$_3$-e-en**

Stop, you idiot! You have fought, but you really should not.

The end of *Edubba'a D* is quite difficult and not well-preserved. The last line is surprising. We read:

f 46. **a-da-min du$_{11}$-ga lu$_2$ lu$_2$-u$_3$ la-ba-ta-la$_2$-la$_2$-a**[55]

A carried-out dispute where no one is inferior to the other.

To the best of my knowledge this is the only Sumerian dispute that ends in a tie.

3 The Functions of School Disputes and School Dialogues

Schoolmasters used the literary form of the dialogue to compose texts that were conceived to improve the Sumerian speaking skills of their pupils. However, the Edubba'a was not just a place of scribal training but also a place for a more general education. Volk (2000) has clearly shown that the schoolmasters intended to

53 Reconstructed text from: TMH NF 3, 42 (HS 1606) rev. vii 18–20 = d 25–27; SLFN 60 (3N-T 904, 170) rev. 7′ = d 25; CBS 13984 + N 2419 (Foto CDLI P268978) rev. ii 19′ = d 25; UET 6/1: 151 rev. 21–23 = d 25–27; PBS 1/2: 96 rev. 2–4 = d 25–27.
54 Reconstructed text after Matuszak 2019: 21.
55 Reconstructed text from: CBS 13872 (Foto CDLI P268887) rev. 22′; CBS 2201 + N 3075 + N 3129 (Foto CDLI P259256) rev. 13′.

teach specific moral values and the right behavior for a human being as well. Among these values we find: to not avoid the assigned work, to strive, to not boast about oneself, to be modest and reliable, to not be lazy, to not fiddle around, to not instigate fights between people but to be able to conciliate them. In *Graduate Student and Supervisor* the correct conduct for a student was expressed by the supervisor, who wants the student to act exactly as he did when he himself was a student (*Graduate Student and Supervisor* 3–8):[56]

3. **za-e-gen$_7$-nam nam-lu$_2$-tur i$_3$-ak ses-gal i$_3$-tuku-am$_3$**
4. **um-mi-a lu$_2$-ta kiĝ$_2$-ĝa$_2$-am$_3$ a$_2$ aĝ$_2$-ĝa$_2$ ĝeš bi$_2$-in-ĝar**
5. **ge al-gu$_4$-ud-da-gen$_7$ i$_3$-gu$_4$-ud-de$_3$-en kiĝ$_2$-ĝa$_2$ bi$_2$-in-si$_3$-ge-en**
6. **enim um-mi-a-ĝu$_{10}$ nu(-un)-taka$_4$ niĝ$_2$ ni$_2$-ĝa$_2$ li-bi$_2$**-AK

3. Like you, I was once young and had a 'Big Brother'.
4. The teacher gave[57] tasks and instructions to each one.
5. Like a springing reed, I sprang around; he put me to work.
6. I did not neglect the teacher's words (told to) me;[58] I did not do anything on my own initiative.

There is also a negative way to point out how a student is supposed to behave: the stigmatization of negative behavior demonstrates that the right to conduct oneself is exactly its opposite; for example, we read in *Enkiheĝal and Enkitalu* 105–107 the following insults:[59]

105. **e$_2$ buru$_3$-buru$_3$ lu$_2$ iri^{ki}-a zi-ir šub-bu**
106. **e$_2$-e šu ša-an-ša lu$_2$ niĝ$_2$ šu ti-a**

56 Reconstructed text after ETCSL 5.1.3.

57 For **ĝeš ĝar** "to give, assign (a task, a work)," see *Sumerian Proverbs* 3.89 **ugula a$_2$ ĝeš ĝar-ra nu-zu** "if an overseer does not know the assigned work"; 11.25 **ugula a$_2$ ĝeš$^?$ ĝa$_2$-ĝa$_2$$^!$ nu-zu$^!$** "if an overseer does not know how to assign a work."

58 I follow here the manuscripts without {n} before the verbal base (**nu-taka$_4$:** TMH NF 3: 38 obv. 6; CBS 15105 [Foto CDLI P269662] obv. 2). **nu-un-taka$_4$:** maybe causative "he (the overseer) let me not neglect the teacher's words (told to) me." Volk (2015b: 111) translates as a causative "Er sorgte dafür, daß ich die mir zuteil gewordenen Worte des Meisters nicht vernachlässigte." However, one would expect a directive 1. sg (**nu-mu-un-taka$_4$**).

59 Reconstructed text from: TMH NF 3 42 (HS 1606) obv. ii 21′-22′ = 105–106; ISET 2 97 (Ni 4056) + ISET 2 108 (Ni 4114+4139) rev. 11′-12′ = 105–106; ISET 1 146 (Ni 4352) obv. 8′-9′ = 105–106; UM 55–21–307 (Foto CDLI P257246) rev. ii 2′-3′ = 105–106; N 4104+4115 (Foto CDLI P278992) obv. ii′ 2′-3′ = 105–106; N 1049+3370 (Foto CDLI P276195) obv. 12′-13′ = 105–106; A 24192 obv. iii 11–12 = 105–106.

105. (You are) one who perforates a house, who makes trouble in the city,
106. who avidly reaches out for the house,[60] one who has snatched things away.

This implies finally that the student being addressed is a thief. The positive moral value is, of course, the opposite of this negative behavior: a good student (like every good citizen) should not steal. In another passage, the stigmatization of excessive alcohol consumption and bad manners shows that a good student (like each true human being) should be moderate and decent (*Enkiheĝal and Enkitalu* 116–118):[61]

116. **kaš un-naĝ eme-sig al-gu$_7$-gu$_7$**
117. **inda$_3$ un-gu$_7$ si sa$_2$-bi nu-ub-be$_2$**

116. After he had drunk beer, he speaks harassingly
117. After he had eaten bread, he cannot speak properly

4 Conclusion: the Context of School Disputes

The didactic function of the disputes goes beyond learning the Sumerian language by heart. We have some hints that *Enkiheĝal and Enkitalu* and *Two Scribes* were staged. Numerous verbal forms, as well as the possessive suffix of the third person, can be easily explained if the speaker is addressing an audience. For example, we read in *Enkiheĝal and Enkitalu:*

112. **a$_2$-ni ĝal$_2$ u$_3$-bi$_2$-in-taka$_4$ ser$_3$ gid$_2$-da nu-ub-be$_2$**[62]
After he opened his arms he sings no sergida-song!

114. **e-lil$_2$-la$_2$ šu-ni-še$_3$ la-ba-ab-du$_7$ / lu$_2$ nu-mu-un(/e)-da-hul$_2$-e**[63]
The *elila*-song is not suitable for his hands; none rejoices over him (/you).

---

60 For **šu ša-an-ša$_{(4)}$-ša$_{(4)}$** see Attinger 2019: n. 350 ad l. 371 "assaillir avec les main = tendre fébrilement, avidement les mains, saisir avidemment."
61 Reconstructed text from: TMH NF 3 42 (HS 1606) obv. ii 32′-33′ = 116–117; ISET 2108 (Ni 4241) rev. 8′ = 116; ISET 1 148 (Ni 4384) obv. ii′ 9′-10′ = 116–117; ISET 2 (Ni 9907) obv. 2′-3′ = 116–117; UM 55–21–307 (Foto CDLI P257246) rev. ii 13′-14′ =116–117; CBS 10397 (Foto CDLI P265614) obv. 3′-4′ = 116–117; A 24192 obv. iii 22–23 = 116–117; UET 6/3: 634:6′-7′ = 116–117.
62 Reconstructed text from: TMH NF 3 42 (HS 1606) obv. ii 28′; ISET 2 97 (Ni 4056) + ISET 2 108 (Ni 4114+4139) + ISET 2 108 (Ni 4241) rev. 17′+6′+5′; ISET 1 148 (Ni 4384) obv. ii′ 5′; UM 55–21–307 (Foto CDLI P257246) rev. ii 9′; N 4104+4115 (Foto CDLI P278992) obv. ii′ 9′; N 1049+3370 (Foto CDLI P276195) rev. 7; A 24192 obv. iii 18; UET 6/3: 634:2′.
63 Reconstructed text from: TMH NF 3 42 (HS 1606) obv. ii 30′; ISET 2 108 (Ni 4114+4139) + ISET 2 108 (Ni 4241) rev. 7′ + 6′; ISET 1 148 (Ni 4384) obv. ii′ 7′; UM 55–21–307 (Foto CDLI P257246) rev.

The verbal forms in the second person plural reinforce this assumption. For example:[64]

> 74. **niĝ$_2$ na-me ba-an-tum$_3$ igi he$_2$-na-bar-re-en-ze$_2$-en**[65]
> He takes everything for himself; you (2. pl.) have seen him.
>
> 108. **niĝ$_2$-gurud-da ab-zi-zi-i igi he$_2$-en-ne-bar-re-en-ze$_2$-en**[66]
> He will pick up what is fallen; you (2. pl.) have seen him.

School disputes are modelled on real disputes between students or, more generally, young boys; they have a framework that consists of onset (– *casus litigandi*) – dispute – conclusion (– consequences), which the teacher filled with pedagogical content. The *casus litigandi* resembles events which are still common in schools today: the insult to and accusation of a student in front of others (as in *Enkiheĝal and Enkitalu*) or the claim to be the best student (as in *Enkimanšum and Ĝirinisa*). The conclusions to these disputes also resemble everyday life in a school. It is not surprising that a supervisor or a teacher is called to reconcile quarreling students. *Enkiheĝal and Enkitalu* and *Ĝirinisa and Enkimanšum* demonstrate that the masters would not tolerate quarrels and disputes if they escalated and involved a challenge to the established hierarchy within the Edubba'a. On the other hand, the other disputes suggest that they were carried out as a form of contest, without a specific *casus litigandi* but simply with the wish to debate and to demonstrate their ready wit. An especially positive attitude to debate is quite evident in the opening line of *Two Scribes* and *Edubba'a D*. The beginning of the *Dispute between two Women B* also shows this attitude. Woman A wishes to start a dispute with Woman B, and she is disappointed by Woman B's refusal (*Dispute between two Women B* 1–3):[67]

---

ii 11′; N 4104+4115 (Foto CDLI P278992) obv. ii′ 11′; A 24192 obv. iii 20; CBS 10397 (Foto CDLI P265614) obv. 1′; UET 6/3: 634:4′.

64 For more examples see Ceccarelli 2018: 134 note 9 and 10.

65 Reconstructed text from: ISET 1 123 (Ni 9497) obv. ii 18; ISET 2 97 (Ni 4056) + N_{D2} ISET 2 108 (Ni 4114+4139) obv. 7′+9′; SLTN 132 obv. 1′; ISET 1 148 (Ni 4384) i′ 9′; UM 55–21–307 (Foto CDLI P257246) rev. i 5′; A 24192 obv. ii 27.

66 Reconstructed text from: TMH NF 3 42 (HS 1606) obv. ii 24′; ISET 2 97 (Ni 4056) + ISET 2 108 (Ni 4114+4139) + ISET 2 108 (Ni 4241) rev. 14′+3′+2′; ISET 1 148 (Ni 4384) obv. ii′ 1′; UM 55–21–307 (Foto CDLI P257246) rev. ii 5′; N 4104+4115 (Foto CDLI P278992) obv. ii′ 5′; N 1049+3370 (Foto CDLI P276195) rev. 3; CBS 15004 (Foto CDLI P269583):1′-2′; A 24192 obv. iii 14.

67 Reconstructed text from the edition of Jana Matuszak (2017), who kindly shared her manuscript with me.

1. **me-ta-am$_3$ am$_3$-di-di-in**
2. **ga-ba-al nam-mu-du$_3$-en a$_2$-zu na-ma-tur**
3. **ta(-a)-aš ga-ba-al nu-e-du$_3$-e-en ta-am$_3$ i-ri-**AK

1. Woman A: "Where are you coming from?"
2. Woman B: "You should not debate with me, your ready wit is insufficient for me!"
3. A: "Why should I not debate with you? What did I do to you?"

Two Scribes and *Edubba'a D*, which contain no particular *casus litigandi*, support the possibility that debate contests were performed in the school. In other words, they could have emulated real debate contests among students.[68] The teacher may have used such debate contests to not only improve the students' Sumerian speaking skills but also to stimulate each student's ambition to surpass his classmates and be the best pupil in the class. An analogy can be found in the first book of Quintlian's *Institutio oratoria*. Quintilian reports on debate contests between students which were performed every 30 days and were judged by the teacher (*Institutio oratoria* 1.2.23–25).

I suggest the following context for the school disputes: on one side the students did not just copy these compositions over and over again to learn them by heart, it is also quite probable, that they performed the disputes in front of an audience; on the other side it is possible that they carried out debates without following a script, but simply improvising, similar to modern debate competitions in which numerous debate teams at almost every university take part.

Bibliography

ETCSL = Electronic Text Corpus of Sumerian Literature (etcsl.orinst.ox.ac.uk)
CAD = A. L. Oppenheim/E. Reiner et al. (ed.), The Assyrian Dictionary of the University of Chicago. Chicago 1956 ff.
CDLI = Cuneiform Digital Library Initiative (cdli.ucla.edu)

Attinger, Pascal. 2002/2019. Edubba'a A (5.1.1). Online translation. DOI: 10.5281/zenodo.2599583 (last accessed November 2019).
Attinger, Pascal. 2010/2015. La houe et l'araire (5.3.1). Online translation. DOI: 10.5281/zenodo.2600239 (last accessed November 2019).
Attinger, Pascal. 2013/2019. ANL 9: Nabi-Enlil-Anum-pīšu (3.3.18). Online translation. DOI: 10.5281/zenodo.2585818 (last accessed November 2019).

68 If these disputes are actually written records of original debates, something comparable – *mutatis mutandi* – to the medieval *questiones disputatae*, cannot be proved. For the didactic value of the *questiones disputatae*, which, however, were not redacted in dialogue form and concerned more serious themes than the Sumerian school dispute, see Lawn 1993.

Attinger, Pascal. 2019. La lamentation sur Ur (2.2.2). Online translation. DOI: 10.5281/zenodo.2599623 (last accessed November 2019).

Cardelle de Hartmann, Carmen. 2007. *Lateinische Dialoge, 1200–1400. Literaturhistorische Studie und Repertorium.* Mittellateinische Studien und Texte 37. Leiden/Boston: Brill.

Cavigneaux, Antoine. 2019. dumu é-dub-ba-a! – u_4-ul-la-àm.... *Nouvelles Assyriologiques Brèves et Utilitaires* 2019/59: 102.

Ceccarelli, Manuel. 2018. Der Umgang mit streitenden Schülern in dem Edubba'a nach den sumerischen *Schulstreitgesprächen Enkiḫeĝal und Enkitalu* und *Ĝirinisa und Enkimanšum. Altorientalische Forschungen* 45: 133–155.

Civil, Miguel. 1976. 'Lexicography'. Pp. 123–157 in *Sumerological Studies in Honor of Thorkild Jacobsen on his Seventieth Birthday, June 7, 1974*, ed. Stephen J. Lieberman. Assyriological Studies 20. Chicago: The University of Chicago Press.

Civil, Miguel. 1985. Sur les "livres d'ecolier" a l'epoque paleo-babylonienne. Pp. 67–78 in *Miscellanea babylonica: Melanges offerts a Maurice Birot*, ed. Jean-Marie Durand and Jean-Robert Kupper. Paris: Éditions Recherche sur les civilisations.

Civil, Miguel. 1992. Education (Mesopotamia). Pp. 301–305 in *The Anchor Bible Dictionary* 2, ed. David Noel Freedman. New York: Doubleday.

Cunningham, Graham. 2007. A catalogue of Sumerian literature (based on Miguel Civil's catalogue of Sumerian literature). Pp. 351–412 in *Analysing Literary Sumerian. Corpus-Based Approaches*, ed. Jarle Ebeling and Graham Cunningham, London/Oakville: Equinox.

Delnero, Paul. 2010a. Sumerian Literary Catalogues and the Scribal Curriculum. *Zeitschrift für Assyriologie und Vorderasiatische Archäologie* 100: 32–55.

Delnero, Paul. 2010b. Sumerian Extract Tablets and Scribal Education. *Journal of Cuneiform Studies* 62: 53–69.

Friberg, Jöran. 2010. Mathematics at Ur in the Old Babylonian Period. *Revue d'Assyriologie et d'archéologie orientale* 94: 97–188.

Gadotti, Alhena. 2014. *'Gilgamesh, Enkidu and the Netherworld' and the Sumerian Gilgamesh Cycle.* Untersuchungen zur Assyriologie und Vorderasiatischen Archäologie 10. Berlin: De Gruyter.

Gadotti, Alhena and Alexandra Kleinerman. 2017. The rules of the School. *Journal of the American Oriental Society* 137: 89–116.

George, Andrew R. 2005. In Search of the e_2.dub.ba.a: the Ancient Mesopotamian School in Literature and Reality. Pp. 127–137 in *An Experienced Scribe Who Neglects Nothing: Ancient Near Eastern Studies in Honor of Jacob Klein*, ed. Yitshak Sefati et al. Bethesda: CDL-press.

Johnson, J. Cale and Mark J. Geller. 2015. *The Class Reunion – An Annotated Translation and Commentary on the Sumerian Dialogue Two Scribes.* Cuneiform Monographs 47. Leiden/Boston: Brill.

Klein, Jacob and Yitshak Sefati. 2014. The "Star (of) Heaven" and Cuneiform Writing. Pp. 85–102 in *He Has Opened Nisaba's House of Learning. Studies in Honor of Åke Waldemar Sjöberg on the Occasion of His 89th Birthday on August 1st 2013*, ed. Leonhard Sassmannshausen. Cuneiform Monographs 46. Leiden/Boston: Brill.

Koslova, Natalia. 2014. Zu den Anfangszeilen einiger Edubba'a-Kompositionen. Pp. 305–326 in *Studies in Sumerian Language and Literature. Festschrift für Joachim Krecher*, ed. Natalia Koslova et al. Babel und Bibel 8. Winona Lake: Eisenbrauns.

Kramarczyk, Andrea and Oliver Humberg (eds.) 2013. *Paulus Niavis. Spätmittelalterliche Schülerdialoge (lateinisch und deutsch). Drei Chemnitzer Dialogsammlungen mit Einführungen zur Person des Autors, zu seinen Schülerdialogen und zu den Möglichkeiten ihres Einsatzes im Unterricht heute.* Chemnitz: Kunstsammlung Chemnitz – Schloßbergmuseum.

Lämmerhirt, Kai. 2010. *Wahrheit und Trug. Untersuchungen zur altorientalischen Begriffsgeschichte.* Alter Orient und Altes Testament 348. Münster: Ugarit-Verlag.

Lawn, Brian. 1993. *The Rise and Decline of the Scholastic 'Quaestio Disputata': with Special Emphasis on its Use in the Teaching of Medicine and Science, Education and Society in the Middle Ages and Renaissance.* Leiden/Boston: Brill.

Ludwig, Marie-Christine. 1990. *Untersuchungen zu den Hymnen des Išme-Dagan von Isin.* Santag 3. Wiesbaden: Harrassowitz.

Matuszak, Jana. 2017. "Und du, du bist eine Frau?!" Untersuchungen zu sumerischen literarischen Frauenstreitgesprächen nebst einer *editio princeps* von *Zwei Frauen B.* Dissertation Universität Tübingen (unpubliziert).

Matuszak, Jana. 2019. Es streite, wer kann! Ein neuer Rekonstruktions- und Interpretationsversuch für das sumerische Schulstreitgespräch ‚Dialog 1'. *Zeitschrift für Assyriologie und Vorderasiatische Archäologie* 109: 1–47.

Michalowski, Piotr. 2010. Learning Music: Schooling, Apprenticeship, and Gender in Early Mesopomia. Pp. 199–239 in *Musiker und Tradierung: Studien zur Rolle von Musikern bei der Verschriftlichung und Tradierung von literarischen Werken*, ed. Regine Pruzsinszky and Dahlia Shehata. Wiener offene Orientalistik. Vienna: Lit Verlag.

Mittermayer, Catherine. 2009. *Enmerkara und der Herr von Arata. Ein ungleicher Wettstreit.* Orbis Biblicus et Orientalis 239. Fribourg/Göttingen: Acad. Press Fribourg/Vandenhoeck & Ruprecht.

Mittermayer, Catherine. 2019. *‚Was sprach der eine zum anderen?' Argumentationsformen in den sumerischen Rangstreitgesprächen.* Untersuchungen zur Assyriologien und Vorderasiatische Archäologie 15. Berlin: De Gruyter.

Ohgama, Naoko and Eleanor Robson. 2010. Scribal Schooling in Old Babylonian Kish: The Evidence of the Oxford Tablets. Pp.217–246 in *Your Praise is Sweet: A Memorial Volume for Jeremy Black from Students, Colleagues, and Friends*, ed. Heather D. Baker et al. London: British Institute for the Study of Iraq.

Peterson, Jeremiah. 2011. *Sumerian Literary Fragments in the University Museum, Philadelphia.* Biblioteca del Proximo Oriente Antiguo 9. Madrid: Consejo Superior de Investigaciones Científicas.

Peterson, Jeremiah. 2015. An Archive of Simple Ledgers Featuring the é um-mi-a(k), "House of the Master," at Old Babylonian Nippur: The Daily Rosters of a Scribal School? *Aula Orientalis* 33: 79–114.

Quintilianus, Marcus Fabus. [3]2006. *Institutionis Oratoriae Libri XII. Erster Teil: Buch I–VI*, ed. H. Rahn. Darmstadt: WBG-Verlag.

Robson, Eleanor. 2001. The Tablet House: A Scribal School in Old Babylonian Nippur. *Revue d'Assyriologie et d'archéologie orientale* 95: 39–66.

Römer, Willem H. Ph. 1990. Aus dem Schulstreitgespräch zwischen Enkimansum und Girine'isa. Pp. 91–98 in *Weisheit, Mythen, Epen. Weisheitstexte* I, ed. Otto Kaiser. Texte aus der Umwelt des Alten Testaments III/I. Gütersloh: Gütersloher Verlagshaus.

Rubio, Gonzalo. 2009. Sumerian Literature. Pp. 11–75, 446–462 in *From an Antique Land: An Introduction to Ancient Near Eastern Literature*, ed. Carl S. Ehrlich. New York: Rowman & Littlefield.
Rubio, Gonzalo. 2016. The inventions of Sumerian: Literature and the Artifacts of Identity. Pp. 231–257 in *Problems of Canonicity and Identity Formation in Ancient Egypt and Mesopotamia*, ed. Kim Ryholt and Gojko Barjamovic. Copenhagen: Museum Tusculanum Press.
Shehata, Dahlia. 2009. *Musiker und ihr vokales Repertoire. Untersuchungen zu Inhalt und Organisation von Musikerberufen und Liedgattungen in altbabylonischer Zeit.* Göttinger Beiträge zum Alten Orient 3. Göttingen: Universitätsverlag.
Sjöberg, Åke. 1973. Der Vater und sein missratener Sohn. *Journal of Cuneiform Studies* 25: 105–169.
Sjöberg, Åke. 1975. Der Examentext A. *Zeitschrift für Assyriologie und Vorderasiatische Archäologie* 64: 137–176.
Sjöberg, Åke. 1976. The Old Babylonian Eduba. Pp. 159–179 in *Sumerological Studies in Honor of Thorkild Jacobsen on his Seventieth Birthday, June 7, 1974*, ed. Stephen J. Lieberman. Assyriological Studies 20. Chicago: The University of Chicago Press.
Tinney, Steve. 1999. On the Curricular Setting of Sumerian Literature. *Iraq* 61: 159–162.
Tinney, Steve. 2011. Tablets of Schools and Scholars: A Portrait of the Old Babylonian Corpus. Pp. 577–596 in *The Oxford Handbook of Cuneiform Culture*, ed. Karen Radner and Eleanor Robson. Oxford: Oxford University Press.
Vanstiphout, Herman L. J. 1997a. The Dialogue between two Scribes. Pp. 589–590 in *The Context of Scripture. Canonical Compositions from the Biblical World*, ed. William Hallo. Leiden/Boston: Brill.
Vanstiphout, Herman L. J. 1997b. The Dialogue between a Supervisor and a Scribe, Pp. 590–592 in *The Context of Scripture. Canonical Compositions from the Biblical World*, ed. William Hallo. Leiden/Boston: Brill.
Vanstiphout, Herman L. J. 2004. Eduba. Amsterdam: SUN.
Veldhuis, Niek. 1997: *Elementary Education at Nippur.* Groningen: Rijksuniversiteit Groningen.
Veldhuis, Niek. 2000. Sumerian Proverbs in Their Curricular Context. *Journal of the American Oriental Society* 120: 383–99.
Volk, Konrad. 1996. Methoden altmesopotamischer Erziehung nach Quellen der altbabylonischen Zeit. *Saeculum* 47: 178–216.
Volk, Konrad. 2000. Edubba'a und Edubba'a-Literatur: Rätsel und Lösungen. *Zeitschrift für Assyriologie und Vorderasiatische Archäologie* 90: 1–30.
Volk, Konrad. 2011. Über Bildung und Ausbildung in Babylonien am Anfang des 2. Jahrtausends v. Chr. *Orientalia Nova Series* 80: 269–299.
Volk, Konrad. 2011–13. Streitgespräch. Pp. 214–22 in *Reallexikon der Assyriologie und Vorderasiatischen Archäologie* 13, ed. Michael P. Streck. Berlin: De Gruyter.
Volk, Konrad. 2015a. Aus dem Leben eines Schülers der altbabylonischen Zeit. Pp. 101–107 in *Erzählungen aus dem Land Sumer*, ed. Konrad Volk. Wiesbaden: Harrassowitz.
Volk, Konrad. 2015b. Der Dialog zwischen Schulaufseher und Schulabsolvent. Pp. 109–116 in *Erzählungen aus dem Land Sumer*, ed. Konrad Volk. Wiesbaden: Harrassowitz.
Waetzoldt, Hartmut. 1989. Der Schreiber als Lehrer in Mesopotamien. Pp. 33–50 in *Schreiber, Magister, Lehrer. Zur Geschichte und Funktion eines Berufsstandes*, ed.

Johann Georg Prinz von Hohenzollern and Max Liedtke. Bad Heilbrunn: Verlag Julius Klinkhardt.

Waetzoldt, Hartmut and Antoine Cavigneaux. 2009. Schule. Pp. 294–309 in *Reallexikon der Assyriologie und Vorderasiatischen Archäologie* 13, ed. Michael P. Streck. Berlin: De Gruyter.

Wilcke, Claus. 2002. Konflikte und ihre Bewältigung in Elternhaus und Schule im Alten Orient. Pp. 10–31 in *Schau auf die Kleinen … Das Kind in Religion, Kirche und Gesellschaft*, ed. Rüdiger Lux. Leipzig: Evangelische Verlagsanstalt.

Wilcke, Claus. 2014. Gesetze in sumerischer Sprache. Pp. 455–633 in *Studies in Sumerian Language and Literature. Festschrift für Joachim Krecher*, ed. Natalia Koslova et al. Babel und Bibel 8. Winona Lake: Eisenbrauns.

Wilson, Mark. 2008. *Education in the Earliest Schools: Cuneiform Manuscripts in the Cotsen Collection*. Los Angeles: Cotsen Occasional Press.

Jana Matuszak*

4 "She was dumbstruck and took it to heart"

Form and Function of Insults in Sumerian Literary Disputations between Women

Ever since the pioneering efforts by Miguel Civil, disputations between women have been established as a small but distinct sub-category of Sumerian literary debates.[1] While they were naturally perceived to resemble the disputations between male students (or future Edubba'a graduates) more than the ones between non-human protagonists, the disputations between women were generally regarded as inferior in structure, content, and style. Bendt Alster (1990: 8), for instance, arrived at the conclusion that a specific disputation between women, which forms the main focus of the present paper, had a comparatively unsophisticated structure and was "just [...] a model composition in which all possible insults are collected, without any specific reference to the actual speaker," while Herman Vanstiphout (1993: 322–23) regarded all of what he called "essays and dialogues" as inferior to the precedence disputations: "It seems that the essays and dialogues are fairly unformed pieces, [... while] the Dispute Poems [...] are generally well-composed."

On the basis of these dismissive assessments, the present paper seeks to prove that, in fact, the disputations between women are highly complex literary compositions too, and not just a random collection of insults. In order to do so, I will first briefly introduce the best-preserved Sumerian disputation between women, a composition known by the modern titles *Two Women B* or *Dialogue*

* SOAS, University of London.

1 Within the scope of the present paper, I will use the term 'Sumerian literary disputations' to refer to a select number of compositions. For the precedence disputations, I follow the definition of Mittermayer (2019: 13), who lists 8 /adamin/. By 'disputations between male students' I mean *Dialogues 1–3*. While *Dialogue 1* has been edited recently by Johnson and Geller (2015), editions of *Dialogues 2* and *3* are currently being prepared by M. Ceccarelli (cf., however, the partial edition of *Dialogue 3* by Römer 1988). To date, the only known disputations between women are *Two Women B* or *Dialogue 5* (henceforth *2WB*) and "*Two Women A*" or *Dialogue 4* (henceforth "*2WA*"). A comprehensive edition of *2WB* can be found in Matuszak (forthcoming) and a text reconstruction and score transliteration of "*2WA*" as well as copies of unpublished manuscripts of "*2WA*" in the appendix to Matuszak (2017). The title has been put in inverted commas, as it is unclear how many individual compositions are among the fragments assembled under the umbrella term "*2WA*."

https://doi.org/10.1515/9781501510274-004

5 (henceforth *2WB*), and then present the results of an in-depth study of the form and function of the insults employed in this text. This will then allow me to address broader questions concerning the nature of the disputation and its didactic motives, and close with some deliberations on its ancient 'Sitz im Leben.'

1 Content and Structure of *Two Women B*

2WB bears the typical tripartite structure of disputations. 1) Beginning with an opening scene, in which one of the two contestants provokes her rival and thus initiates the debate, 2) the main part consists of alternating speeches, in which the two women hurl insults and reproaches against one another; each trying to prove that the other is not a 'good woman,' or more precisely, not a 'good (house)wife.' The housewife is indeed presented as *the* female profession par excellence, in parallelism to the scribe as the only profession befitting a man.[2] The disputation breaks off rather abruptly after a fatal accusation has been uttered by one of the contestants, and 3) the final part, in which the quarrel is settled, takes place at court. Indeed, we find here the longest and most detailed literary account of a lawsuit known in Sumerian literature – which alone could falsify assertions of an unsophisticated plot structure.

But who are the two contestants, and why does the quarrel get so terribly out of hand that a jury and a judge need to be consulted?

2 The Two Contestants, or: Sumerian "Rules for Ritual Insults"

It is true that, unlike some of the Sumerian precedence disputations, the two rivals are not properly introduced at the beginning. Only one of them is identified by the Sumerian name Ninkuzu (Emesal: Gašankuzu) towards the end of the text (l. 173); her rival remains anonymous throughout the entire composition. I will refer to her as Mrs. A – A for Anonymous, but also because she is the first speaker.[3]

2 For a more detailed discussion, see Matuszak 2016: 250 f.

3 The fact that only one of the two contestants is named is unusual, since in other Sumerian disputations between two human peers either both are identified by name (as in *Dialogue 2* [Enkita and Enkiheĝal] and *Dialogue 3* [Enkimanšum and Ĝirini'isa]) or both remain anonymous (as in *Dialogue 1* and all known fragments of "*2WA*"). While it cannot be excluded entirely that Mrs.

Despite the lack of an introduction, however, one can still glean enough information to get a general idea of their personalities and physical characteristics, both from their behavior towards one another, and from certain telling accusations in the main part of the dispute. Thus, we learn that both women are married,[4] and both women belong to the same social class.[5] However, Mrs. A is portrayed as a self-confident, assertive and authoritative person, who not only initiates the debate, but also dominates the disputation, and even ends the text with her final speech. Ninkuzu, on the contrary, is in a defensive position from the very beginning. Her attempt at averting the quarrel fails, and she has to argue her case as best she can. Despite the fact that her professional and rhetorical skills are inferior to those of her rival, she displays utmost contempt towards Mrs. A. This obvious imbalance between the two contestants is, however, typical for Sumerian literary disputations. Catherine Mittermayer (2019: 26 ff. *et passim*) has convincingly demonstrated that Sumerian precedence disputations both anticipate and support the winner throughout the text, and use different techniques in doing so. The same can be observed in *2WB:* While nobody, neither the ancient nor the modern audience, could or can be surprised by the fact that Mrs. A is ultimately going to triumph, the entertaining – and instructive – factor

A's name is lost in a lacuna, the protocol of the lawsuit only necessitates the identification of the defendant (Ninkuzu), not the plaintiff (Mrs. A).

4 Contra Alster (1990: 8 n. 18), who assumed that one contestant is married and the other is not. Mrs. A mentions Ninkuzu's husband in l. 42 (**dam-a-ni in-**TAR "she keeps her husband short [or: she puts her husband to flight]"), l. 51 (**dam-zu tu$_9$ nu-um-mu$_4$** "your husband has no clothes to wear") and indirectly in l. 99, where she calls Mrs. A "spouse of a slave" (**dam e-re-da**), while Ninkuzu denigrates Mrs. A and her husband in l. 140 (**mu-ud-na arkab^{mušen}-a** "husband of a bat"). Moreover, the court case revolving around Ninkuzu's slander of Mrs. A, which had resulted in Mrs. A being repudiated by her husband, leaves no doubt about her marital status. Mrs. A's prosecution speech finally offers further evidence of both contestants being married: she points out their equal social status by stating: **dam-ĝu$_{10}$ dam-a-ni-gen$_7$** "My husband (is) like her husband" (ll. 159 // 167).

5 The women are designated as "neighbors" (**ušur**; ll. 206, 220) and as "social peers" (**dumu lu$_2$-tab-ba**; ll. 180, 196), but it is not entirely clear to which class they belonged. The corresponding Akkadian term *mārti awīlim* found in the bilingual manuscript **X$_6$** (IM 13348 [TIM 9, 6]) rev. 8 (= *2WB* 180) seems to be a misinterpretation of the Sumerian line (**dumu lu$_2$-tab-ba** has been broken up into **dumu lu$_2$** = *mārti awīlim* "daughter of a free citizen" and **tab-ba** = *tappātiki* "your equal"), and thus offers no conclusive evidence that the women belong to the class of free citizens (*awīlū*). The sum of the divorce payment stated in l. 189, 1/3 mina of silver, corresponds to the sum prescribed for a *muškēnum* in § 140 of Hammurapi's law code. However, in practice the sum varied considerably (cf., e.g., Westbrook 1988: 23, 78 and CAD U–W 371 s.v. *uzubbû*), which again does not allow for a definite conclusion about the two women's social status.

lies in discovering *how* she prevails over her rival.[6] This is directly linked to questions of content, style, and function of the insults exchanged during the debate.

In order to understand the relationship between the two adversaries better, and to comprehend why the quarrel gets out of hand, it is necessary to take a closer look at the content of their mutual insults and reproaches. It needs to be established if there are any insults that provide information about the two protagonists relevant to the progression of the dispute, or insults that directly influence the course of events. For this, a hermeneutic tool is needed to distinguish the "telling" accusations from those which fulfill other functions within the text, and William Labov's (1972: 297–353) differentiation between "ritual" and "personal" insults proved useful in this context. In his study of "Rules for Ritual Insults" in Black English vernacular, he observed that in verbal contests, "ritual," i.e. "non-personal," insults are generally grossly exaggerated and thus discernibly untrue, wherefore the addressee need not reply, deny or defend him- or herself against the allegation. If he or she does take the insult personally and reacts correspondingly, it normally amounts to an admission of guilt – as if there were some truth in the insult.

In the case of *2WB*, this can explain why most of the insults exchanged in the main part are never commented upon, but simply ignored. At the same time, the "ritual" insults are also among the funniest, since the absurdity of the exaggeration is likely to arouse laughter and applause by the audience. Consider, for instance, l. 51 f.: "Your husband has no clothes to wear, you yourself are wearing rags: your butt sticks out from them!"[7] Surely, Ninkuzu's husband was not walking about completely naked, and who knows if Ninkuzu's bottom was really visible through her clothes, but readers or listeners – then as now – probably gleefully exulted in the idea. Another malicious exaggeration is found in l. 98, and again it is Mrs. A speaking: "The lower millstone is her husband, the upper millstone is her child."[8] While the metaphor reflects the proportions of the big lower millstone and the small upper grinding stone, it alleges that Ninkuzu is all but married to her slave work, and has no time for a real family. This stands in obvious contradiction to the quips mentioning Ninkuzu's husband, but

6 It must be conceded, however, that due to several lacunae in the final part of the text it remains unclear if she wins in all respects. Note that part of the preliminary verdict against Ninkuzu (ll. 188–96) is later contested by an unknown party (ll. 205 // 209) and that the payment of the divorce money imposed on Ninkuzu (l. 189 f.) might imply the divorce was not or could not be annulled, whence the monetary compensation for Mrs. A. In any case, it is apparent despite the lacunae that the verdict does not mark the end of the lawsuit.

7 *2WB* 51 f.: **dam-zu tu$_9$ nu-um-mu$_4$ ze$_4$-e ^{tu9}aĝ$_2$-dara$_2$ mu$_4$-mu$_4$ / gu-du-zu am$_3$-ta-la$_2$.**

8 *2WB* 98: **^{NA4}kinkin dam-a-ni(-im) ^{NA4}šu-šu$_2$ du$_5$-mu-ni(-im).**

the power of the image, denigrating Ninkuzu to the rank of a slave, apparently was deemed more important than the veracity of the assertion. The remark certainly hurt, but Ninkuzu did not feel compelled to reply. She could feel safe in the knowledge that she had a husband, and that the audience – thanks to other insults that presuppose her being married – knew that too.

“Personal” insults, on the contrary, whether they were intended or perceived as such,[9] provoke reactions in the addressee. The most obvious example of an insult that was probably intended, but certainly perceived as a “personal” insult is the allegation of adultery in Ninkuzu’s final speech to Mrs. A.[10] She calls her a “whore” and a “liar, who’s in constant pursuit of men,” which is why the young men in the neighborhood get no rest at night. The disputation breaks off abruptly after this speech, and the text sets in again with Mrs. A trying to clear her reputation and seeking satisfaction at court. She describes how Ninkuzu slandered her as a “whore,” which reached the ears of her – Mrs. A’s – husband, who consequently divorced her. Apparently, several people interpreted the insults not as exaggerated, untrue, “ritual” insults, but as “personal” ones, which gave rise to fatal rumors. Therefore, Mrs. A wants to defend herself, and since a divorce is a legal issue, she has to convince the authorities of her innocence. This also implies that Ninkuzu, if found guilty of slander, has to face the consequences.

Two aspects are of interest in this context.

(1) First, one needs to understand what drove Ninkuzu to utter the fatal accusation. The key to this question seems to lie in her last speech, as it contains a curious and seemingly ridiculously exaggerated insult that might be the key to the conflict between the two women. Ninkuzu calls Mrs. A a “mother giving birth on a daily basis” (see above n. 10). This seems to be a direct reply to an insult Mrs. A had uttered in her previous speech, where she had mocked Ninkuzu as infertile: “(Too) small vulva, (but) very long pubic hair! Swollen genitals; person (with) a blocked, sick uterus!”[11] Interestingly, there is another instance

9 Cf. Kochman’s (1975: 115) critique of Labov (1972: 297–353), who points out the fluid boundaries between “ritual” and “personal” insults and emphasizes the crucial importance of the addressee’s interpretation of an insult, which determines his or her reaction.

10 *2WB* 152–56: **kar-ke$_4$ eš$_2$-dam-ma še-en lul mu-du$_{11}$-*š*.-du$_{11}$-*š*. dam tuku dam taka$_4$ / lu$_2$-tu-mu ga-ab-us$_2$ mu-tin-e-ne / galla$_4$^{la}-bi-še$_3$ e$_{11}$-da ama gan u$_4$-šu$_2$-⸢uš⸣-[(...)]-a / u[r] šu ziga egir mu-lu-ne-k[a (x)] / m[u-r]u-uš tur dag-ge$_4$-a til$_3$-la u$_3$ n[u-mu-u]n-ši-ku-ku** “The whore was constantly *disseminating* lies in the tavern (which also included facilities for prostitution). (Whenever) she’s married, she’s (quickly) divorced (again). / Liar, in (constant) pursuit of men. / It is this vulva which is being mounted – mother giving birth on a daily basis! / Dog raising (its) paw, (constantly) *pursuing* men. / The young men who live in the city quarter cannot sleep because of her.”

11 *2WB* 148: **galla$_4$^{la} tur siki galla$_4$^{la} gid$_2$-gid$_2$ / pe-zi$_2$-ir** HAR **lu$_2$ ša$_3$ la$_2$ pa$_4$-hal-la.**

where accusations of adultery promptly elicit allegations of infertility: In l. 47, Ninkuzu had said to Mrs. A: “Now (look!) You crept in through the window to (meet) men!,” to which Mrs. A had replied directly: “(Her ever so) pure womb is finished: (it means) loss for her house.”[12]

Throughout the text, it is always Mrs. A who mocks Ninkuzu as infertile and always Ninkuzu who accuses Mrs. A of adultery, and never the other way around. Despite the fact that some of the accusations sound very exaggerated and could thus be interpreted as “ritual” insults if taken out of context, the protagonists’ reactions show that they took them personally, and these reactions subsequently determine the course of events. While attempts at denial or aggressive “personal” counter-attacks are normally an admission of guilt, this – conspicuously – does not seem to be the case with Mrs. A. In the construed scenario of a literary composition, which was *supposed* to end in a court case for didactic reasons, Ninkuzu was apparently already so clearly marked as the ‘bad woman’ that nobody doubted Mrs. A’s innocence. Conversely, the audience was (and is) likely to believe that Ninkuzu, whom Mrs. A kept accusing of failing at every aspect of womanhood, was also infertile, and thus not a good wife. This unequal treatment of the two protagonists thus constitutes one of many examples for the text’s favoritism towards the winner.

In any case, Ninkuzu’s jealousy of her fertile rival seems to lie at the heart of the slander. We are hence dealing with an initially playful verbal contest about who’s the better wife, which slowly turns into a serious relationship conflict based on long-standing personal grudges.[13] The text, far from being a random collection of insults, thus provides us with psychological explanations of the protagonists’ behavior and displays a logical progression of events unfolding on the basis of the two women’s feelings towards one another.

(2) The second aspect of interest is how the two adversaries argue their case at court. Mrs. A states in her prosecution speech that Ninkuzu and she quarreled (ll. 161–62 // 169–71), but implies that Ninkuzu went too far when she called her

12 *2WB* 47 (Ninkuzu): **u$_4$-da-am$_3$ lu$_2$ ab-ba ba-an-ku$_4$-re-en.** *2WB* 48 (Mrs. A): **ša$_3$ ku$_3$ til i-bi$_2$-za e$_2$-a-na.**

13 The introductory part of the text seems to allude to a certain conflict-laden pre-history. While Mrs. A seems to be greatly annoyed by Ninkuzu’s arrival (possibly at Mrs. A’s own house), which surfaces in her irritable initiatory question “Where are you coming from again?!” (*2WB* 1: **me-ta-am$_3$ am$_3$-di-di-in**), Ninkuzu states a few lines later: “You have *used violence* (before), (but) I have paid you back. (Still,) I cannot sleep because of you” (*2WB* 4: **a$_2$ mu-e-a-**AK **šu-bi na-ri-ge$_4$ u$_3$ ba-ra-ra-ku-ku-un**).

a whore, since this caused her – Mrs. A's – husband to demand a divorce.[14] In other words, she appeals to the rule that in a verbal contest one should consciously exaggerate insults to mark them as "ritual" or "non-personal," and thus prevent fatal misunderstandings and an escalation of conflict. As a matter of fact, she had announced her strategy of uttering false, i.e. "ritual," accusations already in the initiation of the debate: "From now on I will make use of my falseness."[15]

Ninkuzu in her defense (ll. 182–85) also stresses that they had a mutual fight, but points out that Mrs. A – unlike herself – took the insults personally: "She spoke to me: I didn't take it to heart. I spoke to her: she was dumbstruck (and) took it to heart."[16] She thus tries to downplay the slander and put the blame on Mrs. A for not knowing how to comport herself in a disputation. Interestingly, the judge does not seem to take Ninkuzu's attempt at self-defense into consideration at all – possibly another instance of favoritism towards the ultimate winner, Mrs. A.[17] Since Ninkuzu did not deny the slander as such, the judge accepts it as a fact that she called Mrs. A a whore – regardless of context. Now his only duty is to find out if Mrs. A is innocent of adultery or not, and if the divorce should consequently be annulled or compensated. This suggests that the unwritten "rule of ritual insults" to which Ninkuzu appeals, namely the one that says one should not react to insults, is not valid at court. Mrs. A's strategy hence has been wiser, since she had indirectly appealed to the universal rule that one should not slander a person in any given context: neither in a verbal contest by means of "personal insults," nor in real life. Ninkuzu's rule, however, is no longer applicable, because the insult has long left the confines of the verbal contest and entered real life, where it has assumed a new dimension. By taking the matter to court, Mrs. A has both ended the disputation and assured that the issue will be settled by higher authorities. Therefore, the rule that the one who speaks

---

14 *2WB* 161–62 // 169–71: **me e-ne-gen$_7$ in mu-un-tub$_2$ / kar-ke$_4$ ma-an-du$_{11}$ (/) dam mu-un-taka$_4$** "We mutually insulted each other. (But) she called me a 'whore' (and thus) caused me to leave (my) husband."
It is interesting to observe that she expressly states that she herself left her husband, although in reality she was repudiated by him. The logic behind this curious phrasing seems to be grounded in the fact that it was Mrs. A's alleged adultery that prompted the divorce, making her the (unintentional) initiator.

15 *2WB* 6: **a-da-lam na-aĝ$_2$-lu$_2$-tu-mu-ĝu$_{10}$ al-ĝa$_2$-ĝa$_2$-ĝa$_2$-an.**

16 *2WB* 182–85: **u$_3$-mu-un-ĝu$_{10}$ ĝe$_{26}$-e e-ne-bi du$_{14}$ i$_3$-**AK**-en-de$_3$-en / in in-gen$_7$ in-tub$_2$-tub$_2$-bu-(un-)de$_3$-en / e-ne ma-an-du$_{11}$ ša$_3$-še$_3$ nu-gid$_2$ / ĝe$_{26}$-e in-na-du$_{11}$ zu$_2$ ba-an-keše$_2$ ša$_3$-še$_3$ ba-an-gid$_2$** "My lord! Me and her, we had a fight. We exchanged insult with insult. She spoke to me: I didn't take it to heart. I spoke to her: she was dumbstruck (and) took it to heart."

17 See, however, the remarks in n. 6.

the last speech wins the disputation does not apply to *2WB* – precisely because the dispute is not finished yet, but is continued in a different setting. Rather than losing the verbal contest, as one might have assumed by Mrs. A's silence after Ninkuzu's last speech, Mrs. A proceeds to win it on a higher level.

To sum up the first part of this study, I would like to distinguish the different functions of insults in *2WB*.

(1) First, we have seen that certain insults were intended or perceived as "personal insults." They determine the course of action, and provide information about the protagonists.

(2) Related to them are allusions to the lawsuit and the outcome of the quarrel, which have been inserted for the information of the audience at various places in the introduction and the main part of the text.[18]

(3) By contrast, the majority of insults and reproaches in the main part of the text aim at indirectly defining an ideal wife. These fall roughly within the category of "ritual insults," and will be studied in the second part of the paper.

3 Form and Function of Insults in *Two Women B*

Before studying the form and function of the insults in the main part of the text, I would like to take one step back and look at the overall structure of *2WB* again, where one thing immediately becomes apparent. Although the entire text consists of nothing but direct speech, and contains no narrative passages whatsoever, the three parts of the text outlined in section 1 form three distinct units, both stylistically and with respect to content. This is also reflected on the layout of the tablets.

The first fifteen lines of the introductory part consist of a series of quick provocations and rebuffs, aimed at initiating the dispute. In sometimes quite long and complex assertions and questions, the two women threaten and provoke each other, and twice – for the information of the audience – allude to the outcome of the dispute. Apart from possible asides to the audience,[19] the

---

18 For constraints of time, they have not been studied here. For an example, see the next footnote.

19 Cf. *2WB* 7–8: **tukum-bi na-aĝ$_2$-lu$_2$-tu-mu-zu ni$_2$ ba-e-ĝ[a$_2$-ĝ]a$_2$-ĝa$_2$-an / ze$_4$-e-me-en e$_2$-a(-) na(-)te-ĝe$_{26}$-en [n]a-aĝ$_2$-lu$_2$-tu-mu-ĝu$_{10}$ [x]**-NE **al-la$_2$-e** "If you yourself (want to) make use of your falseness, you'll be the one who won't be allowed to approach (your) house – (*but*) *she will charge me with mendacity.*" Ninkuzu obviously alludes to the repudiation of Mrs. A by her husband and the ensuing lawsuit, in which Mrs. A accuses Ninkuzu of slander. The change from direct address in the 2nd singular to the 3rd person singular could indicate that the second part of the prediction (here in italics) was intended as an aside to the audience.

heated dialogue seems to go its natural course, and Mrs. A succeeds in drawing Ninkuzu into a quarrel. Once it becomes clear that Ninkuzu must submit to her rival's desire to fight, they transition to the main part, or the disputation proper, which is set off from the introductory scene by means of double rulings.

The main part of the text differs considerably from both the introduction and the conclusion. Each of the two contestants gets ten speeches of varying length, and they are again marked by double rulings. The study of the more regulated, or – if you will – ritualized disputation will comprise most of the remainder of the present paper.

In the final part, both longer speeches and shorter exchanges of words follow the protocol of a court case. However, it still resembles the introduction with its natural dialogues and longer, more complex sentences, and thus stands in contrast to the main part. As in the introduction, double rulings marking the different speakers are largely missing due to the natural flow of the discourse. Information about the identity of the speakers can be derived from appellations[20] and the use or non-use of Emesal, a special socio- or genderlect of Sumerian, which in non-cultic literary compositions was restricted to female speakers.[21]

As indicated above, the remainder of the paper will focus on the disputation proper in the main part of the text – the most striking feature of which, perhaps unexpectedly, is the lack of any characteristics of a dialogue. Instead, we find a multitude of impersonal expressions, mainly in the form of non-finite verbal forms and nominal phrases. If we do come across 'complete' sentences, they are mostly descriptions of the opponent phrased in the 3rd person singular – and not, as would be customary in a dialogue, direct addresses to the opponent in the 2nd. The designation of the disputations between women as "dialogues,"

---

20 The judge is addressed as "my lord" (**u_3-mu-un-ĝu_{10}** by female speakers in ll. 165 and 182; **lugal-ĝu_{10}** // *bēlī* by male speakers such as the herald in l. 176). The herald is called by his professional title **niĝir** // *nāgir* in ll. 174 and 197. Ninkuzu is being addressed with her full name and patronymic in l. 207 (**^{I}[ni]n-ku_3-zu ⸢dumu-munus lugal-nir⸣-ĝal_2**). Finally, one of the two women ironically addresses her rival as "my dear neighbor" (**ušur kal-la-ĝu_{10}**) in l. 220.

21 The use of Emesal in Dumuzi's speech in *Dumuzi-Innana H* 15 – 18, where he is instructing Innana about the "lies of women" (**lul-la munus-e-ne**), actually proves rather than contradicts this point, as he provides Innana with a ready-made excuse for her mother, using Emesal forms. The fact that Dumuzi knows Emesal and speaks it openly has important ramifications for a possible performance of *2WB*, as it shows that it was not taboo for men to speak Emesal or play the part of women (suggestion by P. Attinger; see also section 4). For *Dumuzi-Innana H* see Sefati 1998: 185 – 93 and Attinger 2010/2015.

which is even found in the most recent overviews,[22] is therefore misleading and should be reconsidered.

Consider, for example, Mrs. A's first speech (ll. 16–22):

uru$_2$ niĝen$_2$ kar niĝen$_2$ e$_2$-e$_2$-a ku$_4$-ku$_4$
e$_2$ in-ku$_4$-ra šu bi$_2$-in-si
e$_2$-ba e-ne-eĝ$_3$ bi$_2$-in-tuku
dam dam-da im-da-an-kur$_2$
du$_5$-mu ama-da im-da-ri
e$_2$-ge$_4$-a da ušbur-ra-na-ka du$_{14}$-da mu-ni-in-ku$_4$
im-me(-a)-e$_{11}$-de$_3$-en

Roaming the city, roaming the harbor, entering all houses!
Of the house *she* entered *she* took charge;
In this house *she* took over command.
Spouse *she* alienated from spouse;
The children *she* snatched from (their) mothers.
The daughter-in-law *she* made enter into conflict with her mother-in-law.
For that reason (alone) you are already *defeated!*

While she sets the scene by means of general, non-finite phrases, she then describes the wrongdoings of her rival in a series of quick, succinct assertions, which display an inherent logical progression. From "all houses" the focus zooms in onto one specific house, at the center of which stands the married couple – mentioned in the center of the speech, l. 19. The focus then widens again and finally encompasses the in-laws, who assume their position at the periphery of the core family. The only direct address to Ninkuzu is found in the final line of the speech, in which Mrs. A presents herself as self-confident about her ultimate triumph before Ninkuzu has even uttered a word.

Mrs. A maintains this general structure of 1) general statement employing non-finite verbal forms, 2) concrete accusations in the form of complete, descriptive sentences, and 3) a concluding direct address to the rival even in shorter speeches, such as her third (ll. 40–43):

tu$_7$ gu$_7$ ^{ĝeš}ĝušur BIL$_2$ **u$_5$ gu$_7$ ka tal$_2$**
ame$_2$ nu-mu-un-ge-en e$_2$ a-ra$_2$-še$_3$ nu-mu-ĝar

22 See, for instance, Rubio 2009: 58 and Volk 2012: 220 f. § 10.1. Both designations ultimately go back to the terminology employed in M. Civil's *Catalogue of Sumerian Literature*, a revised version of which can be found in Cunningham (2007). "*2WA*" likewise contains mainly impersonal expressions and descriptions in the 3rd person singular, but an in-depth analysis needs to await the comprehensive edition of the individual text segments.

dam-a-ni in-TAR **gu-ne$_2$ gu tab-ba li-bi$_2$-in-tuku**
ta(-a)-aš ša$_3$-zu al-kur$_4$

Devouring soup, burning (entire) timber beams, wasting oil, opening the mouth wide!
She hasn't administered the women's quarters reliably. *She* hasn't run the household properly.
She kept *her* husband short; *she* only let him have clothes of bad quality.[23]
Why are you (then) so arrogant?!

and her fifth (ll. 61–65):

a si a lu$_3$-lu$_3$(-a) zi$_3$ ar$_3$-ar$_3$-ar$_3$-ar$_3$-ra
in-us$_2$ in-tur-tur in-ar$_3$-ar$_3$-...[24]
i-ni-in-du$_8$ i-ni-in-bil$_2$-bil$_2$
aĝ$_2$ šu du$_{11}$-ga-ni a-ra$_2$-še$_3$ nu-mu-un-ĝar
ma-ni-ib$_2$-gi$_4$-gi$_4$(-gi$_4$)-in

Drawing water, muddying water! Grinding flour non-stop!
She pounded (the grain), *she* shredded it, *she* ground it.
She wanted to bake (bread), (but) *she* burned it completely.
She hasn't ever done anything properly.[25]
(Can) you answer me anything at all to that?

While the third speech contrasts Ninkuzu's greediness with the stinginess she shows her husband, the fifth speech sneers at her incompetence. Her frequent failures are aptly expressed through reduplicated verbal bases (**lu$_3$-lu$_3$, tur-tur, ar$_3$-ar$_3$, bil$_2$-bil$_2$**), lending additional weight to the allegations – they are the Sumerian equivalent of exaggerated modern reproaches containing adverbs such as "always," "constantly," etc. The quadruplication of the verbal base "to grind" (**ar$_3$-ar$_3$-ar$_3$-ar$_3$-ra**), however, not only highlights the repetitive, strenuous task, but also has onomatopoeic qualities, and was surely employed for comic effect.

By contrast, the speeches of Ninkuzu are stylistically far less coherent. She freely mixes complete and truncated sentences, and some of her speeches even consist of nothing but non-finite verbal forms and nominal phrases without copula.

Compare, for instance, her first speech (ll. 23–28), where the use of phrases and complete sentences seems comparatively unsystematic, although she undeniably employs several interesting metaphoric expressions for alleging theft.

---

23 Literally: She did not let his thread have a double thread.
24 Cf. X$_4$ (MS 3228) rev. 7: **mu-na-ar$_3$-ar$_3$-ar$_3$-ar$_3$-ra.**
25 Literally: She has not put the thing she touched on its (right) path.

mu-zuh e$_2$-a-na ur ^{ĝeš}SUG-da-na
še-en-ka$_6$ ^{ge}bešeĝ-a-na šu-HA-da ba-an-du$_8$
mu-KEŠ$_2$ du$_9$-du$_9$ šu urin-(n)a an-su$_3$-a
e$_2$-kišeb-ba du$_8$-du$_8$ e$_2$-a saĝ-e mu-te-te
^{ĝeš}kun$_4$ ^{ĝeš}bala-gen$_7$ e$_2$-a ga-ga-ga
u$_4$-da-am$_3$ su ba-e-sis

Robber of *her* own house! Dog of *her* own trough!
Mongoose of *her* own basket – *she* has heaped up the (catch) of the fisherman (in it)![26]
Rocking the ..., (her) hand has been besmirched with blood.
Opening the storehouse; *she* repeatedly approached the slaves in the house.
Always bringing the ladder instead of the spindle into the house.[27]
Now you are vexed by this![28]

Ninkuzu's seventh speech (ll. 103–109), by contrast, contains next to no complete verbal clauses. The use of short phrases in quick progression documents an increasing loss of self-composure. The use of two enclitic demonstratives (**ka-bi** "*this* mouth" in l. 105; **gar$_3$-bi** "*this* slave hairstyle" in l. 108) moreover suggests that she accompanied her rant with wild pointing gestures.

She rages at her rival as follows:

ni$_2$-su-ub mu-lu e$_{11}$-⌜de$_3$ al$^{?}$⌝-e$_{11}$-de$_3$ bala-bala
ka kur$_2$ igi bala lu$_2$ aĝ$_2$-erim$_2$-ma
in tub$_2$-tub$_2$-bu e-ne-eĝ$_3$ ka-bi šub-ba
ga-ab-du$_{11}$ ga-ba-gaz šaha$_2$ mu-ge ur-gi$_7$ lu$_2$ tar-tar-re
ka sun$_7$-na bala-bala al-IGI.IGI du$_5$-mu lu$_2$ nu-zu
gar$_3$-bi e-ne-eĝ$_3$ ba-ab-be$_2$
in tub$_2$-tub$_2$-bu-ĝu$_{10}$-gen$_7$-nam ba-de-eĝ$_3$-en

Lunatic, completely crazy imbecile, turning everything topsy-turvy!
Mouth changer, eye roller, person of evil!
Insulter! The word in *this* mouth is 'discarded.'
Informant, murderer, pig from a canebrake! Dog putting people to flight!
Uttering arrogant words, she is restless; a bastard child!
This slave hairstyle is being addressed.
(Can) you invent something like my insults?!

26 Since mongooses are portrayed as hungry and greedy in Sumerian literature (compare, e.g., the Sumerian proverbs SP 1.9, SP 8 sect. B 36, and SP 10.12 in Alster 1997), the idea could be that she ate the contents of her basket and then filled it up with the fisherman's catch, which again would imply theft.

27 This line seems to contrast the expected care for the family by means of textile work (symbolized by the spindle) with the actual robbery of her own household (symbolized by the ladder, with which she can access things beyond her reach). Alternatively, the ladder could have been used to climb to the roof of the house in order to rest and hide from work.

28 Literally: Now (your) flesh is bitter because of it.

Ninkuzu’s tendency to get carried away, and her incapability of composing her speeches as coherently as her rival, however, also becomes apparent in her fifth speech (ll. 66–73), which – on the surface – looks less intemperate than her seventh. However, it is the only speech that consists exclusively of complete sentences, and it is the only speech in which the audience is being addressed throughout, as Ninkuzu forgets that she should turn to her rival and speak to her directly in the concluding line.

ki-še-er nu-tuku na-aĝ$_2$-munus-e la-ba-DI**(sa$_2$)/du$_7$**
siki nu-mu-un-da-peš$_6$-e ^{ĝeš}bala nu-mu-un-da-nu-nu
kiĝ$_2$-e šu nu-mu-un-da-sa$_2$ ku$_4$-ku$_4$ e$_3$-de$_3$ (a-)ab-la$_2$
e-sir$_2$-ra u$_3$-ba-gub in al-tub$_2$-tub$_2$-bu
ka-tar-ra un-bala ĝiri$_3$ KU …
pu-uh$_2$-ru-um-še$_3$ an/un-us$_2$ mu-un-zi$_2$-id-e-ne
u$_3$-um-gur teš$_2$ nu-tuku ⸢di ku$_5$-ru$^{?}$⸣-me-en zu$_2$ al-bar$_7$-re
in-na-am$_3$ mu-un-tub$_2$-tub$_2$-be$_2$-en

She knows no limit; *she* is not fit for womanhood.[29]
She cannot comb wool, *she* cannot operate a spindle.
Her hand can’t keep up with *her* work: (the minute she’s) entered, (she’s already) leaving. (The result) is of poor quality.
Whenever *she’s* standing on the street, *she* insults.
Whenever *she* has inversed praise, […].
Whenever *she* has turned to the assembly, they will beat her.
Whenever *she* has contested the verdict,[30] *she* (says) shamelessly: “I’m the one who renders the verdict,” (and) laughs.
This is the insult I utter about her.

Since the second part of the speech alludes to Mrs. A’s improper behavior at court, it possibly informs the audience about events yet to come.[31] Incidentally, most allusions to the outcome of the quarrel are phrased as complete sentences, and all of them are describing the actions of the rival to a third party. One reason for this might be that they fall into the category of ‘concrete accusations,’ which are generally expressed in full sentences. Indeed, there is a certain pattern according to which non-finite verbal forms and nominal phrases on the one

29 Thus N_{14}, N_{21} and U_3 (**du$_7$**). K_1, N_8 and X_4 write **sa$_2$:** “she has not (yet) reached womanhood.”
30 Literally: when she returns.
31 Since the final part of the text contains several lacunae, this is, however, not entirely clear and no correspondences between reproaches and actual events described in the final part can be identified with certainty. Considering that it is the ‘loser’ Ninkuzu speaking, some of the apparent predictions could also be wrong (for instance, in l. 191 the judge orders Ninkuzu to be flogged and not Mrs. A).

hand and complete sentences with finite verbal forms on the other are being used, clearly showing that content determines style.

Non-finite verbal forms and nominal phrases are suitable for:
permanent conditions, such as:

- character traits
  e.g. *2WB* l. 58: **aĝ$_2$-kur$_2$ du$_{11}$-du$_{11}$ ka lul-la bala-bala** "constantly uttering hostilities, always telling lies"; **hulu de-ĝa$_2$ nu-ga nu-nus-e-ne** "evil one, unworthiest of women"
- physical characteristics
  e.g. 2WB l. 139: **saĝ-du kur$_4$ siki šal** "square head (but) thin hair"
- status in society
  e.g. *2WB* l. 45: **lu$_2$ kiĝ$_2$-ša$_4$ (a-)AK ... mu uku$_2$-re-ne** "lowly worker, ... offspring of paupers"

as well as

- repeated actions
  often expressed by means of multiple verbal bases: e.g. *2WB* l. 61: **zi$_3$ ar$_3$-ar$_3$-ar$_3$-ar$_3$-ra** "grinding flour non-stop"

Finite verbal forms are suitable for:

- concrete accusations
  e.g. *2WB* l. 67: **siki nu-mu-un-da-peš$_6$-e ^{ĝeš}bala nu-mu-un-da-NU-NU** "She cannot pluck wool, she cannot operate a spindle."
- descriptions of a logical sequence of actions
  e.g. *2WB* ll. 62–63: **in-us$_2$ in-tur-tur in-ar$_3$-ar$_3$-... / i-ni-in-du$_8$ i-ni-in-bil$_2$-bil$_2$** "She pounded (the grain), she shredded it, she ground it. / She wanted to bake (bread), (but) she burned it completely."

4 Conclusion

Comparing the composition of Mrs. A's deliberate and well-structured speeches with Ninkuzu's less coherent and more intemperate ones, one can arrive at a set of rules governing form and style of *2WB:*

(1) Accusations and insults should generally be phrased as descriptions of the rival in the 3rd person singular and thus only indirectly be addressed to her.

The insults and reproaches are aimed at both informing the audience and influencing their opinion on the respective opponent negatively. At the same time, the indirect mode of communication between the two contestants hardly allows for direct replies or attempts at defending oneself against accusations and slander, since the affected person only *overheard* what her rival told the audience. However, with the comparatively rare, but nevertheless systematic direct addresses to the rival, the contestants do acknowledge each other's presence, and thus *want* their opponents to overhear their scathing remarks.[32] In the case of *2WB*, the only way of winning the favor of the audience is by fighting back in the same manner. As a result, only the contestant who can denigrate her rival most convincingly will triumph in the end.

(2) Speeches should consist of a balanced choice of complete sentences and succinct phrases.

Ideally, a speech should begin with a more general or abstract remark using non-finite verbal forms or nominal phrases, and proceed with more concrete accusations in the form of complete sentences. Short phrases with multiplied verbal bases can be used effectively, as we have seen in the example of **zi$_3$ ar$_3$-ar$_3$-ar$_3$-ar$_3$-ra** "grinding flour non-stop," but long sequences of short insulting expressions at the expense of complete, coherent sentences are a mark of bad style.

3) The last line, or 'punchline,' of a speech must be phrased in the 2nd person singular and thus directly addressed to the opponent.

While the 'punchline' can be used to deliver a fatal blow, sum up the argument, provoke the rival further, make statements about the disputation performed so far, or settle the power relations between the two speakers to the detriment of the opponent, the direct address also fulfills the discourse-structuring role of regulating the *turn-taking*.[33] By finally turning to face the rival and addressing her directly, the speaker signals that her speech has ended and invites her rival to take her turn.

Out of these three rules, at least the first seems to be specific to *2WB* ("*2WA*" still awaits in-depth analysis in this regard). The Sumerian precedence disputations in particular contain far more direct accusations and insults in the 2nd person singular. However, this need not be altogether surprising, since they seem to have been composed for the entertainment of an audience who is invited to observe which of the complementary, non-human contestants can prove their greater utility. In other words: there the joy lies primarily in sitting back and watching, without the immediate urge to judge fellow human beings and contemplating what lesson can be learned for one's own conduct. By this, I do not at all want to exclude the possibility that the precedence disputations also teach moral values, which they certainly do. It just seems to be a little less pronounced

32 Incidentally, this seems to fit the concept of "dropping remarks" on the Barbados described by Irvine (1993: 127), who observed: "The target is supposed to overhear what is said but, being excluded from the conversation, cannot easily protest."

33 For turn-taking see, e.g., Sachs et al. 1974.

than in the disputations between male students and women, as the identification with non-human protagonists is less straight forward. In any case, the fact that the two protagonists of *2WB* systematically avoid addressing each other directly during the actual verbal contest unless they utter their final 'punchlines,' speaks against classifying the main part of the text as a dialogue. Instead, the speeches are designed to inform the audience about the misconduct of the respective rival.

Moreover, the different styles of the disputation proper on the one hand, and the introduction and conclusion on the other, had a direct effect on the audience. While the natural dialogue and interaction between the speakers at the beginning and the end of the text force them into the role of a passive observer, the direct address to the audience in the main part invites them to form an opinion on the two contestants, and lets them assume the role of a judge. This invitation to active mental participation also strengthens the didactic purposes of the text: the audience as a moral judge is indirectly encouraged to lead moral lives themselves. The exaggerated nature of the "ritual" insults and allegations in particular makes it easy to condemn the behavior of the protagonists, and the condemnation of the protagonists by the audience should henceforth prevent them from committing similar lapses in return.

But who was the audience? All we know for sure is that the *2WB* had its 'Sitz im Leben' in the Old Babylonian school. It is attested on over 60 exercise tablets from the first half of the 2nd millennium BCE, copied out by students in the advanced stage of the curriculum. Moreover, we have seen the text's immense didactic potential: teaching students rhetoric, the specific socio- or genderlect spoken by female protagonists in Sumerian literature, the characteristics of an ideal wife, and the procedure of a lawsuit in all its different stages. Furthermore, striking similarities with the Sumerian school disputations in terms of content and structure,[34] combined with the fact that girls rarely enjoyed a scribal education,[35] make male authors and a predominantly male audience very likely. In other words: despite the fact that the text features two housewives as its main protagonists, it was probably written by male teachers for mainly male students. Finally, since the manuscripts we have stem from a time when Sumerian was no longer spoken, the relevance and accessibility of the text outside of the school, where Sumerian was learned as a dead language, was probably negligible. However, it is precisely the lack of natural dialogue between the protagonists in the

34 For an assessment of the similarities between Sumerian disputations between women and those between male students, see Matuszak (2018).

35 The scarce evidence for girls learning how to read and write in the Old Babylonian period has been assembled by Lion and Robson (2005).

main part, presupposing an audience as the real addressee of the speeches, which constitutes the most salient indicator that the text had at least the *potential* to be performed on stage.[36] It therefore seems legitimate at least to *entertain the idea* of a scholastic stage production, enacted by schoolboys, of the fateful dispute between Mrs. A and Ninkuzu, the incompetent and infertile housewife, who is convicted for her jealous slander of the competent and fertile Mrs. A, who – understandably – took the insults to heart.

Bibliography

CAD = A. L. Oppenheim/E. Reiner et al. (ed.), The Assyrian Dictionary of the University of Chicago. Chicago 1956 ff.

Alster, Bendt. 1990. Sumerian Literary Dialogues and Debates and their Place in Ancient Near Eastern Literature. Pp. 1–16 in *Living Waters: Scandinavian Orientalistic Studies Presented to Professor Dr. Frede Løkkegaard on his Seventy-fifth Birthday, January 27th 1990*, ed. Egon Keck et al. Copenhagen: Museum Tusculanum Press.

Alster, Bendt. 1997. *Proverbs of Ancient Sumer. The World's Earliest Proverb Collections.* Bethesda, Md.: CDL-Press.

Attinger, Pascal. 2010/15. Dumuzi Innana H (4.08.08), online-translation. DOI: 10.5281/zenodo.2599581 (last accessed November 2019).

Cunningham, Graham. 2007. A Catalogue of Sumerian Literature (based on Miguel Civil's Catalogue of Sumerian Literature). Pp. 351–412 in *Analysing Literary Sumerian. Corpus-based Approaches*, eds. Jarle Ebeling and Graham Cunningham. London: Equinox.

van Dijk, Johannes J. A. 1953. *La sagesse suméro-accadienne. Recherches sur les genres littéraires des textes sapientaux.* Leiden: Brill.

Irvine, Judith T. 1993. Insult and Responsibility: Verbal Abuse in a Wolof Village. Pp. 105–34 in *Responsibility and Evidence in Oral Discourse*, eds. Jane H. Hill and Judith T. Irvine. Studies in the Social and Cultural Foundations of Language 15. Cambridge: University Press.

Johnson, J. Cale, and Markham J. Geller. 2015. *The Class Reunion – An Annotated Translation and Commentary on the Sumerian Dialogue Two Scribes.* Cuneiform Mononographs 47. Leiden/Boston: Brill.

Kochman, Thomas. 1975. Grammar and discourse in vernacular Black English (review of Labov 1972). *Foundations of Language* 13: 95–118.

36 Further indicators are the use of demonstratives, which could have been accompanied with pointing gestures (already mentioned in section 3), as well as changes of scene (from Mrs. A's house, where the dispute likely took place, to the meeting place of the city assembly in the final part of the text) and gaps in the text that needed to be filled with gestures in order to ensure a logical progression of events. Despite the text-immanent evidence suggesting that the text could have been performed, external evidence is lacking. A comprehensive assessment, taking into account previous studies by van Dijk (1953: 76), Römer (1990: 22), Wilcke (2012) and Mittermayer (2019: 159 f.), can be found in Matuszak (forthcoming, chapter 4.3).

Labov, William. 1972. *Language in the Inner City. Studies in Black English Vernacular.* Philadelphia: University of Pennsylvania Press.

Lion, Brigitte, and Eleanor Robson. 2005. Quelques textes scolaires paléo-babyloniens rédigés par des femmes. *Journal of Cuneiform Studies* 57: 37–54.

Matuszak, Jana. 2016. "She is not fit for womanhood": The Ideal Housewife according to Sumerian Literary Texts. Pp. 228–54 in *The Role of Women in Work and Society in the Ancient Near East*, eds. Brigitte Lion and Cécile Michel. Studies in Ancient Near Eastern Records 13. Boston/Berlin: De Gruyter.

Matuszak, Jana. 2017. *"Und du, du bist eine Frau?!" Untersuchungen zu sumerischen literarischen Frauenstreitgesprächen nebst einer* editio princeps *von* Zwei Frauen B. Diss. Univ. Tübingen.

Matuszak, Jana. 2018. Assessing Misogyny in Sumerian Disputations and Diatribes. Pp. 259–272 in *Gender and Methodology in the Ancient Near East*, eds. Stephanie L. Budin et al. Barcino Monographica Orientalia 10. Barcelona: Edicions de la Universitat de Barcelona.

Matuszak, Jana (forthcoming). "Und du, du bist eine Frau?! Editio princeps und Analyse des sumerischen Streitgesprächs 'Zwei Frauen B'. Untersuchungen zur Assyriologie und Vorderasiatischen Archäologie 16. Berlin/Boston: De Gruyter.

Mittermayer, Catherine. 2019. *‚Was sprach der eine zum anderen?' Argumentationsformen in den sumerischen Rangstreitgesprächen.* Untersuchungen zur Assyriologie und Vorderasiatischen Archäologie 15. Berlin/Boston: De Gruyter.

Römer, Willem H. P. 1988. Aus einem Schulstreitgespräch in sumerischer Sprache. *Ugarit-Forschungen* 20: 233–245.

Römer, Willem H. P. 1990. "Weisheitstexte" und Texte mit Bezug auf den Schulbetrieb in sumerischer Sprache. Pp. 17–109 in *Weisheitstexte, Mythen und Epen. Weisheitstexte I*, eds. Willem H. P. Römer and Wolfram von Soden. Texte aus der Umwelt des Alten Testaments III, 1. Gütersloh: Gütersloher Verlagshaus Gerd Mohn.

Rubio, Gonzalo. 2009. Sumerian Literature. Pp. 11–75 in *From an Antique Land. An Introduction to Ancient Near Eastern Literature*, ed. Carl S. Ehrlich. Lanham [et al.]: Rowman & Littlefield.

Sachs, Harvey et al. 1974. A Simplest Systematics for the Organization of Turn-Taking for Conversation. *Language* 50: 696–735.

Sefati, Yitzhak. 1998. *Love Songs in Sumerian Literature. Critical Edition of the Dumuzi-Inanna Songs.* Ramat Gan: Bar-Ilan University Press.

Vanstiphout, Herman L. J. 1993. "Versed Language" in Standard Sumerian Literature. Pp. 305–29 in *Verse in Ancient Near Eastern Prose*, eds. Johannes C. de Moor and Wilfred G. E. Watson. Alter Orient und Altes Testament 42. Kevelaer: Butzon und Bercker – Neukirchen-Vluyn: Neukirchener Verl.

Volk, Konrad. 2012. Streitgespräch. Pp. 214–22 in *Reallexikon der Assyriologie und Vorderasiatischen Archäologie* 13, ed. Michael P. Streck. Berlin: De Gruyter.

Westbrook, Raymond. 1988. *Old Babylonian Marriage Law.* Archiv für Orientforschung Beiheft 23. Horn: Verlag Ferdinand Berger & Söhne GmbH.

Wilcke, Claus. 2012. *The Sumerian Poem Enmerkar and En-suḫkeš-ana: Epic, Play, Or? Stage Craft at the Turn from the Third to the Second Millennium B.C. With a Score-Edition and a Translation of the Text.* American Oriental Series Essay 12. New Haven, Conn.: American Oriental Society.

A. R. George*

5 The Tamarisk, the Date-Palm and the King

A Study of the Prologues of the Oldest Akkadian Disputation

The Babylonian poem *Tamarisk and Date-Palm* is rightly described as "perhaps the best known of all Akkadian disputations" (Jiménez 2017: 28).[1] It has had the benefit of one hundred years of scholarly attention, during which the periodic accrual of new fragments has sustained interest.[2] As in some other disputations, the action in *Tamarisk and Date-Palm* is retrojected into the remote past, when the gods first organized human life on earth. In the garden of the first king, a tamarisk and a date-palm fall to quarreling over which is more useful to man and god. According to the usual pattern of a disputation, each in turn states his own importance and derides his opponent. A judgement would have followed, in favour of one or the other, but the end of the poem is missing and so prevents us knowing both judge and verdict. Probably the king was the judge, and probably his verdict fell in favour of the date-palm, for a Babylonian fable reckons it *šar iṣṣī* "king of trees."[3]

With a composition that is so well known, it would seem otiose to add another general study to those that already exist. However, like many Babylonian literary compositions the text of *Tamarisk and Date-Palm* still contains passages in need of clarification. It also retains, upon close reading, a capacity to spring surprises. One such surprise is an outcome of this contribution.

---

* School of Oriental and African Studies, University of London.

1 I owe more than this quotation to Enrique Jiménez: as organiser of the Madrid conference he was instrumental in making it a success, and as co-editor of this volume he made valuable comments on this paper.

2 The *editio princeps* of Ebeling (1917: 32–34; 1927: 6–12) was brought up to date first by Lambert (1960: 151–64) and then by Wilcke (1989). Further studies by Cavigneaux (2003), Streck (2004), Cohen (2013) and Jiménez (2017) have added to the understanding of details and contributed to knowledge of its subject matter.

3 Wilcke (1989: 169). See in addition the many entries **gišimmar** (^{giš}**nimbar**) "date-palm" = *šarru* "king" in lexical texts collected by *CAD* Š/2, the sign's use as a logogram for *šarru* "king" in a Nineveh colophon (Borger 1973: 171 iv 48; Roaf and Zgoll 2001: 286), and the date-palm's epithets in an incantation that records its function in exorcism (*Udug-ḫul* XIII–XV 124, ed. Geller 2016: 469): **bala níg-kèš-da me-te nam-lugal-la-ke$_4$** // *markas palê simat šarrūti* "bond of sovereignty, symbol of kingship." Other grounds for the date-palm's triumph are adduced by Cohen (2013: 196).

https://doi.org/10.1515/9781501510274-005

Tamarisk and Date-Palm is written in poetry. Babylonian poetry is marked by considerable formality.[4] Ideas are presented in units of sense that coincide with units of verse: cola, half-lines, lines, couplets and, sometimes, larger stanzas. This structural architecture is carefully composed, so that meaning comes not only from the semantic load of a poem's vocabulary but also from its formal structure. While a general study of the congruence of prosodic structure and meaning in Babylonian poetry is not yet written, individual case studies (e.g. George 2010) have revealed some of the gains to be made by paying close attention to a poem's architecture. The new knowledge claimed in the present paper arises in part from a close reading of structure as well as language.

1 The Prologues of Tamarisk and Date-Palm

Tamarisk and Date-Palm opens with a prologue, which sets the scene in remote antiquity, when the world was young. This prologue survives in three different versions on three different tablets: (a) an Old Babylonian tablet of the mid-eighteenth century BC, from Tell Harmal, a site in modern Baghdad (Fig. 1); (b) a Middle Assyrian tablet of about the thirteenth century BC, from Assur on the river Tigris below Mosul; and (c) another tablet of about the thirteenth century BC, from Emar in Syria, on the river Euphrates upstream of Raqqa. The existence of these versions allows study of the evolution of the composition as a whole over time and space. More importantly for the present purpose, it allows a comparison of the different versions of the prologue, their vocabulary, prosody, structure and other formal features. Parts of the two prologues of (a) and (b) have already been compared as examples of prosody by Jiménez (2017: 35); the verse structure of the prologue of (c) has not been subjected to examination.

In many periods and places those who wrote out Babylonian poetry on clay tablets did so in such a manner that the ends of lines on the tablet coincided with boundaries between units of verse. This custom makes it easy to identify the poetic line or verse. It so happens, however, that none of the three surviving witnesses to the prologue of *Tamarisk and Date-Palm* is so organized. Accordingly, the first task of one studying their prosody is to identify where the beginnings and ends of the lines of verse fall on the tablets. Enough is known of the formal features of Babylonian poetry to make this a productive exercise, though there are some places where debate might remain open.

4 On some of the many formal features of Babylonian poetry see most recently Lambert 2013: 17–34 and Wisnom 2015: 487–89.

Fig. 1: Old Babylonian Manuscript of *Tamarisk and Date-Palm* (IM 53946 obverse). Photograph by Anmar Fadhil

The prologue of the oldest witness, Old Babylonian tablet (a), is set out on the first six lines of the tablet as follows:[5]

1 *[i-n]a ú-mi-{im} ul-lu-tim i-na ša-na-tim ru-qa-tim i-nu-ma*
2 *[i-lu] iz-zi-qú ù-ki-nu ma-tam i-ta-an-ḫu i-lu a-na* ⌜*a-we*⌝*-lu-tim*
3 *[ú]š-bu ip-ša-ḫu ù-*<*še*>*-ri-du-ši-im nu-uḫ-ša-am da-i[a]-*<*na*>*-ni*
4 *[a-n]a šu-te-ši-ir ma-tim gu-šu-úr ni-ši i-bu-*<*ú*> *ša-ra-am*
5 *[ma-t]a-am ki-ši a-na ša-pa-ri-im ṣa-al-ma-at qa-qa-di ni-ši ma-da-tim*
6 *[ša-ru-u]m i-na ki-*⌜*sà*⌝*-li-šu i-za-qa-ap gi-ši-*⌜*ma-ra*⌝*-am i-ta-tu-ša*
7 *[um-ta-al-l]i bi-na-am . . .*[6]

5 IM 53946 obv. (cuneiform text Lambert 1960 pl. 39).

6 Philological notes: l. 2 *iz-zi-qú* with the copy (so too Bottéro 1991: 14 n. 18); others have sought here the name of the Igīgū-gods, emending to *i-gi!-ku* (Wilcke 1989: 183; Heimpel 1997: 556; Jiménez 2017: 35), which would be an unconventional spelling, even for an Old Babylonian manuscript. l. 3 *[ú]š-bu:* Wilcke suggested *[pu-u]ḫ-rum* "in einer (Rats)versammlung;" *ušbū ipšaḫū* exhibit asyndeton: with similar vocabulary cf. OB Etana i 2 *ušbū imlikū* "they sat, they took counsel," Agušaya B vi 23 *inūḫ ipšaḫ libbaša* "her mood grew calm, became at ease." l. 3 *ù-*<*še*>*-ri-du-ši-im:* emended in the light of the mythology elaborated in *Ewe and Grain*, where the gods "sent down" sheep and cereals from the Holy Mound (Alster and Vanstiphout 1987: 17; Wilcke 2007: 22). l. 3 *da-i[a]-*<*na*>*-ni:* Wilcke "am Anfang," i.e. reading *i+na! p[a!]-ni*, at the start of a new clause. *dayyānāni* is less serious an emendation; if it is correct it joins the growing number of adverbs in *-āni* (most recently Mayer 2015: 192). l. 5 *[māt]am* not *[āl]am*, with the Emar version's prologue, (c) l. 8: *ša māt*(KUR) *kiš*.

When the sequences of syllabic signs are interpreted as words and those words placed in units of verse, the following passage of ten lines of poetry emerges:

1 *[in]a ūmī | ullûtim || ina šanātim | rūqā́tim*	*-ātim* 2:2
inūma 2 *[ilū] | izziqū || ukinnū | mā́tam*	*-tam* 2:2
ītanḫū | ilū | ana awēlū́tim	*-tim* 3
3 *[u]šbū | ipšaḫū || ušēridūšim | núḫšam*	*-šam* 2:2
dayyānāni | 4 *[an]a šutēšur | mā́tim*	*-tim* 3
gušūr | nišī || ibbû | šárram	*-ram* 2:2
5 *[māt]am | Kiši | ana šapā́rim*	*-rim* 3
ṣalmāt | qaqqadim || nišī | mādā́tim	*-ātim* 2:2
6 *[šarru]m | ina kisallīšu || izzaqap | gišimmā́ram*[7]	2:2
itātušša | [umtalli] | bī́nam	3

The first eight lines of poetry make a set of four couplets of two verses each. Each line ends with the most characteristic feature of Babylonian poetry, the "trochaic" pattern of stress, in which stress (′) falls on a long penultimate syllable (cv̄́, cv́c). As can be seen from the data presented to the right of the transcription, other formal patterns are present. The passage opens and closes with lines ending in the bisyllable *ā́tim*. The ends of the six lines inside this frame repeat three times the pattern *am—im*. Rhyme is a very rare feature of Babylonian poetry, but it is impossible to deny that here the composer imposes a deliberate pattern of sounds on the final syllables of his verses.

There is also a pattern in rhythm. Much Babylonian poetry is constructed in a combination of two basic structures: lines of four cola ("Vierheber" lines) divided midway by a caesura (1 | 1 || 1 | 1 = 2:2), and lines of three cola (1 | 1 | 1 = 3). Each colon is defined by a single stress. Variation between lines of three and four cola has the effect of slowing and accelerating the rhythm. In the present passage the first couplet comprises two equal lines, each of four cola and each divided by a caesura (2:2). The next three couplets alternate three-cola lines (3) and four-cola lines (2:2). This is very carefully structured poetry.

Translation reveals further patterning:

---

7 This word, a loan from Sumerian **g̃iš nimbar**, is booked in the Akkadian dictionaries as *gišimmarum*. The dictionaries are inconsistent in normalizing loanwords ending in /ar/. Examples with a long vowel include *appārum* "marsh" from **ambar**, *igārum* "wall" from **é-gar$_8$**, and *ugārum* "arable land" from **a-gàr.** These suggest that the word conventionally rendered *gišimmarum* might just as probably be normalized *gišimmārum*, with the penultimate stress suited to line-final position in poetry.

In the far-off days, in the far-away years,
    when [the gods] ached with pain,[8] they established the people.
The gods had toiled instead of mankind,
    they sat down (and) rested, they <sent> down to them plenty.

To bring justice to the people <like> a judge,
    they named as king Gušūr-nišī –
To govern the [people] of Kiš,
    the black-headed race, the numerous folk.

The [king] planted a date-palm in his courtyard,
    around it [he filled in with] tamarisk ...

It can be seen that the first two couplets of the Old Babylonian prologue (a) are bound together by their subject matter. They introduce an episode in mythical time and make reference to well-known mythology (see already Cohen 2013: 193). In the first couplet the gods had "ached with pain, they established the people," a very clear allusion to the mythology of human creation. After eons of doing hard labour in the fields, suffering under their elders' yoke, the junior deities had mutinied, and the senior gods had to create mankind to take over the burden of work. The second couplet clarifies the import of the first, that the gods had originally done mankind's work, but then moves on to what they did in their newly idle state: they ensured that mankind had enough to eat and drink. The mythical episode referred to here is also found in the Sumerian disputation between Ewe and Grain, which begins with a prologue in which the gods, dwelling high up on their holy *tell* (city mound), send down to mankind these two staples of the Babylonian economy (n. 6).

Being united by the theme of the creation of human society the first and second couplets may be considered a four-line stanza or quatrain. Four-line stanzas are a prominent feature of other Babylonian poetry.[9] The next two couplets are

---

8 The verb *nazāqum* "to squeak, creak etc." is a verb of noise most recently discussed by Mayer (2017: 20 – 21). It often denotes mental anguish and emotional suffering, but can also describe physical suffering, particularly of those who bear a heavy burden; see Veenhof 2005: 94 – 95 no. 105: 22 – 24 *aššum* GUD.EGIR *lā teggi ukullâm damqam šukunma šīrūšu lā inazziqū* "don't neglect the rear ox: give it good fodder so it doesn't suffer physical harm;" Nabopolassar C12: 18 // 32 i 31 *aššurû ša ... ina nīrīšu kabti ušazziqu nišī māti* "the Assyrian who ... made the people of the land suffer harm under his heavy yoke;" *Poor Man of Nippur* 103 // 134 *minâtēšu urassiba nazāqu ēmissu* "he thrashed his limbs, inflicted pain on him."

9 e.g. Ammiditana's praise-poem to Ištar (Thureau-Dangin 1925), Old Babylonian *Gilgameš* (George 2003: 163), *Ludlul bēl nēmeqi* (George and Al-Rawi 1998: 194 – 97) and *Enūma eliš* (Talon 2005: ix–x; otherwise Lambert 2013: 29 – 30); cf. Hecker 1974: 146 – 51.

also united by theme, and so form a second four-line stanza. The topic is now the creation of a king. His name is sandwiched between two infinitive constructions that act as purpose clauses describing his function. That function is to bring just government to the people, so that they will serve the gods effectively. Here again, the statements tally with well-known mythology, in this case the idea that the gods created kingship subsequent to the first creation of mankind, and gave the people into the new king's care, to organize their labour in the service of the gods.[10]

The two opening quatrains of highly structured poetry are followed by a couplet in which the king plants a date-palm in his palace garden and surrounds it with tamarisks. This passage acts as a narrative bridge to the disputation, in which the two brother trees, having grown up together, engage in their quarrel.

The king Gušūr-nišī in the second quatrain is the surprise advertised at the outset of this paper. His emergence is supported by the verse division. As understood here, the phrase written *gu-šu-ur ni-ši* is the first half of a 2:2 line that ends *ibbû šarram* "they named the king." Previously it has been taken as an infinitive construction, *guššur nišī*, governed by the preposition *ana* that introduces the infinitive construction *šutēšur*[11] *mātim* in the previous line. Lambert (1960: 155) translated *ana šutēšur mātim guššur nišī* as "to guide the land and establish the peoples." Others followed, but with more literal translations of the putative *guššur:* Wilcke (1989: 183) "auf daß er das Land in Ordnung halte, das Volk stärke;" Heimpel (1997: 556) "who would keep order and strengthen the people;" Streck (2004: 255) "[z]ur Leitung des Landes, zur Stärkung der Menschen;" Cohen (2013: 191) "to govern correctly the land and strengthen the people." Despite this unanimity a reading (*ana*) *guššur nišī* "to make the people strong" is semantically implausible. It was not a function of Babylonian royal ideology that the king should make his people *gašrum* "strong": the adjective describes a violent state, and was used of all-powerful kings and gods, of fierce enemies and of wild animals like lions and wild bulls. The dominant ideology was quite the opposite: the people were to be a docile flock, and a king's duty was to protect and lead them like a shepherd, and to give them peace and justice. To turn his people into a violent force would not be in a king's interests, and that is probably why Lambert sought a way out by translating *guššur nišī* as "establish the peoples."

---

10 As recorded in the *Sumerian Flood Story* (now Peterson 2018), the bilingual *Dynastic Chronicle* (Finkel 1980: 66–67), and a late narrative (Mayer 1987, Cancik-Kirschbaum 1995; otherwise Jiménez 2013).

11 *šutēšur* is erroneously written *šu-te-ši-ir.*

As set out above, a verse boundary falls between *šutēšur* and *gu-šu-ur* in the Old Babylonian prologue, which makes the rather awkward twinning of infinitives improbable on structural grounds and commends to the reader the understanding of *gu-šu-ur ni-ši* adopted here: it is the king's name. The matter is clinched by the variant wording of the prologue preserved on the Middle Assyrian tablet, where *ana šutēšur mātim* is lacking entirely and *gušūr niš* occurs without a preposition.

The Middle Assyrian prologue (b) reads as follows:[12]

1 *ina u$_4$-me-el-lu-te* <*ana*> ÙG.MEŠ *ru-qat-*{*u*}*-te*[13]
2 ÍD.MEŠ *iḫ-re-ú* ZI KUR.MEŠ
3 UKKIN *iš-ku-nu* DINGIR.MEŠ KUR.MEŠ ^{d}*a-nu* ^{d}IDIM ^{d}*é-a*
4 *iš-*⌜*ti*⌝*-ni-ši id-da-al-gu*
5 *ina be-er-šu-nu a-ši-be* ^{d}*šá-maš*
6 KIMIN-*i-it be-la-at* DINGIR.MEŠ GAL *us-*⌜*ba*⌝*-at*
7 *ina* IGI-*na šar-ru-tu ina* KUR.MEŠ *ul* <*ib*>*-ba-ši*
8 *u be-lu-tu a-na* DINGIR.MEŠ *šar-ka-at*
9 GIŠ.ÙR.MEŠ *niš* DINGIR.MEŠ *ra-mu-ni-šu*
10 *ṣa-lam* SAG.MEŠ *iq-bu-ni-šu*
11 LUGAL *ina* É.GAL-*lim-šu*
12 *e-za-qa-ap* ^{giš}NIMBAR.ME[14]
13 *e-da-te-šu* KIMIN *ma-li* ^{giš}*bi-nu*

Only slight adjustments are required to organize this thirteen-line passage in units of poetry. We get the following twelve verses:

1 *ina ūmē* | *ellûte* || <*ina*> *nišē* | *rūqāte* 2:2
  2 *nārāte* | *iḫre'ū* || *napulti* | *mātāte* 2:2
3 *puḫra* | *iškunū* || *ilū* | *mātāte* 2:2

12 VAT 8830 (cuneiform text Lambert 1960 pl. 43).

13 Wilcke (1989: 171) emended to *ru!-qe!-te*, which matches the Emar prologue (c) but is not Middle Assyrian. A masculine adjective in *-ūte* (Cohen 2013: 192) is ruled out because the preceding noun ÙG.MEŠ = *nišī* is feminine. Accordingly the *u* is rejected as a corrupt insertion arising from a misreading of the sign *qat* in its more common value *šu*. The resulting spelling *ru-qat-te* for *rūqāte* is so far unparalleled in Middle Assyrian but not unexpected. In discussing "metathesis of quantity" (v:C > vC:) in Middle Assyrian, de Ridder (2018: 73 §113) notes that since the affix *-ūtV-* is commonly written *-ut-tV*, "the feminine plural marker *-āt* > *-att* would be expected, but is not attested." It seems to be now.

14 Singular, as in the Old Babylonian prologue (a). ME is an example of a redundant plural determinative, as found (rarely) in other Middle Assyrian texts (de Ridder 2018: 53 §80); see more generally the discussion of Worthington 2012: 284–87, citing this instance among others.

Anu Ellil Ea | [4] *ištīniš* | *iddálgū* 3
[5] *ina bērīšunu* | *ašibe* | *Šámaš* 3
[6] *ina bērīt bēlat-ilē* | *rabītu* | *úsbat* 3
[7] *ina pāna* | *šarrūtu* || *ina mātāte* | *ul ibášši* 2:2
[8] *u bēlūtu* | *ana ilē* | *šárkat* 3
[9] *gušūr niš* | *ilū* | *rāmūníššu* 3
[10] *ṣalam* | *qaqqade* | *iqbûníššu* 3
[11] *šarru* | *ina ekallēšu* || [12] *ezzaqap* | *gišimmára* 2:2
[13] *edātēšu* | KIMIN || *mali* | *bínu* 2:2

Previously this passage has been taken as more marred by corruption than it actually is. It can now be seen to be mostly in good order, leaving aside the omission of three whole verses (see below) and the obvious errors of the opening line.[15] It is not marked by a regular vocalic patterning comparable with the older prologue, but is organized in conventional lines of verse, each composed of three or four cola. Once again the number of cola forms a pattern, as can be seen from the summary at the right margin. This pattern will be analysed after the translation.

Translation reveals that the text is organized by theme. In the Old Babylonian prologue (a) we proposed a division of the text into stanzas that were coterminous with topics. If the same coincidence of topic and stanza occurs here, the passage falls into four stanzas:

In the far-off days, [among] the far-away folk,
    they dug the rivers, the life of the lands.

The gods of the lands held a meeting,
    Anu, Enlil and Ea took counsel together.
Among them was seated Šamaš,
    between was seated the great Lady of the Gods.

Formerly there was no kingship in the lands,
    and power to rule was bestowed on the gods.
The gods so loved him, Gušur-nišī,
    they decreed for him the black-headed folk.

The king planted a date-palm in his palace,
    around the date-palm, tamarisk was filled.

The first stanza is a couplet consisting of two lines of four cola each (2:2 lines). As in the Old Babylonian version it sets the scene in mythical time, but where the

15 *ūmē-ellûte* instead of OB *ūmī ullûtim* can be explained as crasis; *nišē rūqāte* for OB *šanātim rūqātim* is corrupt (Lambert 1960: 329).

former dwelt on the creation of mankind as the result of the junior gods' mutiny, the Middle Assyrian prologue cites only the task that led to the mutiny: the digging of the rivers that irrigated the lands and made them fertile.

After this introductory couplet a new topic is presented in two couplets, i. e. a four-line stanza. The stanza consists of a single four-cola line (2:2) followed by three lines each of three cola. Its topic is a meeting at which the senior gods gathered for counsel, attended also by the sun-god and the mother-goddess. The 2:2 line puts across the bustle of gods' gathering; the three slower lines of three cola each describe the more stately process of their deliberations.

A second four-line stanza follows, constructed on the same pattern as the first: a single 2:2 line and three slower lines of three cola each. Again, the quatrain is coterminous with a topic, now the creation of kings to rule men. The first couplet states that power was formerly under the gods' control. The second describes the appointment of the king.

The second quatrain is followed by the narrative bridge to the disputation. It is a couplet comprising two 2:2 lines, so making a structural frame with the opening couplet.

Where the Old Babylonian prologue (a) expressed the gods' choice of Gušūr-nišī as king with the clause "they named him king," the Middle Assyrian version (b) has "they loved him." The object is the king's name, restated as a pronoun. A former interpretation, that the gods loved the people and so gave them a king (unnamed), relied on a false word division and can be rejected.[16] The topos is thus one repeated over and again in ancient Mesopotamian royal presentation, from Enmetena to Cyrus: the gods chose from the human crowd a righteous individual, whom they loved and made king to rule the others.

The topos of the gods' love for the chosen ruler recurs in the Emar prologue (c), which reads as follows:[17]

1 *i-na* u_4*-mi-e[l-lu-ti] i-na mu-[ši ul]-lu-ti i-na* MU.ME[Š *ul-la-ti i-na*] ÙG.MEŠ *ru-qè-t[i]*
2 *e-nu-ma* DINGIR.[MEŠ *ú-k*]*i-in-nu* KUR-*ta* URU.DIDLI *e-pu-šu* [*a-na* ÙG.MEŠ]
3 *e-nu-ma uš-[ta]-⌜ap⌝-pí-ku* ḪUR.SAG.MEŠ ÍD.DIDLI *iḫ-[ru-ú na-piš-ti]* KUR-*ti*
4 *pu-uḫ-ra iš-[k]u-nu* DINGIR.MEŠ *ša* KUR-*ti* [*Anu Ellil u Ea il-te*]*-ni-iš*
5 *im-tal-ku-ma i-na bi-ri-šu-nu a-ši-⌜ib* ^{d}UTU⌝ [*Bēlet-ilī bi-ra*]*-a*[18] *uš-ba-<at>*

16 Wilcke 1979: 171 l. 7 Ac *ra-mu ni-šu* = 179 "Die Götter aber gewannen das Volk ... lieb"; Heimpel 1997: 556; also Streck 2004: 255. But nominative *nišū* cannot express the object of such a clause.

17 Msk 7480j=c+74143n+74158 g(+)7490 g(+)74345c (cuneiform texts Arnaud 1985–87, I).

18 The restoration of *birâ* (not "everywhere" but "between," as in SB *Gilgameš* X 84; *AHw* 127) matches the probable intent of the counterpart line in the MA prologue (b). Arnaud and Cohen

6 *i-na pa-na-ma* LUGAL-*ut-tu i-na* KUR-*ti ul i-ba-aš-ši u* [*be-lu-ut-tu a-na* LÚ *u*]*l*[19] *šar-ka-a*[*t . . .*]
7 DINGIR.MEŠ *ir-a-mu-š*[*u*]*-ma* ÙG.MEŠ *ṣa-al-ma-ti* SAG.DU *id-*[*di-nu-šu*[20] . . .]
8 *ša* KUR *kiš ú-*[*g*]*a-am-mi-ru-ni-iš-šu a-na* ⸢KÁ*-šu*⸣[21] [...]

These eight lines of tablet comprise sixteen lines of regular poetry in three or four cola:

1 *ina ūmi* | *u*[*llûti*] || *ina m*[*ūšī* | *ul*]*lûti* 2:2
ina šanāti | [*ullâti* || *ina*] *nišī* | *rūqēt*[*i*] 2:2
2 *enūma* | *ilū* || [*uk*]*innū* | *māta* 2:2
ālī | *ēpušū* | [*ana nišī*] 3
3 *enūma* | *uš*[*ta*]*ppikū* | *ḫursānī* 3
nārāti | *iḫ*[*rû* || *napišti*] | *māti* 2:2
4 *puḫra* | *iš*[*k*]*unū* || *ilū* | *ša māti* 2:2
[*Anu Ellil u Ea* | *iltē*]*niš* | 5 *imtalkūma* 3
ina bīrīšunu | *ašib* | *Šámaš* 3
[*Bēlet-ilī* | *bir*]*â* | *úšbat* 3
6 *ina pānāma* | *šarruttu* || *ina māti* | *ul ibášši* 2:2
u [*bēluttu* | *ana amēli* | *u*]*l šárka*[*t*] 3
[*Gušur-nišī*] | 7 *ilū* | *ir'amūš*[*ū*]*ma* 3
nišī | *ṣalmāti qaqqadi* | *id*[*dinūšu*] 3
[...] | 8 *ša māt kiš* || *u*[*g*]*ammerūniššu* | *ana bābīšu* 2:2
[...]

Again, thematic stanzas—couplets and quatrians—emerge in translation:

In the far-[off] days, in the [far]-off nights,
in the [far-off] years, [among] the far-away folk —

when the gods established the people,
built towns [for the folk,]
when they heaped up the mountains,
dug the rivers, [the life of] the land,

the gods of the land held a meeting,

---

have instead Šamaš's bride, Aya ([^{d}*a*]-*a*). The Mother Goddess and Šamaš are attested participants in divine assemblies (Lambert 1960: 329; SB *Gilgameš* X 319–20); Aya not so.

19 The trace in Msk 7490 g l. 5 (Arnaud 1985–87, I: 224, coll. March 2001) is not the end of DINGIR.MEŠ, *pace* Wilcke 1989: 171; Dietrich 1995: 62.

20 Compare the *Dynastic Chronicle* l. 5 (Finkel 1980: 66–67): **ùg nam-sipa-e-dè mu-un-šúm-mu-[uš]** // *ni-ši a-na re-é-*<*ú*>*-ti id-di-nu-*[*šu*] "they (Anu, Enlil and Ea) gave over [to him (the king)] the people to shepherd."

21 So Msk 7480j=c l. 8 (Arnaud 1985–87, I: 212, coll. March 2001); cf. the sign KÁ in Msk 731064+ rev. i' 13'–15' (Arnaud 1985–87, I: 141, ed. IV: 23).

[Anu, Enlil and Ea] took counsel together,
among them was seated Šamaš,
[between] was seated [the Mistress of the Gods.]

Formerly there was no kingship in the land,
and [power to rule] was not bestowed [on a man.]
The gods so loved [Gušūr-nišī,]
[they] gave [to him] the black-headed folk.

They gathered at his gate the whole [. . .] of the land of Kish.

The kinship between this prologue (c) and the Middle Assyrian prologue (b) is near, for their texts are in close agreement after the phrase *nārāti iḫrû* "they dug the rivers." Before that the Middle Assyrian prologue lacks the lines describing the gods' fashioning of people, cities and mountains. The two prologues also differ in their elaboration of the formulaic invocation of mythical time. The formula is adapted from Sumerian literature, where the norm is a statement in a three-unit pattern (days—nights—years).[22] The two-unit version of the Old Babylonian prologue (days—years) is a reduction of these three units in order to fit a 2:2 line pattern. The Middle Assyrian text has only two units (days—folk), also in a 2:2 verse, but comparison with the Emar prologue would suggest that this is an incomplete rendering of the Emar text's four-unit pattern (days—nights—years—folk) in two 2:2 verses. Both post-Old Babylonian versions give space to *nišī rūqāti* "far-away folk." This is an improbable idea in itself, and a clear incongruity at the end of a sequence of units of time. Presumably it arose through corruption (n. 15). The error evidently become so embedded in the tradition that the verse structure of the Emar prologue has been adapted to accommodate it.

The couplet setting the poem in mythical time in the Emar prologue is followed by three four-line stanzas, each dedicated to a separate topic. The first relates the process by which the junior gods fashioned the surface of the earth. The second and third stanzas exactly match the Middle Assyrian prologue (b), respectively describing the meeting at which the gods had to find a solution to the mutiny (only implicit here), and reporting the institution of kingship.

The arrangement of the verses of the Emar prologue (c) in couplets and quatrains that coincide with units of meaning has the further ramification, that a new topic begins with the clause containing the verb *ugammerūniššu* "they gathered all for him." A break intervenes in the Emar tablet at this point, but it seems that this clause must introduce the narrative bridge which connected the mythological prologue with the disputation. In the other versions this bridge comprises

22 Dietrich 1995. See also George 2009: 81–82 (*Scholars of Uruk*), Cavigneaux 2014: 17 (*Adapa*).

the bare statement that the king planted a date-palm in his palace and surrounded it with tamarisks. The latter part of such a statement occurs in l. 9 of the Emar prologue, but the only secure word is *idātīšu* "around it." This is obviously the counterpart of *itātušša* and *edātēšu* in the other prologues, but the loss of much of the bridging passage in the Emar prologue precludes an analysis of its formal structure and content.

It has long been known that units of Babylonian verse, in particular the line and the couplet, coincide with units of sense, and that the identification of line and couplet in particular is fundamental to comprehension. This analysis of the formal structure of the three prologues of *Tamarisk and Date-Palm* shows that other techniques of prosody could also be used to organize the text. Among these are the grouping of couplets in larger units of poetry (four-line stanzas), patterns made by varying between lines of three (3) and four (2:2) cola, and (in (a) only) the construction of patterns of sound in line-final syllables (rhyme). The clarification that structural analysis brings to the three prologues has the additional result of bringing to light the name of the king in whose palace the disputation between tamarisk and date-palm took place. It is to him that we now turn.

2 The First King of Kiš

King Gušūr-nišī in the Old Babylonian and Middle Assyrian prologues is to be equated with Gušur, in Babylonian tradition the first king of Kiš. In the Sumerian King List his name is written GIŠ.ÙR (i.e. ^{giš}gušur), but for many years it remained without clear decipherment because the first sign of the spelling was uncertain on what was then the sole extant witness, the Weld-Blundell prism. In his critical edition of the *Sumerian King List*, Jacobsen (1939: 76 – 77 n. 39) read gá(?)-[. .]-ùr, based on Langdon's copy (1923 pl. 1 i 43) and a photograph of the prism. The signs in question were correctly read by Hallo as GIŠ.ÙR in 1971, but his collation was not made public until nineteen years had passed, when Douglas Frayne and Lynne George (1990) cited it in their discussion of the omen apodosis *amūt gu-šu-ur ša māta ibēlu* "Omen of Gušur, who ruled the land" (cf. Weidner 1952: 74). Within two decades of their revelation, three more manuscripts of the *Sumerian King List* came to light. Two of them exactly confirmed Hallo's reading of the Weld-Blundell prism and the third offered a variant. The four sources read as follows:

(a) **kiš^{ki} ^{giš}gušur lugal-àm mu gêš-u+gêš-u ì-ak** "(In) Kish Gušur was king and reigned 1,200 years" (Weld-Blundell prism i 43 – 45)

(b) **kiš^{ki}-a ^{giš}gušur-e mu géš-u+géš-u+géš-u 6 ì-na** "In Kish Gušur reigned 2,160 years" (Steinkeller 2003: 269 i 3–4)
(c) **kiš^{ki}-a ^{giš}gušur-e géš-u+géš-u mu ì-ak** "In Kish Gušur reigned 1,200 years" (Klein 2008: 80 i 4–5)
(d) **kiš^{ki}-a lú-^{giš}gušur-ra lugal-àm mu géš-u+géš-u ì-ak** "In Kish Lu-Gušurra was king and reigned 1,200 years" (George 2011: 203 ii 45–46)

The name of the first king of Kish thus exists in three variant forms: (i) Gušur, (ii) Lu-Gušurra, and (iii) Gušūr-nišī. The spelling GIŠ.ÙR (= ^{giš}gušur) points to an interpretation of these variants as: (i) Roof-Beam, (ii) Man of the Roof-Beam, and (iii) Roof-Beam of the People. The image is of the king as one who provides shelter for his subjects, a facet of Old Babylonian royal ideology apparent in Hammurapi of Babylon's epithet *CH* ii 48: *ṣulūl mātim* "roof of the land." An alternative etymology, obscured by the logographic spelling, would be Akkadian *guššur* (< *gašārum* II/1) "Most Powerful." As has often been observed, many of the names of the first kings of Kish are Semitic, and Guššur "Most Powerful" would be a suitable fit at the top of the list. The spelling GIŠ.ÙR would then be a secondary development.

King Gušur (or Guššur) of Kiš, previously attested in the *Sumerian King List* and the Babylonian omen tradition, now takes his place in *Tamarisk and Date-Palm* as the king who planted the eponymous trees and thus provided the arena for their quarrel. In one Babylonian understanding of history, in which kingship was not an antediluvian creation but was bestowed first on Kiš,[23] Gušur was the first king of all. He was thus the first to organize human labour in the service of the gods, not only through agriculture but also through arboriculture. Placing the disputation between tamarisk and date-palm in his reign has the effect of retrojecting their quarrel to the very first exemplars of their two species (so already Bottéro 1991: 20). The quarrel is accordingly inherent and innate in all later specimens. In the Babylonian imagination, wherever tamarisk and date-palm were planted together, the dispute between them continued.

Bibliography

CAD = A. L. Oppenheim/E. Reiner et al. (ed.), *The Assyrian Dictionary of the University of Chicago*. Chicago 1956 ff.

23 Such is the view of the Ur III period copy of the Sumerian King List published by Steinkeller (2003).

Alster, Bendt, and Herman Vanstiphout. 1987. Lahar and Ashnan: Presentation and Analysis of a Sumerian Disputation. *Acta Sumerologica* 9: 1–43.
Arnaud, Daniel. 1985–87. *Recherches au pays d'Aštata: Emar* VI. 4 vols. Paris: Editions Recherche sur les Civilisations.
Borger, Rykle. 1973. Die Weihe eines Enlil-Priesters. *Bibliotheca Orientalis* 30: 163–83.
Bottéro, Jean. 1991. La "tenson" et la réflexion sur les choses en Mésopotamie. Pp. 7–22 in *Dispute Poems and Dialogues in the Ancient and Medieval Near East: Forms and Types of Literary Debates in Semitic and Related Literatures*, ed. Gerrit J. Reinink and Herman L. J. Vanstiphout. Orientalia Lovaniensia Analecta 42. Leuven: Peeters Press.
Cancik-Kirschbaum, Eva. 1995. Konzeption und Legimitation von Herrschaft in neuassyrischer Zeit. Mythos und Ritual in VS 24, 92. *Welt des Orients* 26: 5–20.
Cavigneaux, Antoine. 2003. Fragments littéraires susiens. Pp. 53–62 in *Literatur, Politik und Recht in Mesopotamien. Festschrift für Claus Wilcke*, ed. Walther Sallaberger, Konrad Volk and Annette Zgoll. Orientalia Biblica et Christiana 14. Wiesbaden: Harrassowitz.
Cavigneaux, Antoine. 2014. Une version sumérienne de la légende d'Adapa (Textes de Tell Haddad X). *Zeitschrift für Assyriologie* 104: 1–41.
Cohen, Yoram. 2013. *Wisdom from the Late Bronze Age.* Writings from the Ancient World 29. Atlanta, Ga: Society of Biblical Literature.
Dietrich, Manfried. 1995. *ina ūmī ullûti* "An jenen (fernen) Tagen." Pp. 57–72 in *Vom Alten Orient zum Alten Testament. Festschrift für Wolfram Freiherrn von Soden zum 85. Geburtstag am 19. Juni 1993*, ed. Manfried Dietrich and Oswald Loretz. Alter Orient und Altes Testament 240. Kevelaer: Butzon & Bercker, Neukirchen-Vluyn: Neukirchener Verlag.
Ebeling, Erich. 1917. Aus den Keilschrifttexten aus Assur religiösen Inhalts. *Mitteilungen der Deutschen Orient-Gesellschaft* 58: 22–50.
Ebeling, Erich. 1927. Die babylonische Fabel und ihre Bedeutung für die Literaturgeschichte. *Mitteilungen der Altorientalischen Gesellschaft* 2, III: 3–53.
Finkel, Irving L. 1980. Bilingual Chronicle Fragments. *Journal of Cuneiform Studies* 32: 65–80.
Frayne, Douglas, and Lynne George. 1990. The "Rake's" Progress: A Phantom King of Kiš. *Nouvelles assyriologiques brèves et utilitaires* 1990: 24–25 no. 30.
Geller, Markham J. 2016. *Healing Magic and Evil Demons: Canonical Udug-hul Incantations.* Die babylonisch-assyrische Medizin 8. Berlin: de Gruyter.
George, A. R. 2003. *The Babylonian Gilgamesh Epic: Introduction, Critical Edition and Cuneiform Texts.* 2 vols. Oxford: Oxford UP.
George, A. R. 2009. *Babylonian Literary Texts in the Schøyen Collection.* Cornell University Studies in Assyriology and Sumerology 10. Bethesda, Md: CDL Press.
George, A. R. 2010. The Assyrian Elegy: Form and Meaning. Pp. 203–16 in *Opening the Tablet Box: Near Eastern Studies in Honor of Benjamin R. Foster*, ed. Sarah C. Melville and Alice L. Slotsky. Culture and History of the Ancient Near East 42. Leiden: Brill.
George, A. R. 2011. *Cuneiform Royal Inscriptions and Related Texts in the Schøyen Collection.* Cornell University Studies in Assyriology and Sumerology 17. Bethesda, Md: CDL Press.
George, A. R. and F. N. H. Al-Rawi 1998. Tablets from the Sippar Library VII. Three Wisdom Texts. *Iraq* 60: 187–206.
Hecker, Karl. 1974. *Untersuchungen zur akkadischen Epik.* Alter Orient und Altes Testament: Sonderreihe 8. Kevelaer: Butzton & Bercker; Neukirchen-Vluyn: Neukirchener Verlag.

Heimpel, Wolfgang. 1997. Mythologie (mythology). A.1. In Mesopotamien. *Reallexikon der Assyriologie* 8: 534–64.
Jacobsen, Thorkild. 1939. *The Sumerian King List.* Assyriological Studies 11. Chicago, Ill.: University of Chicago Press.
Jiménez, Enrique. 2013. "The Creation of the King:" A Reappraisal. *Kaskal* 10: 235–54.
Jiménez, Enrique. 2017. *The Babylonian Disputation Poems: with Editions of the Series of the Poplar, Palm and Vine, the Series of the Spider, and the Story of the Poor, Forlorn Wren.* Culture and History of the Ancient Near East 87. Leiden/Boston: Brill.
Klein, Jacob. 2008. The Brockmon Collection Duplicate of the Sumerian King List (BT 14). Pp. 77–91 in *On the Third Dynasty of Ur: Studies in Honor of Marcel Sigrist*, ed. Piotr Michalowski. Journal of Cuneiform Studies Supplemental Series 1. Boston, Mass.: American Schools of Oriental Research.
Lambert, W. G. 1960. *Babylonian Wisdom Literature.* Oxford: Clarendon Press.
Lambert, W. G. 2013. *Babylonian Creation Myths.* Mesopotamian Civilizations 16. Winona Lake, Ind.: Eisenbrauns.
Langdon, Stephen. 1923. *The Weld-Blundell Collection, vol. II. Historical Inscriptions.* Oxford Edition of Cuneiform Texts 2. Oxford: Oxford University Press.
Mayer, Werner R. 1987. Ein Mythos von der Erschaffung des Menschen und des Königs. *Orientalia* 56: 55–68.
Mayer, Werner R. 2015. Nachlese II: zu Wolfram von Soden, Grundriß der akkadischen Grammatik (^{3}1995). *Orientalia* 84: 177–216.
Mayer, Werner R. 2017. Zum akkadischen Wörterbuch: M–S. *Orientalia* 86: 1–41.
Peterson, Jeremiah. 2018. The Divine Appointment of the First Antediluvian King: Newly Recovered Content from the Ur Version of the Sumerian Flood Story. *Journal of Cuneiform Studies* 70: 37–51.
de Ridder, Jacob Jan. 2018. *Descriptive Grammar of Middle Assyrian.* Leipziger Altorientalische Studien 8. Wiesbaden: Harrassowitz.
Roaf, Michael and Annette Zgoll. 2001. Assyrian Astroglyphs: Lord Aberdeen's Black Stone and the Prisms of Esarhaddon. *Zeitschrift für Assyriologie* 91: 264–95.
Steinkeller, Piotr. 2003. An Ur III Manuscript of the Sumerian King List. Pp. 267–92 in *Literatur, Politik und Recht in Mesopotamien. Festschrift für Claus Wilcke*, ed. Walther Sallaberger, Konrad Volk and Annette Zgoll. Orientalia Biblica et Christiana 14. Wiesbaden: Harrassowitz.
Streck, Michael P. 2004. Dattelpalme und Tamariske in Mesopotamien nach dem akkadischen Streitgespräch. *Zeitschrift für Assyriologie* 94: 250–90.
Talon, Philippe. 2005. *The Standard Babylonian Creation Myth Enūma eliš.* State Archives of Assyria. Cuneiform Texts 4. Helsinki: Neo-Assyrian Text Corpus Project.
Thureau-Dangin, François. 1925. Un hymne à Ištar de la haute époque babylonienne. *Revue d'Assyriologie* 22: 169–77.
Veenhof, K. R. 2005. *Letters in the Louvre.* Altbabylonische Briefe in Umschrift und Übersetzung 14. Leiden: Brill.
Weidner, Ernst. 1952. Keilschrifttexte aus Babylon. *Archiv für Orientforschung* 16: 71–75.
Wilcke, Claus. 1989. Die Emar-Version von "Dattelpalme und Tamariske" – Ein Rekonstruktionsversuch. *Zeitschrift für Assyriologie* 79: 161–90.

Wilcke, Claus. 2007. Vom altorientalischen Blick zurück auf die Anfänge. Pp. 3–59 in *Anfang und Ursprung. Die Frage nach dem Ersten in Philosophie und Kulturwissenschaft*, ed. Emil Angehrn. Berlin: de Gruyter.

Wisnom, Selena 2015. Stress Patterns in *Enūma Eliš:* A Comparative Study. *Kaskal* 12: 485–502.

Worthington, Martin 2012. *Principles of Akkadian Textual Criticism*. Studies in Ancient Near Eastern Records 1. Berlin: De Gruyter.

Enrique Jiménez*

6 Antiques in the King's Libraries

Akkadian Disputation Poems at Nineveh

The literary form to which the present volume is devoted, disputation texts, represents one of the most remarkable genres in world literature. Its uncanny ability to percolate down the millennia, defying the boundaries established by language, religion, and literary tradition means that it is present, in one way or another, in virtually every civilization that flourished in Land Between the Rivers. The most distinguished authors in every Mesopotamian culture were assiduous cultivators of literary disputations: Ephrem in Syriac (4th c. CE), al-Jāḥīẓ in Arabic (8th–9th c. CE), Asadī Ṭūsī in Persian (11th c. CE) and Fużūlī in Turkish (16th c. CE). Yet, in spite of their astounding ubiquity and popularity among the most celebrated figures, disputations remained something of a rarity. They were always a marginal genre, the poor sister of loftier religious and secular compositions.

The case of Akkadian literature is paradigmatic in this respect. Akkadian is by far the language in which literary disputations are attested over the longest time period: for some sixteen centuries, from the first quarter of the second millennium until the second century BCE. Yet, these sixteen centuries of history have yielded only six very fragmentary disputations:

1. *Tamarisk and Palm* (see Jiménez 2017: 28–39 and George in this volume), attested between the 18th and the 12th centuries BCE.
2. *Series*[1] *of the Fox* (see Jiménez 2017: 39–57, with previous literature), attested from the last quarter of the second millennium BCE to the last quarter of the first.
3. *Series of Ox and Horse* (see Jiménez 2017: 57–63, with previous literature), attested only in 7th-century manuscripts, but probably composed in the second half of the second millennium BCE.
   3.1. *Donkey Disputation* (see Jiménez 2017: 63–64, with previous literature), known from only one 7th-century fragment, represents perhaps a section of *Ox and Horse*.

* Ludwig Maximilian University of Munich.

1 In Assyriological jargon, the word "series" (Sumerian **éš.gàr** > Akkadian *iškāru*) is used to designate a text composed of more than one "tablet" (i.e., more than one chapter). It is unknown exactly how many chapters each of the known Akkadian disputations had.

https://doi.org/10.1515/9781501510274-006

4. *Series of the Poplar* (edition Jiménez 2017: 157–227), probably composed in the second half of the second millennium BCE, but known only in 7th-century and later manuscripts.
   4.1. *Palm and Vine* (edition Jiménez 2017: 231–87 and Jiménez 2018a), attested in Hellenistic-period manuscripts, might be an episode of the *Series of the Poplar.*
5. *Series of the Spider* (edition Jiménez 2017: 291–323, see Jiménez 2018a), known from 7th-century manuscripts, but composed perhaps around the turn of the first millennium BCE.
6. *Nissaba and Wheat* (see Jiménez 2017: 65–68, with previous literature), known only from one manuscript from the 7th century BCE.

It is unfortunately not a very impressive yield: six poems in sixteen centuries. It is reasonable to assume that other, hitherto unknown poems await discovery in museum cabinets or in the ground of Iraq, but it seems unlikely that our current picture will be dramatically altered by such discoveries. Indeed, compared to other genres bequeathed to us by ancient Mesopotamia, such as wisdom and hymnic compositions, disputation poems represent a minority: whereas several wisdom dialogues, dozens of hymns to gods, and numerous epics are known in many manuscripts, only a few very fragmentary disputation poems have been found so far.

Moreover, if one looks at the timeline of disputation poems, it is revealing that only two of them (*Tamarisk and Palm* and the *Series of the Fox*) are attested in second-millennium manuscripts. It is likely that others (*Series of Ox and Horse*, *Series of the Poplar*, and perhaps the *Series of the Spider*) were second-millennium compositions as well, but they are known only from first-millennium manuscripts. In all cases, only scattered fragments of once long texts survive: the *Series of the Fox*, for instance, was probably 1,500 lines long in Antiquity, but only 300 fragmentary verses have so far been recovered (Jiménez 2017: 45). This circumstance prompted one of the first editors of disputation poems, Erich Ebeling, to state that "as far as fables are concerned, fortune has not been very propitious to the Assyriologists."[2] However, when one studies the history of the transmission of Akkadian disputation poems in detail, the opposite impression seems unavoidable: only a smiling fortune has bestowed upon us these rarities.

2 "[L]eider ist nun gerade, was die Fabel anlangt, Fortuna den Assyriologen nicht sehr hold gewesen" (Ebeling 1927: 3).

1 Disputation Poems in Nineveh

Most of the Akkadian disputation poems known to us today are attested in manuscripts dating to the seventh century BCE: thus, the *Series of the Fox* (no. 2), the *Series of Ox and Horse* (no. 3), the *Donkey Disputation* (no. 3.1), the *Series of the Poplar* (no. 4), the *Series of the Spider* (no. 5), and *Nissaba and Wheat* (no. 6). In total, 6 of the 8 known texts, or 75 %. Only two are hitherto unattested in 7th-century manuscripts: *Tamarisk and Palm* (no. 1, known from earlier manuscripts) and *Palm and Vine* (no. 4.1, attested only in later manuscripts). Four of these texts (i.e., 50 % of all known disputations) are, in fact, attested exclusively in 7th-century manuscripts: this is the case of nos. 3, 3.1, 5, and 6.

The majority of these 7th-century manuscripts stem, of course, from the Libraries of king Assurbanipal of Assyria (r. 669 – 631 BCE), the largest assemblage of literary texts from ancient Mesopotamia, and one of the most important discrete repositories of texts from the entire ancient world.[3] Nineveh is the Mesopotamian library that has yielded the largest number of 'canonical' cuneiform tablets: an estimated 5,000, more than double the amount of Babylon.[4] It is, therefore, no surprise that disputation poems are attested chiefly there, along with dozens of other literary texts known mainly or exclusively from Nineveh manuscripts. The following fragments of disputation poems are known from Nineveh (the numbers in parenthesis represent the total number of manuscripts from sites other than Nineveh):[5]

1. *Tamarisk and Palm:* 0 (6)
2. *Series of the Fox:* 9 (16)
3. *Series of Ox and Horse:* 14 (0)
   3.1. *Donkey Disputation:* 1 (0)
4. *Series of the Poplar:* 4 (3)
   4.1. *Palm and Vine:* 0 (4)
5. *Series of the Spider:* 2 (1)
6. *Nissaba and Wheat:* 0 (1)

---

3 On the libraries of Assurbanipal, see Parpola 1983, Reade 1998/2000, Fincke 2003/2004, George and Frame 2005.

4 Information from Streck 2010: 50 – 51.

5 The present tally counts the number of fragments, and not the number of manuscripts. Most of the fragments of *Ox and Horse*, for instance, may belong to the same manuscript, and indeed several of them have been 'joined' to each other. The numbers have been collected from Lambert 1960: 150 – 211 and Jiménez 2017. Rm.2,228 (Jiménez 2017: 398 – 399) is taken as a manuscript of *Ox and Horse*, although the identification is far from certain.

In total, 30 fragments of disputation poems have been identified in the Libraries of Assurbanipal, whereas 31 come from other findspots. Two disputations (*Ox and Horse* = no. 3 and *Donkey* = no. 3.1) are known exclusively from manuscripts in Assurbanipal's libraries, others mainly from there, but not exclusively (*Poplar* = no. 4, *Spider* = no. 5). In relation to the estimated 31,341 tablets and fragments found at the Nineveh libraries and currently kept at the British Museum, disputations represent an extreme minority: only 0,09 % of the total.

There are several peculiarities about the Ninevite manuscripts of disputation poems. First, all 30 known fragments represent *unique* copies. This situation starkly contrasts with that of most 'canonical' texts from Assurbanipal's libraries, which were, as a rule, preserved in more than one copy, probably to facilitate their use by scholars. However, in the case of disputation poems, not a single case of duplication can be detected: as far as we can ascertain, each chapter of each disputation was represented in the royal libraries by only one manuscript.

On the other hand, all 30 fragments are written in Assyrian script, and none of them in Babylonian script. The rebellious southern neighbor of Babylonia was, *volens nolens*, one of the main suppliers for Assurbanipal's libraries, and indeed around one seventh of all Ninevite tablets are written in the Babylonian script (Fincke 2003/2004). In the case of disputation poems, however, no Babylonian manuscript has so far been identified, which means that not a single manuscript of disputations from Assurbanipal's libraries can be demonstrated to stem from a Babylonian library.[6]

As discussed above, the composition of most disputation poems can be dated to the time before Assurbanipal. A case in point is *Ox and Horse:* the poem was probably composed in the second half of the second century BCE, since some rare hippological words it contains are otherwise only attested in texts from the Middle Babylonian period (Jiménez 2017: 59). However, only Nineveh manuscripts of it are known: according to the Nineveh colophons, the text was subdivided into a series of "extracts" (*nisḫus*), perhaps upon arrival to the royal libraries. Be that as it may, the text is, therefore, attested only in manuscripts that long postdate its likely composition. The fragmentary state of most manuscripts preclude any further attempt to elucidate the process by which a text written several centuries earlier, and otherwise unattested in any library,

6 Not that not all tablets from Nineveh written in Babylonian script stem from Babylonia: the colophons of some of them represent them as originating in Assyria (Fincke 2014: 272–273). On the other hand, many Assurbanipal tablets written in Assyrian script are, according to their colophons, copies of Babylonian originals, but this fact cannot be established in the case of manuscripts of disputation poems.

found its way into the libraries at Nineveh. However, an important document, discussed below, will shed some light on the process.

2 An Assyrian Consignment of Tablets

The small cuneiform tablet Rm.618 (copied in Jiménez 2017: 120) contains a total of twenty-one lines, each of which contains the title of one composition. The tablet is clearly hastily written, with several mistakes and a complete line after l. 1 erased. This suggests that it represents not a library catalogue, but rather some sort of an accession record: as suggested by Lambert (1956: 320 fn. 10), "[i]t probably served some temporary purpose such as accompanying a group of tablets being sent to the Assurbanipal libraries." This accession record reads:

1. *˹šū˺ridam ki ...* [...]	"*Bring down* ... [...]"
2. *adāpa ana qereb šam*[*ê*]	"Adapa to the middle of the s[ky]"
3. *enūma anu enlil*	"When Anu and Enlil"
4. *šarru-ukīn šūpû*	"Sargon the splendid"
5. *enūma purattu iššâ*	"When the Euphrates lifted up"
6. *agālu annīta ina šemêšu*	"Donkey, on hearing this"
7. *enūma ana nuḫuš nišī*	"When, for the abundance of the people"
8. **^{lú}kaš$_{4}$ lugal-e**	"Royal courier"
9. *iškar* ^{d}*atūdi*	The Series "Atūdu" (?)
10. *ēnu marduk ina māt šumeri u akkadi*	"When Marduk in the land of Sumer and Akkad"
11. *iškar bīni*$^{!}$(^{d}NISSABA) *u gišimmari*	The series "Tamarisk (!)[7] and Palm"
12. *iškar ṣarbati*	The series "Poplar"
13. *iškar alpi u sīsê*	The series "Ox and Horse"
14. *alpu dāpinu*	"Savage Ox"
15. *bulṭī lū balṭāti*	"Live (fs.), yes, live!"
16. *ina māt māḫāzi*	"In the land of the shrine"
17. **^{d}nin-ì-si-in-na dumu saĝ an-na-ra**	"To Ninisinna, first-born of An"
18. *mukallimtu ša ludlul bēl nēmeqi*	Commentary on "Let me praise the lord of wisdom"
19. *iškar* ^{d}*etana*	The series "Etana"
20. *ūm isḫur māda*	"When *isḫur māda*"
21. *šarru-ukīn šarru dannu*	"Sargon, the mighty king"

7 The line reads in fact "Nissaba (i.e., the grain goddess) and Palm," but, as discussed in Jiménez (2017: 34), the title is probably a mistake for "Tamarisk and Palm," prompted by the similarity between the signs for "Tamarisk" and "Nissaba."

The most arresting feature of this library record is the large number of disputation poems mentioned: seven or eight,[8] i.e., between 33% and 38% of all the titles. This figure starkly contrast with the 0,09% given above as the total of fragments of disputation poems in Assurbanipal's libraries. In practical terms, what this means is that this very record witnessed in all likelihood the accession of most disputation poems into the Ninevite collections. It is therefore probable that most disputation poems arrived in the royal libraries at the same time.

Several other titles mentioned in this register are also relevant for establishing the nature of the lot. First, the incipit "Royal courier" (l. 8) corresponds to the text otherwise known as *Message of Lu-dingira to his mother*, an Old Babylonian Sumerian text that was copied also in Ḫattuša and Ugarit in Middle Babylonian times.[9] The text was not known to have survived beyond its Ugarit manuscript, and is in fact not attested in first millennium manuscripts. The entry in the catalogue, however, shows that it reached Assurbanipal's collections, and one should expect to find remains of it among the thousands of unidentified bilingual fragments in the Kuyunjik collection.

Secondly, the incipit "To Ninisinna, first-born of An" (l. 17) corresponds to a Sumerian letter to that goddess composed in all likelihood under the auspices of king Sîn-iddinam (1850 – 1844 BCE), but attested only on a single manuscript from Nineveh, 80 – 7 – 19,126.[10] The tablet represents a startling case of survival: it is uncertain how a Sumerian text composed at the beginning of the second millennium BCE found its way into Assurbanipal's libraries without leaving any detectable trace in the intervening centuries. The fact that the first millennium version of the text has an interlinear Akkadian translation suggests that the letter underwent a long process of transmission, which has slipped under the radar.

---

8 Lines 5 – 7 and 11 – 14. The case of l. 9 (The Series "Atūdu" (?)) is doubtful. *atūdu* in Akkadian means "ram," and the title was subsequently interpreted by Landsberger (1934: 97 fn. 1) as referring to an otherwise unattested god Atūdu. The line might be corrupted.

9 See Civil 1964 and Arnaud 2007: 179 – 185 no. 50. See also Gadotti 2010. The Ugarit tablet RS 25.421, which contains also a Hittite version, is in all likelihood an import from Hatti (Nougayrol 1968: 310), but a small duplicating fragment may belong to a local Ugarit copy (see Arnaud 2007: 179).

10 Copied in Craig 1897: 220 and Macmillan 1906: 644 – 645, edited by Nikel 1918: 29 – 31 and Peterson 2016: 78 – 79 The incipit should be read as ^{d}**nin-ì-si-in-na du[mu saĝ an-na-ra]** / *a-na* ^{d}*gu-la ma*[*r**-*tu*$_{4}$ *reš-ti-tu*$_{4}$ *šá* ^{d}*a-nim*]. Contrary to what is suggested in Jiménez (2017: 119), the identification of the manuscript 80 – 7 – 19,126 as the one referred to in the catalogue entry seems to rule out the identification of the entry as a first-millennium version of the letters (1) ^{d}**nin-in-si-na dumu ki-áĝ an maḫ**, "To Ninisina, beloved child of august An" (edited in Brisch 2007: 142 – 156) and (2) ^{d}**nin-ì-si-in-na dumu-saĝ an kù-ga**, "To Ninisinna, foremost of holy An" (*TCL* 16, 60).

Where it not for the existence of the first millennium manuscript and its mention in the catalogue, we would be forced to assumed that the letter ceased to be copied over a millennium earlier than it actually was.[11]

The catalogue lists, therefore, two certain cases of 'antiques', i.e., of second-millennium texts that found their way into Assurbanipal's libraries, but which are otherwise not known from first-millennium manuscripts, and only occasionally from Middle Babylonian tablets. Two more texts mentioned in the library record fulfil these criteria, although their classification as 'antiques' may seem surprising. One of them is the *Epic of Etana* (l. 19), a text known only from Old Babylonian, Middle Assyrian, and Neo-Assyrian manuscripts, but which is so far unattested in Middle or Neo Babylonian tablets. Similarly, *Adapa* (l. 2) is attested in an Old Babylonian Sumerian version (Cavigneaux 2014), transmitted into Middle Babylonian times (Peterson 2017); a Middle Babylonian Akkadian version and at least two manuscripts from Nineveh, broken into several fragments.[12] Were it not for Assurbanipal's libraries, we would not suspect that either of these ancient texts were known during the first millennium BCE. Both texts are, indeed, only known from Neo-Assyrian manuscripts, not Neo-Babylonian.[13]

Can these texts be considered canonical? Can one consider them full members of the select club of the "stream of tradition"? The "stream of tradition" was defined by the coiner of the expression, A. Leo Oppenheim, as "the corpus of literary works of various types that was maintained, controlled, and carefully kept alive by a tradition served by successive generations of learned and well-trained scribes" (Oppenheim 1960: 410 – 11). Not every ancient text that was copied by later generations could, therefore, be considered to belong to this "stream of tradition": only those for which a history of transmission by "successive generations of scribes" can be reconstructed should be included in this category. If that is not the case, in most instances there is no compelling argument for clas-

---

11 A similar case of startling survival is represented by another letter of king Sîn-iddinam, to the god Utu, which has survived in a Kuyunjik copy in Assyrian script (Borger 1991: 58 – 81, Brisch 2007: 158 – 178, and Peterson 2016: 48 – 54). That letter is, however, also attested in a Middle Babylonian manuscript from Emar.

12 On the Akkadian versions of Adapa, see Izreel 2001. On the transmission of Adapa, see Milstein 2017.

13 If the identification of l. 4 as the *King of Battle* Epic, suggested by Lambert (1976: 316) is correct, that text, known only in Old Babylonian forerunners, Middle Babylonian versions, and a Ninevite fragment would also fall into this category. Extracts of the so-called *Sargon's Birth Legend*, mentioned in l. 21, have, however, now been found by the author in two school tablets from Neo-Babylonian Nippur, which shows that the text enjoyed a certain circulation. The Nineveh manuscripts of the text should, therefore, not be regarded as relics.

sifying a text as bequeathed by an undetectable "stream of tradition," rather than by a one-off act of antiquarianism. In particular, texts known to have been composed in earlier periods but attested only in Assurbanipal's libraries, and without any attestable Middle or Neo-Babylonian transmission, are better considered 'antiques' brought to the royal libraries by the antiquarian interests of their librarians, until further evidence shows otherwise.[14]

This is the situation of all disputation poems mentioned in the catalogue: except for *Poplar* (l. 12), none of the disputations are known from anywhere but the Nineveh libraries. Thus, *Donkey, on hearing this* (l. 6) and *Ox and Horse* (l. 13 and 14) are known exclusively from Assurbanipal manuscripts. On the other hand, *Tamarisk* (!) *and Palm* (l. 11) is known only from manuscripts from the second millennium BCE, although its appearance in the present catalogue promises that Neo-Assyrian fragments of this text still await identification.

In other words, by the first millennium BCE most Akkadian disputations were relics of old times. Were it not for Assurbanipal's libraries, most of them would be unknown. Moreover, since all manuscripts of disputations are unique copies, it seems certain that, were it not for the consignment of tablets recorded in Rm.618, only *Fox* and *Spider* would have found their way to Nineveh.

* * *

In order to investigate the origins of this peculiar consignment, one has to look at the other texts listed in Rm.618. Many of the texts mentioned there are attested in multiple manuscripts at Nineveh: this is the case, for instance, of the *Epic of Etana* (l. 19) and the astrological series *Enūma Anu Enlil* (l. 3). In these cases, it seems impossible to decide which specific manuscript of the text belongs to the lot. There are, however, several texts mentioned in the catalogue that are known from only one manuscript from Assurbanipal's libraries: in these cases, those manuscripts can be safely identified with the ones referred to in Rm.618. Those texts are: *Donkey* (l. 6), *Poplar* (l. 12), *Ox and Horse* (l. 13), *To Ninisinna* (l. 17), and the commentary on *Ludlul* (l. 18). All these manuscripts are written in Assyrian script, none in Babylonian script, although at least two different scribal hands are detectable.[15] Moreover, one entry of the commentary on *Ludlul* ex-

---

14 Note, however, that some texts that may be classified as "antiques" in Neo-Assyrian times certainly underwent a long transmission: this is the case of *Adapa*, *Etana*, and *Tamarisk and Palm*, texts attested in several second-millennium versions.

15 At least two types of Assyrian hands are detectable in the Nineveh manuscripts of disputations: 'type 1' is the most common one, 'type 2' appears only in the manuscripts of *Ox and Horse*. 'Type 2' uses ranges of four wedges in signs that in conventional Neo-Assyrian script have only three, such as the second range of ṢI and the ŠE- and ḪI-elements of signs such as NAM and IT

plains a dialectal Babylonian word by means of its Assyrian equivalent, which means that it was either composed or adapted by an Assyrian scholar.[16] Be that as it may, it is clear that all tablets cited in Rm.618 stem from an Assyrian, perhaps Ninevite, scriptorium. Although it is seems impossible to locate such a scriptorium, several of the tablets have Assurbanipal colophons,[17] which means that they were copied expressly for the king's libraries.

Whoever selected the tablets had a clear weak spot for rarities and antiques. Both categories describe well texts such as *To Ninisinna* and *Message of Lu-dingira*, texts composed many centuries earlier, and which find little or no echo in other first millennium assemblages of tablets. The label 'rarity' and 'antique' also describes well Akkadian disputation poems as a whole during the first millennium BCE: at that point, Akkadian disputations were an all but dead genre, a relic kept alive only by antiquarian interests.

3 Reading and Learning

How did a genre as buoyant as disputation literature come to be an obscure, learned artifact? As discussed in Jiménez (2017: 69–108), the language of Akkadian disputation poems represents a parody of the highly literary, baroque style of some traditional Babylonian poetry, and in particular of the so-called *Theodicy* (Jiménez 2018b). In Akkadian disputations, idiosyncratic formulae found only in 'serious' poetry are placed in the mouths of farcical characters, such as insects and trees. The most traditional definition of parody represents it as a form that achieves hilarity by contrasting an old literary form with new, somewhat inappropriate characters.[18] The greater the historical distance from the composition of the parody, the more difficult it becomes to ascertain how exactly the contrast is achieved. Hence, it is often problematic to detect parody in ancient texts, and the classification of certain Mesopotamian texts as such is often disputed.[19] There is, however, one Akkadian text whose parodic character is beyond doubt: the so-called

(see Jiménez 2017: 398). Note that the 'Type 2' manuscript K.3456+ (Lambert 1960: pl. 47, MS B of *Ox and Horse*) preserves a one-line Assurbanipal 'Typ a' colophon. Interestingly, the commentary on *Ludlul* (K.3291 = Lambert 1960: pls. 15–17, *CCP* 1.3) displays 'Type 2' palaeography.

16 See the author's note *apud* Lenzi 2015 rev. 42 (*aspu* explained as *uspu*) and Gabbay and Jiménez 2019: 59: fn. 29.

17 One of the manuscripts of *Ox and Horse* has a 'Typ a' colophon (see above fn. 15), whereas 80-7-19,126 ('To Ninisinna') has a 'Typ d'.

18 For the traditional definition of parody, and for criticism of it, see Dentith 2000: 11–21.

19 See the discussion of a few cases in Jiménez 2017: 100–101.

Aluzinnu Text which has been described as an 'Omnibus Parody' (Jiménez 2017: 103), inasmuch as it parodies texts of several genres.[20] Given the parodic character of both this text and disputation poems, it is no surprise that the *Aluzinnu Text* is also cited among the works recorded in Rm.618 (l. 15).

The *Aluzinnu Text* is well represented at Nineveh, where at least three copies of it were kept.[21] The fact that at least some manuscripts of it arrived at Nineveh together with most disputation poems might reflect an emic category of "parody": both texts use highly literary language and apply it to absurd characters and situations. Although the evidence for reconstructing such a category is admittedly scant, the *Aluzinnu* and disputation literature share a further feature: they both are among the very few texts copied by students at the elementary level of their education.[22] It may seem surprising that texts that parody Akkadian literature consecrated by tradition were also enshrined in the school curriculum. Mesopotamians pedagogues would seem to agree on this point with W. H. Auden, according to whom an ideal university for poets would contain in this library "no books of literary criticism, and the only critical exercise required of students would be the writing of parodies" (Auden 1962: 77).

The pedagogical character of disputation poems is clear not only from the parodic nature of their language, but also from their eristic configuration, which would have made them perfect school exercises. Whereas the parodic language would have taught the students how to use literary language, and in particular how not to use it, the carefully constructed series of speeches and rejoinders would have render them capable of building strong arguments and avoiding rhetorical weaknesses.[23] Disputation literature was, therefore, useful for learning, but it probably stopped being useful thereafter.

The didactic nature of these poems explains only partially their absence from most tablet collections and their rather patchy transmission. Indeed, only a few school exercises with disputations are known, while texts that played a much bigger role in elementary education are ubiquitous in Mesopotamian libraries. There must be other reasons that explain the limited number of manuscripts of disputations, but only new evidence will shed light on them. The fact that the

---

20 See the description of the contents of the *Aluzinnu Text* (*2R* 60, with many duplicates) in Veldhuis 2003: 23–27 and Jiménez 2017: 101–103.

21 It is, of course, uncertain exactly to which copy of the text the record's entry refer. A new edition of the *Aluzinnu Text* by the author is in preparation.

22 Four school tablets with extracts of the *Aluzinnu Text* are listed in Gesche 2001: 178 fn. 687. School tablets with extracts of disputations are published in Jiménez 2017: 289–395 and *id.* 2018a.

23 See also Mittermayer in this volume.

consignment recorded in the tablet Rm.618 arrived in the Nineveh libraries should be a matter of congratulation, for without it the Akkadian tradition of disputation poems –the most long-lived in world literature– would be virtually undetectable.

Bibliography

CCP = Cuneiform Commentaries Project (http://ccp.yale.edu)

Arnaud, Daniel. 2007. *Corpus des Textes de Bibliothèque de Ras Shamra-Ougarit (1936–2000) en sumérien, babylonien et assyrien.* Aula Orientalis Supplementa 23. Sabadell: Ausa.

Auden, Wystan H. 1962. *The Dyer's Hand and Other Essays.* London: Faber and Faber.

Borger, Riekele. 1991. Ein Brief Sin-idinnams von Larsa an den Sonnengott sowie Bemerkungen über Joins und das Joinen. *Nachrichten der Akademie der Wissenschaften in Göttingen. I. Philologisch-historische Klasse* 1991/2: 39–84.

Brisch, Nicole M. 2007. *Tradition and the Poetics of Innovation. Sumerian Court Literature of the Larsa Dynasty (c. 2003–1763 BCE).* Alter Orient und Altes Testament 339. Münster: Ugarit-Verlag.

Cavigneaux, Antoine. 2014. Une version sumérienne de la légende d'Adapa (Textes de Tell Haddad X). *Zeitschrift für Assyriologie* 104: 1–41.

Civil, Miguel. 1964. The Message of "Lú-Dingir-ra to His Mother" and a Group of Akkado-Hittite "Proverbs." *Journal of Near Eastern Studies* 23: 1–11.

Craig, James A. 1897. The Pa-še (Išin) Dynasty. *The American Journal of Semitic Languages and Literatures* 13: 220–221.

Dentith, Simon. 2000. *Parody.* The New Critical Idiom. London: Routledge.

Ebeling, Erich. 1927. Die babylonische Fabel und ihre Bedeutung für die Literaturgeschichte. *Mitteilungen der Altorientalischen Gesellschaft* 2/3: 3–53.

Fincke, Jeanette. C. 2003/2004. The Babylonian Texts of Nineveh. *Archiv für Orientforschung* 50: 111–149.

Fincke, Jeanette. C. 2014. Babylonische Gelehrte am neuassyrischen Hof: zwischen Anpassung und Individualität. Pp. 269–292 in *Krieg und Frieden im Alten Vorderasien. 52e Rencontre Assyriologique Internationale. International Congress of Assyriology and Near Eastern Archaeology Münster, 17.–21. Juli 2006*, ed. Hans Neumann et al. Alter Orient und Altes Testament 401. Münster: Ugarit-Verlag.

Gabbay, Uri, and Enrique Jiménez. 2019. Cultural Imports and Local Products in the Commentaries from Uruk. The case of the Gimil-Sîn family. Pp. 53–88 in *Scholars and Scholarship in Late Babylonian Uruk*, ed. Christine Proust and John M. Steele. Cham: Springer.

Gadotti, Alhena. 2010. A Woman Most Fair: Investigating The Message Of Ludingira To His Mother. Pp. 115–129 in *Why Should Someone Who Knows Something Conceal It? Cuneiform Studies in Honor of David I. Owen on His 70th Birthday*, ed. Alexandra Kleinerman and Jack M. Sasson. Bethesda: CDL Press.

George, Andrew R., and Grant Frame. 2005. The royal libraries of Nineveh: New evidence for King Ashurbanipal's tablet collecting. *Iraq* 67: 265–284.

Gesche, Petra D. 2001. *Schulunterricht in Babylonien im ersten Jahrtausend v. Chr.* Alter Orient und Altes Testament 275. Münster: Ugarit-Verlag.

Izreel, Shlomo. 2001. *Adapa and the South Wind. Language Has the Power of Life and Death.* Mesopotamian Civilizations 10. Winona Lake: Eisenbrauns.

Jiménez, Enrique. 2017. *The Babylonian Disputation Poems. With Editions of the Series of the Poplar, Palm and Vine, the Series of the Spider, and the Story of the Poor, Forlorn Wren.* Culture and History of the Ancient Near East 87. Leiden: Brill.

Jiménez, Enrique. 2018a. New Fragments and Extracts of Akkadian Disputation and Fables Chiefly from Babylonian Schools. *Orientalia* 87: 157–167.

Jiménez, Enrique. 2018b. An Almost Irresistible Target. Parodying the Theodicy in Babylonian Literature. Pp. 124–133 in *Teaching Morality in Antiquity: Wisdom Texts, Oral Traditions, and Images*, ed. Takayoshi Oshima. Tübingen: Mohr Seibeck.

Lambert, Wilfred G. 1956. An Address of Marduk to the Demons. *Archiv für Orientforschung* 17: 310–321.

Lambert, Wilfred G. 1960. *Babylonian Wisdom Literature.* Oxford: Clarendon Press.

Lambert, Wilfred G. 1976. A Late Assyrian Catalogue of Scholarly and Literary Texts. Pp. 313–318 in *Kramer Aniversary Volume. Cuneiform studies in honor of Samuel Noah Kramer*, ed. Barry L. Eichler. Alter Orient und Altes Testament 25. Neukirchen-Vluyn: Butzon & Bercker Kevelaer.

Landsberger, Benno. 1934. *Die Fauna des alten Mesopotamien nach der 14. Tafel der Serie Ḫar-ra=ḫubullu.* Abhandlungen der Sächsischen Akademie der Wissenschaften 42/6. Leipzig: Hirzel.

Lenzi, Alan. 2015. Commentary on Ludlul (*CCP* 1.3). *Cuneiform Commentaries Project.*

Macmillan, Kerr D. 1906. Some Cuneiform Tablets Bearing on the Religion of Babylonia and Assyria. *Beiträge zur Assyriologie* 5: 531–712.

Milstein, Sara J. 2017. Insights into Editing From Mesopotamian Literature: Mirror Or Mirage? Pp. 81–97 in *Insights into Editing in the Hebrew Bible and the Ancient Near East*, ed. Reinhard Müller and Juha Pakkala. Leuven: Peeters.

Nikel, Johannes. 1918. *Ein neuer Ninkarrak-Text.* Studien zur Geschichte und Kultur des Altertums X/1. Paderborn

Nougayrol, Jean. 1968. Textes suméro-accadiens des archives et bibliothèques privées d'Ugarit. Pp. 1–447 in *Ugaritica V. Nouveaux textes accadiens, hourrites et ugaritiques des archives et bibliothèques privées d'Ugarit*, ed. Jean Nougayrol et al. Mission de Ras Shamra 16. Paris: Paul Geuthner.

Oppenheim, A. Leo. 1960. Assyriology– Why and Who? *Current Anthropology* 1: 409–428.

Parpola, Simo. 1983. Assyrian Library Records. *Journal of Near Eastern Studies* 42: 1–29.

Peterson, Jeremiah. 2016. The Literary Corpus of the Old Babylonian Larsa Dynasties. New Texts, New Readings, and Commentary. *Studia Mesopotamica* 3: 1–89.

Peterson, Jeremiah. 2017. A Middle Babylonian Sumerian Fragment of the Adapa Myth from Nippur and an Overview of the Middle Babylonian Sumerian Literary Corpus at Nippur. in *The First Ninety Years. A Sumerian Celebration in Honor of Miguel Civil*, ed. Lluis Feliu et al. Studies in Ancient Near Eastern Records 12. Boston, Berlin: De Gruyter.

Reade, Julian E. 1998/2000. Ninive (Nineveh). *Reallexikon der Assyriologie* 9: 388–433.

Streck, Michael P. 2010. Großes Fach Altorientalistik: Der Umfang des keilschriftlichen Textkorpus. *Mitteilungen der Deutschen Orient-Gesellschaft* 142: 35–58.

Veldhuis, Niek. 2003. Mesopotamian Canons. Pp. 9–28 in *Homer, the Bible, and Beyond: literary and religious canons in the ancient world*, ed. Margalit Finkelberg and Guy G. Stroumsa. Leiden: Brill.

Bernard Mathieu*

7 La «fable» égyptienne du Corps et de la Tête (tablette Turin CG 58004)

Un *procès* littéraire au temps des Ramsès

La composition présentée ici est connue par un document unique: une tablette en bois stuqué inscrite en hiératique, provenant de la collection Drovetti, et conservée aujourd'hui au musée égyptien de Turin (inv. 16355 = cat. 6238 = CG 58004). Une bonne édition (photographie et transcription hiéroglyphique) est désormais disponible grâce à J. López (1984) [fig. 1].

De 9,3 cm de haut sur 35 cm de large, seule la moitié supérieure de la tablette est préservée; la hauteur totale devait être de 19 cm. Le document n'étant pas opistographe, on peut donc en déduire que les huit lignes subsistant constituent la première moitié du texte inscrit initialement. Plusieurs auteurs ont daté la tablette de la XXe dynastie (1185–1070 av. J.-C.) ou de la XXIe dynastie (1069–945 av. J.-C.). Sur des critères paléographiques qu'il ne précise pas, J. López ferait volontiers remonter le document à la XVIIIe dynastie (1540–1292 av. J.-C.), plus précisément aux règnes d'Amenhotep III ou Amenhotep IV-Akhénaton (López 2000: 477; 2005: 147). Mais la nature du néo-égyptien littéraire utilisé invite résolument à dater le texte de l'époque ramesside (XIXe – XXe dynasties), et plutôt de la XXe dynastie, tant sa rédaction que sa copie.[1]

L'originalité de cette pièce, dont le caractère littéraire est spécifié par la présence d'une ponctuation rouge servant à délimiter des stiches groupés en distiques (Mathieu 1988), explique qu'elle ait fait l'objet d'assez nombreuses traductions: (chronologiquement) Maspero 1879, Maspero 1883, Erman 1927: 173–74, Donadoni 1959: 281–82, Brunner-Traut 1963: 126 (n° 18), Donadoni 1967: 339–40, Brunner-Traut 1968: 40–41, Kammerzell 1995: 951–54, Donadoni 1997: 115, López 2000, López 2005: 147–52, Burkard et Thissen 2009: 137–40.

* Université Paul Valéry, Montpellier (France). CNRS – UMR 5140 « Archéologie des Sociétés Méditerranéennes », Équipe « Égypte Nilotique et Méditerranéenne ».

1 Parmi les arguments grammaticaux et lexicaux favorisant cette datation: l'emploi du *yod* prothétique dans le participe perfectif (l. 1: *j.jrw*) et les «temps seconds» ou formes «emphatiques» (l. 2: *j.jr=tw;* l. 6: *j.šm s*), l'emploi du conjonctif *mtw=tw* (l. 1), du perfectif (l. 2: *ḏd;* l. 3: *sbḥ*), de la négation *bn* (l. 8), le neutre rendu par le masculin (l. 8: *p3 ḏd*), ou encore la formation composée *sp-ʿḏ3w* (l. 2), connue par ailleurs dans le *Poème de Qadech* (§ 108, 174, 186 = K*RI* II, 39, 1–5; 57, 1–5; 60, 6–10; 62, 1–4).

https://doi.org/10.1515/9781501510274-007

La difficulté du texte a été récemment soulignée: «Depués de Maspero, pocos autores han intentado traducir este texto particularmente difícil» (López 2000: 477), difficulté tenant pour une grande part à l'attribution des différents propos à l'un ou l'autre des protagonistes. Je me risque toutefois à en proposer ici une traduction inédite, à la faveur d'analyses grammaticales et lexicales nouvelles, tout en faisant miennes les précautions de son éditeur: «esta traducción pretende sólo ser una contribución a la comprensión de un escrito particularmente oscuro.» (López 2000: 478).

Turin CG 58004, 1.

< ḥꜣ.t-ʿ m pꜣ > wp(w) Ḫ.t ḥnʿ Tp • r wḥʿ j.jrw=w •
sḏd qy=w m-bꜣḥ Mʿbꜣ.yt • (r) pt{r}j pꜣy=sn tp •

< Début du > procès entre Corps et Tête
pour expliquer leurs fonctions;
exposé de leur nature devant la cour des Trente
pour examiner leur primauté.

Bien que formulé dans une version abrégée, l'intitulé du texte le range dans la catégorie littéraire des *procès* (voir *infra*, Commentaire général). La dispute oppose en l'occurrence «Corps» à «Tête». D'un point de vue anatomique, le terme *ḫ.t*, en égyptien, désigne précisément le tronc (thorax + abdomen + pelvis); la *ḫ.t* contient ainsi l'ensemble trachée-poumons (*smꜣ*), le cœur (*ḥꜣty*), le foie (*mjs.t*), l'estomac (*mnḏr*), les reins (*gg.t*), la rate (*nnšm*), la vessie (*špt.yt*) et les intestins (*mḫtw*). On pourrait admettre ici que *ḫ.t* désigne, par extension, tout ce qui n'est pas la tête.

L'absence d'article défini, usuel en néo-égyptien (**tꜣ ḫ.t*, **pꜣ tp*), confère à ces deux acteurs un statut de *personae* à part entière. Le terme pour «corps» est féminin en égyptien (*ḫ.t*), tandis que celui pour «tête» est masculin (*tp*). L'opinion de Posener (1981), qui considérait que *tp* était traité dans ce texte comme un féminin, a été à bon droit révisée par J. López (2000: 479) et Fr. Kammerzell (1995). En effet, dans les deux cas où l'article féminin *tꜣ* est utilisé (l. 7 et 8), le mot ainsi déterminé n'est pas *tp*, «tête», mais *tp(y.t)*, «première». Le débat oppose donc ici deux adversaires sexuellement différenciés, comme dans le cas du *Procès entre Vin et Bière*, connu par l'O. DeM 10270, dont nous ne possédons hélas que les premiers mots (Grandet 2010: 153, 377; Mathieu 2011: 164). Pour conserver les genres égyptiens, inversés en français, nous pouvons, le cas échéant, parler de la «personne du Corps» et du «personnage de Tête».

Les deux distiques de l'intitulé sont parallèles: l'enjeu du procès est d'expliquer l'action (*wḥʿ j.jrw=w*) de chacun des acteurs pour les départager, et d'exposer leur nature (*sḏd qy=w*)[2] afin d'établir une hiérarchie. Une fois admis ce parallélisme sémantique, l'interprétation de J. López «El cuerpo disputó con la cabeza para exponer sus respectivas funciones, hablando a gritos ante los Treinta Jueces» (López 2000: 478) me paraît devoir être écartée.

Corps et Tête s'affrontent devant la «cour des Trente», ou Mâbayt, une très ancienne institution héliopolitaine qui n'avait sans doute plus de compétence juridictionnelle réelle depuis au moins le Moyen Empire (Caminos 1954: 234; Konrad 2003; Enmarch 2008: 120). Auréolé de son antique prestige, ce tribunal fait donc ici fonction d'arbitre suprême d'un procès fictif.

Il s'agit d'examiner (*ptr*) la *primauté* respective des protagonistes. Le terme égyptien utilisé pour «primauté» (*tp*), dont la graphie est strictement identique à celle de «Tête», implique aussitôt un vice de forme flagrant, dès l'énoncé de ce débat contradictoire, la primauté (*tp*) revenant nécessairement à Tête (*Tp*). Nul doute que l'affichage linguistique – et humoristique – de ce vice de forme est tout à fait délibéré et qu'il constitue un message à l'endroit du lecteur / auditeur: l'issue du procès est suggérée dès son ouverture, l'intérêt devant être porté sur le débat lui-même. J. López comprend différemment: «Su presidente se preocupaba de que se descubriera al mentiroso» (López 2000: 478), en liant le dernier vers au suivant, mais la ponctuation ne valide guère cette solution. Par ailleurs, l'*incipit* de la fable d'Ésope *L'Estomac et les Pieds* – «L'estomac et les pieds disputaient de leur force (*péri dunaméôs*)» – oriente elle aussi vers cette interprétation de l'égyptien *tp* (Chambry 1927: 70; Rodríguez Adrados 1979: 343–45; 2003: 170, H. 132).

Turin CG 58004, 1–2.

mtw=tw sḥ3w p3 ʿḏ3w • jr.ty=f jw ø m {jr} rmw
r-mn • j.jr=tw m3ʿ.t n p3 nṯr <•> bw.t=f spy.w-ʿḏ3w •

L'on devra révéler celui qui est en faute,
ses yeux, ils seront en pleurs,
jusqu'à ce que pour le dieu justice (maât) *soit faite,*
car son abomination, ce sont les cas de faute.

Le conjonctif *mtw=tw* a valeur modale (Polis 2009: I, 424–30), d'où ma traduction «l'on devra révéler». J'analyse la construction *jr.ty=f jw ø m rmw*, «ses yeux, ils seront en pleurs», comme un Futur III. On ne peut totalement exclure la possibilité d'un emploi cataphorique du pronom suffixe *=f*, qui renverrait dans ce cas au «dieu» évoqué dans le vers suivant: «les yeux du dieu, ils seront en

2 Le groupe déterminatif, comme l'envisage J. López (1984: pl. 184a), doit être lu . La traduction «ihres Status» (Burkard et Thissen 2009: 138) est aussi recevable.

pleurs, jusqu'à ce que pour lui justice soit faite». Le motif des pleurs (*rm.wt*) du créateur, à l'origine de la création des hommes (*rmṯ*), est bien connu dans la documentation égyptienne (Mathieu 1986; Caron 2014). Le dieu en question est vraisemblablement Rê (ou Rê-Atoum), le créateur héliopolitain, plutôt que son correspondant dans l'au-delà, Osiris. Ce dernier est toutefois susceptible lui aussi de présider la cour des Trente, comme on peut l'inférer du nom de l'un de ses quarante-deux assesseurs, dans le chapitre 125 du Livre des Morts: *Wnm(w)-bsk.w pr(w) m Mꜥbꜣ.t*, «Mangeur-d'entrailles issu de la cour des Trente» (Lapp 1997: pl. LXVI).

Le contenu des deux distiques est particulièrement pertinent dans le cadre du genre littéraire des *procès*, puisque ces derniers mettent toujours en scène une confrontation entre la *maât* et l'*iséfet*, entre justice et crime, chaque œuvre constituant une actualisation différente de ce conflit fondamental (Mathieu 2011: 165). La *maât*, rappelons-le, résume l'ensemble des règles présidant à la vie sociale, qu'il s'agisse des relations humaines, de celles entre les générations, entre les vivants et les morts ou entre les hommes et les dieux (Assmann 1989; Menu 2005).

Turin CG 58004, 2–4.

ḏd H̱.t snty=s ø • Tp sbḥ r(ꜣ)=s (r-)jqr •
jr jnk jnk tꜣy sꜣw(.t) • n(y.t) pꜣ pr (r-)ḏrw=f •
sbw sꜣ.y nḥbw sꜣ.w • ꜥ.t nb.t r (= ḥr) ḥb ḥr=j <•>

Corps affirma que Tête était son second,
et sa bouche cria fort:

«Quant à moi, je suis cette poutre,[3]
celle de la maison tout entière,
qui répartit les poutrelles et qui relie les poutrelles,
et toutes les parties du corps s'agitent grâce à moi.

Il n'y a pas lieu de s'étonner qu'on prête une «bouche» à la personne du Corps dans ce débat imaginaire. La formulation est proche de ce qu'on peut lire dans un cycle de chants d'amour ramesside, à peu près contemporain, où des arbres prennent la parole: *jw wḏ nh.ꜣ-d(ꜣ)b r(ꜣ)=s pꜣy=s šꜣ jw=w r ḏd*, «le figuier ayant ouvert la bouche, son feuillage est venu dire» (P. Turin cat. 1966, 1, 11: Mathieu 1996: 85); *tꜣ nh.ꜣ šrj(.t) j.dg=s m ḏr.t=s wḏ=s r(ꜣ)=s r md.t*, «le jeune sycomore qu'elle a planté de sa main, il a ouvert la bouche pour parler» (P. Turin cat. 1966, 1, 15–2, 1: Mathieu 1996: 85).

3 La ponctuation se devine encore sur la photographie (Lopez 1984: pl. 184). Je lis *tꜣy* (démonstratif), plutôt que le simple article défini *tꜣ*.

La personne du Corps se considère comme «la maîtresse poutre» (Maspero 1879: 261) de l'édifice anatomique, c'est-à-dire l'élément central, d'où «partent» tous les autres et auquel tous les autres sont reliés. La même métaphore apparaît dans un texte magique ramesside, le P. Leyde I 343 + I 345, r° VII, 12–13: *t3y=f j3.t p3 syw ʿ.wt*, «sa colonne vertébrale, la poutre des parties du corps» (Massart 1954: 19, 71). L'affirmation de Corps se fonde sur une conception essentielle de la physiologie du corps dans la pensée égyptienne: toutes les parties du corps humain, en effet, passent pour être reliées au cœur (*ḥ3ty*), situé dans la poitrine (*r(3)-jb*), elle-même située dans le tronc (*ẖ.t*), par l'intermédiaire de «conduits» nommés *métou*. C'est ce qu'énonce explicitement le papyrus médical Ebers, 854a (= 99, 2–5): «Chez lui (l'homme), toutes les parties du corps ont des conduits *métou*. Ce sur quoi tout médecin, tout prêtre *ouâb* de Sekhmet ou tout guérisseur doit placer les mains et les doigts, c'est sur la nuque, sur les poignets, à l'emplacement du cœur, sur les bras, sur les jambes. Il peut mesurer le cœur parce que ses conduits *métou* mènent à toutes ses parties du corps; c'est qu'il (le cœur) s'exprime par les conduits *métou* de toutes les parties du corps» (Wreszinski 1913: 205; Bardinet 1995: 84–85). Corps, qui abrite le cœur, est donc en droit de revendiquer sa position centrale.

Dans le dernier vers de ce passage, le verbe *ḥb* a posé problème aux traducteurs. Une possibilité sérieuse à envisager est de le faire dériver de la racine √ḤB signifiant «trembloter», «s'agiter», qui peut s'appliquer aux eaux primordiales comme au blanc d'œuf (Meeks 1981: 245 [78.2642–2644]).

Turin CG 58004, 4–5.

< ḥr > wnf=w jw ḥ3ty wnf=w • jw ʿ.wt srwd=tw •
jw nḥb smn(=w) ẖr Tp • jr.t (ḥr) gmḥ m w3y <•>
šr(.t) (ḥr) srq (r) jtḥ ṯ3w • (m)sḏr (hr) wn {r) sḏm •
r(3) (ḥr) ng (r) gm wšb=f • ʿ.wy=fy srwd=w (r) b3k •

Le visage est gai lorsque le cœur est gai [4]
et que les parties du corps sont fermes;
lorsque la nuque est bien fixée sous Tête,
l'œil observe loin;

la narine respire pour inspirer l'air,
l'oreille s'ouvre pour entendre,[5]
la bouche s'écarte pour trouver sa réponse,
et ses deux parties sont fermes pour œuvrer.[6]

4 La ponctuation se devine encore sur la photographie (López 1984: pl. 184).

5 La ponctuation est visible sur la photographie (López 1984: pl. 184).

6 La ponctuation est visible sur la photographie (López 1984: pl. 184).

Je suggère la présence d'une haplographie de *ḥr* au début de la ligne 4. Comme l'envisage J. López lui-même (1984: pl. 184a), bien qu'il ne retienne pas cette option, le groupe  peut être lu  dans la séquence *jw ʿ.wt srwd=tw*, «lorsque les parties du corps sont fermes». La graphie du verbe *ng*, «s'écarter» (l. 5), a probablement été influencée par celle du verbe *ng(g)*, «caqueter», d'où le groupe déterminatif. Les «deux parties» (*ʿ.wy*) de la bouche se réfèrent non pas aux bras (Burkard et Thissen 2009: 138), mais aux lèvres, ou aux mandibules, comme l'a bien vu J. López (2000: 480).

L'argumentation de la personne du Corps est claire: c'est grâce à elle que le personnage de Tête, qui lui est rattaché par la nuque (*nḥb*), peut afficher une apparence joviale (*wnf*) et remplir son office. Le bon fonctionnement des sens et la faculté du langage en dépendent. On comparera, dans l'autobiographie du nomarque Pahéry (tombe d'Elkâb, XVIIIe dynastie, *temp.* Thoutmosis III): *d=tw n=k jr.ty=ky r mꜣꜣ ʿnx.wy=ky r sḏm ḏd(w).t r(ꜣ)=k ḥr md.t rd.wy=k ḥr šm pẖr n=k ʿ.wy=ky rmn.wy=ky ø rwd(=w) jwf=k ø nḏm(=w) mt.w=k*, «On te donnera tes yeux pour voir et tes oreilles pour entendre ce qu'on dit, ta bouche parlant, tes jambes marchant, tes bras et tes épaules te servant, tes chairs étant fermes, tes conduits *métou* étant souples» (l. 7; Tylor, Griffith 1894: pl. IX; Sethe 1907: 114, 10–16).

Turin CG 58004, 6–7.

j.šm s jw=f wḏr(=w) • jw ḥꜣty=f ṯs=y •
jw pt{r}j=f bwꜣw • mj šwꜣw <•> jw=j mḥ=kw m mꜣʿ.t •
jꜣd.t jm=f ḥr {•} m snd m qntj • ʿ.t nb.t (ḥr) bꜣk m sp.w •
jnk tꜣy=w ḥnw.t jnk • tꜣ tp(y.t) (ny.t) nꜣy=s sn.w [•]

C'est dans son intégrité qu'un homme doit aller,
avec le cœur dressé,
capable de considérer le supérieur comme l'inférieur,
car je suis emplie de justice (maât).

Lorsque les miasmes sont en lui, le visage est dans la crainte et dans l'accablement,[7]
car toutes les parties du corps œuvrent ensemble.
Je suis leur maîtresse, je suis la première,
celle dont les seconds [...] !«

La forme *j.šm* est un «temps second» prospectif, ou forme «emphatique» à valeur modale (Winand 1992: 265–78). J'interprète *wḏr* comme une graphie phonétique du parfait *wḏꜣ(=w)*, à moins qu'il ne s'agisse du parfait *ḏr(=w)*, ce qui ne modifie pas foncièrement le sens: «c'est dans sa force que l'homme doit aller».

7 La ponctuation se devine encore sur la photographie (López 1984: pl. 184).

Ce passage est traduit par G. Burkard, et H.J. Thissen, à la suite de Fr. Kammerzell: «Jetzt kommt jemand, der anmaßend und dessen Herz hochmütig ist, weil er die Vornehmen für Geringe ansieht» (Burkard et Thissen 2009: 138). Il est en effet tentant d'y voir une allusion, de la part de Corps, à l'attitude hautaine de Tête, qui regarderait les êtres supérieurs comme des inférieurs. Mais 1) cette traduction ne rend pas compte de la valeur modale de la forme *j.šm*; 2) elle donne à l'expression *jw ḥ3ty=f ṯs=y*, litt. «alors que son cœur est dressé», une valeur péjorative à ma connaissance non attestée (Mathieu 1996: 78, n. 251).

La personne du Corps rappelle que la *maât* est en elle. On songe à ces nombreuses formulations, attribuées à des êtres divins, il est vrai, où il est question de «vivre de la *maât*» (*ʿnḫ m m3ʿ.t*), c'est-à-dire de s'en nourrir. Ainsi, par exemple, Hatchepsout déclare en parlant d'Amon: *sʿ3~n=j m3ʿ.t mr(w).t~n=f jw rḫ~n=j ʿnḫ=f jm=s*, «j'ai fait grandir la *maât* qu'il avait désirée, car j'ai appris qu'il s'en nourrissait» (Grande Inscription du Spéos Artémidos, col. 9: Allen 2002). Il faut surtout rappeler que, selon les conceptions égyptiennes, la conscience morale était censée émaner du foie (*mjs.t*), dans la mesure où là réside la nature (*qdw*) de l'individu (Meeks 1995). Grâce à la *maât* placée en son sein, l'homme est doté du discernement lui permettant de distinguer le bien du mal; ce serait le sens de l'expression «capable de considérer le supérieur comme l'inférieur».

La suite est délicate à interpréter. La phrase «lorsque les miasmes (*j3d.t*) sont en lui, le visage est dans la crainte et dans l'abattement» semble s'opposer directement à «Le visage est gai lorsque le cœur est gai» (l. 4). Le groupe transcrit  par J. López (1984: pl. 184a; 2005: 151–52, n. 10) est à lire , ce qui modifie naturellement la traduction. Sous toute réserve, je relie le mot suivant *qntj* à la racine √GNN, «défaillir»; on rapprochera par exemple, dans le P. Lansing 4, 2–3: *wrš p3 rḫty (ḥr) ṯs h3y ḥʿw nb gnn(=w)*, «le blanchisseur passe la journée à monter et descendre, et tout son corps est éreinté» (Gardiner 1937: 103, 2–3; Caminos 1954: 385).

Turin CG 58004, 8.

ø ʿḏ3=w wsy p3 ḏd(w) n=f Tp <•> r(3) bn sw m ḏ3w=f •
jm ḏd=tw n=j t3 tp(y.t) • jnk sʿnḫ(w) mt[n (?) •]

C'est totalement faux, ce que lui [8] *dit Tête !*
La bouche, n'est-elle pas son contradicteur ? [9]
Qu'on me nomme, moi, la première,
car c'est moi qui fais vivre [...] !«

8 Au dieu qui préside la cour des Trente.

Une interprétation, qu'on ne peut totalement exclure, est de faire du premier distique le corrélat du distique introduisant le discours de Corps: *ḏd Ḫ.t sn.t=s (n) Tp sbḥ r(ꜣ)=s (r-)jqr*, «Corps affirma que Tête était son second, et sa bouche cria fort». Dans les deux cas, en effet, le locuteur est explicitement nommé (*Ḫ.t* / *Tp*), et le mot «bouche» (*r(ꜣ)*) est employé. On comprendrait dans ces conditions: «»C'est totalement faux !«, c'est ce que lui dit Tête, »La bouche, n'est-elle pas son contradicteur ?«)», et viendrait ensuite l'argumentation de Tête. Mais cette solution se heurte à un obstacle grammatical. En effet, l'énoncé «Qu'on me nomme, moi, la première» ne peut guère être prononcé par Tête, qui, en sa qualité de personnage *masculin*, aurait dit plutôt: **jm ḏd=tw n=j pꜣ tp(y)*, «Qu'on me nomme, moi, le premier».

Ne s'adressant pas directement à son adversaire, mais aux membres du tribunal, Corps réfute vigoureusement les prétentions de Tête en utilisant la formulation juridique consacrée: «C'est totalement faux !». On comparera, par exemple, dans le *Procès d'Horus et Seth*, 13, 2: *mꜣʿtw Ḥr ø ʿḏꜣ=w Stẖ*, «Horus a raison et Seth a tort» (Gardiner 1932: 54, 10 – 11). Il faut reconnaître, après *ʿḏꜣ=w*, le morphème ou «suffixe intensif» *wsy* (< *wy sw*), bien attesté en néo-égyptien littéraire (Neveu 1996: 234, n. 1).

Le mot *ḏꜣw* fait probablement paronomase avec *ʿḏꜣ=w*, mais son sens n'est pas assuré; pour *ḏꜣw*, «opposant», avec ici le sens de «contradicteur», étant donné le déterminatif de l'homme portant la main à la bouche, cf. *Wb* V, 517, 10 – 12.

La moitié inférieure de la tablette étant perdue, la lacune est sans doute de huit lignes, ce qui correspond à une bonne quinzaine de distiques. Cette moitié manquante devait comporter la réponse argumentée de Tête, constituée peut-être de douze distiques, à l'instar du discours de Corps, suivie du verdict de Rê et de la cour des Trente qui, finalement, accordait gain de cause à Tête.

Traduction suivie

(1) < *Début du* > *procès entre Corps et Tête*
pour expliquer leurs fonctions;
exposé de leur nature devant la cour des Trente
pour examiner leur primauté.

9 La présence d'une ponctuation n'est pas exclue (López 1984: pl. 184).

L'on devra révéler (2) *celui qui est en faute,*
et ses yeux, ils seront en pleurs,
jusqu'à ce que pour le dieu justice (maât) *soit faite,*
car son abomination, ce sont les cas de faute.

Corps affirma que Tête était son second,
(3) *et sa bouche cria fort:*

«Quant à moi, je suis cette poutre,
celle de la maison tout entière,
qui répartit les poutrelles et qui relie les poutrelles,
et toutes les parties du corps s'agitent grâce à moi.

(4) *Le visage est gai lorsque le cœur est gai*
et que les parties du corps sont fermes;
lorsque la nuque est bien fixée sous Tête,
l'œil observe loin;

la narine (5) *respire pour inspirer l'air,*
l'oreille s'ouvre pour entendre,
la bouche s'écarte pour trouver sa réponse,
et ses deux parties sont fermes pour œuvrer.

(6) *C'est dans son intégrité qu'un homme doit aller,*
avec le cœur dressé,
capable de considérer le supérieur comme l'inférieur,
car je suis emplie de justice.

Lorsque les miasmes (7) *sont en lui, le visage est dans la crainte et dans l'accablement,*
car toutes les parties du corps œuvrent ensemble.
Je suis leur maîtresse, je suis la première,
celle dont les seconds [...] !

(8) *C'est totalement faux, ce que lui dit Tête !*
La bouche, n'est-elle pas son contradicteur ?
Qu'on me nomme, moi, la première,
car c'est moi qui fais vivre [...] !«

Commentaire général

Ce n'est pas le lieu ici d'entreprendre un commentaire approfondi de ce texte et de sa riche postérité. Aussi m'en tiendrai-je à quelques brèves remarques.

Comme cela a été reconnu très tôt (Maspero 1879; 1883), le *Procès du Corps et de la Tête* offre la plus ancienne attestation d'une *disputatio* dont il existe de nombreuses versions, notamment une fable d'Ésope,[10] *L'Estomac et les Pieds*

10 Ésope, mentionné déjà par Hérodote (II, 134), vécut au VIe s. av. J.-C., mais on ne connaît de

(Chambry 1927: 70), et l'apologue des membres et de l'estomac de Ménénius Agrippa, rapporté par Tite-Live au tournant des Ier s. av. – Ier s. apr. J.-C. (*Histoire romaine* II, XXXII, 9 – 12). Ces œuvres inspirèrent à leur tour le début du *Coriolan* de Shakespeare (Acte I, scène 1), écrit vers 1609, et la fable de La Fontaine des *Membres et de l'Estomac*, dans la deuxième moitié du XVIIe siècle (*Fables* III, 2).

Au-delà de la diversité des variantes, toutes ces versions ont en commun, outre ceux qu'a mis en évidence J. López (2000: 480), un trait qu'il est important de souligner: le point de départ qu'est *la révolte* des gouvernés, numériquement majoritaires, contre l'autorité légitime, unique, et la conclusion par la justification de l'ordre établi. Dans la fable d'Ésope, les pieds revendiquent leur supériorité physique, oubliant qu'ils sont alimentés par l'estomac (*koilia*), ce qui permet à l'auteur de conclure: « Il en va ainsi dans les armées: le nombre le plus souvent n'est rien, si les chefs n'excellent pas dans le conseil ». Dans l'apologue de Ménénius Agrippa, ce sont toutes les parties du corps qui conspirent contre l'estomac (*venter*) et cessent leur activité, avant de comprendre que l'estomac ne se contentait pas de jouir de leur travail: « (les membres et le corps tout entier) virent alors que l'estomac ne restait point oisif, et que si on le nourrissait, il nourrissait à son tour, en renvoyant dans toutes les parties du corps ce sang qui fait notre vie et notre force, et en le distribuant également dans toutes les veines, après l'avoir élaboré par la digestion des aliments ». Ainsi Ménénius Agrippa apaisa-t-il la colère du peuple contre le sénat.

Or c'est bien ainsi que se présente le *procès* de la tablette de Turin, le texte débutant par l'indignation du corps contre la préséance de la tête. Bien que la réponse de Tête soit perdue, il fait peu de doute que l'intention du texte était de justifier la hiérarchie instituée pour désamorcer toute velléité de rébellion de la part des gouvernés. Le *Procès du Corps et de la Tête*, comme les autres *procès* littéraires contemporains et ses lointains épigones, avait nécessairement des fins politiques, tout particulièrement dans une Égypte ramesside secouée par les scandales et affaires de corruption (Vernus 1993), et dans un contexte sociopolitique où pouvait poindre la critique ouverte d'une autorité défaillante.

Le contenu et la forme des nombreux parallèles du texte égyptien ont conduit les commentateurs, depuis Maspero, à le considérer comme une *fable*, voire à en faire le prototype même, sinon l'origine, de ce genre littéraire (Maspero 1879; Williams 1956; López 2000; 2005). Or les termes de l'intitulé (*< ḥ3.t-ˁ m p3 > wp(w) H̱.t ḥnˁ Tp, < Début du > procès entre Corps et Tête*) permettent de classer le texte dans un genre littéraire spécifique, dont j'ai présenté ailleurs les

ses fables que des transcriptions postérieures; cf. Rodríguez Adrados 1979: 343 – 345, Rodríguez Adrados 2003: 170, H. 132.

principaux critères de définition (Mathieu 2011). On comparera notamment la formulation des intitulés d'œuvres contemporaines que sont le *Procès entre Horus et Seth* (*pꜣ wpw Ḥr ḥnʿ Stẖ:* Gardiner 1932: 37) et le *Procès entre Vin et Bière* (*pꜣ wpw Jrp jrm Ḥ(n)q.t;* Grandet 2010: 153, 377). La composition égyptienne n'est donc pas une «fable», au sens formel du terme, même si elle a pu constituer une source majeure des fabulistes de l'Antiquité classique.

Cette mise au point me paraît importante, dans la mesure où elle favorise une meilleure intégration de ce texte, et, plus généralement du genre littéraire des *procès*, dans le contexte global des *débats* sumériens et akkadiens (Reinink et Vanstiphout 1991, Vanstiphout 1992, Jiménez 2017). La richesse de ce fonds littéraire autorise sans doute de fructueux termes de comparaison avec la documentation égyptienne. On notera en particulier le motif du statut des protagonistes, présenté initialement comme *équivalent*, avant que la querelle ne soit tranchée par une instance divine établissant une hiérarchie de référence: «Les personnages (...) ne sont jamais hétérogènes mais toujours complémentaires, et appartenant l'un et l'autre à la même catégorie (...) un arbitre – on dirait que c'est, plus volontiers, une divinité – tire la conclusion du débat en proclamant vainqueur un des deux champions» (Bottéro 1991: 13). Ce schème général s'applique strictement au genre égyptien.

Je laisse aux spécialistes le soin d'approfondir ces questions (cf. déjà Herrmann 2008, Jiménez 2017: 128–30), en espérant que la présente étude pourra alimenter leur réflexion. On prendra garde toutefois à ne pas surestimer l'influence de la tradition proche-orientale sur le texte du *Procès entre Corps et Tête*. Ce dernier, on l'a vu, reflète, sur le fond, des conceptions authentiquement égyptiennes, et, sur la forme, une structuration métrique qui recourt à des règles de composition on ne peut plus «classiques». Il demeure que la faveur du genre des *disputes* dans le Proche-Orient ancien a certainement joué un rôle décisif dans la diffusion des *procès* de l'Égypte ramesside.

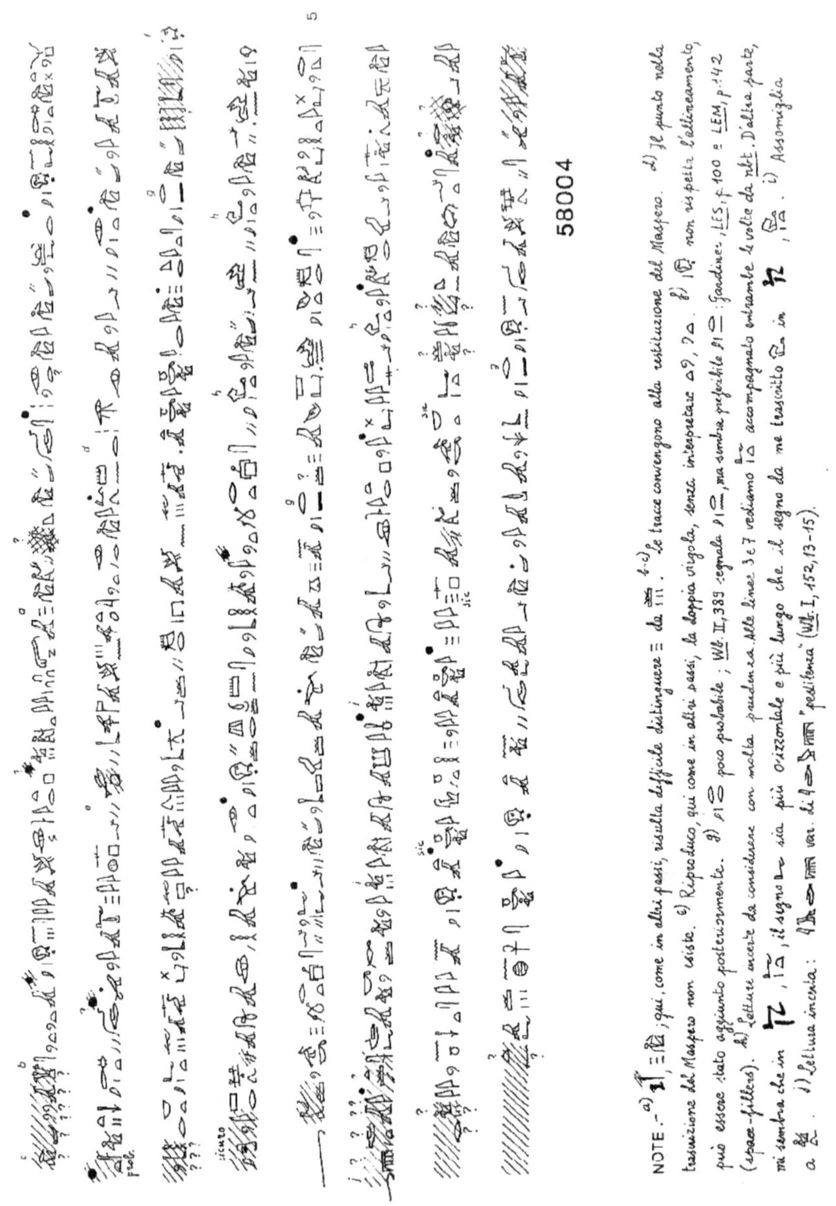

Fig. 1. Tablette Turin CG 58004 (d'après J. López, *Ostraca ieratici. Catalogo del Museo Egizio di Torino, Serie seconda, Collezioni*, III/4, Milano, 1984, pl. 184a).

Bibliographie

KRI II = Kenneth A. Kitchen, *Ramesside Inscriptions. Historical and Biographical* II. Oxford 1979.

Allen, James P. 2002. The Speos Artemidos Inscription of Hatshepsut. *Bulletin of the Egyptological Seminar* 16: 1–17 et pl. 1–2.
Assmann, Jan. 1989. *Maât, l'Égypte pharaonique et l'idée de justice sociale.* Paris: Julliard.
Bardinet, Thierry. 1995. *Les papyrus médicaux de l'Égypte pharaonique*, Coll. «Penser la médecine». Paris: Fayard.
Bottéro, Jean. 1991. La «tenson» et la réflexion sur les choses en Mésopotamie. Pp. 7–22, dans *Dispute poems and dialogues in the Ancient and Mediaeval Near East. Forms and types of literary debates in semitic and related literatures*, éd. Gerrit J. Reinink et Herman J. L. Vanstiphout. Orientalia Lovaniensia Analecta 42. Leuven: Peeters Press.
Brunner-Traut, Emma. 1963. *Altägyptische Märchen.* München: Diederichs.
Brunner-Traut, Emma. 1968. *Altägyptische Tiergeschichte und Fabel. Gestalt und Strahlkraft.* Darmstadt: Wissenschaftliche Buchgesellschaft.
Burkard, Günter et Thissen, Heinz J. 2009. *Einführung in die altägyptische Literaturgeschichte II. Neues Reich.* Berlin: LIT Verlag.
Caminos, Ricardo A. 1954. *Late Egyptian Miscellanies.* London: Oxford University Press.
Caron, Cloé. 2014. *Des hommes de larmes, des hommes de tristesse ? La conception anthropogonique dans les Textes des Sarcophages du Moyen Empire égyptien (2040–1785).* Mémoire de l'Université du Québec à Montréal.
Chambry, Émile. 1927. *Ésope. Fables.* Paris: Les Belles Lettres.
Donadoni, Sergio. 1959. *Storia della letteratura egiziana antica*, Milano: Nuova Accademia Editrice.
Donadoni, Sergio. 1967. *La Letteratura egizia.* Firenze/Milano: Sansoni.
Donadoni, Sergio. 1997. Disputa tra il corpo e la testa. Pp. 115–116, dans Anna M. Donadoni-Roveri (dir.), *La scuola nell'antico Egitto.* Torino: Museo egizio di Torino.
Enmarch, Roland. 2008. *A World Upturned. Commentary on and Analysis of The Dialogue of Ipuwer and the Lord of All.* Oxford: Griffith Institute Publications.
Erman, Adolf. 1927. *Die Literatur der Aegypter* (1923); trad. anglaise par Aylward M. Blackman, *The Literature of the Ancient Egyptian*, London: Methuen & co. Ltd.
Gardiner, Alan H. 1932. *Late Egyptian Stories* (réimpr. 1981). *Bibliotheca aegyptiaca* I. Bruxelles: Fondation égyptologique Reine Élisabeth.
Gardiner, Alan H. 1937. *Late-Egyptian Miscellanies, Bibliotheca aegyptiaca* VII. Bruxelles: Fondation égyptologique Reine Elisabeth.
Grandet, Pierre. 2010. *Catalogue des ostraca hiératiques non littéraires de Deîr el-Médîneh, Tome XI (n°s 10124–10275)*, Documents de fouilles de l'Institut français d'archéologie orientale 48. Le Caire: Institut français d'archéologie orientale.
Herrmann, Sabine. 2008. Altorientalische und griechische Rangstreitgespräche. *Saeculum* 59: 201–212.
Jiménez, Enrique. 2017. *The Babylonian Disputation Poems. With Editions of the Series of the Poplar, Palm and Vine, the Series of the Spider, and the Story of the Poor, Forlorn Wren.* Culture and History of the Ancient Near East 87. Leiden/Boston: Brill.

Kammerzell, Frank. 1995. Vom Streit zwischen Leib und Kopf. Pp. 951–954 dans *Texte aus der Umwelt des Alten Testaments* III/5. *Mythen und Epen* 3, éd. Otto Kaiser et Rykle Borger. Gütersloh: Gütersloher Verlagshaus.

Konrad, Kirsten. 2003. Zur kosmischen Konnotation des Zahlenwertes Dreißig, *Zeitschrift für ägyptische Sprache und Altertumskunde* 130: 81–87.

Lapp, Günther. 1997. *Catalogue of Books of the Dead in the British Museum*. I. *The Papyrus of Nu (BM EA 10477)*. London: British Museum Press.

López, Jesús. 1984. *Ostraca ieratici. Catalogo del Museo Egizio di Torino, Serie seconda, Collezioni*, III/4. Milano: Istituto Editoriale Cisalpino – La Goliardica. Pp. 50–51 et pl. 184–184a.

López, Jesús. 2000. Los origenes de la fábula: la disputa del cuerpo y la cabeza. *Aula Orientalis* 17–18: 475–482.

López, Jesús. 2005. *Cuentos y fábulas del antiguo Egipto*, Pliegos de Oriente. Madrid: Trotta Editorial.

Maspero, Gaston. 1879. Fragment d'une version égyptienne de la fable des membres et de l'estomac. *Études égyptiennes* I (réimpr. 1886): 260–264.

Maspero, Gaston. 1883. Fragment d'une version égyptienne de la fable des membres et de l'estomac. *Comptes rendus de l'Académie des inscriptions et belles-lettres* 27/1: 4–5.

Massart, Adhémar. 1954. *The Leiden Magical Papyrus I 343 + I 345*. Oudheidkundige Mededelingen vit het Rijksmuseum van Oudheden 34. Leiden: Rijksmuseum van Oudheden.

Mathieu, Bernard. 1986. Les hommes de larmes: à propos d'un jeu de mots mythique dans les textes de l'Ancienne Égypte. Pp. 499–509 dans *Hommages à François Daumas*, Orientalia Monspeliensia III. Montpellier: Université Paul Valéry.

Mathieu, Bernard. 1988. Études de métrique égyptienne. I. Le distique heptamétrique dans les chants d'amour. *Revue d'Égyptologie* 39: 63–82.

Mathieu, Bernard. 1996. *La poésie amoureuse de l'Égypte ancienne. Recherches sur un genre littéraire au Nouvel Empire* (réimpr. 2008). Bibliothèque d'Étude 115. Le Caire: Institut français d'archéologie orientale.

Mathieu, Bernard. 2011. Les «Procès». Un genre littéraire de l'Égypte ancienne. Pp. 161–166 dans *From Illahun to Djeme. Papers presented in Honour of U. Luft*, éd. E. Bechtold, A. Gulyás, A. Hasznos. *British Archaeological Reports, International Series* 2311. London: BAR Publishing.

Meeks, Dimitri. 1981. *Année lexicographique*, tome 2, Paris: éd. D. Meeks.

Meeks, Dimitri. 1995. Le foie, Maât et la nature humaine. Pp. 145–156 dans *Hermes Aegyptiacus, Egyptological Studies for B.H. Stricker*, éd. Terence DuQuesne. Discussions in Egyptology, Special Number 2. Oxford: DE Publications.

Menu, Bernadette. 2005. *Maât, l'ordre juste du monde* (réimpr. 2010). Paris: Michalon.

Neveu, François. 1996. *La Langue des Ramsès. Grammaire du néo-égyptien* (réimpr. 2010). Paris: Khéops.

Polis, Stéphane. 2009. *Étude de la modalité en néo-égyptien*, 2 vol. Thèse de l'Université de Liège.

Posener, Georges. 1966. Quatre tablettes scolaires de Basse Époque (*Aménémopé* et *Hardjédef*). *Revue d'Égyptologie* 18: 47.

Posener, Georges. 1981. Notes de transcription. *Revue d'Égyptologie* 33: 140.

Reinink, Gerrit J. et Herman J. L. Vanstiphout (éd.) 1991. *Dispute poems and dialogues in the Ancient and Mediaeval Near East. Forms and types of literary debates in semitic and related literatures.* Orientalia Lovaniensia Analecta 42. Leuven: Peeters Press.
Rodríguez Adrados, Francisco. 1979. *Historia de la fábula greco-latina*, vol. 1. Madrid: Editorial de la Universidad Complutense.
Rodríguez Adrados, Francisco. 2003. *History of the Graeco-Latin Fable* III. *Inventory and Documentation of the Graeco-Latin Fable.* Leiden: Brill.
Sethe, Kurt. 1907. *Urkunden der 18. Dynastie* IV (réimpr. 1984). Leipzig: J. C. Hinrichs'sche Buchhandlung.
Tylor, Joseph J. et Francis Ll. Griffith. 1894. *The Tomb of Paheri at El Kab*, Egypt Exploration Fund 11. London: Egypt Exploration Fund.
Vanstiphout, Herman J. L. 1992. The Mesopotamian Debate Poems: A General Presentation (Part II: The Subject). *Acta Sumerologica* 14: 339–367.
Vernus, Pascal. 1993. *Affaires et scandales sous les Ramsès.* Paris: Pygmalion, Coll. Bibliothèque de l'Égypte ancienne.
Williams, Ronald J. 1956. The Fable in the Ancient Near East. Pp. 3–26 dans *A Stubborn Faith. Papers on Old Testament and Related Subjects Presented to Honor W.A. Irwin*, éd. Edward C. Hobbs. Dallas: Southern Methodist University Press.
Winand, Jean. 1992. *Études de néo-égyptien* I. *La Morphologie verbale.* Aegyptiaca Leodiensia 2. Liège: Centre informatique de philosophie et lettres.
Wreszinski, Walter. 1913. *Die Medizin der alten Aegypter*, vol. III. Leipzig: J. C. Hinrichs'sche Buchhandlung.

Andréas Stauder*

8 Opposing Voices in Ancient Egyptian Literature

Two types of Egyptian literature are of direct interest in the context of the present volume: Late Egyptian disputes that pit personifications against one another, and Middle Egyptian "discourses," as these are referred in Egyptology. After briefly presenting the former, which are sparsely documented and may or may not reflect an initial influence by Mesopotamian disputes, I concentrate on the latter. Whether formally dialogues or monologues, these integrate multiple voices or attitudes to a question and are therefore strongly dialogic in a Bakhtinian sense. In two appendices, I briefly refer Middle and Late Egyptian satires of professions and Demotic dialogues concerned with the initiation into restricted sacerdotal knowledge.

1 Late Egyptian Disputes

Dating to the New Kingdom, three disputes pit personifications against one another (Mathieu 2011: 162–64; Jiménez 2017: 128–30; López 2005a). Among all Egyptian texts, these come closest to the Mesopotamian disputes. All three are fragmentarily documented in single witnesses:

– *Trial of Head and Belly* (the original incipit): the beginning of the composition is preserved on T. Turin 58004, a writing board of unknown origin, of which only the upper half (eight lines) is preserved.[1] T. Turin 58004 has been dated to the times of Amenhotep III-Akhenaten (ca. 1350 BCE; López 2000; see Jiménez 2017: 129 and n. 351) or to the late Twentieth Dynasty (ca. 1100 BCE, Burkard & Thissen 2008: 137). In the composition, Head and Belly vie as to whose function is more vital than the other. Parallels in Esop, Titus Livius, and beyond have been noted (Mathieu 2011: 163–64; Burkard and Thissen 2008: 139–40).

* École Pratique des Hautes Études, Université Paris Sciences et Lettres (EPHE, PSL, UMR 8546 AOrOc).

1 Text: López 1984: 50–51, pl. 184–184a; edition and translation: López 2000; translation and discussion: Burkard and Thissen 2008: 137–40; Kammerzell 1995. See also the contribution by Mathieu in the present volume.

https://doi.org/10.1515/9781501510274-008

- *Trial of Wine and Beer* (the original incipit): only the incipit and first sentence are preserved on O. DeM 10270, a Twentieth Dynasty (ca. 1190 – 1070 BCE) ostracon from the workmen's village of Deir el-Medineh.[2] The text appears to begin with a recrimination of Wine against Beer. Based on the grammatical genders in Egyptian, it has been tentatively suggested that Wine could stand for a man working in the hardships outside, and Beer for a woman staying inside (Mathieu 2011: 164).
- A dispute between trees, fragmentarily preserved on P. Turin 1966 ro, an early Twentieth Dynasty papyrus also from Deir el-Medineh.[3] As the dispute takes places in an orchard inhabited by lovers, this composition has often been related to Ramesside love poetry.

In relation to these three fragmentary compositions, two Late Egyptian narrative compositions are to be mentioned. Both consist largely of dialogues:
- *Truth and Falsehood* (modern title, based on the two main protagonists), partially preserved on P. Chester Beatty II, a Twentieth Dynasty papyrus from Deir el-Medineh (ca. 1190 – 1070 BCE).[4] The narrative and dialogues oppose Truth (*Mꜣʿt*) to his younger brother Falsehood (*Grg*), the latter having falsely accused the former of having robbed him of an extraordinary dagger.
- *Trial of Horus and Seth* (original incipit), or (*Contendings of) Horus and Seth* (as the composition is more commonly referred to), a lengthy composition fully preserved on P. Chester Beatty I, a Twentieth Dynasty papyrus from Deir el-Medineh.[5] The narrative and dialogues pit Horus and Seth against one another over a period of some eighty years as to whom of the two will inherit the royal function from Osiris.

All preserved incipits—in two of the three disputes and in one of the two narrative compositions—include the word *wpw* "Trial," which appears to be a generic marker (Mathieu 2011):
- *wpw ẖt ḥnʿ tp r wḥʿ i͗.i͗r=w sḏd ḳi͗=w m-bꜣḥ mʿbꜣyt (r) ptri͗ pꜣy=sn tp mtw.tw sḥꜣ pꜣ ʿḏꜣ (...)* "Trial between Head and Body until the resolution that was made, announcing their nature before the Court of Thirty to see their chief (*scil.* who is chief among the two) so that the one who was wrong was revealed."

2 Text: Grandet 2010: 153, 377.

3 Text: López 1992; edition and translation: López 2005b; see also Lopéz 2005a: 137–46; Jiménez 2017: 128 – 30.

4 Text: *LES* 30 – 36; among translations, e.g., Wente 2003a.

5 Text: *LES* 37–60; monographic study: Broze 1997; among other translations, e.g., Wente 2003b; further references in Burkard and Thissen 2008: 35 – 47.

- *p3 wpw ỉrp ḥnʿ ḥnḳt* "The trial between Wine and Beer."
- *[ḥ3tỉ-ʿ] m p3 wpw ḥr ḥnʿ stẖ (...)* "[Beginning] of the trial between Horus and Seth (...)"

Among these five texts, three pit personifications against each other: among the disputes, *Belly and Head, Wine and Beer* (the third features talking trees, *Sycamore and Fig Tree*); and among the narrative compositions, *Truth and Falsehood* (the second features gods, *Horus and Seth*). This raises the question of possible connections with the Mesopotamian genres of disputes. While actual influence remains difficult to demonstrate, a possible context for such is given by intensified cultural contacts between Egypt and the Levant and the Near East beginning in the mid-Eighteenth Dynasty (Jiménez 2017: 128–30). As the presence of other Mesopotamian literary works at Amarna, Akhenaten's new capital, illustrates, tokens of the Mesopotamian genre could have reached Egypt possibly by the times of Amenhotep III-Akhenaten, for example along with foreign wives married to the Egyptian king and their retinues (e.g., Kemp [2]2006: 292–96). As the preserved incipits demonstrate, the Egyptian compositions reflect the importance of judicial matters in Ramesside times. If, therefore, there was an initial outside influence, the Mesopotamian model would have been rapidly integrated and re-framed in specifically Egyptian terms in compositions such as *Trial of Head and Belly* and *Trial of Wine and Beer.* As the small number of texts suggests, Egyptian disputes may never have gained broad popularity. Based on what is preserved, they could also have been much shorter and simpler than Mesopotamian ones. Whether they should be seen as relating to any educational context remains entirely unclear given the evidence at hand.

An altogether different development is seen in the narrative compositions, *Truth and Falsehood* and *Trial of Horus and Seth*, with the latter standing out by its sheer length and multi-layered complexity.[6] The two compositions belong squarely to the group of Late Egyptian tales, integrating the model of the "Trial" with this tradition. The figures are allegorical, and a mythical background underlies both compositions, possibly pointing to models of royal succession. More fundamentally, the compositions are deeply humorous and entertaining, and provide a ferocious parody of judicial procedures in Ramesside times. In *Truth and Falsehood*, Truth wins, not because he is right, but only because he has managed to trick his opponent rhetorically before the tribunal. In *Trial of Horus and Seth*, the issue is solved after endless contradictory debates, argumentation, and exchanges of letters, only when Isis tricks Seth rhetorically into performative

6 See the detailed discussion of Broze 1997.

self-contradiction through wordplay—the duration of the whole process, dragging on over some eighty years, being parodic in itself. The two compositions stage rhetoric as a tool by which the protagonists, rather than working toward establishing the truth, trick, trap, and deceive one another. Both are expressive of a bleak view of rhetoric as a tool for manipulation at the hands of the powerful, in utter disconnect from any ethic value (Coulon 1999: 117–27).

2 Middle Egyptian "Discourses" and their Social Settings

In altogether different ways and reflecting different social settings, rhetoric is even more central to Middle Egyptian literature, particularly of the Middle Kingdom (2000–1700 BCE).[7] Among the various types of Middle Egyptian literature are compositions referred in modern scholarship as "discourses."[8] One of these "discourses" is a dialogue (*Debate of a Man and his Ba*; all titles are modern ones); another is a very long monologue followed by a dialogue (*Dialogue of Ipuwer and the Lord of All*); and the others are monologues addressed to an interlocutor who remains silent (most notably *Eloquent Peasant*, *Discourse of Khakhaperreseneb*; also *Discourse of a Fowler*, and *Discourse of Sasobek*). Whatever their format, these "discourses" stage different voices with high performative effect and virtuosity. Of the three main types of Middle Egyptian literature, "teachings" (*sbꜣyt*) and tales would continue, taking new forms, into Late Egyptian and Demotic literature; "discourses," by contrast, would not, and are therefore specific to Middle Egyptian literature.[9]

Prior to illustrating Middle Egyptian "discourses," aspects of the social and cultural settings of Middle Egyptian literature and rhetoric more broadly should be briefly outlined. Middle Kingdom elite society has been variously characterized as a court society, a petitioning society, and/or a society in which face-to-face interaction was paramount in determining an individual's advancement or fate. In this context, Middle Egyptian literature was not oral (it was transmitted in writing, and its very high degree of internal patterning points to composition in writing), yet fundamentally aural (formal features and high verbal vir-

---

7 On Middle Egyptian literature, see Parkinson 2002.

8 Parkinson 1996; 2002: 193–234. In the following, the type of Egyptian literary text is set in inverted commas, to distinguish it from other uses of the common English word.

9 On the issues raised by the discontinuation of "discourses," see Parkinson 2002: 226–234.

tuosity point to performance, which, furthermore, is staged, reflexively, in compositions such as *Neferti*). Primary settings were performative, in the royal court and in other elite contexts.[10]

Verbal etiquette and rhetoric are amply thematized in autobiographical self-presentations inscribed on stone, as well as in literature of all types. Middle Egyptian literary teachings abound in metapragmatic statements on the importance of rhetoric, for example, a king advising his son and successor-to-be: "Be skillful with words, and you will be victorious [...] The strong arm of a king is his tongue, words are stronger than any fight" (*Teaching a Merikare* E 32–33).[11] The most culturally central teaching of all, *Teaching of Ptahhotep*, concerns notably proper (verbal) etiquette, and defines itself as a teaching into the "norm" or "standard" (*tp-ḥsb*, on which see Coulon 1999: 112–14) of "accomplished/perfect speech" (*mdt nfrt*). The last expression, which is central to Middle Egyptian literature in general,[12] has dimensions that are at once ethic, rhetoric, and aesthetic in *Ptahhotep* (Hagen 2012). In a composition that is not a teaching, *Neferti*, "accomplished/perfect speech" is "choice verses" performed to distract the king and, by extension, the elite. In addition, poetic language in *Neferti* is also a verbal figuration of order, set against the anomic world that Neferti presentifies to the king, and at once contains in and through his "choice verses."

The importance of rhetoric is also manifest in dialogues in narratives (on which see also Worthington 2004). In *Tale of a Shipwrecked Sailor* (ca. 1950–1850 BCE), for example, a low-level official attempts to dispel a higher official's terror of reporting to the king what seems to have been an unsuccessful expedition. The former tells the latter: "Wash yourself, put water on your fingers, so that you can answer when addressed. You shall speak to the king with your mind with you, you shall answer without stammering. A man's mouth (*r3*) saves him, his speech (*mdt*) gives veiling of the face to him (i.e. makes that one be lenient for him)" (*Shipwrecked Sailor* 13–19). The low-level official goes on telling the frightened official a lengthy story of his own experience to illustrate, by analogy, that all will be well. The composition ends abruptly with the higher official's response: "Don't act brilliant, friend! What is the point of giving water to a fowl at the dawn of its slaughter in the morning?" (*Shipwrecked Sailor* 183–86). Besides the explicit thematization of rhetoric in face-to-face interaction, note the shattering brevity of the frightened high official's dismissal, consisting of just

---

10 In much later Ramesside times (1300–1070 BCE), one of several contexts for the reception and cultivation of Middle Egyptian literature would be educational, but no similar educational contexts can be made out for the Middle Kingdom itself.

11 See, e.g., Coulon 1999: 103.

12 E.g., Moers 2001: 167–91, with references to previous literature; Coulon 2004: 128–29.

two clauses. Note, furthermore, how the high official takes up the mid-level official's very opening words about pouring water, and reverses these to signify the exact opposite of their original meaning. Such a maximization of the intratextual gap will also be one central rhetorical strategy in the "discourses" to be discussed now.

3 *Eloquent Peasant*

The ambivalent relationship of "perfect speech" to "Order" (Maat), is at the core of one the most rhetorically complex "discourses" of Middle Egyptian literature, *Eloquent Peasant.*[13] The composition, which dates to around 1850 BCE, is documented in a series of four Middle Kingdom manuscripts, the two earliest of which derive from the so-called Berlin Library, a collection of literary texts deposited in a Theban tomb around 1800 BCE (Parkinson 2009: 77–112).

The opening narrative section stages a peasant from Wadi Natrun—an outsider, therefore—who is robbed of the goods he had come to trade in the Valley. The Peasant then addresses nine successive petitions to the king's deputy, the high steward Rensi son of Meru, who remains silent. It finally turns out that the authorities have remained intentionally unresponsive so that the Peasant may keep deploying his out-of-the-ordinary eloquence, which is subsequently written down on a roll under the king's own order. During his nine petitions, the Peasant, in increasing despair, moves from the specific situation of his being denied justice to broader social, political, and ultimately cosmic, levels in questioning Maat, thus raising the theodic question. The composition thereby stages a metapragmatic commentary on the social role and effects of rhetoric, addressing the problematic link between discourse and reality, and the question whether rhetoric can be reconciled with the model of Maat (Parkinson 1990; Coulon 1999).

Among the various rhetorical strategies deployed by the Peasant, the direct iteration of words is revelatory of a possibly unstable relation between the word and what it should stand for. The Peasant thus urges the king's deputy Rensi: "Do Maat for the Lord of Maat of whose Maat there is (real) Maat" (*ỉr mꜣꜥt n nb mꜣꜥt nty wn mꜣꜥt nt mꜣꜥt=f*, B1 334–35).[14] Playing on the different associations of the repeated word, the king's deputy is here to judge ("do Maat") for Thoth

13 Photographs and text: Parkinson 2012b and 1991, respectively; translation and commentary: Parkinson 2012a; see, further, the analyses in notably Parkinson 1990; 2002: 168–82; and Coulon 1999: 104–109, 114–17.

14 All translations after Parkinson 2012a, some slightly adapted.

("the Lord of Maat"), who functions as a divine model of justice and has "(real) Maat," implying, by contrast, that others, such as possibly Rensi himself, have Maat only in name or form (Coulon 1999: 108–109, 115; Parkinson 2012a: 271–72). Inasmuch as the various significations of words are themselves intertextually determined, wordplay becomes a maximally condensed mode for exploring the fissures in normative discourse.

Such fissures are also expressed through directly antithetical statements. For example: "The measure of heaps now defrauds for himself; the filler for another now despoils his surroundings; he who leads lawfully now commands theft—who then will beat off wretchedness? when the dispeller of infirmity is going wrong; (...)" (B1 135–38). A nominal pole, the subjects consisting of participial constructions, refers to the situation as it should be, and therefore to what, normatively, should be Rensi's behavior. This clashes with a verbal pole, referring to the here and now of the speech situation, the petitions the Peasant addresses to the same Rensi, and thereby to the situation as it is empirically found to be.[15] The following is even more subtly insinuating: "Does the scale wander (*ỉn ỉw ỉwsw nnm=f*)? *Is* the balance *being* partial (*ỉn ỉw mḫ3t ḥr rḏt ḥr gs*)? And is Thoth lenient (*ỉn ỉw rf ḏḥwtỉ sfn=f*)? Then you may do evil!" (B1 179–81). The three rhetorical questions in sequence call for "of course not" denials to each. In the first and third questions, the constructions SUBJECT *sḏm=f* express general or habitual unaccomplished aspect, referring to the normative state-of-affairs, how things should be. In the second question, by contrast, the construction SUBJECT *ḥr sḏm* expresses progressive aspect, pointing to the speech situation, to how things actually are. Through contrasts in verbal aspect, the Peasant here insinuates that the normative values that Rensi as a deputy to the king should embody (first and third questions, habitual or general aspect) stand in direct conflict to his actual observed behavior (second question, progressive aspect).

The disconnect between the normative and the actual is expressed, furthermore, through the subversion of imagery that recurs as long-distance echoes.[16] For example, Rensi is addressed as a cosmic "rudder" (B1 122–23) and as a Nile flood (B1 173), both pointing to the most normative sphere of all, the king's. But the image of the rudder then also becomes one of a helmsman whose boat had gone adrift (B1 157–58), a ferry that has sunk (B1 229), and a boat that runs out of control (B1 252), while the image of Rensi as the Nile flood gives way to one as a destroyer of fish in the river (B1 257–62) (Parkinson 2012a: 211). Such strategies of rhetorical subversion extend to official discourse

15 Coulon 1999: 107–108, with a discussion of the similarly patterned B1 165–69.
16 See the detailed commentary by Parkinson 2012a.

that the Peasant keeps alluding to in his petitions. In the first petition, the Peasant eulogizes Rensi. He does so first through a series of epithets directly reminiscent of formulations in contemporary autobiographies, a highly topical inscriptional genre: "For you are a father to the orphan, a husband to the widow, a brother for the repudiated woman, a kilt to who has no mother" (B1 93–95). He pursues the eulogy with a series of five epithets that is modelled on nothing less than the five-fold royal titulary: "Let me make your name in this land according to good rule: Guide free of greed, Great one free of lowliness, who terminates falsehood, who brings about *Maat*, who comes to the one whose voice babbles in fear" (B1 95–99). Rensi's five-fold titulary is subsequently echoed by a similarly five-fold mock titulary in the fourth petition (B1 252–55), which, in the immediately following fifth petition, is itself "debased into a series of derogatory statements" to do with fishing (B1 257–61; Parkinson 2012a: 211). The normative formulations inspired by the autobiographies, for their part, are made to stand in an increasingly stark contrast with actuality as the Peasant goes on with his petitions. Through what amounts to an *Entfremdung* avant la lettre, the Peasant presents the elite with its normative discourse about itself, destabilizing the same discourse (Coulon 1999: 107). Like direct juxtaposition, antithetical formulations, and long-distance modulations of imagery, the maximization of intertextual gaps reveals the fissure between the normative and the actual. In and through "accomplished/perfect speech" (*mdt nfrt*), in principle an index of Maat, the Peasant questions the relation between the two—reflexively, because "accomplished/perfect speech" is made to bear on itself.

4 *Dialogue of Ipuwer and the Lord of All*

A core concern of Middle Egyptian literature is the theodic question (Parkinson 2002: 130–38; Enmarch 2008: 55–58): suffering and imperfection is experienced in the world and actuality is divorced from ideality, raising the question how this can accord with the creator's justice. The theodic argument, which is central to the Peasant's questioning of Maat (see above), receives its most extensive, and at once darkest, expression in the *Dialogue of Ipuwer and the Lord of All.*[17] The composition is preserved in a single manuscript, P. Leiden I 344 ro, from the late Nineteenth Dynasty (ca. 1200 BCE; Enmarch 2005) but is much earlier, arguably dating to the late Middle Kingdom (ca. 1800–1700 BCE).[18]

17 Edition and study: Enmarch 2008, on which the following is based.
18 Enmarch 2008: 20–22; secondarily, Stauder 2013: 463–68.

After the lost beginning, which may or may not have included an opening narrative frame, much of the composition consists of a series of anaphoric stophes spoken by Ipuwer, otherwise known as an Overseer of Singers (Laments I-III, 1.1–10.3; Injunctions I-III, 10.3-ca.11.9). In the following section, Ipuwer and the Lord of All—the king, and as such a figure solidary with the creator god himself—take turns (Enmarch 2008: 28–33). This discursive section consists of a direct Reproach by Ipuwer to the Lord of All, a Meditation by Ipuwer, a Reply of the Lord of All, a second Reproach, and a second Reply (ca.11.10-ca.17.3). Like the beginning, the end of the composition is lost.[19] In the Laments and Injunctions, Ipuwer develops images of general misery and the disruption of order, and topics of social inversion, including the collapse of royal authority, of correct ritual procedure, and of elite written culture. In the following Reproaches, Ipuwer denounces the negligence of the creator god and the inaction of the Lord of All, his deputy. The Lord of All replies by pointing to the imperfect nature and evil behavior of humanity as responsible for its own suffering.

Through poetic imagery, the Laments and Injunctions move from one thematic complex to the next and meander back to ones previously evoked. The divorce between the world as it should be and as it is observed is often couched in the *Sonst-Jetzt* scheme (Schenkel 1984; Parkinson 2002: 58–60), a one-sentence format common in Middle Egyptian "discourses" and laments, which sets a(n ideal) past situation in an antithetical contrast with the (problematic) present. Like in *Eloquent Peasant*, wordplay is directly expressive, for instance: "O, but now Maat is through this land in this its name (only), but it is wrongdoing that they do, building (*grg*) on it (*scil.* Maat)" (5.3–4): "building" (*grg*) on Maat is homophonous with *grg* "lie, falsehood," and thereby inherently vitiated (Coulon 1999: 109–10; Enmarch 2008: 105–106). Like in *Eloquent Peasant*, too, normative discourse is intertextually evoked and made to clash with vivid images of disorder and counter-normative situations: the disconnect between ideality and actuality is brought to the fore through a maximization of intertextual gaps.[20] In the Reproaches and Replies, Ipuwer and the Lord of All do not oppose one another through direct counter-arguments but voice their adverse positions by taking up motifs and imagery from the preceding Laments and Injunctions or their opponents' preceding speeches, re-contextualizing these so that they express diverging significations. The speakers' opposed positions are thus articulated through a maximization of intratextual gaps as much as intertextual ones. The poem does not drive toward a discursive solution of the contradiction. Rather,

19 For the overall structure, see Enmarch 2008: 56.
20 Compare Enmarch 2008: 36–42, 49–52, and the commentary.

"th(e) modulation of tone and accretive treatment of themes has a baroque, contrapuntal, quality" (Enmarch 2008: 55). This semantic intensification is dramaticized through the long-delayed response of the Lord of All, then through the dialogue structure of the second part, and leads to an increasingly resonant and multiply-voiced vision of Egypt engulfed in chaos.[21]

5 *Debate of a Man and His Ba*

Different attitudes toward death are staged in the Middle Egyptian *Debate of a Man and His Ba*.[22] The *Debate* is known from a single manuscript, P. Berlin 3204, dating to ca. 1800 BCE, and may have been composed a few decades or generations earlier during the Twelfth Dynasty. P. Berlin 3204 derives from the "Berlin Library," a group of literary texts deposited in a Theban tomb, and including notably the two earliest known copies of *Eloquent Peasant* (see above). Fragments of the lost beginning of P. Berlin 3204 have recently resurfaced in altogether unexpected places (P. Mallorca II and P. Amherst III).[23]

Uniquely in Middle Egyptian literature, a man addresses his Ba, an aspect of the person and a mode of existence also associated with mobility in the afterlife.[24] P. Mallorca II and P. Amherst III, the recently recovered initial fragments of P. Berlin 3024, demonstrate that, as had long been hypothesized, the dialogue between the Man and the Ba was preceded by a narrative frame of uncertain length. Tantalizing as they are, these fragments show that this staged a Man, referred as "The sick one" (*mr*), who reports his conversation with his Ba to an audience that includes a woman called "The living one" (*ʿnḫt*). In this liminal situation, the Man can either go to death or back to life, this alternative being the topic of the Debate (Escolano-Poveda 2017: 36–37). The overall structure of the composition can be schematized as follows (with "Ba 1" for the first speech of the Ba, "Man 1" for first speech of the Man, and so forth):

- narrative frame (uncertain length, fragmentary);
- Ba 1 (fragm.) – Man 1 (fragm.) – Ba 2 – Man 2;

---

21 See Enmarch 2008: 45–55, 60–64, with an analysis of style and performative aspects.

22 Text and study: Allen 2011; see also Parkinson 2002: 216–26; other modern titles include *Gespräch eines Lebensmüden mit seiner Seele* or *The Man who was tired of Life*.

23 See Escolano-Poveda 2017 and Parkinson 2003, respectively.

24 In *Discourse of Khakheperreseneb* (text: Parkinson 1997; interpretation: Parkinson 2002: 200–204), a monologue is addressed to the "heart" or "mind" (*ib*), the seat of mental ability and agency.

- Ba 3, the Ba's longest speech, culminating in parables 1 and 2 – Man 3, the longest speech of all, consisting of litanies 1–4;
- Ba 4, a short final reconciliation.

Throughout their speeches, the Man and the Ba display consistent, yet opposed, perspectives on death. The Ba emphasizes the horror of death, as an end to a transient life. The Man stresses the blessings of death, associated with the afterlife and funerary provisions, and as a release of life. The poem thus stages two voices: the Man's, tending to espouse a more normative cultural discourse, and the Ba's, tending to a more counter-cultural one (Parkinson 2002: 218) also found in some Harpists' songs.

While the Man's and the Ba's perspectives on death remain constant throughout the *Debate*, their positions as to whether death should be wished for immediately or waited for to come in its proper time are reversed in the course of the poem.[25] In his first two speeches, the Ba advocates for immediate death, considering the Man's sorry state. The Man, to the contrary, underscores that an untimely death will deprive him (and thereby the Ba as well) of the opportunity to provide for the afterlife. In a dramatic reversal, the Ba in his third speech makes a tableau of the ephemeral nature of life, and urges the Man to enjoy life. The Man responds through a picture of the wretchedness of his situation and his social isolation, advocating immediate death. The short final speech of the Ba is reconciliatory, proposing to accept death as the ultimate end, so that the Man and the Ba can reach the West in harmony.

Throughout their speeches, the Ba and the Man develop common imagery.[26] The speakers take up imagery from their opponent's or their own previous speeches, subverting, reversing, or assimilating it. A case of direct reversal is at the crucial juncture between Man 2 and Ba 3. Arguing against untimely death, the Man had concluded with a normative vision of burial associated with the proper funerary rites: "Set your heart, my soul, my brother, until the heir has grown up *who will present offerings*, who will attend to the tomb *on burial* (*qrs*) *day*, and will transport *a bed for the necropolis*" (Man 2, 60–62).[27] In his rebuttal, the Ba takes up the very word *qrs* to paint a bleak vision in which the "offerings" (to be presented) have become "tears" (to be brought), while the "bed in the necropolis" is echoed with a corpse "on the hill": "As for your bringing to

25 I follow Allen's (2011: 137–60) interpretation; see, however, Parkinson 2002: 218 and 219–226, reading differently.

26 The following is based on the very rich commentaries by Allen (2011) and Parkinson (2002: 219–27), to which the reader is referred for much further elaboration.

27 All translations after Allen (2011), some slightly adapted; emphasis mine.

mind *burial*, this is heartache; it is *bringing tears*; it is taking a man from his house so that he is *left on the hill* (...)" (Ba 3, 56–59). He who was supposed to be "in a pyramid" and have heirs to attend for his funerary service (Man 2, 42–43) has, in the Ba's speech, become one who "has died on the riverbank for lack of a survivor," one "to whom the fish and the lip of the water speak" (Ba 3, 64–66).

In the Ba's and the Man's speeches, imagery goes through successive modulation, thus the image of a journey through the whole second part of the composition. In the Ba's third speech, it is first a metaphor of life, its transience and unpredictability (Ba 3, 1st parable, 68–80). In the Man's response, it is recast positively as a coming home from an expedition, an image of death as a release from a painful life (Man 3, 3d litany, 130–42, in particular tercets 1, 4, 6), then as one of a man standing in the bark, in a vision of the afterlife (Man 3, 4th litany, 143–45). It is finally taken up by the Ba in his closing reconciliatory speech: "(...) Reject the West, but desire that you reach the West when your body touches the earth, and I will alight after your weariness, thus we will make harbor together" (Ba 4, 151–54). The image of the riverbank has an even longer history of successive modulations. The riverbank is first a part of the Man's vision of funerary bliss: "I will *drink water at the flood* and shall lift away dryness, and you will make jealous another *ba* who is hungry" (Man 2, 47–49). The Ba reverses the image into one of being abandoned and lacking proper funerary rites: "like *the inert who have died on the riverbank* for lack of a survivor, the waters having taken his end, or Sunlight similarly––to whom the fish and the lip of the water speak" (Ba 3, 63–67). The Ba then modulates the image into one of life often interrupted before time, and therefore to be lived and enjoyed now: "(...) disembarked with his wife and his children, and *they perished atop a depression ringed by night with riverbankers.* (...) But I care about her children, broken in the egg, who saw the face of Khenti before they lived." (Ba 3, 1st parable, 73–80). The Man responds by the same image, asking why stay alive given his dire condition: "Look, my name reeks: look, more than crocodile's smell, *at a site of slaughter with riverbankers*" (Man 3, 1st litany, 95–97). Moving to increasingly loftier levels (compare also stench becoming myrrh), the Man then transforms the image into one of death as coming home: "Death is in my sight today, like myrrh's smell, like sitting under sails on a windy day. Death is in my sight today, like the lotuses' smell, *like sitting on the Bank of Inebriation*" (Man 3, 3d litany, 132–36). Joining the previously evoked thematic thread of the journey, the riverbank, finally, becomes a harbor, a normative image of harmonious death, in the closing verse of the composition: "(...) Then we will *make harbor* at the same time" (Ba 4, reconciliation, 154).

At the level of the overall poetic form, while the initial exchanges (Ba 1, Man 1, Ba 2, Man 2) are terse and interrupting, the much longer speeches that follow (Ba 3, Man 3) are based on more densely patterned modes of discourse, parables (Ba 3, second part) and litanies (the whole of Man 3). The four litanies in Man 3 move from descriptions of the Man's wretchedness on a personal level ("Look, my name reeks ...") and social isolation ("To whom can I speak today ...") to visions of death as a coming home ("Death in my sight today ...") and eternal bliss ("Surely, he who is there will be a living god ..."). The metric structure of the four litanies is highly patterned (8 < 16, with increasingly repetitive imagery, then 6 > 3 tercets, see Allen 2011: 124) and contributes to the ultimate sense of release in the third and fourth. Throughout the composition, common imagery is subverted, and also increasingly assimilated and integrated, by the two parties; the resolution is brought about in and through poetic language itself (Parkinson 2002: 226).

6 Conclusion

While composed and transmitted in writing, Middle Egyptian literature is fundamentally geared at performance (education, in particular, is only one secondary, much later, setting). *Debate of a Man and his Ba* stages different attitudes toward death, while *Eloquent Peasant* and *Dialogue of Ipuwer and the Lord of All* center around the theodic question and, particularly the former, the problematic relation between words and what these stand for. Being the products of a society in which face-to-face verbal interaction were of central importance, the compositions are highly rhetorical; they often concern, and stage, rhetoric itself, reflexively. The compositions do not consist of directly discursive expositions of arguments and counter-arguments leading to a resolution that would have one position win over another. Rather, they portray different aspects of, or attitudes to, a question through what has been described as accretive thematic modulation.

Within one sentence, one turn, in turn-taking, and over longer distance, iteration cum variation is central to the rhetoric of the compositions presented above. The repetition of a word, with or without wordplay, makes the different significations of that word clash. Similar imagery is taken up, with different and often opposed significations. Segments of normative discourse are extracted from their original places, notably in inscriptions, and inserted into the literary contexts in which their original significations become problematic. Through such indirect citationality at all levels, both intratextual and intertextual gaps are maximized, revealing the fissures of discourse itself. Complexly voiced iteration accumulates over the course of a performance, building up a resonant and increasingly polyphonic space.

Formally, *Debate of a Man and his Ba* is a dialogue with an introductory narrative frame; *Eloquent Peasant* is a monologue with a narrative frame; and *Dialogue of Ipuwer and the Lord of All* is a very long monologue followed by a dialogue (the beginning and end, where a narrative frame may have been located, are lost). Despite such formal differences, the compositions are much closer than they may seem at first, not only thematically and rhetorically, but also in terms of their voicing. While *Debate* stages a dialogue, both speakers ultimately stand for the same individual, a man experiencing near-death. The Man speaks of the Ba mostly in the third person, addressing him directly only at the crucial turn of Man 2 to Ba 3. Throughout the composition, the Man and the Ba do hardly respond to one another directly but develop common imagery in ways that counter their opponent's speeches with high effect. Conversely, the monologues are themselves strongly addressive. Ipuwer's anaphoric Laments and Injunctions are addressed to the Lord of All. When they finally come, the long-delayed Replies of the Lord of All draw on imagery previously developed by Ipuwer and therefore respond to Ipuwer's earlier Laments and Injunctions as much as to his immediate Reproaches. In *Eloquent Peasant*, the petitions are even more strongly interlocutive in their address to, and even apostrophe of, Rensi son of Meru. The dramatic progression of the Peasant's petitions is entirely in response to Rensi's continued, and increasingly louder, silence, which becomes itself a major topic of the petitions.

The compositions discussed above are strongly dialogic in a Bakhtinian sense: they include other voices. In *Eloquent Peasant*, high-cultural discourses are intertextually evoked, and questioned, by the speaker in his petitions to an unresponsive deputy of the king, himself a figuration of these same high-cultural discourses. A similar comment applies to Ipuwer's densely intertextual addresses to the long silent Lord of All. In *Debate of a Man and his Ba*, various voices receive what would seem to be a direct figuration in the two speakers, yet each speaker also individually stands for multiple voices. Whether formally dialogues, monologues, or combining both, the compositions bring these various voices together, with the effect of foregrounding intratextual and intertextual gaps. Through the rhetoric of iteration and indirect citation, they integrate, rather than discursively resolve, the multiple voices they stage.

Appendix 1: Satires of Professions

Some Sumerian disputes make satires of professions. The very small group of Egyptian disputes does not include any, but satires of professions are prominent in another type of literature of the same period (Dynasties 19 – 20, ca. 1300 – 1075 BCE) and are therefore mentioned here for the sake of reference. These compositions (Jäger 2004: 193 – 304) espouse the ethos of the scribal milieus from which they arguably derive, and deride notably the military profession. Formally, they adopt the general format of the "teaching" (*sbꜣyt*), which consists of a direct address to a son, or a younger man, who is instructed but does not respond.[28] The Ramesside satires of professions have a major antecedent in the Middle Egyptian *Teaching of Dua's son Khety* (also referred to as the *Satire of Trades*).[29] In this, the father presents the son with a series of tableaus of the hardships or unworthiness of various trades, leaving him to contemplate the uniquely blessed status of the scribe. Satire is also central in the Ramesside literary *Satirical Letter*, or *Satirische Streitschrift* (main manuscript ca. 1200 BCE; Fischer-Elfert [2]1992; 1986). In this, a military scribe, Hori, accuses his addressee, a fellow scribe, of gross incompetence at extensive lengths. Like in the satires of professions (couched in the teaching format), the addressee does not respond in the *Satirical Letter*.

---

28 The format of the "teaching" (*sbꜣyt*), which is highly productive in Middle Egyptian, Late Egyptian, and Demotic literature alike, has the addressee, the son, remain silent. In one case only, the son responds: in the early Ramesside *Teaching of Ani* (ca. 1250 BCE (?); text: Quack 1994), the teaching on ethical and religious values and behavior is followed by a dialogue between Ani and his son Khonshotep, who questions the value of the instructions he has just received (see Burkard and Thissen 2008: 104 – 108; for the tentative possibility of a Near Eastern influence, Quack 1994: 218 – 19). A dialogue between a father and his son is probably also featured in a short Ramesside ostracon from Deir el-Medineh (Posener 1951: 30, pl. 50 – 50a. Fischer-Elfert 1997: 10 – 16; Burkard and Thissen 2008: 136 – 137), where the son, quite to the contrary, praises the instructions.

29 Jäger 2004: 1 – 192, I-XCIV; see also Widmaier 2013. The dating of the composition has traditionally been to the Middle Kingdom, ca. 2000 – 1750 BCE but remains uncertain, with a low dating to the early New Kingdom, ca. 1550 – 1450 BCE, not to be excluded (provisionally, Stauder 2013: 468 – 76).

Appendix 2: Demotic Dialogues and Initiation into Restricted Sacerdotal Knowledge

Two of the most massive preserved Demotic compositions consist of dialogues, embedded into a narrative frame for the second: the *Ritual for Entering the Chamber of Darkness* or *Book of Thoth*, and the *Myth of the Sun's Eye* or *Return of the Goddess* (all titles are modern ones). Both compositions are about restricted sacerdotal knowledge. They are presently documented in a relatively high number of manuscripts, suggesting that they may have been more widely circulated than Demotic literary compositions in the narrower sense.[30] As these sacerdotal dialogues are entirely different from Mesopotamian disputes, the following is kept maximally succinct, the interested reader being referred to the studies cited below.

The *Book of Thoth* (thus named by the editors of the text, Jasnow and Zauzich 2005) or *Ritual for Entering the Chamber of Darkness* (thus Quack forthc.) is documented in a still growing number of manuscripts dating from the first century BCE to the second century CE and is one of the most complex and difficult surviving ancient Egyptian texts.[31] The composition consists of a dialogue between one, or possibly several, masters, and a disciple.[32] The scene is the "Chamber of Darkness" (*ʿ.t-kky*), probably referring to the House of Life, with strong underworldly connotations. The dialogue centers around esoteric sacerdotal knowledge, the sacred names of entities and beings (Jasnow and Zauzich 2005: 38–65), and very much writing itself (Quack 2007) with rich figurative imagery (Jasnow 2011). The indications of speakers could be interpreted as pointing to a performance, the setting of which has been sought in connection with rituals of initiation into the House of Life (Quack 2007).

The *Myth of the Sun's Eye* is documented in manuscripts from the second century CE (as well as in a Greek translation dating to the third century CE) and represents another highly complex composition.[33] The composition consists mostly of dialogues, embedded in a narrative frame. The narrative frame is based on the myth of the Return of the Goddess, documented in a variety of sources

30 For an overview of Demotic litterature in general, see Quack 2009.

31 Edition and study: Jasnow and Zauzich 2005; translation with introductory commentary: Jasnow and Zauzich 2014; additions notably by Quack 2006; 2007; and forthc.; a revised edition is in preparation by Jasnow and Zauzich.

32 Different interpretations in Jasnow and Zauzich 2005: 3–17; 2014: 30–37; and Quack forthc.

33 Edition: de Cenival 1988; recent translation: Quack and Hoffmann 2007: 195–229, with further references on pp. 356–58; for an introduction, Quack 2009: 128–40.

from earlier times on: a goddess, often Re's daughter or "Eye," had retreated to the South in anger, and is propitiated to return to Egypt, appeased and bringing welfare to the land. In the Demotic composition, the angry goddess is the "Nubian Cat," standing for the goddess Tefnut, and speaks with the "Little Dog-Monkey," a son of Thoth, who tries to appease the goddess and persuade her to return to Egypt. The narrative ends with the protagonists' successful return to Egypt culminating in the celebration of a festival. As part of the argument, the dialogues include animal parables, some with parallels in other literary traditions such as the Mesopotamian Etana and the Indian Pancatantra, as well as the elucidations of signs of writing in reference to esoteric sacerdotal knowledge (Von Lieven 2010). The sacerdotal dimension of the text is also manifest in the multiple layers of commentary with which the manuscripts are interspersed, bearing testimony to a highly complex textual tradition. Possible indications for performance have been noted and it has been proposed that settings for this could have been at the end of festivals, in relation to sacerdotal practices of a collective elucidation of complex texts (Quack and Hoffmann 2007: 198).

In both the *Book of Thoth* or *Ritual for Entering the Chamber of Darkness*, and the *Myth of the Sun's Eye*, the dialogue format relates to the initiation into, or elucidation of, restricted sacerdotal knowledge, including writing itself. An outwardly similar association between the dialogue format and the initiation into esoteric knowledge recurs in the Corpus Hermeticum, even if there does not seem to be any strong direct link between this and the Demotic composition.[34] The association also has much earlier antecedents in the Egyptian tradition itself: in the Coffin Texts already (ca. 2000 BCE), the speaker (the deceased) finds himself in dialogue with various assemblies or guardians and must demonstrate his mastery of esoteric knowledge during his funerary journey.[35] It has been suggested that this dialogue format in the Coffin Texts may itself have a background in entry examinations into professional guilds, during which one would have had to demonstrate a mastery of a restricted professional knowledge (Fischer-Elfert 2002: 30–35).

34 Jasnow and Zauzich 2014: 49–50; Quack 2007: 261; Jasnow and Zauzich 2005: 65–71.
35 E.g., Coulon 2004: 134–36, with further discussion of debates in assemblies and councils.

Bibliography

LES = Gardiner, Alan H. 1932. *Late Egyptian Stories.* Bibliotheca Aegyptica I. Bruxelles: Fondation Reine Élisabeth.

Allen, James. 2011. *The Debate Between a Man and His Soul. A Masterpiece of Ancient Egyptian Literature.* Culture and History of the Ancient Near East 44. Leiden/Boston: Brill.

Broze, Michèle. 1996. *Mythe et roman en Égypte ancienne: les aventure d'Horus et Seth dans le Papyrus Chester Beatty I.* Orientalia Lovaniensa Analecta 76. Leuven: Peeters.

Burkard, Günter, and Heinz Thissen. 2008. *Einführung in die altägyptische Literaturgeschichte II. Neues Reich.* Einführungen und Quellentexte zur Ägyptologie 6. Münster: LIT Verlag.

Coulon, Laurent. 1999. La rhétorique et ses fictions. Pouvoirs et duplicités du discours à travers la littérature égyptienne du Moyen et du Nouvel Empire. *Bulletin de l'Institut français d'archéologie orientale* 99: 103–32.

Coulon, Laurent. 2004. Rhétorique et stratégies du discours dans les fomules funéraires: les innovations des Textes des Sarcophages. Pp 119–42 in *D'un monde à l'autre. Textes des pyramides, Textes des sarcophages*, ed. Susanne Bickel and Bernard Mathieu. Bibliothèque d'étude 139. Cairo: IFAO.

de Cenival, Françoise. 1988. *Le mythe de l'œil du soleil.* Demotische Studien 9. Sommerhausen: Gisela Zauzich Verlag.

Enmarch, Roland. 2005. *The Dialogue of Ipuwer and the Lord of All.* Griffith Institute Publications. Oxford: Griffith Institute.

Enmarch, Roland. 2008. *A World Upturned: Commentary on and Analysis of The Dialogue of Ipuwer and the Lord of All.* Oxford: Oxford University Press.

Escolano-Poveda, Marina. 2017. The Missing Beginning of the Debate of a Man and his Ba and the Continuation of the Tale of the Herdsman (P. Mallorca I and II). *Zeitschrift für ägyptische Sprache und Altertumskunde* 144: 16–54.

Fischer-Elfert, Hans-Werner. 1986. *Die satirische Streitschrift des Papyrus Anastasi I. Übersetzung und Kommentar.* Ägyptologische Abhandlungen 44. Wiesbaden: Harrassowitz.

Fischer-Elfert, Hans-Werner. ^{2}1992. *Die satirische Streitschrift des Papyrus Anastasi I.* Kleine Ägyptische Texte. Wiesbaden: Harrassowitz.

Fischer-Elfert, Hans-Werner. 1997. *Lesefunde im literarischen Steinbruch von Deir el-Medineh.* Kleine ägyptische Texte 12. Wiesbaden: Harrassowitz.

Fischer-Elfert, Hans-Werner. 2002. Das verschwiegene Wissen des Irtisen (Stele Louvre C14). Zwischen Aracanum und Preisgabe. Pp. 27–35 in *Ägyptische Mysterien?*, ed. Jan Assmann and Martin Bommas. München: Fink.

Grandet, Pierre. 2010. *Catalogue des ostraca hiératiques non littéraire de Deîr el-Médineh, Tome XI (nos. 10124–10275).* Documents de fouilles de l'Institut français d'archéologie orientale 48. Le Caire: IFAO.

Hagen, Fredrik. 2012. *An Egyptian Literary Text in Context: The Instruction of Ptahhotep.* Orientalia Lovaniensia Analecta 218. Leuven: Peeters.

Jäger, Stephan. 2004. *Altägyptische Berufstypologien*. Lingua Aegyptia Studia Monographica 4. Göttingen: Seminar für Ägyptologie und Koptologie.
Jasnow, Richard. 2011. 'Caught in the Web of Words' – Remarks on the Imagery of Writing and Hieroglyphs in the Book of Thoth. *Journal of the American Research Center in Egypt* 47: 297–317.
Jasnow, Richard, and Karl-Theodor Zauzich. 2005. *The Ancient Egyptian Book of Thoth: A Demotic Discourse on Knowledge and Pendant to the Classical Hermetica*. Wiesbaden: Harrassowitz.
Jasnow, Richard, and Karl-Theodor Zauzich. 2014. *Conversations in the House of Life. A New Translation of the Ancient Egyptian Book of Thoth*. Wiesbaden: Harrassowitz.
Jiménez, Enrique. 2017. *The Babylonian Disputation Poems*. Culture and History of the Ancient Near East 87. Leiden/Boston: Brill.
Kammerzell, Frank. 1995. Vom Streit zwischen Leib und Kopf. Pp. 951–54 in *Mythen und Epen. Texte aus der Umwelt des Alten Testaments III*, ed. Elke Blumenthal et al. Gütersloh: Gütersloher Verlagshaus Mohn.
Kemp, Barry. ²2006. *Ancient Egypt. Anatomy of a Civilization*. London and New Work: Routledge.
López, Jesús. 1984. *Ostraca ieratici N. 57450–57568. Tabelle lignee N. 58001–58007*. Catalogo del Museo Egizio di Torino, Seria Seconda, Collezioni, III.4. Milano.
López, Jesús. 1992. Le verger d'amour (P. Turin 1966, recto). *Revue d'Égyptologie* 43: 133–43.
López, Jesús. 2000. Los orígenes de la fábula: la disputa del cuerpo y la cabeza. *Aula Orientalis* 17/18: 475–82.
López, Jesús. 2005a. *Cuentos y fábulas del Antiguo Egipto*. Pliegos de Oriente. Barcelona: Trotta.
López, Jesús. 2005b. La Disputa de los árboles del huerto. Pp. 19–25 in *Actas del segundo congreso ibérico de egiptología*, ed. J. Cervelló Autuori, M. Díaz de Cerio Juan, and D. Rull Ribó. Bellaterra: Universitat Autònoma de Barcelona.
Mathieu, Bernard. 2011. Les "Procès". Un genre littéraire de l'Égypte ancienne. Pp. 161–66 in *From Illahun to Djeme. Papers Presented in Honour of Ulrich Luft*, ed. Eszter Bechtold, András Gulyás, Andrea Hasznos. BAR International Series 2311. Oxford: Archeopress.
Moers, Gerald. 2001. *Fingierte Welten in der ägyptischen Literatur des 2. Jahrtausends vor Christus: Grenzüberschreitung, Reisemotiv und Fiktionalität*. Probleme der Ägyptologie 19. Leiden/Boston: Brill.
Parkinson, Richard B. 1990 Literary Form and the "Tale of the Eloquent Peasant." *Journal of Egyptian Archaeology* 78: 163–78.
Parkinson, Richard B. 1991. *The Tale of the Eloquent Peasant*. Oxford: Griffith Institute Publications.
Parkinson, Richard B. 1996. Types of Literature in the Middle Kingdom. Pp. 297–312 in *Ancient Egyptian Literature: History and Forms*, ed. Antonio Loprieno. Probleme der Ägyptologie 10. Leiden/Boston: Brill.
Parkinson, Richard B. 1997. The Text of *Khakheperreseneb:* New Readings of EA 5645, and an Unpublished Ostracon. *Journal of Egyptian Archaeology* 83: 55–68.
Parkinson, Richard B. 2002. *Poetry and Culture in Middle Kingdom Egypt: A Dark Side to Perfection*, London/New York: Continuum.

Parkinson, Richard B. 2003. The Missing Beginning of 'The Dialogue of a Man and His Ba': P. Amherst III and the History of the 'Berlin Library'. *Zeitschrift für ägyptische Sprache und Altertumskunde* 130: 120–33.
Parkinson, Richard B. 2004. 'The Discourse of the Fowler': Papyrus Butler verso (P.BM EA 10274). *Journal of Egyptian Archaeology* 90: 81–111.
Parkinson, Richard B. 2009. *Reading Ancient Egyptian Poetry. Among Other Histories.* Malden/Chichester: Wiley-Blackwell.
Parkinson, Richard B. 2012a. *The Tale of the Eloquent Peasant: A Reader's Commentary.* Lingua Aegyptia Studia Monographica 10. Hamburg: Widmaier Verlag.
Parkinson, Richard B. 2012b. *The Ramesseum Papyri.* British Museum Online Research Catalogues. http://www.britishmuseum.org/research/publications/online_research_catalogues.aspx (last accessed November 2019).
Posener, Georges. *Catalogue des ostraca hiératiques de Deir el-Médineh.* Documents de fouilles de l'Institut français d'archéologie orientale 18. Le Caire: IFAO.
Quack, Joachim F. 1994. *Die Lehren des Ani. Ein neuägyptischer Weisheitstext in seinem kulturellen Umfeld.* Orbis Biblicus et Orientalis 141. Fribourg: Universitätsverlag, and Göttingen: Vandenhoeck & Ruprecht.
Quack, Joachim F. 2006. Review of R. Jasnow and K.-Th. Zauzich, The Ancient Egyptian Book of Thoth: A Demotic Discourse on Knowledge and Pendant to the Classical Hermetica. *Orientalistische Literaturzeitung* 101: 610–15.
Quack, Joachim F. 2007. Die Initiation zum Schreiberberuf im Alten Ägypten. *Studien zur Altägyptischen Kultur* 36: 249–95.
Quack, Joachim F. 2009. *Einführung in die altägyptische Literaturgeschichte III: Die demotische und gräko-ägyptische Literatur.* Einführungen und Quellentexte zur Ägyptologie. Münster: LIT Verlag.
Quack, Joachim F. Forthc. Review of R. Jasnow and K.-Th. Zauzich, Conversations in the House of Life. A New Translation of the Ancient Egyptian Book of Thoth. To appear in the next issue of *Enchoria.*
Quack, Joachim F., and Friedhelm Hoffmann. 2007. *Anthologie der demotischen Literatur.* Einführungen und Quellentexte zur Ägyptologie. Münster: LIT Verlag.
Schenkel, Wolfgang. 1984. Sonst-Jetzt: Variationen eines literarischen Formelementes. *Welt des Orients* 15: 51–61.
Stauder, Andréas. 2013. *Linguistic Dating of Middle Egyptian Literary Texts.* Lingua Aegyptia Studia Monographica 12. Hamburg: Widmaier Verlag.
Von Lieven, Alexandra. 2010. Wie töricht war Horapollo? Die Ausdeutung von Schriftzeichen im Alten Ägypten. Pp. 567–74 in *Honi soit qui mal y pense. Studien zum pharaonischen, griechisch-römischen und spätantiken Ägypten zu Ehren von Heinz-Josef Thissen*, ed. Christian Leitz, Daniel von Recklinghausen and Hermann Knuf. Orientalia Lovanensia Analecta 194. Leuven: Peeters.
Wente, Edward F. 2003a. The Blinding of Truth by Falsehood. Pp. 104–107 in *The Literature of Ancient Egypt. An Anthology of Stories, Instructions, Stelae, Autobiographies, and Poetry*, ed. William K. Simpson. Yale: Yale University Press.
Wente, Edward F. 2003b. The Contendings of Horus and Seth. Pp. 91–103 in *The Literature of Ancient Egypt. An Anthology of Stories, Instructions, Stelae, Autobiographies, and Poetry*, ed. William K. Simpson. Yale: Yale University Press.

Widmaier, Kai. 2013. Die *Lehre des Cheti* und ihre Kontexte. Zu Berufen und Berufsbildern im Neuen Reich. Pp. 483–557 in *Dating Egyptian Literary Texts*, ed. Gerald et al. Lingua Aegyptia Studia Monographica 11. Hamburg: Widmaier Verlag.
Worthington, Martin. 2004. Question and Answer in Middle Kingdom Dialogues. *Journal of Egyptian Archaeology* 90: 113–21.

Andrés Piquer Otero*

9 Those Who Cannot Do, Reign?

The Sources of the Fable of Jotham

1 Foreword

The Hebrew Bible is famous or infamous for opening a window into the literary traditions of the Ancient Near East. The window is, nevertheless, not a very diaphanous one. Like latticework, subtle veil or, at times, the cracks or stains of age, we are invited to a broken or distorted view of topics, genres, myths, and even particular episodes and formulae. Much of this muddling of sources and contexts (at times available to us in other textual traditions, from Mesopotamia to Syria and Egypt) can be put down to the ideological re-shaping of Hebrew literary traditions which progressively transformed them into the different books of the Bible in the second half of the First Millennium BCE. These different "layers of intent" by a series of editors or redactors, together with the growing temporal distance and de-contextualisation of elements and themes which had a living role in the period of the kingdoms of Israel and Judah (plus likely earlier forefathers), make placing biblical texts in their Ancient Near Eastern coordinates a daunting task. And even after a partial decoding or retracing of a late-elaborated passage or motif to earlier periods, one of the recurring conundrums in our field is to determine how and when these pieces came into the knowledge of Hebrew writers. Some of these topics of the biblical microcosm are clearly linked to wider-scope debates that are addressed elsewhere in this volume, namely orality versus written transmission, or importation of genres versus parallel developments throughout the area. For these issues, the *Fable of Jotham* generates more questions than it answers,[1] but, as it stands now, constitutes a good example of how biblical redactors attempted to incorporate literary traditions of their cultural background with varying degrees of adroitness.

> (7) *wayyaggiḏ lᵉyôṯām wayyēleḵ wayyaʿᵃmōḏ bᵉrōʾš har-gᵉrizîm wayyiśśāʾ qôlô wayyiqrāʾ wayyōʾmer lāhem šimʿû ʾēlay baʿᵃlê šᵉḵem wᵉyišmaʿ ʾᵃlêḵem ʾᵉlōhîm:* (8) *hālôḵ hālᵉḵû hāʿēṣîm limšōaḥ ʿᵃlêhem meleḵ wayyōʾmrû lazzayiṯ mᵉlôḵāh [molḵāh] ʿālênû:*
> (9) *wayyōʾmer lāhem hazzayiṯ heḥᵒḏaltî ʾeṯ-dišnî ʾᵃšer-bî yᵉḵabbᵉḏû ʾᵉlōhîm waʾᵃnāšîm wᵉhā-*

* Universidad Complutense de Madrid.

1 See the general presentation in Schipper 1997: 23–40.

https://doi.org/10.1515/9781501510274-009

laḵtî lānûa‘ ‘al-hā‘ēṣîm:
(10) *wayyō’mrû hā‘ēṣîm latt$^{e’}$ēnāh l^{e}ḵî-’at molḵî ‘ālênû:*
(11) *wattō’mer lāhem hatt$^{e’}$ēnāh heḥ^{o}ḏaltî ’eṯ-moṯqî w$^{e’}$eṯ-t^{e}nûḇāṯî haṭṭôḇāh w^{e}hālaḵtî lānûa‘ ‘al-hā‘ēṣîm:*
(12) *wayyō’mrû hā‘ēṣîm laggāp̄en l^{e}ḵî-’at m^{e}lôḵî [molḵî] ‘ālênû:*
(13) *wattō’mer lāhem haggep̄en heḥ^{o}ḏaltî ’eṯ-tîrôšî hamśammēaḥ ’^{e}lōhîm wa’^{a}nāšîm w^{e}hālaḵtî lānûa‘ ‘al-hā‘ēṣîm:*
(14) *wayyō’mrû ḵol-hā‘ēṣîm ’el-hā’āṭāḏ lēḵ ’attā m^{e}lāḵ-‘ālênû:*
(15) *wayyō’mer hā’āṭāḏ ’el-hā‘ēṣîm ’im be’^{e}meṯ ’attem mōš^{e}ḥîm ’ōṯî l^{e}meleḵ ‘^{a}lêḵem bō’û ḥ^{a}sû ḇ^{e}ṣillî w$^{e’}$im-’ayin tēṣē’ ’ēš min-hā’āṭāḏ w^{e}ṯō’ḵal ’eṯ-’arzê hall^{e}ḇānôn:*
(16) *w$^{e‘}$attā ’im-be’^{e}meṯ ûḇ^{e}ṯāmîm ‘^{a}śîṯem wattamlîḵû ’eṯ-’^{a}ḇîmeleḵ w$^{e’}$im-ṭôḇāh ‘^{a}śîṯem ‘im-y^{e}r-*
ubba‘al w$^{e‘}$im-bêṯô w$^{e’}$im-kigmûl yāḏāyw ‘^{a}śîṯem lô: (17) *’^{a}šer-nilḥam ’āḇî ‘^{a}lêḵem wayyašlēḵ*
’eṯ-napšô minneged wayyaṣṣēl ’eṯkem mîad miḏyān: (18) *w$^{e’}$attem qamtem ‘al-bêṯ ’āḇî hayyôm*
wattahargû ’eṯ-bānāyw šiḇ‘îm ’îš ‘al-’eḇen ’eḥāṯ wattamlîḵû ’eṯ-’^{a}ḇîmeleḵ ben-’^{a}māṯô ‘al-
ba‘^{a}lê š^{e}ḵem kî ’^{a}ḥîḵem hû’: (19) *w$^{e’}$im-be’^{e}meṯ ûḇ^{e}ṯāmîm ‘^{a}śîṯem ‘im-y^{e}rubba‘al w$^{e‘}$im-bêṯô hay-*
yôm hazzeh śimḥû ba’^{a}ḇîmeleḵ w^{e}yiśmaḥ gam-hû’ bāḵem: (20) *w$^{e’}$im-’ayin tēṣē’ ’ēš mē’^{a}ḇîme-*
leḵ w^{e}ṯō’ḵal ’eṯ-ba‘^{a}lê š^{e}ḵem w$^{e’}$eṯ-bêṯ millô’ w^{e}ṯēṣē’ ’ēš mibba‘^{a}lê š^{e}ḵem ûmibbêṯ millô’ w^{e}ṯō’-
ḵal ’eṯ-’^{a}ḇîmeleḵ: (21) *wayyānās yôṯām wayyiḇraḥ wayyēleḵ b$^{e’}$ērāh wayyēšeḇ šām mipp^{e}nê*
’^{a}ḇîmeleḵ ’āḥîw:

(7) And tidings were brought to Jotham and he set off to stand upon the summit of Mount Gerizim, raised his voice and cried, saying to them: “Hearken to me, lords of Shechem, and
may God hearken to you: (8) Once upon a time, the trees came to anoint a king over them,
and they said to the olive: Be king over us.
(9) And the olive said to them:

Would I leave my fat which brings me honour among gods and men
To go and sway over the trees?
(10) And the trees said to the fig: Lo, you be queen over us.
(11) And the fig said to them:
Would I leave my sweets and my good fruit
To go and sway over the trees?
(12) And the trees said to the vine: Lo, you be queen over us.
(13) And the vine said to them:
Would I leave my fresh squeeze
Which rejoices gods and men
To go and sway over the trees?
(14) And all the trees said to the thorn-bush: Lo, you be king over us.
(15) And the thorn-bush said to the trees:
If you truly want to anoint me as king over you, come shelter in my shade;
And if not, may fire spring from the thorn-bush and devour the cedars of Lebanon.
(16) And now, if with truth and honesty you have acted when appointing Abimelech as king and acted well with Jerubbal and his house; and if you did to him according to the
merit of his hands (17) (for my father fought for you and risked his life, and delivered you
from the power of Midian; (18) but you have risen against my father’s house today, killing
his sons, seventy men upon a single stone, and appointing Abimelech as king). (19) And
now, if with truth and honesty you have acted with Jerubbal and his house today, rejoice
in Abimelech and let him also rejoice in you. (20) But if not, may fire spring from Abimelech

and devour the lords of Shechem and the house of Millo and may fire spring from the lords of Shechem and from the house of Millo and devour Abimelech." (21) And Jotham fled and ran away to Beer and lived there because of Abimelech, his brother.

2 The *Fable* in the Context of *Judges* 9

In this sense, a first glance at the *Fable* at large and, in particular, at the small section which contains the "dispute" between trees is very meaningful, because, even before delving into redactional details, a sensitive reader is struck by the remarkable awkwardness of the passage: The "dispute" is ancillary to Jotham's demands of justice and to the negative judgment he is levelling on Abimelech, so the redactor is mixing a philosophical reference on the nature, limitations, and risks of kingship with a more straightforward situation of a people and a king not honoring loyalties and alliances in the past and, prospectively, in the future.[2] Thus, the *mašal* here stands in the realm of the general, the sort of inquiry on world-order associated frequently with wisdom literature, whereas the reality it illustrates (or anticipates) belongs to the particular, to the triangle of tension between the people of Shechem, Abimelech and the legacy of Jerubbal. This tension or incongruity is further exacerbated by the author's (or redactor's) attempt to create an overarching and multi-layered literary connection between Jotham's speech (including the *Fable*) and the grisly fate of Abimelech and the Shechemites. Thus, the text should to be analysed as a form of speech – fulfilment correlation which, clearly, has parallels in the prophetic genre, besides its recurring usage as a compositional device in Northwest Semitic narrative texts (cf. Parker 1997). From this point of view, Jotham's speech could be (and has been) interpreted in two ways; first, as a form of oracle, albeit, so to speak, a "conditional" one: a fateful doom is prognosticated on Shechem and Abimelech if they do not act in a faithful way; then, as an active form of curse,[3] where the speech itself would actually be working as a binding proclamation where the wronged party (Jotham) levels an implicit accusation of injustice against the Shechemites (and, in turn, Abimelech) which brings forth the negative conclusion detailed in the final narrative. This double meaning of the passage would not be unheard of, as prophetic oracles in other passages of the

2 See, e.g., Soggin 1981: 173–74; Boling 1975: 175.
3 See Schipper 1997: 23–40. *Contra*, Soggin 1981: 175, who considers the curse function a later development and thus does not seem to take into account earlier parallels for ritual speech-curses in the Hebrew Bible.

Bible are susceptible to acquire an implicit or explicit function of cursing their object to the spelled doom. That would be the case, saliently, of the Oracles of Balaam (*Num* 22–25) or of Elijah's prediction / curse of draught in 1*Kgs* 17.[4] In the present state of the chapter, verse 57 explicitly states, as a closure to the passage, that Jotham did in fact curse the Shechemites.

Taking this pattern as the basis for an analysis of the passage, its structure is quite straightforward:

1. Narrative Introduction (**v. 7**)
2. Jotham's Speech (**vv. 8–20**)
   A. *The Disputation of Trees* (**vv. 8–15**):
      a. Petition to olive and refusal (**vv. 8–9**)
      b. Petition to fig and refusal (**vv. 10–11**)
      c. Petition to vine and refusal (**vv. 12–13**)
      d. Petition to thorn-bush (**v. 14**)
      e. Thorn-bush' acceptance, conditional to fidelity; *menace of destruction by fire* (**v.15**)
   B. Exhortation to the lords of Shechem (**vv. 16–20**):
      a. Protasis: condition of fidelity (**v. 16**)
      b. Excursus on Jerubbal's virtue and his betrayal by the lords of Shechem (**vv. 17–18**)
      c. Recapitulation of protasis + apodosis on positive outcome (**v. 19**)
      d. Protasis: unfaithfulness + apodosis on negative outcome: *mutual destruction of king and lords by fire* (**v. 20**)
3. Narrative Section: Jotham's escape; Abimelech king; treason by the lords of Shechem (**vv. 21–30**)
4. Narrative Section: Abimelech's victory over Shechem: *burns the lords in the tower* (**vv. 31–49**)
5. Narrative Section: Abimelech slain in Thebez (**vv. 50–55**)
6. Recapitulation and assessment of events as *retribution*, specifying Jotham's "curse" (**vv. 56–57**)

The author (or likely a redactor) of the passage has connected all sections with each other with a recurring leitmotiv based on punishment and retribution by fire: First featuring in the thorn-bush' words within the disputation of trees (2.A.e), it reappears as the threat of retribution levelled by Jotham to the lords of Shechem (2.B.d). Though steeped in formulaic language, as I will detail further

4 For the relevance of the ritual usage off a mountain for this sort of proclamation, see Niditch 2008: 116.

later, the resort to fire in the speech is picked up in the narrative as the literal way in which Abimelech brings doom on the Shechemites, by burning the tower or keep where they had retreated during the siege of the city (4). In turn, Abimelech meets his fate while trying to follow an identical procedure in the siege of Thebez against the rebels, when a woman cracks his skull by dropping a millstone (6). This narrative device clearly creates a bond in the speech-fulfilment pattern which is structured, in Jotham's speech, around a long protasis-apodosis period, where alternatives are given for fidelity and righteousness vs. unfaithfulness and wickedness. This is a known pattern in the Historical Books. It appears, e.g., in 1*Kgs* 1:51–53, where it involves an oath[5] to God.[6] In Jotham's speech, the oath element is not explicit in the protasis-apodosis structure, but it does feature at the beginning of his words in v. 7: (*šimʿû ʾēlay baʿᵃlê šᵉḵem wᵉyišmaʿ ʾᵃlêḵem ʾᵉlōhîm, Hearken to me, o lords of Shechem; and God will hearken to you*). These sentences may be understood in a formal and legal context: Jotham begs permission to plead his case before the Lords of Shechem and God is added to the equation with a petition for reciprocity (listening to Jotham's words is the rightful thing to do, so that God listening to the lords of Shechem becomes conditional to it). This oath context is further underscored by the setting of the speech: talking from the summit of a mount involves an appeal to the divine (again, see the parallel situation in the Oracles of Balaam, among others).

3 Sources of Discourse

With these general ideas in mind, I will try to focus on the sources of discourse in Jotham's speech, particularly in vv. 8–15, the "Fable of Trees." I will begin with a series of observations on thematic elements which involve a continuity with other ancient Near Eastern writings, particularly in the area of Mesopotamia and Syria-Palestine, but also within the biblical tradition itself, to then move to a structural analysis of the *Fable* itself as a form of disputation, though likely a modified or reworked one.

5 I have discussed the syntax of protasis-apodosis oaths in Piquer Otero 2008.

6 See *Ruth* 3:13 for a similar structure of two alternatives defined by protasis-apodosis patterns and strengthened by an oath.

3.1 Trees and Kings

One of the most striking features of the chapter and the *Fable* is the usage of trees as a leitmotif, as I have already mentioned. This can hardly be attributed exclusively to the writer or redactors of *Judges* 9, as we have another meaningful case of a tree-based *mašal* in the Bible: 2*Kgs* 14:9 and its parallel in 2*Chr* 25:18:

> *wayyišlaḥ y*^{e}*hô'āš melek̲-yiśrā'ēl 'el-'*^{a}*maṣyāhû melek̲-y*^{e}*hûd̲āh lē'mōr haḥôaḥ '*^{a}*šer ball*^{e}*b̲ānôn šālaḥ 'el-hā'erez '*^{a}*šer ball*^{e}*b̲ānôn lē'mōr t*^{e}*nāh-'et̲-bitt*^{e}*k̲ā lib̲nî l*^{e}*'iššā watta'*^{a}*b̲ōr ḥayyat̲ haśś ād̲eh '*^{a}*šer ball*^{e}*b̲ānôn wattirmōs 'et̲-haḥôḥa:*

> And Jehoash king of Israel sent to Amaziah king of Judah, saying: "The thistle in Lebanon sent to the cedar in Lebanon saying, 'give your daughter to my son as a wife.' And a beast of the field in Lebanon came by and trode on the thistle."

This brief "fable of trees" is invoked by Jehoash of Israel as a rebuke to Amaziah of Judah after he threatened the king of Israel, emboldened by his victory against Edom. Here, the parable-analogy value of the fable of thistle and cedar is clear (see Boling 1975: 174): those who boast and try to bite more than they can chew are destined to a fateful and shameful end. The imagery used, as in the *Fable of Jotham*, is centered in the world of trees and is based on an indirect form of confrontation: a small and unworthy plant (the thistle, which shares with the bush in *Judg* 9:15 thorns as a defining characteristic) challenges one of the trees archetypal to greatness and power, the cedar of Lebanon. The short passage then creates a polar model: the largest vs. the smallest. A polar image or merism is also associated with trees in other characterisations of royalty which involve the depiction of totality or universality. Such is the case of Solomon's depiction as the ideal king in 1*Kgs* 5, namely in v. 13:

> *way*^{e}*d̲abbēr 'al-hā'ēṣîm min-hā'erez '*^{a}*šer ball*^{e}*b̲ānôn w*^{e}*'ad̲ hā'ēzôb̲ '*^{a}*šer yōṣē' baqqîr*

> And he talked about trees, from the cedar in Lebanon to the hyssop which grows on the wall.

Again, cedar of Lebanon against a small plant (hyssop in this case) features in association with royalty in a polar image of singular knowledge and encyclopaedic lore, a well-known feature of ideal models of kingship in the ancient Near East, where universal (and hence god-like and god-given) knowledge would go hand in hand with universal rulership.

These two passages are relevant for the cultural context of the *Fable of Jotham* inasmuch as they define two usages of tree imagery within the Hebrew Bible which: 1) belong to the narrative tradition of the Historical Books (whether that means a connection to the so-called Deuteronomistic History will be addressed in the final section of this paper); 2) they involve a literary relationship between the world of trees and the world of kings in two distinct ways: whereas 2*Kgs* 14:9 constitutes a form of invective or provocation between kings before a battle,[7] 1*Kgs* 5 resorts to wisdom (and its implied mastership over nature) as a positive element of characterisation. In a wider Near Eastern setting, this has to be connected to a larger identification between king and tree, which has been studied textually and iconographically in scholarly literature since the last century. One of the grounds for this connection lies in the concept of "shadow of the king," *i.e.*, the protective and life-giving area of royal control and power.[8] Some authors[9] remark the more pervasive relationship between tree and king, in connection with the tree symbolising (as the king embodies) cosmic world order. It is therefore possible to conclude that the composer of *Judges* 9 had a certain degree of knowledge of the importance of trees in typical discourses related to the sphere of royalty of the Near East, likely from traditions inherited or developed by Israelite scribal circles of the monarchic period. Thus, the presence of the *Fable* cannot be casual, but would be an easy fit into the author's intention of presenting an invective or challenge against an unworthy king and an unworthy people. To what point the material in vv. 8–15 is recovered from a different composition, original to the author / redactor of the chapter or something in between (creative adaptation of an existing source) will be discussed below.

3.2 Forest Fires

Before, I will examine another relevant element in the construction of the chapter and its cultural context: references to burning fire. They feature both within the *Fable* (in the thorn bush' speech, v. 15) and in Jotham's words on Abimelech and the Shechemites (v. 20) and, of course, in the narrative fulfilment of the curse/oracle. At first sight, it is tempting to understand this reference to "consuming fire" within the parameters of biblical ideology and imagery (Dtr[10] or Yahwistic in a more generic way) as a canonical form of divine wrath or retribution (see, e.g. the references to the burning wrath of God in *Ex* 15:7 or Elijah's

7 A practice attested in other passages of the Bible, without tree imagery, such as 1*Kgs* 20:10–11.

8 Cf. Oppenheim 1947; more recently, Ruprecht 2003: 17–25.

9 Cf. Parpola 1993: 167–68; Jiménez 2017: 37 f, 71, 193, 231, 257 n. 651, 262, 284.

10 The relationship of the Fable with Dtr redaction layers of biblical redaction has been largely discussed and a pre-Dtr ascription seems possible and even likely. Cf. Wong 2006: 9.

summoned fire in *2Kgs* 1:10,12,14). Though that can be the basic cultural coordinate behind the allusion, it is remarkable that a comparison between *royal* (evidently analogous to divine) wrath or military power and fire is attested in neighbouring literary corpora. A revealing example can be found in the Kilamuwa Inscription (*KAI* 24 1:5–7):

> *bt ʾby bmtkt mlkm ʿdrm wkl šlḥ yd lhl[ḥ]m wkt byd mlkm kmʾš ʿklt zqn w[km]ʾš ʿklt yd*
>
> My father's house was amidst powerful kings and they all extended their hand to fight; but I was against the hand of kings like fire which devours a beard or like fire which devours a hand.

The king's retaliation against invaders or conquerors, a rightful wrath, is depicted as consuming fire in a rather graphical way (consuming the hands stretched against the kingdom but also beards in a more wild and intense conflagration). Given the context of *Judges* 9 in relationship with an unfaithful king and rebellious people, it is again quite possible that Jotham's usage of fire as the physical element of punishment and destruction is not only part of the Yahwistic stock imagery, but explicitly related to royal language of the period.

3.3 Redaction Between Thorn and Cedar

Thus, the ingenuity of the composition (though at times it can result slightly overbearing due to the accumulation of allusions) lies in connecting these two features of kingly parlance in a movement from the symbolic to the concrete: trees and consuming fire, given that trees are prone to catch fire, as the thorn bush threatens, as Jotham threatens, and as it finally happens in the siege of Shechem. Further, the author manages to pile up references which, though linked to royal discurse in the parameters I have outlined above, feel quite at home with Yahwistic (and potentially Deuteronomitic) codes. This requires, of course, adaptation, and this is more visible in the last verse of the *Fable*, v. 15. As it has been noted by quite a few commentators of *Judges* (Boling 1975: 174; Soggin 1981: 173), this verse and the thorn bush' words does not seem to fit in the overall structure of vv. 8–15: First, rhythm seems to change and, whereas the other verses have a slightly rough but distinct metric poetic pattern, v. 15 is closer to prose and definitely too long to fit within the rhythmic structure of the section. Second, thematically it seems to be quite unconnected to the previous lines of discussion between trees (see Schipper 1997: 28; Lindars 1973): whereas in 9, 11 and 13 each tree gives a reason to decline kingship by explicitly listing its well-known virtues with a recurring formula, the thorn bush says nothing of that sort and just gives the other trees the alternative of obeying (coming under his "royal" shade) or being consumed by the fire of his wrath. Further, there is a reference to the cedars of Lebanon here which strikes as puzzling, as the cedar does not feature at all in the previous disputation, which seems to restrict itself to trees prized by their fruits (olive, vine, and fig). It seems that, as in the short fable in *2Kgs* 14:9 discussed above, the author chose to include (shoehorn?) a reference to the cedars of Lebanon as they are associated with power and nobility recurrently in the Bible and in Northwest Semitic literature of the period.[11] This again creates a layered accumulation of allusions: on one hand, the smaller unworthy plant which destroys the powerful; on the other hand, the unworthy king who destroys treacherous lords, as it comes to happens in the narrative. The metaphor of cedars as lords faced with an (unrighteous) king can be also find in Isa 14:8, the satirical dirge for the king of Babylon:

> *gam-b*^{e}*rôšîm śām*^{e}*ḥû l*^{e}*ḵā ʾarzê l*^{e}*ḇānôn mēʾāz šāḵaḇtā lōʾ-yaʿ*^{a}*leh hakkōrēṯ ʿālênû*
>
> Also fir rejoiced for you, cedars of Lebanon: "Since you lied down, the cutter will not come up against us."

Although maybe not as clear and prevalent in ancient Near Eastern literature as the cedar, the thorn-bush also seems to have a role in literary traditions in the ancient Israelite background. For instance, the portracted dialogue exchange between the thorn and the pomegranate in Ahiqar:

> *snyʾ šdr lrmnʾ lm snyʾ lrmnʾ mh ṭb šgyʾ kbyk lpgʿ bʾbyk ʿnh rmnʾ wʾmr lsnyʾ ʾnt klk kbn ʿm zy pgʿ bk*
>
> The bramble sent to the pomegranate: "Bramble to Pomegranate: 'What use are the thorns which hurt the one who touches your fruit?'" The pomegranate answered and said to the bramble: "you are all thorns hurting anyone who touches you."

Though in a different setting and topic, the text indicates (together with *2Kgs* 14:9), the frequent usage of spiked plants and bushes (thorn, bramble, thistle) to indicate unworthy or valueless (but boastful) characters in a discussion.[12]

All in all, the composer seems to have created a conclusion which is a perfect match for the following development of Jotham's rebuke against Abimelech and the Shechemites in structure, as it is clearly seen by the parallel beginning of the protases:

---

11 For the inclusion of this symbolic value into *Judges* 9, see Oeste 2011: 86.

12 For further parallels between Ahiqar and the *Fable of Jotham*, see Kottsieper 1997.

v. 15:	*ʾim beʾ*^{e}*meṯ*	*if in truth*
	w^{e}*ʾim-ʾayin tēṣēʾ ʾēš*	*and if not let fire come out*
vv. 16 + 19:	*w*^{e}*ʿattā ʾim-beʾ*^{e}*meṯ*	*And now if in truth*
v. 20:	*w*^{e}*ʾim-ʾayin tēṣēʾ ʾēš*	*and if not, let fire come out*

Also, the connection between v. 15 and the previous part of the *Fable* is managed through thematic affinity by resort to "tree language" in a wide sense, adopting recurring stock elements (cedars and thorns) in a (rather clumsy, if I may judge) attempt to keep a unity of sorts.

3.4 Why and What Disputation?

Thus, this evidence points in the direction that a disputation (vv. 8–14) was inserted or used to craft the beginning of Jotham's speech and then contextually adapted to fit with his curse/oracle of vv. 16–20. The main issue then, at least for the purpose of this paper and volume, is to determine what kind of composition it is, its possible connection to similar literature[13] and the reasons for its insertion into the passage. At first sight, some features are relevant for this topic:

(1) Debate between trees, with each of them presenting its own merits, is a recurring topic in Mesopotamian disputation literature[14] (e.g. Sumerian *Tree and Reed*; Akkadian *Tamarisk and Palm*, *Palm and Vine*, or the *Series of the Poplar*). The three trees included are well-known and appreciated for the value of their fruits, which they themselves expose in a straightforward way.

(2) Without delving too deep into formal aspects, vv. 8–14 present a poetic structure, again, a feature of disputation literature in the ancient Near East.

---

13 Recent bibliography has pointed out the similarities between the Greek text of the Fable and one of Aesop's fables (see Römer 2015; Kellenberger 2018), which would open up the scope of this research to the wider and far-reaching problem of possible influences of Greek literature in biblical books in general and in the Historical Books in particular (see, e.g., the seminal work of Van Seters 1983; Garbini 1988). Nevertheless, the present case is quite weak, for two reasons already outlined in Kellenberger 2018: the high number of Semitic calques (or, more specifically) LXX-style "Hebraisms" (see Piquer Otero 2016) in that particular Greek text ascribed to Aesop and the presence of that fable only in late Byzantine collections (Kellenberger 2018: 133, 136). This would indicate that, in this case, the "fable of trees" would be actually an inclusion of the LXX version of the *Fable of Jotham* into the Aesopian corpus at some point during Christian Late Antiquity or medieval transmission of Aesop.

14 See Jiménez 2017. A proposal for a Mesopotamian origin of the *Fable* was already brought forward in Diels 1910; more recently, see also Tatu 2006; Mengozzi 2016.

(3) As discussed in literature, both olive and vine speak in terms which have been defined as "blatant polytheism[15]": oil and wine respectively honoring and cheering "gods and men." This, at the very least, would imply a re-utilisation of an extant composition of the monarchic period, either Israelite or inter-/transnational.
(4) On the other hand, the interest of the trees is not being proclaimed winner of a contest (and hence prove themselves worthy of kingship) but to claim that their "natural role" is too important to forsake it in favor of rulership. That would be definitely a quite original proposal in the disputation tradition, although not unheard of in fables (*The Story of the Poor Forlorn Wren* [Jiménez 2017: 327–76] would involve the anticlimactic success in competition of an unworthy candidate).
(5) Also, for a list of important fruit-bearing trees, the palm, given its centrality in other disputation compositions and in the Akkadian tradition at large, is strikingly missing. This could suggest that the 3-speaker discussion was part of a larger composition which the composer of *Judges* 9 adapted in order to create (by the inclusion of v. 15, as commented above) a modified or transformed fable, where disputation is, in the end, secondary to a moral lesson on rulership and unworthiness. If v. 15 is hiding the remains of another old independent fable or proverb with thorn and cedars on boastful insignificant leaders (as opposed to it being a new creation by the redactor of *Judges* 9, cf. Lindars 1973), most traces of this have been erased or thoroughly transformed in order to make the thorn bush anticipate Jotham's own words in the curse/oracle against Abimelech and the Shechemites.

4 Conclusions

These five short ideas are the basis for proposing, as has been the majority tendency in scholarship on the passage, that the *Fable of Jotham* does use an earlier (or at least an independent) text with traits similar to disputation poetry of the Near East, but, on the other hand, shows in its present state some re-working (or at least abridgement) of that source in order to make it fit in the overarching discourse-narrative structure and in the ideological framework of the story. This shall be the object of my final observations, a proposal on the reasons behind the inclusion of such short piece of disputation literature. The topic has been treated recurrringly in commentaries of *Judges*, where one basic point of argu-

15 See Jiménez 2017: 130; Crüsemann 1978: 15; Dubach 2009: 166–67.

mentation has been the presence or absence of an anti-monarchic element, connected to the Deuteronomistic assessment of monarchy at large.[16] I think that this sort of debate leads to a pretty unsolvable conundrum, as the passage is open enough to accept an overlaying array of meanings and senses, as I have outlined above when talking of the prophecy-curse ambivalence of Jotham's words.[17] Nothing in *Judges* 9 indicates clearly whether the negative outlook implicit to becoming king among the trees is pointed at a general appreciation of kingship, though that could be the case. On the other hand, the chapter is quite clear in having as a grounding theme the retribution which an unfaithful ruler and the unfaithful people who bring him to power are bound to suffer. Why then to include verses 8–14? My proposal is that the excerpt of disputation was used by the redactor of the passage within the parameters of a form of legal disputation of sorts, a form of *rîb*, well-known in biblical tradition and quite at home both in prophetic and wisdom genres,[18] genres which could be indeed far from unrelated: resort to a wisdom text which deals with a form of archetypal example or "case" (the *mašal sensu stricto*) which reinforces the position of the speaker. In that sense, the short list of three worthy trees that decline kingship and the *ad hoc* words of the unworthy tree that accepts it under threat are, although clumsily, offering a "universal" analogue for the dispute or challenge with the Shechemites. In that sense, it would be a more sophisticated form of pre-conflict short story or fable (such as those founds in exchanges between kings in the Bible and in letters of the ancient Near East), but one endowed with the authority of a wisdom text, which, as such, reflects knowledge of world-order, and makes the conclusion (doom of the unfaithful) bound to a form of "cosmic justice."

This has been, at least, the way the *Fable* has been interpreted in part of the literary tradition which derives from it. Briefly, I would like to mention two works which are likely inspired by it: Qumran Cave 4 fragments labelled as *Four Kingdoms*[19] (where the huge tree which symbolises Babylon in *Dan* 4 is extended as the succession of empires in dispute) and the disputation of trees contained in the 13th century collection of fables by the Armenian author Mkhitar Gosh[20]: In

16 In modern times, the interpretation of the Fable as an anti-monarchic text was held by Martin Buber (1967: 75); the same opinion is held in commentaries such as Soggin 1981: 177; or Niditch 2008: 114, 116. For a critical view of this interpretation, see Maly 1960; Lindars 1973.
17 Such view is also present in Lyke 1997: 138; Schipper 1997: 26.
18 See the general taxonomy and reflections on genre and function in Schipper 1997:12–20.
19 4Q552–553; see the detailed commentary in Reynolds 2011: 191–205.
20 See the comments in Jiménez 2017: 283–284 and, in this volume, the paper by Sergio La Porta.

this text, the trees again dispute and they seem to decline themselves being fit for kingship, having other virtues. The final conclusion, led by the palm, is to create a form of order with each type of tree specialised (as a "prince") in a function of administration (building, prisons, etc.) Although there is some likely Christian influence in this arrangement (one may think of Pauline conceptions of the Church as the "body of Christ" see e.g. 1 *Cor* 12:12–31; *Col* 1:18; 2:18–20; *Eph* 1:22–23; 3:19; 4:13) the text derives from the *Fable* in form and contents and, I would say, shares with it the basic principle of using the "type of trees" for defining a problem which has to be solved by wisdom and leads to a vision of ideal world-order. It is possible that the stories and poems on trees debating known by Hebrew writers were read in a similar spirit since the first millennium BCE and that the tampered version adopted into *Judg* 9 was playing with the genre in order to define the dystopian model which was in turn thrown as accusation at Abimelech and the Shechemites.

Bibliography

KAI = H. Donner/W. Röllig, Kanaanäische und aramäische Inschriften Bd. 1–3. Wiesbaden 1962–64.

Boling, Robert. 1975 *Judges*. Anchor Bible Commentary 6 A. Garden City NY: Doubleday.

Buber, Martin. 1967. *Kingship of God*. London: Humanities.

Crüsemann, Frank. 1978. *Der Widerstand gegen das Königtum: die antiköniglichen Texte des Alten Testamentes und der Kampf um den frühen israelitischen Staatt*. Wissenschaftliche Monographien zum Alten und Neuen Testament. 49. Neukirchen-Vluyn: Neukirchener.

Diels, Hermann. 1910 Orientalische Fabeln im griechischen Gewande. *Internationale Wochenschrift für Wissenschaft, Kunst und Technik* 4: 993–1007.

Dubach, Manuel. 2009 *Trunkenheit im Alten Testament. Begrifflichkeit—Zeugnisse—Wertung*. BWANT 184. Stuttgart: Kohlhammer.

Garbini, Giovanni. 1988. *History and Ideology in Ancient Israel*. New York: Crossroad.

Jiménez, Enrique. 2017 *The Babylonian Disputation Poems. With Editions of the Series of the Poplar, Palm and Vine, the Series of the Spider, and the Story of the Poor, Forlorn Wren*. Culture and History of the Ancient Near East 87. Leiden: Brill.

Kellenberger, Edgar. 2018. Once Again: The Fable of Jotham (Judg 9) and Aesop. *Semitica* 60: 131–137.

Kottsieper, Ingo. 1996. Die alttestamentliche Weisheit in Licht aramäischer Weisheitstraditionen. Pp. 128–62 in *Weisheit außerhalb der kanonischen Weisheitsschriften*, ed. Bernd Janowski. Veröffentlichungen der Wissenschaftlichen Gesellschaft für Theologie 10. Gütersloh: Christian Kaiser.

Lindars, Barnabas. 1973. Jotham's Fable – A New Form-Critical Analysis. *Journal of Theological Studies* 24: 355–66.

Lyke, Larry. 1997. *King David with the Wise Woman of Tekoa: The Resonance of Tradition in Parabolic Narrative.* The Library of Hebrew Bible / Old Testament Studies 255. Sheffield: Sheffield Academic.

Maly, Eugene. 1960. The Jotham Fable – Anti-Monarchical? *Catholic Biblical Quarterly* 22: 299–305.

Mengozzi, Alessandro. 2016. Foglie di fico, spine di rovo e cedri del Libano. Piante silenti e dialoganti nella Bibbia e dintorni. *Kervan* 20: 63–79.

Niditch, Susan. 2008. *Judges.* Louisville, KY: Westminster John Knox.

Oeste, Gordon. 2011. *Legitimacy, Illegitimacy, and the Right to Rule: Windows on Abimelech's Rise and Demise in Judges 9.* Library of Hebrew Bible/Old Testament Studies 546. New York: T&T Clark.

Oppenheim, Leo. 1947. The Shadow of the King. *Bulletin of the American Schools of Oriental Research* 107: 7–11

Parker, Simon. 1997. *Stories in Scripture and Inscriptions: Comparative Studies on Narratives in Northwest Semitic Inscriptions and the Hebrew Bible.* New York: Oxford University.

Parpola, Simo. 1993. The Assyrian Tree of Life: Tracing the Origins of Jewish Monotheism and Greek Philosophy. *Journal of Near Eastern Studies* 52: 161–208.

Piquer Otero, Andrés. 2008. An Old Greek Reading Attested in the Sahidic and Old Latin Fragments of 1Kgs 1:52. Text-critical Analysis and Relationship with the Hebrew Text. *Hénoch* 30: 80–93.

Piquer Otero, Andrés. 2016. Hebraisms. Pp. 182–192 in *Handbuch zur Sepguaginta 3. Die Sprache der Septuaginta.* eds. Eberhard Bons and Jan Joosten. Gütersloh: Gütersloher.

Reynolds, Bennie. 2011. *Between Symbolism and Realism: The Use of Symbolic and Non-Symbolic Language in Ancient Jewish Apocalypses 333–63 BCE* Journal of Ancient Judaism Supplements 8. Göttingen: Vanderhoeck und Ruprecht.

Römer, Thomas. 2015. The Hebrew Bible and Greek Philosophy and Mythology. Some Case Studies. *Semitica* 57: 185–203.

Ruprecht, Eberhard. 2003. *Die Jothamfabel und außerisraelitische Parallelen.* Göttingen: Vanderhoeck und Ruprecht.

Schipper, Jeremy. 1997. *Parables and Conflict in the Hebrew Bible.* Cambridge: Cambridge University.

Soggin, Alberto. 1981. *Judges.* Philadelphia: Westminster.

Tatu, Silviu. 2006. Jotham's Fable and the Crux Interpretum in Judges ix. *Vetus Testamentum* 56: 105–124.

Van Seters, John. 1983. *In Search of History. Historiography in the Ancient World and the Origins of Biblical History.* New Haven: Yale University.

Wong, Gregory. 2006. *Compositional Strategy of the Book of Judges.* Vetus Testamentum, Supplements 111. Leiden: Brill.

Section II Eastern Disputations during the Middle Ages

Sebastian Brock*

10 Disputations in Syriac Literature

The incorporation of disputations and dialogues of one sort or another into Syriac poetry, both narrative and stanzaic, is extremely common and can take on a variety of different forms,[1] just one of which will be the focus of the present contribution, namely the distinctive genre of the dispute poem, where two protagonists argue in alternating stanzas. The genre has its roots in the precedence disputes of ancient Mesopotamian literature, composed in Sumerian and Akkadian and normally involving personifications;[2] it has continued right up to modern times to be popular, whether it be in Jewish Aramaic, Syriac,[3] Middle Persian, Persian or Arabic.[4] In Syriac it is first attested in the mid fourth century CE in three poems by Ephrem (d.373) where Death and Satan argue over which of the two has the greatest influence over human beings.[5] The first of these opens:

> 1. I heard Death and Satan loudly disputing
> which was the strongest of the two among humankind.
>
> 2. Death has shown his power in that he conquers all,
> Satan has shown his guile in that he has made all to sin.
>
> 3. (Death) Only those who want to, O Evil One, listen to you,
> but to me they come, whether they will it or not.
>
> 4. (Satan) You just employ brute force, O Death,
> whereas I use traps and cunning snares.

The final verse very clearly points to the deliberately semi-humorous character of these poems: they are meant for amusement as well as for instruction:

> 27. Our laughing at them now, my brethren, is a pledge
> that we shall be enabled again to laugh, at the Resurrection. (Nisibene Hymns 52)

* University of Oxford.

1 See in general Ruani 2016, with the Clavis de textes syriaques de Controverse (by M. Debié), 385–446; and more specific, Brock 1987; 2010b.

2 See the volumes in which Drijvers (1991) and Butts (2017) appear.

3 Murray 1995; Brock 2001.

4 Wagner 1962. There are also examples in Modern Syriac (Mengozzi 2013 and especially Mengozzi in this volume) and Modern Arabic.

5 Carmina Nisibena 52–54; translation of no. 53 in Brock and Kiraz 2006: 155–67.

https://doi.org/10.1515/9781501510274-010

Elsewhere Ephrem implies the existence of a dispute between Body and Soul, and one between the Months, although it is unlikely that either of these is among the several extant dispute poems on these two topics, on both of which more will be said below. Although personifications of this sort continue to be found, in the majority of the fifty-odd surviving Syriac poems[6] belonging to the genre the protagonists have become biblical characters, and the nature of the dispute has shifted from an argument over precedence to one of a theological nature.

1 Form and Structure

In their form the dialogue poems constitute a sub-category of the *soghitha* (plural *soghyatha*), or stanzaic poem where the verses all have the same simple syllabic structure (very often two lines consisting of 7+7 7+7 syllables). In many cases the name of the melody (*qala*), to which the poem should be sung, is provided, and a Refrain is also given, suggesting that the stanzas were sung by a solo voice, while a chorus would sing the Refrain, probably after each stanza. The normal structure of the dialogue poem follows a threefold pattern: a brief introduction provides the setting; this is followed by the main body of the poem, consisting in the dialogue between the two characters; this often has an alphabetic acrostic which requires that the poem will consist of at least 22 stanzas, or 44 if (as is more often the case) the acrostic progresses by pairs of stanzas. Finally, there is a brief judgement or resolution pronounced by a third character who acts as judge. As will be seen below, a number of variations on this general pattern are to be found. A distinctive feature of quite a number of these poems, which very effectively brings out the element of repartee, is the direct picking up of the first speaker's words by the second speaker who then reverses the sense. Several examples of this rhetorical device are to be found in the *Dispute between the Two Thieves* hanging on crosses beside Jesus:

> 48. (Bad Thief) I am quite amazed that you should believe
> in a man put to death, who is now dead and gone.
> Who would be attracted by what you have said,
> apart from you who have fallen in love with him!
>
> 49. (Good Thief) I am quite amazed that you blaspheme against the Son of God
> who has died of His own volition.

6 A list is given in Brock 1991; an updated one is provided in Brock (forthcoming).

Let your mouth be silent, for it is full of offence.
Blessed is the Crucified One whom I have confessed.

2 The Protagonists

The protagonists in the precedence disputes of ancient Mesopotamia were inanimate objects, animals, or concepts, but never individual human beings. The earliest Syriac examples, Ephrem's three disputes between Death and Satan, continue with this tradition, and quite a number of later cases can be adduced, such as *Gold and Wheat*,[7] or *Cup and Wine* by the medieval poet Khamis. In other cases, such as *Grace and Justice*, the personifications reflect the Christian context to which they belong. An exceptional case is provided by the *Dispute of the Months* (see Brock 1991) where all twelve speak, each presenting its wares before the Year, who sits there as the Judge:

1. The Months of the year gather together
to present the beauty of their produce;
the Year sits there as mistress
to hear the case between them.
(Refrain) Come and listen to what the months have to say, and give praise to the Creator.

Each month, starting with Nisan (~ April), then presents its produce, having first dismissed its predecessor with the words 'Be off with you, N, you have done no better than I'. No verdict is given, but in the Jewish Aramaic counterpart, preserved in the Palestinian Targum at *Exodus* 12:2, it is a question of in which month the Exodus will take place, a scenario also alluded to by Ephrem in his allusion to a similar contest:

Nisan, the victorious month, who was sent by the Victorious One,
was resplendently victorious in Egypt, delivering and escorting out the Bride of the King.
(Hymns on the Resurrection 3:1)

One might have expected this to have been replaced by the Resurrection in the Syriac poem, but instead its boast is in its mountains decked with flowers and swallows. An intriguing feature of the Syriac poem is that it provides a fusion of the ancient Mesopotamian precedence dispute with the Greek ekphrasis tradition, which also lies behind the medieval western theme of the Labours of the Months.

7 Translation in Brock 1991.

The most popular subject for a dispute poem was Body and Soul. Again, Ephrem already attests to the existence of this theme when he wrote:

> Body and Soul go to court
> to see which had caused the other to sin. (Nisibene Hymns 69:5)

No less than four different dialogues on this topic are to be found in Syriac.[8] The imagined scenario has them arguing in the presence of the Judge over which of the two least deserves punishment. The first (and perhaps the oldest) of these poems opens:

> 1. Soul and Body fell into dispute
> and became engaged in a great struggle.
> Let us listen to what they are saying
> in that great contest in which they are involved.

From the outset the soul takes a haughty stance of superiority, no doubt reflecting the Greek and especially the Platonic tradition, of regarding the incorporeal as superior to the corporeal. Very soon the Soul is on the attack:

> 5. It was in you, Body, that all the evil passions
> sprang up: they did not touch me.
> The lusts issued from you,
> that is why you are to be chastised.
>
> 6. (Body) It was in you, Soul, that I was aroused,
> I received my sensation in you;
> had your stirrings not come down to me
> passions would never have harmed me.

Eventually they both appeal to the Judge:

> 43. (Soul) Listen, O Judge, and settle the case all at once
> between me and the Body which utters such threats.
> Let truth shine out, O You who examine all,
> and grant me the crown which I expect.
>
> 44. (Body) Listen, Lord, and see: if the Soul receives a crown,
> do not deprive me;
> and if I am beaten, strike the Soul too,
> for without it I would never have sinned.

---

8 See Brock 1995/1999, which contains a translation of IV; a translation of I is included in Brock 2012: 282–89.

The Judge's final words are in fact a tacit rebuke to the Soul:

> 46. (Judge) Both of you now have acted together,
> and a single judgement is reserved for you.
> Join one another and do not be separated,
> for there is no division between you.

In the other three disputes the Soul and the Body speak more from a position of parity, and indeed in the second poem, attributed to Jacob of Serugh (d.521),[9] where the scenario is the imminent approach of death, the mutual recriminations with which they start out eventually are replaced by a shared lamentation over their separation at death.

The third *Dispute between Body and Soul* is by the learned author, 'Abdisho' of Soba (Nisibis; d. 1318) who incorporated it into his collection entitled *The Paradise of Eden*, a work which (to judge by the large number of manuscripts and several printed editions) has always remained extremely popular, despite the difficulty and obscurity of some of its constituent poems. The scene is evidently before the Judge, and the poem opens:

> 1. I heard report of a battle
> taking place between Body and Soul;
> I desired, like some sage
> to see which one would hit the mark.

Accusation and counter-accusation then follow one another, although towards the end (stanzas 38 ff.) the mood changes, as in Jacob's poem, and the Soul invites the (dead) Body to receive healing and life.

In common with Jacob's poem, the fourth *Dispute between Body and Soul* commences, after a brief preface, with the Body opening the attack on the Soul, rather than the other way round, which is the case in the other two disputes. Near the end, instead of any judgement, the authorial voice prays:

> 22. Have mercy on us, O Compassionate One,
> make quarrels to cease from our midst;
> in Your mercy, act as peacemaker between us
> lest Satan get too much pleasure out of us.

Body and Soul then end up speaking together and putting the blame on Satan:

---

9 Translation in Drijvers 1991.

23. We used to be neighbours, like brothers,
but Satan laid traps for us
and made us audacious
like ravening wolves.

The topic provided authors with ample scope for dealing with the proper interrelationship between body and soul, along with issues involving the function of free will.

3 Biblical Characters

The adaptation of the genre to include biblical characters has also occurred in Jewish Aramaic where several examples are preserved in the Palestinian Targum tradition. Unfortunately the dating of this material is very uncertain, but it seems likely that the incorporation of biblical protagonists into the Syriac tradition of dialogue poems had its roots in Jewish Aramaic, even if the extant Jewish examples may only be contemporary with their Syriac counterparts. Although the Syriac *Dispute between Abel and Cain*[10] shares its subject with one of the Jewish Aramaic disputes, the nature of the dispute is very different: in the latter the issue is a theological one, freewill or predestination, whereas in the Syriac poem the focus is more on the importance of intention. Cain, in anger and envious that Abel's sacrifice has been accepted, but not his, claims:

15. (Cain) I am the eldest, and so it is right
that God should accept me, rather than you,
but He has preferred yours, and mine He has abhorred:
He has rejected my offering and chosen yours.

16. (Abel) In all offerings that are made
it is love that He wants to see,
and if good intention is not mingled in,
then the sacrifice is ugly and so gets rejected.

Next in biblical sequence is the *Dialogue between Abraham and Isaac*,[11] based on *Genesis* 22. Whereas almost all other dialogue poems take just a single verse in the biblical text as their starting point, that on Abraham and Isaac not only follows the chronological sequence of the biblical narrative, but also introduces two other speakers, first Sarah at the outset, and then finally God. The introduc-

10 Edition with translation Brock 2000; translation also in Brock 2012: 51–60.
11 Translation in Brock 2012: 65–75.

tion of Sarah is to be found in a number of Syriac verse retellings of *Genesis* 22,[12] and she likewise features in some Jewish and Greek texts, her intervention being treated in various different ways.

Three further Old Testament episodes were provided with dialogue poems: *Joseph and Potiphar's Wife*, *Joseph and Benjamin*, and *Job and his Wife*. Not surprisingly, it was the Gospels which provided the source for the majority of the dialogues involving biblical characters, and in some cases there are more than one on the same topic (as was also the case with a few of the Old Testament ones); this applies, for example, to the dialogues of the Angel Gabriel, first with Zacharias (*Luke* 1:11–20), and then with Mary (*Luke* 1:26–38). Mary also features in two further dialogues, one with Joseph, the other with the Magi, both episodes being based this time on the *Gospel of Matthew*.[13] Joseph's arrival back home to find his fiancée pregnant (*Matthew* 1:18–19) is the starting point of one of the most dramatic of these poems, as can be seen from the opening of the dialogue:

> 4. Joseph was dumfounded at Mary,
> seeing her pregnancy of which he knew nothing.
> He began to chide and reproach her,
> saying, Listen, girl,
>
> 5. (Joseph) Reveal to me the secret of what has happened to you;
> it is greatly shocking what you speak of;
> who has led you astray, virgin,
> and snatched away your wealth, chaste girl?
>
> 6. (Mary) I will disclose to you how it all happened,
> says Mary, So listen, Joseph:
> a man of fire came down to me,
> he gave me a greeting – and this took place.
>
> 7. (Joseph) That I should believe this is hard:
> it is not good, so do not repeat it.
> If you are willing, speak to me
> about what took place: who has led you astray?

It is only Mary's persistence in her endeavour to persuade him that she is telling the truth which finally (over more than twenty stanzas later!) leads Joseph to concede that she is not lying. Underlying the whole dialogue is the conflict between Faith and Reason: it is only when Joseph's reason concedes there might be

12 One of these is translated in Brock 2012: 76–84 (see also Brock 1999, chapter VI).
13 All three dialogues involving Mary are translated in Brock 2010a: 125–45. *The Angel and Zacharias*, and the first two dialogues involving Mary are translated in Brock 2012: 127–151.

something in Mary's faith that the angel comes to Joseph by night to reassure him (*Matthew* 1:20).

It so happens that among the rare examples of the genre in Greek there are two pairs of dialogues between Mary and the Angel and Mary and Joseph, the older of which is attributed to Proclus (d.446/7).[14] Although there are no direct literary borrowings either way, the Syriac and Greek poems share many *topoi*, as well as literary form.

The hesitation on the part of John the Baptist to baptise Christ in the Jordan (*Matthew* 3:14–15) supplied a natural starting point for a development into a dialogue poem.[15] Among the various objections that John proffers is the following:

> 19. (John) The river You have come to is far too small
> for You to stop there for it to contain You.
> Heaven cannot suffice for Your might,
> so how can the water of baptism hold You?
>
> 20. (Jesus) The womb is yet smaller than the Jordan,
> yet of my own will I dwelt in the Virgin.
> Just as I was born from the womb,
> so shall I be baptized in the Jordan.

Christ's baptism in the River Jordan also plays a central role in the dialogue between the personified rivers, Pishon and Jordan (*Genesis* 2:11, *Matthew* 3:13),[16] which constitutes a genuine precedence dispute.

The episode of the Sinful Woman who anointed Jesus in the house of Simon the Pharisee (*Luke* 7:36–50) has caught the imagination of many Syriac authors, as well as those writing in other languages. While in the western Christian tradition the woman has usually been identified as Mary Magdalene, this is only very rarely the case with Syriac writers, by whom the woman is normally left unnamed. A narrative poem attributed (perhaps rightly) to Ephrem introduces two characters absent from the biblical text, the seller of the unguent, and Satan.[17] The latter figure is given a very much more prominent role in the *Dispute of Satan and the Sinful Woman*,[18] which constitutes a particularly fine example of the genre, presenting the listener/reader with a psychological drama between the woman's old self (externalized as Satan) and her new resolve to go and anoint the feet of Jesus and ask his forgiveness. Satan voices her all inner hesi-

14 La Piana 1971: 110–23, 212–19.
15 Translation in Brock 2012: 176–84.
16 Translation in Brock 2012: 31–35.
17 Translation in Brock 2012: 185–201.
18 Published in Brock 1988; translation also in Brock 2012: 201–10.

tations, providing the many sensible reasons why she should not burst into and interrupt a lunch party in the house of a stranger.

14. (Satan) If you listen to my advice
you won't disturb that gentleman:
he is sitting with the nobility,
and if he sees you he may well be angry.

15 (Woman) I'm not taking your advice
for you greatly dislike those who repent.
Up till today I have been with you,
but from today on it is to Mary's Son that I belong.

16. (Satan) He is God's Son, and if you go in
he's not going to receive you as you would like to suppose;
he will hold you in abhorrence because of your deeds,
and you will be an object of shame when you come back.

Among the several other dialogue poems based on the New Testament, three may be singled out. That between the Two Thieves crucified alongside Jesus is based on the account in *Luke* 23:39–41, where one of the thieves repents.[19] From the sixth-century onwards they were accorded names, Dumachus and Titus, and these are sometimes supplied in the manuscripts containing the dialogue. The poem opens:

1. There fell on my ears the sound of the two thieves
disputing on Golgotha;
let us listen, my brethren, to what they are saying
as they stand in this wondrous judgement court.

As in the *Dialogue between Mary and Joseph*, the dispute turns out to be Faith and Reason, the latter based on the evidence of outward circumstances:

12. (Bad Thief) It is astounding on your part that you do not see
the flail-marks all over his back,
yet here you are proclaiming that it is glory that he possesses!
Who will believe what you are saying today?

13. (Good Thief) It is folly on your part that you do not notice
how the departed, in groups, clap their hands
leaving their place to go out to meet Him (Mt 27:51);
but your heart is hardened and you do not give your assent.

19 Translation in Brock 2012: 211–19.

The Good Thief (Titus) reappears in what is the best known and most popular of these poems, the *Dialogue between the Cherub and the Repentant Thief.*[20] In the Syriac translation of *Genesis* 3:24 it is a single Cherub who is stationed at the Gate of Paradise in order to prevent Adam and Eve, representing fallen humanity, from re-entering. In response to the Good Thief's request to be remembered by Jesus when he came to his kingdom, Jesus promises him 'This day you shall be with me in Paradise (*Luke* 23:43). The Cherub, however, obedient to his original instructions, is firm in refusing entry to the Thief:

> 20. (Cherub) Be off with you, man, and don't argue any further
> for this is what I have been ordered:
> to guard from your race, by means of the sword,
> the Tree of Life that is to be found in here. (cf. *Genesis* 3:22)
>
> 21. (Thief) Be off with you, angel; you should learn and see
> that I've left behind, hanging on Golgotha,
> that very Fruit of Salvation that is in your garden
> – so that our race may now enter without any hindrance.

It is not until twenty stanzas later that, on the Thief's producing the Cross, that the Cherub is won over:

> 41. (Thief) O agent for the King, do not be upset;
> your authority is repealed, for your Lord has willed it so.
> It is His Cross that I have brought to you as a sign:
> look and see if it is genuine, and do not be so angry.
>
> 42. (Cherub) This Cross of the Son which you have brought to me
> is something I do not dare to look upon at all.
> It is both genuine and awesome; no longer will you be debarred
> from entering Eden, seeing that He has so willed it.

The poem, which is the nearest that Syriac authors ever got to producing liturgical drama, is still sometimes acted out by two deacons in a liturgical context.[21] In the medieval West it was the Resurrection scene of the visit of the women to the tomb, and the angel's question to them 'Whom is it you seek', which provided the stepping-stone, as it were, to the development of liturgical drama. In the Syriac tradition the Resurrection scene also produced a couple of dialogue poems, but based instead on chapter 20 the Gospel of John; there the woman who encounters Jesus (whom she imagines to be the Gardener) is Mary Magda-

20 Translation in Brock 2012: 220–29.
21 See Mengozzi 2013. There are several Modern Syriac versions of the poem.

len. In an early Syriac tradition, however, the woman was identified as Mary, the mother of Jesus, and this is presupposed in both of the dialogues between Mary and the Gardener.[22]

A small number of the dialogue poems involve the rivalry between Christianity and Judaism; the most striking among these is that between the Church and the Synagogue[23] which, unlike most Syriac literature involving Jews and Judaism, is remarkably even-handed. The issue is a basic one: which of the two is the true 'heir' and 'bride'?

3. The Daughter of the Hebrews is boasting
that she is heir to the House of God,
but the Church says, in opposition,
that 'I am the daughter and true heir'.

4. Judge between them, all you who listen
with open and unerring judgment,
and once their words have reached an end,
give the victory to her who proves true.

Bridal imagery is quite prominent throughout the poem:

9. (Synagogue) A bridal bower for me in the wilderness did God construct,
a cloud of light above my head He suspended;
a pillar of fire He took as well
to illumine me, since it is me He loved.

10. (Church) Your bridal bower would have been spacious and glorious
if the Calf had not defiled you.
Look how your adultery is marked out in your very bridal chamber!
May the Father have mercy on both you and me.

At the end, and against all expectation (and the words of stanza 4), no verdict is given, although of course for the audience it would have been a foregone conclusion.

Another case where the topic is presented in an unexpectedly even-handed way is the *Dispute between Cyril and Nestorius*,[24] one of a small number of dialogues where the protagonists are non-biblical figures. This poem, which is of East Syriac origin sets out, in a simple manner, the two contrasting positions on Christology.

22 Translations in Brock 2010a: 146–50.
23 Translation in Brock 2017; 2019.
24 Translation in Brock 2004.

Two other dialogues involving non-biblical protagonists deserve particular mention. The first concerns Helena, mother of Constantine, and her encounter with the Jews of Jerusalem when she was in search of the true Cross.[25] As in the case of Abraham and Isaac, this poem does not strictly follow the normal pattern: because it is closely based on the prose narrative of the *Finding of the Cross*, elements of narrative are interspersed in the poem, and there are three speakers, not two: Helena, the Jews of Jerusalem, and Judas, their representative (who eventually converts to Christianity).

The second poem is the *Dispute between St Marina and Satan*,[26] one of a small number of dialogue poems which involve saints. When her widowed father decided to enter a monastery Marina was determined to enter with him, but of course had to pose as a eunuch. In due course she/he gained the reputation as a model monk, but then one day she is falsely accused of having fathered the child of a local inn-keeper's daughter. Firm in her monastic vocation, she refuses to reveal her true identity, and so is expelled from the monastery. Patiently bearing all sorts of insults and accusations, she brings up the child outside the monastery gate. Only after her death does her identity (and the falsehood of the accusation) come to light. The dispute between her and Satan is clearly modelled on that of Satan and the Sinful Woman, and represents her interior struggle when she is accused of fathering the child: should she, as Satan points out, make things so much easier for herself by simply revealing her identity, or should she silently and in great humility adhere to her monastic vocation despite all the ignominy involved.

4 Liturgical Context

Most of the dispute poems involving biblical characters came to be associated with different parts of the liturgical year, even if they may well not have been originally written with this in mind. The two main seasons to which they are associated are Nativity-Epiphany, and Holy Week; for the latter the allocation in the liturgical tradition is as follows:

Palm Sunday: *Church and Synagogue*, *Church and Sion*
Monday: *Abel and Cain*
Tuesday: *Abraham and Isaac*

25 Translation in Brock 1999, chapter XI (along with a narrative poem on the same subject, but also including Constantine).
26 Translation in Brock 2008.

Thursday:	*Satan and the Sinful Woman*
Friday:	*The Two Thieves*
Saturday:	*The Cherub and the Thief, Death and Satan*
Resurrection:	*Mary and the Gardener*

Normally they feature in the course of the Night Office (Lilyo). This may suggest that at least some of the Dialogues may have been originally written for Vigil services for certain popular commemorations at which there was a considerable presence of laity: the combination of good instruction conveyed in a lively and gently humorous manner would have served as a good recipe for retaining the congregation's attention.

5 Authorship and Transmission

The majority of the dialogue poems are anonymous, and it is only in rare cases that the author's name is known for certain: this is definitely the case with Ephrem's three precedence disputes between Death and Satan, and the same applies to the sixth of the Discourses against the Jews by Jacob of Serugh (d.521) and to the *Dispute between the Cedar and the Vine*, by David bar Paulos (8th/9th century).[27] Actually, neither of these two dialogues strictly follows the standard pattern since the protagonists speak in alternating blocks of verses, and not in alternating stanzas.

As frequently happens with anonymous works, there is a strong temptation on the part of scribes to provide attributions. Thus, for example, one of the several manuscripts transmitting the dialogue between Satan and the Sinful Woman (of Luke 7) ascribes the poem to Jacob of Serugh, while in the East Syriac tradition a number of the dialogue poems are transmitted together with the Verse Discourses by the fifth-century poet Narsai, but it is very unlikely that any of them are genuinely by Narsai. A more dramatic case concerns the *Dispute of the Months*, which is anonymous in the two manuscripts (dating from almost a millennium apart!) which form the basis of the published text; subsequently, however, the poem turned up incorporated into a collection of poems by the fourteenth-century poet Khamis bar Kardahe. The eighth- or ninth-century date of the earlier manuscript used in the edition at once makes it clear that the attribution to Khamis is erroneous.

27 Translation in Butts 2017.

In the case of the majority of the dialogue poems the absence of a reliable attribution makes any attempt to date a particular poem hazardous, the only reliable criteria being the *terminus ante quem* provided by the date of the earliest manuscript (this will rarely be earlier than about the ninth century), and the absence or presence of the use of rhyme (which only came into regular use under the influence of Arabic poetry, especially from about the twelfth century onwards). A further criterion might be added, namely the transmission of the poem in both East and West Syriac liturgical tradition, for this would suggest that the poem dates from before the end of the sixth century, by which time the two ecclesiastical and liturgical traditions had effectively separated, with only rare subsequent interaction.[28] On the basis of this last criterion, it would seem fairly well assured that the following belong to the fifth or early sixth century: *Abel and Cain*, *Angel and Mary*, *Mary and the Magi*, *John the Baptism and Christ*, *The Cherub and the Thief*, and *The Months*. Less certain is the case of two further Old Testament dialogues, between Joseph and Potiphar's wife, and between Joseph and Benjamin.

Most of the dialogue poems are transmitted in liturgical manuscripts, of which the earliest date from about the ninth century. The earlier manuscripts, which in many cases are the only ones to provide the complete text of a poem, may either be collections of liturgical hymnology arranged according to the liturgical year, or the liturgical services themselves, in which the dialogue poems find their place. Since many churches had two choirs (*gude*), and since parchment and paper were expensive, economies could be made if each choir used pairs of manuscripts in each of which only alternate verses, one with odd- and the other with even-numbered verses, had been copied. This of course provides a problem for modern scholars when only one half of the text survives, and sometimes it involves a hunt for a number of different manuscripts as being necessary before a complete poem can be put together, especially as abbreviation is another hazard to which the poems were often subjected. In the modern printed liturgical books the dialogue poems have often suffered badly, and the preservation of complete poems in them is rare.

28 The case of the dispute between Body and Soul by 'Abdisho ', mentioned above, is exceptional: his immensely popular Paradise of Eden, to which the dispute belongs, was transmitted in both East and West Syriac manuscripts.

6 By Way of Conclusion

These dispute and dialogue poems, with their stylised character, constitute a distinctive contribution of the Syriac literary tradition to the transmission, from past to present, of this long-lived Middle Eastern literary genre. Although the genre never seems to have caught on in Greek, it found a new home in the medieval West as the tenson or tenzone, no doubt having travelled by way of Arabic through Sicily and/or Spain. One result of this migration of the genre was the contemporary appearance in the thirteenth century of two separate Disputes between Body and Soul, one produced in Mesopotamia by 'Abdisho' of Nisibis, and the other in Italy by Jacoponi da Todi.[29] Vivacious, instructive, and often possessing an element of humour, it is perhaps not surprising that these dispute poems have enjoyed such longevity.

Bibliography

Brock, Sebastian. 1985. A dispute of the months and some related Syriac texts, *Journal of Semitic Studies* 30: 181–211. Reprinted in Brock 1999, chapter VIII.

Brock, Sebastian. 1987. Dramatic dialogue poems. Pp. 135–47 in *IV Symposium Syriacum,* ed. Corrie Molenberg and Gerrit J. Reinink. Orientalia Christiana Analecta 229. Rome: Pontificio Istituto Orientale.

Brock, Sebastian. 1988. The Sinful Woman and Satan: two Syriac dialogue poems, *Oriens Christianus* 72: 21–62.

Brock, Sebastian. 1991. Syriac dispute poems: the various types. Pp. 109–119 in *Dispute Poems and Dialogues in the Ancient and Mediaeval Near East: Forms and Types of Literary Debates in Semitic and Related Literatures*, ed. Gerrit J. Reinink and Herman L. J. Vanstiphout. Orientalia Lovaniensia Analecta 42. Leuven: Peeters. Reprinted in Brock 1999, chapter VII.

Brock, Sebastian. 1995. Tales of two beloved brothers: Syriac dialogues between Body and Soul. Pp. 29–38 in *Studies in the Christian East in Memory of Mirrit Boutros Ghali*, ed. Leslie S. B. MacCoull. Society for Coptic Archaeology, North America. Reprinted in Brock 1999, chapter IX.

Brock, Sebastian. 1998. A Syriac dispute Poem: the River Pishon and the River Jordan, *Parole de l'Orient* 23: 3–12.

Brock, Sebastian. 1999. *From Ephrem to Romanos. Interactions between Syriac and Greek in Late Antiquity.* Aldershot: Ashgate Variorum.

Brock, Sebastian. 2000. Two Syriac dialogue poems on Abel and Cain, *Le Muséon* 113: 333–75.

29 The openings of both poems are quoted in Brock 1995: 30.

Brock, Sebastian. 2001. The dispute poem: from Sumer to Syriac, *Journal of the Canadian Society for Syriac Studies* 1: 3–20.

Brock, Sebastian. 2004. Syriac Dialogue: an example from the past, *Journal of Assyrian Academic Studies* 18/1: 57–70.

Brock, Sebastian. 2008. St Marina and Satan. A Syriac dispute poem, *Collectanea Christiana Orientalia* 5: 35–57.

Brock, Sebastian. 2010a. *Bride of Light. Hymns on Mary from the Syriac Churches.* Moran Etho 6. Piscataway NJ: Gorgias.

Brock, Sebastian. 2010b. Dramatic narrative poems on biblical topics in Syriac, *Studia Patristica* 45: 183–96.

Brock, Sebastian. 2012. *Treasure-House of Mysteries. Explorations of the Sacred Text through Poetry in the Syriac Tradition.* Yonkers NY: St Vladimir's Seminary Press.

Brock, Sebastian. 2017. Synagogue and Church in Dialogue: a Syriac poem. Pp. 525–40 in *"Lampada per I miei passi è la tua parola, luce sul mio cammino": Studi offerti a Marcello del Verme,* ed. Pasquale Giustiniani and Franceso del Pizzo. Bibbia e Oriente, Suppl. 27. Bornato in Franciacorte (BS): Sardini.

Brock, Sebastian. 2019. *The People and the Peoples. Syriac Dialogue Poems from Late Antiquity.* Journal of Jewish Studies, Supplement 3. Oxford.

Brock, Sebastian. forthcoming. Biblical dialogues in Syriac: texts and contexts. In a forthcoming volume, ed. Peter Toth.

Brock, Sebastian, and George Kiraz. 2006. *Ephrem the Syrian. Select Poems.* Provo, Utah: Brigham Young University Press.

Butts, Aaron. 2017. A Syriac dialogue poem between the Vine and the Cedar by Dawid bar Paulos. Pp. 462–73 in *The Babylonian Disputation Poems: with Editions of the Series of the Poplar, Palm and Vine, the Series of the Spider, and the Story of the Poor, Forlorn Wren,* by Enrique Jiménez. Culture and History of the Ancient Near East 87. Leiden: Brill.

Drijvers, Han J. W. 1991. Body and Soul: a perennial problem. Pp. 121–34 in *Dispute Poems and Dialogues in the Ancient and Mediaeval Near East: Forms and Types of Literary Debates in Semitic and Related Literatures*, ed. Gerrit J. Reinink and Herman L. J. Vanstiphout. Orientalia Lovaniensia Analecta 42. Leuven: Peeters.

La Piana, Giorgio. 1971. *Le rappresentazioni sacre nella letteratura bizantina.* London: Ashgate Variorum Reprints.

Mengozzi, Alessandro. 2013. The Cherub and the Thief on the You Tube: an Eastern Christian liturgical drama and the vitality of the Mesopotamian dispute, *Annali del Istituto Orientale di Napoli* 73: 49–65.

Murray, Robert. 1995. Aramaic and Syriac dispute poems and their connections. Pp. 157–87 in *Studia Aramaica*, ed. Markham J. Geller et al. Journal of Semitic Studies Supplement 4. Oxford: Oxford University Press.

Ruani, Flavia (ed.). 2016. *Les controverses religieuses en syriaque.* Études syriaques 12. Paris: Geuthner.

Geert Jan van Gelder*

11 The Debate of Spring and Autumn in Arabic Literature

The great Iraqi prose writer al-Jāḥiẓ, who died at an advanced age in December 868 or January 869, was fond of opposites and debates. He wrote books, treatises, and epistles on many serious subjects and also on more frivolous topics, often using a mixture of jest and earnest, notably in "The Superiority of the Belly to the Back" (*Tafḍīl al-baṭn ʿalā l-ẓahr*), "The Superiority of Blacks to Whites" (*Tafḍīl al-sūdān ʿalā l-bīḍ*), and "The Boasting Contest of Girls and Boys" (*Mufākharat al-jawārī wa-l-ghilmān*). These and other debates in al-Jāḥiẓ's oeuvre may be called literary, but they are not "literary debates" in the more restricted sense used here, for they lack an element that is a striking feature already of the earliest debates, in Sumerian and Babylonian: the prosopopoeia, or *fictio personae*, whereby objects, substances, or concepts are personified or humanized and introduced as speaking. This element is not found in early Arabic poetry or prose before the contact with other cultures in Iraq, Syria, and Persia.[1] It is not certain that al-Jāḥiẓ used it. Among his preserved debates, "The Boasting Contest of Girls and Boys," a highly entertaining text about sex, has a misleading title, for it is not boys and girls who speak but a boy-lover and a girl-lover.[2] The same goes for the lengthy, sprawling debate about dog vs. cock, part of his great *Kitāb al-Ḥayawān*, "The Book of Living Beings,"[3] where the speakers are "the man of the dog" and "the man of the cock."[4] Likewise, belly and back are not made to speak in the "The Superiority of the Belly over the Back"[5] nor do blacks and whites directly confront one another in "The Superiority of Blacks over Whites."[6] Unfortunately, of some other debates by al-Jāḥiẓ we only have the titles. One of them is *Mufākharat al-misk wa-l-zabād*, "The Boasting Contest of Musk and Civet" (see Pellat 1984: 148 no. 142); we don't

* University of Oxford.

1 On the classical Arabic literary debate, see e.g. Wagner 1962 and 1993; Van Gelder 1987 and 1991; Heinrichs 1991; Mattock 1991; al-Sawāḥilī [2007?]; Naẓarī and Fūlādī 2015.

2 al-Jāḥiẓ [1964]–79, II: 87–137, English translation in Colville 2002: 202–30.

3 Or "The Book of Life," as argued in Montgomery 2013: 10–11.

4 al-Jāḥiẓ 1965–69, I: 222–389, II: 5–375 (interrupted by numerous digressions).

5 al-Jāḥiẓ [1964]–79, IV: 153–66, English translations in Colville 2002: 62–69 and Hutchins 1989: 163–67.

6 al-Jāḥiẓ [1964]–79, I: 173–226; English translations in Colville 2002: 25–52, Hutchins 1989: 139–66 and Khalidi 1981: 3–51.

https://doi.org/10.1515/9781501510274-011

know if the perfumes are speaking themselves, as they do in much later Arabic texts.[7]

In one of his epistles al-Jāḥiẓ says that he, in his earlier works, "mentioned the quarrel (*ikhtiṣām*) of winter and summer and the argumentation of each of them to the other, and the argumentation of the man of the goat and the sheep."[8] The latter is apparently preserved in his *Book of Living Beings*, and it does not contain speaking goats or sheep. The other is not preserved. The title seems to suggest that winter and summer are actually speaking, for "the argumentation of each of them" can only apply to winter and summer, grammatically speaking. This tempted me to write, in my 1987 article, that "the wording of this title make[s] it almost certain that the seasons are speaking themselves." I should have remembered, however, that the title of the debate "of girls and boys" is misleading, for it is a debate *about* girls and boys, so it is possible that summer and winter are not speaking either.

There is in fact a text that is extant, ascribed to al-Jāḥiẓ in the sources, entitled *Salwat* [or *Sulwat*] *al-ḥarīf* [or *al-ḥirrīf*] *bi-munāẓarat al-rabīʿ wa-l-kharīf*, "The Friend's Comfort: On the disputation of Spring and Autumn," in which the seasons are personified and speak.[9] However, even if we only had the title this would suggest that the text is spurious, for titles in rhymed prose (*sajʿ*) belong to a somewhat later time than that of al-Jāḥiẓ. It is one of a number of false attributions to al-Jāḥiẓ. The text itself makes this even more abundantly clear, for the style is very un-Jāḥiẓian; it uses *sajʿ* consistently, whereas al-Jāḥiẓ rarely used it, and there are numerous quotations from poetry and prose dating from the late ninth and the tenth centuries. As Oskar Rescher demonstrated, it was written by a Persian in the middle of the eleventh century;[10] I shall come back to it presently. It is not the only Arabic text on this and related seasonal topics. A book on Winter and Summer, *Kitāb al-Shitāʾ wa-l-ṣayf*, is attributed to a contemporary of al-Jāḥiẓ, Abū Ḥātim al-Sijistānī (d. 864)[11] and another with the same title to

7 Van Gelder 1991 (with a translation of a 15th-century literary debate in which musk, ambergris, saffron, and civet speak).

8 al-Jāḥiẓ [1964]–79, II: 95 (*ikhtiṣām al-shitāʾ wa-l-ṣayf wa-iḥtijāj aḥadihimā ʿalā ṣāḥibihī*), cf. Yāqūt 1936–38, XVI: 107 (quoting al-Jāḥiẓ listing his books): *Iftikhār al-shitāʾ wa-l-ṣayf*, the same al-Ṣafadī 1931–2005, XXIII: 197.

9 Published together with al-Sharīf al-Murtaḍā, *al-Shihāb fī l-shayb wa-l-shabāb*. See Pellat 1984: 173.

10 Rescher 1931: 526 (with a shortened translation of the debate, 498–526). See also al-Sawāḥilī [2007?]: 17–19.

11 *K. al-shitāʾ wa-l-ṣayf*, mentioned in Ibn al-Nadīm 1871–72, 58, = Ibn al-Nadīm 2009, I: 168; Ibn Khallikān 1968–72, II: 433 and al-Ṣafadī 1931–2005, XVI: 15.

Ibn al-Marzubān (d. 921);[12] they are not preserved and it is uncertain if they were proper debates. We have some other texts, however, from the very short to longer compositions.[13]

Literary texts on the comparison of the seasons or the months are ancient. There is one in Syriac, a poem dating probably from the fifth or sixth century (Brock 1985: 188). The months are personified and speak. There are Hebrew poems, also probably from the fifth and sixth centuries, on the months vying for Pesach/Passover or on the dispute between summer and winter.[14] In one of Aesops *Fables*, Winter mocks Spring (it is not a proper debate). Spring and Winter speak in what is perhaps the oldest European literary debate, *Conflictus veris et hiemis*, attributed to Alcuin (d. 804).[15] Much older is a debate in Sumerian, between summer and winter.[16] There is a difference with the Arabic tradition, for the Sumerian, Latin, and Syriac texts, as well as the English *The debate and stryfe betwene somer and wynter* of 1528[17] (going back to a French model) and the early 15th-century Dutch text *Een abel spel van den winter ende van den somer*[18] are all in verse,[19] whereas the Arabic tradition favors prose for the literary debate, normally the ornate, rhymed and rhythmical but unmetered kind called *saj*ʿ, which does not count as verse to the Arabs because it lacks

12 Muḥammad ibn Khalaf ibn al-Marzubān, *K. al-Shitā*ʾ *wa-l-ṣayf*, mentioned in Ibn al-Nadīm 1871–72, 150 = Ibn al-Nadīm 2009, I: 461, al-Ṣafadī 1931–2005, III: 45.

13 Brockelmann (1937–49, Suppl. I: 521) attributes a "Wettstreit zwischen Herbst und Frühling" ("Contest between Autumn and Spring") to the well-known writer and critic Ḍiyāʾ al-Dīn ibn al-Athīr (d. 1239). He refers to al-Nuwayrī's *Nihāyah* (al-Nuwayrī 1923–, I: 175–76), but this is merely a short passage in rhymed prose, in which Autumn boasts to Spring: "I am the one who brings the disappearance of poisons, the departure of clouds, the pressing of vine's daughters, and a multitude of various dishes and drinks ..." It is not a debate.

14 van Bekkum 1991: 80–81; Klein 1989.

15 Waddell 1948: 82–87 (Latin and English translation), and Cristóbal López and Arcaz Pozo in this volume.

16 Vanstiphout 2004; a Dutch translation in Vanstiphout, 2004: 167–79.

17 *The debate and stryfe betwene somer and wynter with the estate present of man*, London: Laurence Andrew for [R. Wyer?], 1528?

18 Text in dbnl (digitale bibliotheek voor de Nederlandse letteren), from A. H. Hoffman von Fallersleben, A. H. *Horae Belgicae*, 1968; accessible at http://www.dbnl.org/tekst/hoff004hora01_01/zoek.php?page=1&pageSize=50&categorie=titel&fq=ti_id%3Ahoff004hora01&zoek=somer (last accessed November 2019). For German "folkloristic" versions, see Liungman 1941.

19 The Persian and Turkish *munāẓarah* traditions also regularly employ verse. There is anonymous debate between summer and winter in Eastern Turkish from the 2nd half of the 11th century, see Brockelmann 1924: 32–34 and Aynur in this volume.

the strict quantitative meters of true poetry. The typical classical Arabic literary dispute is written in rhymed prose and there are only a few debate-like poems.[20]

One can only speculate about why *saj*ʿ is preferred to poetry (*shiʿr*), for classical Arabic literary debates. It is different for vernacular Arabic: the modern texts studied by Enno Littmann and Clive Holes are poems.[21] Poetry is certainly the dominant literary form in Classical Arabic. In the European tradition with its Homer, Virgil, Dante, Milton and others, narrative poetry has a very high status, and the same applies to Persian, where literary debates are usually in verse form. It is different in Arabic, where poetry is predominantly lyrical and descriptive and narrative verse ranks lowly. Stories are told mostly in prose, and a debate, after all, is a narrative. To make it properly "literary" the medium of rhymed prose is suitable; it accommodates narrative as well as ekphrasis, which is an important element of the debate texts. Sebastian Brock has described the Syriac literary debate "as a fusion of two originally separate genres, the precedence dispute and the ἔκφρασις or description, the one essentially Mesopotamian, the other Greek" (Brock 1985: 184). The same could be said of the Arabic literary *munāẓarah*, only I would not maintain that the description or ekphrasis in it is of Greek origin, for that element seems authentically Arabic. The earliest and most highly esteemed Arabic poetry, from pre-Islamic times, is full of description of nature and animals. Descriptions of the seasons, especially of Spring, are very common in Arabic poetry especially from the early Abbasid period onward.[22] The Egyptian poet and literary critic Ibn Wakīʿ al-Tinnīsī, who died in 1003, composed a poem on the four seasons;[23] but it is not a debate.

Before discussing this poem and other literary texts on the seasons I should mention that the customary division of the year into four seasons as we know them is not found in pre-Islamic Arabic. The word used for "spring," *rabī*ʿ, is particularly interesting and if the reader finds the following somewhat confusing I have succeeded, for it *is* confusing. In early Arabic, *rabī*ʿ meant the "season in

20 An early instance is a poem of six lines by al-Ṣanawbarī (d. 945), with a debate between rose and narcissus (al-Ṣanawbarī 1998, 448); see Schoeler 1974: 313–15; a late example is a poem of 28 lines with a dispute between olive oil and meat by Nīqūlā al-Turk (d. 1828), in Shaykhū 1897: 249–50, anonymously in al-Hāshimī [1901]: 182–83. Jiménez 2017: 138, 150 mentions disputation "poems" by al-Jāḥiẓ, but all works by al-Jāḥiẓ are in prose.

21 Littmann 1951; Holes 1995, 1996, 1998, and see his contribution to the present volume.

22 See e. g. Schoeler 1974, which deals with nature poetry from the pre-Islamic period until mid-Abbasid times (al-Ṣanawbarī, who died in 945 or 946). Numerous anthologies contain chapters on spring and spring flowers; the Andalusian Abū l-Walīd al-Ḥimyarī (d. 1048) wrote *al-Badīʿ fī waṣf al-rabīʿ* (Wonderful Descriptions of Spring), an anthology of poetry and prose.

23 al-Thaʿālibī 1947, I: 363–68, also, somewhat shortened, in the 14th-century encyclopedia by al-Nuwayrī, (al-Nuwayrī 1923–, I: 179–83, in a chapter on the seasons, I: 169–83.

which, as a result of the rains, the earth is covered with green" (Plessner 1995). In Lane's *Lexicon*, which is based on the mediaeval Arabic dictionaries, one reads that the word refers to seasons and to two months: the first *rabīʿ* is "*the season in which the truffles and the blossoms come*, and this is [also called] *the rabeeạ of the herbage*" and the second *rabīʿ* is "*the season in which fruits ripen.*" Confusingly, we read that "all of them (i.e., the early Arabic lexicographers) agree that the *kharīf* (or *autumn*) is called *al-rabīʿ* . . . *the two divisions of the winter* [by which he means *the half-year commencing at the autumnal equinox*] are called *rabīʿān* (two *rabīʿ*s) . . . *rabīʿ* is applied by the Arabs to the whole *winter* . . . *the year consists of six seasons* ..." Thus far Lane's *Lexicon* (which has much more).[24] In pre-Islamic Arabic there were two months called *rabīʿ*;[25] they became part of the Muslim calendar as the first and the second *Rabīʿ*. But because the Islamic calendar from the very beginning was a lunar calendar without intercalation, the connection of these month with spring, or any other season, was lost. When not referring to the calendar the word *rabīʿ* is always the normal word for spring, as one of the four seasons we know—unless it is a personal name, to add to the potential confusion. In the Arabic literary debates between *al-rabīʿ* and *al-kharīf* we can interpret the former always as "Spring."

The poem on these four seasons by Ibn Wakīʿ consists of 108 couplets (rhyming *aa bb cc dd* ..., whereas normally Arabic poems employ monorhyme, *aaaaaa* ...); it opens as follows:

> You ask me about the best time:
> You've asked the right person.
> You asked which time is most pleasant,
> which is most suited to revelry.
> I have to say something describing the four seasons,
> which will not fail to convince any astute person.

Then there follow sections on Summer (*al-ṣayf*), Autumn (*al-kharīf*), Winter (*al-shitāʾ*), and Spring (*al-rabīʿ*). It soon becomes clear that the poet's idea of revelry is drinking wine, and that in his view wine could be drunk in any season except perhaps summer. Spring, coming last, is the obvious winner, although it is not a proper contest and the seasons do not speak.

---

24 Lane 1863–77, III: 1018–19; see also the entry on *kharīf*, II: 726.

25 There existed different sets of pre-Islamic Arabic names for the months; see al-Marzūqī 1996: 207–10.

The above-mentioned debate between Spring and Autumn, entitled *Salwat al-ḥarīf*, falsely ascribed to al-Jāḥiẓ, on the other hand, is a true literary debate.[26] It is long, perhaps some 7,000 words, written in rhyming prose interspersed with poetry by various poets, often without attribution. At the beginning the author says that he is in the service of Qawām al-Mulk wa-Niẓām al-Dīn Abū Yaʿlā Aḥmad ibn Ṭāhir, a vizier of the Seljuqs who died in 1052 or 1053.[27] At the end the unnamed author says: "It was written on Thursday on the twelfth of the month Rabīʿ II of the year 441,"[28] which corresponds with 9 September 1049. I said that the seasons are personified; in fact, the debate is carried out by fictional but "real" human persons representing Spring and Autumn. The author tells us that one day he went out to seek solitude. He finds a pleasant spot, a typical *locus amoenus*. Some well-behaved people appear, one of them being a handsome young man called al-Rabīʿ ibn al-Ṭayyib. This could be a real name, for as said above al-Rabīʿ is also a man's name, as is al-Ṭayyib, but like many Arabic names it could be translated, and in English this would be "Spring, son of Pleasant." Another is a venerable old man called al-Kharīf ibn al-Munʿim, which translates as "Autumn son of Bringer or Blessing." Unlike the other, this name does not have the ring of realism, for real people are not called al-Kharīf, which has unfortunate connotations, such as *kharif*, "dotard, senile, feebleminded" and *khurāfah* "superstitious or fictitious story, fable." As for the patronymic, at least in pre-modern times no human could properly be called al-Munʿim, "Bringer of Blessing," because it is one of the many epithets of God, sometimes included in the list of God's "most beautiful names."[29]

Al-Rabīʿ and al-Kharīf speak in turn, each producing five lengthy and somewhat repetitive monologues about the blessings of Spring and Autumn. Much of the debate is about medical matters, about Galenic humors and temperaments, sicknesses and diseases prone to happen, about healthy and unhealthy aspects of the seasons and the food or drinks produced in them, about noxious animals and vermin, and so on. Although they strongly contradict each other, the atmosphere remains pleasant and respectful. The text as a whole may be called prolix, yet there are some good pithy sayings, as when al-Rabīʿ quips, "Spring is Time's nut, Autumn is its shell; Spring its marrow, Autumn its bones; Spring its purity, Autumn its grime; Spring its choice wine, [116] Autumn its dregs; Spring its fresh

26 For a recent short discussion of this text see Shuraydi 2014: 68–69.

27 On him see Ibn al-Athīr, 1987–2003, VIII: 278, 282.

28 [ps.-]al-Jāḥiẓ AH 1302: 131.

29 In modern times one finds people called Munʿim, presumably to be taken as a shortened form of ʿAbd al-Munʿim ("Servant/slave of the Bringer of Blessings," often spelled Abdel-Moneim).

draught, Autumn its lees; Spring its nose, Autumn its tail—who would equate a camel's nose with its tail?—; Spring its chest, Autumn its posterior."[30]

Both quote poetry and even though there must be far more Arabic poems in praise of Spring, the old man called Autumn is able to quote some epigrams and longer poems in praise of Autumn.[31] It is al-Kharīf, Autumn, who has the last word; he remarks that the time of the year is in fact Autumn, ready to serve the patron, the vizier Qawām al-Mulk (one will remember that the debate was written in September, in the month called "the second Rabīʿ," where Rabīʿ does *not* mean "spring"), and Mr Autumn ends with quoting a maxim, "The present is better than the absent, the existent is better than the non-existent." This, concludes the author, is the last of what took place between the old man and the young man and each went his separate way.

Autumn, who may be considered the underdog, has been victorious, though by a slender margin and on dubious grounds. A victory of the underdog makes the debate more interesting; similarly, the humble hoe wins the debate with the more sophisticated plough in Sumerian (Vanstiphout 1984). That the Arabic debate between knowledge and ignorance by Muḥammad al-Jazāʾirī (d. 1922) ends in a victory of the former, though expected, is somewhat disappointing from a literary point of view; the loser at least is consoled with being told that his existence is necessary.[32] Often, however, there is no clear winner. This happens often in Arabic literary debates that are written in honor of a patron, who is sometimes the arbiter in the dispute. Pen and sword, who figure in several debates, are both necessary to the ruler and both have to cooperate with each other.

Presenting the abstract contestants as real persons named after the seasons is a ploy to make the debate more realistic. There is a tendency in Classical Arabic literature to look down on fiction, or rather overt fiction. The animal fables in

---

30 [ps.-]al-Jāḥiẓ AH 1302: 115–16. To the present author there is little to choose between the camel's nose and its tail.

31 [ps.-]al-Jāḥiẓ AH 1302: 122–25, poems by Ibn al-Rūmī (d. 896), Ibn al-Muʿtazz (d. 908), a certain al-Bādhānī (not identified), and a short anonymous piece (attributed to an otherwise unknown Abū Saʿd al-Iṣbahānī in al-Tīfāshī 1980: 234, in a chapter on the four seasons). Three longer poems (together 62 lines) are by Abū ʿUmar ʿAbdān al-Farrukhī. In al-Tīfāshī 1980: 233 this poet is called ʿAbdān ibn ʿAbd Allāh al-Iṣfahānī. I have not been able to identify him with certainty, but he may well be identical with ʿAbdān al-Iṣbahānī, known as al-Khūzī, who has an entry in al-Thaʿālibī 1947, III: 296–300.

32 *Munāẓarat al-ʿilm wa-l-jahl*, by Muḥammad ibn Muḥammad al-Daysī (or al-Dīsī?) al-Hāmilī al-Jazāʾirī, in al-Ṭayyān 2000: 185–206. In Hämeen-Anttila 2002: 405–6 a debate with the same title—possibly the same debate—is attributed to Muḥammad ibn Muḥammad ibn al-Mubārak al-Jazāʾirī, who died in 1912.

the early Arabic prose work *Kalīlah and Dimnah*, in which animals speak and act like humans, are accepted, perhaps because it was known they were translated from the Middle Persian. It took a while before new texts were composed of a clearly fictional character, but in due course many literary debates were written where objects or abstract concepts speak: pen and sword, rose and narcissus, chandelier and candelabra, wine and wax candle, perfumes, precious stones, rice and pomegranate seeds, palm tree and vine, fig and grape, water melon and date, apricot and mulberry, cheese and olives, oil and meat, camel and horse, dinar and dirham, gold and glass, hairlocks on the temple and cheek-down, sword and lance, heaven and earth, sun and moon, water and air, land and sea, truth and falsehood, generosity and miserliness, going abroad vs. staying at home; and, moving to modern times, boat and train, donkey and bicycle, tram and bus, telephone and telegraph.[33]

Compared with the Arabic debates between pen and sword, which I studied in some detail in my earlier article (Van Gelder 1987), the debates between the seasons are a bit tame and sedate. The discussion usually consists of a series of monologues, whereas pen and sword sometimes attack each other in quick sallies and repartees, with an element of invective that is lacking in the polite exchanges in the pseudo-Jāḥiẓ text on Spring and Autumn. It is the same in a later text, by Ibn Ḥabīb al-Ḥalabī, from Aleppo, who died in 1377, a section of his book entitled *Nasīm al-ṣabā*, "Breeze of the East Wind" (the East Wind is the Arabic lyrical, if not meteorological, equivalent of the Zephyr). It is a collection of thirty stylistic exercises mostly in lyrical descriptions, written in a highly ornate prose, with prose rhyme interspersed with short bits of poetry. The fifth section,[34] entitled "On the Seasons of the Year," begins with:

> The seasons of the year attended a session of erudition * on a day on which an astute person could attain his highest ambition * in the presence of people of eloquence and elocution * proficient in the art of composition. * Each one of them stood up to express his ideas * and to boast to his peers. *
>
> Spring spoke and said,
> I am the youth of Time, the soul of all that has life, the pupil (*insān*) of the eye of mankind (*insān*), the life of souls, the bridal adornment of all that grows ...

33 The list is not exhaustive. Giving references for each type would swell the notes and the bibliography inordinately.

34 Ibn Ḥabīb AH 1302: 18–23, also in al-Hāshimī n.d., I: 256–59. In the following fragment I have attempted to imitate the prose rhyme, marked with asterisks.

Spring is followed by his three colleagues, but it is not much of a contest, for although each is full of himself they do not attack each other and at the end they have a jolly time together before they disperse. Much livelier is the debate between the seasons in a modern text in verse, in vernacular Iraqi Arabic, composed in 1930.[35]

It may be interesting to compare the Arabic debates on this theme with other traditions. Although I have argued that the Arabic tradition was influenced in a diffuse sense by earlier traditions, it is quite clear that there is no direct influence from texts to texts in the written tradition: there are no translations of Greek, Syriac,[36] or Pahlavi debates into Arabic, let alone Sumerian or Babylonian. There are some obvious differences between the Sumerian disputation of Summer and Winter and the Arabic debates of the seasons. The Sumerian text opens with a cosmogonic introduction in which the god Enlil determines the tasks of Summer and Winter. Before these two speak, they act: they perform a host of labors. It is all about agriculture, horticulture, and livestock, fish, fowl, pigs; about ploughing, building irrigation works, dikes and ditches. When they speak, boasting and insulting each other, it is still about wheat, flax, cattle, reed, fish, vegetables, grapes, wine, and beer. In the end, the god Enlil, while recognizing that the two are complementary and that one cannot be without the other, declares Winter to be the winner. Summer submits, the two are reconciled, and at a banquet with beer and wine peace is restored. It is all very much hands-on; the contestants are laborers. By contrast, in the Arabic tradition the personified seasons are presented more as the consumers rather than the producers of the fruits and products. The pseudo-Jāḥiẓ debate is full or learning, especially on medical matters. In addition to being scholarly, the tone of the Arabic debates is also far more genteel and courtly, more urban and urbane, befitting the language and style, which are polished and ornate, with rhyme, rhetorical figures, metaphors and comparisons. This is not to suggest that the Sumerian debate is devoid of rhetorical figures and comparisons; in the introduction the god Enlil is compared to a mighty bull, Summer and Winter, born from the union of Enlil and Earth, are also presented as large bulls, and Ezina, the goddess of grain, appears as a beautiful girl. When the debate proper begins, however, the language is plain and direct, about concrete things and acts.

As so often in Sumerian literary texts, gods play an active role, as creators and arbiters. Even in a Christian text, the Middle Dutch debate between Summer

---

35 In al-Khāqānī 1962, IV: 73–75.

36 There may be one, of a lost Syriac original, in *al-Filāḥa al-Nabaṭiyya* ("Nabataean Agriculture") by Ibn Waḥshiyya (d. 931), see Hämeen-Anttila 2006: 334–36.

and Winter, the judge is the pagan goddess Venus, who reconciles the contestants. An Arabic literary debate will normally start, as do in fact almost all Arabic texts, with a doxology, a pious introduction mentioning God, who is said to have created everything including the seasons and all they produce; but God is never the judge, let alone an actor, in the debate. If there is an arbiter at the end it is the patron to whom the debate is dedicated.

In Arabic, as we have seen, the seasonal debates are of three kinds: debates between spring and autumn, between summer and winter, and debates between all four seasons. If there are more than two contestants they tend to speak for themselves and boast, without attacking each of the others. A duel between two speakers is livelier, as a general rule. Debates between two consecutive seasons are rare. An Arabic dispute between autumn and winter by an obscure Andalusian writer who died in 1154 is mentioned but is apparently not preserved;[37] there is one in Ottoman Turkish, it seems, between spring and winter,[38] and the poem by Alcuin mentioned before is a quarrel between spring and winter. I do not know the Ottoman text, but in the Latin debate Spring is a clear winner, not surprisingly. The outcome of a dispute between opposite seasons is more in the balance. We saw that in Sumer Winter prevails over Summer.

As for Arabic, although we know of several debates between Summer and Winter, the oldest ones have not been preserved. The theme persisted: an author born in Tunis in 1854 who died in 1916 in Istanbul, Muḥammad Makkī ibn Muṣṭafā, known as Ibn ʿAzzūz, composed a boasting contest between Summer and Winter, but apparently it is not preserved.[39] In the lengthy and erudite debate between Summer and Winter by another very late author[40] from Mecca, Abū Bakr ibn Muḥammad ʿĀrif Khūqīr al-Makkī (d. 1930), composed in 1898 and published in 1902 (al-Makkī 1902: 2–83), the author's persona tries to arbitrate, saying that there is no clear winner (al-Makkī 1902: 68–70), but the contestants protest. They demand another judge. The author suggests a learned authority, a certain

37 *Munāẓarat al-kharīf wa-l-shitāʾ*, by Abū l-Ḥakam ʿAmr ibn Zakariyyā ibn Baṣṣāl al-Burhānī al-Ishbīlī, according to al-Baghdādī 1972, II: col. 558. This is evidently an error for Abū l-Ḥakam ʿAmr ibn Zakariyyā ibn Zakariyyā ibn Baṭṭāl al-Bahrānī, see al-Marrākushī 2002, III: 399–400.

38 Ethé 1882: 76; see also H. Aynur in this volume.

39 Hämeen-Anttila 2002: 408 (where his place of death is said to be "al-Āstāna," which is another name of Istanbul, not the capital of present-day Kazakhstan).

40 I call him "late" because stylistically and in general outlook the author and his text seem to belong to the pre-modern period of Arabic literary history. It uses rhymed prose throughout except in some quoted passages and includes numerous quotations from poetry, mostly unacknowledged.

ʿAbd al-Ḥafīẓ al-Qārī (or al-Qāriʾ) from the nearby town al-Ṭāʾif (al-Makkī 1902: 71), who is accepted. This ʿAbd al-Ḥafīẓ is a real person,[41] probably a friend of the author, so we could say that the text has two authors, an original way of composing a literary debate. His verdict, given as a kind of appendix (al-Makkī 1902: 84–87) and also composed in rhyming prose, is much the same as the earlier one and this time Summer and Winter are reconciled (al-Makkī 1902: 74). ʿAbd al-Ḥafīẓ concludes his verdict with a poem in praise of Abū Bakr Khūqīr. Earlier debates between pen and sword, in which a patron or a ruler is made the arbiter, served as an alternative to panegyric poetry; the Summer vs. Winter debate by the two Arabian writers serves as social intercourse between friends and equals, also as an alternative of poems of the widespread genre called *ikhwāniyyāt*, "brotherly, or friendly matters."

It may surprise us that Summer and Winter are declared to be equals in Arabia, of all places. In the Middle East one would expect Summer to be less popular, as it was for instance in the poem on the season by Ibn Wakīʿ, mentioned earlier. A poem preferring winter over the other seasons, not a debate text, was composed by Abū Hilāl al-ʿAskarī (d. after 1005).[42] A debate between Spring and Autumn, both being more moderate than Summer or Winter, would be more balanced. A very brief summary of the matter is offered in a mini-anecdote quoted towards the end of the tenth century but probably being older:[43]

> Muḥammad ibn Hārūn [whoever he was[44]] was asked: Which is better, Autumn or Spring? He replied, Spring to the eye, Autumn to the mouth.

The popularity of the Spring and Autumn theme could be connected with the importance of the two ancient Persian feasts of the Spring and Autumn equinoxes, Nayrūz (or Nawrūz) and Mihrajān (or Mihragān), respectively, which also often figure in Arabic texts.[45] It was customary to send congratulations, often in the form of poems, or to give presents at these feasts. In one of his speeches in *Salwat al-ḥarīf*, Spring quotes a passage in praise of Nayrūz from a letter by ʿAlī ibn Ḥamzah al-Iṣbahānī (d. *c.* 937),[46] and the two feasts are mentioned at the end of

---

41 ʿAbd al-Ḥafīẓ ibn ʿUthmān al-Qārī, who founded a library in al-Ṭāʾif in 1902, as found in an online source.

42 al-ʿAskarī 1979: 240–41, Yāqūt 1936–38, VIII: 264–67.

43 al-Tawḥīdī 1988, II: 52, al-Azdī 1902: 105 = 1997: 307; al-Rāghib AH 1287, II: 334, al-Zamakhsharī 1976–82, I: 43.

44 There are several Abbasid caliphs or princes called thus and a few others.

45 On Nawrūz see Levy and Bosworth 1993; on Mihrajān see Calmard 1991.

46 [ps.-]al-Jāḥiẓ AH 1302: 126; Nayrūz is also mentioned p. 125 in one of three poems in praise of Autumn, ascribed to Abū ʿUmar ʿAbdān al-Farrukhī.

the debate;[47] but I am not aware of any literary debate between these two feasts, either in Arabic or Persian.

I have sketched the somewhat sketchy history of the debates of the seasons in Arabic, from the beginnings, which we may call its Spring, to around the year 1930 or somewhat later, which I hesitate to call its Winter, firstly because the rather recent vernacular ones are livelier than some earlier ones and secondly because there may be later debates for all we know and the genre may continue to blossom.

Bibliography[48]

al-ʿAskarī, Abū Hilāl. 1979. *Dīwān*, ed. by Jūrj Qanāziʿ. Damascus: Majmaʿ al-Lughah al-ʿArabiyyah bi-Dimashq.

al-Azdī, Muḥammad Ibn Aḥmad Abū l-Muṭahhar. 1902. *Ḥikāyat Abī l-Qāsim al-Baghdādī / Abulḳâsim: Ein bagdâder Sittenbild*, ed. Adam Mez. Heidelberg: Carl Winter.

[al-Azdī, Muḥammad Ibn Aḥmad Abū l-Muṭahhar] [ps.-] al-Tawḥīdī, Abū Ḥayyān. 1997. *Al-Risālah al-Baghdādiyyah*, ed. ʿAbbūd al-Shāljī. Köln: Manshūrāt al-Jamal.

al-Baghdādī, Ismāʿīl (Bağdatlı İsmail Paşa). 1972. *Īḍāḥ al-maknūn fī al-dhayl ʿalā Kashf al-ẓunūn ʿan asāmī l-kutub wa-l-funūn / Keşf-el-zunun zeyli*, ed. Şerefettin Yaltkaya and Rifat Bilge, 2 vols. İstanbul: Milli Eğitim Basımevi.

Brock, Sebastian P. 1985. A Dispute of the Months and Some Related Syriac Texts. *Journal of Semitic Studies* 30: 181–211.

Brockelmann, Carl. 1924. Altturkestanische Volkspoesie, II, *Asia Maior* 1: 24–44.

Brockelmann, Carl. 1937–49. *Geschichte der arabischen Litteratur*, 5 vols. Leiden: Brill.

Calmard, Jean. 1991. Mihragān. Pp. 15–20 in *The Encyclopaedia of Islam*, New [= Second] Edition, vol. 6.

Colville, Jim, 2002. *Sobriety and Mirth: A Selection of the Shorter Writings of al-Jahiz.* London: Kegan Paul.

Ethé, Hermann. 1882. Über persische Tenzonen. Pp. 48–135 in *Verhandlungen des fünften internationalen Orientalisten-Congresses gehalten zu Berlin im September 1881*, Theil 2, Heft 1. Berlin: Weidmann (A. Asher).

Hämeen-Anttila, Jaakko. 2002. *Maqama: A History of a Genre.* Diskurse der Arabistik 5. Wiesbaden: Harrassowitz.

Hämeen-Anttila, Jaakko. 2006. *The Last Pagans of Iraq: Ibn Waḥshiyya and his* Nabatean Agriculture. Leiden/Boston: Brill.

al-Hāshimī, Aḥmad. [1901]. *Jawāhir al-adab fī ṣināʿat inshāʾ al-ʿArab.* Cairo: Maṭbaʿat al-Nīl.

al-Hāshimī, Aḥmad. n.d. *Jawāhir al-adab fī adabiyyāt wa-inshāʾ lughat al-ʿArab.* Beirut: Muʾassasat al-Maʿārif.

47 [ps.-]al-Jāḥiẓ AH 1302: 130.

48 The Arabic definite article al-, in all positions, is ignored for the alphabetical order. If an Arabic title has only a Muslim date of publication (AH = Anno Hegirae) the corresponding Christian year (or years) is (are) given between square brackets.

Heinrichs, Wolfhart. 1991. Rose versus Narcissus: Observations on an Arabic Literary Debate. Pp. 179–98 in *Dispute Poems and Dialogues in the Ancient and Mediaeval Near East. Forms and Types of Literary Debates in Semitic and Related Literatures* ed. G. J. Reinink and H. L. J. Vanstiphout. Orientalia Lovaniensia Analecta 42. Leuven: Peeters.
al-Ḥimyarī, Abū l-Walīd Ismāʿīl ibn ʿĀmir. 1989. *Al-Badīʿ fī waṣf al-rabīʿ*, ed. Henri Pérès. [Casablanca]: Dār al-Āfāq al-Jadīdah.
Holes, Clive. 1995. The Rat and the Ship's Captain: A Dialogue-poem (*muḥāwara*) from the Gulf, with Some Comments on the Social and Literary-historical Background of the Genre. Pp. 101–20 in *Dialectologia Arabica: A Collection of Articles in Honour of the Sixtieth Birthday of Professor Heikki Palva.* Studia Orientalia 75. Helsinki: Finnish Oriental Society.
Holes, Clive. 1996. The Dispute of Coffee and Tea: A Debate-poem from the Gulf. Pp. 302–15 in *Tradition and Modernity in Arabic Language and Literature*, ed. J. R. Smart. Richmond, Surrey: Curzon.
Holes, Clive. 1998. The Debate of Pearl-diving and Oil-wells: a poetic commentary on socio-economic change in the Gulf of the 1930s. *Arabic and Middle Eastern Literatures* 1: 87–112.
Hutchins, William M. 1989. *Nine Essays of al-Jahiz.* London: Peter Lang.
Ibn al-Athīr, ʿIzz al-Dīn. 1987–2003. *Al-Kāmil fī l-tārīkh*, ed. Abū l-Fidāʾ ʿAbd Allāh al-Qāḍī and Muḥammad Yūsuf al-Daqqāq. Beirut: Dār al-Kutub al-ʿIlmiyyah.
Ibn Ḥabīb al-Ḥalabī. AH 1302 [1884–5]. *Nasīm al-ṣabā.* Constantinople: Maṭbaʿat al-Jawāʾib.
Ibn Khallikān, Abū l-ʿAbbās Shams al-Dīn Aḥmad ibn Muḥammad ibn Abī Bakr. 1968–72. *Wafayāt al-aʿyān wa-anbāʾ abnāʾ al-zamān*, ed. Iḥsān ʿAbbās. Beirut: Dār al-Thaqāfah.
Ibn al-Nadīm. 1871–72. *Al-Fihrist*, ed. Gustav Flügel, Johanned Roediger, and August Müller. Leipzig: F. C. W. Vogel, repr. Beirut: Maktabat Khayyāṭ, n.d.
Ibn al-Nadīm. 2009. *Al-Fihrist*, ed. Ayman Fuʾād Sayyid. London: Muʾassasat al-Furqān.
al-Jāḥiẓ 1965–69. *Al-Ḥayawān*, ed. ʿAbd al-Salām Muḥammad Hārūn. 8 vols. Cairo: Muṣṭafā al-Bābī al-Ḥalabī.
al-Jāḥiẓ. 1964 (date of preface)–79. *Rasāʾil*, ed. ʿAbd al-Salām Muḥammad Hārun. 4 vols. Cairo: Maktabat al-Khānjī.
[ps.-]al-Jāḥiẓ AH 1302 [1884], *Salwat* [or *Sulwat*] *al-ḥarīf bi-munāẓarat al-rabīʿ wa-l-kharīf*, together with al-Sharīf al-Murtaḍā, *al-Shihāb fī l-shayb wa-l-shabāb.* Constantinople: Maṭbaʿat al-Jawāʾib [see pp. 105–31].
Jiménez, Enrique. 2017. *The Babylonian Disputation Poems: with Editions of the Series of the Poplar, Palm and Vine, the Series of the Spider, and the Story of the Poor, Forlorn Wren.* Culture and History of the Ancient Near East 87. Leiden/Boston: Brill.
Khalidi, T. (ed. & tr.). 1981. Al-Jāḥiẓ: *Kitāb Fakhr al-Sūdān ʿalā al-Bīḍān* / The Boast of the Blacks over the Whites. *Islamic Quarterly* 25: 3–51.
al-Khāqānī, ʿAlī. 1962. *Funūn al-adab al-shaʿbī.* Baghdad: Maṭbaʿat al-Azhar.
Klein, Michael L. 1989. Months Compete for Passover Honor; Targumic Fragments Reveal How Hebrew Months Vied for Pesach. *Moment* (April 1989) 14–18.
Lane, Edward William. 1863–77. *An Arabic-English Lexicon.* 8 vols. London: Williams and Norgate.
Levy, R., and C. E. Bosworth. 1993. Nawrūz. P. 1047 in *The Encyclopaedia of Islam*, New [= Second] Edition, vol. 7.

Littmann, Enno. 1951. Neuarabische Streitgedichte. Pp. 36 – 66 in *Festschrift zur Feier des zweihundertjährigen Bestehens der Akademie der Wissenschaften in Göttingen, II: Philologisch-historische Klasse*. Berlin: Springer.
Liungman, Waldemar 1941. *Der Kampf zwischen Sommer und Winter*. Helsinki: Academia Scientiarum Fennica (FF Communications, 130).
al-Makkī, Abū Bakr ibn Muḥammad ʿĀrif Khūqīr. 1902. *Musāmarat al-ḍayf bi-mufākharat al-shitāʾ wa-l-ṣayf*. Beirut: s.n.
al-Marrākushī, Abū ʿAbd Allāh Muḥammad ibn Muḥammad 2002. *Al-Dhayl-wa-l-takmilah li-kitābay al-Mawṣūl wa-l-Ṣilah*, ed. Iḥsān ʿAbbās, Muḥammad ibn Sharīfah, and Bashshār ʿAwwād Maʿrūf. 6 vols. Beirut: Dār al-Gharb al-Islamī.
al-Marzūqī, Abū ʿAlī Aḥmad ibn Muḥammad. 1996. *Al-Azminah wa-l-amkinah*, ed. Khalīl al-Manṣūr. Beirut: Dār al-Kutub al-ʿIlmiyyah.
Mattock, J. N. 1991. The Arabic Tradition: Origin and Development. Pp. 153 – 64 in *Dispute Poems and Dialogues in the Ancient and Medieval Near East: Forms and Types of Literary Debates in Semitic and Related Literatures*, ed. Gerrit J. Reinink and Herman L. J. Vanstiphout. Orientalia Lovaniensia Analecta 42. Leuven: Peeters Press.
Montgomery, James E. 2013. *Al-Jāḥiẓ in Praise of Books*. Edinburgh: Edinburgh University Press.
Naẓarī, ʿAlīriḍa (Alireza), and Maryam Fūlādī. 2015. Dirāsat binyat wa-maḍmūn al-ḥiwār al-adabī (al-munāẓarah) fī adab al-ʿaṣr al-Mamlūkī. *Iḍāʾāt Naqdiyyah* (Iran), Year 15, No. 20: 143 – 68.
al-Nuwayrī, Shihāb al-Dīn Aḥmad ibn ʿAbd al-Wahhāb. 1923– . *Nihāyat al-arab fī funūn al-adab*. Cairo: Dār al-Kutub.
Pellat, Charles. 1984. Nouvel essai d'inventaire de l'œuvre ǧāḥiẓienne. *Arabica* 31: 117 – 64,
Plessner, M. 1995. Rabīʿ. P. 350 in *The Encyclopaedia of Islam*, New [= Second] Edition, vol. 8.
al-Rāghib al-Iṣfahānī, *Muḥāḍarāt al-udabāʾ wa-muḥāwarāt al-shuʿarāʾ*. Būlāq: Maṭbaʿat Ibrāhīm al-Muwayliḥī, AH 1287 [1870].
Rescher, Oskar. 1931. *Excerpte und Übersetzungen aus den Schriften des Philologen und Dogmatikers Ǧāḥiẓ aus Baçra (150 – 250 H.) nebst noch unveröffentlichen Originaltexten*. Stuttgart: s.n.
al-Ṣafadī, Ṣalāḥ al-Dīn Khalīl ibn Aybak. 1931 – 2005. *Al-Wāfī bi-l-Wafayāt / Das biographische Lexikon des Ṣalāhaddīn Ḫalīl ibn Aibak aṣ-Ṣafadī*. Bibliotheca Islamica 6. Beirut/Wiesbaden/Berlin: Franz Steiner – Klaus Schwarz.
al-Ṣanawbarī. 1998. *Dīwān*, ed. Iḥsān ʿAbbās. Beirut: Dār Ṣādir, 1998.
al-Sawāḥilī, Muṣṭafā Muḥammad Rizq. [2007?]. *Al-Mufākharāt al-mutakhayyalah fī l-nathr al-ʿArabī: Taʾrīkh wa-taqwīm*. Cairo: Jāmiʿat al-Azhar, Kulliyyat al-Lughah al-ʿArabiyyah, Qism al-Adab wa-l-Naqd.
Schoeler, Gregor. 1974. *Arabische Naturdichtung. Die zahrīyāt, rabīʿīyāt und rauḍīyāt von ihren Anfängen bis Aṣ-Ṣanaubarī. Eine gattungs-, motiv- und stilgeschichtliche Untersuchung*. Beirut/Wiesbaden: Franz Steiner.
Shaykhū, Luwīs (Louis Cheikho). 1897. *ʿIlm al-adab*, vol. I. Beirut: Maṭbaʿat al-Ābāʾ al-Yasūʿiyyīn.
Shuraydi, Hasan. 2014. *The Raven and the Falcon: Youth versus Old Age in Medieval Arabic Literature*. Leiden: Brill.

al-Tawḥīdī, Abū Ḥayyān ʿAlī ibn Muḥammad ibn al-ʿAbbās. 1998. *Al-Baṣāʾir wa-l-dhakhāʾir*, ed. Wadād al-Qāḍī. Beirut: Dār Ṣādir.
al-Ṭayyān, Muḥammad Ḥassān (ed.). 2000. *Al-Mufākharāt wa-l-munāẓarāt*. Beirut: Dār al-Bashāʾir al-Islāmiyyah.
al-Thaʿālibī, Abū Manṣūr ʿAbd al-Malik ibn Muḥammad ibn Ismāʿīl. 1947. *Yatīmat al-dahr fī maḥāsin ahl al-ʿaṣr*, ed. Muḥammad Muḥyī l-Dīn ʿAbd al-Ḥamīd. Cairo: Maktabat al-Ḥusayn al-Tijāriyyah.
al-Tīfāshī, Aḥmad ibn Yūsuf. 1980. *Surūr al-nafs bi-madārik al-ḥawāss al-khams*; in the redaction of Muḥammad ibn Jalāl al-Dīn al-Mukarram Ibn Manẓūr, ed. Iḥsān ʿAbbās. Beirut: al-Muʾassasah al-ʿArabiyyah.
van Bekkum, Wout J. 1991. Observations on the Hebrew Debate in Medieval Europe. Pp. 77–90 in *Dispute Poems and Dialogues in the Ancient and Mediaeval Near East. Forms and Types of Literary Debates in Semitic and Related Literatures*, ed. G. J. Reinink and H. L. J. Vanstiphout. Orientalia Lovaniensia Analecta 42. Leuven: Peeters.
van Gelder, Geert Jan. 1991. Arabic Debates of Jest and Earnest. Pp. 199–211 in *Dispute Poems and Dialogues in the Ancient and Mediaeval Near East. Forms and Types of Literary Debates in Semitic and Related Literatures*, ed. G. J. Reinink and H. L. J. Vanstiphout. Orientalia Lovaniensia Analecta 42. Leuven: Peeters.
van Gelder, Geert Jan. 1987. The Conceit of Pen and Sword: On an Arabic Literary Debate. *Journal of Semitic Studies* 32: 329–60.
van Gelder, Geert Jan. 1991. Four Perfumes of Arabia: A translation of al-Suyūṭī's *al-Maqāma al-miskiyya*. *Res Orientales* 9: 203–12.
Vanstiphout, Herman L. J. 1984. On the Sumerian Disputation between the Hoe and the Plough. *Aula Orientalis* 2: 239–51.
Vanstiphout, Herman L. J. 1997. The Disputation between Summer and Winter. Pp. 584–88 in *The Context of Scripture, I: Canonical Compositions from the Biblical World*, ed. W. W. Hallo *et al.* Leiden: Brill.
Vanstiphout, Herman L. J. 2004. *Eduba: Hoe men leerde schrijven en lezen in het Oude Babylonië. Een bloemlezing van literaire teksten uit de scholen van Sumer.* Amsterdam: Sun.
Waddell, Helen. 1948. *Mediaeval Latin Lyrics*. New York: Henry Holt.
Wagner, Ewald. 1962. *Die arabische Rangstreitdichtung und ihre Einordnung in die allgemeine Literaturgeschichte*. Abhandlungen der Geistes- und Sozialwissenschaftlichen Klasse der Akademie der Wissenschaften und der Literatur in Mainz, 1962, no. 8.
Wagner, Ewald. 1993. Munāẓara. Pp. 565–68 in *The Encyclopaedia of Islam*, New [= Second] Edition, vol. 7.
Yāqūt. 1936–38. *Muʿjam al-udabāʾ*, ed. Aḥmad Farīd Rifāʿī. Cairo: Dār al-Maʾmūn, repr. Beirut: Iḥyāʾ al-Turāth al-ʿArabī, n.d.
al-Zamakhsharī, Maḥmūd ibn ʿUmar. 1976–82, *Rabīʿ al-abrār wa-nuṣūṣ al-akhbār*, ed. Salīm al-Nuʿaymī. Baghdad: Maṭbaʿat al-ʿĀnī.

David Larsen*

12 Night and Day in Islamicate Literary Disputation

Dispute between Night and Day enters the Near Eastern literary record with surprising lateness. Not until the Islamic period can dialogues between the two be found. Absence from the record is of course no proof of absence from performance, and certainty in the history of Night versus Day is an unsustainable pretense. Greek hexameter poetry gives off flashes of a case in point—an Orphic tenet about Night and Day and the convergence of their paths far overseas (*Odyssey* X.86), or in Tartarus (*Theogony* 748–50), or at some other gated boundary between the worlds (Parmenides I.11, *Odyssey* XXIV.12).[1] According to Hesiod, it is at a "bronze threshold" (the fiery sky of sunup and sundown?) that Night and Day approach and address one another, quite like the shepherds of *Odyssey* X.83.[2] The extant literature is silent about what they have to say, but there is reason for imagining that their speech was mimed in Orphic rite.

Apostrophes *to* the night and day are common.[3] Job in Chapter Three curses his day and night (a *hysteron proteron* for the day of his birth and the night of his conception), but in the book of *Job* they do not reply, and nowhere else in the Bible nor in any ancient text does Day or Night return an answer that I can find. The earliest place I find them to speak is *Kalām al-layālī wa-l-ayyām* (The Discourse of Nights and Days) by Ibn Abī l-Dunyā (d. 281/894), a thematic collection of popular Muslim preaching. The book begins with a Prophetic hadith describing two heraldic angels who accompany the sun in its rising and setting, calling out ascetic exhortations;[4] in subsequent reports, the day and the night

* New York University. Delivered in Pittsburgh, Pennsylvania on 16 March 2018 at an A.O.S. panel in honor of Geert Jan van Gelder. Translations from Arabic are mine, and from other languages as marked.

1 See Böhme 1953: 38–41 and Böhme 1970: 35–39, 54, reviewed by Guthrie 1954: 305–6 and summarized by Robbins 1970: 10–11.

2 Hesiod also calls Night the mother of Day (*Theogony* 124), but Heraclitus calls Hesiod ill-informed in the matter (DK 22B57).

3 The *Mercator* of Plautus (d. 185 BCE) mocks the convention in its opening lines; see Handley 2006.

4 Ibn Abī l-Dunyā 1997: 13–14; also in the hadith collection of Ibn Ḥibbān, d. 354/965 (1993, VIII: 121).

https://doi.org/10.1515/9781501510274-012

speak for themselves, as in the sermon of Bakr b. ʿAbd Allāh al-Muzanī (d. ca. 106/724):

> Every day sent by God to the people of the earth calls aloud: "O son of Adam, take best advantage of me! After me, there may not be another day." And every night says: "O son of Adam, take best advantage of me! After me, there may not be another night." (Ibn Abī l-Dunyā 1997: 35)

In the Islamic literary record, pious exhortations like these are not out of the ordinary, nor is their attribution to voiceless speakers. For the discourse of virtually any element or aspect of Creation, there is Qurʾānic precedent: according to *Sūrat al-Isrāʾ* (Q 17:44), "There is nothing that does not praise Him aloud."[5]

It is several generations after Ibn Abī l-Dunyā that disputation about Night and Day enters the record, with *Kitāb al-Layl wa-l-nahār* (The Book of Night and Day) by Ibn Fāris (d. 395/1004). In this debate, the speaking adversaries are not Night and Day, but their partisans (*ṣāḥib al-layl* and *ṣāḥib al-nahār*), and in that strict sense—if the genre be restricted to contests of personified speakers that are non-human and/or abstract—Ibn Fāris's text is no "true" literary debate.[6] It is in any case where scrutiny of Night and Day in Islamicate disputation literature must begin. *The Book of Night and Day* presents some features that set it apart from later texts in the subgenre, and other features that practically define the subgenre. I will discuss these under three headings.

The first is formal. Literary disputation in Arabic (*munāẓara*, *mufākhara*, *muḥāwara*) is overwhelmingly a prosimetrum genre.[7] Not so in Persian, where disputation form is variable, and Night and Day are a case in point: two of our Persian examples are set in different poetic forms (*qaṣīda* and *masnavi*) and a third

5 Van Gelder 1987: 332. There is also *Sūrat al-Naml* (Q 27:16), out of which the rich *manṭiq al-ṭayr* (Language of the birds) tradition arises; see Mārdīnī 2008: 281–93 and the editor's introduction to Ibn Abī Ḥajala (2018: 59–68).

6 "Allegorical" is my preferred designator for disputations of this type; "imaginary," as in as in Mārdīnī (2008), is another. Van Gelder (1987: 333–34) notes that both allegorical and non-allegorical debates are found at the beginning of Arabic *munāẓara* tradition, and do not represent successive stages in the genre's development. Hämeen-Anttila (2014: 263–64) says the distinction is not typologically significant. Meanwhile, Ṣiddīq (2000: 196–97) makes a cogent argument for reclassifying most literary disputations as *mufākharāt* (boasting-matches). *Munāẓara* he defines as a contest of viewpoints and convictions, in which different ideas are weighed against each other; *mufākhara* is the arena for declaring one set of qualities to be superior to another, whether these pertain to animals, plants, cities, races and other ethnic groups, or people as individuals.

7 As a literary mode in Arabic, *munāẓara* can take different forms; as a literary genre, prosimetrum is the norm. See Frow 2006: 65–66 for the distinction, and cf. Wagner 1963: 442.

is prosimetrum. But in all our Arabic examples, the interplay of poetry and prose is essential. Arabic *munāẓarāt* are therefore close to *maqāmāt* (dialogic narratives of "assemblies"), wherein the speaker's rhymed-prose discourse often frames a poem or ends in one.[8] In every Arabic and Hebrew text surveyed here, the overlap between these genres is appreciable.

In Night and Day disputations subsequent to Ibn Fāris, the poetry and prose are composed by the same author. In *The Book of Night and Day*, the verses are not Ibn Fāris's compositions, but testimonia (*shawāhid*) cited by his speech-contestants as evidence for the superiority of Night or Day. As such, their value is rhetorical, which leads to a second aspect of *The Book of Night and Day* I would like to highlight: the text's affiliation to Islamic debate culture.

Constraints of space here forbid an overview of disputation practices in Islam.[9] Makdisi (1981: 108–12) points out that it was only through dialectic (*jadal*, *khilāf*, *naẓar*) that scholarly consensus (*ijmāʿ*) could be reached concerning matters in which no judgment was supplied by scripture or Prophetic example. Furthermore, in the absence of degree-awarding institutions, the scholar's credibility depended on consistent mastery of the art, as Makdisi (1981: 133) says in *The Rise of Colleges:*

> A Muslim scholar, unlike his western counterpart, could not hope for the time when he could receive his doctoral degree and thus come to the end of his struggle to the top. He had to prove himself at every turn. To have a successful academic career, he had first to rise to the top, and then to maintain his position there. His situation was similar to the gunman in the American films called "Westerns" who was a target for all newcomers aspiring to his position; or to the champion boxer, who was to defend his title against all contenders. And this he did in the arena of disputation.

There is no question that the legal-scholarly milieu is near-adjacent to *The Book of Night and Day*. Remembered now as a philologist, Ibn Fāris had a deep and abiding concern for law. He was the first to write a *Fiqh al-lugha* (The Statutes of Language), as well as a *Futyā faqīh al-ʿarab* (*Fatwā*s of the Legal Scholar of the Arabs), which is a book of puzzles designed to improve the linguistic proficiency of judges.[10] He also cared enough about the law to change his allegiance from one school to another (Shāfiʿī to Mālikī; Yāqūt 1993, I: 411). So when we find

---

8 In the words of Mattock (1991: 163). Arabic *munāẓara* is "so closely related to, and perhaps directly descended from, the *maqāma* as to constitute a subclass of the latter"; see n. 14 below.
9 See Ahmed 2016: 146–48, Belhaj 2010, Fallāḥ 2009, Ṣiddīq 2000, Wagner 1993, Jirīsha 1989, Makdisi 1981: 108 ff., and van Ess 1976.
10 Ibn Fāris 1958. The genre is described by al-Suyūṭī (1971, I: 622–37).

Ibn Fāris modeling disputation practices in the *Book of Night and Day*, it is important to have the law and legal education in mind.

If not strictly "of the school, for the school," the *Book of Night and Day* is a para-scholastic exercise.[11] In terms of *sitz im leben* it is comparable to the dispute poems of ancient Babylon, which were composed and copied as school texts (Jiménez 2017: 121–24). Another way in which Ibn Fāris's Islamic-era contribution compares to the Babylonian corpus is its parodic nature—with this key difference. The *Book of Night and Day* is not a parody of higher literary forms and genres, as Jiménez (2017: 97–108) shows the Babylonian poems to be, but a parody of forensic disputation techniques. Mock debate over matters of arbitrary preference is a light-hearted exercise of rhetorical skills that are drawn on in real-life dialectic.[12] The *Book of Night and Day* is a work of rhetoric, more concerned with modeling a learned speech-contest than dispensing information about Night or Day. The cosmological and calendrical information it presents is incidental to the contest at hand.[13]

Geographic origin is the third feature to be highlighted in *The Book of Night and Day*, whose opening lines ground the text in western Iran: "I was asked by a young man from the mountainous area of *al-Māhayn* [the onetime garrison cities of Dinavar and Nahawand] to compose a few reliable pages on the subject of Night and Day, and the grounds on which one might justly be preferred to the other."[14] A glance ahead at the Bibliography will show that four of our first

---

11 The phrase is Werner Jaeger's, revived for Arabic literary history by Schoeler (2002).
12 "Exercises in scholarly frivolity" is Mattock (1991: 163)'s characterization of literary *munāẓara*; van Gelder (1991) shows that the element of jest (*hazl*) is a near-essential of the genre.
13 Ibn Fāris (1993: 23–24) allows the partisan of Night a short lexicographical digression on the taxonomy of nights and their groupings—material of the sort treated by al-Farrā' (1980) and Ghulām Tha'lab (1978), to name only two authorities familiar to Ibn Fāris. Not all areas of Islamic night-and-day research are engaged in *munāẓara*, though. The question of which was created first, treated extensively in al-Ṭabarī's *History* (1968, I: 61–80), tr. Rosenthal (1989: 228–49), scarcely comes up in the texts surveyed here; cf. also Ibn 'Arabī 2001: 55–67. Yet another field apart is that genre of hadith collection called "Actions of the day and night" (*'amal al-yawm wa-l-layla*), detailing what the Prophet used habitually to do and say at different times of day and night, and on other recurrent occasions. Generally speaking, the Night and Day tradition of Islamic *munāẓara* is sparing in its use of Prophetic hadith, but see Ibn Fāris 1993: 39; also, al-Ḥamawī (2016: 715) refers to the very interesting dialogue between Paradise and Hell narrated by the Prophet in al-Bukhārī (2004: 1011) *et alibi* (search indices for the opening words: *Taḥājjat al-janna wa-l-nār*).
14 Ibn Fāris taught for a while in the city of Hamedan, which is as close to Dinavar and Nahawand as they are to each other. One wonders if the "young man" in question isn't Badī' al-Zamān al-Hamadhānī (d. 398/1008), a native of Hamedan who was Ibn Fāris's protégé. If a firm identification were possible, it would bolster Ḥammūdī (1982)'s claim of Ibn Fāris's importance to

six examples were composed in Iran, and that the fifth is by an Arab author with an evident affinity for Persian literature. When Night and Day first quarrel as personified speakers it is in a Persian poem, the *Shab va rūz* (Night and Day) of Asadī Ṭūsī (d. 465/1072–73). Not even from the Hebrew-language disputation by al-Ḥarīzī (who writes elsewhere of a voyage to Susa), can a Persian connection be excluded.[15]

For Iran as the geographical matrix of Night and Day dispute, the literary record offers no clear explanation. There is in extant Middle Persian literature just one example of literary debate: the Parthian-language *Drakht-i Asūrīk* (The Babylonian Tree), a disputation of the ancient kind between a date palm and a goat (Brunner 1980a, *id.* 1980b). The estimation of Firuza Abdullaeva is that the latter-day "reappearance of the debate genre in New Persian literature came as a direct borrowing from Arabic Classical literature"—but also that "The most likely direct influence on the Arabic model is an Iranian one," given how many Persians were writing in Arabic at the time of the genre's emergence.[16] In other words, Iranian influence on *The Book of Night and Day* cannot be excluded, nor can Iran be excluded as an incubator of the form. As for Night and Day themselves as personified speakers, any antecedents in pre-Islamic Iranian tradition are lost to my view.[17]

So much for the origins and forms of Night and Day as a subgenre of disputation literature. In terms of polemical content there no great diversity. For almost a thousand years, Night and Day boast of much the same things—above all, the praiseworthy human activities each makes possible. The texts vary mostly on two points: the outcome of the judgment and the identity of the judge. Not always is either one present. *Occasio litigandi* (the fictive cause of the dispute) tends to be unvivid, and sometimes goes missing along with any prologue to speak of. *Non*-fictive occasion is something else. The Night and Day disputes

the history of the *maqāma*, lately revived by Pomerantz and Orfali (2019). Hämeen-Anttila (2002: 73 n. 32) expresses doubt in Ḥammūdī's thesis, but then summarizes a *maqāma*esque fiction by Ibn Fāris, as transmitted by al-Hamadhānī, just six pages later (2002: 79–80).

15 Mirsky 2007: 656. And the biographical notice of al-Ḥarīzī by Ibn al-Sha‘‘ār al-Mawṣilī (d. 654/1256), ed. Sadan (1996: 52), mentions a trip to Irbil.

16 Abdullaeva 2014: 257. The *Kalīla wa-Dimna* of Ibn al-Muqaffa‘ (d. ca 139/756) and its dialogic beast fables present some elements of disputation, but Mārdīnī (2008: 50) excludes it from the genre's history on structural grounds, saying that it lacks the dialectical framework essential to *munāẓara*. (For a report of Ibn al-Muqaffa‘'s participation in intra-ethnic *mufākhara*, see the sixth night of al-Tawḥīdī 1997: 57).

17 Although the dark-vs.-light dialectic of Zoroastrian cosmology comes naturally to mind, I refrain from drawing a connection. I caution also against facile equation to pairs like dawn and dusk or sun and moon, which lack the nycthemeral plenitude of Night and Day.

of Nezārī Qohestānī and ʿAlwān al-Ḥamawī are circumstanced by moments of personal and political crisis; both authors claim to have written them in a single night. So too was Ibn Fāris's "little book" written extemporarily (*fa-irtajaltu kutayyibī hādhā*), at his student's request. Whether point of fact or literary pretense, extemporaneity itself points back to the *rhetorica umbra* of the schools where debate skills were exercised.[18] Closeness to the legal-scholarly milieu did not, however, remain a constant of the subgenre: all examples after Ibn Fāris appear as variations on a literary theme.[19]

Here follows a descriptive catalogue of extant disputations of Night and Day.

1. *The Book of Night and Day* by Ibn Fāris (d. 395/1004) is easily summarized (Mārdīnī 2008: 319 – 21). The discussants stage various claims and counter-claims about the indicia of Night or Day's superiority, including priority of mention in the Qur'ān, reckonings of the Islamic calendar, and the dictamina of poets. The dispute is not waged on a level field: midway through, the partisan of Night quotes some verses that were recited to him by his father (*Wa-anshadanī abī raḥimahu llāh*). This would seem to be none other than Ibn Fāris's own father, Fāris b. Zakariyā, an Arab scholar of provincial Iran cited only by his son (as far as I have ever seen). The partisan of Night quotes him twice, in what seem like breaks in character. This is the second instance:

> The partisan of Night said: [....] The preference of writers is for night over day, because the heart, which is in motion during the day, is tranquil at night. And that is how they achieve the ordering of their discourse, and bring it within range of the [reader's] understanding.
>
> A judicious ruler can tell his elite subjects from his commoners by the way their nights are spent. "For the educated man, night is day" (*Al-layl nahār al-adīb*) is an old saying—and it is heard in a story my father told me about a certain Barmecide whose son was appointed governor. When news reached him of his son's inattention to those he governed, and of his devotion to frivolous pastimes, he wrote to him [these verses, meter: *sarīʿ*]:
>
> Set up your days for seeking the heights,
> and do without the get-togethers with your friends,
> so that, when the night draws nigh,
> and surfaces of eyes are covered,
> and the night is fast to bring you what you want—
> [you heed instead the maxim:] "For the educated man, night is day."
> Many are the youths of ascetic demeanor

18 The phrase is Juvenal's; see Kaster 2001: 323.

19 The influence of now-lost disputations between Night and Day on our extant examples is a certainty. The likelihood that some now-extant examples have escaped the present catalogue is also great; see Bibliography (I.10).

whose nights you might think spent at admirable tasks
[but] whose secrets are covered over by the night,
as they live richly and at ease the whole night through.
Unconcealed are the delights of a stupid man,
and they are the target of every watchful enemy.[20]

There is no final judgment (and no judge) to uphold the claims of either side, but the partisan of Night gets the last word and seems the predetermined victor in the text, insofar as Night is preferred by writers (*muʾallifū l-kutub*).

2. The *Night and Day* of Asadī Ṭūsī (d. 465/1072–73) is a 41-verse *qaṣīda* in which Night and Day each give one speech. The word of Day is last and longest (twenty-five verses to Night's fourteen), and ends in praise of the poet's father Abū Naṣr Aḥmad Asadī, inviting him to serve as judge.[21] In Arabic *munāẓara*, the panegyric element was a late development; in this early New Persian example, we see it already built in.[22]

There are echoes of Ibn Fāris in Ṭūsī's poem, as in verse 31 where Day says (in the Victorian English translation of Louisa Stuart Costello): "True, death was *first*; but, tell me, who / Thinks life least worthy of the two?" (Asadī Ṭūsī 1978: 94, Costello 1899: 52). Within the poem, there is nothing to provoke this remark; the speech of Night makes no mention of life and death as such. Its antecedent is found in the *Book of Night and Day*, where Night contends that the Qurʾān's habit of mentioning *layl* before *nahār* is a sign of God's preference (Ibn Fāris 1993: 17–18). To this, Ibn Fāris's partisan of Day responds: "Mentioning something first dictates neither preference nor virtue. Do you not see that He also says, magnified be His adoration, that He 'created death and life' (*khalaqa l-mawta wa-l-ḥayāta*, Q 67:2), when the preferability of life is so well known?" In Asadī Ṭūsī's poem, the rejoinder has been cast into verse, leaving the anterior claim of Night up to hearer and reader to supply.

Intertextuality goes by different routes, and in this case a direct citation of Ibn Fāris's text is not necessarily indicated. Q 67:2 could be used to parry any claim of excellence based on priority of mention, and may have been a standard

20 Ibn Fāris 1993: 28; for a comparable narration from the author's father see Ibn Fāris 2007: 214.

21 Abdullaeva (2009: 72) summarizes a modern controversy in which some have reckoned this Abū Naṣr Aḥmad—the senior Asadī—to be the poem's true author. Given the fashion in *ghazal* poetry for incorporating the author's pen-name (*takhalluṣ*) in the last line (already current in the poems of Anṣārī described just ahead), the identification is understandable. But the *Night and Day* of Asadī Ṭūsī is not a *ghazal*.

22 Hämeen-Anttila 2006: 142, Abdullaeva 2009: 79–80.

retort. If Asadī Ṭūsī does not borrow outright from *The Book of Night and Day* (as I believe he does), then he plays on the same conventions of Islamic debate culture as Ibn Fāris.

3. ʻAbd Allāh Anṣārī Harawī (d. 481/1089), the Sufi shaykh of Afghanistan, was called by many honorifics during his lifetime and after.[23] An adherent of the orthodox Ḥanbalī school, he took a leading part in traditionalist opposition to rationalist theology (*kalām*), in particular the Ashʿarism then ascendant in Sunni Islam.

It is remarkable that Anṣārī would adopt the *munāẓara* form at all, given the stance against dialectic taken in his Arabic-language *Dhamm al-kalām* (Condemnation of Rationalist Theology). *Dhamm al-kalām* is a lengthy hadith collection whose contents were chosen to discredit all discursive methods of arriving at knowledge, except what was modeled in Prophetic *sunna* (word and deed) (de Beaurecueil 1965: 209). But in Persian the same author is credited with two literary disputations: a Passion and Intellect (*Maqālat ʿishq va ʿaql*) and a Night and Day (*Mubāḥatha* or *Munāẓara shab va rūz*).[24] These were anthologized in two separate *majmūʿā*s (compilations): one called *Kanz al-sālikīn* (Treasure of the Followers of the Way), and another called *Zād al-ʿārifīn* (Provision for the Gnostics), which present altogether a bibliographic jumble.[25] The *Discussion of Night and Day* appearing in *Zād al-ʿārifīn* lacks the opening section of the text as it appears in *Kanz al-sālikīn*, where the *Discussion of Night and Day* is followed by a short text called *Fazīlat-i shab* (On the Superiority of Night) that shares content with it.[26]

The ramified state of these texts is a sign of their popularity. The demand for books and treatises by Anṣārī seems to have exceeded the supply. As a composer of New Persian prose, he was an early master, just as Asadī Ṭūsī (Firdawsī's teacher) was for New Persian poetry.[27] Anṣārī's is the only Persian *munāẓara*

23 Yazıcı and Uludağ 1988: XVII: 222, Farhâdî 1996: 5.

24 The *Bayān qazā va qadar* (Elucidation of Chance and Destiny) accompanying them in *Kanz al-sālikīn* is not a dialogue, and neither is the *Bayān darwīshān ḥaqīqī va-majāzī* (Elucidation of [the Difference between] a Real Dervish and a Pretend One) in *Zād al-ʿārifīn.*

25 Utas 1988: 85 explains how parts of *Kanz al-sālikīn* were copied into certain Central Asian manuscripts of another text by al-Anṣārī called *Manāzil al-sāʾirīn* (Stations of the Wayfarers).

26 Yazıcı 1964: 67. Between the two modern editions of *Kanz al-sālikīn* there are differences also. Yazıcı (1959) imports a number of passages from *Zād al-ʿārifīn*, and retains other material athetized by Mawlāʾī (1998).

27 Rahman 1995: VIII: 539. Some variation of prose style in his works is to be expected, given that (even before the blindness that overtook him late in life) they were dictated to students; see

of Night and Day to be modeled on the Arabic *maqāma* form (his Night and Day speak for themselves in rhymed prose, interspersed with poems in different forms and meters), and the Arabic *munāẓarāt* of Night and Day subsequent to it seem in turn to follow his pattern. Anṣārī was also an early master of the Persian *ghazal*, which appears fully formed in the *Discussion of Night and Day*, down to the incorporation of the poet's *takhalluṣ* into last lines (see n. 21 above).

Night has the last word and is the disputation's presumed winner. Anṣārī closes with an ascetic warning: "But woe to those who are drunk with exultation in the day, busy with wickedness at night, and pridefully asleep in the morning, who do not know that tomorrow they will be among 'the People of the Graves' (Q 60:13)."[28]

4. The Arabic-to-Hebrew translation by Judah ben Solomon al-Ḥarīzī (d. 622/1225) of the fifty *maqāmāt* of al-Ḥarīrī (d. 516/1122) was completed before al-Ḥarīzī's departure from al-Andalus in 1216 CE. The fifty original *maqāmāt* he composed in Hebrew under the title *Sefer Taḥkemoni* (Book of the Taḥkemonite) are the work of his mature, Eastern period (Drory 1993: 285).[29] While al-Ḥarīrī's *maqāmāt* hew closely to a single narrative template, al-Ḥarīzī's own are a miscellany. He announces as much in the first of the *Taḥkemoni*'s two Hebrew-language dedications, promising the reader an assortment of every genre and theme then current in Islamic literature. The rationale for the wide appeal, he says in a third, Arabic-language dedication, is to promote Hebrew-language competency among eastern Jewry, which in his view was in a disgraceful state (Drory 1993: 289–94).

Among the genres mustered by al-Ḥarīzī, *munāẓara* is represented by a suite of five (nos. 39–43), the first of which pits Night against Day.[30] The occasion for its narration is seemingly retrojected to the period of the Exodus, as the narrator sets the scene at Rimmon-Perez (*Numbers* 33:19–20) where, amid a noble gathering, a sub-narrator stands up to expound some ancestral proverbs and enigmas (*Job* 15:18). The story is called in Hebrew a *mahberet* (the standard translation for *maqāma*), but its Arabic title (*al-Munāzaʿa bayna l-layl wa-l-nahār*) declares it to be a "Contest between Night and Day." The occasion for the contest is the vernal equinox, as the sub-narrator begins:

---

de Beaurecueil (1954: 89–90) and (1982). But *nota bene* that, until the 15th century CE, no mention was made of *Kanz al-sālikīn* nor *Zād al-ʿārifīn* among Anṣārī's works (Farhâdî 1996: 23).

28 Anṣārī Harawī 1998: II: 566: *Amma vaay bar aan kasani keh rooz sarmast-e soroorand o shab mashghool-e sharoorand o sobh dar khaab-e ghoroorand, nemidanand keh farada min aṣḥābi l-qubūri*. Translated by Yass Alizadeh (personal communication, November 2018).

29 For the Taḥkemonite see *2 Samuel* 23:8.

30 See Alba Cecilia in this volume, § 3.5.

> Know that when the sun encamped in the constellation of Aries, and its light grew stronger and was revealed, and darkness lighted up, ...[g]reat pride covered the light of Day. He spoke arrogantly against the Night. He spoke and said:
>
> "I am the prince of princes. Nights are my servants. God has appointed me over them to be their ruler and their governor. For I am white and they are black as coals. I am of the sons of Shem, and they are of the sons of Ham. Therefore, they are my servants all the days of their life, willingly or unwillingly."[31]

The racialized salvo of Day is nothing new; we find it already in the texts of Asadī Ṭūsī and Anṣārī Harawī (where Day calls Night *ḥabashī* "Ethiopic"). Al-Ḥarīzī's *maqāma* is not however the calque of any known Persian text, but a free adaptation of the Islamic form for Hebrew literature, in which Qur'ānic proofs are swapped out for Biblical ones (from Chapter Three of *Job* in particular). Day is made the winner, and Night gives a concession speech.

It is hard to say whether al-Ḥarīzī's 39th *maqāma* is the product of his Eastern residency, as there is ample Iberian precedent for allegorical dispute. There are Andalusian texts with talking flowers as far back as the 4th/10th century, as well as debates between Pen and Sword, Sleep and Wakefulness, and a *mufākhara* among the precious stones (Mārdīnī 2008: 67–69). But in al-Ḥarīzī's lifetime, Night and Day *munāẓara* tradition was still in its Persian phase. In the literature of the Muslim West there is no known contest of Night and Day.

5. *Mufākharat al-layl wa-l-nahār* (The Boasting-Match of Night and Day) by Ibn Ghānim al-Maqdisī (d. 678/1279) is the earliest Arabic text in which personifications of Night and Day argue on their own behalf. That Ibn Ghānim worked after a Persian model is likely, as his best-known work, *Kashf al-asrār ʿan ḥukm al-ṭuyūr wa-l-azhār* (Disclosure of the Secrets of the Wisdom of the Birds and Flowers), is loosely patterned on the Persian-language *Manṭiq al-ṭayr* (Conference of the Birds) of Farīd al-Dīn 'Aṭṭār (d. 618/1221).[32]

The *Boasting-Match of Night and Day* is comparatively obscure. Its appearances in print have been anonymous, and only in one manuscript is attribution to Ibn Ghānim made.[33] It is nonetheless an important text that indicates the pattern for Arabic Night and Day disputes to come, which is the same pattern as Anṣāri

31 Tr. Reichert (1973, II: 242).

32 Wagner 1963: 455 n. 2, *GAL* I 450–51, S I 808–09. For Ibn Ghānim's *mufākharāt* of Cairene neighborhoods see Shishtawī 1999a: 5–49, and perhaps 91–122; the fragmentary *mufākhara* of Mecca and Medina in Beinecke Arabic MSS 206, fol. 47v-48v, seems to be his also.

33 Massé 1961 and Shishtawī 2001, described by Mārdīnī (2008: 324); identified as Ibn Ghānim's in Beinecke Arabic MSS 206, fol. 45v.

Harawī's *Discussion of Night and Day:* its prose is all rhymed prose, and its poems are original compositions by the same author.

It is the first dispute between Night and Day to feature a judge, although the way this happens is elegantly convoluted (and muddled furthermore by text-critical problems). It begins with the pair taking their case before "a practiced judge" (*ilā ḥākimin khabīrin*), saying: "We want you to judge between us fairly and in due measure. Make your judgment accord with Truth, and do not go beyond it, and set us both upon a level path." The judge's identity is never revealed, and in the Cairo manuscript edited by Shishtawī (2001: 16) it is instead "a practiced sage" (*ilā ʿālimin khabīrin*). "Let each of you expound the proofs of your superiority over the other," the judge or sage responds. But there is no further intervention on this speaker's part.

Day and Night each take two rounds, in that order. The second speech of Night makes up the greater part of the text—a speech in which Night recounts all that was said by the attendees of an earlier assembly. A *maqāma* set within the frame of a *mufākhara* is what it is, albeit an open frame: the text ends where the *maqāma* ends, without reverting to disputational form.[34]

The *maqāma* begins with Night's description of the prior assembly:

> If only you could have seen the people of conviviality and nocturnal conversation brought together under the canopy of magic, when they were companionably served with the cup of the blowing breeze! To them was the Beloved made manifest, and things hidden were uncovered and made visible, and the ailing soul was healed by His all-pervading favor. [If you could have seen all that,] then you would be overcome by embarrassment at what I am saying. And if you had any understanding of what I comprehend, you would be checked from speaking by the sight of my companions and my friends, each of them calling at my gate!

The nocturnal gathering is obviously a Sufi gathering, and in the work of a Sufi-identified author (as was Ibn Ghānim) the victory of Night seems assured (as it was in Ibn Fāris), insofar as nighttime is the right time for collective Sufi devotions.

There enters at this point a second judge. It is *lisān al-ḥāl*, translated as the "language of states" or the "language of things," but more literally as "the tongue/language of the current state of affairs."[35] *Lisān al-ḥāl* is a well-known (if insufficiently-documented) trope of Islamic literature: an allegorization of the totality of essences, attributes and acccidents as they happen to be disposed

---

34 Ibn Ghānim's conclusion to the text may be lost to us. Even the most complete version in Shishtawī 2001 ends abruptly.

35 "Language of the states" (*die Sprache des Zustandes*) is Ritter's translation (2013: 3); "inner language of things" (*die innere Sprache der Dinge*) is Rudolph's (1988: 303).

at any given moment—or the moment itself, given a speaking voice. Here, in the *maqāma* of Night, *lisān al-ḥāl* plays a moderator's role, commanding various lovesick speakers—a mourner (*al-nāʾiḥ*), a blabbermouth (*al-bāʾiḥ*), a shouter (*al-ṣāʾiḥ*), etc.—to detail their plights in prose and verse. Their speeches number six, whereupon the text breaks off. No final judgment is pronounced, but Night gets the last word, carries the endorsement of *lisān al-ḥāl*, and is the winner by default.

6. Nezārī Qohestānī (d. 720/1320 – 21), author of *Masnavī-i Rūz va shab* (The Poem of Day and Night), is one of Persian poetry's shaded lights. Few facts of his life can be gleaned outside his body of work, which is large and diverse and spans a career at several Ilkhanid client courts followed by two decades of seclusion in the town of his birth (Bīrjand in Khorasan). A celebrant of the grape, he was recognized as a forerunner of Ḥāfeẓ (d. 792/1390) by Jāmī (d. 898/1492) (Lewisohn 2003: 232).

The *Poem of Day and Night* dates itself to the eve of Nawrūz in the year 699/1300, at the beginning of his seclusion.[36] At 550 *masnavi* lines (only 446 in the edition of Nasrollah Pourjavady), its claim to be one night's work is not totally impossible. It is dedicated to the Mīhrebānid prince of Qohestān, Shams al-Dīn ʿAlī Shāh (r. 688 – 708/1289 – 1308), from whose court the poet had been exiled. The instigator of the dispute is Night, as Pourjavady (2006: iv-v) summarizes:

> Nezārī begins his story by saying that when he was sitting all alone in his room, the Night began to speak to him, asking him to write about the Day's cruelty and injustice to it, and then to send this report to the king. The poet agrees to do that, provided that the Day (or the Sun) can also speak for itself. Since Day and Night cannot be present both at the same time, they choose the Zephyr to act as the messenger. [....] The strife between the Night and the Day continues, and after exchanging seven messages, the Night yields to the Day and admits that the Sun (*shams*) is superior to it, since the king (Shamsoddin) shares the same name or title with it. This brings the poet again to praising his patron, Shamsoddin ʿAlī Shāh, and asking for his forgiveness.

Professedly determined by the name of the poem's dedicant, the victory of Day is telegraphed in the poem's title (the only one in which Day comes before Night).

Scholars have not held back from interpreting Day and Night as Qohestānī's mouthpieces for differing sects: "Sunnism, or exoteric Islam as night" in the reading of Eboo Jamal (2015), "and Shīʿism, particularly its Ismāʿīlī esoteric in-

36 Remarkably close to the fictive date of Dante's *Comedy*, which begins on Maundy Thursday of the Christian year 1300.

terpretation, as day." The difficulty is that more than one esoteric tradition is drawn on in Qohestānī's verse. Also, the poet's own allegiances are variously estimated. Pourjavady proposes a mid-life conversion to mystical Twelver Sh'ism from the charismatic Ismā'īlism of his youth, but Lewisohn (2003: 236) cautions against an overconfident separation, given that in Ilkhanid-era Persia "the amalgamation of Ismā'īlī doctrine with Sufi symbols and concepts is so complete that analysis of the significance of a certain verse, without simultaneous study of both these esoteric traditions, is well-nigh impossible." It is however true that Shams al-Dīn 'Alī Shāh was an adherent of Sunnī orthodoxy, and Qohestānī's sometime Ismā'īlism is a given.Exactly how these positions play out in *The Poem of Day and Night* calls for further study.

7. The *Munāẓara bayna l-layl wa-l-nahār* (Disputation between Night and Day) of 'Alā' al-Dīn 'Alī al-Mārdīnī (d. 750/1349), is none too complicated. Day makes one speech, Night contests it point for point, and the dispute comes to an end without a judgment or a judge. Rated "a middling poet" (*la-hu naẓm wasaṭ*) by Ibn Ḥajar al-'Asqalānī (d. 852/1449), al-Mārdīnī is remembered nonetheless among the *belles-arts* writers of Mamluk Egypt.[37] He was active as a hadith scholar and a jurist of the Ḥanafī school, and wrote an *uṣūl al-fiqh* (Principles of Jurisprudence) in addition to some other literary disputations, most notably a Narcissus versus Rose.[38] In the *Disputation between Night and Day* he works in a range of conventional idioms, as for example Day's catalogue of the planets:

> O Night, although you may boast of your stars and their light and your planets and their night-travels, your Saturn has fallen into a lowly quadrant, and your Jupiter has lost the way to its alignment, and your Mars was scorched as it turned to face the sun, and beneath it your Venus is obscured, and your Mercury cannot close his eyes for sleeplessness. With your planets at their perigees, you are like a sickly invalid.[39]

Astrological banter is a sign of some distance from the law schools. Despite the author's legal background, his text is not grounded in forensics, but in a literary genre that was by then well established.

---

37 Ibn Ḥajar 1993, III: 85. For a bio-bibliography, see the editor's introduction to al-Mārdīnī (2002: 17–28).
38 *GAL* II 161, S II 200, ed. most recently by Shishtawī (1999b: 7–17), discussed by Mattock (1991: 157–60), Heinrichs (1991: 193–95), and Mārdīnī (2008: 222–26, 475–76).
39 Berlin MS Sprenger 1168, fol. 5v.

8. ʿAlwān al-Ḥamawī (d. 936/1530), a Sufi shaykh of Syria, composed *Nuzhat al-asrār fī muḥāwarat al-layl wa-l-nahār* (Divertimento of the Secrets in the Controversy of Night and Day) only days after a local anti-Ottoman uprising was violently quashed.[40] Night and Day do not discuss these events, but the author describes his personal experience of the uprising in the introduction:

> Hearing a report of aromatics surpassing musk and ambergris is nothing like being in their presence and smelling them—which is what happened [to me] after long nights spent in a state of inward contraction (*qabḍ*) whose attacks spread wide their claws. It lasted so long that my soul was on the point of going the way of Ilyās— one of the Emissaries, by permission of the Creator of souls—when thanks to the Gracious and All-Determining I came to a garden of sociability where God's friend al-Khiḍr once tarried, now purified with song by a dove of the precinct, by dint of its skillful vocalization in praise of God the Magnificent and Beautiful, "the Great and Most High." (Q 13:9) Inside of me, there opened up a spreading tree of hidden secrets [—a welcome change,] after the issue of the terrors sent down by the "guests of grey" in trials heaped up like cumulus clouds, befalling the land of Syria on account of Jānbardī al-Ghazālī and the military might of the Ottoman Sultan, God grant him victory—an event that never entered our minds, nor was it in our calculations. (Al-Ḥamawī 2016: 710)

ʿAlwān's pro-Ottoman sympathies are attested elsewhere and are not in doubt.[41] Less obvious are the reasons for his resort to *munāẓara* form in these circumstances. Are his Night and Day competing representatives for Mamluk and Ottoman power? In a word, no. I interpret the text as a politically quietist message to the adepts of his order in the wake of the Ottoman victory.

The opening speeches of Day and Night are very long, and contain long poems. A short exchange between them follows, until the intervention of the Truth (*al-Ḥaqq*, being one of God's ninety-nine names, and a seeming favorite of ʿAlwān's) in the role of judge. The Truth tells Night and Day to cut out the dialectic, and go back to serving the vital functions for which they were created. At this, the heads of Night and Day are bowed (Q 20:111) and the text concludes. The poems are second-rate, but ʿAlwān is a gifted composer in rhymed prose. *Divertimento of the Secrets* is a standout text in his corpus. A prolific writer on Sufism, jurisprudence, and moral subjects, he is not credited with any other works of artistic prose (*adab*).

---

40 Led by Jānbardī al-Ghazālī (a onetime Mamluk governor of Hama, ʿAlwān's home city), the uprising came to an end outside Damascus with the beheading of its principal on 6 February 1521. See Bakhit 1982: 3–33.

41 In an essay dating to the reign of Selim I (1517–20 CE), al-Ḥamawī (2000: 142) calls the Mamluk governors of Syria "those tyrannical despots whom the Truth allowed to carry on before seizing and destroying them."

9. Our last title, *Naḍrat al-bahār fī muḥāwarat al-layl wa-l-nahār* (Blossom of the Desert Aster in the Controversy of Night and Day), was published in two editions during the lifetime of its author, Muḥammad b. Muḥammad al-Mubārak al-Jazāʾirī (1847–1912).[42] In the introduction to the second edition, al-Jazāʾirī (1893: 2) says it was the first *maqāma* he ever composed. Born in Beirut to a family of Algerian immigrants, he was educated at Damascus, where here he tutored the children of the resistance leader Abdelkader ibn Muhieddine El Djezairi (1808–1883) who had moved there in exile from French-occupied Algeria. As an educator and an editor of classical texts for print (including abridgements of al-Hamadhānī and al-Ḥarīrī), al-Jazāʾirī was an energetic representative of the Nahḍa movement (Ḥāfiẓ and Abāẓa 1986, I: 277). He published other original disputation texts in the neo-Classical mode, including one in praise of El Djezairi entitled *Abhā maqāmatun fī l-mufākhara bayn al-ghurba wa-l-iqāma* (A Splendid *Maqāma* of the Boasting-Match between Exile and Staying Put) in an 1879 lithograph edition at Damascus.[43]

Blossom of the Desert Aster is likewise in praise of El Djezairi, and is the longest Arabic disputation surveyed here.[44] Mārdīnī (2008: 322) points out some imitative touches showing that the author knew Ibn Fāris's *Book of Night and Day.* There is also in *Blossom of the Desert Aster* a return to Ibn Fāris's way of quoting verses by earlier poets, as in the introduction's first lines:[45]

> One day, I looked into "the alternation between night and day" (Q 2:164), and the finer points of secret wisdom that God deposited in each of their hours. And to the interpretations of *lisān al-ḥāl* I leant my ear, in order that my links to its chain of transmission be without a gap, and on this authority I narrate here the strange and marvelous things the pair have to say. It has been said that "Night and Day are full of wonders."[46] [And also:] "Whose parents give them no education / will have Night and Day for their teachers."[47]

42 The title of the first version was *Ghināʾ al-hazār fī muḥāwarat al-layl wa-l-nahār* (The Nightingale's Song in the Controversy of Night and Day), and its text is preserved in al-Bayṭār 1993, III: 1355–66. Ziriklī (2002, VII: 77) mentions it by this title also. Mārdīnī (2008: 323–24) mentions a *Munāẓara bayna l-layl wa-l-nahār* in manuscript at Damascus (MS Ẓāhiriyya 5576) that was copied, but not authored, by al-Jazāʾirī's contemporary ʿAbd al-Qādir ʿUmar Nabhān (1845–1912). This text too praises Abdelkader El Djezairi, and seems to be a close emulation of *Blossom of the Desert Aster*, if not yet another version of the *Blossom* dictated by al-Jazāʾirī himself.

43 Sarkis (n.d., I: 695), ed. Ṭayyān 2000: 149–84.

44 According to the biographical notice of al-Ḥāfiẓ and Abāẓa (1986, I: 275), al-Jazāʾirī composed panegyric for no one else.

45 Al-Jazāʾirī 1893: 3–4. Al-Ḥamawī (2016: 710) does this also, with verses quoted from Abū Madyān al-Tilimsānī (d. 594/1198).

46 Ibn Nubāta (d. 768/1366), as in al-Ibshīhī 2008: 375.

47 Abū Muḥallam al-Shaybānī (d. 245/859), as in al-Zamakhsharī 1992, V: 353.

Blossom of the Desert Aster has much in common with *Divertimento of the Secrets* as well. In these late texts, Night and Day are not just disembodied speech-contestants, but actors endowed with form and dynamism. "In the whiteness of its light, Day found me afoot," narrates al-Ḥamawī, "and stroked my face with an outstretched hand of sunlight, and greeted me with the forearm of God's Oneness, in which there is no doubt and no uncertainty" (Al-Ḥamawī 2016: 711). Al-Jazāʾirī elaborates the motif into allegorical battles that ekphrasize the changing skies of dusk and dawn:

> Answering the challenge, Night brought all his force down on the foe, making missiles of his lit stars, and left no visible remains [of Day] and no outline. And when the full moon had embroidered his mantle of darkness, and bedecked his wreathed crown with apogeal flowers, and enraptured the intellects [of its beholders], Night said: "I praise the One who made me to be a refuge for true lovers…."
>
> Day then pounced, and assailed him with the violence of a conquering king, and when he had reascended the pulpit, the plain lit up at the return of his figure. He spoke in praise of the One who dispels the veil of darkness, calling Him by name the Light, and launched into a chapter from the Holy Book, ornamented with a brilliant, blazing lamp. With its glare, he illuminated the path, and the way was lit up with its brilliance. He shouted: "O Night, have you cut short your train of wonders?…." (Al-Jazāʾirī 1893: 5–7)

Night and Day each take the field seven times and give seven speeches (as in Qohestānī's *Poem of Day and Night*). The controversy seems to go on for one week. As in *Divertimento of the Secrets*, the role of judge is played by the Truth, and the judgment is the same: Night and Day are brothers, and should leave aside the dialectic and the controversy. A long moralizing poem at the end develops the theme, and concludes with Abdelkader El Djezairi's praises.

The heavyweights of visionary Islamic literature (Avicenna, Suhrawardī, ʿAṭṭār, *et al*) left behind no disputations of Night and Day. For some authors, it may have been too much a cliché of the schools.[48] All the same, there is cosmic profundity in each answer to the question: If all of sublunary time split itself in two and fell to arguing, what would it sound like? For the set to which Night and Day belong is Time itself. This is the meaning of the verse quoted above by al-Jazāʾirī: to be educated by Night and Day is to learn from Time/Fate, called in Arabic *al-dahr.*[49] Night and Day are a merism of *al-dahr:* two halves constituting

---

48 The poet John Milton (d. 1085/1674) was in his Cambridge days compelled to argue on behalf of Day in a Latin debate on "Whether Day or Night is the More Excellent," for which see Milton (1953, I: 218–33).

49 As in the verse of Nāṣir-i Khusraw (d. 481/1088): "Day and night passed over me / and their changes changed me too…" Tr. Schimmel (2001: 14).

a totality, like land and sea (*barr wa-baḥr*). Or perhaps they belong to fate in a subordinate way, as in the sacred hadith:

> The Prophet, God's blessings and peace be upon him, said: "God, be He exalted and magnified, says: 'The children of Adam complain of Time/Fate (*al-dahr*), when Time/Fate am I, and night and day are in My hand.'"[50]

Bibliography

GAL = Brockelmann, Carl. 1932–49. *Geschichte der arabischen Litteratur.* Leiden: Brill. 5 vols; *S* = Supplementband. The pagination of vols. I and II follows that of the first edition (1898–1902).

1 Disputations of Night and Day in Manuscript and Print

1. Abū l-Ḥusayn Aḥmad IBN FĀRIS (d. 395/1004), *Kitāb al-Layl wa-l-nahār* (The Book of Night and Day)
   - Tehran, Malek National Library MS Majmūʿa 852, fol. 121–26
   - Kitāb al-Layl wa-l-nahār, ed. Ḥāmid al-Khaffāf. 1988. *Turāthunā* 14: 173–99. (Based on a handwritten copy of the Tehran MS made in 1987 by ʿAbd al-ʿAzīz al-Ṭabāṭabāʾī.)
   - Reprinted as *al-Layl wa-l-nahār.* 1993. Beirut: Dār al-Muʾarrikh
2. ʿAlī b. Aḥmad ASADĪ ṬŪSĪ (d. 465/1072–73), *Shab va rūz* (Night and Day)
   - Asadī Ṭūsī (2), ed. Jalal Khaleghi Motlagh. 1978. *Majallah-i Dānishkadah-i Adabīyāt va ʿUlūm-i Insānī, Dānishgāh-i Firdawsī* 14:1: 91–96, 126
   - Tr. von Hammer-Purgstall 1818: 49–50, Rückert 1874: 61–63, Ethé 1882: 83–88, Costello 1899: 47–53
3. Abū Ismāʿīl ʿAbd Allāh b. Muḥammad ANṢĀRĪ HARAWĪ (d. 481/1089), *Kanz al-sālikīn* (Treasure of the Followers of the Way), chapter 2: *Mubāḥathat* (or *Munāẓarat*) *shab va rūz* (The Discussion of Night and Day)
   - ʿAbdullāh-i Anṣāri'nin *Kanz as-Sālikīn* veya *Zād al-ʿĀrifīn'i* (2), ed. Tahsin Yazıcı. 1959. *Şarkiyat Mecmuası* 3: 25–49
   - *Zād al-ʿārifīn*, ed. Murād Awrang. 1974. Tehran: Chāpkhānah-i Firdawsī. 9–19
   - *Majmūʿah-ʾi rasāʾil-i Fārsī-i Khvājah ʿAbd Allāh Anṣārī*, ed. Muḥammad Sarvar Mawlāʾī. 1377/1998. 2nd printing. Tūs: Intishārāt Tūs. II: 551–66
   - Noted by Çelebi (n.d., II: 945) and Ritter (1934: 97)
   - Imitated in the Turkish *Münâzara-i şeb va rūz* of Fasîh Ahmet Dede (d. 1111/1699); see Hatice Aynur in this volume.

50 *Qāla llāh: Yasubbu banū Ādama l-dahra wa-anā l-dahru bi-yadī l-layl wa-l-nahār.* al-Bukhārī (2004: 1264), Muslim (2007: 1051).

4. Judah ben Solomon AL-ḤARĪZĪ (d. 622/1225), *Taḥkemoni*, no. 39: *Maḥberet ha-yom we-ha-layla / Maqālat al-Munāzaʿa bayna l-layl wa-l-nahār* (The Speech-Contest between Night and Day)
   - *Iudae Harizii Macamae*, ed. Paul Lagarde. 1883. Göttingen: Hoyer. 147–49
   - Tr. Reichert 1973, II: 241–46, del Valle 1988: 260–62, Segal 2001: 298–301
5. ʿIzz al-Dīn ʿAbd al-Salām b. Aḥmad IBN GHĀNIM AL-MAQDISĪ (d. 678/1279), *Mufākharat al-layl wa-l-nahār* (The Boasting-Match of Night and Day)
   - Royal Batavian Society MS A 655, fol. 200v-201v
   - Yale Beinecke Arabic MSS 206, fol. 45v-47r
   - Dār al-Kutub MS Adab 1586, ed. Shishtawī 2001: 15–22 as Mufākharat al-layl wa-l-nahār li-Majhūl
   - Partial tr. Massé 1961: 145–46
6. Ḥakīm Saʿd al-Dīn NEZĀRĪ QOHESTĀNĪ (d. 720/1320–21), *Masnavī-i Rūz va shab* (The Poem of Day and Night)
   - St. Petersburg, National Library MS Dorn 415
   - *Masnavī-i Rūz va shab*, ed. Naṣrollah Pourjavady. 2006. Tehran: Nashr-i Nay
7. ʿAlāʾ al-Dīn Abū l-Ḥasan ʿAlī b. ʿUthmān b. Ibrāhīm AL-MĀRDĪNĪ, also known as Ibn al-Turkumānī (d. 750/1349), *Munāẓara bayna l-layl wa-l-nahār* (A Debate Between Night and Day)
   - Dār al-Kutub MS adab Taymūr 834
   - Staatsbibliothek zu Berlin MS Sprenger 1168, fol. 5r–7r
   - Edited for print by an unknown scholar, and posted anonymously to the Internet in Nov. 2007: http://alsada.org/plus/viewtopic.php?f=20&t=49345 (retrieved January 2020)
8. ʿAlī b. Aṭiyya, known as ʿALWĀN AL-ḤAMAWĪ (d. 939/1530), *Nuzhat al-asrār fī muḥāwarat al-layl wa-l-nahār* (Divertimento of the Secrets in the Controversy of Night and Day)
   - Staatsbibliothek zu Berlin MS Wetzstein II 1794, fol. 1r–11v (*GAL* II 333)
   - Universitätsbibliothek Leipzig MS Vollers 0873–02, fol. 11r–18v (*GAL* S II 461)
   - Ed. Kadhim Safi Hussein (from an early 11th/17th c. MS whose photocopy is kept in Najaf at Maktabat Amīr al-Muʾminīn). 2016. *Majallat al-ʿUlūm al-insāniyya* (University of Babylon) 23: 2: 704–19. https://www.iasj.net/iasj?func=fulltext&aId=130033 (retrieved January 2020)
9. Muḥammad b. Muḥammad al-Mubārak AL-JAZĀʾIRĪ (d. 1330/1912), *Naḍrat al-bahār fī muḥāwarat al-layl wa-l-nahār* (The Blossom of the Desert Aster in the Controversy of Night and Day)
   - 2nd ed. 1311/1893. Beirut: al-Maṭbaʿat al-Adabiyya (*GAL* S II 758, S III 379)
   - Reprinted in Hāshimī 1955, I: 263–74, Ṭayyān 2000: 119–48, Shishtawī 2001: 23–43
10. Works that are inextant or out of reach:
   - ʿAlī b. Fatḥ Allāh al-Maʿdānī al-Iṣbahānī (d. 890/1485), a Persian-language *Munāẓarat al-layl wa-l-nahār* (Disputation of Night and Day), noted by al-Bābānī (n.d., I: 391)
   - Jalāl al-Dīn al-Suyūṭī (d. 911/1505), *al-Falak al-dawwār fī faḍl al-layl ʿalā l-nahār* (The Rotating Spheres in Praise of Night to the Detriment of Day), noted by Çelebi (n.d., II: 1291)

– Sharaf al-Dīn Ḥusayn b. Masʿūd al-Shāfiʿī, *Ḥadīqat al-bahār fī l-mufākhara bayna l-samāʾ wa-l-arḍ wa-l-layl wa-l-nahār* (The Garden of Aromatic Plants in the Boasting-Match between Heaven and Earth and Night and Day), noted by Brockelmann, *GAL* S II 908

2 Primary Sources

al-Bayṭār, ʿAbd al-Razzāq. 1993. *Ḥilyat al-bashar fī tārīkh al-qarn al-thālith ʿashar*, ed. Muḥammad Bahjat al-Bayṭār. 2nd printing. Beirut: Dār Ṣādir. 3 vols.

al-Bukhārī. 2004. *Ṣaḥīḥ al-Bukhārī*, ed. Aḥmad Zahwa and Aḥmad ʿInāya. Beirut: Dār al-Kitāb al-ʿArabī. 1 vol.

al-Farrāʾ. 1980. *al-Ayyām wa-l-layālī wa-l-shuhūr*, ed. Ibrāhīm al-Abyārī. 2nd printing. Cairo/Beirut: Dār al-Kitāb al-Miṣrī / Dār al-Kitāb al-Lubnānī.

Ghulām Thaʿlab, Abū ʿUmar al-Muṭarriz. 1978. *Kitāb Yawm wa-layla fī l-lugha wa-l-gharīb*, ed. Muḥammad Jabbār al-Muʿaybid. *Majallat Maʿhad al-Makhṭūṭāt al-ʿArabiyya* 24: 2: 239–338.

al-Ḥāfiẓ, Muḥammad Muṭīʿ, and Nizār Abāẓa. 1986. *Tārīkh ʿulamāʾ Dimashq fī l-qarn al-rābiʿ ʿashar al-hijrī*. Damascus: Dār al-Fikr. 2 vols.

al-Ḥamawī, ʿAlwān. 2000. *al-Naṣāʾiḥ al-muhimma li-l-mulūk wa-l-aʾimma*, ed. Nashwa al-Ḥamawī. Damascus: Dār al-Maktabī.

al-Hāshimī, Aḥmad, ed. 1955. *Jawāhir al-adab fī adabiyyāt wa-inshāʾ lughat al-ʿarab*. [Cairo]: Maṭbaʿat Aḥmad ʿAlī Mukhaymar. 2 vols. in 1.

Ibn Abī l-Dunyā. 1997. *Kalām al-layālī wa-l-ayyām li-bni Ādam*, ed. Muḥammad Khayr Ramaḍān Yūsuf. Beirut: Dār Ibn Ḥazm

Ibn Abī Ḥajala. 2018. *Manṭiq al-ṭayr*, ed. Aḥmad ʿAbd al-Karīm Mashhadānī. Rabat: Dār al-Amān.

Ibn ʿArabī. 2001. *Rasāʾil Ibn ʿArabī*, ed. Muḥammad ʿAbd al-Karīm al-Namarī. Beirut: Dār al-Kutub al-ʿIlmiyya.

Ibn Fāris. 1958. *Futyā faqīh al-ʿarab*, ed. Ḥusayn ʿAlī Maḥfūẓ. *Majallat al-Majmaʿ al-ʿIlmī al-ʿArabī* (Damascus). 33: 1: 443–656.

Ibn Fāris. 2007. *al-Ṣāḥibī fī fiqh al-lugha al-ʿarabiyya wa-masāʾilihā wa-sunan alʿarab fī kalāmihā*, ed. Aḥmad Ḥasan Basaj. 2nd ed. Beirut: Dār al-Kutub al-ʿIlmiyya.

Ibn Ḥajar al-ʿAsqalānī. 1993. *al-Durar al-kāmina fī aʿyān al-mīʾa al-thāmina*. Beirut: Dār al-Jīl. 4 vols.

Ibn Ḥibbān. 1993. *Ṣaḥīḥ Ibn Ḥibbān*, ed. Shuʿayb Arnāʾūṭ. 3rd printing. Beirut: Muʾassasat al-Risāla. 18 vols.

al-Ibshīhī, Shihāb al-Dīn Muḥammad. 2008. *al-Mustaṭraf fī kulli fanni mustaẓraf*, ed. Muḥammad Khayr Ṭuʿmah al-Ḥalabī. Beirut: Dār al-Maʿrifa.

al-Mārdīnī, ʿAlāʾ al-Dīn ʿAlī. 2002. *Bahjat al-arīb fī bayān mā fī kitāb Allāh al-ʿazīz min al-gharīb*, ed. Marzūq ʿAlī Ibrāhīm. Cairo: al-Hayʾa al-Miṣriyya al-ʿAmma li-l-Kitāb.

Milton, John. 1953–82. *Complete Prose Works*, ed. Don M. Wolfe *et al.* New Haven: Yale Univ. Press. 8 vols. in 10.

Muslim b. al-Ḥajjāj. 2007. *Ṣaḥīḥ Muslim*, ed. Khalīl Maʾmūn Shīḥā. Beirut: Dār al-Maʿārif. 1 vol.

al-Shishtawī, Muḥammad, ed. 1999a. *al-Mufākharāt al-bāhira bayna ʿarāʾis mutanazzihāt al-Qāhira*. Cairo: Dār al-Āfāq al-ʿArabiyya.

al-Shishtawī, Muḥammad, ed. 1999b. *Nūr al-nahār fī munāẓarāt al-wurūd wa-l-rayyāḥīn wa-l-azhār.* Cairo: Dār al-Āfāq al-ʿArabiyya.
al-Shishtawī, Muḥammad, ed. 2001. *al-ʿAwn fī mufākharāt al-kawn.* Cairo: Dār al-Āfāq al-ʿArabiyya.
al-Suyūṭī, Jalāl al-Dīn. 1971. *al-Muzhir fī ʿulūm al-lugha wa-anwāʿiha*, ed. Muḥammad Aḥmad Jād al-Mawlā, ʿAlī Muḥammad al-Bajāwī, and Muḥammad Abu 'l-Faḍl Ibrāhīm. Cairo: Dār Iyḥāʾ al-Kutub al-ʿArabiyya. 2 vols.
al-Ṭabarī. 1968. *Tārīkh al-Ṭabarī: Tārīkh al-rusul wa-l-mulūk*, ed. Muḥammad Abū l-Faḍl Ibrāhīm. 2nd ed. Cairo: Dār al-Maʿārif bi-Miṣr. 10 vols.
al-Tawḥīdī, Abū Ḥayyān. 1997. *Kitāb al-Imtāʿ wa-l-muʾānasa*, ed. Khalīl al-Manṣūr. Beirut: Dār al-Kutub al-ʿIlmiyya.
al-Ṭayyān, Muḥammad Ḥassān, ed. 2000. *al-Mufākharāt wa-l-munāẓarāt.* Beirut: Dār al-Bas͟hāʾir al-Islāmiyya.
Yāqūt al-Ḥamawī. 1993. *Muʿjam al-udabāʾ: Irshād al-arīb ilā maʿrifat al-adīb*, ed. Iḥsān ʿAbbās. Beirut: Dār al-Gharb al-Islamī. 7 vols.
al-Zamakhsharī, 1992. *Rabīʿ al-abrār fī nuṣūṣ al-akhbār*, ed. ʿAbd al-Amīr Muhannā. Beirut: Muʾassasat al-Aʿlamī li-l-Maṭbūʿāt. 5 vols.

3 Secondary Sources and Translations

Abdullaeva, Firuza. 2009. The Bodleian Manuscript of Asadī Ṭūsī's *Munāẓara between an Arab and a Persian:* Its place in the transition from ancient debate to classical panegyric. *Iran* 47: 69–95.
Abdullaeva, Firuza. 2014. The Origins of the *Munāẓara* Genre in New Persian Literature. Pp. 249–73 in *Metaphor and Imagery in Persian Poetry*, ed. Asghar Seyed-Gohrab. Leiden: Brill.
Ahmed, Shahab. 2016. *What is Islam? The Importance of Being Islamic.* Princeton: University Press.
al-Bābānī, Ismāʿīl Bāshā al-Baghdādī. N.d. *Hadiyyat al-ʿārifīn: asmāʾ al-muʾallifīn wa-athār al-muṣannifīn.* Beirut: Dār Iḥyāʾ al-Turāth al-ʿArabī. 2 vols.
Bakhit, Muhammad Adnan. 1982. *The Ottoman Province of Damascus in the Sixteenth Century.* Beirut: Librairie du Liban.
de Beaurecueil, Serge de Laugier. 1954. Une ébauche persane des "Manāzil as-sāʾirīn": Le "Kitāb-è Ṣad maydān" de ʿAbdallah Anṣārī. *Mélanges islamologiques* 2: 1–90.
de Beaurecueil, Serge de Laugier. 1965. *Khwādja ʿAbdullāh Anṣārī (396–481 H./1006–1089), mystique hanbalite.* Beirut: Imprimerie Catholique.
de Beaurecueil, Serge de Laugier. 1982 ʿAbdallāh Anṣārī. *Encyclopaedia Iranica.* (Online ed.) http://www.iranicaonline.org/articles/abdallah-al-ansari (retrieved January 2020).
Belhaj, Abdessamad. 2010. *Argumentation et dialectique en islam: Forms et sequences de la munāẓara.* Louvain: Presses Universitaires.
Böhme, Robert. 1953. *Orpheus: Das Alter des Kitharoden.* Berlin: Weidmannsche Verlagsbuchhandlung.
Böhme, Robert. 1970. *Orpheus: Der Sänger und seine Zeit.* Bern/Munich: Francke Verlag.
Brunner, Christopher J. 1980a. The Fable of *The Babylonian Tree.* Part I: Introduction. *Journal of Near Eastern Studies* 39: 3: 191–202.

Brunner, Christopher. 1980b. The Fable of *The Babylonian Tree*. Part II: Translation. *Journal of Near Eastern Studies* 39: 4: 291–302.

Çelebi, Kâtip (= Ḥajjī Khalīfa). N.d. *Kashf al-ẓunūn ʿan asāmī l-kutub wa-l-funūn*. Beirut: Dār Iḥyāʾ al-Turāth al-ʿArabī. 2 vols.

Costello, Louisa Stuart. 1899. (New ed.) *Rose Garden of Persia*. London: Gibbings & Co.

Drory, Rina. 1993. Literary Contacts and Where to Find Them: On Arabic Literary Models in Medieval Jewish Literature. *Poetics Today* 14: 2: 277–302.

Eboo Jamal, Nadia. 2015. Nezāri Qohestāni. *Encyclopaedia Iranica*. (Online ed.) http://www.iranicaonline.org/articles/nezari-qohestani (retrieved January 2020).

van Ess, Josef. 1976. Disputationspraxis in der islamischen Theologie: Einer vorläufige Skizze. *Revue des études islamiques* 44: 23–60.

Ethé, H[ermann]. 1882. Über persische Tenzonen. Pp. 48–135 in *Verhandlungen des V. internationalen Orientalisten-Congresses* 2: 1. Berlin: Asher & Co. / Wiedmannsche Buchhandlung.

al-Fallāḥ, Qaḥṭān Ṣāliḥ. 2009. Madkhal ilā l-ḥiwār wa-l-munāẓara fī l-ʿaṣr al-ʿAbbāsī. *al-Maʿrifa* (Syria) 551: 99–118.

Farhâdi, A. G. Ravân. 1996. *ʿAbdullāh Anṣārī of Herat (1006–1089 C.E.): An Early Ṣūfī Master*. Richmond (Surrey, U.K.): Curzon Press.

Frow, John. 2006. *Genre*. London and New York: Routledge.

van Gelder, Geert Jan. 1987. The Conceit of Pen and Sword: On an Arabic Literary Debate. *Journal of Semitic Studies* 32: 2: 329–60.

van Gelder, Geert Jan. 1991. Arabic Debates of Jest and Earnest. Pp. 199–211 in *Dispute Poems and Dialogues in the Ancient and Mediaeval Near East. Forms and Types of Literary Debates in Semitic and Related Literatures*, ed. G. J. Reinink and H. L. J. Vanstiphout. Orientalia Lovaniensia Analecta 42. Leuven: Peeters.

Guthrie, W. C. K. 1954. Review of Böhme (1953). *Gnomon* 26: 5: 303–307.

Hämeen-Anttila, Jaakko. 2002. *Maqama: A History of a Genre*. Wiesbaden: Harrassowitz.

Hämeen-Anttila, Jaakko. 2006. The Essay and Debate (*al-Risāla* and *al-Munāẓara*). Pp. 134–44 in *Arabic Literature in the Post-Classical Period*, ed. Roger Allen and D. S. Richards. Cambridge: Cambridge Univ. Press.

Hämeen-Anttila, Jaakko. 2014. On the early history of literary debate (*munāẓara*) in Islamic Spain. Pp. 261–73 in *Vivir de tal suerte: Homenaje a Juan Antonio Souto Lasala*, ed. Mohamed Meouak and Cristina de la Puente. Cordoba: Oriens Academic.

von Hammer-Purgstall, Joseph. 1818. *Geschichte der schönen redekünste Persiens*. Vienna: Heubner und Volke.

Ḥammūdī, Hādī Ḥasan. 1982. *al-Maqāmāt min Ibn Fāris ilā Badīʿ al-Zamān al-Hamadhānī*. Beirut: Dār al-Āfāq al-Jadīda.

Handley, E. W. 2006. Dialogue with the Night (PAnt 1.15 = "PCG" VIII 1084). *Zeitschrift für Papyrologie und Epigraphik* 155: 23–25.

Heinrichs, Wolfhart. 1991. Rose Versus Narcissus: Observations on an Arabic Literary Debate. Pp. 179–98 in *Dispute Poems and Dialogues in the Ancient and Mediaeval Near East. Forms and Types of Literary Debates in Semitic and Related Literatures*, ed. G. J. Reinink and H. L. J. Vanstiphout. Orientalia Lovaniensia Analecta 42. Leuven: Peeters.

Jiménez, Enrique. 2017. *The Babylonian Disputation Poems: with Editions of the Series of the Poplar, Palm and Vine, the Series of the Spider, and the Story of the Poor, Forlorn Wren*. Culture and History of the Ancient Near East 87. Leiden/Boston: Brill.

Jirīsha, ʿAlī. 1989. *Adab al-ḥiwār wa-l-munāẓara.* El-Mansoura: Dār al-Wafāʾ li-l-Ṭibāʿa wa-l-nashr wa-l-tawzīʿ.

Kaster, Robert A. 2001. Controlling Reason: Declamation in Rhetorical Education at Rome. Pp. 317–37 in *Education in Greek and Roman Antiquity*, ed. Yun Lee Too. Leiden: Brill.

Lewisohn, Leonard. 2003. Sufism and Ismāʿīlī Doctrine in the Persian Poetry of Nizārī Quhistānī (645–721/1247–1321). *Iran* 41: 229–51.

Makdisi, George. 1981. *The Rise of Colleges: Institutions of Higher Learning in Islam and the West.* Edinburgh: Edinburgh Univ. Press.

Mārdīnī, Raghdāʾ. 2008. *al-Munāẓarāt al-khayāliyya fī adab al-mashriq wa-l-maghrib wa-l-andalus.* Damascus: Dār al-Fikr.

Massé, Henri. 1961. Du genre littéraire “Débat” en arabe et persan. *Cahiers de civilisation médiévale* 4/14: 137–47.

Mattock, John N. 1991. The Arabic Tradition: Origin and Developments. Pp. 153–63 in *Dispute Poems and Dialogues in the Ancient and Mediaeval Near East. Forms and Types of Literary Debates in Semitic and Related Literatures*, ed. G. J. Reinink and H. L. J. Vanstiphout. Orientalia Lovaniensia Analecta 42. Leuven: Peeters.

Mirsky, Aharon, *et al.* 2007. al-Ḥarīzī, Judah ben Solomon. *Enyclopaedia Judaica.* 2nd ed. I: 655–57.

Pomerantz, Maurice, and Bilal Orfali. 2019. Ibn Fāris and the Origins of the Maqāmah Revisited. Pp. 95–114 in *Arabic Belles Lettres*, ed. Joseph Lowry and Shawkat Toorawa. Atlanta: Lockwood Press.

Rahman, Munibur. 1995. Risāla (2). *Encyclopaedia of Islam.* 2nd ed. VIII: 539–44.

Reichert, Victor Emanuel, tr. 1965–73. *The Tahkemoni of Judah al-Harizi: An English Translation.* Jerusalem: Raphael Haim Cohen’s Ltd. Publishers. 2 vols.

Reinink, G.J, and H.L.J. Vanstiphout, eds. 1991. *Dispute Poems and Dialogues in the Ancient and Mediaeval Near East: Forms and Types of Literary Debates in Semitic and Related Literatures.* Leuven: Departement Oriëntalistiek / Peeters.

Ritter, Hellmut. 1934. Philologika VIII: Anṣārī Herewī – Senāʾī Ġaznewī. *Der Islam* 22: 2: 89–105.

Ritter, Hellmut. 2013. *The Ocean of the Soul: Men, the World and God in the Stories of Farīd al-Dīn ʿAṭṭār*, tr. John O’Kane with Bernd Radtke. Leiden: Brill.

Robbins, Emmet. 1970. Famous Orpheus. *Orpheus: The Metamorphosis of a Myth*, ed. John Warden. Toronto: Univ. of Toronto Press.

Rosenthal, Franz, tr. 1989. *The History of al-Ṭabarī*, vol. 1. Albany: SUNY Press.

Rückert, Friedrich, and W[ilhelm] Pertsch. 1874. *Grammatik, Poetik und Rhetorik der Perser.* Gotha: Friedrich Andreas Perthes.

Rudolph, Ekkehard. 1988. Der Wettstreit der Schriftarten: eine arabische Handschrift aus der Forschungsbibliothek Gotha. *Der Islam* 65: 2: 301–16.

Sadan, Joseph. 1996. Rabi Yehudah al-Harizi ke-Tzomit Tarbuti. *Peʿamim: Studies in Oriental Jewry* 68: 16–67.

Sarkis, Joseph Elian. N.d. *Muʿjam al-maṭbūʿāt al-ʿarabiyya wa-l-muʿarraba.* Cairo: Maktabat al-Thaqāfa al-Dīniyya.

Schimmel, Annemarie, tr. 2001. *Make a Shield from Wisdom: Selected Verses from Nāṣir-i Khusraw’s Dīvān.* Rev. ed. London: I. B. Tauris / Institute of Ismaili Studies.

Schoeler, Gregor. 2002. *Écrire et transmettre dans les débuts de l'islam*. Paris: Presses Universitaires de France; tr. Shawkat Toorawa. 2009. *The genesis of literature in Islam: From the aural to the read*. Rev. ed. Edinburgh: Edinburgh Univ. Press.

Segal, David Simha, tr. 2001. *Judah Alḥarizi, The Book of Taḥkemoni: Jewish Tales from Medieval Spain*. London/Portland: Littman Library of Jewish Civilization.

al-Ṣiddīq, Ḥusayn. 2000. *al-Munāẓara fī l-adab al-ʿarabī wa-l-islāmī*. Giza: al-Sharika al-Miṣriyya al-ʿĀlamiyya li-l-Nashr / Longman.

Utas, Bo. 1988. The *Munājāt* or *Ilāhī-nāmah* of ʿAbdu'llāh Anṣārī. *Manuscripts of the Middle East* 3: 83–87.

del Valle Rodriguez, Carlos, ed. and tr. 1988. *Las asambleas de los sabios* (Taḥkĕmonī). Murcia: Universidad de Murcia.

Wagner, Ewald. 1963. *Die arabische Rangstreitdichtung und ihre Einordnung in die allgemeine Literaturgeschichte*. Abhandlungen der Geistes- und Sozialwissenschaftlichen Klasse 8. Wiesbaden: Akademie der Wissenschaften und der Literatur.

Wagner, Ewald. 1993. Munāẓara. *Encyclopaedia of Islam*. 2nd ed. VII: 565–68.

Yazıcı, Tahsin. 1964. ʿAbdullah-i Anṣāriʾnin *Kanz as-Sālikīn* veya *Zād al-ʿĀrifīnʾi* (4). *Şarkiyat Mecmuası* 5: 67–80

Yazıcı, Tahsin and Süleyman Uludağ. 1998. Herevī, Hâce Abdullah. *İslâm ansiklopedisi*. XVII: 222–26.

al-Ziriklī, Khayr al-Dīn. 2002. *al-Aʿlām: Qāmūs tarājim li-ashhar al-rijāl wa-l-nisāʾ min al-ʿarab wa-l-mustaʿribin wa-l-mustashriqīn*. 15th printing. Beirut: Dār al-ʿIlm li-l-Malayīn. 8 vols.

Amparo Alba Cecilia*

13 Disputation Poems in Medieval Hebrew Literature in Spain

Hebrew literature in Spain begins around the 10th century CE, when the Jews started to participate in the intellectual and artistic risorgimento promoted by the Caliphs of Córdoba Abderraman III and Al-Hakam II. Jewish communities quickly adopted Arabic language and culture; at the same time, a renewed interest was stirred in the study of the Hebrew language and in its use for the artistic expression par excellence: poetry. One Dunas ben Labrat, who settled in Cordoba around 950, is reputed to be the first who used the models, literary conventions, and quantitative meter of Arabic poetry in Hebrew.

However, Spanish Hebrew poetry reached its highest peaks two centuries later, during the 11th and first half of the 12th centuries, during the period of the independent Taifa kingdoms and the Almoravid conquest. After the Almohad conquest of Spain, in the mid-12th century, many Jews fled into exile to the Christian kingdoms in the North; this period sees the emergence and flourishing of Spanish Hebrew narrative, which is also based on Arabic models. Most of the Spanish Hebrew narrative works produced from the mid-12th century until the 15th century follow the form and style of the Arabic *maqāma*, composed in rhymed prose with intercalated poems (cf. Schippers 2002). The peculiarity of Spanish Hebrew literature lies mainly in its frequent quotations from the Bible and from Rabbinical literature, wherein lies its originality, in spite of its stylistic and formal dependence of the Spanish Arabic literature.

The debate is undoubtedly a minor genre among the literary works cultivated by Hispanic authors during the Middle Ages. As such, we find it, with very few exceptions, always embedded into works of narrative character, especially in collections of *maqāma*s or stories. It is therefore no surprise that the study of the Spanish Hebrew debates has not sparked a great deal of interest among researchers. I first started to work on these texts some twenty-five years ago (Alba Cecilia 1993, *ead.*1997, and *ead.* 2008), fascinated by the topics and treatment that literary debates had in the three cultures that coexisted in the Iberian Peninsula during the Middle Ages.

Already in the mid-20th century Menéndez Pidal (1948: 13) stated that "the dispute as a framework to develop a literary theme" is a genre common to all

* Universidad Complutense de Madrid.

https://doi.org/10.1515/9781501510274-013

literatures.[1] In the Middle Ages, debates were composed in Latin (*disputatio*), in Romance languages (*tenso*, *disputa*, and *partiment*), in Arabic (*mufākhara*), and in Hebrew (*milḥemet*, *vikuaḥ*).[2] Literary debates or dialogues between two contenders who defend opposing points of view is, therefore, a widespread genre in the Middle Ages. The reason is probably that it offers a pleasant way of teaching, and represents a poetic-rhetorical device for poets to exert their skills in praising and vituperating the same matter, or one thing and its opposite. These debates or disputes could be held between different types of rivals, such as people of different gender, age, and social status (e. g. clergyman, poet, scribe, soldier, warrior, man and woman, young and old, and master and pupil), as well as objects that represent them (e. g. pen, blade, scissors). Debates between concepts and allegorical entities also exist (e. g. wealth and wisdom, vice and virtue, soul and body, intellect and heart), as well as between animals or plants and between personified inanimate entities (e. g. day and night, wine and water, summer and winter).

From a literary point of view, these debates use both prose and rhyme, are usually written as a dialogue, and often feature, in addition to the litigants, a judge who is knowledgeable in the subject under debate, and who settles the question by making one of the contenders the winner. From the point of view of their contents, the issues covered are varied, but by far the most common categories in the Middle Ages are the following:

1. Debates of body and soul, or of heart and soul, or other members of the body.
2. Discussions of arms and letters, sometimes represented by a clergyman and a soldier, or by a sword and a pen.
3. Debates of wine and water, of summer and winter, of night and day, of wealth and wisdom, etc.

1 Disputations in Medieval Spanish-Language Literature

In medieval literature in Spanish language there are debates belonging to each of the three thematic categories outlined. I will refer to them only very briefly as a way of contextualizing their Hebrew counterparts:

1 See, more recently, Reinink and Vanstiphout 1991: 1.

2 See the contributions to sections III and IV of the present volume.

(1) Debate between Body and Soul (García Solalinde 1933). The oldest version of a debate between the Body and the Soul in Spanish dates to the 12th century (Franchini 2001: 23–42 and 215–17). It consists of 37 couplets, and is inspired by the French poem *Débat du Corps et de l'Âme*,[3] which is in turn probably a version of the Latin poem *Rixa animae et corporis*. It contains a discussion in which the soul and body of a deceased person blame each other for his sins. This theme became widespread in all languages,[4] and different versions of it are known in Spanish literature.[5]

(2) The debate between Arms and Letters, or between the Knight and Clergyman, is represented by the *Dispute between Elena and María*,[6] written in 1280 by an author who, judging from the words he uses, must have hailed from León, Zamora, or Salamanca. This text presents a dispute between two noble sisters: María, mistress of an abbot, and Elena, lover of a knight. Each one sets forth the advantages of one's life and the disadvantages of the other's life. Their arguments are based on material considerations, such as the quiet and easy life of the clergy against the harsh and uncertain one of the knight. The two sisters engage in an intense and virulent dialogue, in which they once and again present arguments for and against their beloved ones.

The tone of the discussion rises and it turns into insults. The sisters cannot agree, so they decide to take their case to court of king Oriol, "great judge of cases of love," to settle the issue. The manuscript breaks when they are presenting their arguments, so the outcome is unknown.[7]

(3) The debate between water and wine is a topic often found in medieval literature; *Los denuestos del agua y el vino* ("The insults between water and wine") can be dated to the early 13th century. This debate has parallels in

---

3 Batiouchkof 1891, Kastner 1905, and Franchini 2001: 40–42.

4 An extensive bibliography on the topic can be found in the article by Bossy 1976.

5 The theme reappears in the allegorical-Dantesque school (end of 16th century) with the title *Revelación de un ermitaño* ("Revelation of a hermit," see Franchini 2001: 133–150 and 253–258); it influences the *Farsa racional del libre albedrío* ("Rational farce of free will," by Diego Sánchez de Badajoz, 15th c.) and reaches down to Calderón's time, who uses it in one of his "sacramental plays" of his first phase, entitled *El pleito matrimonial del cuerpo y el alma* ("The marriage lawsuit of body and soul"), see Alborg 1972: I, 100.

6 The work is published, with a comprehensive study, by Menéndez Pidal 1914. Cf. also Menéndez Pidal 1948, Alvar 1974: 159–177, and Franchini 2001: 95–122 and 229–234.

7 Several versions of this debate are known in European literature; it was also picked up by Latin literature, sometimes in blatantly satirical poems; others, in a more measured and courteous manner: see Tavani 1964.

French and Latin debates.[8] In the Spanish version, water and wine discuss on their respective benefits and mock the enemy's defects. The dispute ends jokingly when both contenders ask for wine to drink.

2 Types of Debates in the Hebrew Hispanic Literature

Although traditional Jewish literature could have provided models to medieval Hebrew authors,[9] their immediate models were Arabic. From Arabic literature they borrow their aesthetic and formal patterns, and its various religious and secular themes.

The influence of genres, themes and motifs of Andalusian Arabic literature started to leave its imprint on Hispanic Hebrew poetry during the 11th century CE onwards. During this period several renowned Hebrew poets, such as Shemuel ha-Nagid, Yosef Ibn Hasday, Shelomoh ibn Gabirol, Mosheh ibn Ezra, and Yehudah ha-Levi, borrowed some of motifs from Spanish Arabic poetry that can be considered forunners to the debates. For instance, the praise of the pen and its qualities is one of the favorite and most frequent motifs both in laudatory poems and in poetic riddles.

In the mid-12th century, after the Almohads had taken control of most cities of Al-Andalus, large groups of Jewish population emigrate to Christian kingdoms in the north. Consequently, cities like Toledo, Zaragoza, and Barcelona become the new Jewish cultural centers. A feature of this new phase of Jewish literature is the rise of Hispanic Hebrew narrative, which also follows the general features of Arabic narrative. The literary genre of the debate, either independent or included in larger works, reaches its zenith in this period. The form of expression it adopts is the *maqāma*, which, as stated above, consists of alternating rhymed prose and verse.

8 The Castilian text forms a whole together with *Razón de Amor*. Menéndez Pidal 1919 offers an edition of the work. Other editions can be found in Alvar 1974: 141–157 and Franchini 2001: 43–80 and 219–225. On other debates between water and wine, see Hanford 1913 and McFie 1981.

9 For example, the book of Job, in which the protagonist's friends speak alternately in a debate of high theological content about divine justice, reward and punishment, sin, etc. Also, some discussions appear sporadically in Rabbinic literature, such as disputes between the mountains for God to deliver the Law on them, or between the Hebrew letters that appear before God asking Him for the world to be created by them, among others. See van Bekkum 1991.

In the following, I will adopt the tripartite typology exposed above to present the main themes and authors of Hispanic Hebrew literature: first, I will speak about the debates between body and soul; then on the debates between arms and letters; and in the third place on debates on other topics.

2.1 Debates between Body and Soul

2.1.1 The oldest Spanish Hebrew debate is probably the one composed by the poet and philosopher Shelomoh ibn Gabirol (Málaga? ca. 1022 – Valencia? ca. 1058).[10] The debate presents a disputation between the soul and the body, who mutually accuse each other of being the cause of man's sins. The disputation is part of a larger religious poem of clear neo-Platonic influence, which consists of 34 verses divided into three hemistiches each and contains the following sections:

Verses 1–7: Introduction: the poet reflects on the day of his death, when soul and body are required to submit to the trial of their Creator (v. 5) and feels terrified for his sins.

(...) Terror overwhelmed me
When I thought of the day of (my) death
And I trembled with fear.
(...) Day of devastation for the wicked
Who for his sins is summoned
And examined by his Creator.
(...) When the Soul together with the Body
Appear to be condemned.

Verses 8–19: The soul begins its plea: it pleads not guilty (v. 8) and declares itself a victim, since it has spent his life locked up in a dark prison (v. 10), inhabiting a corpse (v. 11), a body that has caused it to commit all kinds of sins (lust, gluttony) and which, therefore, deserves to be punished (v. 18).

I am tired of the body's filth,
I want to escape
The foul stench of the corpse,
(...) (The body) gets into every sin
And drags me (into it) by force,
(...) He is tied to all lust,
And never stops eating and drinking.

10 Yarden 1971: vol. I, no. 20, 31–34.

Verses 20–28: The body speaks up: it declares itself innocent. It argues that, without the soul, it is worth nothing, it is like a house without an owner, a sterile being, like a rolling stone or the shoots of the vine (v. 22). It is, in sum, as innocent or as guilty as the soul is, and it is the soul who should be judged for the body's actions.

(...) I too am deprived of children
Like the shoots of the wine,
Which are useless;
Without a soul, I am
Like a house without its owner
(...) Remove, my soul, your bitterness,
And eat the fruits of your actions,
"And pay your debts." (2 Kings 4:7)
I have no evil desires,
Since I am just like you –
"How can you say: 'I am not defiled'?" (Je 2:23)

Verses 29–30: A new character appears offstage: it is the poet himself who describe the despair of body and soul, both doomed to be united forever.

They are dejected beings who agitate
and find no reconciliation
"joined one to another" (Job 41:17)
(...) both are forever bound to each other –
"both will burn together" (Is 1:31)

Verses 31–34: The poem ends with a penitential prayer in which the deceased person (the poet, again) begs for compassion and forgiveness from the Supreme Judge.

The arrogant loves arrogance
"If you kept a record of sins,
Lord, who could stand?" (Palm 130:3)
Sooth your fearful anger (...)
"so that your maid's son may be refreshed" (Ex 23:12)
Have mercy on me,
and on the day of judgment,
do not punish me in your anger.

2.1.2 Yehudah al Harizi (ca. 1170–1230) is the main responsible for the introduction of the *maqāma* in Spanish Hebrew literature: he was an expert in Arabic literature and had previously translated Al-Hariri's *maqāmas* into Hebrew (Schippers 2002: 305–306). He himself composed a collection of *maqāmas* entitled

Sefer Taḥkemoni ("Book of the Sages"),[11] which includes the largest collection of Hispanic Hebrew debates. Many topics are covered; in many cases, the debate is a literary joust in which poets praise the most diverse and colourful things, such as ants and fleas.[12] All the debates are embedded within the framework of a fictional trip to the East undertaken by the two main characters: Heman the Ezraḥite (the narrator) and Ḥever the Kenite (his friend, a well-educated tramp). The collection is composed in the *maqāma*-format, in which rhymed prose and metric poems alternate.

Chapter XIII of the work contains a "Dialogue between Soul and Body, Intellect and Desire."[13] Ḥever the Kenite introduces this "dialogue" at the request of his partner as a "pleasant story" and places it in the Day of Judgment, a day of terror for sinners, in which body and soul will together stand before God. The insults that the two contenders hurl at each other follow very closely the model of the poem of Ibn Gabirol. However, Al Harizi further complicates the story by introducing two new characters: Intellect, who encourages the soul to be purified and cleansed of the filth of its body; and Desire, who spurs the soul to pursue happiness in this life and to enjoy its body. Intellect argues that there is hope for the soul as long as it frees itself from the yoke of Desire, and thus persuades soul to rely on the forgiveness of God. The story concludes with a self-praising poem by Ḥever, who adjudicates the debate, in a way, by impersonating the Heavenly Judge:

I save the frail flesh from the cauldron's fire,
the soul from the Pit's conflagration.
The evil desire, the body in lust,
are but straw or a smoking brand.
Then happy the man who for Father takes God
and is led by that Father's firm hand.

11 Translations in del Valle 1988 and Segal 2001.

12 Thus, in chapter 4, "The ant and the flea," two poets appear before a judge to decide which of the two is better and, to that effect, they challenge each other to compose poems in praise of these insects. Something similar occurs in the next chapter, in which twelve poets have to praise one month each. Chapters 12 and 42 contain disputes between greed and generosity; chapter 17 is a dispute between a non-believer (karaite) and a believer (Rabbanite). Chapter 39 presents a dispute between day and night; chapter 40, between the sword and the pen; chapter 41, between a man and a woman "on who offers more for the world and its fire"; chapter 43, between the sea and the land.

13 Translated by del Valle 1988: 132–138 and Segal 2001: 134–142.

He shall root from his heart transgression and sin,
plant contrition and right in their place.
Then shall he bask in Eternal Light
and look on his Maker's face.[14]

2.1.3 The third debate on this issue can be found in the *Sefer ha-Mešalim*, "Book of Tales" (David 1992/1993),[15] a collection of ten stories on different subjects, written around 1233 by Jacob ben Eleazar of Toledo – a grammarian, translator, and poet – following the formal techniques of the *maqāma*. The first chapter is entitled "allegorical tale about the soul and the body" (David 1992/1993: 15–22). The main character is the fictional author-narrator, Lemuel ben Itiel, who is sometimes called by his real name, Jacob.[16] The poem is presented as a love story whose main characters are different parts of the narrator's body: thus, his rational soul is portrayed as a passionate and temperamental young aristocrat; his intellect is the soul's beloved, embodied by a handsome general. Wisdom appears as the general's lover, and the heart (a metonym for the body) imprisons the soul and prevents it from joining its lover, the intellect.

The first scene is set outdoors, in a street frequented by, among others, "chariots of love," troops of warriors, "and leading them all, the love of my soul, the general of an army *outstanding among ten thousand*" (*Song of Songs* 5:10). On seeing the narrator, all passers-by run to hug and kiss him, but his soul is plunged into a deep erotic dream in which he sees how "the sun hugs the moon."

(...) I was strolling down the avenues used by chariots of love and the chariots of love came down running, like armies of countless warriors, with banners and flags fluttering in the wind, and behind them, the chariots of love, one after the other, and at the head of all, the love of my soul, the general of the army, "outstanding among ten thousand" (Song of Songs 5:10).

---

14 Translation by Segal 2001: 142.

15 The "Book of Tales" has not yet been translated in its entirety, but Spanish translations of some chapters are available: chapters 4 (Alba Cecilia 2008: 291–311), 6 (Díez Macho 1952: 39–45), and 7 (Navarro 1982).

16 For instance, in l. 77, in a quotation from *Genesis*.

When they saw me, they ran to meet me, hugged me and kissed me and, then, my soul fell asleep. And it dreamed that the sun was hugging the heart of the moon [...]
And he sang his poem saying:
"I slept but my heart was awake" (Song of Songs 5:2)
And I heard the voice of my beloved calling me:
My beloved, wake up,
Come with your beloved and rest.
When I heard it, my heart trembled,
"And could no longer control myself" (Ge 45:1)[17]

This erotic dream of the soul makes the heart "angry and agitated in his chamber." Consequently, the heart locks up in this chamber both the soul and the narrator, so that they become invisible to the intellect, "the general of love."

In the next scene, the soul looks out the window "to see the deer, bright as the sun," and then, dressed in its finest clothes and accompanied by its maids, goes up to an upper chamber, where "the deer of his love" appears to it. While the soul is dazzled by the light of its lover's face, the lover gets angry at the soul for not having come to welcome it and have remained hidden, causing him great pain and anguish. Then the soul "prostrated itself to its lover, began to mourn and begged him saying" that it was the heart's fault and asks, "can, perchance, a man live without a heart?" (l. 60). However, the lover leaves, and the soul is left "shrouded in bitterness of separation."

In the third scene, the wily heart makes the soul believe that the narrator was the one who caused the separation of the lovers. The soul, therefore, refuses to talk to him. At this point, the narrator Jacob awakens from his sleep and implores the soul be reconciled with him "as is customary among humans"; but this offends the soul even further, as the soul considers itself far superior to man.

In the next scene, the heart, irritated by the arrogance of the soul, becomes the defender of the narrator. Heart admits the superiority of the soul, as well as its beauty and purity, but reminds it that:

"If your origins and the origins of your origins are lofty, there are others that are loftier (...) and if you were not resting on your earthly body, you would be hidden (...) you are mine in the presence of God and I am your anointed; Why do you offend me and despise me?" (l. 100)

Upon hearing this speech, the narrator takes the soul's side and accompanies it in its quest for the "general of love" who lives in the Garden of Delight, whose owner is Wisdom. The soul finally joins the narrator, and the story concludes with the soul giving a philosophical speech on the creation of the world.

---

17 All translations from the *Sefer ha-Mešalim* are the author's own.

In this story the relationship between soul and body is presented in Neo-platonic terms, and expressed in the form of an erotic story with all the typical elements of the genre: a beautiful lady who hides from her beloved, rivals (heart, wisdom) that prevent the meeting of lovers, jealousy, anger, lust, crying... The purpose of the tale is, as the author himself states at the beginning of the chapter, to entertain the reader:

I composed the story of the intellect / as a (tale) of love to amuse
Now, read it and enjoy / its delights, which are plentiful!

This idea is repeated in the poem that closes the story:

The story of the intellect concludes here. / It was composed as a poem of love
Think of it kindly, my friend, / and do not consider its defects.

2.1.4 Among the debates between body and soul we should also include the work of Yom Tob Soriano, *Milḥemet ha-ebarim* ("disputation between the members").[18] There is little information on this author, whose name appears in the form of an acrostic in this poem. He seems to have lived in the fifteenth century in the city of Soria. Written in rhymed prose, the poem contains a dispute between members of the body (including the soul) who each tries to defend that its function is the most important. The soul participates in the dispute as one of the members of the body, not only because without soul there is no life, but also because soul is, just like them, responsible for the actions of humankind.

This debate shows many similarities with a midrash story in which the king of Persia, at the end of his days, sets off to find a drug that could keep him alive. After having overcome many an obstacle in his quest, all the members of his body, except the soul, argue over which one has contributed more to the success of the enterprise. In the end, language is the winner.[19]

In Soriano's debate, the members of the human body, aware of its value and virtue, start a debate to determine which one is superior and should therefore be recognized by the others as the lord of all of them. The head, hands, heart, legs and soul speak in turn. In the end, God intervenes declaring His omnipotence; He is the creator of all beings, who orders their death and can resuscitate them. All the body members unanimously declare that God is their Lord (Klein 2007: 123–26).

---

18 Haberman 1936 and van Bekkum 1991: 89.
19 *Midrash Tehillim* to Psalms 39:2, see Haberman 1936 and van Bekkum 1991: 89.

2.2 Debates between Arms and Letters

One the most common types of debates in Medieval Arabic literature is the debate between Arms and Letters.[20] In medieval Spanish Hebrew literature, this type of debate is represented by three major works: two of them are sections of larger works, whereas another is an independent composition. The earliest example of a debate between the arms and the letters in Spain can be found in the *Risalat al Sayf wa-l-Qalam* (Epistle on Sword and Pen), composed by Cordoban poet Ahmad ibn Burd al-Asgar around 1040.[21] The introductory verses stress the importance of both arms and letters:

> *Because sword and pen[22] are two torches that guide him who, in the middle of the night, pursues glory, and two ladders leading to the stars for him who seeks the highest honors (...) they rivaled in praising themselves and sought merit, disputing it with haughtiness and pretending each that its arrow was the winning one.*[23]

Sword and Pen present arguments based on antitheses: Pen represents the truth against the injustice of Sword, justice against its violence, Pen's humble origins against Sword's noble cradle; Pen's nudity (the bare cane) against the luxurious garments (sheath, precious stones) of Sword. In sum, the intellectual, internal strength of writing is opposed to the physical, external strength of the sword, each representing one social class competing for preeminence: poets and court scribes against rulers and soldiers.

The debate ends in a draw: it is ruled that the two contenders are equally important for the good governance of the court, so they regain their sanity and stop fighting. "What an ugly thing is that our affects walk apart and our ideas are discordant, when God had united us in such noble friendship!" They then unite to sing the praises of king Muyahid of Denia, an accomplished soldier and patron of literature:

---

20 See the seminal study by van Gelder 1987.

21 A translation and study can be found in de la Granja 1976: 3–44.

22 Already in the early Abbasid era, literary praises of the pen started to gain popularity. Andalusian poets incorporated many of their images into their own compositions. I. Levin collects and translates fragments of the major Arab poets from the ninth and tenth centuries such as Abu Tamamand Al Mutanabbi in Levin 1977 (in Hebrew).

23 The following translations from the *Risalat al Sayf wa-l-Qalam* are based on the translation of de la Granja 1976: 3–44.

> *He has put us both on the same footing in his days of war and peace, and with you he has gone beyond peace and with me beyond violence, and he did not spare you until he had attained his desire and did not neglect me until he found his love.*

2.2.1 Chapter XL of Yehudah al Harizi's *Sefer Taḥkemoni* is a "Battle of Sword and Pen for Mastery of Men."[24] This time, the scene is set at the home of the narrator Heman the Ezraḥite, who tells how, in a night of insomnia, was visited by a traveler dressed in rags, whom he recognized as his "teacher and friend" Ḥever the Kenite. Having Ḥever eaten everything that was served, he started to recite poems: "now when he could gorge no more, he began to display his wisdom's store," whereupon the narrator "seized scroll and pen to set his baubles down." But, as soon as he starts writing, his pen breaks twice, so he throws it away. Ḥever then berates him to treat so a blessed object, chosen by God, and begins to tell a story in which the scribes of the king and the generals of his armies discuss their respective preeminence. After a verbal dispute between them, the objects themselves (the pen and the sword) take the floor and start praising themselves and mocking the rival:

> *Then the Sword and Pen spoke, giving stroke for stroke. Said the Sword, I am the warrior's might and creed, eagle and lion I feed. (...) Then the Pen answered, saying, I am the prophet who dwells in Wisdom's tent, Jacob upright and excellent: he who clasps me tight grasps true delight.*[25]

The arguments pleaded by either litigant are not entirely new. In fact, as mentioned above, the author, Judah Al Harizi, had translated the *maqāma*s of Al Hariri of Basra and was well versed in Arabic language and culture. Consequently, he uses many of the literary images that had previously been introduced by Hispanic Arabic poets, such as the strength of the sword and the terror it inspires, and the humble beginnings and fragility of pen. All this is, however, furnished with a generous amount of Biblical quotations.

As was the case of the *Risala* of Ibn Burd, there is no clear outcome in the present poem, although the superiority of the pen seems to be implied in its last plea. The narrator intervenes after pen's last speech, praising his friend's eloquence and copying his words down with a pen, thus closing the debate.

2.2.2 Pen is also the winner of the debate between Pen and Sword in the fourth chapter of the *Sefer ha-Mešalim* of Jacob ben Eleazar, entitled "[Debate be-

24 del Valle 1988: 263–266 and Segal 2001: 302–306 (the latter is followed here).
25 Translation from Segal 2001: 304.

tween Pen and Sword], the Sword is defeated and listens to questions of ethics and philosophy from the mouth of the pen."[26]

This text is a composition of about two hundred lines in rhymed prose with intercalated poems. It has three clearly differentiated parts: the first is an allegorical introduction that situates the story in an age where "the generation of fools grew and multiplied," to the extent that it cornered Wisdom. Wisdom had to remain hidden in caves until a new king, named "eloquent prophet," a lover of science and poetry, rose to the throne, restored wisdom, and persecuted the fools. The narrator, who is the protagonist of the events, describes his encounter with Wisdom, a young maiden "who knows no man," and whom he marries.

The second part of the poem, which contains the actual discussion, is introduced rather abruptly: "When Wisdom went to the study house in the company of her husband [...] she saw two men fighting." These two men will be the main characters of the *maqāma:* "one was a brave warrior; his face was like a lion's, he wore a sword fastened to his hips." The other had nothing but a humble cane in his hand; however, he accepted the warrior's challenge. These two contestants are immediately replaced by instruments that represent them, and which start praising their own virtues. The arguments presented by the pen follow closely the topics and motifs introduced by the previous generations of poets, and in particular by Yehudah Al-Harizi. Thus, the sword mocks the pen for its humble origins and for its weakness:

> *How can the pen boast among the reeds, if it is just the same? (...) Once uprooted, it loses its scent, consistency and green color, and becomes yellow and negligible. If it is not sharpened, its body swells like a wineskin; it is thanks to the sword, who sharpens its tip, that it has a heart.*[27]

The pen, on the other hand, defends itself from these attacks by accepting its humble cradle and reproaching the sword for its lack of wisdom and for its origins:

> *If I tell you how you were born, that will not contribute to your glory: remember your birth, and do not forget: iron comes from dust.*

Sword then boasts of its strength:

26 Translation and study in Alba Cecilia 2008: 291–314.
27 Translations are the author's own.

A sword is the ornament of kings, the servant of the princes and the protector of the wanderers; it revives the one who wields it and is aid against its enemies; if my enemies pay no attention to me, they will be chopped off.

Pen reproaches the violence and injustice that Sword brings and urges it to learn from Pen's words. Pen recites a poem, the final one, which convinces Sword:

I am strong and have marks of my strength,
My enemy is terrified by my mouth's saliva,
Because, though low in height, is it not true that
The edge of my mouth reaches to the far corners of the country?
I am Wisdom, I dwell together with Cunning;
My mouth will reveal to you hidden secrets
And will inform you of what was before,
But what will happen, I do not know.

Sword then declares itself defeated and asks to be instructed by Pen.

Here begins the text's third part, which consists of some sort of philosophical-theosophical treatise on the unicity of God and on His qualities. These qualities are explained by Pen, who humbly recognizes that God alone is the owner of true Wisdom. The debate ends with Sword's acknowledgment that Wisdom is superior to everything else, since, as Qohelet states, *Wisdom makes one wise person more powerful than ten rulers in a city* (Qo 7:19) and *Wisdom is better than weapons of war* (Qo 9:18).

2.2.3 The third exemplar of the debates between Pen and Sword considered here is Sem Tob Ardutiel's *Debate between Pen and Scissors* (Nini and Fruchtman 1980), one of the works that the famous author of *Moral Proverbs,* Don Santo de Carrión, composed in Hebrew. It dates to the first half of the 14th century, and is different from all previous Hebrew debates in that it is an independent unit, and not part of a larger work. It was composed following the same literary technique of the above-discussed poems, i. e. in rhymed prose with intercalated poems. The text is written in first person, as an autobiography, whence its secondary title: *Ma'ase ha-Rav* (Tale of the Rabbi). For this reason, some scholars have interpreted it as an allegorical story related to the socio-political context of the author's time.[28] The debate is divided into four parts:
(1) Debate between the author and his pen.
(2) Dialogue between the author and the scissors
(3) Debate between scissors and pen
(4) Denouement in the presence of a judge.

28 See, for instance, Shepard 1978, Colahan 1979, Einbinder 1994, and Zackin 2008.

The action is set in the author's home, on "a cold winter day" in which everyone remains locked in their houses. In the absence of friends with whom to chat, he decides to spend the day writing and starts to compose a eulogy of Pen, in which he compares it with the staff of Moses, "whoever has pen and ink has enough, since they are worth more than all peers." Many of the images in praise of the pen were already classic in the Andalusian poems: "it knows my thoughts without me revealing them and shapes them; it hears every secret without having ears; it perceives everything hidden without having eyes" (Nini and Fruchtman 1980: 41–42) But there are also some new and highly complex images, such as the comparison of a paper with a valley and the pen with the cloven hooves of an ox plowing it: "with its footsteps it traces a path, plowing the paper as a valley with its foot, like the cloven hoof of an ox" (*ibid.* 45). This image of the cloven hoof evokes, on the one hand, the tip of the pen, split in two; on the other, it is a clear reference to animals that, according to the Bible, are ritually clean.

In order to write down these praises of the pen, the author tries to wet the tip in the ink, but the ink is frozen and the pen gets blunt. This causes a debate between the author and his pen, whom the author accuses of being a traitor and ungrateful for having abandoned him after having been so generously praised:

> *Is this my reward for having honored you, and for having called you the rod of the Lord, for having praised you seven times a day, for having given to you the highest and most noble praise of mouth and tongue? (...) Where is the rock that you penetrated? For is it not said that "a soft tongue breaketh the bone?" (Proverbs 25: 15) And Moses, did he not stretch forth his hand and raise it up to strike twice with his rod, and did "he not cleave the rock and did not the waters gush out?" (Isaiah 48:21) But you turned back in the face of soaked chaff. What would you have done against resistance? Your teeth bit into absorbent cotton and your vigor fled from you. "If thou goest limp in the day of need thy strength is small indeed" (Deuteronomy 34:7) And my complaint be upon my soul and my violence upon my head because I chose you from among all my friends and companions to be daily delight. You put my hopes to shame, and now you offer me naught but vain emptiness. This is the reward of one who abandons the cyprus and seeks refuge under a worthless bramble. "The staff upon which I lean is a broken reed" (Isaiah 36:6).*[29]

Pen responds to the author's accusations and invites him to press hard into the inkwell with his finger; however, when he does so, he gets hurt.

In the second section, which begins at this point (Nini and Fruchtman 1980: 53–60), the author appears silent, staring out the window of his room: he has lost all hope of spending that day pleasantly writing. Suddenly, he hears a

29 Nini and Fruchtman 1980: 46–47. Translation from Shepard 1978: 82, 89–90.

voice urging him to cut out letters and thus compose a text. Then a dialogue begins between the author and his scissors, who praise themselves. The author is pleased to have found a substitute for the pen and decides to use the scissors. After he does so, the scissors begin to boast, despising pen and ink, and initiate their own debate, in which the sword —a representative of the noble warrior – is replaced by the humble, though arrogant, scissors (*ibid.* 61–72).

Scissors boast of the magnificence of the letters produced by them, whereas the work of Pen is as superficial as the colors it produces. Pen pleads its case against Scissors, which, it claims, are very useful to shear and cut hair and nails, but useless for writing for its slowness: "Before concluding a word, one has already forgotten the beginning!"; "While you write a line, I can write the books of Daniel and Ezra!" (*ibid.* 1980: 63). Whereas in the debates of Sword and Pen, Pen typically reproaches Sword for the violence it exerts on men, in this debate, Pen reproaches Scissors for the violence they exert on the paper, which is destroyed beyond repair. Pen claims to slide affectionately on the paper's surface, touching only a part of it.

To end the discussion, Pen suggests that they seek an impartial judge who can rank all household utensils by their usefulness (*ibid.* 73–76). The judge thus decides on the outcome, a rare fact in debates of Semitic origin, but quite frequent in the Castilian debates. The judge puts each instrument in its proper place: he writes with the pen and cuts nails, beard and mustache with the scissors. The triumph of the pen is total, as well as the defeat of the scissors, who are unable to speak. To celebrate his victory pen throws a party "in honor of the day in which the Lord saved him from the hands of its enemies."

The debate ends with the intervention of the narrator, no longer as a fictional character, but as the author Sem Tob ben Isaac, who claims to have composed this satire in the month of Tammuz of the year 5105 (July 1345) (*ibid.* 76). At the beginning of the poem the author had already explained his intention to compose a work with cutout letters "with the blade of a sword with two edges," and had highlighted the beauty of these letters, "more beautiful than brocades and garlands, and than the most beautiful girls."

2.3 Debates on Various Topics

2.3.1 Wine and Water: In Yosef ben Meir ibn Zabarra's *Sefer Saʾasuʾim* ("Book of Delight")[30] (Barcelona, 12th century) there is a debate between two diners on the excellences of water and wine (chapter I). After having attacked each other, they reach a compromise: both are good; "A little is helpful, but much is harmful."

Chapter XXVII of *Sefer Taḥkemoni* is a "Praise and reproach of wine";[31] the narrator, tired of leading an abstemious life, joins a group of young drinkers who praise wine. An old man berates them for not having mentioned the best qualities of the wine, and begins to praise wine himself for its color, its flavor, the effects that it produces and even the glass from which it is drunk. The young people encourage him to go on further and list negative aspects of wine. He complies so well that "cups were emptied with assiduity as many swore off wine in perpetuity" (Segal 2001: 237). When the narrator asks the old man his name, he immediately recognizes his old friend Ḥever the Kenite.

2.3.2 Poetry and Prose: Mosheh Ibn Ezra (11th/12th centuries) mentions in his work on poetics some Arabic disputations that dealt with the superiority of poetry over prose (Abumalham Mas 1985/1986: II 67–70). In the second chapter of the *Sefer ha-Mešalim* of Jacob ben Eleazar there is a dispute between poetry and prose, "About the qualities of both, which ends with the victory of the poet" (David 1992/1993: 23–27). The poem begins with a discussion at a meeting of lawyers: one defends prose and accuses poetry of being based on lies and stupidity; another praises poetry and its rules. Seeing himself defeated, the defender of the prose leaves the meeting.

2.3.3 Wisdom and Wealth (*Milḥemet ha-Ḥokhma we-ha-ʿoser*) by Yehudah ibn Sabbetay (late 12th century); it is a satirical work written in 1214 in honor of Todros ha-Levi Abulafia of Burgos; it discusses the advantages and qualities of wisdom and wealth, which are alternatively presented by two knights (Salvatierra 2014).

2.3.4 Dispute between Winter and Summer: a poem by Abraham ibn Ezra (1092–1167)[32] appears to be the oldest text that addresses this issue.

2.3.5 Day and Night: This is the title of the XXXIX *maqāma* of Al Harizi's *Taḥkemoni*;[33] the narrator sets the scene at the Biblical place of Rimon Perets

30 Forteza Rey 1983: 67–70. A translation and commentary of the book, with a selection of texts, can be found in Abrahams 1912: 9–61 and Schippers 1999.

31 Segal 2001: 233–237 ("Of the Cup's Joys and Other Allows").

32 It is poem No. 122 of Abraham ibn Ezra's 'Diwan' (see van Bekkum 1991). See the edition in Egers 1886.

33 Segal 2001: 298–301 ("The Debate of Day and Night: Whose the Greater Might and Delight").

at a meeting of scholars, in which one of them, who turns out to be the narrator's friend Ḥever, tells how, during the summer solstice, Day "put on the cloak of pride and did the Night deride" (Segal 2001: 298).[34] After discussion between the two, Night recognizes the superiority of Day.

2.3.6 Old and Young Man (or Religion and Philosophy). I will refer, in the last place, to one of the "dialogues" that appear in the apologetic work of Yishaq ben Yosef Pulgar (first half of 14th century), entitled *Ezer ha-Dat* ("The Support of Faith"). As in the previous examples, Pulgar uses also rhymed prose.[35] In the second treatise of the work, he deals with the subject, by then already old, of how to harmonize Philosophy and Faith. This topic takes the shape of a debate between an old man, representing the traditional religion, and a young man, a philosopher. The narrator sets the scene on a journey that he undertakes with the aim of finding the truth. After leaving his city, "the wind carries him on its wings to Jerusalem." Walking through the streets of the city, he sees a crowd gathered around two individuals: a tall old man, wrapped in his prayer shawl, and a handsome young man, whose "countenance shone like pearls, his complexion like roses and whose lips were of a beautiful red color." Both discuss life after death (*Olam ha-ba*): in the old man's opinion, such life is reserved to him who observes the Torah's commandments, and it is not attainable for heretics who, like the young man, read books of Greek philosophy and other non-Jewish works. The young man replies angrily by mocking his opponent's lack of intelligence despite his advanced age. According to him, religion does not give wisdom, but serves a social need: it is necessary for the safety of the community, while philosophy alone aims to discover truth. As here seems to be no clear winner, and the discussion heats up, with continuous insults from the young to the old man, the community decides to go to the king of Israel and to ask him to intervene and pronounce a verdict. The solution is conciliatory: "both paths are needed to reach perfection: the religious observance and theoretical knowledge. Wisdom cannot exist outside of the Torah. A religious person without philosophy in his soul is lost because, as the Mishnah says (*Abbot* 2:5), the ignorant (*ʿam ha-arets*) cannot be just (*ḥasid*); the Torah is therefore a prelude and a preparation for bringing the intellect from potential to action, and for joining it and joining [the Active Intellect]. All who rise to this level shall reach eternity, and this is the afterlife (*Olam ha-ba*)."

I would like to conclude stressing once again the idea that, although Spanish Hebrew debates, especially those from the 12th and 13th centuries, follow the top-

---

34 See also del Valle 1988: 260–262.
35 Levinger 1984. See Haliva 2015.

ics and formal conventions of Arabic debates, their dependence on Hebrew models is also clear. This Hebrew identity stems, first, from the frequent insertion of Biblical and Rabbinic quotations. Secondly, it comes from the clear dependence of the poetic imagery upon the texts' Jewish religious context. This adaptation is particularly clear in Sem Tob de Carrion's "Debate between the Pen and the Scissors," riddled with images from and references to Rabbinical *Halakha* and *Haggada*.

It is interesting to note also that the Spanish-Hebrew debates draw from their own tradition: their arguments, motifs and images would be reused by Jewish authors of later centuries. This is the case, for example, of the "Debate between body and soul" of Ibn Gabirol (11th century), which became a source of inspiration for the "Dialoge between soul and body, intellect and desire" in chapter XIII of the *Sefer Taḥkemoni* of Al-Harizi (13th century), as well as for the "Allegorical tale about the soul and the body" in the first chapter of Jacob ben Eleazar's *Sefer ha-Mešalim* (13th century) and for Yom Tov Soriano's *Disputation between the members* (*Milḥemet ha-ebarim*, 15th century).

Bibliography

Abrahams, Israel. 1912. *The Book of Delight and Other Papers*. Philadelphia: The Jews Publication Society of America.

Abumalham Mas, Montserrat. 1985/1986. *Moše Ibn 'Ezra, Kitāb al-Muḥāḍara wal-Muḏākara*. Madrid: CSIC.

Alba Cecilia, Amparo. 1993. Debate de la espada y el cálamo. *Proyección Histórica de España en sus Tres Culturas: Castilla y León, América y el Mediterráneo III*: 7–14. Ed. E. Lorenzo Sanz. Valladolid.

Alba Cecilia, Amparo. 1997. Espada vs. cálamo: debates hispánicos medievales. *Thélème* 11: 47–56.

Alba Cecilia, Amparo. 2008. El "Debate del cálamo y la espada," de Jacob ben Eleazar de Toledo. *Sefarad* 68: 291–314.

Alborg, Juan Luis. 1972. *Historia de la literatura española*. Madrid.

Alvar, Manuel. 1974. *Antigua poesía española lírica y narrativa (siglos XI-XIII)*. México: Porrúa.

Batiouchkof, Theodor. 1891. Le Débat de l'Âme et du Corps. *Romania* 20: 1–55.

Bossy, Michel-André. 1976. Medieval Debates of Body and Soul. *Comparative Literature* 28: 144–163.

Colahan, Clark. 1979. Santob's Debate: Parody and Political Allegory. *Sefarad* 39: 87–107 and 265–398.

David, Yonah. 1992/1993. *The Love Stories of Jacob ben Eleazar. Critical Edition with Introduction and Commentary*. Tel Aviv. [In Hebrew]

de la Granja, Fernando. 1976. *Maqāmas y risalas andaluzas. Traducciones y estudios*. Madrid: Hiperión.

del Valle, Carlos. 1988. *Judá ben Shelomo Al-Harizi, Las asambleas de los sabios*. Murcia: Universidad de Murcia.

Díez Macho, Alejandro. 1952. *La novelística hebraica medieval*. Barcelona.

Egers, Jacob. 1886. *Diwân des Abraham ibn Esra mit seiner Allegorie Hai ben Mekiz*. Berlin.

Einbinder, Susan. 1994. Pen and Scissors: A Medieval Debate. *Hebrew Union College Annual* 65: 261–276.

Forteza Rey, Marta. 1983. *Yosef ben Meir ben Zabarra. Libro de los entretenimientos*. Madrid: Editora nacional.

Franchini, Enzo. 2001. *Los debates literarios en la Edad Media*. Arcadia de las letras 9.Madrid: Laberinto.

García Solalinde, Antonio. 1933. La disputa del alma y el cuerpo. *Hispanic Review* 1: 196–207.

Haberman, Abraham Me'ir. 1936. Milḥemet ha-ʾAvārīm le-Yōm Ṭōv Sōryānō. *Yedīʿōt ha-Mākhōn le-Ḥēqer ha-Shīrāh ha-ʿIvrīt* III: 133–150. [In Hebrew]

Haliva, Rachel. 2015. *Isaac Polqar – A Jewish Philosopher or a Philosopher and a Jew? A Study of the Relationship between Philosophy and Religion in Isaac Polqar's ʿEzer ha-Dat [In Support of the Law] and Teshuvat Apikoros [A Response to the Heretic]*. Unpublished PhD dissertation: McGill University.

Hanford, James Holly. 1913. The Mediaeval Debate Between Wine and Water. *Publications of the Modern Language Association* 28: 315–367.

Kastner, Leon Emile. 1905. Débat du corps et de l'âme in provençal. *Revue des langues romanes* 48: 30–64.

Klein, Joel T. 2007. *Body-Soul-Spirit: Journey with Sages Across Stages Through the Ages Into Holistic Therapy*. New York: iUniverse.

Levin, Israel. 1977. The Pen and the Rider. in *A.M. Habermann Jubilee Volume. Studies in Medieval Hebrew Literature*, ed. Z. Malachi. Jerusalem. [In Hebrew]

Levinger, Jacob. 1984. *Ezer hadat*. Tel Aviv. [in Hebrew]

McFie, Helen. 1981. *The Mediaeval Debate Between Wine and Water in the Romance Languages: Tradition and Transformation*. Unpublished PhD dissertation: University of Pennsylvania.

Menéndez Pidal, Ramón. 1914. Elena y María. *Revista de Filología* 1: 52–96.

Menéndez Pidal, Ramón. 1919. *Poema de Mío Cid y otros monumentos de la primitiva poesía española*. Madrid.

Menéndez Pidal, Ramón. 1948. *Tres poetas primitivos*. Buenos Aires: Espasa Calpe Argentina.

Navarro, Ángeles. 1982. Un cuento de Jacob ben Eleazar de Toledo. *El Olivo* 15: 49–82.

Nini, Yehudah, and Maya Fruchtman. 1980. *Maʾase ha-Rav: Milḥemet ha-ʾEt ve-ha-Misparayim*. Tel Aviv: Tel Aviv University.

Reinink, Gerrit Jan, and Herman Vanstiphout. 1991. *Dispute Poems and Dialogues in the Ancient and Mediaeval Near East. Forms and Types of Literary Debates in Semitic and Related Literatures*. Orientalia Lovaniensia Analecta 42. Leuven: Peeters.

Salvatierra, Aurora. 2014. "*Milḥemet ha-Ḥokhma we-ha-ʿoser de Yehudah Ibn Šabbetay:* Propuesta de lectura, edición y traducción" *Miscelánea de Estudios Árabes y Hebreos, sec. Hebreo*, 63: 243–283.

Schippers, Arie. 1999. Ibn Zabara's Book of Delight (Barcelona, 1170) and the Transmission of Wisdom From East to West. *Frankfurter Judaistische Beiträge* 26: 149–161.

Schippers, Arie. 2002. The Hebrew *maqāma* (Chapter 8.1–8.1.8.3). Pp. 302–327 in *Maqāma: A History of a Genre*, ed. J. Hämeen-Anttila. Diskurse der Arabistik 5. Harrassowitz: Wiesbaden.

Segal, David Simha. 2001. *Judah Alḥarizi, The Book of Taḥkemoni: Jewish Tales from Medieval Spain.* London, Portland: Littman Library of Jewish Civilization.

Shepard, Sanford. 1978. *Shem Tov: His World and His Words.* Miami: Ediciones Universal.

Tavani, Giuseppe. 1964. Il dibattito sul chierico e il cavaliere nella tradizione mediolatina e volgare. *Romanistisches Jahrbuch* 15: 51–84.

van Bekkum, Wout Jacques. 1991. Observations on the Hebrew Debate in Medieval Europe. Pp. 77–90 in *Dispute Poems and Dialogues in the Ancient and Medieval Near East*, ed. G. J. Reinink and H. L. J. Vanstiphout. Orientalia Lovaniensia Analecta 42. Louvain: Peeters.

van Gelder, Geert Jan. 1987. The Conceit of Pen and Sword: On An Arabic Literary Debate. *Journal of Semitic Studies* 9: 329–360.

Yarden, Dov. 1971. *The Liturgical Poetry of Rabbi Shelomoh ibn Gabirol.* Jerusalem. [In Hebrew]

Zackin, Jane Robin. 2008. *A Jew and his Milieu: Allegory, Polemic, and Jewish Thought in Sem Tob's Proverbios Morales and Ma'aseh Ha Rav.* Unpublished PhD dissertation: The University of Texas at Austin.

Firuza Abdullaeva-Melville*

14 Debate in Iranian Literary Culture[1]

The origins of the debate genre in the history of Persian literature are most likely related to the shared literary cultures of ancient Mesopotamia, although the earliest surviving dispute belongs to the pre-Islamic period, specifically to the reign of the Parthian and Sasanian dynasties. The Arab invasion of the 7th century changed the direction of its development by adopting, adapting and absorbing the features of Arabic court poetry, which had a strong influence of pre-Islamic Bedouin traditions that carried the elements of much earlier mixed Semitic traditions. Such a fertile liaison produced a most impressive fruit, which spread its seeds not only among the neighbouring literatures of the Muslim East, but has survived until our days although in a different form. It should not be a surprise that pre-election campaigns organised by various political parties in contemporary Iran use not only the same literary paradigm in producing their propagandistic texts, but even the term, *monazere*, which is also used for other kinds of discussion, not necessarily scholarly.

Enrique Jiménez (2017) in his comprehensive comparative survey of the history of the genre suggests a chart according to which the earliest and the only known pre-Islamic Iranian disputation, *The Goat and the Assyrian Tree*, could have its origin linked to the Sumerian tradition, moderated by Akkadian.[2] It seems that we would need to add one more moderator, Old Persian, as the only surviving pre-Islamic Iranian tenzone seems to have its roots traced back to the Achaemenid period.[3] The debate poetry in the New Persian language, especially that by Ahmad b. ʻAlī Asadī Ṭūsī (999 – 1072), had a much more complicated cross-cultural influence.[4]

---

* University of Cambridge.

1 This essay is based on two my previous studies of the genre: Abdullaeva 2009 and Abdullaeva 2011.

2 According to Areg Bayandur, the text of *The Goat and Palm Tree tenzone* was reconstructed on the basis of the Sumero-Akkadian paradigm using the contemporaneous Middle Persian sources (Bayandur 2013 [unpublished], I thank Artur Ambartsumyan for sharing with me the abstract of this dissertation). However, this does not exclude the idea that one of the originals was compiled in Parthian, and the attempt to drastically refurbish it was a part of the Sassanian anti-Parthian propaganda campaign, which resulted in the absence of any traces of the Parthians in the *shahnama* ('royal chronicle') texts of the pre-Islamic period.

3 See my discussion below in the section on *The Goat and the Babylonian Tree*, and Chunakova 2001: 20.

4 Jiménez 2017: 125 – 153, especially p. 150, fig. 6.

https://doi.org/10.1515/9781501510274-014

Literary debates, compared with the situation in the Ancient world, were not as popular as one might expect in New Persian literature, and when they did enter the palace from the bazaar, they immediately acquired the status of high literature, albeit not in its original form. When it appeared at court, it was impregnated with the features of another genre, which was dominant during the entire Classical period: namely the *qasīda*, with a very well developed panegyric part.

In other words, the marriage of the old Semito-Iranian *tenzone* and the young Arabic *qasīda* resulted in a baby whose nature was inherited from his young (Arabic) mother, enhanced by a rather strong pedigree of the old (pre-Islamic Iranian) father. As a result, we have a *qasīda*, which is formally organized as a debate and only in the finale reveals its 'qasidian' features. *Munāzara* had also a younger and slightly more gentrified sister serving mainly at court – *lughz* (riddle) although it would also have a strong link with its folklore roots. Its normally long introduction aimed to puzzle the reader/addressee elegantly and its conclusion to dissolve the riddle, deciphering the *mamdūh* (dedicatee) in a powerful apotheosis.[5]

For two centuries, the Iranian literary tradition was cultivated in the fresh and fertile soil of the 'green house' of the New Persian language under the lid of the Arabic linguistic and more generally cultural domination. When the lid was lifted, the genre of debate had the hybrid seeds of self-destruction, whereas the seeds of the other genre (ode) was more popular and sustainable, and later devoured disputation.[6]

1 Persian *munāzara* in the Context of the Debate Literature of the East

The evolution of the genre went through two main stages: the first evidence from antiquity in almost all languages of the Near and Middle East (Sumerian, Akkadian, Egyptian, Aramaic, Syriac, Middle Persian/Pahlavi, or Parthian, and Arabic) represents the debate between two sides. The range of opponents juxtaposed against each other does not have any visible restrictions: they could be different natural phenomena and seasons (summer and winter, months of the year),[7] the

5 One of the best examples is Manūchihrī's poetic puzzle of *Candle* dedicated to 'Unsūrī.

6 It would be fair to mention that the genre of *munāzara* has not disappeared without a trace. It still exists in Modern Persian literature, especially in poetry following the rules of *'arūz*.

7 Brock 1985. See more bibliography on this subject in van Gelder 1987 and *id.* in this volume.

same class of objects (ladder and staircase), or flora and fauna (goat and palm tree, as in the above-mentioned Parthian/Pahlavi text, or grain and sheep, as in the Sumerian one).[8] They could be different plants (rose and narcissus), animals (sheep and goat) or birds (owls and nightingales), or their combinations, i.e. birds contesting other types of animals (dogs and cockerels). They could be countries or geographical places (Egypt and Syria, East and West), or even more abstract ideas, like human features (miserliness and generosity), or literature (prose and poetry), and parts of the human body (mouth and anus). One can see no particular difference between the behaviour of personified birds, flowers, animals or objects and human beings, in the debates between the lovers of girls and boys, or blacks and whites.

1.1 Pen, or Sword – Who is Mightier?

Literary debate existed in Iranian court culture in other capacities. One of them was to display eloquence as a verbal part of the battle skills during the ceremonial parley before the knightly single combat. Such skills of *bazm-u razm* ('[art of] feasting and fighting') were among compulsory parts of the chivalric code of a properly educated young mediaeval Iranian aristocrat.[9] This could be the reason why one of the most popular pair of contestants in a standard debate would be the Pen and the Sword. The idea that both skills are attributes of one educated nobleman is expressed in the finale of Asadī Tusī's Fifth *munāzara*, who as a real peace maker suggests that they should not fight but reconcile in one person, especially if he is a king, or a patron:

> *A nobleman whose courage increased danger [for enemies] and justice*
> *By means of a shining sword and a gold-scattering pen*[10]

Asadī's contemporary, Qatrān Tabrīzī (1009–1072) was writing in a similar manner:

8 See the editions by Alster and Vanstiphout 1987, Cunningham and Black 2000, Mittermayer 2019.

9 One of the most detailed manuals of such kind is the Mirror for Princes, compiled by the Ziyarid King Kaykāvūs for his son in 1082: Qābūs b. Vashmgīr 1082 [1951]. This book could be a continuation of the pre-Islamic tradition, reflected in the Pahlavi text *The King and his Page* (Unvala 1921).

10 Asadī Tusī, *The Debate between the Iranian and the Arab*, Bodleian Library, Ms. Elliott 37, f. 236r.

There was always rivalry between the sword and the pen
Now they have united in the good fortune of the king.[11]

However, if contested, the pen is always superior to the sword, as allegedly stated by the greatest conqueror of all time, Alexander the Great.[12]

This could be another explanation for the ritual of public parley as part of a knightly single combat, which would be performed as a verbal rehearsal before the actual battle.[13] The weaponry of two knights was eloquence, their audience, apart from the opponent, was their soldiers and generals, to be inspired to victory. In some cases, such verbal debates could decide the outcome of the battle for both armies. This could be one of the reasons why, for example, the overwhelming majority of the battle illustrations of Firdousī's *Shahnama* would depict throughout the centuries the single combats of two noble knights in front of their armies (Fig. 1).

In the Arabic Bedouin tradition, this seems to be developed into a parley between the representatives of two tribes, tribal poets, mastering their skills in public before the battle. Gradually in the time of peace, these performances would move to the bazaar, where the poets would expect a rather similar reaction from their audience. The history of the genre shows that this is one of the most ancient surviving literary forms, which is witnessed by the literatures as early as those of Sumer and Babylon (Asmussen 1968).

The tradition of poetic competitions in the New Persian language was no less popular at the Persian courts, most likely, during 'two centuries of silence',[14] for which we do not have many written sources. However, by the start of the 'five centuries of glory'[15] there are plenty of evidence of such public contests between the court poets as a common royal entertainment. It seems that Sultan Mahmud (971–1030), having introduced at his court in Ghazna a regimented hierarchy of

11 Qatrān Tabrīzī [1362/1983]: 23.
12 Detailed bibliography in van Gelder 1987: 337 fn. 29.
13 Cf. F.B.J. Kuiper's idea of the ritual contests in the ancient Indian tradition in Kuiper 1960.
14 The term 'two centuries of silence', or in Persian 'do qarn-e sokut' (7th-9th cc. CE), was introduced by A. Zarrinkoub. *Two Centuries of Silence*, originally published in in 1957 in Tehran (Amir Kabir), also transl. into English by Paul Sprachman (Zarrinkoub 1957 [2017]). This is the period between the Arab invasion and the rise of the Samanid dynasty in Bukhara, on the most far-flung periphery of the Caliphate, where and when the New Persian language emerged as the written language of religion and administration but also literature and first of all poetry of the highest standards. For this reason, Rudaki, the chief poet of the Samanid court, was crowned with the title 'Adam of Poets' (i.e. the first among the [great] poets).
15 This is roughly the period identified as the Golden age of Persian poetry: 9th-15th centuries CE (between Rudaki and Jami).

Fig. 1: Parley between Human and Piran, attributed to Muhammad Qasim, Firdawsi, Shahnamah, Mashhad, 1648, Ms Holmes 151 (A/6), f. 331recto. Royal Collection Trust / © Her Majesty Queen Elizabeth II 2018

the highly populated guild of professional poets, only developed the idea of the poetic competitions at his *majlis*, while such tradition had already fully shaped during the reign of the Samanids in Bukhara (819 – 999).[16]

2 The Iconic Survivor: The Goat and the Babylonian (Assyrian) Tree

Compared with the views of the colleagues working with the Arabic material, there is little difficulty in tracing the appearance of the debate in Persian literature directly back to the pre-Islamic period, as witnessed by the only survivor of this period, the well-known *Buz ud Drakht-i Assurīk* ([The Debate between] the Goat and the Assyrian, or Babylonian/Date Palm Tree),[17] the poem[18] with some loan words of Parthian origin,[19] written in Book Pahlavi script (Henning 1950; Lazard 2006). The text is incomplete: both the beginning and the end (altogether about 120 verses) are missing (Tafażżolī 1995). It is possible that the surviving text is the Middle Persian version of a much earlier poem compiled in Old Persian (Chunakova 2001: 20), as witnessed in Strabo's *Geography:*

> 'The country produces larger crops of barley than any other country (bearing three hundredfold, they say), and its other needs are supplied by the palm tree; for this tree yields bread, wine, vinegar, honey, and meal; and all kinds of woven articles are supplied by that tree; and the bronze-smiths use the stones of the fruit instead of charcoal; and when soaked in water these stones are used as food for oxen and sheep which are being fattened. There is said to be a Persian song wherein are enumerated three hundred and sixty uses of the palm tree; and, as for oil, the people use mostly that of sesame, but this plant is rare in all other places'[20]

---

16 Nizami 'Aruzi Samarqandi 550-552/1155 – 1157 [1910]. English translation in Muḥammad 1919.

17 BNF Supplément Persan 1216; published facsimile by Blochet 1895. See the Russian translation of this tenzone by Chunakova 2001: 159 and Ambartsumian 2000. For an English translation, see Brunner 1980a and *id.* 1980b, see also Unvala 1923. See Brunner 1980a: 191 fn. 1 on the name of the tree. On its possible Akkadian precursor, *The debate between the Palm and the Tamarisk*, see Vogelzang 1991: 48 – 9 and Jiménez 2017: 133. On the possible influence of the *Debate between Palm and Vine*, a Babylonian text attested only in Hellenistic manuscripts, see Jiménez 2017: 282 – 83.

18 É. Benveniste was the first who identified the text as a poem, see Benveniste 1930. See also Lazard 2002/2003 and de Fouchécour 2005.

19 C. Bartholomae was the first who identified some of its vocabulary as Parthian, see Bartholomae 1922.

20 Jones 1930: 216. I am grateful to Artur Ambartsumyan for this reference. On this passage, see also Jiménez 2017: 133.

It is possible to guess that the Old Persian song was much longer as it had to include the 360 features of the palm tree, or perhaps this figure is just a metaphoric trope. It is notable that both Strabo and the author of the *tenzone* call it a song, which indicates its oral circulation (Chunakova 2001: 91 and 160).

If we compare two rather similar pieces, the Parthian/Pahlavi debate *The Goat and the Assyrian [Palm] Tree* and the Sumerian *The Sheep and the Grain,*[21] we will see that in the Sumerian version the priority shifts from the nomadic cattle breeders to the agricultural society: Grain's victory is legitimised and sanctioned by the supreme god Enki. On the contrary, in the Iranian debate it is still the Goat who overwhelms the Palm Tree. This can be either a witness of its even more ancient origin, or the increasing role of religion: the Goat's superiority is linked through her milk with the sacred objects, like *homa*, which was associated with a special drink prepared by the Zoroastrian priests to go into ecstatic trance during the religious ceremonies.

The contesting parties in this debate might have also represented the opposition between the two faiths, with the Goat representing Zoroastrianism and the Palm tree representing the pagan religions of Assyria and Babylonia, in which the cult of the tree formed an important part (Smith 1926/1928). However it is more likely that here we have the same manifestation of the contrast between pastoral life, personified by the Goat, and the agricultural life, symbolized by the Palm tree (Rūh-al-Amīnī 1369/1990) as in the Sumerian *Debate between Grain and Sheep.*

3 The Classical [New] Period

The question of the origin of the genre in Arabic and Persian literature would not be so complex if the two traditions had not been so much intertwined at the stage of the so-called early New or Classical period of their development. For Arabic, this period starts mostly with the beginning of the Muslim era, whereas for Persian it starts only with the "Renaissance" of Persian literary culture after 'two centuries of silence', or non-existence / other-existence under the lid of the Arabic linguistic and partial cultural domination, and the change of alphabet from Pahlavi to Arabographic.

The most crucial role in the formation of the debate (*munāzara)* genre in classical [New] Persian literatures was played by the court poets, among

21 Tafażżolī 1995: 548; editions in Alster and Vanstiphout 1987, Cunningham and Black 2000, Mittermayer 2019, and *ead.* in this volume.

whom Asadī Tūsī (ca. 999 – 1072/73), should be mentioned the first as it was his series of *munāzara* that became the earliest survivors. These poems are now in the unique manuscript of the *Anthology of Persian poetry* in the Bodleian Library.[22] This manuscript is remarkable for several reasons; one of them is that it contains the only copy of his so-called fifth *munāzara*,[23] the *Debate between the Arab and the Iranian*,[24] which has received a surprisingly mixed attention from the scholars – from deliberate neglect to exclusive interest.[25]

---

22 Bodleian Library Ms. Elliott 37, ff. 233r-234v, 236r. The title and the name of the author are not mentioned in the manuscript, but are identified by one of its previous owners, Sir Gore Ouseley, who wrote in Persian inside the front cover: *Daqā'iq al-Ash'ār* by 'Abd al-Wahhāb (Ethé 1889: no. 1333) suggests that the author could be 'Abd al-Wahhāb Bukhārī Dawlatābādī (d. 1190/ 1766), who compiled a *Tazkira-yi Bīnazīr*. In the chapter dedicated to the *Tadhkira-yi Bīnazīr*, Ahmad Gulchin Ma'ānī mentions the Bodleian manuscript as a *jung*, with reference to the copy of *Mu'nis al-Ahrār* by Muhammad b. Badr al-Jājarmī from the Tehran University library. He also mentions the opinion of Mirzā Muhammad Qazvinī, who thought that at least half of the Bodleian *Daqā'iq al-Ash'ār* was borrowed from the *Mu'nis al-Ahrār* (Golčin-Ma'āni 1348/ 1969: 200 – 201).

23 In the past, some doubt has been expressed about the identity of Asadī Tūsī, thought by Hermann Ethé to be two separate authors, father and son (Ethé 1882: 48 – 49). Constantin Chaykin, however, demonstrated that there was only one Asadī (Chaykin 1934: 119 – 161), and since then this has been the common opinion among scholars (de Blois 2004: 77 – 78, Khaleghi-Motlagh 1977). However, some (for example, F. Mojtabā'ī) still consider that there were two authors with the same name: Pourjavādī 2006: 99 fn. 11.

24 Ms. Elliott 37, ff. 233r-234v, 236r. Asadī Tūsī (ca. 1010 – ca. 1070) is known as the author of five debates: *Munāzara-yi rumh-u qous*, ('the Debate between Lance and Bow') and *Munāzara-yi āsmān-u zamīn* ('Debate between Heaven and Earth'), *Munāzara-yi musalmān-u gabr* ('Debate between the Muslim and the Zoroastrian'), *Munāzara bā 'Arab kunad ba fazl-i 'ajam* ('Debate between the Arab and the Iranian') and *Munāzara-yi Shab-u Ruz* ('Debate between Night and Day').

25 Both Ethé (1882: 48 – 135) and Hedāyat (1878: 110) did not include it in their editions of Asadī's *munāzaras*. Ethé published three Asadī's debates using the text of the Bodleian library, considering the debate under discussion the earliest one (Ethé 1882: 70). Reza Quli Khan's neglect might be due to the fact that the poem existed only in one copy, which he could consider to be rather suspicious. Bertels's supposition was that they both thought that the quality of the poem was not good enough to ascribe it to Asadī. E. Wagner followed Ethé in ignoring these two poems, though indicating no reason why he did so (Wagner 1993). Nevertheless, it then attracted special attention from C. Salemann and E. Bertels (Bertels 1988) and Dj. Khaleghi-Motlagh published his version of the full text together with the other four *munāzaras* (Khaleghi-Motlagh 1977). More recently, N. Pourjavadi published fragments of all Asadī's *munāzaras* (Pourjavādī 2006: 430, 444, 527, 627 – 632).

3.1 Asadī Tūsī's Debate between the Arab and the Iranian[26]

The poem is a typical contest between two parties which are represented in this poem by an Arab and an Iranian (*'ajam* generally means a non-Arab, but usually as it is here an Iranian), each of whom tries to prove their superiority, sometimes using the vocabulary which now would be styled 'politically incorrect'. In the very first *bayt* the poet introduces himself as the Iranian,[27] describing the situation as a real event:

> *Once upon a time I and several Arabs, fast and eloquent in speech*
> *Were at a party of a nobleman, happy and joyful from wine...*

Such promising start, when everyone was enjoying the conversation and music, however, suddenly (after several goblets of wine) takes a dangerous turn, when one of Arab companions suddenly exclaims: *'ajam chīst?! Fakhr ahl-i 'arab-rā rasad ay ablah-i nādān* – "What is Iranian? Glory belongs to Arabs only, you, ignorant idiot."

This declaration introduces a twenty-one-*bayt*-long monologue, in which the Arab contestant mentions all the advantages of his people, such as their religion, language, skills, crafts and features of national character in particular hospitality, courage and generosity.

The author reciprocates with a long soliloquy, consisting of 80 *bayts*, and invaluable information about all fields of human life from dress fashion to gastronomy, where the Persians are superior to the Arabs. In quite a direct manner he abuses and accuses his opponents of uncivilised behaviour, like eating lizards, insects and mice, smelling of camel excrement, murdering newly born girls and selling the children of their female slaves, which could mean their own children. He boasts of Iran's natural resources, literature and poets, mentioning Rūdakī as the author of a divan of 180,000 bayts (sic) as well as 'Unsurī, 'Asjadī and probably Kisā'ī.[28] However, he completely ignores Firdousī, even when he mentions the stories of Rustam, Sām, Bizhan and, of course, Garshasp.[29] This could be an indication of his rivalry with Firdousī, unless he seri-

---

26 On Asadī's debate between the Arab and the Iranian, see also Seyed-Gohrab in this volume.
27 Asadī plays here both roles, first putting on the mask of the Arab and then taking it off. The part that he is performing on behalf of the Arabs helps to reveal his sound knowledge and sincere interest in Islamic and pre-Islamic Arab history and culture.
28 It is not clear from the ms, it could be: *kasān-i ki* – those from [other parts of the country].
29 Asadī Tūsī wrote his own epic poem *Garshaspnama* ('Book of Garshasp') about one of the characters of the *Shahnama* ('Book of Kings'), emulating the style of one of his predecessors Firdousī, who completed his *magnum opus* about 1010.

ously considered the above-mentioned legends as purely folk and hence anonymous. However, as the author of the Persian dictionary *Lughat-i Furs* with strong component of poetic anthology, it is very unlikely that he would be unaware of the contribution of his predecessor. It is probably not a total coincidence that in a very similar manner Rustam (Roystakhm) and Isfandiyar (Spandyad) are mentioned in the much earlier *Goat and Palm Tree* (see above).

The poem has a very peculiar conclusion: having expressed these numerous killing arguments, which were bound to bring victory to the author and humiliate his opponents, the poet suddenly proposed peace: "We are both," – says he, "Muslims who, according to the order of God, are like brothers. We should not pay so much attention to our material life, we are equal before God, and we should remember that we will have nothing but our good deeds and faith on the Day of Resurrection."[30]

After a couple of verses praising Islamic virtues, the author moves on to express the main purpose of the poem (*qasd*, or *du'a*): praise of two Muhammads, due to one of whom the Ka'ba is flourishing, and due to the other, whose name is *'amīd* Muhammad Abū Ja'far, the Mashhad of Nuqān[31] [is prospering] (*bayts* 105–106). In the very last verse one more dedicatee is mentioned: *Khwāja* Abū Nasr, who was identified by Khaleghi-Motlagh as the Amir of Jastan, or probably his son Shams ad-Dīn, with the *kunya* Abū'l-Ma'ālī and the *laqab* Tāj al-Mulk.[32] However, it is more likely that this poem was still written in Asadī's native Tūs, maybe in his birthplace Nuqān, which could explain the rather immature quality of the poem and hence it being disregarded as composed by Asadī (Bertels 1988: 226–27). Note, however, in another Asadī's poem of similar nature, *the Debate between the Zoroastian and the Muslim,* it is the Muslim who defeats the Zoroastrian.

---

30 A very similar finale was supplied for the first Turkish opera Özsoy (Fereydun), which Mustafa Kemal commissioned Ahmet Adnan Saygun to produce for the occasion of the official visit of Reza Shah in June 1934. According to its libretto by Münir Hayri Egeli, Ferdowsi's original story was drastically 'improved'. The ruthless murder of Iraj by his jealous brothers Tur and Salm in the Shahnama, was replaced by a happy reunion and reconciliation between Tur (the King of Turan, i.e. the Turkic lands) and Iraj (the King of Iran) on the basis of their common faith, despite their different ethnic origin.

31 Tūs consisted of two parts, Tabaran and Nuqann (Minorsky and Bosworth 2000, Bertels 1988: 26).

32 The name of Abū Nasr's son was taken from the *musammat*, which is ascribed to Asadī again only in the Bodleian manuscript of *Daqā'iq al-Ash'ār*. Other anthologies have this *musammat* as belonging to Qatrān, for which reason it is usually included in his *Dīvān:* Khaleghi-Motlagh 1977: 658–659.

Asadī's debates are a good example of the literary reflection of the *shuʿū-biyya* movement.[33] He plays quite an unusual role of peacemaker between the different sides: the Arabs, carriers of Islam, and the Iranians, representatives of the ancient pre-Islamic tradition but rejecting the faith of his ancestors. Excellent quality literary works on this topic had been produced by representatives of both sides,[34] whose attitude towards their opponent would be clear and unchangeable.[35]

In the case of Asadī, his conformist suggestion to put aside the ethnic and cultural conflicts between the Arabs and the Persians and consider only their confessional brotherhood would be similar to his betrayal of the ideals of the *shuʿūbiyya*, which would provide good evidence of the maturing integration of Iranian society into the Muslim community.

4 Genres of Ode and Debate: One, Two in One, or Three in One?

As far as Asadī's poem is one of the earliest surviving pieces combining the features of both the debate and the ode, the question arises: should we agree with the definition of Persian traditional poetics, suggesting that *munāzara* by the 11th century was simply a kind of *qasīda?*

Going back to the earlier examples of the *munāzara* genre, it seems that the origins of the *munāzara* and *qasīda* are the same. The *qasīda* gradually incorporated poems of different purpose with one main aim: to praise or to mock a tar-

33 See Bosworth 1998/2000, Enderwitz 1997: 513–516, Norris 1990, Sourdel and Sourdel 2004: 753–54.

34 On the superiority of Arabs over the Iranians see *Anthology of Classical Arabic Poetry and Prose*, selected and translated by Geert Jan van Gelder in 2013: Abū Hayyān at-Tawhidi's *al-Imtāʿ wal-muʾānasah* (van Gelder 2012: 195–207 and 386–89), and a brilliant example of anti-Arab polemics in Arab verse by Bashshār b. Burd (van Gelder 2012: 34–36 and 360–61). Some other older texts are known only by their titles, as given in Ibn al-Nadim's *Fihrist:* Ibn Abī Tāhir Tayfūr (d. 280/893), *Fadl al-ʻarab ʻalā l-ʻajam* (Ibn-an-Nadīm 938 [1871]: 146); Saʻīd ibn Humayd (d. *c.* 257/871), *Intisāf al-ʻajam min al-ʻarab* and *Fadl al-ʻarab wa-ftikhāruhā* (Ibn-an-Nadīm 938 [1871]: 123); Is'hāq ibn Salama, *Fadl al-ʻajam ʻalā l-ʻarab* (Ibn-an-Nadīm 938 [1871]: 128); Al-Madā'inī (d. 228/842–43), *Mafākhir al-ʻarab wa-l-ʻajam* (Ibn-an-Nadīm 938 [1871]: 104).

35 One of the best examples could be the verses attributed to Firdousī (*Shahnama*, ed. Bertels, reign of Yazdagird III, bayt 24,600), which is not included in other critical editions:

From drinking camel's milk and eating locusts
Arabs reached [the stage of] producing laws.

geted person. For this reason, we identify as *qasīdas* the poetry of *madh* (praise), *fakhr* (self-praise) and *hajv/hijā* (anti-praise > satire) as well as elegy, which is the best expression of the idea of 'le roi est mort, vive le roi!'[36] If *qasīda* is indeed the collective term for *madh, fakhr and hijā,* Asadī's Fifth *munāzara* represents all three in one in the final stage of its development.

It seems that the literary form of *qasīda* was borrowed from Arabic literary tradition into Persian already with fully shaped features, the main one of which was praise (see de Fouchécour 2006: 419). Used mostly as panegyric, it could also take a shorter form, like *ghazal*, or *rubāʿī.*[37]

Some of the ancient samples of literary debate did not have the main panegyric aspect; it could end abruptly, with the author's assumption that it is clear who the winner is. This could be the indication that originally *qasīda* and *munāzara* were most likely two different genres, which then merged into one.

The definition of literary debate in Arabic literature, suggested van Gelder (1987: 330), is very similar to what Persian *munāzara* would be, with the only distinction: the Persian poetic debates could be judged by a third party, whose opinion would normally coincide with that of the author.[38] However, there could be more than two participants, or there could be no judge to nominate the winner. It is rarely a dialogue: the participants often have only one chance to express themselves in a monologue so the weakest starts and the strongest concludes the dispute on a very high note, so that nobody would have any doubt who deserves the prize and the praise.

---

36 When a king dies poets compile elegy to mourn his death, however, quite often those elegies would contain a prominent panegyric part praising the new king succeeding his deceased predecessor. Both elegy and panegyric parts would be the components of one piece, which has a structure of a classical qasida (ode). The main body of a standard *marthīya* (elegy) usually contains a description of poet's grief and sorrow and praise of the late king and the detailed list and description of his qualities. In the finale the author mentions the name of the new king, who is actually already replacing the previous *mamduh*, sometimes even surpassing him in his qualities. But of course the elegy could be written in memory of a friend, teacher, or other official.

37 This is very close to one of the panegyric functions of the oldest full-fledged *munāzara maqāma* in Arabic, one of the best examples of which could be the debate by Ahmad b. Burd al-Asghar (first half of 11th century), see van Gelder 2012: 224–54 and 399–401.

38 For example, in the *Debate between the Cup and the Water-Pipe* the judge was a Serving Table, who was not given any features of either a dedicatee or an author, see: Jang-i Jām-u Qalyān (*The Debate Between a Goblet and a Water-Pipe*), in Zhukovsky 1901: 22–23.

5 Religious Component as a Secret of Survival: Or God as Patron

There is no doubt that the Persian Classical *munāzara* was influenced by the Classical Arabic debate tradition; however, this process most likely was mutual, being a part of a shared literary culture. This means that we should consider the common features that were borrowed from the Arabic debate literature. Some of them have already been discussed, including the influence of *maqāmas*, mostly compiled in *saj'*,[39] and of the Qur'ān (van Gelder 1987: 329–30).

The genre of *munāzara* was borrowed into the New Persian literature from Arabic, but the subsequent influence on both of them was mutual. The main development of the genre happened during the 9th-10th centuries, when the Arab dominance over the conquered Iranian territories penetrated the substrate cultures, and the Iranian in the first instance. Iran's literary traditions obviously did not disappear altogether but went to a deeply dormant state. Two centuries in the Persian history of debate literature compared with half a millennium of interruption in the Akkadian tradition seems nothing (Jiménez 2017: 126).

As mentioned above, there is only one surviving debate example in Middle Persian. There are none surviving in any other Iranian languages of the pre-Islamic period, including Old Persian, Avestan, Median, Soghdian, Khwarazmian, or Bactrian. In fact we do not have any evidence of secular literature *per se* of the Achaemenid period apart from the above-mentioned quotation from Strabo's *Geography,* which only supports Ph. Huyse's idea that pre-Islamic Iran until the late Sasanian period was mainly an oral society (Huyse 2006: 410). This could be also the result of the bias against poetry displayed by the Zoroastrian priests, who adhered for a long time to an oral tradition of transmitting religious texts (Boyce 1957, De Bruijn 1997: 54). Later, during the Arab invasion, the Zoroastrian clergy felt responsible for preserving the religious texts, which could be the reason why the surviving texts of that period are predominantly religious. It is not thus surprising that the only surviving pre-Islamic Iranian disputation has a strong religious connotation: the Goat wins mainly because she proves her association with the sacred Zoroastrian rituals as well as her closeness to the rulers.

39 According to John Mattock, 'it (*munāzara*) is really so closely related to, and perhaps directly descended from, the *maqāmah* as to constitute a subclass of the latter. It cannot, frankly, be said to be an important genre within Arabic literature. The authors from whose hands we possess *munāzarat* are in many cases obscure and, in others, not those who are noted principally for their "literary" writings, however distinguished they may be in other spheres' (Mattock 1991: 163).

The similar rivalry between poetic and religious texts, caused by their almost equal influence on human nature, can be seen in the polemics of Muhammad with his audience in the earliest Sūrahs of the Qur'ān, where he explains the difference between prophet and poet,[40] the origin of the opinion in early Islam of poetry being the Qur'ān of Satan (Bürgel 1988: 11).

The mythological mentality seen here witnesses not only the very ancient origin of this literary genre, but links it to other literary traditions of personification of non-humans, as in the Sanskrit *Animal Fables*, continued in the *Kalīla and Dimna* cycle, or represented in the Qur'ān by speaking mountains, heaven, earth,[41] or thunder.[42]

The genre evolved through many cultural and linguistic traditions, enriching itself with more details in every particular case but keeping its structure basically intact from its very origin. Indeed, most of its elements and characters are already present in the earliest Sumerian examples: the author, who introduces the situation, the two arguing counterparts, and the judge. The most striking transformation to occur during the four millennia can be associated with the figure of the judge.[43]

In the Sumerian debates the judge was the god, who in many cases was the creator of the contesting personages, or the king. In the earliest New Persian *munāzaras* the god is replaced by the patron. So we can identify the debate and the *qasīda* as having the same origins, which through a gradual transformation, boosted by the formation of Classical Arabic poetry, developed into a genre more suitable and necessary for the new conditions of life. The genre of the literary debate in its pure form dissolved into other genres, which became more popular and came to replace it: *qasīda*, *ghazal*, romantic epics.

6 Form of Dialogue in New Persian Poetry

The structure of a dialogue became very popular in Persian court poetry throughout the whole Classical period. The poets of the Ghaznavid court, especially such prominent panegyrists as 'Unsūrī, Farrukhī, Manūchihrī, and later Hāfiz, the

40 Qur'an: 36.69, 69.41, 21.5, 37.36, 52.30.

41 The debate between the heaven and the earth in particular was popular among other authors, see Ethé 1882: 55–59, 74–75, Wagner 1963, van Gelder 1987: 334, Pourjavādī 2006: 430.

42 For more examples see van Gelder 1987: 332.

43 Ch. Brunner mentions the verbal contest in the Iranian tradition in the context of the judicial process, which links it with the didactic literature of so-called *andarz* genre (Brunner 1980a: 193).

master of the *ghazal*, actively used the figure *su'āl-u javāb* ('question and answer') in both *qasīda*s and *ghazal*s. Most of them represent a dialogue between a lover (in panegyrics – a poet) and beloved (a patron).[44] However, some of them would follow the idea of a poet expressing his own doubts, arguing with himself or with some real or imagined speaker. One of the first and the most brilliant examples is Rūdakī's *Qasīda on old age*, when Rūdakī is 'talking' to his young friend:[45]

Oh thou moon faced,[46] *musky tressed one, how cans't thou e'er know or deem*
What was once thy poor slave's station – how once held in high esteem?[47]

Pure anaphoric dialogue, where every new *bayt* or sometimes even *misrā'* has an accentuated incipit, like "Said he..., Said I," was very often used as an independent poem or a part of a bigger work, as for example in long epic poems, like the verbal contest of Farhād and Khusraw in Nizami's Sufi interpretation of *Khusraw-u Shīrīn*,[48] juxtaposing *bātin* and *zāhir*, spiritual and material:[49]

First he [Khusraw] asked: Where are you from?
Said he [Farhād]: From the land of love
Said he [Khusraw]: What are they doing there?
Said he [Farhād]: They buy grief and sell their souls.
Said he [Khusraw]: It is not good to sell your soul!
Said he [Farhād]: For those who are in love it is not surprising.
Said he [Khusraw]: You are so much in love in your heart!
Said he [Farhād]: It is you who speak of "the heart," I [speak] of the soul
Said he [Khusraw]: What is the love for Shīrīn to you
Said he [Farhād]: It is more than my sweet life...

Sometimes even one *misrā'* can contain both a question and an answer, as in the *ghazal* by Hafiz, starting with, 'Said I: "I grieve for you"; said he: "Your grief will

44 See Julia Meisami's example of Farrukhī's panegyric dedicated to Amir Yusuf on the birth of his son in Meisami 2003: 217. It is also noticeable that the Arabic word *harīf*, borrowed into Persian, was in heavy use in such poems in both meanings: enemy, rival and friend, beloved.
45 *Māhrūy-i mishkīn-mūy* – "Musk-haired moon-face [youth]" could be of course a sequence of standard epithets for a beloved.
46 Mahruy ('Moon-faced') could be his personal name.
47 Translation by A.V. William Jackson in Arberry 1967: 35.
48 Two other examples of debates incorporated into bigger *masnavi* works, Mahmud 'Ārifī's *Gūyu Chougān* and Badr ad-Dīn Hilalī's *Shāh-u Gadā*, can be found in Ethé 1882: 123–35.
49 Niẓāmī n.d.: 56.

end"...'[50] or even the whole dialogue, where the action is extremely compressed in such a masterpiece as the *dubaytī* ascribed to Rūdakī:

She came. Who? My beloved. When? At dawn.
She was frightened. By whom? By her enemy. Who was her enemy? Her father...
I gave her... What? A kiss. Where? On her juicy lips.
Were they lips? No! What was it? Carnelian. Like what? Like sugar.

Farrukhī, a great master of panegyric poetry was able to create both qasidas and ghazals in the form of a dialogue. In one of his short masterpieces, he managed to narrate a whole love story in five-*bayt ghazal* (Farrukhī 1378/1999: 435) where his feelings go through the whirlpool of emotions: from misery of begging to anger and threatening by God and then complete frustration and depression:

You are leaving, I hate you leaving!
Oh, look at me to say at least goodbye...
Don't go! As if you do – my own soul will leave with you!
How unhappy I am with you, and so is God!
...You've left, and after you've left because of this longing for you
God knows what will become of me!

In his Sada *qasīda*, starting with the standard description of the cruel beloved who has just left, Farrukhī finds consolation talking to the flowers in the winter garden (Farrukhī 1378/1999: 157):

The violet said: if your beloved has left, maybe
To replace her in your memory you'll take and keep me?
What did the daffodil say? She said: for the eyes of the friend who is far away
Accept my eyes for the grief her eyes [caused you]...[51]

50 Translation by Meisami 2003: 218.

51 A far-fetched but striking comparison could be made with the poem by Vladimir Kirshon (1902–1938), known for being both tool and victim of Stalinist repression. This poem was turned twice to a song by Tikhon Khrennikov and then Mikael Tariverdiev for Eldar Ryazanov's iconic Soviet film *The Irony of Fate* (1975). In this poem the author tries to find his suddenly disappeared beloved, asking the ash tree, poplar, autumn, rain, moon and cloud about her whereabouts. None of them can help. In the last stanza the poet asks his only trusted friend about his beloved, who eventually replies by saying: 'She was your beloved, now she is my wife'.

7 Reception and Audience of Debate Poetry: From Bazaar to Court

There could be another criterion by which to identify the difference between the ancient debate and a *munāzara* of the Muslim era: the audience. Persian poetic disputations of the Classical era were catering for the taste of a king and his entourage.

The authors and their audience were obviously different for the Sumerian *Goat and Grain*, Parthian/Pahlavi *Goat and Assyrian Tree*, and many others in Akkadian, Syriac, Greek, Arabic. According to several definitions, disputations were only partly considered as "exercises in scholarly frivolity" (Mattock 1991: 163), "erudite learning, or homiletic piety" (van Gelder 1991: 209), or "rhetorical skill" (Vanstiphout 1991: 24). Most of them did not have a very high status although they had both didactic and entertaining qualities. However, when the debate acquired the features of the *qasīda* it entered the court triumphantly, not through the secret back door as a part of jest's equipment but through the glorious front door as a sparkling tool of the professional panegyrist. Its status changed completely, and this seems to have happened at the Persian court. Before that the debate would live either in the bazaar square of a big and noisy Mesopotamian town, school, battle field, or in the cell of a Syrian scholar, carefully choosing Biblical topics for his poem.[52]

Most of them, especially the earliest, were certainly designed to be performed orally in public. In the Middle Persian poems we can see traces of such orality in the words by means of which the author/the wandering story-teller addressed the people gathered around him to see the performance: 'O men, the tree of even dry wood, whose top was golden...' (Unvala 1923: 650).

According to Marianna E. Vogelzang, in the Akkadian debate literature, for example, the role of the audience must have been especially significant, as the winner would be identified as "the speaker most loudly applauded."[53]

---

52 Brock 1991: 114. Cf. Bayandur's idea that the Middle Persian *tenzone* is the list of words compiled for teaching purposes to train professional scribes, secretaries, and other administrative staff (Bayandur 2013).

53 Vogelzang notes that the endings of all the disputes are missing but that 'direct address to the audience is particularly appropriate to oral literature' (Vogelzang 1991: 56). However, there is no evidence of the audience in Akkadian literature, and very little in Sumerian literature (Jiménez 2017: 108–11 and Veronica Afanasyeva in personal discussion).

8 Wordless Debates

There are also some examples of surviving non-textual examples of the debate literature in the form of visual continuous narrative, similar to the Rustam cycle, or Aesop-like Soghdian parables in the Penjikent frescos now in the Hermitage Museum, tale of Bizhan and Manizha in the Freer beaker, or Bahram Gur and his lute player in the tiles from the Takht-i Sulayman complex, and several others.

One of such examples, possibly illustrating the Goat and Palm Tree debate could be the bowl which represents the earliest ever depicted continuous narrative with the animation effect (Fig. 2). The second one was published recently in a completely different context (Askari Alamouti 2018: 156 fig. 4), could be the visual representation of the debate between the Goat and the Dove judged by the Ibex who is turning towards the Dove to announce its victory (Fig. 3).

Fig. 2: Bowl with the Goat and the Palm Tree motif, Shahr-i Sukhta, *3rd millennium B.C.* © National Museum of Iran, photography by Firuza Melville 2010

Fig. 3: Bowl with the Dove, Goat and Ibex motif, Nishapur, 9–10th century, Reg. No. 22113 © National Museum of Iran, photography by Hojjatollah Askari Alamouti 2017

Bibliography

Abdullaeva, Firuza. 2009. The Bodleian Manuscript of Asadī Ṭūsī's Munāẓara Between an Arab and a Persian: Its Place in the Transition from Ancient Debate to Classical Panegyric. *Iran* 47: 69–95.

Abdullaeva, Firuza. 2011. The Origins of the *Munāẓara* Genre in New Persian Literature. Pp. 249–273 in *Metaphor and Imagery in Persian Poetry*, ed. A.-A. Seyed-Gohrab. Leiden: Brill.

Alster, Bendt, and Vanstiphout, Herman L.J. 1987. Lahar and Ashnan. Presentation and Analysis of a Sumerian Disputation. *Acta Sumerologica* 9: 1–43.

Ambartsumian, Arthur A. 2000. “Асурийское, Ассирийское, Вавилонское дерево” или “Финиковая пальма” [Драхт-и-Асурик]. *Зороастрийские тексты на пехлеви.* https://www.zoroastrian.ru/node/806 (last accessed November 2019).

Arberry, Arthur. 1967. *Classical Persian Literature.* London: G. Allen & Unwin.

Askari Alamouti, Hojjatollah. 2018. Conceptual Analysis of the Dove and Goat Motif on a Nishapur Pottery Vessel in Light of Roland Barthes’ Approach to Mythology. *Iran* 56: 148 – 160. DOI: 10.1080/05786967.2017.1388679

Asmussen, Jes P. 1968. Ein iranisches Wort, ein iranischer Spruch und eine iranische Märchenformel als Grundlage historischer Folgerungen. *Temenos* 3: 7 – 18.

Bartholomae, Christian. 1922. Zur Kenntnis der mitteliranischen Mundarten IV. *Sitzungsberichte der Heidelberger Akademie der Wissenschaften. Phil.-hist. Klasse* 6.

Bayandur, Areg. 2013. *The Language of the Middle Persian monument Drakht-i Asūrīg.* Moscow: PhD dissertation.

Benveniste, Émile. 1930. Le texte du Draxt Asūrīk et la versification pehlevie. *Journal asiatique* 218: 193 – 225.

Bertels, Evgeny Eduardovich. 1988. Пятое муназере Асади Тусского. Pp. 207 – 241 in *Ученые записки. История литературы и культуры Ирана. Избранные труды*, Москва

Blochet, Edgard. 1895. Textes pehlevis inédits relatifs à la religion mazdéenne. *Revue de l’Histoire de religions* 32: 18 – 23.

Bosworth, Clifford Edmund. 1998/2000. Shuʿūbiyya. P. 717 in *Encyclopedia of Arabic Literature*, ed. J. S. Meisami and P. Starkey. Abingdon/New York: Routledge.

Boyce, Mary. 1957. The Parthian gōsan and Iranian Minstrel Tradition. *Journal of the Royal Asiatic Society:* 10 – 45.

Brock, Sebastian P. 1985. A Dispute of the Months and Some Related Syriac Texts. *Journal of Semitic Studies* 30: 181 – 211.

Brock, Sebastian P. 1991. Syriac Dispute Poems: The Various Types. Pp. 109 – 119 in *Dispute Poems and Dialogues in the Ancient and Medieval Near East*, ed. G. J. Reinink and H. L. J. Vanstiphout. Orientalia Lovaniensia Analecta 42. Louvain: Peeters.

Brunner, Christopher J. 1980a. The Fable of the Babylonian Tree. Part I: Introduction. *Journal of Near Eastern Studies* 39: 191 – 202.

Brunner, Christopher J. 1980b. The Fable of the Babylonian Tree. Part II: Translation. *Journal of Near Eastern Studies* 39: 291 – 302.

Bürgel, Johann Christoph. 1988. *The Feather of Simurgh: The “Licit” Magic of the Arts in Medieval Islam.* New York: New York University Press.

Chaykin, Konstantin Ivanovich. 1934. *Асади-старший и Асади-младший:* ’в Фердовси (934 – 1034), Москва-Ленинград.

Chunakova, Olga. 2001. *Пехлевийская Божественная комедия.* Москва: Восточная литература.

Cunningham, Graham, and Black, Jeremy A. 2000. The debate between Grain and Sheep. *The Electronic Text Corpus of Sumerian Literature* 5.3.2. http://www-etcsl.orient.ox.ac.uk/ (last accessed November 2019).

de Blois, François. 2004. *Persian literature. A bio-bibliographical survey (Volume V).* London: Routledge.

De Bruijn, J.T.P. 1997. Iran VI. Religions. in *Encyclopaedia of Islam, Second Edition*, ed. P. Bearman, T. Bianquis, C. E. Bosworth, E. van Donzel and W. P. Heinrichs. Leiden: Brill.

de Fouchécour, Charles-Henri. 2005. Review of "Le mètre du Draxt asûrîg." *Abstracta Iranica* 26: no. 362. http://abstractairanica.revues.org/1933 (last accessed November 2019).
de Fouchécour, Charles-Henri. 2006. Iran viii. Persian Literature (2) Classical. Pp. 414–432 in *Encyclopaedia Iranica*, ed. E. Yarshater. New York: Encyclopaedia Iranica Foundation.
Enderwitz, Susanne. 1997. al- Shuʿūbiyya. in *Encyclopaedia of Islam, Second Edition*, ed. P. Bearman, T. Bianquis, C. E. Bosworth, E. van Donzel and W. P. Heinrichs. Leiden: Brill.
Ethé, C. Hermann. 1882. Über persische Tenzonen. Pp. 48–135 in *Verhandlungen des fünften Internationalen Orientalisten-Congresses. Zweiter Theil*, Berlin: Asher.
Ethé, C. Hermann. 1889. *Catalogue of the Persian, Turkish, Hindustani and Pushtu Manuscripts in the Bodleian Library.* Oxford: Clarendon Press.
Farrukhī. [1378/1999]. *Dīvān.* ed. M. S. Dabīr Siyāqī. Tehran.
Golčin-Maʿāni, A. 1348/1969. *Tārīkh-i tazkirahā-yi Fārsī, jild-i 1, Intishārāt-i Dānishgāh-i Tihrān, 1/1236.* Ganjīna-yi fihrist-u kitābshināsī 12. Tehran.
Hedāyat, Reżāqoli Khan. 1878. *Majmaʿ al-foṣaḥā.* Tehran.
Henning, Walter Bruno. 1950. A Pahlavi Poem. *Bulletin of the School of Oriental and African Studies* 13: 641–648.
Huyse, Philip. 2006. Iran viii. Persian Literature (1) Pre-Islamic. Pp. 410–414 in *Encyclopaedia Iranica*, ed. E. Yarshater. New York: Encyclopaedia Iranica Foundation.
Ibn-an-Nadīm, Muḥammad Ibn-Isḥāq. 938 [1871]. *Kitāb al-Fihrist.* ed. G. L. Flügel. Leipzig.
Jiménez, Enrique. 2017. *The Babylonian Disputation Poems. With Editions of the Series of the Poplar, Palm and Vine, the Series of the Spider, and the Story of the Poor, Forlorn Wren.* Culture and History of the Ancient Near East 87. Leiden: Brill.
Jones, Horace Leonard. 1930. *Strabo, Geography, Volume VII: Books 15–16.* Loeb Classical Library 241. Cambridge: Harvard University Press.
Khaleghi-Motlagh, Djalal. 1977. Asadi Tusi. Pp. 643–678 in *Majalla-i Dānishgāh-i Adabiyāt-u ʿUlūm-i Insānī-i Dānishgāh-i Firdawsī*, Mashhad.
Kuiper, Franciscus B.J. 1960. The Ancient Aryan Verbal Contest. *Indo-Iranian Journal* 4: 217–281.
Lazard, Gilbert. 2002/2003. Le mètre du Draxt asûrîg. *Orientalia Suecana* 51/52: 327–336.
Lazard, Gilbert. 2006. Prosody III. Middle Persian. *Encyclopædia Iranica.* http://www.iranicaonline.org/articles/prosody-middle-persian (last accessed November 2019).
Mattock, John N. 1991. The Arabic Tradition: Origin and Developments. Pp. 153–163 in *Dispute Poems and Dialogues in the Ancient and Medieval Near East*, ed. G. J. Reinink and H. L. J. Vanstiphout. Orientalia Lovaniensia Analecta 42. Louvain: Peeters.
Meisami, Julia Scott. 2003. *Structure and Meaning in the Medieval Arabic and Persian poetry.* London: Routledge.
Minorsky, Vladimir, and Bosworth, Clifford Edmund. 2000. Ṭūs. in *Encyclopaedia of Islam, Second Edition*, ed. P. Bearman, T. Bianquis, C. E. Bosworth, E. van Donzel and W. P. Heinrichs. Leiden: Brill.
Mittermayer, Catherine. 2019. *Was sprach der eine zum anderen? Argumentationsformen in den sumerischen Rangstreitgesprächen.* Untersuchungen zur Assyriologie und Vorderasiatischen Archäologie 15. Berlin: De Gruyter.
Muḥammad, Mírzá. 1919. *Revised translation of the Chahár Maqála (Four Discourses) of Niẓámí-i ʿArúḍí of Samarqand.* ed. E. G. Browne. London.
Niẓāmī, Jamal ad-Dīn Abū Muḥammad Ilyās ibn-Yūsuf ibn-Zakkī. n.d. *Kahmsa.* Teheran.

Nizamī-i Arūzī-i Samarqandī. 550-552/1155–1157 [1910]. *Chahār Maqāla*. ed. M. Qazvini. Tehran.

Norris, Harry T. 1990. Shuʿūbiyyah in Arabic Literature. Pp. 31–47 in *The Cambridge History of Arabic Literature. Abbasid Belles Lettres*, ed. J. Ashtiany, T. M. Johnstone, J. D. Latham and R. B. Serjeant. Cambridge: Cambridge University Press.

Pourjavādī, Nasrollah. 2006. *Zabān-i ḥāl dar ʿIrfān-u adabīyāt-i pārsī*. Tehran.

Qābūs b. Vashmgīr, Kay Kāʾūs b. Iskandar b. 1082 [1951]. *The Naṣīḥat-Nāma known as Qābūs-Nāma of Kay Kāʾūs b. Iskandar b. Qābūs b. Vashmgīr. Edited with critical notes by Reuben Levy.* Gibb Memorial Series, New Series 18. London.

Qatrān Tabrīzī. [1362/1983]. *Dīvan-i Qatrān-i Tabrīzī*. ed. B. oz-Zaman Foruzanfar, Z. Safa and S. H. Taqizadeh. Tehran.

Rūh-al-Amīnī, M. 1369/1990. Justārī mardum-shenasī az manzuma-yi drakht-i asurig. Pp. 323–336 in *Haftād maqāla. Armaghān-i farhangī ba duktur-i Ghulāmhusayn Sādiqī*, ed. Y. Mahdawī and Ī. Afšār. Tehran.

Smith, Sidney. 1926/1928. Notes on 'The Assyrian Tree'. *Bulletin of the School of Oriental and African Studies* 4: 69–76.

Sourdel, Janine, and Sourdel, Dominique. 2004. *Dictionnaire historique de l'islam*. Paris: Presses Universitaires de France.

Tafażżolī, Aḥmad. 1995. Draxt ī āsūrig. Pp. 547–549 in *Encyclopaedia Iranica*, ed. E. Yarshater. New York: Encyclopaedia Iranica Foundation.

Unvala, Jamshedji Maneckji. 1921. *The Pahlavi Text "King Husrav and His Boy." Published With its Transcription, Translation and Copious Notes*. Paris: Geuthner.

Unvala, Jamshedji Maneckji. 1923. Draxt-I Asurīk. *Bulletin of the School of Oriental and African Studies* 2: 637–678.

van Gelder, Geert Jan. 1987. The Conceit of Pen and Sword: On An Arabic Literary Debate. *Journal of Semitic Studies* 9: 329–360.

van Gelder, Geert Jan. 1991. Arabic Debates of Jest and Earnest. Pp. 198–211 in *Dispute Poems and Dialogues in the Ancient and Medieval Near East*, ed. G. J. Reinink and H. L. J. Vanstiphout. Orientalia Lovaniensia Analecta 42. Louvain: Peeters.

van Gelder, Geert Jan. 2012. *Classical Arabic Literature: A Library of Arabic Literature Anthology*. New York: NYU Press.

Vanstiphout, Herman L.J. 1991. Lore, Learning and Levity in the Sumerian Disputations: A Matter or Form, or Substance? Pp. 23–46 in *Dispute Poems and Dialogues in the Ancient and Medieval Near East*, ed. G. J. Reinink and H. L. J. Vanstiphout. Orientalia Lovaniensia Analecta 42. Louvain: Peeters.

Vogelzang, Marianna E. 1991. Some Questions about the Akkadian Disputes: Dispute Poems and Dialogues. Pp. 47–57 in *Dispute Poems and Dialogues in the Ancient and Medieval Near East*, ed. G. J. Reinink and H. L. J. Vanstiphout. Orientalia Lovaniensia Analecta 42. Louvain: Peeters.

Wagner, Ewald. 1963. Die arabische Rangstreitdichtung und ihre Einordnung in die allgemeine Literaturgeschichte. *Abhandlungen der Geistes und Sozialwissenschaftlichen Klasse. Akademie der Wissenschaften und der Literatur* 1962/8: 437–476.

Wagner, Ewald. 1993. Munāẓara. Pp. 565–569 in *The Encyclopaedia of Islam. Volume 7*, Leiden: Brill.

Zarrinkoub, Abdolhossein. 1957 [2017]. *Two Centuries of Silence. An Account of Events and Conditions in Iran During the First Two Hundred Years of Islam, From the Arab Invasion to the Rise of the Tahirid Dynasty.* Bethesda: Mazda Publishers.
Zhukovsky, Valentin. 1901. *Сказки попугая. Спор чашки с кальяном. Сост. В.А.Жуковский.* St Petersburg.

Asghar Seyed-Gohrab*

15 The Rhetoric of Persian Verbal Contests

Innovation and Creativity in Debates between the Persians and the Arabs

1 Introduction

Persian literary tradition is extremely rich in the genre of debates. It would not be an exaggeration to state that one can find virtually debates between any conceivable object or idea. These debates can be categorized in different groups depending on their subject-matter. Debates on heavenly bodies (Earth and Heaven, Moon and Sun, Spring and Autumn), members of the body, (Eye and Heart, Vagina and Penis), ethico-philosophical concepts (Love and Reason, Body and Soul), musical instruments (Trumpet and Lute), daily life objects (Needle and Thread), socio-political issues (the Labourer and the Rich).[1] This list can go on for many lines cataloguing all types of subjects treated in Persian debate literature. The question is why this genre has become a favourite of poets and writers for more than one millennium. What are the cultural background of such poems? What are the characteristics of the Persian debate genre?

In discussions on Persian debate literature, reference is usually made to the Middle Persian (or Pahlavi) text *Drakht ī asūrīk* (*The Assyrian Tree*).[2] With the advent of New Persian literature in the ninth century, this genre appeared to be popular, first as a rhetorical device in various literary forms and later as an independent literary form in which two objects or ideas dispute on a subject, trying to prove their superiority. Debates appear in both poetry and prose, but debates in poetry are more common. The Persian debate poems are didactic while entertaining elements are always present. This genre could be seen as a repository of rhetorical techniques to outshine an opponent, making of disputation a

* Leiden University.

1 Pūrjavādī (1385/2006) has presented in his excellent book, *Zabān-i ḥāl*, a large number of examples of various types of debates in Persian literature; see also de Bruijn 2006–2007. Also in Arabic, the genre of poetic disputation is rich, see e.g. van Gelder 1987; 1991; 1998 and his contribution in the present volume.

2 On this text see Tafażżolī 1996b; 1376/1997; see also Abdullaeva-Melville's contribution in the present volume.

https://doi.org/10.1515/9781501510274-015

verbal art (Belhaj 2016: 291–307). Debate poems appear in different literary forms, especially panegyrics (*qaṣīda*) and rhyming couplets (*mathnavī*) used in epic poetry. Debates in the form of a panegyric are meant to praise the qualities of a patron. After two or three couplets, establishing the occasion for which the poem is composed (usually a convivial courtly setting), the poet starts his debate. The first speech turn is commonly given to the adversary who elaborates in praising the subject in question for several couplets. Afterwards the proponent who is usually identified with the poet himself takes over and refutes what he has heard. The final part of the poem is reserved to praise the name and excellent qualities of the patron.

Perhaps the first poet who wrote several long poems in the form of the dispute is Asadī from Tus in Khurasan (ca. 1000–1072) who is famous for his 9,000 couplets long epic poem *Garshāsp-nāma* (completed around 1065–66), which he dedicated to Abū Dulāf Shaybānī, the ruler of Nakhjavan.[3] Asadī's name is associated with the genre of *munāẓarāt* ('debates'), five of which are extant. These poems are couched in the form of a panegyric (*qaṣīda*) and deal with the following subjects: The Arab and the Persian (*ʿarab-u ʿajam*), the Zoroastrian and the Muslim (*mugh-u musalmān*), the Lance and the Bow (*nayza-u kamān*), Night and Day (*shab-u rūz*), and the Heaven and the Earth (*āsmān-u zamīn*). Each of these poems possesses their own specific literary merits but the first two poems introduce socio-political and religious dimensions, which have made them intriguing for more than one millennium. The first debate between the Arab and the Persian consists of hundred and twenty couplets. It is a praise poem dedicated to Abū Jaʿfar Muḥammad.[4] The poet identifies himself with the Persian defending his superiority against the Arab. It has many features of being a Shuʿūbiyya ("confessors of equality") discourse in which the Persians voiced their superiority with references to their ancient culture and glory.[5] In the other debate between the Zoroastrian and the Muslim, the poet identifies himself with the Muslim and can be regarded as an anti-Shuʿūbiyya statement.

---

3 On the biography and works of Asadī see Khaleghi-Motlagh 1987.

4 For Asadī's patron's see Khaleghi-Motlagh 1356/1977: 665–71; 1357/1978.

5 The term Shuʿūbiyya comes from the Koran (49:13) "O you men! Surely, We have created you of a male and a female, and made you tribes (*shuʿūb*) and families (*qabā'il*) that you may know each other…"; see Shakir N.D.: 773. In some Koran translations such as M. Pickthall, *shuʿūb* is translated with 'nations' and *qabā'il* with 'tribes', which becomes politically loaded. In this essay, I follow the translation of Ignaz Goldziher. There are a large number of studies on this topic; see Enderwitz 1997; Goldziher 2009; Gibb 1962; Mottahedeh 1976; Richter-Bernburg 1974; Pourshariati 2010. Most recent studies to my knowledge are Dabiri 2013; Webb 2016; and Savant 2013.

Discussions on the superiority of one culture over another point at the Shuʿūbiyya movement which reached its zenith in the ninth century.[6] The goals of this movement vary in its development from the equality of all Muslims in comparison to the Quraysh family's claim of leadership, to the equality between the Arabs and non-Arabs, usually Persians who voiced their superiority over the Arabs. The movement could not be seen as a nationalist movement trying to overthrow the central government but more emphasizing the Persian cultural supremacy, yet movements such as the revolt of Bābak al-Khurramī (d. 838) appeared during the reign of Caliph al-Maʿmūn in 816–817 (Yūsofī 1989).[7] The Shuʿūbī movement had different purposes for different hierarchies in the society. The class of secretaries (*dabīr*s or *kātib*s), who were mostly the Persians, supported the Shuʿūbī's to "close their profession to non-Persians" (van Berkel 2003: 80). These Persian secretaries played a central role in the translation movement in the eighth and ninth centuries, translating works from various languages into the Arabic. Such debates offered them an opportunity to voice religious and cultural aspects of Persian culture.[8] The interesting thing is that they did not turn their back on the Islam but tried to integrate Islam within the Persian cultural context. Richard N. Fry assesses that Islam developed within the continuity of Persian culture, becoming "a truly universal culture and religion" (Fry 1975: xii). This Islam which was created during the tenth and eleventh centuries was an "Iranian Islam using the Arabic language" (Fry 1975: 165).

The second debate on the Zoroastrian priest and a Muslim is interesting as it transcends ethnicity and concentrates on the superiority of the Muslims over non-Muslims, especially the Zoroastrians. In such poems, as in the European counterpart debates between Christians and Jews studied by Thomas Reed, the poem is "essentially didactic and requires a clear resolution to confirm its doctrinal values" (Reed 1990: 136). As we shall presently see, in such poems, being a true Muslim is based on piety and not on ethnicity. Although Islam ignored ethnicity, taking all Muslims as one community (*umma*, Koran 3:106), there was still tensions among different ethnic groups in early centuries of Islam, where the colour of skin and blood-ties played a role (Lewis 1990). The emergence of such poems is motivated by the challenges of superiority between Arab Muslims and Persian Muslims. In Arabic sources such as Ibn Qutayba's *Excellence of the Arabs*, Persians are blamed for "opening the door" to integration of the foreign elements in Islam (Ibn Qutayba 2017: xv).

6 See Norris 1990; Zarrīnkūb 1368/1989: 384–87; Agius, 1980; Webb 2016: 246–49.
7 On Zandaqa and its followers see de Blois 2002; Madelung 1986.
8 Duri 1987, see chapter 3 "The Arab Nation and its Sense of Identity" (Duri 1987: 84–133).

It is indeed true that the Persians introduced new readings of Islam and even of the holiest laws and rituals. In several of such debates, the Persian poet even defies the Islamic rules on drinking wine. Elsewhere I have discussed how in Persian courtly circles, the wine contests against the rose, listing its medicinal, comradely and pleasing qualities (Seyed-Gohrab 2013).[9] The wine also blames the Arabs for the fact that Prophet Muḥammad forbade it, because the Arabs were not moderate users. In this particular contest, the wine wins the contest, and the entire Muslim courtly gathering toasts with a glass of wine. Such debates show how the Islamic rules are negotiated, stretched and even transgressed in a culture where wine-drinking constitutes an integral part of social and political experience.[10]

While Asadī's first debate on the Arab and the Persian can be defined as a remnant of a Shuʿūbiyya statement, the second debate on the Muslim and the Zoroastrian hails Muḥammad and Islam. Based on such contradictory positions in these two poems, scholars such as Furūzānfar (1369/1980: 452 n. 1)[11] and Ethé (1881) have doubted the attribution of the two poems to one poet. Khaleghi-Motlagh (1987) gives another possibility by saying, it "may be that Asadī, like others, reasoned that an Iranian Muslim was superior to an Arab Muslim, but a Muslim, whatever his nationality, was superior to an Iranian Zoroastrian." Bertel's (1374/1995: 20–22) believes that all the debate poems are written by a single poet: Asadī wrote these poems for specific people to win a Muslim Persian patron (see also Abdullaeva 2009; 2012).

2 Debates between the Persians and the Arabs

Asadī is the first poet to devote a single debate poem to the contest between the Arabs and the Persians. The subject has been so popular in the history of the Persian literature that several poets and writers tried their hand in highlighting the excellence of the Persians over the Arabs for various purposes. As we will see later on in this essay, the subject is popular in modern Iranian society where the political tensions between the Arab Sunnites and the Shiite Persians exist.

Praising Persian culture and pre-Islamic kings appear extensively in early Arabic poetry, especially in the poetry of poets such as Abū Nuwās (747–813), who praised their Persian ancestry. As Richard A. Serrano (1997) says, Abū

9 For a comparable topic see Heinrichs 1991.

10 One of Shahab Ahmed's theses which he successfully discusses is that wine is constitutive of Islam; see Ahmed 2016.

11 For the entire section see Furūzānfar 1369/1980: 438–491.

Nuwās was not alone among the Arab-speaking Persians in disdaining the Arab culture. Serrano relies on Goldziher's research who states "that there were probably a great many more Shuʿūbiyya ("confessors of equality")" (Goldziher 2009: 137). Even poets writing in Arabic praised Pre-Islamic Persian kings, their exploits and justice. A representative example is al-Buḥtūrī (821–897), who turned his attention in one of his famous panegyrics towards the Persian past, criticizing the Arab culture of his day. Such praises have different functions and could not be simply interpreted as a cultural supremacy of one culture over another.

Asadī's poem takes place at a feast in the palace of an Iranian aristocrat where people are drinking wine and listening to music. At this gathering, a discussion is opened about the superiority of Persians over the Arabs. Suddenly an Arab intervenes in fury, "What is a Persian? Pride belongs only to Arabs, O ignorant idiot!" (l. 4) listing the excellence of the Arabs over the Persians, emphasizing the nobility of the prophet's tribe Quraysh, the Arab's eloquence referring to several Arab poets such as al-Mutanabbī, al-Buḥtūrī, and Jarīr.[12] Afterwards he refers to the learned Arabs such as Nuʿmān.[13] The Arab emphasizes the hospitality and courage of his culture, the Arab horse and camel husbandry. He is proud that the Prophet Muḥammad was an Arab and that the Koran is written in Arabic and that Mecca, and the Zamzam spring belong to the Arabs:

> The tomb of the excellent Prophet is propitiously in our land,
> So are all the men who were the leaders of religions.
> So is Mecca, which is the valley for the pilgrims, and the spring of Zamzam;
> So is Kaʿba which is the Kiblah of all practising Muslims.
> Also Muḥammad the Prophet of God belongs to our stock,
> Also the Koran is revealed to the world in our language.
> Mankind is superior over all other living beings due to speech;
> Therefore, there is no better language than ours.
> Things that have a single name in your language,
> have three hundred different names[14] in our language.
> I have argued the qualities of the Arabs, which I have revealed to you,
> O, show your arguments on the qualities of the Persians.[15]

After these catalogues of praises, which takes twenty-two couplets, the Persian starts to speak in seventy-nine couplets, calling Arabs as demons of the desert,

12 For a list of these poets see Khaleghi-Motlagh 1357/1978: 69.

13 It is not clear which Nuʿmān the poet is referring to as there are several learned men with the same name.

14 The word used here is *alvān* which literally means 'colours' or 'shades.' An alternative translation would be 'connotations.'

15 Khaleghi-Motlagh 1357/1978: 70–71, ll. 21–25.

as camel drivers while the Persians have brought forth mighty kings such as Kayūmarth, Hūshang, and Jamshīd. Afterwards he boasts of the champions of Iranian culture such as Sām, Garshāsp and Rustam. The poet then refers to the Persians as learned people referring to the achievements of Muḥammad Zakarīyā Rāzī[16] (see Goodman 1995). Afterwards he names Persian poets such as Rūdakī (860 – 940), ʿUnṣurī (c. 9610 – 1039), ʿAsjadī (11th century) and Kisāʾī (c. 953 – 1001).[17]

The poet also enters religious field, challenging the identity of the Prophet Muḥammad. A heated subject in the debates between the Arabs and the Persians is the attribution of a prophet to the Persians. Apparently, the Persians wanted to provoke their Arab opponents through such claims. Ibn Qutayba (828 – 889) reports in his *Excellence of the Arabs*, how the Persians appropriate biblical prophets to their own genealogy. He feverishly rejects the idea that Adam could have belonged to the Persian descent:

> It is hard to credit the Easterners' inclusion of Adam in their boast against the Arabs. (...) they also lay claim to the prophets, saying that only four of them – Hud, Salih, Shu'ayb and Muhammad – were Arabs. This claim is an empty boast: it has no substance and is a flagrant injustice to the Arabs. Their arguments are built on falsehood and delusion and can therefore be knocked over with a feather. Such unjust claims against the Arabs are truly obscene. Adam! As if the Arabs were not also Adam's descendants! And then to say that Moses, Jesus, Zechariah, john the Baptist, and other Children of Israel are theirs! As I have explained to you, there is no genealogical bond between Persia and the Children of Israel. (Ibn Qutayba 2017: 27)

Such provocative attributions belong to the genre. It is also interesting to note that Ibn Qutayba, a polygraph, descended in the "second or third generation from an Arabicized Iranian family" (Lecomte 1971), creates different identities among Persians. He distinguishes between the probably Persians from the province of Khurasan and others, and the translators have chosen to distinguish this by the word 'Easterners.'[18]

Asadī says that the Prophet Muḥammad was originally of Persian stock because he was an offspring of Abraham, who was also a Persian. He emphasizes that the Prophet chose two groups: the Quraysh tribe from the Arabs and the Per-

16 Known to the Latins as Rhazes, ca. 854 – 925 or 935.

17 It is interesting that he says that the collected work of Rudaki amounts to 180.000 couplets, whereas the number of couplets survived the teeth of time is considerably fewer; see Khaleghi-Motlagh 1357/1978: 119.

18 Ibn Qutayba 2017: xviii. See also Lecomte 1971; Rosenthal, 1998; Ashraf 2006.

sians from the rest of non-Arabs. He continues that the Persians appear in the Koran. The People of the Cave (*aṣḥāb al-kahf*), which refers to the seven sleepers at Ephesus were also Persians. He emphasizes how the Prophet Muḥammad has praised the Persians.[19] The poet then points at Persian words in the Koran. One such word is *sajjil* which in his view is a compound of the Persian words *sang* ('stone') and *gil* ('mud' or 'clay'). The word appears in the Koranic Sūra *The Elephant* 105:4.[20]

Another subject the poet dwells upon is the treatment of baby girls and how the pre-Islamic Arabs buried their newly born daughters immediately after birth. This is a recurring theme in Persian sources till modern times, condemning the Arabs of this practise, called *wa'd al-Banāt* and is disapproved of in the Koran (81:8):[21]

> You drank blood when a girl was born
> You hid her alive under the earth.[22]

Another subject Asadī introduces to attack the Arabs is their mistreatment of the Prophet. In other debates, the Arabs are often criticized for their mistreatment of the Prophet and his family. Asadī states that the Arabs mistreated the Prophet, throwing him out of the city of Mecca, insulting him, and even breaking his teeth. In his view, the Arabs called the Prophet a poet, a demon and a sorcerer and instead of accepting his faith, they worshipped other gods. He continues to state how the Arabs have killed the third and the fourth caliph ʿUthmān (d. 656) and ʿAlī Ibn Abī Ṭālib (c. 600–661). The poet then underscores how Persians love the house of God, journeying hundreds of kilometres across deserts, mountains and steppes to reach the Kaʿba. Once at the Kaʿba, the Persians kiss the house, walk around it, weep and ask forgiveness from God. While the Persians are devoted to the religion and come to Mecca to renew their love and devotion to God, the Arabs rob the pilgrims who have come from a far distance. They steal their clothes and provisions. One is not even safe to take off one's shoes because the Arabs will immediately steal them:

> For the sake of pilgrimage, we journey one thousand kilometres
> To come to the Kaʿba from the borders of Balkh and Balkhān.

---

19 The legend of the seven sleepers appears in the Koran as *Aṣḥāb al-kahf* (18:8–26); see Sims-Williams 1998.

20 The citation goes as follows: "Casting them against stones of baked clay."

21 For modern examples of Persian poets condemning the Arab practice see Seyed-Gohrab 2015: 63–4.

22 Khaleghi-Motlagh 1357/1978: 73, l. 51.

> We kiss her [the Ka'ba] stones with our hearts and we walk around her;
> We weep and ask forgiveness from the exalted God. (...)
> When a pilgrim comes to the desert from a far off place,
> You seize him, and strip him of his dress and bread.
> He is not safe if he puts off his shoes,
> For you will steal the shoes the moment you get an opportunity.[23]

Another category of praise concerns the geographical setting of Iran, her natural resources and gentle climate. The poet states that compared to the Arab lands, the soil of Persia is fertile. Persia is rich in having mines of lapis lazuli, gold and silver. While a gentle and fragrant breeze blows through Persia, the wind in Arabia is hot and poisonous.[24] Persia is rich in generating fruits in any size and colour, even incomparable to the fruits promised to believers in Paradise. Arabia lacks the many rivers running through Persia. The sun (*khur*) casts its rays to Persia first, because it comes out of the province of Khurasan. Later on the day the sun reaches Arabia.

Next item of praise relates to the textile. Here the poet emphasizes that the Persians wear dresses made of silk, brocade and fur while the best clothes the Arabs wear are made of cotton. The fragrance exuding from the garments of the Persians are musk and ambergris, while the smell wafting from the Arab clothes is the stunk of a mange camel. The Arabs spend their lives in tents filled with sands while the Persians mostly spend their times in gardens. When they go into a building, the Arabs sit on carpets made of camel hair while the Persians sit on carpets made of silk and wear thrones made of gold.

Another category concerns the eating habits of the Persians contrasted to the Arabs. This is a subject which is repeatedly discussed in other Persian sources, which usually go back to Middle Persian sources in which diets are related to modes of purity and impurity (see Touraj Daryaee 2012: 229–42). The poet states that the Persians eat fowls and lambs while the Arabs eat snakes, locust, mice, and dead lizards. The eating habit of the Arabs is a topical issue in Iran and is unfortunately used in pejorative racial references in contemporary Iran.[25] Persian literature is full of such passages, which are often later interpolations. One example is the occurrence of the following piece in the epic poem *Shāh-nāma*

23 Khaleghi-Motlagh 1357/1978: 74, ll. 64–65, 67–68.

24 The hot and poisonous wind has also become a type of *topos* in Persian poetry when describing Arabian deserts. For such description of Manūchihrī (d. ca. 1040) see Seyed-Gohrab 2017: 14–36.

25 After sexual harassment of two young Iranian men, the anti-Arab sentiment intensified and people used racist insults to refer to the Arabs. Zimmt (2015) refers to some of the derogatory epithets among which "lizard- and grasshopper-eaters."

or *The Book of the Kings*, composed in 1010 by Ferdowsi. The poet describes the fall of the Sasanian Empire (224 CE–650 CE) at the end of the epic by the Muslim Arabs. Here it is mentioned that before the great battle in the seventh century, the Persian general Rustam Farrukhzādān wrote a letter to his enemy Saʿd b. Vaqqās, warning him of the Persian power. The following lines are so popular with contemporary Iranian nationalists that they recite them on any occasion which might slightly have to do with the Arabs, be it a political disagreement or football match:

> From feeding on camel's milk and lizards,
> the Arabs' hopes have come so far
> as to aspire to the Persian Empire,
> spit on you, O revolving Wheel, spit on you!

Scholars of Persian literature have shown that these and similar lines are later interpolations and could not be written by Ferdowsi.[26]

Another field of contest concerns the personal names. According to the poet, the way the Persians choose a name is to emphasize their servanthood to God such as ʿAbdullāh ('Servant of God') or ʿAbd al-Ṣamad ('Servant of the Eternal') while the Arabs have names such as ʿAbd al-Ṣanam ('Servant of the Idol') or ʿAbd al-Manāf ('Servant of Manāf,' a pagan idol), revealing their sympathy with their pagan past. The poet highlights that such names are chosen to serve Satan and that giving such names to individuals derive from ignorance and blindness. The words such as Manāf refer to idols the Arabs worshipped before the advent of Islam.[27]

Before turning to the panegyric part of his poem, praising Sayyid Abū Jaʿfar Muḥammad, the poet concludes that being a good Muslim does not depend on one's origin and ethnicity because the divine law is for all Muslims and the one who is more pious, will be superior to others:

> For you and for us, God has decreed the divine law
> Which is one, because pious believers are like brothers.
> On Resurrection Day, neither possessions, nor means, nor houses
> Are of any use except good deeds and good faith. (...)

---

26 See Daryaee 2012: 231–32, and the literature Daryaee refers to.

27 Manāf is the name of a deity of ancient Arabia; see Fahd 1991 (http://dx.doi.org/10.1163/1573-3912_islam_SIM_4901, last accessed November 2019). On the authority of al-Ṭabarī, Fahd (1991) states "One of the most famous is that of ʿAbd Manāf, one of the four sons of Ḳuṣayy, reformer of the cult in Mecca. His mother had promised him to the god, so as to protect him from the evil eye, for he was so handsome that he was surnamed al-ḳamar 'the moon'."

A person is better at all times in God's eye,
Who is God-fearing; this makes all hard things easy.[28]

In the Persian contest poems, there is usually a judge to safeguard impartiality but in this case the poet leaves this part and starts praising his patron Abū Jaʿfar Muḥammad who is a Persian. The poet presupposes that the Persians are naturally better than the Arabs. The poet takes the position of a Persian distancing himself from the Arabs by using 'we' (*mā*) and 'you' (*shumā*). Moreover, the lack of arbitration confirms the poet's partiality. This poem is a good example of debates on ethnicity showing how paradigms of 'we' versus 'the other' work. Promotion of identity and otherness cannot exist without praising one and refuting the other. P. Voestermans (1991: 219–21) distinguishes between 'alterity' as "discourse on the otherness of people" and 'identity' as "the affirmation of who we are by contrasting nearly every element of our way of life with that of others" creating a self-other dialectics (Voestermans 1991: 219). To define one's identity, one needs difference which is often interpreted as the other. Difference turns into otherness in a process of drawing a boundary between the self and the other. The poet's role in such cultural time-frame, in which the Persian language wanted to assert itself, was to define and enforce the boundaries to protect his own identity. To define such boundaries, the poet thinks of conflictive elements within one's culture to exclude the other, ideally naming the other's qualities in an eloquent fashion, magnifying the differences. Many of the boundaries easily shift, depending on the poet's purpose, literary, political, religious, and social codes.

When it concerns discussions on the superiority of Islam, the poet says that the rules and principles of Islam are equal to all people. Religion can remove otherness. He says, that in God's view, a person is more pious who is more fearful of God. Asadī wrote another debate poem of 108 couplets between a Muslim and a Zoroastrian, dedicating the poem to the just king (*shāh-i ʿādil*) and then to the Vizier, Abū Naṣr Aḥmad ibn ʿAlī. It is fascinating to examine how the poet treats Islam and Muslims against Zoroastrianism. In this poem, the two parties promise each other to convert to the other's religion depending on the convincing and forceful reasons offered by each party. Such debating poems between Muslims and the followers of other religions make sure that the Persians can confirm their Islamic faith while maintaining their ethnic background.

Contrary to the previous poem, the poet identifies himself with the Muslim contesting against the Zoroastrian, emphasizing in the opening lines that he is a

28 Khaleghi-Motlagh 1357/1978: 77, ll. 97–97, 100.

true Muslim, devoted to the Prophet Muḥammad. The Zoroastrian starts the contest by emphasizing the superiority of the fire over the earth, using the Empedocles' (c. 490 – c. 430 BC) theory of the Four Elements, i.e., fire, air, water, and earth. According to this theory the fire is put in the highest position while the earth is the lowest, and water and air are in the middle at either side. Their corresponding qualities are hot-dry, cold-moist, hot-moist and cold-dry respectively. According to Zoroastrian cosmogony, creation of the world is emanated from the divine essence, the Endless Light, through the omnipresent fire. The centrality of the fire in Zoroastrianism is a reason for the Zoroastrian to start his arguments by describing the qualities of the fire and why they venerate the fire. He identifies Islam with the earth and in the second part of the debate, the Muslim defends the earth's position by cataloguing the earth's qualities. The Zoroastrian alludes to cosmological aspects of the fire and how through the fire's warmth and light the clouds are made and how winds flow through the effect of hotness. Without the warmth of the fire nothing can grow. It is worth mentioning here that the Zoroastrian's use of the word fire includes a constellation of allusions, which metonymically refer to anything associated to fire and warmth.[29]

> The priest said: "My Kiblah is better than yours."
> because it brings fire from the earth with much excellence
> It is through the warmth of fire that clouds rise and the wind[30] moves;
> The earth allows trees to grow through fire's power.[31]

After these references, the Zoroastrian points to the ritual use of the fire in different cultures. He refers to the practice of burning corpses in fire in India but also to the Zoroastrian practice of putting a belt before the sacred fire:

> The Indians burn proudly their bodies in fire;
> the Zoroastrian priests girdle themselves with a belt before the fire. (...)
> It is through fire that the sky is illumined and the world is bright
> It is through fire that all people pass through this world to the other. (...)
> Death derives from coldness, and the earth has a cold temperament the soul derives from warmth, and the fire holds the warmth.[32]

29 On the veneration of fire by Zoroastrians see Boyce 1989.
30 Khaleghi-Motlagh has chosen for the variant *āb* 'water', but another variant reading is *bād* 'wind'.
31 Khaleghi-Motlagh 1357/1978: 80, ll. 4–5.
32 Khaleghi-Motlagh 1357/1978: 80, ll. 6, 9, 11.

The Zoroastrian then refers to the fire in the Islamic tradition. It is commonly believed that Abraham invited the people of Nimrod, who is the epitome of infidelity, to worship his God, Nimrod threw him into fire. Due to his faith to God, Abraham came unscathed from Nimrod's fire (Renard 1986). Persian poets such as Jalāl al-Dīn Rūmī (1207–1273) refer to this episode, stating that the fire changed into a garden.[33] Trials by fire is a recurring topic in Persian literary tradition, especially the trial of Siyāvash, who was accused of having sex with his step-mother. He had to go through a fire ordeal but he came out of it safely, proving his innocence. In the case of Abraham, he came out of the fire due to his trust in God. Interestingly, the Zoroastrian argues that Abraham proudly choose the fire:

> God made the fire one of the miracles of Abraham;
> Was the voice speaking to its friend Abraham or to the fire?
> Abraham rose from the fire and grow into a prophet with a mission,
> proudly choosing the fire, the kiblah of Zarathustra.[34]

Then, the Zoroastrian focuses on the hierarchy among the four elements, arguing the superiority of fire and why the other three elements owe their existence to the fire:

> The earth is lower than water and air and again fire
> Is on the top, below this Whirling dome.
> These three [elements] subsists through fire in whatever form,
> therefore, these three must accept their low positions.[35]

The Zoroastrian speaks of the fire's utilitarian role in daily life, pointing at how it burns incense and ambergris, as well as how fire is used to gauge the value of gold and silver:

> In the censer, the fire is the judge of ambergris and incense
> In the oven, the fire is the money-checker of gold and silver.
> Its flames are tongues, longing for gold and silver;
> In speaking the truth, the fire is like the pointer of the scale.[36]

---

33 See Renard 1986: 637 where he summarizes how Rūmī refers to the fire. Abraham was "like a gold coin, tested and proven; like a horseman he held the reins of the fire; like a moth he rested content in the flames. For Abraham, the fire became coolness and safety, his nurse, his wine. It was a delightful garden full of every kind of blossom and tree."

34 Khaleghi-Motlagh 1357/1978: 80, ll. 8–9.

35 Khaleghi-Motlagh 1357/1978: 81, ll. 13–14.

36 Khaleghi-Motlagh 1357/1978: 81, ll. 20–21.

In the next passage, the Zoroastrian praises the qualities of the sun. In many Persian poems, the qualities of the sun are enumerated. Here the poet only refers to several traits of the sun such as its central position in the firmament, by virtue of whose light people are able to see, the animals can exist, and the plants can grow:

> If I kneel before the sun, it is not a wonder,
> for I see the sun in the heat of the fire as friend.
> Also the sun is a messenger, sent by God of heavens.
> The Sun's miracle is that it gives sights to the eyes;
> From the sun, all hearts receive their lives;
> From the sun, all stars receive their lights. (...)
> When the sun rises, the animals start to move in cheers;
> When the sun sets, the animals will disappear again.
> The sun is like God's ambassador, decreeing
> two hundred thousand plants and branches to grow. (...)
> The sun is like a reviewer of the army, watching the march of plants;
> at spring time, it comes to the plains, mountains and dales. (...)
> If these virtues all belong to the sun and the fire,
> My kiblah is better [than yours] and you should not deny this.[37]

By identifying his faith with the sun, the Zoroastrian gives a final punch to the Muslim, whom he equates with the earth and how it depends on the warmth, light, and growing quality of the sun. The Muslim's response is rhetorically strong, listing a constellation of qualities attributed to the earth. He starts by stating that the reason why the earth is positioned the lowest among the four elements is because the earth is humble. The fire was not friendly to Abraham as it injured his tongue. This reference is probably wrong as fire burned Moses' tongue and not Abraham. The Muslim refers to the fire on the day of Resurrection and how it will burn the sinners in the hell. The fact that the earth is suspended in the heavens is through God's power and have nothing to do with the power of fire. The Muslim concentrates on the position of man on earth by referring to Adam's creation. Islamic tradition is rich with references to Adam as God's beloved, how he asked all angels to kneel before Adam, and how he appointed Adam as his vice-regent on the earth. Alluding cryptically to this event, the Muslim shows the centrality of the earth. As mankind is made of the clay, the earth has become the direction of worship of the whole world.

> What is the earth if it will be beneath the fire
> For it is humble and it is not a fault to be humble.

---

37 Khaleghi-Motlagh 1357/1978: 82–3, ll. 24–28 and 33.

If Abraham grow to a prophet by searching the fire,
it was the same fire that injured his tongue.
And if God talked to him through a voice,
didn't he say to the earth at Noah's deluge: "bring forth water!"
The believer and the unbeliever will see the fire on the Resurrection Day,
yet the fire is with the unbelievers in the hell. (...)
The earth has become the Kiblah through the virtue of Adam's clay;
God's angels are kneeling to it, while the prophets are its visitors.[38]

The Muslim sees the earth as a living creature. While it is a caravanserai housing people for a while, it is a rich table feeding all animals.

Food, cloth and all minerals come from the earth;
the colourful fruits of trees and the gems from the stones.
The earth is like a mother, while plants are the breast
The animals are like her children that she is embracing. (...)
The world is like a caravanserai, God is the host,
The earth is like a table for animals sitting to feed.
The earth is the spot of prostration so that you see how on her surface
All the world prays to God and asks forgiveness.
The wild beasts are kneeling while man is standing,
The trees are kneeling to praise God.[39]

After this reference to the lofty position of the earth, the Muslim gives a sweeping rebuttal on the Zoroastrian argument of the superiority of the fire among the four elements. The Muslim turns the quality of the earth as a passive element into a dynamic quality. The immovability of the earth is compared to the centrality of a medieval king's court around which the entire world revolves. The king is appointed by God and his court is the centre of the world. The geocentric position of the earth is here utilized to underscore how the other planets are leaning on the earth. The splendid image of the earth as a dot in the centre and the spheres moving in lines drawn by a pair of compasses is powerful. The fact that the fire, water, and wind can move are interpreted as the earth's servants, coming and going like servants at a court. Through the revolution of the planets, the seasons appear, which are in turn at the earth's service, offering specific colours to each

38 Khaleghi-Motlagh 1357/1978: 83, ll. 35–39, 43.
39 Khaleghi-Motlagh 1357/1978: 84, ll. 45–46; 85, ll. 48–50. The word *tashahhud* means "making a profession of religion by testifying the unity of God and the apostleship of Mouhammad" (Steingass 1963: 304). In this line the poet is depicting the posture of a person during the five times compulsory prayer. The posture of the trees is compared with the kneeling during the prayer.

season. The Muslim compares the earth to a book, and the trees as letters. The Muslim highlights man's close connection to the earth. Not only man is made of the earth, but his departure also depends upon the earth.

> The spheres are like a court while the earth is a king
> Firmly leaning on the earth, the elements are its servants.
> To serve the earth, they constantly come and go
> Whether they are day and night, the elements, or the moving stars.
> The seasons are all serving the earth because at good moments,
> it offers each of them attires, like donned idols.
> Sheer white for the winter, a two-coloured robe for the summer;
> Yellow silk for autumn, new brocade for spring. (...)
> The earth is like a book, the trees the letters of speech.
> The earth is like a dot, the spheres the lines of the compass. (...)
> Our coming is through the earth, our going is also through the earth;
> On Resurrection Day, we, small and big, rise from the earth.[40]

The final rebuttal of the Muslim corresponds to the Zoroastrian's praise of the sun. It is fascinating how the qualities of the sun are used to praise the earth's superior traits. One cannot look at the sun because its sharp rays will blind the eyes, and even the turning of the earth around the sun, creating day and night, is rather due to the earth. The Muslim uses a cliché image of the sun as the candle of the earth whose light is entirely for the sake of the earth:

> I also heard your speech about the sun:
> The sun is also occupied with the earth as long as it revolves.
> Although the eyes see things through its light,
> Yet if they look at the sun, they will destroy their eyes.
> If days appear through the rays of the sun, what is it
> that the dark night is from the shadow of the earth if looked well.
> The earth is the spread of God, the sun is its candle,
> Constantly shining upon the earth, upon the seas and deserts.
> The earth does not exist because of the candle but the candle
> has always existed for the earth's sake.[41]

After this speech turn, the Zoroastrian accepts the Muslim's superior arguments and converts to Islam, acknowledging that Islam is the true faith and that "Muḥammad is the best among the prophets and the saints" (l. 73). Of course, such poems have a ritually initiatory value to give space to people of other religions to voice their opinions about their own religions and criticize Islam. The audiences

40 Khaleghi-Motlagh 1357/1978: 85–86, ll. 51–54; 86, ll. 57, 59.
41 Khaleghi-Motlagh 1357/1978: 86, l. 65; 87, ll. 66–69.

of both of the poems analysed here are Persian Muslims. They present themselves as superior to the Arabs but more Muslims than the Arabs. This is a strategy to integrate Islam as a religion in the Persian culture and at the same time, emphasizing the differences between the Persians and the Arabs. In the early centuries of Islam, the Arabs considered themselves superior based on their religions, colour and bloodline, but the rise of several movements in Persian cultural areas was to challenge this superiority, longing for equality among all Muslims. It is certainly a strategy deployed by Asadī not fully exploiting the rich poetic repertoire associated with the sun in Persian poetry, instead giving much room to the Muslim to enumerate the qualities of the earth. The Zoroastrian is allowed to formulate his flow of arguments in thirty couplets while the Muslim does this in forty-one couplets, and the remaining thirty-five couplets praise his patron. Asadī's poem does not give an intricate technique of argumentation, but he rather catalogues qualities and virtues of religious hierarchies, determining the Persian Muslim position both ethnically (against the Arabs) and religiously (against the Zoroastrians).

3 A Debate Poem on the Persians and the Arabs in 20th-Century Iran

Asadī's poems belong to the category of texts that are still used in the Persian-speaking countries to emphasize the 'we' and 'other' paradigm. Nationalists and religious fanatics use such texts to provoke anti-Arabic and anti-Sunnite sentiments. Doing a google search on Asadī and *Munāẓarāt*, one can immediately find websites in which specific lines of his poetry are recited for nationalist agenda.[42]

An example of a modern debating context is the poet cleric Mishkāt, the pen name of Ḥājj Shaykh ʿAlī Imāmī Nūrī, also known under the name 'Friday Prayer of Kāshmar.' He was born in the city of Kāshmar in 1910 and died in 1996. He has written many poems on the Shiite saints, especially on the mourning of the third Shiite Imam Ḥusayn (killed 680). In his poem of thirty-three couplets, he names the qualities of the Persians, commencing with the pre-Islamic Persian kings, their justice and victories, but then he gives the speech turn to an Arab who refers to the Prophet Muḥammad, his offspring and several saints of the Arab origin. Afterwards he stresses how God chose to reveal his message in the Arabic

42 See, for instance, https://www.youtube.com/watch?v=7Xu5e_uugv0 (last accessed November 2019).

language through the Koran. The Persian admits all these and says that all of your arguments are certainly true but according to your own Arabic sources when the Persian king Bahman departed this ephemeral world, he had a daughter named Humā. All Persian nobles gathered at the court around this princess like moths fluttering lovingly around a candle light. With full devotion, they offered her the crown and the kingly ring. But now you should hear about manner and culture of the Arabs. Mishkāt continues that when Muḥammad, the pride of mankind, passed away, he had a daughter named Fāṭima al-Zahrā (606–632). The poet emphasizes that she was the lord of womankind, the envy of the sun and the moon, words fail to catch her qualities. Instead of honouring her, the Arab mobs rushed to her house, setting her door to fire, pushing the door's shaft on her, piercing it through her side, and killing her unborn baby Mohsen who was six months old:

> When Bahman departed this transient world,
> He had a daughter whose name was Humā.
> All Persian nobles and elites
> Went to the court, the sanctify place.
> They formed a circle around their princess;
> All became moths around that candle.
> In full contentment and satisfaction,
> They entrusted the crown and the ring to her.
> Listen to the manner and behaviour of the Arabs!
> I will explain how the Arabs's ways are.
> When the pride of the universe departed from this world,
> He left a daughter with the name of Fatima.
> What a daughter, she was the pride of the world.
> She was the lady and the leader of all women;
> Her brilliance had embarrassed the sun and the moon;
> The jinns and mankind were unable to praise her qualities.
> Instead of respecting her, the oppressing [Arab] tribe
> Rushed to her house
> Setting the door of her house in fire,
> Burning her heart through sorrow and tribulations.
> When the shaft of the door reached her side,
> Her six months old baby died as a martyr.
> She saw so much oppression from this folk
> That her tomb has become invisible from your eyes.[43]

Mishkāt's poem is interesting as it gives a new turn to the racial discussion. In this poem, the Persians are depicted as a people proud of their pre-Islamic her-

43 See http://meshkatkashmari.blogfa.com/category/6 (last accessed November 2019).

itage, associating the Persian kings with justice, and honouring women as their leader. Humā is one of the many legendary women whose exploits are recounted in lengthy medieval narratives (Hanaway 1989; Tafażżolī 1996a). The poet's reference to Humā is interesting as she is reported to be the daughter of Bahman but the same woman is also reported to become pregnant by her father in the ancient tradition of next-of-kin marriages common in Persia and Egypt.[44] The poet, a Shiite cleric, does not allude to such reference and simply emphasizes how the Persians hailed Humā as their queen, respecting her after the death of her father. The poet puts Humā's treatment in shrill contrast to the manner how the Arabs treat the daughter of the Prophet. While one becomes a queen, the other is beaten so badly that her unborn baby is killed. The poet uses these differences for his Persian Shiite audience to enlarge the hatred and enmity between the Shiites Persians and the Sunnite Arabs. This difference is further amplified by alluding to the 'invisible' grave of the unborn baby, pointing at the Wahhabi inhibition of worshipping the saints' mausoleums, which in Persian and Shiite context is very central.

In addition to its racial designation, this poem is probably used at Shiite mourning sessions on the death of Fāṭima.[45] She is the wife of the first Shiite Imam ʿAlī ibn Abī Ṭālib, and the mother of the second and the third Shiite imams Ḥasan, and Ḥusayn, who together with the Prophet form the *Ahl al-bayt*, 'the people of the house.' Also she is one of the fourteen 'immaculate beings' (*maʿṣūm*) in Shiite tradition. Moreover, like the other Shiite imams and saints, she will act as the intercessor (*shafīʿ*) on the Resurrection Day. She was deeply revered in Iran before the Islamic Revolution (1979) as the ideal mother and wife, who actively helped her husband in socio-political matters. Her position has become very prominent after the Revolution, as the Iranian Women's Day is on 20 Jumāda al-Thānī, Fāṭima's birthday. The death of her unborn baby Muḥsin struck her with such a sorrow that she wept for years that she received the title 'the Eternal Weeper.' At the annual mourning sessions of Fāṭima, people weep for the injustice and the violence inflicted upon her. The reference to Fāṭima and the violence to a pregnant woman would rouse the audience's emotions, which is the goal of such Shiite mourning sessions, offering them good reasons to openly weep for Fāṭima.

---

44 Perhaps the most extensive prose narrative on Homa is *Dārāb-nāma by the 12th century author* Abū Ṭāhir Muḥammad b. Ḥasan b. ʿAlī b. Musā Tarsūsī (or Tarṭūsī), in which the exploits of the legendary Kayanid king *Dārāb*, son of Bahman and Humā are recounted; see Hanaway 1996; Ṭarsūsī 1374/1995.

45 See Rosiny 2001; Sered 1991: 131–146. On Fatima's life see Veccia Vaglieri, 1965; Shariati 1983; Badry 2000; Nashat 1990.

4 Conclusion

Although Persian contest poetry is a favourite genre with much literary merits and flavour, the underlying motives to write many of such poems with themes which are related to race or moral virtues are to emphasize the supremacy of Persian culture over the Arabs or to challenge certain Islamic rules to criticize Islam, presenting new reasons why for instance drinking of wine is laudatory for Muslims or that being a good Muslim is based on piety and not on ethnicity. Asadī even denies Arab descent of the Prophet Muḥammad, declaring him a Persian. The same applies for the Shiite religious poets such as Mishkāt who give the example of Humā as the Persian queen, condemning the Arab's treatment of women in general, and especially the Prophet's daughter Fāṭima. The underlying message of several of the Persian contest poems are anti-Arab verbiage to secure the continuity of Persian pre-Islamic culture. In several of such poems, we also see strong anti-Sunnite sentiments, praising the Shiites, stressing the supremacy of Shiism over Sunnism. Debate poetry is a lucid example exhibiting how literary works serve political and cultural agendas, throughout one millennium. While Asadī's poems stress the Persian cultural and religious superiority in the eleventh century, Mishkāt's poem follows the same trace, adding Shiism and female veneration of the Shiites and the Persians at the centre.

Bibliography

Abdullaeva, Firuza. 2009. The Bodleian Manuscript of Asadī Ṭūsī's Munāẓara between an Arab and a Persian: Its Place in the Transition from Ancient Debate to Classical Panegyric. *Iran* 47: 69–95.

Abdullaeva, Firuza. 2012. The Origins of the *Munāẓara* Genre in New Persian literature. Pp. 249–273 in *Metaphor and Imagery in Persian Poetry*, ed. Ali Asghar Seyed-Gohrab. Leiden/Boston: Brill.

Agius, Dionisius A. 1980. The Shuʿūbiyya Movement and its Literary Manifestation. *The Islamic Quarterly* 24: 76–88.

Ahmed, Shahab. 2016. *What is Islam: The Importance of Being Islamic*. Princeton: Princeton University Press.

Ashraf, Ahamd. 2006. Iranian Identity, iii. Medieval Islamic Period. Pp. 507–522 in *Encyclopaedia Iranica*, ed. Ehsan Yarshater. New York: Encyclopaedia Iranica Foundation.

Badry, Roswitha. 2000. Zum Profil weiblicher ʿUlamā in Iran: Neue Rollenmodelle für 'islamische Feministinnen'. *Die Welt des Islams* 40/I: 7–40.

Belhaj, Abdessamad. 2016. Ādāb Al-Baḥth w-al-Munāẓara: The Neglected Art of Disputation in Later Medieval Islam. *Arabic Sciences and Philosophy* 26: 291–307.

van Berkel, Maaike. 2003. *Accountants and Men of Letters: Status and Position of Civil Servants in Early Tenth Century Baghdad*. PhD Dissertation University of Amsterdam.

Bertel's, Yevgeny E. 1374/1995. *Tārīkh-i adabiyyāt-i Fārsī: az dowrān-i Firdowsī tā 'ahd-e saljūgiyyān* (trans. Sirus Īzadī). Tehran: Hīrmand.

de Blois, François C. 2002. Zindik. Pp. 510–513 in *Encyclopaedia of Islam, Second Edition*, ed. Peri Bearman et al. Leiden: Brill.

Boyce, Mary. 1989. *Ātaš*. Pp. 1–5 in *Encyclopaedia Iranica*, ed. Ehsan Yarshater. London/New York: Routledge & Kegan Paul.

de Bruijn, Johannes T. P. 2006–2007. Spring versus Autumn: A Dispute in the Meadows of Thoughts. *Persica* 21: 1–8.

Dabiri, Ghazal. 2013. Historiography and the Shoʿubiya Movement. *Journal of Persianate Studies* 6: 216–234.

Daryaee, Touraj. 2012. Food, Purity and Pollution: Zoroastrian Views on the Eating Habits of Others. *Iranian Studies* 45/2: 229–242.

Duri, Abd al-Aziz. 1987. *The Historical Formation of the Arab Nation: A study in Identity and Consciousness* (trans. L. I. Conrad). London: Croom Helm.

Enderwitz, Susanne. 1997. Al-Shuʿūbiyya. Pp. 513–516 in *Encyclopaedia of Islam, Second Edition*, ed. Peri Bearman et al. Leiden: Brill.

Ethé, Carl H. 1881. Über persische Tenzonen. Pp. 48–135 in *Verhandlungen des fünften internationalen Orientalisten-Congresses* Vol. I, Berlin: A. Asher & Co Weidmannsche Buchhandlung.

Fahd, Toutic. 1991. Manāf. Pp. 349 *Encyclopaedia of Islam, Second Edition*, ed. Peri Bearman et al. Leiden: Brill.

Fry, Richard N. 1975. *The Golden Age of Persia* (reprinted 2003). London: Phoenix.

Furūzānfar, Badi al-Zamān Z. 1369/1980. *Sukhan wa sukhanvarān* (fourth print). Tehran: Khʷārazmī.

van Gelder, Geert Jan. 1987. The Conceit of Pen and Sword: On an Arabic Literary Debate. *Journal of Semitic Studies* 32/2: 329–360.

van Gelder, Geert Jan. 1991. Arabic Debates of Jest and Earnest. Pp. 199–211 in *Dispute Poems and Dialogues in the Ancient and Medieval Near East: Forms and Types of Literary Debates in Semitic and Related Literatures*, ed. Gerrit J. Reinink and Herman L. J. Vanstiphout. Orientalia Lovaniensia Analecta 42. Leuven: Peeters Press.

van Gelder, Geert Jan. 1998. Debate Literature. Pp. 186 in *Encyclopedia of Arabic Literature* 1, ed. Julie S. Meisami and Paul Starkey. London: Routledge.

Gibb, Hamilton A. R. 1962. The Social Significance of the Shuʿubiya. Pp. 62–73 in *Studies on the Civilization of Islam*, ed. Stanford J. Shaw and William. R. Polk. London: Routledge & Kegan Paul.

Goldziher, Ignaz. 2009 (third print). *Muslim Studies*, ed. Samuel M. Stern (trans. C. R. Barber and Samuel M. Stern). New Brunswick/London: Aldine Transaction.

Goodman, Len E. 1995. Al-Rāzī. Pp. 474–477 in *Encyclopaedia of Islam, Second Edition*, ed. Peri Bearman et al. Leiden: Brill.

Hanaway, William L. 1989. *Bahman-nāma*. Pp. 499–500 in *Encyclopaedia Iranica*, ed. Ehsan Yarshater. London/New York: Routledge & Kegan Paul.

Hanaway, William L. 1996. *Dārāb-nāma*. Pp. 8–9 in *Encyclopaedia Iranica*, ed. Ehsan Yarshater. Costa Mesa, California: Mazda Publishers.

Heinrichs, Wolfhart. 1991. Rose versus Narcissus. Observations on an Arabic Literary Debate. Pp. 179–198 in *Dispute Poems and Dialogues in the Ancient and Medieval Near East: Forms and Types of Literary Debates in Semitic and Related Literatures*, ed. Gerrit J.

Reinink and Herman L. J. Vanstiphout. Orientalia Lovaniensia Analecta 42. Leuven: Peeters Press.
Ibn Qutayba. 2017. *The Excellence of the Arabs by Ibn Qutaybah*, ed. James E. Montgomery and Peter Webb (trans. by Sarah B. Savant and P. Webb). New York: New York University Press.
Khaleghi-Motlagh, Djalāl. 1356/1977. Asadī-yi Ṭūsī. *Majalla-yi dānishkada-yi adabiyyāt va ʻulūm-i insānī-yi dānishgāh-i Firdowsī* 13/4: 643–678.
Khaleghi-Motlagh, Djalāl. 1357/1978. Asadī-yi Ṭūsī II. *Majalla-yi dānishkada-yi adabiyyāt va ʻulūm-i insānī-yi dānishgāh-i Firdowsī* 14/1: 68–130.
Khaleghi-Motlagh, Djalāl. 1987. Asadī Ṭūsī. Pp. 699–700 in *Encyclopaedia Iranica*, ed. Ehsan Yarshater. London/New York: Routledge & Kegan Paul.
Lecomte, Gérard. 1971. Ibn Ḳutayba. Pp. 844–847 in *Encyclopaedia of Islam, Second Edition*, ed. Peri Bearman et al. Leiden: Brill.
Lewis, Bernard. 1990. *Race and Slavery in the Middle East: An Historical Enquiry.* Oxford: Oxford University Press.
Madelung, Wilferd. 1986. Khurramiyya. Pp. 63–65 in *Encyclopaedia of Islam, Second Edition*, ed. Peri Bearman et al. Leiden: Brill.
Mottahedeh, Roy P. 1976. The Shuʿubiyah Controversy and the Social History of Early Islamic Iran. *International Journal of Middle East Studies* 7: 161–182.
Nashat, Guity. 1990. Women in the Islamic Republic of Iran. *Iranian Studies* 13, No. 1/4: 165–194.
Norris, Harry T. 1990. Shuʿūbiyya in Arabic Literature. Pp. 31–47 in *Cambridge History of Arabic Literature: Abbasid Belles-Letters*, ed. Julia Ashtiany et al. Cambridge: Cambridge University Press.
Pourshariati, Parvaneh. 2010. The *Akhbār al-Tiwāl* of Abū Ḥanīfa Dīnawarī: A *Shuʿūbī* Treatise on Late Antique Iran. Pp. 201–289 in *Sources for the History of Sasanian and post-Sasanian Iran*, ed. Rika Gyselen. *Res Orientales* 19. Bures-sur-Yvette: Groupe pour l'Étude de la Civilisation du Moyen-Orient.
Pūrjavādī, Nasrollāh. 1385/2006. *Zabān-i ḥāl*, Tehran: Hermes.
Reed, Thomas L. 1990. *Middle English Debate Poetry and the Aesthetics of Irresolution.* Columbia/London: University of Missouri Press.
Renard, John. 1986. Images of Abraham in the Writings of Jalāl ad-Dīn Rūmī. *Journal of the American Oriental Society* 106/4: 633–640.
Richter-Bernburg, Lutz. 1974. Linguistic Shuʿūbīya and Early Neo-Persian Prose. *Journal of the American Oriental Society* 94/1: 55–64.
Rosenthal, Franz. 1998. Ebn Qotayba, Abū Moḥammad ʿAbd-Allāh. Pp. 45–47 in *Encyclopaedia Iranica*, ed. Ehsan Yarshater. Costa Mesa, California: Mazda Publishers.
Rosiny, Stephan. 2001. The Tragedy of Fāṭima al-Zahrā' in the Debate of two Shiite Theologians in Lebanon. Pp. 206–219 in *The Twelver Shia in Modern Times; Religious Culture & Political History*, ed. Rainer Brunner and Werner Ende. Leiden: Brill.
Savant, Sarah B. 2013. Shuʻubis. P. 513 in *The Princeton Encyclopedia of Islamic Political Thought*, ed. Gerhard Bowering. Princeton: Princeton University Press.
Sered, Susan. 1991. Rachel, Mary, and Fatima. *Cultural Anthropology* 6/2: 131–146.
Serrano, Richard A. 1997. Al-Buḥturī's Poetics of Persian Abodes. *Journal of Arabic Literature* 28/1: 68–87.

Seyed-Gohrab, Ali A. 2013. The Rose and the Wine: Dispute as a Literary Device in Classical Persian Literature. *Iranian Studies* 47/1: 69–85.
Seyed-Gohrab, Ali A. 2015. Poetry as Awakening: Singing Modernity. Pp. 30–132 in *Literature of the Early Twentieth Century: From the Constitutional Period to Reza Shah*, Vol. 11, ed. Ali A. Seyed-Gohrab. London/New York: I. B. Tauris.
Seyed-Gohrab, Ali A. 2017. Manūchihrī's The Raven of Separation: Arabic Poetic Topoi and the Persian Courtly Tradition. *Iran-Namag* 2/3: 14–36.
Shakir, Mohammad H. No Date. *The Holy Qoran: Arabic Text and English Translation* (by M. H. Shakir). Tehran: Esmaʿilian, n.d.
Shariati, Ali. 1983. *Fatima is Fatima* (trans. Laleh Bakhtiar). Tehran: Shariati Foundation.
Sims-Williams, Nicholas. 1998. Ephesus, Seven Sleepers of. Pp. 474 in *Encyclopaedia Iranica*, ed. Ehsan Yarshater. Costa Mesa, California: Mazda Publishers.
Steingass, Franz. 1963 (fifth reprint). *Persian-English Dictionary.* London: Routledge & Kegan Paul.
Tafażżolī, Ahmad. 1996a. i.*DĀRĀ(B)* I. Pp. 1 in *Encyclopaedia Iranica*, ed. Ehsan Yarshater. Costa Mesa, California: Mazda Publishers.
Tafażżolī, Ahmad. 1996b. Draxt ī Āsūrīg. Pp. 547–549 in *Encyclopaedia Iranica*, ed. Ehsan Yarshater. Costa Mesa, California: Mazda Publishers.
Tafażżolī, Ahmad. 1376/1997. *Tārīkh-i adabiyyāt-i Īrān pīsh az islām.* Tehran: Sukhan.
Ṭarsūsī (or Tarṭūsī), Abū Ṭāhir Muḥammad b. Ḥasan b. ʿAlī b. Musā. 1374/1995. *Dārāb-nāma-yi Ṭarsūsī*, 2 vols. (third print), ed. Dhabih-Allāh Ṣafā. Tehran: ʿIlmī va Farhangī.
Veccia Vaglieri, Laura. 1965. Fāṭima. Pp. 841–850 in *Encyclopaedia of Islam, Second Edition*, ed. Peri Bearman et al. Leiden: Brill.
Voestermans, Paul. 1991. Alterity/Identity: A Deficient Image of Culture. Pp. 219–250 in *Alterity, Identity, Image: Selves and Others in Society and Scholarship*, ed. Raymond Corbey and Joep Leerssen. Amsterdam: Rodopi.
Webb, Peter. 2016. *Imagining the Arabs: Arab Identity and the Rise of Islam.* Edinburgh: Edinburgh University Press.
Yūsofī, Ḡolām-Ḥoseyn. 1989. Bābak Ḵorramī. Pp. 299–306 in *Encyclopaedia Iranica*, ed. Ehsan Yarshater. London/New York: Routledge & Kegan Paul.
Zarrīnkūb, ʿAbd al-Ḥoseyn. 1368/1989. *Tārīkh-i Īrān baʿd az islām.* Tehran: Amīr Kabīr.
Zimmt, Raz. 2015. Beehive: 'Arab Lizard and Grasshopper Eaters:' Incitement and Expressions of Racism on Iranian SNS. *Beehive: Middle East Social Media* (online available at https://dayan.org/content/beehive-arab-lizard-and-grasshopper-eaters-incitement-and-expressions-racism-iranian-sns; last accessed November 2019).

Hatice Aynur*

16 A Survey of Disputation Texts in Ottoman Literature

The literary debate genre is one that has been widespread and popular in Turkish literature, as it has been in so many other literary traditions around the world. The earliest known disputation poems in Turkish literature are found in the *Dîvânu Lugati't-Turk* (*Compendium of Turkic Dialects*),[1] an Arabic-Turkish dictionary written between 1072 and 1074 in Baghdad by Kaşgarlı Mahmûd (d. 1074). Ever since, disputation texts[2]—whether in prose, poetry, or a mix of the two—have remained popular in both Eastern and Western Turkish literature.[3]

Despite the popularity of the genre, disputation texts in Turkish literature have attracted relatively little scholarly interest. This is unfortunate, not only because they make for great reading, but also because they have the potential to offer a great deal to scholars in a wide number of fields. I aim, in the pages that follow, to rectify this state of affairs by providing a survey of these texts that I hope will serve both to promote awareness about them and to make them more accessible to other researchers. But before moving on to my survey of the texts themselves, a few words are in order on what has been written about them to date.

The origin and history of Turkish disputation texts and their possible links to Persian and Arabic disputation texts are poorly understood. In Turkey, it is widely accepted that debate poems developed out of the earlier literary debate tradition in Central Asia and that the Ottoman disputation genre is directly linked to these early Eastern Turkish examples.[4]

* İstanbul Şehir University.

1 For an English translation of the text, see Maḥmūd al-Kāšġarī 1985.

2 Most disputation texts in Turkish literature are in verse, but examples in prose can be found as well. Here, I use "text" to refer to both forms.

3 Different approaches exist to the classification and division of the Turkish language. In this article, I prefer to use the general division of Eastern Turkish and Western Turkish, with the former covering the Turkish used in Central Asia until the rise of the Central Asian states in the late nineteenth and early twentieth centuries and the latter covering the Turkish used in the Ottoman Empire and in modern Turkey. The writing of debate texts in both Eastern and Western Turkish has continued uninterrupted until today. For a scholarly evaluation of disputation texts in Eastern Turkish, see Jarring 1981.

4 The well-known scholar of Turkish literature Fuad Köprülü (1934: 22) wrote that the disputation genre spread to Persian and Arabic literature from Turkish folk literature. It was Turkish-origin Persian poets from Central Asia who wrote the earliest Persian debate poems, and poets from

https://doi.org/10.1515/9781501510274-016

The earliest such examples that we know of today are contained in Kaşgarlı Mahmûd's dictionary, a number of the entries in which include illustrative poetry excerpts of unknown authorship.[5] Among these excerpts, eight fall into the debate genre.[6] The inclusion of these disputation poems indicates that the genre was already well established in Turkish literature by the eleventh century, suggesting that the roots of the genre in Turkish go back to the pre-Islamic period. The topic of the eight quatrains (*dörtlük*) in Kaşgarlı Mahmûd's dictionary is a debate between summer and winter, with each season criticizing the other in an effort to establish its own superiority:

> Summer says to Winter: "The bullfinch flees from you, the swallow ... rests in me, the nightingale sweetly sings his songs, male and female couple" – that is to say, in summer (Maḥmūd al-Kāšġarī 1985, I: 387; III: 308).
> Winter says to Summer: "In you there arise scorpions; flies, gnats, (harmful worms) and snakes; [thousands and tens of thousands]; they tie their tails and attack."[7]

There are several disputation poems that date from the period between *Dîvânu Lugati't-Turk* and the earliest example of Ottoman Turkish disputation poems. Of these, three are particularly well known both inside and outside of Turkey. All three date from the first half of the fifteenth century: Ahmedî's *The Dispute between Musical Instruments* (*Sazlar Münâzarası*),[8] Yûsuf Emîrî's *The Dispute between Hashish and Wine* (*Beng ü Çağır*),[9] and Yakînî's *The Dispute between Arrow and Bow* (*Münâzara-i Ok ve Yay*).[10]

Once we reach the Ottoman period, the number of disputation texts increases dramatically. Though there are few in-depth studies of the genre, a number of smaller studies on individual texts do exist, especially in the form of a transcription of the text into the Latin alphabet with a brief introduction to the particular

---

the Khorasan region who wrote the earliest Arabic debate poems. For the beginnings of Persian debate poems and their connections to Arabic literature, see Abdullaeva [Melville] 2012: 249–73 and [Abdullaeva] Melville in this volume.

5 These poems are written in the form of quatrains or couplets. Dankoff and Kelly offer a list of the poems organized by topic at the end of their edition of the *Compendium of Turkic Dialects*. See Maḥmūd al-Kāšġarī 1985, III: 290–310.

6 The precise number of disputation poems in Kaşgarlı Mahmûd's work is the subject of some debate. Here, I accept the number that Robert Dankoff and James Kelly offer in their index to the *Dîvânu Lugati't-Turk:* Maḥmūd al-Kāšġarī 1985, III: 308–09.

7 Maḥmūd al-Kāšġarī 1985, II: 336; III: 309. Brackets and parentheses in the original. On debates between Spring and Winter, see also van Gelder in this volume.

8 For Ahmedî's book, see Bodrogligeti 1987: 55–88.

9 For Yûsuf Emiri's book, see Alpay 1973: 103–25.

10 For Yakînî's book, see İz 1962: 267–87.

text in question and the wider disputation-text genre. Most of the introductory parts of such studies repeat the classification Fatih Köksal offers in his article in the *Türkiye Diyanet Vakfı İslam Ansiklopedisi*, in which he groups the texts in the genre into a varying number of thematic categories arranged according to chronological order (Köksal 2006: 580–81). While Köksal's article took into account many previously unconsidered or unknown debate texts and was a valuable contribution to the literature at the time, the publication of a number of new edited texts and studies on the genre in the years since has left it somewhat dated in terms of its comprehensiveness and approach.

This paper aims to offer a more up-to-date survey of the texts in the genre, but not a comprehensive one. It will be confined to two main types of texts: stand-alone texts and texts that are part of larger works. Texts of the second type are mostly found in *mesnevî* works (in other words, a section of long versified stories). Unfortunately, I will not be able here to focus on disputation texts in folk literature or those that are part of a divan (the collected poems of a poet), with the exception of one qasida I deal with in the section on the Sword and the Pen below. My reason for excluding the folk texts is that their structure and form are slightly different from those of the other texts I discuss here; coupled with this is the sheer number of these folk texts, which would make it impossible to do them justice here even were it not for the methodological difficulties involved.[11] As for the poems in divans, I have left them out because very little research has been done on them, and the few random examples that have been studied provide insufficient grounds to say anything conclusive.[12]

The titles of Turkish disputation texts generally begin with the Arabic term *munâzara* or, in a few cases, the Arabic term *mubâhasa*, both of which mean disputation, debate, or discussion. In the Ottoman context, these two terms' Turkish cognates, *münâzara* and *mübâhase*, are slightly different from each other. The parties involved in a *münâzara* work collaboratively to reach the truth. To that end, they do not oppose the evidence the other parties bring forward. In a *mü-*

11 Debate poems in folk literature are poorly studied. It is not clear how many such texts there are, though there are clearly many. I am thus reluctant to go into too much detail about them here, but one thing it is possible to say is that in Turkish folk poems, the use of question-and-answer forms is popular. In some cases, virtually every new couplet or sometimes line has an accentuated incipit like "Said he ..., Said I," which gives many folk poems a disputational aspect even when they do not overtly embrace a disputational theme or otherwise follow the patterns of the other poems I discuss here. Including them would thus have introduced problems of definition and categorization that I prefer to avoid. For question-and-answer poems, see Günay 1976: 253–57; İvgin 1982, II: 255–64; Tuncalp 1969: 7–9.

12 For an example of a disputation poem in a divan, see Hayâlî Bey's (d. 1557) eleven-couplet ghazel entitled *The Debate of Sun and Moon* (*Münâzara-i Mihr ü Mâh*) in Tarlan 1945: 83.

bâhase, however, the parties involved are characterized by animosity towards one another, and their discussions involve sarcasm. Turkish texts, like Arabic and Persian disputation texts, are in verse, in prose, in rhymed prose, or in combination of the three (in rhymed prose interspersed with poetry).

In my research, I have come across thirty-six Ottoman-Turkish disputation texts,[13] which I have classified according to their topics under fifteen thematic headings: the Contest of Pleasurable Substances (twelve texts), the Sword and the Pen (seven texts), the Parrot and the Crow (three texts), Spring and Winter (two texts), Earth and Sky (two texts), Pederasts and Womanizers (two texts), Contest of the Fruits (one text), Man and Beast (one text), Contest of the Birds (one text), the Ball and the Polo Stick (one text), Sugar and Salt (one text), Day and Night (one text), the Candle and Censer (one text), and Candle and Moth (one text).

In this paper, I offer a brief overview of the debate texts in each of the categories listed here, except for those in the first category, which I discuss at slightly greater length. While it is impossible to focus on any of the texts in detail, I do

13 There are a number of additional texts I have encountered that I do not include in this total, as they are either inaccessible or else defy easy categorization. What follows is a list of these poems, with a brief description for each. *Lutfî's Münâzara:* The subject of the poem and the identity of the poet Lutfî are obscure. The sources that mention the poem do not give any information as to whether this *münâzara* belongs to the famous fifteenth-century poet Lutfî from Central Asia. *Necâtî's (d. 1508) Münâzara-i Gül ü Hüsrev:* The only available five couplets from the text suggest that the topic of the contest could be the arrow and the bow. *Celâl Bey's (d. after 1571) Sa'd u Sa'îd:* The only information about this work is contained in Ahdî's *Tezkire* (Solmaz 2005: 121). Ahdî (d. 1593/94) mentions in his entry on Celâl Bey that he wrote a book called *Sa'd u Sa'îd* in the *münâzara* style. The subject of the disputation is unknown. *Latîfî's (d. 1582) Fusûl-i Erbaa:* This book has long been categorized as part of the *münâzara* genre, but this seems untenable. Latîfî wrote this book in four separate parts, each with its own title. In each part, a single narrator (Latîfî) explains the characteristics of a particular season in prose interspersed with poetry, but nowhere does one find anything resembling a *münâzara*. However, the word itself does appear at a number of points in the text. At the beginning of the part on spring, for example, the narrator says that while strolling through a garden, he engaged in a *münâzara* with a nightingale, but there is no actual *münâzara* text. Elsewhere in the book, *münâzara* is used in two subheadings, but again, there is no *münâzara* text. Also, it is unclear whether these headings belong to Latîfî himself or whether they were added later. The latter seems more likely, as other copies of the book use the word *menkabet* instead of *münâzara* for these headings. Since nothing in the text itself could have led to its being categorized as a work in the *münâzara* genre, it seems most likely that the reason for this mischaracterization is that when the four parts of this work were brought together and printed as a single volume in Istanbul 1870, they were published under the title *Münâzara-ı Latîfî*. Later researchers seem to have read much of the title but little of the actual book, thus leading them to repeatedly cite it as an example of a genre of which it is not, in fact, a part. For the text of *Fusûl-i Erbaa*, see Sevgi 1987: 137–221.

offer basic information on each text, where available, including its title, author, date of composition, the names of the contenders in the debate, and the result of the debate. I also review and comment on the secondary sources on the given texts where applicable.

1 The Contest of Pleasurable Substances

The sixteenth-century Ottoman biographical dictionaries of poets (*tezkires*), such as those of Âşık Çelebi (d. 1572; Âşık Çelebi 2010) and Latîfî (d. 1582; Latîfî 2000), are full of anecdotes and details on how Ottoman poets enjoyed themselves and spent time together, the places where they socialized,[14] and what they ate and drank during these gatherings (*meclis*).[15] Mind-altering substances seem to have been a fixture in many of these gatherings, with wine, opium, hashish, and several others particularly popular. Less popular, or at least mentioned less frequently in the *tezkires*, were coffee and tobacco. According to Kâtib Çelebi (d. 1657; Kâtib Çelebi 1972: 39) and the historian Peçevî (d. 1651; Peçevî 1283 [1866], I: 363–64), coffee was first imported to Istanbul in 1543. Gelibolulu Âlî (d. 1600; Mustafâ Âlî 1997: 363–64) and Peçevî (1283 [1866], I: 363–64) mention that the first coffeehouses were later opened in Tahtakale by Hekîm from Aleppo and Şems from Damascus. According to Âşık Çelebi's *tezkire*, the earliest poem on coffee was written before 1570 by the poet Belîğ (d. 1572/73? Âşık Çelebi 2010, I: 427). Other substances, too, were also a popular topic for poems. From the late sixteenth century onward, these substances found their way into the debate genre and seem to have become the single most popular theme among Ottoman poets and writers, with twelve separate texts discovered so far. These texts can be divided into two groups.

The texts in the first group focus on only two substances—or, we can say, they have only two main characters—which they refer to in their titles. Examples of this sort of poem were penned by Yusuf Emiri (*Beng ü Çagır/Hashish and Wine*) and the renowned poet Fuzûlî (d. 1556). Fuzûlî wrote *The Debate of Hashish and Wine* (*Beng ü Bade*) in Turkish between the years 1510 and 1514 and dedicated the poem to Shah Ismail (d. 1524). It was in mesnevî form with 445 couplets.[16]

14 For meeting places in Istanbul in the sixteenth century, see Aynur 2018.

15 For these, especially Ottoman courtly gatherings, see İnalcık 2011.

16 There are around seventy manuscript copies of *Beng ü Bâde*, most of which are in Turkey and Iran. The work has also been published eight times in Tabriz, Tashkent, and Istanbul in Arabic letters. Many scholarly editions of the text have also been published with introductions in Turkey and abroad. For detailed information and a copy of the text in English, see Gibb 1904,

The winner of the debate is wine. In 1931, the literary historian Tahir Olgun declared, in an assumption that has been widely accepted ever since, that hashish represented the Ottoman sultan Bâyezîd II (d. 1512) and wine represented the Persian Shah Ismail.[17]

Gâzî Giray (d. 1607), the khan of Crimea, was an admirer of Fuzûlî's poem[18] and wrote *The Dispute between Coffee and Wine* (*Kahve ve Bâde*) in verse when he was in the city of Pecs in Hungary around 1603.[19] Unfortunately, no copy of the manuscript is known to have survived. Nevertheless, the title marks this poem as coffee's first appearance as a contender in a debate text in world literature.[20]

Another significant disputation poem in this group is *Münâzara-i Kahve vü Bâde* by Nağzî (Nağzî 2014). It was written in mesnevî form with more than 4,300 couplets and 266 subtitles in 1625/26. Nağzî took part in the war between the Ottomans and Persians in 1615 and was held captive in Iran. Finally able to return to Istanbul ten years later, Nağzî found his homecoming bittersweet. Upon his return, he discovered that he had lost his family. He had no job, and he soon fell into poverty. His friends proved to be of little help. He seems to have turned to pleasurable substances as a means of consolation. To further amuse himself, he decided to compose a poem on an original theme. Unaware of Gâzî Giray's work, he thought that no one had written about coffee and wine before and set the two as his theme. The story begins with a portrayal of spring and a pan-

III: 88–89. For a German version of the text, see *Des türkischen dichters Fuzûlî: poëm "Laylâ-Meğnun" und die gereimte Erzählung "Benk u Bade"* (Haşiş und Wein) 1943: 150–204.

17 [Olgun], 1931: 54–55. This assumption needs further research. It is not grounded in the text itself, but rather in the historical context of the period. When Fuzûlî was writing his debate, Bâyezîd II—known as Bâyezîd the Pious—was in his sixties and Shah Ismail was a young man, and the power struggle between the Ottomans and Safavids was just beginning. Both characters (wine and hashish) in the text also have strong personalities and so can be taken to represent real persons. Additionally, Shah Ismail was fond of wine and Bâyezîd II fond of hashish in his youth.

18 It should be mentioned here that another admirer of Fuzûlî, Hâcî Mehdî Şukûhî (d. 1896), who was born in Tabriz and wrote in Azeri Turkish, wrote a parallel text to *Beng ü Bâde*. It was in *mesnevî* form, with 516 couplets. He called his poem *Münâzara-i Akl u Aşk* (The disputation between reason and love).

19 The only available information on the text is in Peçevî's (d. 1649) history. See Peçevî, 1283 [1866/67], II: 251; Peçevi İbrahim Efendi 1982, II: 236.

20 Coffee's appearance in other branches of this genre outside Turkish literature occurs later. The next that I am aware of is from the Yemeni literary tradition of debates over pleasurable substances and was written later in the seventeenth century: a poetic debate between coffee and *qāt* written in Judeo-Yemeni and attributed to Rabbi Sālim al-Shabazī (d. c. 1679). See Tobi 2008: 301–10; Wagner 2005: 121–49.

egyric qaside to Sultan Murâd IV (r. 1623–1640), who two years earlier had ascended to the throne at the age of eleven. Later, Murâd IV would be remembered for the severe restrictions he placed on the consumption of alcohol, tobacco, and other pleasurable substances while he was on the throne. In the introduction to his poem, Nağzî states that his work reflects his personal experience. The text is significant for its detailed depictions of the origins, the spread, and the contemporary vogue of coffee drinking. The narrative also includes descriptions of the entertainment practices and centers of the capital. At the end of the text, there is no winner and, with the help of the cupbearer, coffee and wine make peace.

The second, and perhaps more interesting, group of Contest of Pleasurable Substances texts has more than two characters. In this group, there are nine texts, the writers of seven of which are unknown. Most of these texts are written in prose interspersed with poems.

Mübâhasât-ı Mükeyyefât:[21] The first text of this type was written by the famous Ottoman physician Nidâî Efendi (d. after 1567), who was also the author of a popular rhymed work on medicine. This is the earliest example of a text in Ottoman Turkish that features a debate between more than two pleasure-giving substances. The beginning and the end of the work are in verse and the other parts are in prose. The author says he wrote the text as a humorous way of entertaining and alleviating the sorrow of those suffering from quitting pleasurable substances. In the text, six contenders—opium, *bersh* (a compound drug apparently of varying composition, containing opium and sometimes cannabis),[22] hashish, *boza* (a fermented beverage made from malted millet or other grains), wine, and mead (honey wine)—argue over which one of them is superior. Among the contenders, mead is the winner.

Mahzenü'l-Esrâr/Dâfi'ü'l-Hüzn: This was written by Vardarlı Fazlî (d. after 1636) in mesnevî form with 764 couplets. There are six contenders: hashish, *bersh*, opium, coffee, wine, and *boza*.[23] The text is divided into eighteen sections.

---

21 Büyükkarcı Yılmaz 2013: 681–704.

22 Ahmet Talât Onay (1992: 77) mentions that in Ottoman coffeehouses, patrons would be served one cup of *bersh* "syrup" before they were served their coffee. This one cup of *bersh* was apparently enough to make them "drunk." During the month of Ramadan, after the breaking of the fast at sunset, drinkers reportedly preferred to drink *bersh* in place of wine.

23 İ. Hakkı Aksoyak published two articles on Fazlî's disputation text in 2016 and 2018. In the first, he introduced the content of the text; in the second, he published the text itself. See Aksoyak 2016: 223–43; Aksoyak 2018: 78–137. In the 2016 article, Aksoyak lists the number of contenders as eight. The two additions he makes to the six I list above are *beng* and *fünûniyyâ*. This seems to be a mistake, as *beng* was another term Ottoman authors used for cannabis or hashish, and it is likely as a synonym for hashish that Fazlî used the term here. Likewise, Fazlî seems to have used *fünûniyyâ* as a kind of nickname for *bersh* in reference to its composite composition,

Throughout the poem, especially from sections nine to eighteen, each contender enumerates the proofs of its superiority or insults the other contenders. At the end of the dispute, *bersh*, opium, and hashish throw their support behind coffee and unite against wine. Wine then quits the debate and goes to Europe, leaving coffee the winner.

Two years before Fazlî wrote the poem, on 2 September 1633, a great fire tore through Istanbul and burned down roughly one-fifth of the city. The sultan, Murâd IV, apparently believing that the fire had started in a coffeehouse and fearing another, demolished coffeehouses across the city—with the help of the famous preacher Kâdîzâde Mehmed Efendi (d. 1635), who viewed both coffee and tobacco as haram—and built in their place special rooms for singles, blacksmiths, and tanners (Yılmazer 2006: 179). The sultan also forbade the smoking of tobacco.[24] Sections four and five of Fazlî's poem describe how the severity of Murâd IV's severe restrictions on the consumption of tobacco affected peoples' lives.

When Coffee arrives in at the session, a member of the *meclis* wants to ask him what happened to his friend Tobacco, but is afraid to say his name:

> You had a very close friend—more than a friend,
> You were confidants and soulmates.
> Wherever you would go, he would go too;
> Wherever you would sit, he would sit too.
> ...
> Do not speak his name to me!
> Mention not his moniker or description!
> Were you to speak and the qadi to hear,
> They would come for you, and then for me.
> Those who speak his name are hanged,
> Their houses and their business attacked.
> Those who love him risk their teeth,
> Their noses, and their ears.
> Some are even dragged by horses.
> Or have reeds jammed under their nails.
> They have raised the world against him,
> And procured a fatwa that he be burned.

---

as indicated by couplet 166, where he describes bersh as "a young person [who is] steeped in the sciences [*zû-fünûn*] and elegant" (*Bir civân-ı zû-fünûn u hem zarîf*). However, also see Aynur and Schmidt (2007: 69 n. 46), where the same term is used in reference to opium specifically. In either case, it seems that *fünûniyyâ* is being used here as a synonym for another substance else rather than as a substance in its own right.

24 Although Murâd IV indulged in wine, he hated opium and tobacco (Yılmazer 2006: 179). Kâdîzâde Mehmed Efendi supported the tobacco ban of the sultan as well.

And then, on the sultan's order,
They burned my friend like so much wood.

In the following section of the poem, Coffee offers an elegy for his friend Tobacco.

[Letâif]: No title or author are available in the text. It was most probably written in the middle of the seventeenth century.[25] There are seven participants: opium, *bersh*, hashish, *boza*, wine, mead, and coffee. At the end of the debate, coffee is the winner.[26] One of the important features of this debate is the place of coffee. In the session where coffee comes to the gathering, all contenders salute him with a great respect:

> Welcome, O most distinguished and well-known person of our time; after you came to the world, no place remained for us here. Your fame is too great, and we can do naught but accept it.[27]

Menâkıb-ı Mükeyyefât-ı Âlem: This was written by Sıhhatî Çelebi (d. 1692/93). The number of contenders in this text is seven. Compared to the protagonists in Nidâî's text, here, coffee and arak (modern *rakı*, an anise-flavored liquor) replace mead. Tobacco joins the sessions with coffee, but remains silent during the debate.[28] One of the important features of this debate is the place of coffee. Like the previous text, in the session where coffee comes to the gathering, all contenders salute him with great respect.

Although the debate continues, we understand that coffee is going to win. At the end of the dispute, coffee exiles wine and arak to Europe and *boza* to Tataristan, while opium, *bersh*, and hashish stay with coffee.[29]

---

25 The manuscript copy of the text is in the Süleymaniye Library: Tercüman no. 361. For an analysis of this text, see Aynur and Schmidt 2007: 69–73.

26 Imported from Yemen by way of Egypt, coffee was consumed privately and publicly in coffeehouses in the Ottoman Empire from the second half of the sixteenth century onward. In the late sixteenth and seventeenth centuries, some sultans prohibited coffee as a deplorable innovation, the substance not having existed in the prophet Muhammad's time. See Aynur and Schmidt 2007: 55.

27 Büyükkarcı Yılmaz 2013: 689. Translation is mine.

28 In some texts, tobacco joins the sessions with coffee but remains silent during the debate. The silence of tobacco needs further research, but it is likely related to Murâd IV's harsh measures against tobacco, mentioned in the poem above.

29 Here, and in a number of other texts, coffee exiles some of the substances abroad after its victory. Although no work has been done on this subject, we can assume that these exile locations are not chosen by accident. A close reading of each substance's presentation of itself offers a clue of the connection between the substance and its place of exile. For example, in his study

Hikâyet-i Cem'iyyet-i Mükeyyefât-ı Âlem ve Mübâhase ve Mücâdele:[30] The writer and date of completion of this text are unknown, but it was copied in 1737.[31] There are fourteen protagonists: opium, *bersh*, hashish, *boza*, wine, mead, arak, tobacco, apple wine, *müselles* (syrup or wine, reduced to a third distillation), *mukim* (?), *mâddetü'l-ferah* (exhilarating medicine), "musky ... [illegible]," and coffee.

According to text, coffee's arrival at the gathering is similar to that of a sultan arriving with grand viziers, ulema, and military men. All contenders stand up and salute him with great respect: "Welcome, O most distinguished and well-known person of our time" (Büyükkarcı Yılmaz 2013: 690). At the end of the session, hashish and wine fight, and hashish is defeated and runs away. Among the remaining contenders, opium, *bersh*, *mukim*, *mâddetü'l-ferah*, and tobacco throw their support behind coffee and the rest do so for wine. There result is a stalemate between wine and coffee.

Muhâleme-i Mükeyyefât: The author and date of composition of this text are unknown, but it was copied in 1750 in Istanbul. There are similarities between Sıhhatî Çelebi's text and this one, perhaps indicating that this is a shortened version or imitation of that text. The name and number of the contenders are the same. At the end of the debate, coffee exiles wine and arak to Europe and *boza* to Tataristan, while opium, *bersh*, and hashish stay with coffee, as in Sıhhatî Çelebi's text.

[Münâzara-i Mükeyyefât]: Its title, author, and date of composition are unknown. It was in a scrapbook preserved in the manuscript collection of the University Library of Leiden.[32] The text is in written prose with the interpolation of verse in the narration. The author was likely an inhabitant of Istanbul, as the text contains several references to districts and institutions of the Ottoman capital (Aynur and Schmidt 2007: 56). The text might have been written in the seventeenth century, or perhaps later. The number of the contenders is six: hashish, *bersh*, opium, *boza*, wine, and coffee. At the end of the debate, wine, *boza*,

on *Hikâyât-ı Mükeyyefât-ı Âlem*, Fatih Ülken wrote a chapter on the geographical regions and places where pleasurable substances were consumed. According to *Hikâyât-ı Mükeyyefât-ı Âlem*, *boza* was associated with Tataristan and Crimea; beer, with Transylvania and Erdel; mead, with Rumelia, Bosnia, and Erdel; cherry liqueur, with Edirne and Belgrade; *müselles*, with Gallipoli and Erdel; wine and arak, with Europe; hashish, with frontier lands; and opium, *bersh*, tobacco, and coffee, with Istanbul. See Ülken 2017a: 271–72.

30 Büyükkarcı Yılmaz 2013: 690.

31 The manuscript copy of this text is in the Atatürk Library (Istanbul): Belediye K. 633/6, 35v-49r.

32 The text was published with a detailed study by Hatice Aynur and Jan Schmidt. See Aynur and Schmidt 2007.

and hashish are respectively exiled to Europe, the land of the Tatars, and Khorasan, while opium, *bersh*, and coffee, the clear winners of the debate, remain together.

[Mükeyyefât-ı Âlem]: This work's title, author, and date of composition are unknown. A facsimile edition with an introduction was published by Hans Joachim Kissling (d. 1985; Kissling 1971: 285 – 303). Kissling mentioned that it was in a scrapbook preserved in his collection. Prior to that, the manuscript was in the collection of the famous German Turcologist and Orientalist Theodor Menzel (d. 1939). The number of contenders is seven: *bersh*, opium, hashish, *boza*, arak, wine, and coffee. Tobacco joins the sessions with coffee, but remains silent during the debate. This seems to resemble Nidâî's text, but further research is needed to draw any connection between the two texts or any others.

Hikâyât-ı Mükeyyefât-ı Âlem: This work is written in prose with only one couplet of poetry; its author and date of composition are unknown (Ülken 2017a: 261 – 76). There are twelve contenders: hashish, *bersh*, opium, *boza*, wine, beer, mead, cherry liqueur, *müselles*, arak, coffee, and tobacco (which does not join the debate). Compared to the previous texts, beer and cherry liqueur here become contenders for the first time. The winner of the debate is coffee. Coffee sends wine and arak to Europe, *boza* to Tataristan, beer to Wallachia, mead to Bosnia, cherry liqueur to Edirne and Belgrade, and *müselles* to Gallipoli and Transylvania, while he makes opium and *bersh* his siblings and tobacco his servant.

⋆ ⋆ ⋆

It is not surprising that after Nidâî Efendi's work in the late sixteenth century, there were an increasing number of Contest of Pleasurable Substances texts with more than two characters in the Ottoman world. The consumption of mind-altering substances—especially wine, opium, hashish, *bersh*, *boza*, tobacco, and coffee—was popular,[33] and the places where these substances were consumed, especially coffeehouses, was an important issue in Ottoman times.

---

33 For example, in *Hikâyât-ı Mükeyyefât-ı Âlem*, different substances are associated with the particular groups of people who use them: opium is associated with witty and elegant persons; bersh, with witty and elegant *çelebi*s (gentlemen of status); hashish, with madrasa students and Bektashis; *boza*, with Tatars, ghazis in border regions, torchbearers, mule drivers, stablemen, and servants; beer, with poor people and nobles; mead, with the elite circle of Rumelia, chiefs, ghazis, and Bosnian dignitaries; cherry liqueur, with the ruling elites and members of the palace; wine, with the common people; and coffee, with both poor people and rich people. Ülken 2017a: 270 – 71.

2 The Sword and the Pen (*Kılıç ve Kalem*)

The Sword and the Pen was one of the most popular debate themes in pre-modern literature and the second most important dispute subject for Ottoman writers.[34] I have identified seven texts in this category.

Kasîde fî Bahsi's-Seyf ve'l-Kalem: The earliest available example of the debate between sword and pen was written in qaside form (eighty-one couplets) by one of the most prolific authors in Anatolia in the fourteenth century, Ahmedî (d. 1413).[35] The composition date must have been before 1410, because it was presented to Emir Süleymân (d. 1410) and also has Emir Süleymân as an arbiter in the text.[36] In the text, the pen and the sword try to justify their superiority over each other using many different arguments. Neither accepts the other's superiority, so both the pen and the sword go to Emir Süleymân to decide which of them is superior. He says that the pen and the sword both belong to him and that he does not want them to fight, thus declaring no winner.

Münâzara-i Seyf ü Kalem: This was written in prose interspersed with verse in 1485 in Balıkesir by Uzun Firdevsî (d. after 1517), who is known for his multi-volume work *Süleymânnâme-i Kebîr* on the life of the philosopher-king Solomon (Firdevsî-i Rûmî 2017). He dedicated it to Bâyezîd II (r. 1481–1512). The debate takes place in King Solomon's palace during a *meclis*. In this *münâzara*, two fictional characters represent the sides in the debate. The pen is voiced by the Scribe Nasir bin Feylesof and the sword by the Arab commander Ra'd bin Berk. The two engage in a debate to decide who should be King Solomon's grand vizier. Both the sword and the pen make claims of superiority with reference to verses of the Koran and the hadith and sayings of the prophet Muhammad, and each tries to refute the claims of the other. In the end, King Solomon, acting as arbiter, reconciles the adversaries, saying that both are indispensible: the realm cannot exist without the pen, and no king can reign without the sword.[37]

---

34 In his article, Geert Jan Van Gelder (1987: 337) details the historical background of debates between the pen and sword. According to his research, the pen and sword theme appeared for the first time in Arabic literature.

35 Ahmedî is famous for his *İskendernâme* (The story of Alexander) mesnevî, and he was also the first author to compose a book on the history of the Ottoman dynasty, *Tevârîh-i Âl-i Osmân* (The histories of the dynasty of Osman), written before 1410.

36 Fort the text, see Kadıoğlu 2011: 161–80.

37 In Gelder's article, there is a similar quotation, but from Arabic primary sources and with a clear hierarchy: "Alexander the Great or another Greek ruler or sage said: 'This world's affairs

Risâle fî Mufâharâtı's-Seyf ve'l-Kalem: According to most relevant secondary sources, the famous sixteenth-century scholar and poet Kınalızâde Alî Çelebi (d. 1572) wrote a debate text in Turkish on the sword and the pen, entitled *Seyf ve Kalem (*Köksal 2006: 581*).*However, Hasan Aksoy's study on Alî Çelebi's works has shown that his book was written in Arabic, in verse with the interpolation of Koranic verses, and that its actual title is *Risâle fî Mufâharâtı's-Seyf ve'l-Kalem.*[38] The two available copies of the text are in Istanbul.[39]

Münâzara-i Seyf ü Kalem: This text was written by Naîmî-i Hâmidî in the sixteenth century. No known copy of the text exists. The only information on the text—the writer, the title, and six couplets from the text—is available in Latîfî's biographical dictionary of poets, *Tezkiretü'ş-şu'ârâ* (Latîfî 2000: 163–64).

Münâzara-i Tîğ u Kalem: This text was written in verse interspersed with rhymed prose by Şabânzâde Mehmed Muhteşem (d. 1708/09) in 1683.[40] There are two contenders (the sword and the pen) and a judge (*Akl*/Reason). In thirty-six sections, both the sword and the pen make claims of superiority and try to point out the shortcomings of the other. At the end of the debate there is no winner; the two contenders then approach Reason to decide the victor, and he chooses the pen over the sword. According to Reason, the world is conquered by the sword, but the well-being of the state is made perennial by the pen.

Muhâverât-ı Seyf u Kalem: This text was written in prose by Cemâl Efendi, who was acting second secretary of the Council of Education.[41] Although there is no information on its exact date of composition, we can assume from Cemâl Efendi's position that it was written between 1845 and 1856. No manuscript copy of text exists, but there is a printed version of the text with no details about its date or place of publication. The text is very similar to Muhteşem's text in terms of its structure and content. There are two contenders in text, the sword and the pen, with Reason as arbiter. Again, there is no ultimate winner,

---

are determined by two things only, and one of them is inferior to the other: they are the sword and the pen, and the sword is inferior to the pen'." See Gelder 1997: 337 n. 29.

38 Aksoy 1976: 42. For a detailed account of his life and works, see Oktay 2002: 207. Apart from this disputation poem, Alî Çelebi wrote two widely circulated treatises on the sword and the pen in Arabic. One of them praises the qualities of the pen (*Risâle-i Kalemiyye*), while the other praises the qualities of the sword (*Risâle-i Seyfiyye*). The writing of treatises on qualities of the pen and the sword was popular among Ottoman authors, most of whom were scholars or members of the bureaucratic class. For a brief evaluation of these treatises, see Tuşalp Atiyas 2017: 131–33.

39 Süleymaniye Library-Esad Efendi Collection- 3724/3, 3^{v}-4^{v}; Ali Emiri Library-Millet Genel-433/2, 4^{v}-5^{r}.

40 For a study on the social and intellectual context of the text, see Tuşalp Atiyas 2017: 113–55.

41 For the text, see Ülken 2017b: 278–83.

so they go to Reason to decide which is superior. But in this case, Reason demands that they make peace and declares no winner. Fatih Ülken, however, proposes that there are two possible readings of the result in the text. The first one is the explicit one: that there is no winner. The second one is that the actual winner is the pen, because in text the first speaker was the pen, the pen spoke longer than the sword, and all the verses in the text were about the pen's qualities. There is no poetry whatsoever in the text.

Münâzara-i Seyf ü Kalem: The last example of this type of text was published in 1920.[42] Its author, Mehmed Bahâeddîn, was an Arabic and Persian teacher at Amasya High School. It was written in prose interspersed with verse. Like the texts of Şabânzâde Mehmed Muhteşem and Cemâl Efendi, this one again has Reason serve as arbiter. And again, the debate is inconclusive, so the contenders ask Reason to declare the victor. Reason talks about their virtues and elaborates on their similarities rather than their differences, then has them make peace without declaring a winner.

It is interesting that the theme of the Pen and the Sword appears to have remained popular and ultimately much longer-lived than that of the Contest of Pleasurable Substances. I have been unable to find any disputation texts on pleasurable substances from the nineteenth through the early twentieth century. This might be related to changes in how these substances were perceived in the Ottoman Empire in later periods.

3 The Parrot and the Crow (*Tûtî ve Zâğ*)

There are three Parrot and Crow texts written in Turkish. In these texts, the parrot represents the soul and the crow represents the body. The reason the parrot represents the soul is that it, like the soul in the body, lives in a cage. The crow is clever and free, but its voice and appearance are ugly. People accept it as an ill omen and a harbinger of disaster. In all three texts, the winner is the parrot.

The first of these texts is the *Dâsitân-ı Tûtî vü Karga-i Alâeddîn*, written by Filibeli Alâeddîn Alî Çelebi (d. 1499) in the late fifteenth century (Tan 2015: 353–74). The text tells the story of two characters—a parrot and a crow—and it consists of 118 verses. The dispute ends with the parrot declared superior.

42 For the text, see Çakıcı 2010: 110–30.

The other two texts dealing with a parrot and crow are based on a Persian text entitled *Mübâhase-i Tûtî bâ-Zâğ.*[43] Until Serap Arslan's 2016 postgraduate thesis, each of these two texts was treated separately. She found the Persian source material for the two texts in Istanbul at the Süleymaniye Library[44] and revealed the relationship between the three texts. In the Persian original, there is no record about the name of the author or the place and date of composition. One of the two Ottoman texts is written in prose, the other one is in verse, and both are translations. Both were translated from the Persian text and have similarities between them in terms of structure and subject. The biggest difference is in their form (prose and verse).

The first translation was produced in 441 verses in 1558 by Nev'î (d. 1599), a poet and the teacher of Suleyman the Magnificent's children. The dispute ends with the victory of the parrot and the defeat of the crow (Gürer 2005: 85–179; Taş and Zülfe 2007: 660–96).

Although it is impossible to tell the exact date of the second translation, it was carried out at the behest of Sultan Mehmed III, so it is possible to estimate a date. It was translated by a person named Şerîf Efendi between the years 1595 and 1603. All that is known about Şerîf Efendi is that he worked under the patronage of Gazanfer Agha (d. 1602), one of the famous Darüssade Aghas (heads of the white eunuchs of the Imperial Harem). Şerîf Efendi presented his translation to the sultan with the help of Gazanfer Agha. As he intended it as a gift for the sultan, he used very ornamental language in his translation. There are some poems and verse fragments in Persian and Turkish in the text.

4 Spring and Winter (*Bahar ve Kış*)

Besides the 11th-century disputation recorded in Kaşgarlı Mahmûd's dictionary discussed at the beginning of this article, there are two stand-alone written texts on debates between spring and winter in the Ottoman period. The first one belongs to Lâmiî Çelebi (d. 1532), who was the most prolific writer of Ottoman literature in the first half of the sixteenth century. Among his over forty-

43 There seem to be no signs of any other disputation poem in Persian literature with a parrot and a crow as its subject. It should be noted that the story of this text is much different from that of the crow and parrot in Sadi of Shiraz's *Gülistân* and *Bostân*, and the Persian text was thus not inspired by Sadi's works. As Serap Arslan (2016: 15) has suggested, this text was most likely written by an Ottoman author who knew and wrote Persian very well, and later, both Nev'î and Şerîf Efendi translated it into Turkish.

44 Süleymaniye Library (Istanbul), Reşid Efendi Collection, no. 1036–37.

five works, four—each mentioned here under the relevant subheading below—involve a debate between different characters.

Münâzara-i Sultân-ı Bahâr Bâ-Şehriyâr-ı Şitâ: Lâmiî Çelebi wrote *Münâzara-i Sultân-ı Bahâr Bâ-Şehriyâr-ı Şitâ* between 1522 and 1527 in highly complex rhymed prose interspersed with poems and verse fragments in Turkish and Persian. The text depicts the struggle between spring and winter on Uludağ (Mount Olympus) in Bursa, the earliest capital of the Ottoman Empire. In this text, rich in secondary characters, each party takes turns extolling the virtues of either spring or winter. Uludağ is symbolized by an old man, summer is the ally of spring, and autumn acts as the harbinger and ally of winter. The text also features as characters a variety of animate and inanimate objects, ranging from rain and clouds to the sun and moon and flowers, plants, and animals.

Berf ü Bahâr (Winter and Spring): This text on spring and winter was written by Sıdkî Pasha. He presented his work to Sultan Murâd IV. Sıdkî Pasha's text has some similarities to Lâmiî Çelebi's work. He certainly read Lâmiî Çelebi's text and was influenced by him. Sıdkı Pasha's language is ornamental in style. He inserts couplets from famous Turkish and Persian poets such as Bâkî (d. 1600), Assâr-ı Tebrîzî (d. 1382), Hafez of Shiraz (d. 1390), and Selmân-ı Sâvecî (d. 1376). The winner of the debate is the spring.

5 Earth and Sky (*Yer ve Gök*)

Two poems are known to depict a debate between earth and sky. The first occupies two chapters of Baba Yûsuf's (d. 1512?) mesnevî *Mevhub-ı Mahbub.* It was written in 1507/08, and does not contain the word *münâzara* in its title. Sky (sixteen couplets) and earth (twenty-seven couplets) each make claims of superiority and point out the shortcomings of the other (Şeyh Baba Yûsuf Sivrihisârî 2000: 214–17).

The other disputation between earth and sky is found at the beginning of Lâmiî Çelebi's *Gûy u Çevgân* mesnevî. It was inspired by the Persian poet Ârifî's (d. 1449) *Hâlnâme/Gûy u Çevgân* text, but Lâmiî expanded upon and used new imagery in the debate in his text. Sky (fifty-two couplets) and earth (forty-two couplets) make claims of superiority and try to refute the other (Tezcan 1981: 53–59). Ârifî's *Hâlnâme/Gûy u Çevgân* was translated with commentary in the late sixteenth century by İlhâmî (Ebadi 2013: 45–53).

6 Disputation between Pederasts and Womanizers

A debate between pederasts and womanizers occupies the third chapter of the famous author Deli Birâder (Crazy Brother) Gazâlî's (d. 1534/36) *Dâfi'ü'l-Gumûm ve Râfi'ü'l-Humûm* (The repeller of sorrow and remover of anxiety).[45] It is titled "Gulâm-pâre yârânlar ve zen-pâre birâderlerin mâbeyninde olan münâzarât ve mufâhirât" (Contest and boast between pederasts and womanizers).[46] The pederasts take offense at a comment made by the womanizers and provoke a war. Satan intervenes and convinces both groups to have a verbal duel in order to prevent a disastrous war among his followers. As the plot illuminates, the two groups take opposite sides in a debate over the most favorable parts of the human body, comparing the male buttocks to the female vagina. The winning side at the end of the dispute is the pederasts, and the two sides draw up a treaty declaring that the pederasts shall thenceforth have a right to all the illegitimate boys born of the womanizers' adulterous relationships (Kuru 2000: 18–19).

The second example of this type of text belongs to Sünbülzâde Vehbî (d. 1809). His *Şevk-engîz* narrates arguments between two men—one a womanizer and the other a homosexual.[47] It is in mesnevî form with 777 couplets. At the end of the debate, the two protagonists go to an old sage (*pir*) and ask him his opinion on their behavior. The old man responds that only spiritual love provides deliverance, whereupon the two debauchers repent (Schmidt 1993: 17).

7 Contest of the Fruits

Sohbetü'l-Esmâr: The title of this disputation poem makes it clear that it is a conversation between fruits. It was written in mesnevî form, and the story starts with Huceste-Simâ's (Wise-Man) paying a visit to a garden. It is springtime, and as soon as he enters the garden and vineyard he hears the voice of each fruit making claims of its own superiority and trying to refute the claims of the others. In two hundred couplets, more than thirty fruits make boasts about themselves and criticize the others, in the following order: *âlûçe* (sour plum), *âlû* (plum), *kilâs*

45 For the text and a detailed analysis, see Kuru 2000.

46 Kuru suggests that the message readers were possibly meant to take away from this is that the "society of sinners" is to be kept contained and separated from the "society of believers." For a transcription and translation of the debate, see Kuru 2000: 57–71, 169–82.

47 For detailed information on the text, see Schmidt 1993: 9–37.

(cherry), *zerdâlû* (apricot), *elma* (apple), *emrûd* (pear), *engûr* (grape), *heyvâ* (quince), *nârinç* (orange), *nâr* (pomegranate), *hurmâ* (date), *bâdâm* (almond), *piste* (pistachio), *şeftâlû* (peach), *suncud* (silverberry), *şahpâlûd* (chestnut), *innâb* (red date), *fındık* (hazel nut), *tût* (mulberry), *âlubâlû* (sour cherry), *zogal* (cornelian cherry), *incir* (fig), *cevz* (walnut), *lîmû* (lemon), *hıyar* (cucumber), *germek* (a kind of melon that grows early in the season), *karpuz* (watermelon), *şemmame* (a kind of melon that is inedible but displayed at home because of its fragrance), and *kavun* (melon). At the end of the dialogue there is no clear winner, and Huceste-Simâ leaves the garden after listening to the fruits' boasting and accusations.

Since the first publication of the text in 1927 in Azerbaijan by Emîn Âbid under the title "Fuzuli'nin Malum Olmayan bir Eseri" (An unknown book of Fuzûlî), a great deal of debate has surrounded the question of this text's true author. Emîn Âbid attributed the text to the famous Fuzûlî. However, many scholars from Fuad Köprülü on have raised doubts about this claim.[48]

There is another disputation poem on the Contest of the Fruits that was likely written in the nineteenth century in Eastern Turkistan. This text was written in Eastern Turkish and was published by Gunnar Jarring (1936). A new edition of this text was published by A. Deniz Abik (2005). Abik compared this text with the one above and suggests that while they have many similarities in terms of topic and characters, both texts are dissimilar in a number of ways, including their meter and the names of the fruits involved in the debate, though both use Persian names for the most part.[49] More research is needed to reach a conclusion on any possible relationship between the two texts.

8 Man and Beast (*İnsan ve Hayvan*)

Şerefü'l-insân: Lâmiî Çelebi's *Şerefü'l-insân*, despite being a disputation text, does not have "disputation" in its title. It was written in prose interspersed with poetry in 1526/27. Lâmiî Çelebi presented his work to Suleyman the Magnificent (r. 1520–1566), and it was his most copied, and thus most popular, piece.

The disputation ends with Man's superiority over Beast. Nonetheless, the text advises that animals should not be harmed. Gibb, in his famous *History*

48 Because the debate concerns Fuzûlî, one of the most famous poets in the Turkish literary world, the question of whether this book truly belongs to him is a hot topic. For the most recent article on this debate and an explanation of each participant's views, see Hüseyinoğlu 2017: 57–67. For the text of the poem itself, see Yüksel 1972: 216–23.

49 For the comparison, see Abik 2005: 34–6.

of Ottoman Poetry (Gibb 1904, III: 21) contends that this piece of Lâmiî Çelebi's is a free translation of *Resâilü İhvânü's-Safâ*. But Sadettin Eğri, in an extensive doctoral dissertation on the subject, has proven this not to be the case and has shown that the similarities between the two works were the result of the authors' use of similar sources (Eğri 1997: 83). In the text, men from seven different nations dispute against seven animals (a bull, leopard, parrot, hawk, fish, snake, and bee) in front of seven judges in seven sessions. There are many side characters in the text. The text was very popular, and more than one hundred copies can be found in various libraries.

9 Contest of the Birds

Deh Murg (Ten Birds): This work was written in 1513 by Dervîş Şemsî (d. after 1513) in mesnevî form (1,053 couplets) and dedicated to Selim I (r. 1512–1520).[50] As its title makes clear, the book depicts a conversation between ten birds: an owl, crow, parrot, vulture, nightingale, hoopoe, swallow, peacock, partridge, and stork. Although the title brings to mind Ferîddîn Attâr's (d. c. 1221) famous *Mantık al-Tayr*, it was not translated from or inspired by that work. There is no story in the book. Each of the ten birds talks, making boasts and criticizing what the previous bird said about itself. Each bird represents a particular type of person. The owl, for example, represents mystics/Sufis, while the peacock represents merchants.

10 The Ball and the Polo Stick (*Gûy u Çevgân*)

This disputation poem, like the one on Earth and Sky, is found at the beginning of Lâmiî Çelebi's *Gûy u Çevgân* mesnevî. In the poem, a ball (twenty-seven couplets) and a polo stick (thirty-six couplets) each make claims of superiority and point to the shortcomings of the other (Tezcan 1981: 59–63).

50 There are twelve available manuscript copies of the text. For an introduction and a critical edition of the text, see Kaya 1997.

11 Sugar and Salt (*Şeker ve Tuz*)

As mentioned above, Firdevs-i Tavîl (d. after 1517) is known for his multi-volume *Süleymânnâme-i Kebîr*. The topic of the forty-fifth volume of that work is a debate between sugar, salt, honey, and syrup, and it was written in prose interspersed with poetry. The first chapter is an argument between sugar and salt ("Der-beyân-ı mübâhase-i şekker ve milh"). The second chapter is debate between sugar, honey, and syrup ("Dâsitân-ı münâzara kerden-i şekker ve 'asel ve dûş-âb der pîş-i Süleymân 'aleyhisselam") (Usta 2009: 61–93). According to the title of the second chapter, the debate takes place in King Solomon's palace during a *meclis*.

12 Day and Night (*Rûz u Şeb*)

Münâzara-i Şeb u Rûz was written by Fâsihî (d. 1699), and is similar in content to "Şeb u Rûz," a disputation poem by the Persian writer Abdullâh b. Muhammed el-Ensârî el-Herevî (d. 1089) in *Kenzü's-Sâlikîn*. It was written in prose interspersed with poetry. At the end of the disputation, no one party emerges as superior: day and night accept each other.[51]

13 Candle and Censer (*Şem' ile Micmer*)

Münâzara-i Pervâne bâ-Şem' was in Ahmedî's famous *İskendernâm*e (The story of Alexander) mesnevî, mentioned above. It is the second chapter of the book and it is only twenty-two couplets. Some sources state that Ahmedî's *İskendernâme* was a translation of Nezâmî Ganjavî's (d. 1209) *İskendernâme*. However, after an extensive study of Ahmedî's *İskendernâme*, İsmail Ünver showed that while Ahmedî was influenced by Ferdowsî and Nezâmî in terms of the topic and some events of İskender's life, his work was distinct from theirs (Aḥmedī 1982: 11–13). One of the important differences between Ahmedî's work and those others is its *münâzara* sections. There are no *münâzara*s between candle and censer or candle and moth in Nezâmî's text. These two *münâzara*s in Ahmedî's text are the first such examples in Turkish literature. Ahmedî first completed his book in 1390, and he completed his last-known addition to it in 1410.

---

51 For an introduction and a critical edition of the text, see İçli 2014: 513–37. On disputations between Day and Night in Islamicate literature, see Larsen in this volume.

14 Candle and Moth (*Pervane ile Şem'*)

Like Candle and Censer, *Münâzara-i Şem' bâ-Micmer* occupies a chapter of Ahmedî's *İskendernâme*, the third. The twenty-two couplets of this poem follow the above-mentioned candle and censer poem in the *İskendernâme*.

15 Conclusion

Disputation texts have been a popular genre in the Turkic literary world ever since, and perhaps even before, Kaşgarlı Mahmûd wrote his *Dîvânü Lugati't-Turk* in the late eleventh century. In the Ottoman world, we can see early examples of such texts in the first half of the fifteenth century. In my research, I have come across more than thirty-six such texts. But very few scholars have devoted much serious attention to the genre.[52] We thus have only a very incomplete picture of the nature and number of such texts by Ottoman poets and writers, and of how many may have survived and where.

In this paper, I have offered a brief survey of disputation texts in Turkish, grouped according to their themes and main characters. This classification reveals that the most popular subjects are the Contest of Pleasurable Substances, the Debate of the Sword and the Pen, and the Contest between the Parrot and the Crow, followed by those between Spring and Winter, Earth and Sky, the Fruits, Pederasts and Womanizers, Man and Beast, the Birds, the Ball and the Polo Stick, Sugar and Salt, Day and Night, Candle and Censer, and Candle and Moth.

Turkish disputation texts were often inspired by Persian texts on the same subject, but were usually not direct translations. The texts in the most popular category, that of the Contest of the Pleasurable Substances, seem to be unique to the Ottoman Empire. I have not come across any such texts with as many mind-altering substances elsewhere.

Texts written about mind-altering substances reveal close observations of the everyday life of the Ottomans, with references to coffee consumption and the dangers of tobacco serving as clear examples. These call out for closer scholarly attention and promise to reveal much about life and literature in the Ottoman Empire that we are only dimly aware of now. What might a closer study of the inter-textual relations among the twelve texts on this theme discussed here tell us? What was the relation between the growing number of these

52 A PhD dissertation was completed on debates in classical Turkish literature after I submitted my article. See Şeyma Benli. 2019. *Klasik Türk Edebiyatında Münazara*. İstanbul University.

texts from the seventeenth century onward and the severe restrictions placed on mind-altering substances during the reign of Murâd IV? Who were the audience for these texts? What was their purpose? Were they meant to be didactic, or entertaining, or both? Close and comparative study of these texts has the potential to answer these and many other questions, all of which will expand our understanding of the Ottoman world in important ways.

Bibliography

Abdullaeva, F. 2012. The Origins of the Munāzara Genre in New Persian Literature. Pp. 249–73 in *Metaphor and Imagery in Persian Poetry*, ed. Ali Asghar Seyed-Gohrab. Leiden: Brill.

Abik, A. Deniz. 2005. *Meyveler Münazarası: Doğu Türkçesi.* Ankara: Seçkin Yayıncılık.

Aḥmedī. 1982. *İskender-nāme: İnceleme – Tıpkıbasım* ed. İsmail Ünver. Ankara: TDK.

Aksoy, Hasan. 1976. Kınalı-zâde Ali Çelebi: Hayatı, İlmî ve Edebî Şahsiyeti, Arapça Eserlerinin İstanbul Kütüphanelerinde Mevcut Yazma Nüshaları. Bachelor's Thesis. İstanbul University.

Aksoyak, İ. Hakkı. 2016. XVII. Yüzyıl Şairlerinden Vardarlı Fazlî ve Mahzenü'l-Esrâr (Dâfi'ü'l-Hüzn) Mesnevisi. Pp. 223–243 in *14. yy.dan 19. yy.'a Anadolu ve Rumeli'de Yazılmış Türkçe Edebî Metinler Üzerine Söylenmemiş Sözler.* Ankara: Grafiker Yayınları.

Aksoyak, İ. Hakkı. 2018. XVII. Yüzyıl Şâirlerinden Vardarlı Fazlî'nin Mahzenü'l-Esrâr (Dâfi 'ü'l-Hüzn) Mesnevisi. *Akademik Dil ve Edebiyat Dergisi* 2/2 (Summer): 78–137.

Âlî, Gelibolulu Mustafa. 1997. *Mevâ'idü'n-Nefâis fî Kavâ'idi'l-Mecâlis.* Edited by Mehmet Şeker. Ankara: TTK.

Alpay, Gönül. 1973. Yusuf Emiri'nin Beng ü Çagır adlı Münazarası. *Türk Dili Araştırmaları Yıllığı Belleten 1972:* 103–25.

Arslan, Serap. 2016. A Transcription and Textual Analysis of Münazara-i Tuti vü Zağ Tercemesi. MA Thesis. Boğaziçi University.

Âşık Çelebi. 2010. *Meşâirü'ş-Şu'arâ: İnceleme–Metin.* ed. Filiz Kılıç. 3 vols. Istanbul: İstanbul Araştırmaları Enstitüsü.

Aynur, Hatice. 2018. Representations of Istanbul as a Literary and Cultural Space in Ottoman Texts (1520–1560). Pp. 245–56 in *An Iridescent Device: Premodern Ottoman Poetry.* ed. Christiane Czygan / Stephan Conermann. Göttingen: Bonn University Press.

Aynur, Hatice and Jan Schmidt. 2007. A Debate between Opium, Berş, Hashish, Boza, Wine and Coffee: The Use and Perception of Pleasurable Substances among Ottomans. *Journal of Turkish Studies I: In Memoriam Şinasi Tekin I = Türklük Bilgisi Araştırmaları Şinasi Tekin Armağanı I: In Memoriam Şinasi Tekin I* 31/1: 51–117.

Bodrogligeti, Andras J. E. 1987. A Masterpiece of Central Asian Turkic Satire: Ahmadi's A Contest of String Instruments. *Ural-Altaic Yearbook* 59: 55–88.

Büyükkarcı Yılmaz, Fatma. 2013. Nidayi el-Ankaravi'nin Bilinmeyen Bir Eseri: Mübahasat-ı Mükeyyefat ve Aynı Konudaki Diğer Eserler. *Turkish Studies* 8/3: 681–704.

Çakıcı, Bilal. 2010. Mehmed Bahâeddin'in 'Münâzara-ı Seyf ü Kalem'i. *Acta Turcica Çevrimiçi Tematik Türkoloji Dergisi* 2/3 (January): 110–30.

Des türkischen dichters Fuzûlî: poëm "Laylâ-Meğnun" und die gereimte Erzählung "Benk u Bade" (Haşiş und Wein). 1943. Pp 150–204. Nach dem Druck Istbl. 1328 übersetzt von Nedjati Hüsnü Lugal, O. Reşer. Istanbul.

Ebadi, Gheis. 2013. Osmanlı-Türk Edebiyatında İlginç Bir Çeviri Örneği: İlhâmî'nin Gûy u Çevgân Çevirisi. MA Thesis. İhsan Doğramacı Bilkent University.

Eğri, Sadettin. 1997. Lami'i Çelebi, Şerefü'l-İnsan. PhD diss. Gazi Üniversitesi.

Emin Âbid. 1927. Fuzuli'nin Malum Olmayan bir Eseri. *Hayat Mecmuası* 1/16 (March): 314–15.

Firdevsî-i Rûmî. 2017. *Kalem ile Kılıcın Münâzarası: Münâzara-i Seyf ü Kalem*. ed. Ahmet Tanyıldız. Istanbul: Büyüyen Ay.

Gelder, Geert Jan Van. 1987. The Conceit of Pen and Sword: On an Arabic Literary Debate. *Journal of Semitic Studies* 32/2: 329–60.

Gibb, E. J. W. 1904. *A History of Ottoman Poetry*. Ed. Edward G. Browne. vol. III. London: Luzac &Co.

Günay, Turgut. 1976. Türk Halk Şiirinde İlk Deyişme (Müşâare) Örnekleri. Pp 253–57 in *Uluslararası Folklor ve Halk Edebiyatı Semineri Bildirileri*. Ankara: Konya Turizm Derneği.

Gürer, Abdülkadir. 2005. Nev'i'nin Kayıp Sanılan İki Eseri: 'Münâzara-i Tuti vü Zağ' ve 'Gevher-i Raz'. *Türk Dilleri Araştırmaları* 15: 85–179.

Hüseyinoğlu, Ali Şamil. 2017. Sohbetü'l-Esmâr (Meyvelerin Sohbeti) Mesnevisi Konusunda Tartışmalar. Pp. 57–67 in *II. Uluslararası Türk Dili ve Edebiyatları Öğretimi Sempozyumu Bildirileri: Prof. Dr. M. Fuad Köprülü Adına, 17–18 Nisan 2017*. ed. İsmet Çetin and Halil Çeltik. Ankara: Gazi Üniversitesi.

İçli, Ahmet. 2014. Fasîh'in Rûz u Şeb Münâzarası. *EKEV Akademi Dergisi* 18, no 60 (Summer): 513–37.

İnalcık, Halil. 2011. *Has-bağçede 'Ayş u Tarab: Nedîmler Şâirler Mutribler*. Istanbul: Türkiye İş Bankası.

İvgin, Hayrettin. 1982. Halk Şiirinde 'Dedim-Dedi'. *II. Milletlerarası Türk Folklor Kongresi Bildirileri*. vol 2. Ankara: Kültür ve Turizm Bakanlığı.

İz, Fahir. 1962. Yakînî's Contest of the Arrow and the Bow. Pp 267–87 in *Németh Armağanı*. Ankara: TTK.

Jarring, Gunnar. 1936. *The Contest of the Fruits: An Eastern Turki Allergory*. Lunds: Universitets Ärsskrift.

Jarring, Gunnar. 1981. *Some Notes Eastern Turki (New Uighur) Munazara Literature*. Lund: Publications of Royal Society of Letters at Lund.

Kadıoğlu, İdris. 2011. Kılıç Kalem Münâzarası. *CBÜ Sosyal Bilimler Dergisi: Prof. Dr. Mahmut Kaplan'a Armağan* 9/2: 161–80.

Kâtib Çelebi. 1972. *Mîzanü'l-Hak fî İhtiyâri'l-Ehak*. Edited by Orhan Şaik Gökyay. Ankara: MEB.

Kaya, İdris Güven. 1997. *Derviş Şemsi ve Deh Murg Mesnevisi: İnceleme, Tenkidli Metin ve Tıpkıbasım*. Cambridge, MA: Harvard University.

Kissling, Hans Joachim. 1971. Der Wettstreit der Genußgifte. Bemerkungen zu einem türkischen Kunstmärchen. Pp 285–303 in *Asien Tradition und Fortschritt: Festschrift für Horst Hammitzsch zu Seinem 60. Geburststag*, ed. Lydia Brüll and Ulrich Kemper. Wiesbaden: Otto Harrassowitz.

Köksal, M. Fatih. 2006. Münazara, Türk Edebiyatı. In *TDV İslâm Ansiklopedisi*. vol. XXXI. Istanbul: TDV.

Köprülü. 1934. *Türk Dili ve Edebiyatı Hakkında Araştırmaları*. Istanbul: Kanat Kitabevi.

Kuru, Selim Sırrı. 2000. A Sixteenth Century Scholar Deli Birader and his Dâfi'ü'l-Gumûm ve Râfi'ü'l-Humûm. PhD diss. Harvard University.

Latîfî. 2000. *Tezkiretü'ş-Şu'arâ ve Tabsıratü'n-Nuzama.* ed. Rıdvan Canım. Ankara: Atatürk Kültür Merkezi Başkanlığı.

Maḥmūd al-Kāšġarī. 1985. *Compendium of Turkic Dialects (Dīwān Luyāt at-Turk).* 3 vols. Edited and translated with introduction and indices by Robert Dankoff in collaboration with James Kelly. Cambridge, MA: Harvard University.

Nağzî. 2014. *Münâzara-i Kahve vü Bâde.* ed. Hasan Şener. Ankara: Grafiker Yayınları.

Oktay, Ayşe Sıdıka. 2002. Kınalızâde Ali Efendi'nin Hayatı ve Ahlâk-ı Alâî İsimli Eseri. *Dîvân,* no 1: 185–233.

[Olgun], Tahir. 1931. *Manzum Bir Muhtıra: Başlangıcından Tanzimat Devrine Kadar.* Istanbul.

Onay, Ahmet Talât. 1992. *Eski Türk Edebiyatında Mazmunlar ve İzahı.* ed. Cemâl Kurnaz. Ankara: Türkiye Diyanet Vakfı.

Peçevî. 1283 [1866–67]. *Tarih-i Peçevi.* vol. 2. Istanbul: Matbaa-i Amire.

Peçevi İbrahim Efendi. 1982. *Peçevi Tarihi.* ed. Bekir Sıtkı Baykal. vol. 2. Ankara: Kültür Bakanlığı.

Schmidt, Jan. 1993. Sünbülzāde Vehbī's Şevḳ-engīz, an Ottoman Pornographic Poem. *Turcica* 35 (Summer): 9–37.

Sevgi, Ahmet. 1987. Latifi (Hayatı ve Eserleri): İnceleme-Metin. PhD. Thesis. Ankara: Gazi Üniversitesi.

Solmaz, Süleyman. 2005. *Ahdî ve Gülşen-i Şu'ara'sı: İnceleme-Metin.* Ankara: Atatürk Kültür Merkezi Başkanlığı.

Şeyh Baba Yûsuf Sivrihisârî. 2000. *Mevhûb-ı Mahbûb: İnceleme-Metin-Sözlük-İndeks.* ed. Ahmet Kartal. Eskişehir: Eskişehir Yunus Emre Kültür, Sanat ve Turizm Vakfı.

Tan, Bünyamin. 2015. Alaeddin Ali Çelebi'nin Münâzara Türünde Bir Eseri: Dasitan-ı Tuti vü Karga-i 'Alaeddin. *Atatürk Üniversitesi TAED* 54: 353–74.

Tarlan, Ali Nihat. 1945. *Hayâlî Bey Dîvânı.* İstanbul: İÜ Edebiyat Fakültesi Türk Dili ve Edebiyatı Dalı.

Taş, Hakan and Ömer Zülfe. 2007. Nev'i'nin Münâzara-i Tuti vü Zağ Adlı Mesnevisi. *Turkish Studies = Türkoloji Araştırmaları* 2/3 (Summer): 660–96.

Tezcan, Nuran. 1981. Lāmi'ī'nin Gūy u Çevgān'ında İki Münazara. *Türk Dili Araştırmaları Yıllığı-Belleten 1980:* 53–9.

Tobi, Yosef. 2008. Šālôm (Sālim) al-Šabazī's (Seventeenth-Century) Poem of the Debate between Coffee and Qāt. *Proceedings of the Seminar for Arabian Studies* 38: 301–10.

Tuncalp, Enver. 1969. Divan ve Halk Edebiyatı Şiirimizde Dedim-Dedi. *Bayrak* 17/61: 7–9.

Tuşalp Atiyas, Ekin. 2017. Eloquence in Context: Şa'bānzāde Meḥmed Efendi's (d. 1708–1709) Münāẓara-i Ṭīġ u Ḳalem and 'The People of the Pen' in the Late-Seventeenth-Century Ottoman Empire. *Turcica* 48: 113–55.

Ülken, Fatih. 2017a. Müellifi Meçhul Bir Edebî Münazara: Hikâyât-ı Mükeyyifât-ı Âlem. *Uluslararası Sosyal Araştırmalar Dergisi* 10/52 (October): 261–76.

Ülken, Fatih. 2017b. Ondokuzuncu Yüzyılda Kaleme Alınmış Bir Edebî Münazara: Cemal Efendi'nin 'Muhâverât-ı Seyf ü Kalem'i. *Uluslararası Sosyal Araştırmalar Dergisi* 10/ 52 (October): 277–83.

Usta, Halil İbrahim. 2009. Firdevsî-i Rûmî'nin Bir Münazarası. *Ankara Üniversitesi Dil ve Tarih-Coğrafya Fakültesi Dergisi* 49/1: 61–93.

Wagner, Mark. 2005. The Debate Between Coffee and Qāt in Yemeni Literature. *Middle Eastern Literatures* 8/2: 121–49.
Yılmazer, Ziya. 2006. Murad IV. In *TDV İslâm Ansiklopedisi*. vol. XXXI. Istanbul: TDV.
Yüksel, Sedit. 1972. Sohbetü'l-Esmâr Fuzulî'nin Değildir. *Türkoloji Dergisi* 4/1: 216–23.

Sergio La Porta*

17 Dispute Poems in Armenian

From its inception in the fifth century, Armenian literature has adopted and adapted the literary forms, genres, and vocabulary of neighboring cultures, whether of the Greeks to the West, of Syria/Mesopotamia to the South, or of Iran to the East. In other words, writers in Armenian were usually quite familiar with other literatures and comfortable with negotiating between their own literary register and those of another. Given Armenian authors' receptivity to external literary trends and skill at developing them within an Armenian linguistic and poetic idiom,[1] it is not surprising that disputation poems, present in literary cultures across the region, appear in Armenian. To my knowledge, however, recent scholarship has not devoted either extended discussion or systematic analysis to the Armenian articulations of this genre, nor have Armenian cases been brought into any sustained engagement with more familiar examples from other literary cultures.[2]

It should be noted that writing in Armenian was dominated by Christian ecclesiastics until modernity.[3] People outside of the Church did engage in narrative production, but such compositions generally remained oral and reached literary expression through the hand of a monk or priest. Despite periods of ecclesiastical opposition, peripatetic Armenian bards, known as *gusan*-s and later as *ašuł*-s, formed part of the cultural landscape from pre-Christian times until the twentieth century.[4] This being said, one should be careful about drawing too stark a distinction between the secular and religious narrative worlds as there was con-

* California State University, Fresno. I would like to thank my colleague Dr. Michael Pifer for his many insightful comments. I would also like to thank the Provost's Office and the College of Arts and Humanities of California State University, Fresno, for granting me release time to complete this essay. The transliteration of Armenian follows the Hübschmann-Meillet-Bienvensite system.

1 See Pifer forthcoming for a sophisticated elaboration of Armenian literary production as a process of adaptation of modes of composition.

2 So, e.g., none of the articles in Reinink and Vanstiphout (1991) address the Armenian evidence. The most recent authoritative work on debate poetry, Jiménez (2017), as thorough as it is, only mentions the fables of Mxit'ar Goš.

3 The Armenian alphabet itself was invented by Maštoc' in 406 in order to translate the Bible. Soon thereafter, a group of students trained in the alphabet and in Greek and Syriac translated other patristic works. Simultaneously, a native literary tradition emerged that reemployed literary models and styles for Armenian interests. On the Armenian literary tradition, see Thomson 1980.

4 On the *gusan* < Parthian *gōsān*, see Boyce 1957; *ašuł*-s will be discussed further below.

https://doi.org/10.1515/9781501510274-017

siderable slippage between them. The two registers of folk and institutional literature did not occupy hermetically sealed spaces, but engaged in a fluid and mutually reinforcing dynamic.[5]

One immediate problem that the student of the dispute poem faces is that of delineating a discrete corpus of texts to consider, as there are numerous analogous literary forms, not to mention the even greater complexity of handling their relationship to oral composition, development, and transmission. My understanding of the dispute poem follows that of earlier scholarship which identifies five constituent elements to the genre as usefully summarized by Enrique Jiménez (2017: 11–12). The genre may be characterized as consisting of 1) poems or poetic texts, that 2) are tripartite in structure, 3) contain few narrative elements, 4) usually feature inanimate protagonists, and 5) discuss the supremacy of one of the interlocutors over the other.

Dispute poems that strictly conform to the above-given definition may be found among the extensive collection of *Medieval Armenian Folk Songs* Asatur Mnacʻakanyan (1956) culled from manuscripts of the National Armenian Manuscript Archive in Erevan, Armenia (Matenadaran), as well as from earlier publications.[6] Two types of dispute in particular – between Heaven and Earth and between Soul and Body – were first written down in the seventeenth and eighteenth centuries, but exist in multiple versions, and will constitute the focus of this study. Mnacʻakanyan's work is not simply a large anthology. He attempted to produce critical editions of the poems he gathered,[7] supplied a lengthy introduction on Armenian poetics, and provided commentary for each poem. In his commentary, Mnacʻakanyan presented the publication history of and previous scholarship on a poem as well as his philological observations that tried to determine the original period and historical context of a poem's composition and its literary development.

5 See Russell (2004) for a discussion of the intersection between "secular" and "religious" literature in medieval Armenian.

6 For an overview of publications and studies of medieval Armenian poetry, see van Lint 2014.

7 The legitimacy of producing critical editions for inscribed oral literature is questionable. Instead of trying to construct critical editions of these poems, it is preferable that all the variants be published as separate texts and recognized as individual poems in and of themselves. It seems a violation of the integrity of the poems to try and judge "correct" readings when it is almost certain that no single "original version" of the poem existed. Rather, we must imagine the existence of multiple versions of the poem that came into existence through the dynamic relationship of reciter and audience. We may observe a similar problem with the critical edition of the Armenian epic *The Daredevils of Sasun* (*Sasuncʻi cṙer*), where "the variants" of the text provide different iterations of the story. For a valuable reading of "the variants," see Russell 2014.

Mnac'akanyan's work represents the most thorough scholarly treatment of these poems and remains a remarkable achievement, but some of his analysis is marred by Soviet interpretative constraints. Furthermore, he ignored consideration of these poems beyond an Armenian literary context. His conclusions thus warrant reevaluation, particularly in light of concomitant developments in neighboring literary cultures, and in order to assess how Armenian disputation poems offer a different perspective on the genre. Before passing on to the two specific instances of the disputes between Heaven and Earth and Soul and Body, however, it is helpful to provide a general overview of dispute and dialogue literature, both in prose and poetry, in Armenian between the fifth and fifteenth centuries. While this overview will perforce be incomplete, it is meant both to suggest the breadth of disputation literature in Armenian and to bring into relief the very sporadic attestation of precedence dispute poems between the fifth and seventeenth centuries.

1 Disputation poems in Armenian literature

Dispute and debate literature can be traced to the beginning of the Armenian literary tradition. Among the earliest Syriac works to be translated into Armenian in the fifth century were those either genuinely by or attributed to Ephrem (ca. 306–373CE). A collection of fifty-one hymns ascribed to him in Armenian contain three dialogue poems that have been preserved only in that language and have been edited by Mariès and Mercier (1961: 42–56, 72–76). They are found within a grouping of eight hymns that are associated with the theme of virginity and have been translated into English by Mathews (1999; 2001–2). The first of the dialogues is a dispute between Marriage and Chastity, while the other two are between Virginity and Chastity. The latter two contain a lengthy dispute in alternating stanzas of four lines each between the personified states of living. The poems also include an introduction, conclusion, and a refrain, suggesting that the original form was that of the *sugītā*.[8] The Armenian translation, however, does not preserve the name of the meter (*qalā*) used, nor was any attempt to reproduce a metrical patterning made. These "Ephremic" hymns, however, do not seem to have made an impact on the aesthetic or literary choices of writers in Armenian as they did not generate any imitations or adaptations, at least among the corpus of poetic works that have come down to us. Furthermore,

8 On the problem of the definition of the *sugītā*, see Brock 2008. See also Brock's contribution to this volume, as well as his numerous articles on them, including Brock 1984 and 1991.

in contrast to the Syriac *sugītā*, dialogue poems never seem to have been employed for liturgical purposes in Armenian.

In addition to the translation of these dialogue poems strictly defined, other types of prose dialogue or debate literature also entered into Armenian at this time. The *Progymnasmata* of Aphthonios were translated and adapted into Armenian, most likely in the late sixth century. Known as the *Book of Chreiai* (*Girk' Pitoyic'*), these rhetorical exercises exposed students to the comparison between personalities, objects, and animals, similar to those often found in precedence dispute poems. The seventh book of the collection, "Concerning Comparison," contains comparisons of Abraham and Elijah, agriculture and military professions, spring and summer, field and harbor, horse and ox, and olive and palm (Muradyan 1993: 153–83).

A more productive type of prose "dialogue" that occurs in Armenian is *eratopokriseis*, or the "question and answer" form, which appears quite early in both native and translated texts. Again, the genre is one that has only been minimally examined; numerous question and answer texts remain unedited. *The Canon of Grigor Part'ew*, also known as *The Questions and Answers of Grigor and an Angel*, may be the earliest use of the genre in Armenian (Adontz 1925–26), but the frequency with which it is used increases beginning in the twelfth century and particularly within the monastic school system. Yovhannēs Vanakan *Vardapet* Tawušec'i (1180-c.1251) addressed several exegetical problems in this manner (Ervine 2000), as did his student, Vardan Arewelc'I (d. 1271). A commentary on *Genesis* attributed to Ełišē, but more likely by the thirteenth-century Vahṙam Ṙabuni (Vardanean 1929), also approached the biblical text through this method. The monastic teacher Yovhannēs Orotnec'i used the format for a polemic against dyophysites, but it is his student, Grigor Tat'ewac'i (1344–1409), who represents the most extreme adherent to this genre. Nearly every single composition he penned employed this format, including his numerous sermons collected in two volumes. Although the format had a long pedigree within Armenian, interaction with Franciscan and Dominican missionaries in the thirteenth and fourteenth centuries, and the introduction of Latin theological compendia also left their mark on the Armenian question and answer format and enhanced its prestige (La Porta 2015: 292–93).

Besides the use of *eratopokriseis* just mentioned, I have not found the employment of dispute poems or their echoes where one might expect them: Armenian homiletic literature.[9] Likewise, a less than thorough examination of liturgi-

9 For example, none of the collected homilies attributed to Yovhannēs Mandakuni (5th c.), Ełišē (5th-6th c.) nor the collection known as the *Yačaxapatum* (*Stromateis*) attributed to the fourth-cen-

cal hymns did not reveal any dispute or dialogue forms. The famous *Book of Lamentation* (*Matean Ołbergut'ean*) of Grigor Narekac'i (956–1003) presents itself as the words of the author with God and as a spiritual conversation with revelation (Mahé 2009–2010), but it does not constitute a dialogue in the formal sense.[10] And while a number of religious polemics were rendered into Armenian in the fifth to seventh centuries, only one polemic dialogue was apparently translated, a fragment of the anti-Jewish and incorrectly attributed *Dialogue of Athanasius and Zacchaeus* (Calzolari 2000). Its appearance in Armenian seems to be due more to the esteem in which Athanasius was held than for any specific polemic purpose.

We can observe a greater variety of genres in play in written Armenian after the turn of the first millennium. I have already noted the increased usage of the question and answer format, but more significant is the broadening application and appreciation of poetic forms, a phenomenon whose appearance has been associated with intensified relations with Islamicate culture (Cowe 2005). The polymath Grigor Magistros (d. 1058) is credited with having introduced mono-rhyme into Armenian poetics, possibly based on the *qaṣīda*-s of al-Mutanabbi (Cowe 2005: 384–85). His versified version of the Bible in mono-rhyme emerged as the result of a dispute with a Muslim, identified as the 'Abbasid scholar and diplomat Abū Naṣr al-Manāzī (Terian 2012: 10–12), at the court of Constantinople over the qualities of the Qur'ān and the Bible. Magistros also engaged in actual dialogue through epistolary exchanges with Christians and Muslims alike (Weller 2017). To Grigor, too, we may be indebted for the translation of Platonic dialogues into Armenian, although some scholars contend that these may have been completed in the sixth century (Calzolari 2014: 350–51). Five Platonic dialogues are known to exist in Armenian—the *Euthyphro*, the *Apology of Socrates*, the *Timaeus*, the *Laws*, and *Minos*—but the works seem to have exerted only minor influence on Armenian thought.

The earliest example of a dispute poem to have been originally composed in Armenian is the *Discourse on Wisdom Composed as a Diversion* by Yovhannēs the Deacon Philosopher (d. 1129), a monk at the monastery of Hałbat (Cowe 1994–95). The poem contains 189 lines of unrhymed 16 syllables and presents an exchange between the author and a blackbird chick on the reason for the bird's singing talent. The dialogue, however, is not partitioned equally between

---

tury Grigor Part'ew (the Illuminator), contain a dramatized dialogue or dispute; nor do the homilies Catholicos Zak'aria Jagec'i (9th c.). References to editions of these works may be found in Thomson 1995.

10 Nearly each of the 95 prayers begins with the phrase: "From the depths of hearts, word with God" (*I xoroc' srtic' xōsk' ěnd astucoy*).

the contestants. Yovhannēs opens the poem with a 42-line appeal to the blackbird chick to reveal to him the secrets of his music. The blackbird replies in 18 lines of accusation against humanity for having transgressed its natural boundaries. The speaking returns to the poet who both accepts and pushes back against the bird's accusations in 70 lines. The bird then retorts in 55 lines that through their transgressions human beings are the cause of their own alienation from the world in which they live. Moreover, the chick grieves that as a consequence of humanity's sin, the animals, created as their servants, rebelled against their masters, and though innocent, also suffered corruption. Yovhannēs then concedes defeat in the final quatrain, admitting that,

> Truly it spoke this in conformity with events,
> Presenting the elements of its case with wisdom
> By which we sophists and poetasters are trounced,
> Admonished in silence, dispensing with long speeches (Cowe 1994–95: 150).

As S. P. Cowe (1994–95: 137) observes, the poem represents one of our earliest examples of didactic poetry in Armenian and should be read as a spiritual exhortation. Through this dialogue, Yovhannēs holds forth an example from nature for his monastic audience to imitate so that through prayer and renunciation one may achieve direct experience of God.

Although the poem is a dispute between two characters, it does not adhere to the classical form of the genre. The disputants are not two objects, non-human animals, personified character traits, ways of life, or biblical figures, but the author and an animal. Nor is the contest one of precedence. Yovhannēs does not argue for the superiority of human creation over the natural world, nor does the chick contend that the natural world is superior to the human. Rather, the argument revolves around the lack of harmony in the state of the present world and the reason for humanity's distance and alienation from it and the divine. In its complex spiritual argument and self-personification, Yovhannēs Sarkawag's poem seems to articulate a later development that presupposes a tradition of dispute poems whose style would have been recognizable to his audience, despite the fact that there is no textual evidence that this was the case.

Possibly inspired by Yovhannēs' poem is a poetic dispute of Tērtēr Erewanc'i (ca. 1300–1360) which imagines a debate between Grape, Wine, and Philosopher. I am uncertain whether the poem has been published, but a copy of it is preserved in Matenadaran (M) ms. 8029, dated to before 1376. A brief description of the poem's content is given by A. Mnac'akanyan (1976: 865–66) in volume three of the *Hay žołovrdi patmut'yun* (History of the Armenian People). According to this summary, Grape and Wine argue against and defeat contemporary philosophy. Wine explains that it has not come into existence to do evil, but with good intentions—to comfort the mournful, to adorn tables, to relieve depression, and to win over strangers. Philosopher and Wine exchange a set of arguments at the end of which the philosopher concedes in octosyllabic monorhyme:

> Wine! I blamed you,
> O, sweet and fragrant good cup.
> I sinned against the holy Creator
> Who fashioned you a good cup,
> A very desirable, sweet fruit.[11]

Without access to the complete poem, it is hard to judge the nature of its contents, but would seem to promote the idea that humanity, and not God's other creations, is responsible for the former's sinful state. Although apparently much simpler in construction and meaning than Yovhannēs's philosophical discourse, it nonetheless would be consonant with it.

A very popular form of poetic dialogue between two non-human creatures, the nightingale and rose, appears in Armenian beginning in the thirteenth-century, but does not construct a precedent contest. Inspired by *ghazal* poetry, these poems address the longing of the lover for the beloved, whether in a physical or spiritual sense (Cowe 2005: 390 – 96). So, too, the poem of the young priest Yovhannēs and the *mullah*'s daughter Asha, attributed to either Yovhannēs Erznkac'I (d. 1293) or T'lkuranc'i (d. 1535), encapsulates dialogues between the author and his beloved, as well as other characters. Although the poem foregrounds issues of religious conversion, it is not a contest poem between Christianity and Islam. Instead, the poem embodies an artistic model of merging the aesthetics of both traditions as it charts the author's path to "finding Christianity" through engagement with Islam.[12] Finally, the fifteenth-century bishop of Diyarbakir and poet Mkrtič' Nałaš composed a dialogue poem between the *gharīb* (stranger) and his soul which explores the theme of spiritual estrangement in addition to geographical displacement as a common feature of the human condition.[13]

We may further observe that the fables of Mxit'ar Goš (d. 1213) and Vardan Aygekc'i (d. 1235) employed prose dialogue as a means of conveying gnomic wisdom. Some of these compositions include short exchanges between animals,

---

11 *Gini, ězk'ez dsrvec'i, / K'ałc'r ew anuš bažak bari. // Es mełay surb araričʻin, / Or k'ez stełcec' bažak bari, / K'ałc'ěr ptuł yoyž c'ankali:*, Mnac'akanyan 1976: 866.

12 See the interpretations of Cowe 2005: 389 and La Porta 2011: 113 – 114.

13 For a penetrating analysis of the *gharīb* and how it can be considered a productive strategy of cultural engagement, see Pifer 2018.

natural elements, and characteristic human types and therefore bear a resemblance to the dispute poem. Most of them, however, do not include actual debates or dialogues, but only the pronouncements of one character at the end of the scene.[14] These, too, are edificatory and adapt popular narrative forms in order to convey ethical and spiritual prescriptions. It is clear that both authors were concerned with the transmission of such knowledge as they each also composed collections of spiritual counsels (*xratk'*).

Thus, in the first half of the second millennium, we can discern many examples of literary forms related to or associated with the dispute poem, but clear instances of precedence poems *in stricto sensu* are rare. Our closest examples are Yovhannēs the deacon's *Discourse on Wisdom* and, presumably, the *Dispute between the Grape, Wine, and a Philosopher* of Tērtēr Erewanc'i. Both of these are didactic in nature and emphasize human wisdom's limitations as set by humanity's sinful nature.

2 Two Armenian Examples of Dispute Poems

Precedence dispute poems first appear in manuscript anthologies dating to the beginning of the seventeenth century. As noted, Mnac'akanyan (1956) published a number of dispute poems in his collection of *Medieval Armenian Folk Songs*. He divided the entire collection into five "bunches" (*p'unǰer*) according to general categories of his own determination: the first includes love poems; the second, patriotic poems; the third, poems concerning liturgical life; the fourth, social poems; and the fifth, additional poems. The dispute poems are all grouped within the fourth bunch of "social" (*soc'ialakan*) poems. This bunch contains forty poems, of which eight may be considered dialogue or dispute poems. These eight can be further subdivided into three groups according to interlocutors: 1) Heaven and Earth, 2) Soul and Body, and 3) Turtle-dove and another bird or object (Jackdaw and Turtle-dove; Nightingale and Turtle-dove; Plough and Turtle-dove). The poems in the third category, however, are not precedence poems, are very brief, and deal with why one should lament the onset of autumn.

The sudden appearance of dispute poems in manuscripts of the seventeenth and eighteenth centuries coincides with the greater prominence and institutionalization of the itinerant bards called *ašuł*-s in Armenian and *'āšıq*-s in Turkish,

14 Jiménez (2017: 283–284) provides an analysis of one of the fables attributed to Goš inspired by the story of Jotham in *Judges* 9:8–15 that figures a date palm and vine among other vegetation.

both from Arabic *'āshiq*, "lover" (Berberian 1965: 811; van Lint 2005: 339–41; Yang 2016). The figure of the *ašuł* in Armenian possibly emerged around 1500, but over the course of the seventeenth century, Armenian *ašuł*-s became associated with schools in Iran, Anatolia, and the Caucasus. The advent and development of the Armenian *ašuł* overlapped with that of the Tukish *'āšıq*, who similarly occupied a larger cultural space in the seventeenth century and became somewhat institutionalized among dervish orders and the military (Lewis 1986: 697; Yang 2016: 48–50). The inscription of the Armenian precedence dispute poems should be situated within this broader phenomenon of the rising popularity of the *ašuł* / *'āšıq* in the sixteenth and seventeenth centuries. Debates between Heaven and Earth and Soul and Body were recited by the Armenian *ašuł*-s of New Julfa in the eighteenth and nineteenth centuries; and in the 1950s, Mnac'akanyan himself transcribed a variant of both poems from "an old *ašuł*," Mac'ak Mukuč'yan, who lived in the village of Jarxeǰ in Diliǰan province (Mnac'akanyan 1956: 611–12, 623–25). Mukuč'yan's recitation of "Heaven and Earth" is in Turkish (*er, goy*; i.e., *yer, gök*) and the *ašuł* explained that it had been translated because "before it had been in Armenian."[15] G. Lewonyan (1941: 129) reports that *ašuł*-s in the nineteenth and twentieth centuries "also used to sing 'the debate between Heaven and Earth', two people seated across from each other, stanza by stanza."[16] Garegin Yovsēp'ean (1898: 546, 548–49), who published a copy of the poem, recalls that a certain Aslan agha had reported to him that the poem was sung by the people of the region of Moks (*Mokac'ik'*). These attestations of the oral performance of the debate indicate that the poems circulated widely in the oral as well as the written register, and suggest that the impetus to record these poems in writing may be accounted for by the more general trend of the enhanced renown of the bard within the oral culture.

Mnac'akanyan (1956: 381–93) presents three dispute poems between Heaven and Earth in the main body of his collection. The first of them has often been ascribed to the seventeenth-century *vardapet* (monastic teacher) Nersēs Mokac'i, but in his study Mnac'akanyan (1956: 608–609) successfully challenges the attribution by demonstrating that the ascription arose from an unfounded association. The meter of the poem conforms to that of the type of poem called *hayrēn* in Armenian. Each stanza consists of a couplet of two fifteen-syllable lines that are broken into hemistichs. The first hemistich is heptasyllabic and consists of three feet of syllables in a 2–3–2 pattern. The second hemistich is octasyllabic

15 *ařaǰ hayeren a ełel*, Mnac'akanyan 1956: 611.

16 *Ergum ēin naew 'Erkink'i ew erkri večě,' erku hogi mimyanc' dem nstac, p'ox ař p'ox.*

and consists of three feet in a 3–2–3 pattern.[17] Each couplet possesses end-rhyme in –*i*. The poem overall has the following simple tripartite structure:

I. Introduction (1 couplet = 4 hemistichs)
II. Arguments by Heaven and Earth (18.5 couplets + 1 hemistich = 75 hemistichs)
   a. Heaven's concession (2 couplets = 8 hemistichs)
III. Conclusion (2 couplets = 8 hemistichs)

The beginning of each argument for both Heaven and Earth repeats the same line (or two hemistichs). For Heaven, it is:

> Heaven said to Earth— /
> I have something greater than you. //[18]

For Earth it is:

> Earth said to Heaven— /
> The strength of God is greater. //[19]

At the end of this version of the debate, Heaven concedes defeat to Earth. Following Mnac'akanyan, interpreters of the poem have viewed it as favoring a material and physical understanding of the universe against a spiritual one directed towards heaven. While Mnac'akanyan contends that such a terrestrial perspective further militates against attributing the poem to a monastic scholar such as Nersēs Mokac'i and in support of the poem's being a popular song,[20] others used the poem to cast Nersēs as a religious and social activist.[21]

---

17 One wonders if it is to an earlier form of the *hayrēn* that Antony of Tagrit (9th c.) refers when he observes that "Persians, Syrians, Armenians and other nations compose *sogyātā*," although they have not studied Homeric poetry (Watt 1986: 6); also cited in Brock 2008: 368. The most common metrical pattern for a stich of a *sugyātā*, however, is 7+7, rather than 7+8, as is the case with *hayrēn*-s.
18 *Erkink'n getnin asac' / Ban unim k'an zk'ez aweli //.*
19 *Getinn erknuc'n asac' / Astucoy munnat'n aweli //.*
20 As further evidence of anonymous authorship, Mnac'akanyan observes that none of the five copies of this poem preserved in the Matenadaran bears an author, nor do another two copies of the poem preserved elsewhere. Another poem on the same theme, which Mnac'akanyan claims has undergone a "spiritual" development, is again anonymous. A third version of the dispute suggests that it was recited by the *ašuł* Talip, but does not claim any authorship.
21 See for example, Hacikyan et al. 2002: 804–805. An English translation of the entire poem is also provided there; all translations in this essay are my own unless otherwise noted.

Both of these positions, however, assume an incorrect *Weltanschauung* for the poem. Although Heaven concedes at the end of the debate, the poem's thrust does not privilege a materialist understanding of the universe; rather, it presents itself as a didactic poem intended to instruct young people in humility and the transitory nature of this life, as the concluding stanza elucidates:

> Children, wonder! /
> This wonder is awesome. //
> But you, youngsters, humble yourselves, /
> And put your head to the earth. //
> What is higher than heaven, /
> That it lowered its head to the earth? //
> Today, we are walking on top of the earth /
> Tomorrow, we enter within it! //[22]

The word "wonder" (*ačap'*) in the first two verses of the stanza is a loan into Armenian from Arabic, *'ajab*. It echoes the word's use in the first stanza of the poem so that the expression of wonder[23] nicely frames the entire poem:

> Heaven and Earth are brothers /
> I wonder which one is greater? //
> I say the height of heaven, /
> He, the fruit of the earth. //[24]

The use of the loanword may help us more precisely date the poem. The earliest attestations of *ačap'* in Armenian appear in authors of the thirteenth-fourteenth centuries. Another loanword from Arabic that appears in the text, *munat'*, "strength, favor" (<Arab. *munnat*) and is repeated in Earth's responses to Heaven is otherwise only attested in a fourteenth-century colophon. A date of literary composition between the 14th and 16th c. for this articulation of the poem would therefore fit both the linguistic and available manuscript evidence.

---

22 *Mankunk', duk' ačap' arēk', / Ayd ačap'd ē zarmanali: // Duk' ayl c'acac'ēk', manktik', / U glux drēk' i getni. // K'an zerkink'n inč' barjr kay, / Or glux edir i getni, // Aysōr vran ku k'aylemk', / Vałn mtnunk' nerk'ew getni: //* (Mnac'akanyan 1956: 386–87).

23 We may note a similar evocation of wonder at the beginning of the Persian dispute between Heaven and Earth discussed below. The word there, however, is *shigift*, and not *'ajab*, so no textual relation can be posited. The composer of the Armenian poem also develops the theme more fully.

24 *Erkink'n u getink'n ełbark', / Ačap' or k'an zorn aweli. // Zerknic' barjrut'iwnn asem, / Nay getnin ptułn aweli: //* (Mnac'akanyan 1956: 381). The use of *nay*, "he [says]," here may indicate that the poem was intended to be read by two people as reported by Levonyan (1941: 129).

Such a dating for the writing of the poem does not, however, preclude the possibility of an earlier oral stage of composition for the debate.

The second of the Heaven and Earth dispute poems published by Mnac'akanyan is preserved in a manuscript dated to 1784. It has the same meter as the previous, but it is much shorter containing only 8 couplets. The rhyme in *–i* is only maintained in the first two couplets. The third couplet has a semi-rhyme of *–im* and *–i*; the fourth of *–ay* and *–i*; the fifth and sixth couplets do not rhyme; the seventh rhymes in *–aw*; and the eighth has a semi-rhyme of *–ay* and *–i*, but with rhyme of *–i* for the last two hemistichs. In contrast to the first dispute poem, here Earth concedes to Heaven, admitting,

> I have sinned against you, my brother, I have sinned.// I declare you noble./
> You are more praiseworthy than I!//[25]

Because Earth capitulates to Heaven in this way, Mnac'akanyan (1956: 613) considered this version of the poem to have undergone a "spiritualizing development." The third version of the poem printed by Mnac'akanyan was recorded by Łewon P'irłalemyan likely in Van in the nineteenth century from the disciples of the eighteenth-century *ašuł* Talib, who is referred to in the poem as their *p'ir* or spiritual master.[26] The poem ends, like the first, with a call to keep our heads to the ground for although today we are walking on it, tomorrow we will enter into it.

While Mnac'akanyan looks for comparable material written in Armenian, he completely neglects the literature of neighboring cultures. Disputes between Heaven and Earth, although not very common, occur in both Syriac and Persian. The dispute in Syriac is a prose *mēmrā* that appears in a manuscript in the British Library, Add. 14616, that has been dated to the sixth or seventh century. Sebastian Brock, who translated and studied the poem, prefers a sixth-century dating and characterizes it as a "popular piece of literature," whose introduction and conclusion "provide a vague liturgical setting" (Brock 1978: 262). An abbreviated form of the dispute is incorporated within the ninth-c. *Liber Castitatis* of Išo'dnaḥ, metropolitan of Basra. Although it does not seem to fit the context in which it appears, the vague liturgical setting of the dispute and its inclusion within a history of monastic foundations and figures underscores the liquid boundaries between monastic and popular literature.

---

25 *Mełay k'ez, ełbayr im, mełay, // Es k'ez xōrat'ay ari, / Du es mec k'an zis goveli: //* (Mnac'akanyan 1956: 389).

26 Arm. *p'ir* < Prs. *pīr*, "elder," is the equivalent of Arabic *shaykh*, and in a religious context refers to a Sufi master (Bosworth 1995).

The Persian example of the dispute between Heaven and Earth is the well-known *munāẓara* of Asadī Ṭūsī (11th c.), the earliest known user of the genre in Persian (Massé 1961: 137–40). Much about the life of Asadī, who was from Ṭūs in Khorasan, is unknown, but he worked in local courts in Armenia and its environs. One of his patrons was the Shaddādid ruler of Ani, Shujāʿ al-Dawla Manūchihr b. Shāvur (r. 1072–1118), whom he mentions in the colophon to his *munāẓara, The Lance and the Bow.* The *munāẓara* is preserved in an anthology of poetry dated to the eighteenth century contained within the Elliott collection (ms. 37) of the Bodleian Library (Abdullaeva 2009).

The three poems share the argument that heaven is the abode of the angels, while the earth houses the prophets and saints. The Syriac *mēmrā* and the Armenian poem also have a few other isolated points of similarity, but the three poems are quite distinct compositions, and their conclusions differ.[27] As noted above, at the end of the Armenian poem, Heaven concedes to Earth with praiseworthy humility; at the end of the *mēmrā*, Heaven proposes that they be reconciled as sisters just as their respective inhabitants have become reconciled as brothers. In a manner different from both the Armenian and Syriac disputes, in the Persian *munāẓara* it is a third figure, Time, who suddenly appears and imposes peace upon the disputants. We certainly cannot speak of any direct influence or even engagements between the texts themselves, but this clustering of interest in and treatments of a dispute between Heaven and Earth does situate the Armenian poem within a larger regional literary conversation in Anatolia and Mesopotamia. It also sketches a 1,300 year period between the sixth and nineteenth centuries during which the broad theme of a dispute between Heaven and Earth was popular among the Christian and Muslim communities in the region.

The second debate theme first found in Armenian manuscripts of the seventeenth century is that between Soul and Body. Like *The Debate between Heaven and Earth, The Debate between Soul and Body* has the meter of the *hayrēn*, each stanza consisting of a couplet of two fifteen-syllable lines that are broken into hemistichs of seven and eight syllables, but not consistently in the 2–3–2/3–2–3 pattern. The structure, too, is tripartite, although the poem is longer and instead of a concession, there is a lament:

I. Introduction (1 couplet = 4 hemistichs)

27 Cf. the observation of Jiménez (2017: 127), "not a single case of direct translation [of a dispute poem, SL] is known."

II. Alternating discussion between Soul and Body (43.5 couplets = 174 hemistichs)[28]
   a. Soul's lament (1 couplet + 3 hemistichs = 7 hemistichs)
III. Conclusion (2 couplets + 1 hemistich = 9 hemistichs).

The poem begins with an introduction announcing Soul and Body as wealthy brothers who go around with each other. There follows a series of alternating couplets led by Soul who exhorts Body to join it in prayer and seeking forgiveness for sins. Body responds that they are still young and they should eat and drink. Soul warns Body not to keep itself like bronze, which tarnishes, but like gold. Soul responds that it is protecting itself through the accumulation of things. Beginning in the 22nd couplet, Soul launches into a ten-couplet monologue trying to make Body realize that nothing will keep it from death. The first five and a half couplets consist of descriptions of wealthy rulers and biblical figures who are no longer alive. These include "the father of Łarun,"[29] the king of the T'aṙ,[30] baron Shadad,[31] Abraham, Israel, Moses, Solomon, and Askanadar Zullar.[32] The next couplet and a half encourage Body to look in the Gospels to find support for Soul's argument. In the next two couplets Soul provides a list of prohibitions Body should observe,[33] otherwise Body will become like Judas. Body then realizes Soul is leaving it like a swallow from its cage. Soul and Body then lament their fates. Soul cries it is leaving empty-handed, a homeless stranger (*łarib*) to the world; Body, that it is repentant, but buried in a deep prison. Body tells Soul to go "until the Lord will sit in judgment. / May He be merciful to us."[34] Soul then laments that it has no excuse:

> Woe is me, woe unto sinners,
> The Lord will sit in judgment!
> What will I say: I was held, bound?
> Woe is me, woe unto sinners,

28 Stanza 14 consist of a couplet plus one hemistich.
29 Presumably, the Abbāsid Caliph, al-Mahdī, who was the father of Hārūn al-Rashīd.
30 Presumably, the king of the Tatars, so the Mongol Khān.
31 Presumably, a Shaddādid emir.
32 I.e., Alexander *ḏū'l-qarnayn* (of the two horns), Alexander the Great.
33 E.g., Soul advises Body to refrain from eating foods that are *haram*, and reminds it that there are many that are *halal*, using the Armenian transcription of both Arabic terms. It further counsels not to harm friends, or to commit slander.
34 *Minč'ew Tērn darastan nsti, / Na lini zmez ołormac: //*, Mnac'akanyan 1956: 407.

The garden was built for the righteous
Hell of torments, for sinners.[35]

The poem then concludes with the evocation of the singer of the poem, Budał Ōłlin Łazi Xan (Budaq Oğlu Ğazi Xan)[36]:

Budał Ołli Łazi Xan,
Sit and cry your sins.
How many liars like you
Came into this world and left.
Say with one mouth "Father I have sinned,"
Lord God, open the gate of the garden,
To the singers and listeners,
Writers and those who lend their ear
May God be merciful.[37]

As the lack of a concession indicates, the poem is not a true precedence dispute like that between Heaven and Earth. Soul does not argue for its superiority over Body; rather, it repeatedly encourages Body to pray and ask for forgiveness, and reminds it of its temporary nature. The conclusion also differs from that of Heaven and Earth in that it mentions the poem's singer, Budaq Oğlu, about whom we have no information. Mnac'akanyan does not think him the original composer of the poem, but only its developer (*mšakoł*) or transmitter (*taracoł*).[38]

The thematic tension between the body and soul is a longstanding one reflected in many different literary cultures, but had developed particular rele-

35 *Hogin i marmnoyn asac'. / Vay inj, vay inj meławorac'. // Tērn i datastan nsti, / Inč' asem, kalac em, kapuac. // Vay inj, vay meławorac'. // Ardaroc' draxtn ē šinac, / Meławorac' džoxk' tanǰanac': //*, Mnac'akanyan 1956: 407–408.

36 The name Budał is from Turkish *budaq* meaning a branch of a tree. The name is attested among Armenians beginning in the sixteenth century.

37 *Budał Ołli Łazi Xan, / Du nstir u k'o mełk'n lac'. // K'ani k'ez pēs sut mardikk' / Erek ašxarhs u gnac': // Mēk beran Hayr mełay asēk', / Tēr astuac, draxtin duṙn bac'. // Asołac' ew lsołac', / Grołoc' ew akanǰ drołac', // Astuac lini ołormac: //*, Mnac'akanyan 1956: 408.

38 Mnac'akanyan conjectures that the poem, like that between Heaven and Earth, was composed between the tenth and fourteenth centuries, and subsequently spread as a popular poem, one version of which finally achieved written form under the name of Budał Ołlu. He further contends that the majority of the debates between Soul and Body derives from this single text, but that each reciter or copier of it gave it his own emphasis. Such a reductive philological and literary analysis ought to be rejected, but his gathering of analogous material is useful and does attest to the popularity of the debate.

vance in Christian contexts.[39] The tenor of this poem is closest to that of the Syriac dispute attributed to Jacob of Serugh (ca. 451–521) known as *Body and Soul II* (Drijvers 1991). In that poem, too, the shared fate of the body and soul is emphasized over their opposition; Body and Soul do not cast blame upon each other, but lament together. Similar to the Syriac poem, Soul tries to act as a counselor for Body and the theme of exhortation to repentance is present. Han Drijvers has pointed to the Syriac dialogue's affinities with medieval Latin examples of this theme which "leaves us with the question of possible historical links between the Syriac disputes between Body and Soul and their western equivalents" (Drijvers 1991: 129). Although positing contacts between Syriac and Armenian literary cultures poses no difficulties, no direct textual association can be asserted.

3 Classification

There is no indication that these poems were considered to belong to a separate genre within Armenian poetics. They both are included among other poems, known generally as *tał*-s. The compilations in which they were included along with these other poems furnish some indication of how they were conceptualized by their audience. The scribes of two of the manuscripts that contain *The Debate between Heaven and Earth* are known. Both manuscripts were copied in Kaffa in the Crimea and by ecclesiastics in the seventeenth century. In one (M7709), copied by the annalist and priest Xač'atur of Kaffa (also known as Xač'ġuz; Bardakjian 2000: 70–71), the poem is found among a collection of poetry that has been compiled along with works of entertainment literature, such as the *History of the Youth Farman* (Russell 1997), the *Story of a boy and a girl*,[40] the *Tale of the City of Bronze* (Russell 1983), as well as the author's own Chronicles. In the other (M3081), copied by the monk Zak'aria Erznkac'I in 1617, it is found along with other dialogic texts that served didactic purposes, such as *The Wisdom of*

39 Although Mnac'akanyan does not engage in any comparative analysis himself, he was well aware of the long and broad interest in the problem and refers the reader to F. Batyushkov's early comparative study of legends on the body and soul published in 1890, *Сказания о споре души с телом в средневековой литературе*. From Mnac'akanyan's remarks, it is clear that Batyushkov included this poem in his study, although I have not been able to check the work.

40 This story contains a series of questions or riddles in the middle of it that bear affinities with the story of Tawaddud in *The Thousand and One Nights*.

Ahikar, and the *Questions and Answers of Basil and Grigor*, as well as the *Story of a boy and a girl*, and the book of fevers.[41]

The Debate between Soul and Body is included in more varied miscellanies, but they reflect a general paraenetic orientation. One (M8443), produced in New Julfa in 1687 by the *dpirapet* (chief scribe, protonotary) Kostandin Jułayec‘i, also contains *The Wisdom of Ahikar*, prayers, as well as Kostandin's *Questions and Answers on the Bible*, his instruction in accounting and weights and measures, and his verse exhortation to children. Another (M3445, 17th-c.) includes the *Vision of St. Grigor Lusaworič‘*, sermons, a history, Proverbs, and counsels, including one against the drinking of wine. A third (M4285, 17th-18th c.) situates the poems among parts of a ritual book, a long poem known as *The Book of Adam* by Aṙak‘el Siwnec‘i (Stone 2007), riddles by Nersēs Šhnorhali, omens, a sermon on health, and a brief history of the economy of Christ. The collections in which the debate poems are found, then, corresponds to the didactic intent of their contents.

4 Dating

Although these two debate poems are first attested in manuscripts in the seventeenth century, the linguistic evidence supports an earlier dating for their written composition between the fourteenth and sixteenth centuries.[42] Mnac‘akanyan (1956: 613, 620 – 22) argues that both poems were originally composed as folk poems between the tenth and fourteenth centuries. He locates them within the intellectual debates that were taking place in the eleventh century, and contextualizes the contest between Heaven and Earth among the other types of debate literature mentioned above, namely, the poem of Yovhannēs Sarkawag, the fables of Mxit‘ar Goš and Vardan Aygekc‘i, and the dispute of Tērtēr Erewanc‘i. He similarly bases his dating of *The Debate between Soul and Body* on the existence in Armenian of prose disputes between Body and Soul from the period as well as the appearance of arguments between the soul and body incorporated within other poems.[43]

---

41 Zak‘aria seems to have been fond of this type of paraenetic literature, cf. M84.

42 *The Debate between Soul and Body* attests similar linguistic features as that between Heaven and Earth and likewise suggests a date of written composition between the fourteenth and sixteenth centuries.

43 So, for example, he cites a medieval vision attributed to Grigor Lusaworič‘ (Gregory the Illuminator), and poems by Xač‘atur Keč‘aṙec‘i (d. ca. 1330) and Yovhannēs Erznkac‘i. He also points to the evocation of this "Baron Shadad" as support for his dating since the Shaddādids control-

Undoubtedly, however, other manifestations of these debates circulated prior to that period. As indicated in the brief overview of debate literature in Armenian, Mnac'akanyan is correct that there is a marked increase in the written attestation of forms affiliated with the debate poem after the turn of the first millennium, but this does not mean that we should identify this intensification of attestation with the point of origination. Indeed, our earliest known dispute poem by Yovhannēs Sarkawag suggests that dialogue poems were familiar enough to his audience that he could adapt the form for his own purposes.

This burst of poetic argumentation in the eleventh century recalls that of Asadī Ṭūsī's composition of dispute poems. Scholars have speculated that Ṭūsī drew upon an Iranian pre-Islamic tradition as witnessed by the *Draxt ī āsūrīg* (The Assyrian Tree) composed during the Parthian period.[44] The Parthian Arsacid dynasty and elites ruled Armenia, too, from the first century CE to 428, surviving some two centuries after their cousins in Iran had been replaced by the Sasanians. It is not difficult to imagine Armenian *gusan*-s (< Parthian *gōsān*) performing debate poems either at court or in villages at feasts and commemorative occasions, much as Strabo (*Geog.* 16.1.14) reports the singing of a song about the uses of the palm tree in the Sasanian period or as illustrated in the Middle Persian *Khusro the son of Kawād and the Page* (*Ḵusraw ī Kawādān ud rēdak-ēw*).[45] In contrast to the Syriac tradition in Mesopotamia, which comes to prominence in the fourth century, this literature was not translated into the liturgical life of the Church. A possible explanation for this divergence may be that the genre was too closely associated with Armenia's Parthian pre-Christian past to be assumed into liturgical and homiletic composition. It perhaps continued to survive outside of the official canon of literature, performed in the banqueting halls of the noble families, at gravesites, and in public spaces on feast days by *gusan*-s for the entertainment and edification of all. Antony of Tagrit cited above (n. 17) may have

---

led the city of Ani in the late eleventh and twelfth centuries. Yet the poem seems to recall Hārūn al-Rashīd as well, and the 'Abbāsid court of the late eighth and ninth centuries was also renowned for its culture of debate. It is thought, e.g., that the genre existed in Arabic by the ninth century, Mattock 1991:155–56. Nonetheless, we may ask if there may be something more to the connection with the Shaddādids given that the Shaddādid emir Shujā' al-Dawla Manūchihr b. Shāvur patronized Asadī Ṭūsī's composition of dispute poems.

44 So already Massé 1961: 138.

45 See Asmussen 1973: 52–56; Jimeńez 2017: 133. We may also compare the Sadjid emir of Azerbaijan's reception of Prince Gagik Arcruni in ca. 907 as depicted by the first continuator of T'ovma Arcruni's *History of the House of Arcrunik'*. According to the anonymous tenth-century author, the former engaged the future Armenian king with numerous questions, Thomson 1985: 346.

had such performances of precedence poems in mind when he referred to the production of *sugyātā* in Armenian in the ninth century.

Why some representatives of the genre enter the literary record in the eleventh century is up to further speculation. The increased prevalence of dispute literature at the turn of the millennium is likely tied to larger issues such as the enhanced literary appreciation for non-liturgical poetry generally that warranted its written expression and collection. This desire may have been partially motivated by the prestige poetry held in the Islamicate world, but it may have been facilitated by technologies of writing and book production. The emergence and common usage of miniscule writing as well as the introduction of paper as a writing material certainly reduced the cost of producing manuscripts and allowed for the copying and dispersion of numerous non-canonical texts.[46]

It may also be linked to the development and proliferation of monastic schools whose teachers practiced the question and answer method in their pedagogy and required texts to facilitate instruction. The availability of fables, popular poems, and straightforward *eratopokriseis* in addition to direct paraenesis provided ecclesiastical educators with tools of instruction for students of all ages and various social backgrounds (see, e.g., Manukyan 1997). The interweaving of folk and didactic literature proved to be an effective and productive literary and pedagogic practice.

As suggested above, the inscription of these debate poems in codices occurred simultaneously with the rise of the *ašuł* and possibly in response to it. In the decentered world of early modernity in which Armenian populations were widely dispersed, both clerics and bards had to compete for their audiences. The debates between Heaven and Earth and Soul and Body provided both entertainment and edification to its readers and listeners, whether they be in the Crimea or Iran.

5 Conclusion

The Armenian debate poems and their traces challenge us to transcend the boundaries that often circumscribe our understanding of these poems. In them, just as within the debates between Heaven and Earth and Soul and

46 The dating of the creation of Armenian miniscule letters (*bolorgir*) is debated, but it seems likely that there was a gradual process from the tenth to the thirteenth centuries in which miniscule came to supplant uncial *(erkat'agir)* as the dominant form of writing. The earliest paper manuscript, which is written in a mixed *erkat'agir-bolorgir* script dates to 971/981. See Stone-Kouymjian-Lehman 2002: 69–71, 99–103.

Body, it is clear that the oppositions set between written versus oral and religious versus secular literature are false binaries. Instead, they should be regarded as siblings who share similar fates. The Armenian evidence attests to the fact that the highly literary style of the debate was generated and promoted in a popular register, and could move in and out of the medium of writing.[47] Likewise, "religious" and "secular" literatures were generally engaged in a fruitful dynamic, often at the hand of the same author. Moreover, the linguistic fluidity observed within the poems themselves, where Armenian, Arabic, Persian, and Turkish slip into each other,[48] suggests that treating each linguistic iteration of these poems as a defined set is deceptive. This shifting movement between languages, registers, and contexts complicates any attempt to discern clear lines of transmission. The question seems less one of determining cultural influence than of listening to conversations across cultures whose polyphony nonetheless reveals a shared aesthetic in which the dispute poem bore currency.

Bibliography

Abdullaeva, Firuza. 2009. The Bodleian Manuscript of Asadī Ṭūsī's Munāẓara Between an Arab and a Persian: Its Place in the Transition from Ancient Debate to Classical Panegyric. *Iran* 47: 69–95.

Adontz, Nicholas. 1925–26. Le questionnaire de Saint Grégoire l'Illuminateur et ses rapports avec Eznik. *Revue de l'Orient Chrétien* 25: 309–357.

Asmussen, Jes P. 1973. *Studies in Judeo-Persian Literature.* Leiden: Brill.

Bardakjian, Kevork. A Reference Guide to Modern Armenian Literature, 1500–1920. With an Introductory History. Detroit: Wayne State University Press.

Berberian, Haig. 1965. La littérature arméno-turque. Pp. 809–819 in *Philologicae turcicae fondamenta*, vol. 2, ed. Louis Bazin, Pertev N. Boratav, and Jean Deny. Wiesbaden: Steiner.

Bosworth, Clifford. E. 1995. Pīr. P. 306 in *The Encyclopaedia of Islam. New Edition. Volume VIII*, ed. Clifford E. Bosworth, Emeri van Donzel, Wolfhart Heinrichs, and Gérard Lecomte. Leiden: Brill.

Boyce, Mary. 1957. The Parthian Gōsān and Iranian Minstrel Tradition. *Journal of the Royal Asiatic Society* 1–2: 10–45.

Brock, Sebastian. 1978. A Syriac dispute between Heaven and Earth. *Le Muséon* 91: 261–270.

---

47 The Armenian evidence would thus support the suggestion of Holes (1995: 103) that disputation poems "may have oscillated between the sphere of 'low' (i.e. unrecorded) and 'high'; (=i.e. literate and recorded culture," cited by Jiménez (2017: 128), who, however, is more cautious.

48 See Russell 1994 for other examples.

Brock, Sebastian. 1984. Syriac Dialogue Poems: Marginalia to a Recent Edition. *Le Muséon* 97: 29–58.
Brock, Sebastian. 1991. Syriac Dispute Poems: The Various Types. Pp. 109–119 in *Dispute Poems and Dialogues in the Ancient and Mediaeval Near East: Forms and Types of Literary Debates in Semitic and Related Literatures*, ed. Gerrit J. Reinink and Herman L. J. Vanstiphout. Orientalia Lovaniensia Analecta 42. Leuven: Peeters.
Brock, Sebastian. 2008. Dialogue and other sughyotho. Pp. 363–384 in *Mélanges Offerts au Prof. P. Louis Hage à l'occasion de son 70e anniversaire*, ed. Ayoub Chahwan. Kaslik: PUSEK.
Calzolari, Valentina. 2000. La version arménienne du Dialogue d'Athanase et Zachée du Pseudo-Athanase d'Alexandrie: Analyse linguistique et comparaison avec l'original grec. *Le Muséon* 113: 125–147.
Calzolari, Valentina. 2014. Philosophical Literature in Ancient and Medieval Armenia. Pp. 349–376 in *Armenian Philology in the Modern Era: From Manuscript to Digital Text*, ed. Valentina Calzolari with the collaboration of M.E. Stone. Handbuch der Orientalistik 23/1. Leiden/Boston: Brill.
Cowe, S. Peter. 1994–95. Armenological Paradigms and Yovhannēs Sarkawag's *Discourse on Wisdom. Revue des études arméniennes* 25: 125–156.
Cowe, S. Peter. 2005. The Politics of Poetics: Islamic Influence on Armenian Verse. Pp. 379–403 in *Redefining Christian Identity: Cultural Interaction in the Middle East since the Rise of Islam*, ed. Jan J. van Ginkel, Heleen L. Murre-van den Berg, and Theo M. van Lint. Orientalia Lovaniensia Analecta 134. Leuven/Paris/Dudley: Peeters.
Drijvers, Han J. W. 1991. Body and Soul: A Perennial Problem. Pp. 121–134 in *Dispute Poems and Dialogues in the Ancient and Mediaeval Near East: Forms and Types of Literary Debates in Semitic and Related Literatures*, ed. Gerrit J. Reinink and Herman L. J. Vanstiphout. Orientalia Lovaniensia Analecta 42. Leuven: Peeters.
Ervine, Roberta. 2000. Antecedents and parallels to some questions and answers on Genesis in Vanakan Vardapet's "Book of Questions." *Le Muséon* 113: 417–28.
Hacikyan, Agop, Gabriel Basmajian, Edward S. Franchuk, and Nourhan Ouzounian (eds.). 2002. *The Heritage of Armenian Literature. Volume II: From the Sixth to the Eighteenth Century.* Detroit: Wayne State University Press.
Holes, Clive. 1995. The Rat and the Ship's Captain: A dialogue poem from the Gulf, with some comments on the social and literary-historical background of the genre. Pp. 101–120 in *Dialectologia Arabica. A Collection of Articles in Honour of the Sixtieth Birthday of Professor Heikki Paiva.* Studia Orientalia 75. Helsinki: Finnish Oriental Society.
Jiménez, Enrique. 2017. *The Babylonian Disputation Poems: With Editions of the* Series of the Poplar, Palm and Vine, *the* Series of the Spider, *and the* Story of the Poor, Forlorn Wren. Culture and History of the Ancient Near East 87. Leiden/Boston: Brill.
La Porta, Sergio. 2011. Conflicted Coexistence: Christian-Muslim Interaction and its Representation in Medieval Armenia. Pp. 103–23 in *Contextualizing the Muslim Other in Medieval Judeo-Christian Discourses*, ed. Jerold Frakes. New York: Palgrave Macmillan.
La Porta, Sergio. 2015. Armeno-Latin intellectual exchange in the fourteenth century: Scholarly traditions in conversation and competition. *Medieval Encounters* 21: 269–294.
Levonyan, Garegin. 1941. *T'atronĕ Hin Hayastanum: Patma-banasirakan tesut'yun.* Erevan: Haypethrat.

Lewis, Bernard. ʻĀs̲h̲iḳ. P. 697 in *The Encyclopaedia of Islam. Volume 1. New Edition*, ed. Hamilton A. R. Gibb, Johannes H. Karmers, Évariste Lévi-Provençal, and Joseph Schacht. Leiden: Brill.

Mahé, Jean-Pierre. 2009–2010. Paroles à Dieu et Dialogue avec l'Écriture. *Revue Théologique de Kaslik* 3–4: 259–274.

Manukyan, Nona. 1997. Interrelation Between Scholarship and Folklore in Medieval Armenian Culture. *Le Muséon* 110: 81–89.

Mariès, Louis and Charles Mercier. 1961. *Hymnes de Saint Ephrem conservées en version arménienne: Texte arménien, traduction latine et notes explicatives.* Patrologia Orientalis 30.1. Paris: Firmin-Didot.

Massé, Henri. 1961. Du genre littéraire " Débat " en arabe et en persan. *Cahiers de civilisation medieval* 4(14): 137–147.

Mathews, Edward G. 1999. Armenian Hymn IX, *On Marriage*, by Saint Ephrem the Syrian. *Journal of the Society for Armenian Studies* 9: 55–63.

Mathews, Edward G. 2001–2002. Saint Ephrem the Syrian. Armenian Dispute Poems Between *Virginity and Chastity. Revue des études arméniennes* 28: 143–169.

Mattock, John N. 1991. The Arabic Tradition: Origin and Development. Pp. 153–163 in *Dispute Poems and Dialogues in the Ancient and Mediaeval Near East: Forms and Types of Literary Debates in Semitic and Related Literatures,* ed. Gerrit J. Reinink and Herman L. J. Vanstiphout. Orientalia Lovaniensia Analecta 42. Leuven: Peeters.

Mnacʻakanyan, Asatur. 1956. *Haykakan Miǰnadaryan Žołovrdakan Erger.* Erevan: HSSṘ GA.

Mnacʻakanyan, Asatur. 1976. Gełarvestakan grakanutʻyun. Pp. 851–79 in *Hay žołovrdi patmutʻyun*, vol. 3, ed. Čatur P. Ałayan et al. Erevan: HSSṘ GA.

Muradyan, Gohar (ed.). 1993. *Girkʻ Pitoyicʻ.* Erevan: HGAS.

Pifer, Michael. 2018. The Age of the Gharīb: Strangers in the Medieval Mediterranean. Pp. 13–37 in *An Armenian Mediterranean: Words and Worlds in Motion*, ed. Kathryn Babayan and Michael Pifer. Mediterranean Perspectives. Cham, Switzerland: Palgrave Macmillan.

Pifer, Michael. Forthcoming. Armenian Adaptations: Rethinking Comparison in Literary History.

Reinink, Gerrit J. and Herman L.J. Vanstiphout (eds.). 1991. *Dispute Poems and Dialogues in the Ancient and Mediaeval Near East: Forms and Types of Literary Debates in Semitic and Related Literatures.* Orientalia Lovaniensia Analecta 42. Leuven: Peeters.

Russell, James R. 1983. The Tale of the Bronze City in Armenian. Pp. 250–61 in *Medieval Armenian Culture*, ed. Thomas J. Samuelian and Michael E. Stone. University of Pennsylvania Armenian Texts and Studies 6. Chico, CA: Scholars Press.

Russell, James R. 1997. The History of the Youth Farman (Patmutʻiwn Farman Mankann), a Medieval Armenian Romance. *Acta Orientalia* 50: 203–244.

Russell, James R. 2004. Khachʻatur Kechʻaretsʻi: A Guide to Christianity. Pp. 1455–1462 in *Armenian and Iranian Studies*, ed. James R. Russell. Harvard Armenian Texts and Studies 9. Cambridge, MA: Dept. NELC, Harvard University and Armenian Heritage Press.

Russell, James R. 2014. The Epic of Sasun: Armenian Apocalypse. Pp. 41–77 in *The Armenian Apocalyptic Tradition: A Comparative Perspective*, ed. Kevork Bardakjian and Sergio La Porta. Studia in Veteris Testamenti Pseudepigrapha 25. Leiden: Brill.

Stone, Michael E. 2007. *Adamgirkʻ: the Adam Book of Aṙakʻel of Siwnikʻ.* Oxford: Oxford University Press.

Stone, Michael E., Dickran Kouymjian, and Henning Lehman. 2002. *Album of Armenian Paleography.* Aarhus: Aarhus University Press.

Terian, Abraham. 2012. *Magnalia Dei: Biblical History in Epic Verse by Grigor Magistros. The First Literary Epic in Medieval Armenian. Critical Edition with Introduction, Translation and Commentary.* Hebrew University Armenian Series 14. Louvain: Peeters.

Thomson, Robert W. 1980. The Formation of the Armenian Literary Tradition. Pp. 135–150 in *East of Byzantium: Syria and Armenia in the Formative Period*, ed. Nina Garsoïan, Thomas Mathews, and Robert W. Thomson. Washington, D.C.: Dumbarton Oaks Research Library and Collection.

Thomson, Robert W. 1985. *Thomas Artsruni. History of the House of Artsrunik'. Translation and Commentary.* Detroit: Wayne State University Press.

Thomson, Robert W. 1995. *A Bibliography of Classical Armenian Literature to 1500 AD.* Corpus Christianorum. Tournhout: Brepols.

van Lint, Theo M. 2005. The Gift of Poetry: Khidr and John the Baptist as Patron Saints of Muslim and Armenian Āšiqs – Ašułs. Pp. 335–378 in *Redefining Christian Identity: Cultural Interaction in the Middle East since the Rise of Islam*, ed. Jan J. van Ginkel, Heleen L. Murre-van den Berg, and Theo M. van Lint. Orientalia Lovaniensia Analecta 134. Leuven/Paris/Dudley: Peeters.

van Lint, Theo M. 2014. Medieval Poetic Texts. Pp. 377–413 in *Armenian Philology in the Modern Era: From Manuscript to Digital Text*, ed. Valentina Calzolari with the collaboration of M. E. Stone. Handbuch der Orientalistik 23/1. Leiden/Boston: Brill.

Vardanean, Aristakēs. 1929. Ełišēi Vardapeti Harc'munk' ew Patasxanik' i Girs Cnndoc'. *Handēs Amsorya* 43: 1–10, 65–79.

Watt, John W. (trans.). 1986. *The Fifth Book of the Rehetoric of Antony of Tagrit.* Corpus Scriptorum Christianorum Orientalium 481, *scriptores syri* 204. Louvain: Peeters.

Weller, AnnaLinden. 2017. Byzantophilia in the letters of Grigor Magistros? *Byzantine and Modern Greek Studies* 41(2): 167–181.

Yang, Xi. 2016. Sayat'-Nova: Within the Near Eastern bardic tradition and posthumous. PhD diss., UCLA.

Yovsēp'ean, Garegin. 1898. Žołovrdakan banahiwsut'ean hetk'er miǰnadarean tałaranneric'. *Ararat* 11–12: 544–551.

Section III Western Disputations during the Middle Ages

Vicente Cristóbal and Juan Luis Arcaz Pozo*

18 Tradition and Innovation in the Early Medieval Latin Debates

Alcuin's Conflictus veris et Hiemis, Scottus' Rosae liliique certamen, and the Eclogue of Theodulus

1 Debate in Greco-Roman Literature

In the literature of ancient Greece and Rome there is no autonomous genre of debates,[1] but debates do feature frequently, in various forms and in varying degrees of evolution, subsumed in other genres that were very popular. Debates, understood as a verbal confrontation between two characters, contain, in their simplicity and in elementary dramatic form, the seed of the theater, and even of choral poetry. According to Francisco R. Adrados (1972: 142–213), the *agṓn* or "verbal confrontation" would be the seminal form of both genres. The *agṓn* is a key ingredient in the rituals of primitive agrarian cultures, in which it is related either to the cult of the dead, to triumph ceremonies or weddings, or to the worship of the gods. Adrados (1972: 69) believes, against theories that define the *agṓn* as Attic or Sicilian in origin, that it is Panhellenic, while also recognizing that "it is an element that we will find again and again in Greek and non-Greek rites of pre-theatric character" (Adrados 1972: 173). The influence of Mesopotamian traditions on the development of the Greek *agṓn* is widely recognized by modern scholars.[2] *agṓnes* feature frequently in Greek tragedy and comedy: there is, for instance, an *agṓn* between Just and Unjust Argument in Aristophanes' *Clouds*, and between Hecuba and Helena in Euripides' *Trojan Women*. It is also a common device in Roman theater, for instance in the confrontation

---

* Universidad Complutense de Madrid. The authors would like to express their gratitude to Enrique Jiménez for translating and revising the present article, as well as for his valuable remarks.

1 As noted by Vanstiphout 2004: 155, "The strange thing is not so much the great spread of the genre [*sc.* of disputations]: it arose in ancient Mesopotamia, is prominent in Syrian Christian literature and is still very popular in Arabic to this day, both in classical literature and in folk traditions; and in Latin and various vernacular languages it flooded Europe in the Middle Ages and afterwards. The strange thing is that it is almost non-existent in the Greek and Latin classical tradition" (original Dutch cited in Jiménez 2017: 131 n. 359).

2 See e. g. Wagner 1963: 460–462; Froleyks 1973: 418, Murray 1995: 164, and Jiménez 2017: 131.

https://doi.org/10.1515/9781501510274-018

between the slave Toxilus and the pimp Dordalus in Plautus' *Persa* (vv. 406–426), in which both insult each other using almost the same number of verses.

Choral lyric can also have an agonal structure. Thus, in Catullus' *Poem* 62, two choirs take part, one of girls and another one of boys, who defend opposite views: the boys praise marriage as a necessary social institution, whereas girls prefer their maidenhood.[3]

In addition, the fable, a genre that personifies non-human entities, contains some conspicuous examples of *agṓn*, as has frequently been acknowledged. Thus, among the fables attributed to Aesop – an author whose historical existence is dubious, but who, according to the Greek tradition, lived in Phrygia or Tracia around the 6th century BCE – there is one (No. 346) that contains a verbal disputation between winter and spring (Jiménez 2017: 131–32 with n. 361). Similarly, Phaidros, a 1st century CE Latin poet who hailed from Macedonia, wrote a fable on the Fly and the Ant (No. IV 25), in which the two personified insects speak defending their respective merits.[4] The moral of the fable, put in the poet's mouth, gives victory to the Ant.

Many scholars[5] believe that in bucolic poetry, both in Theocritus (3rd century BCE) and Vergil (1st century BCE), there are also vestiges of debates that hark back to archaic rituals. According to these authors, Theocritus found a model for his *Idylls* in the folklore of Sicily: he would have adapted pre-existing short and simple pastoral songs, perhaps similar to Amoebaean singing (Petropoulos 1960). Perhaps as an echo of their ancient folk foundations, Theocritus' *Idylls* and Vergil's *Eclogues* have compositional schemes similar to those of the literary debates in other cultures – for example, in the singing joust from *Idyll* V, vv. 80 ss., in which one of the contenders is proclaimed winner.[6] Similarly, Vergil's *Eclogues* III and VII are composed as short alternating stanzas – what we call "Amoebaean singing" – while *Eclogue* VIII has long songs and one of the singers is proclaimed the winner by a referee. The same scheme can be found in later Latin bucolic poets, such as Calpurnius (1st century CE) and Nemesian (probably 3rd century CE). These examples, and in particular Vergil, provide a model for the Medieval poets that will be studied below: Alcuin, Sedulius Scottus, and the

3 See Latin text and English translation in Cornish, Postgate and Mackail 1913: 84–85.
4 See Latin text and English translation in Perry 1965: 340–343.
5 Thus Petropoulos 1960 and, more recently, Horowski 1973. Discussions on the origins of the genre can be found in Teijeiro 1972 and Cristóbal 1980: 29–39. Note that Duchemin 1960 does not believe that Theocritus was the inventor of the genre; he tracks down its origins in pre-historic cattle breeding cultures and, after studying the relationship between shepherding and music, concludes that all poetry has its origins in shepherding.
6 See Greek text and English translation in Hopkinson 2015: 92–103.

mysterious Theodulus (see Schäfer 2001). If *eclogues* indeed derive from folk debates, it would be remarkable that, in the Middle Ages, such *eclogues* provided in turn the framework for the newly born genre of the debate.

Before turning to these Medieval debates, a few of their ancient forerunners will be considered. First and foremost, the fable, for it is in fact a fable what is inserted into the *Fourth Iamb* of the Greek poet Callimachus, who lived in the 3rd century BCE and was an approximate contemporary of Theocritus. Although as fragmentary as the rest of Callimachus' *Iamboi*, it is, in both its structure and its setting, a full-fledged debate. The *Fourth Iamb* is an *agṓn* between a Laurel and an Olive.[7] The two trees ponder their virtues and list their rival's demerits. The laurel boasts of its relationship with Phoebus, through prophecy and worship, whereas the olive tree counters with allusions to its mythical origins, and statements about its superiority over Laurel. A Bramble-Bush is the arbiter of the dispute, but the conclusion is missing. Callimachus himself states at the beginning that this fable was told by the ancient Lydians, and locates the discussion on Mount Thymus of Lydia: this important element suggests an Eastern origin.

Two distinct traits of Callimachean poetry can be found in this poem: first, the mention of the source has the purpose of fulfilling Callimachus' self-imposed requirement of never singing anything unattested (cf. *Fragmenta* 612, *amártyron oudèn aeídō*, "I sign nothing that is not attested" and Hymn V 56: *mŷthos d' ouk emós, all' hetérōn*, "the story is not mine but told by others").[8] Secondly, the typically Alexandrian *mise en abyme:*[9] the conversation between trees is inserted inside a conversation between birds. The olive tree, in its speech, is actually conveying the conversation of two crows perched on its branches, a conversation that happens to deal with the respective merits of the olive and the laurel.

Many scholars have pointed out that the *Saturae* by the early Latin author are clearly inspired by Callimachus' *Iamboi.*[10] Ennius is, in fact, reputed to be

7 Jiménez 2017: 132. The Greek text and an English translation can be found in Trypanis, Gelzer and Whitman 1973: 118 – 127.

8 Greek text and English translation in Trypanis, Gelzer and Whitman 1973: 270 – 271 and 116 – 117, respectively.

9 The same technique that Catullus puts into play in his *Carmen* 64 (Latin text and English translation in Cornish, Postgate and Mackail 1913: 98 – 127: the abandonment of Ariadna is inserted as an ekphrasis in the bridal quilt within the story of the wedding of Peleus and Thetis.

10 Rostagni 1964: 216 – 217: "È probabile che, pur senza compromettere i rapporti con usi e tradizioni indigene, entrasse nelle *Saturae* l'influenza dei *Giambi* di Callimaco, il maestro della letteratura ellenistica; poichè, tra l'altro, nei *Giambi* callimachei i motivi favolistici (...) avevano parte rilevante." See also von Albrecht ³2012: 115: "Ob Ennius des Vorbilds der kallimacheischen Iamben bedurfte, um auf den Gedanken zu kommen, in seine *satura* Fabeln einzuschließen (...), muß ganz offen bleiben, zumal die Verwendung des *versus quadratus* in Fabeln ungriechisch ist.

the author of a now lost *Iudicium Vitae et Mortis*,[11] which we may assume to have been influenced by Callimachus's *Iamboi*.[12]

The famous Augustan poet Ovid (43 BCE – 17 CE) includes in his first work, *Amores*, a remarkable example of agonal literature. Contained within the first elegy of the third book of *Amores*, Ovid refers to a vision: Tragedy and Elegy presented themselves to him personified as women and each tried to convince Ovid to cultivate their respective genres.[13] Each of them pleads her case in one speech (vv. 20–30, Tragedy; vv. 35–60, Elegy), so the composition has a great metaliterary density. The two figures are entirely personified, with physical details that symbolize their literary character (v. 7–14). Thus, for instance, Elegy is dressed in a fine tunic and has perfumed hair, so that her attire and cosmetics suggest the erotic seduction of her literary content; but has one leg longer than the other, which refers to the metrical form of the elegy (elegiac couplet), composed of two verses, one longer than the other. The vision occurs in a *locus amoenus* with an untouched forest, a fountain, a cave and birdsong. In the epilogue (v. 61–70), the poet decides to continue for the moment to cultivate the Elegy – not surprisingly, since the speech of Elegy was notably more verbose, and she spoke last. He also states that he will devote himself soon to tragedy. Both the structure and the character of the composition resemble the features of the Oriental genre of the debate. It is possible that Ovid, who knew Callimachus' poetry well, was inspired by the Alexandrian poet.

Another Ovidian passage reminiscent of the structure of Medieval debates, in particular of the debates between Arms and Letters, is the judgment of the arms held between Odysseus and Ajax recorded in *Metamorphosis* XIII 1–381.[14] In this passage, both heroes vie over the right to inherit Achilles' weapon-

Mit dem *Kampf zwischen Tod und Leben* (*sat*. 20 V.) eröffnet Ennius die allegorische Poesie in Rom, der eine große Zukunft beschieden ist. Das Gewicht der literarischen Reflexion in der Satura läßt an Kallimachos denken."

11 Quintiliano, *Inst. orat.* IX 36: *Sed formas quoque fingimus saepe, ut Famam Vergilius, ut Voluptatem ac Virtutem, quem ad modum a Xenophonte traditur, Prodicus, ut Mortem ac Vitam, quas contendentes in satura tradit Ennius.*

12 *Iudicium Vitae et Mortis* is also the title of the *Fabulae Atellanae* (dramatic farces of popular origin) of the 2nd century BCE Latin author Novius, although this title differs from other preserved from that author, such as *Agricola*, "the farmer," *Andromacha* (parody of a tragedy), *Duo Dosenni*, "the two hunchbacks," *Gallinaria*, "comedy of chickens," and *Virgo praegnans*, "pregnant girl."

13 The Latin text and an English translation can be found in Goold 1914: 444–449.

14 Latin text and English translation in Miller 1916: II 228–255.

ry.[15] The structural affinities of this episode with the genre of debates are clear: in the text, mythical characters argue their own cases; they are not personifications, however, they symbolize something more than themselves: this is, in fact, a confrontation between *fortitudo* (bravery), embodied by Ajax, and *sapientia* (intelligence), the essential attribute of Ulysses. Moreover, this is a debate between the old Homeric *Virtus*, based solely on physical strength, and the new *Virtus*, with philosophical, particularly Stoic, overtones. The winner is, of course, Ulysses, who had spoken, naturally, in second place. The text is therefore a forerunner of the Medieval debates between the Knight and the Clergyman.[16]

The latest example of the genre of debate in ancient Latin literature is the poem entitled *Iudicium coci et pistoris*, "Dispute between the cook and baker," which probably dates to the third century CE. The text, attributed to a mysterious poet called Vespa ("wasp"), otherwise entirely unknown, is included in the omnibus work known as *Anthologia Latina*.[17] The text has 99 hexameters, and its structure is similar to the other examples seen so far: a brief presentation and an epilogue provide a frame for two speeches, the first by a baker, the second by the cook. There is no victor, but the referee, the god Vulcan (a fire god, very fitting because of the litigants' job), declares a tie. As in the other cases studied, each of the speakers ponders their respective achievements and merits, in both cases with burlesque references to mythology. The parodic tone of the text is widely recognized by scholars:[18] it is clear, for instance, in the initial invocation of the Muses: "Ladies thrice three, who all give us different arts, leave the hills of Pieria and write with me..." (*Ter ternae, varias cunctae quae traditis artes, / linquite Pierios colles et scribite mecum*).

The last dispute from Antiquity worth mentioning is Prudentius's Psychomachia (end of the 4th century CE), a Christian war epic with Homeric-Virgilian echoes, but whose characters are personifications of vices and virtues. The work contains eight battles in which actions alternate with speeches. The Psychoma-

15 Ovid may have had many ancient rhetorical and dramatical sources as models; among them the two plays on the topic written by the Roman playwrights Pacuvius and Accius under the title *Armorum iudicium*. For a more detailed analysis, see Cristóbal 1994.

16 Other passages in the *Metamorphoses* also have an agonal structure. This is the case of the contest between Pan and Apolo, celebrated in the Tmolo mount with the mount itself as the arbiter (*Metamorphoses* XI 150 – 173, see Latin text and English translation in Miller 1916: II 130 – 133). Two types of music and two musical instruments vie in this passage: the syrinx or flute of seven reeds, invented and played by Pan; and the lyre, Apollo's instrument. Instead of speeches, there is musical disputation. The referee, again, rules the second participant the winner.

17 Socas Gavilán's recent Spanish translation (Socas Gavilán 2011) discusses further details about the history of the *Antologia*'s genesis, its literary features and its many authors and genres.

18 See e.g. Milazzo 1980 and Rabuzzi 1991.

chia's personification of moral concepts and representation of them as litigants provided a model for medieval disputation literature.

2 The *Conflictus Veris et Hiemis* Attributed to Alcuin of York

After these forerunners of the genre in Antiquity, the Early Middle Ages have yielded three unique Latin debates: the *Conflictus Veris et Hiemis,* attributed to Alcuin of York (eighth century), the *Rosae liliique certamen,* attributed to Sedulius Scottus (ninth century), and the so-called *Ecloga Theoduli* (9th or 10th century). These three poems are composed as Amoebaean singing, i.e., the central part is built as a series of short couplets recited alternately by the two litigating characters, rather than as two successive interventions. Moreover, in the three poems we find elements typical of the classical bucolic genre, and in particular clear echoes of Vergil's *Eclogues.* In fact, Alcuin's poem and the *Ecloga Theoduli* can be styled hybrids of bucolic and debate, and even the *Rosae liliique certamen* as been called "a charming Eclogue" (Raby 1927: 195).

It is not entirely certain that the *Conflictus Veris et Hiemis,* attributed to Alcuin, Charlemagne's main court poet, was actually written by Alcuin (see Raby 1927: 160 – 61). Carmen Castillo, after a detailed grammatical analysis, concludes that its author could not be the erudite monk, since the poem displays a confusion of genres unexpected in a teacher; it must instead be, she argues, attributed to someone close to him, a pupil (Castillo 1973).

As already mentioned, the text is a hybrid between the "eclogue" and the "debate," in which the bucolic genre provides a framework for the verbal contest between Spring and Winter, a contest adjudicated by the shepherd Palaemon in favor of the Spring. It all starts, as in the Virgilian *Eclogues,* with a landscape setting with especial mention of tree shade:

Conveniunt subito cuncti de montibus altis
pastores pecudum vernali luce sub umbra
arborea, pariter laetas celebrare Camenas.
Adfuit et iuvenis Daphnis seniorque Palaemon.
Omnes hi cuculo laudes cantare parabant.

All the shepherds of the flocks suddenly gathered
from the mountain-tops on a bright spring day,
to sing joyous poetry together in the shade of the trees.
Young Daphnis was there, as was aged Palaemon,
all of them making ready to sing the cuckoo's praises.

Conflictus Veris et Hiemis vv. 1–5[19]

Some unnamed (vv 1–2: *Conveniunt ... pecudum pastores)* and other named shepherds (v. 4: *Adfuit et iuvenis Dafnis seniorque Palemon*) congregate: two of them, Daphnis and Palaemon, bear Virgilian names. They gather, we are told, in order to sing the praises of the cuckoo, harbinger of the spring (v. 3: *pariter celebrare Camenas,* and v. 5: *Omnes hi cuculo laudes cantare parabant*). This prologue closely follows the pattern of classical bucolic, which at the beginning always mentions the landscape, the shade of a tree, and the song of the shepherds.[20] But then two peculiar characters join the human participants, as two more shepherds: the seasons Spring or Summer (*Ver*)[21] and Winter (*Hiems*). The contestants accuse each other, defend themselves from their rival's accusations, and boast of their respective merits in a succession of short speeches inspired by the Amoebaean singing of the classical bucolics.[22]

What is different from the classical tradition is that good weather is epitomized here in the image of the cuckoo, the harbinger of the spring in Northern countries. W. P. Ker pointed out that, in Anglo-Saxon poetry, the cuckoo breaks the silence of winter, and is thus considered a bird of good omen.[23] While ostensibly trying to decide whether to support or reject the cuckoo, the two seasons are thus in fact pondering their own merits.[24]

There are two levels to this poem: a deeper and intrinsic one, which is the conflict between the two opposite seasons, i.e., good and bad weather; and another more superficial and explicit, which is the dispute over whether or not the cuckoo bird should be allowed to return. The debate is thus focused on the return of the bird, which distinguishes it from its Latin forerunners and from other similar texts. On the other hand, Winter's portrayal as a vicious character has clear Christian overtones: Winter is lazy, does not want the cuckoo to come because it brings with it activity and effort (verses 19–21), is also given to gluttony and drinking (verses 23–24), and is greedy and covetous (verses 32 and 35): it therefore accumulates three capital sins. Moreover, Spring calls Winter an ar-

19 Latin text from McEnerney 1981, English translation from Godman 1985: 145–149.

20 On these elements, see Cristóbal 1980: 143–322.

21 In the text, *Ver* refers to a period that goes beyond our "spring" and includes the "summer" as well (only in v. 36 is it possible to distinguish "spring" from "summer"). It refers to good weather in general as opposed to the winter.

22 Vergil's *Eclogues* III and VII are good examples of Amoebaean singing.

23 Ker 1904: 152–153, quoted by Raby 1927: 161.

24 A similar case is that of the 'Swallow song of Rhodes', a paean to the arrival to the swallow, a bird that is harbinger of the good weather, and thus greeted as if it were a god.

rogant person who could not survive without the work of the other seasons (verse 40), thus adding a new capital sin. Now Spring's victory is certain, and so it is recognized by the referee of the event, the shepherd Palaemon. This shepherd, who was qualified as a *senior* in the first verses, i.e., as the voice of experience, delivers the concluding speech (vv. 45–55), in which the panegyric of the cuckoo is resumed and turns almost into a divine hymn. The final verses of the poem may well reflect the Passover, since the resurrection of Jesus is also celebrated in the spring:

> *Tu iam dulcis amor, cunctis gratissimus hospes:*
> *Omnia te expectant, pelagus tellusque polusque,*
> *Salve, dulce decus, cuculus, per saecula salve!*
>
> Sweet love, everyone's most welcome guest,
> everything awaits you – the sea, earth and heavens –
> greetings sweet beauty! Cuckoo, greetings forever!
>
> *Conflictus Veris et Hiemis* vv. 53–55[25]

In conclusion, the *Conflictus Veris et Hiemis* is a hybrid of an ecloga and a debate, but one with a clear insular flavor, and an implicit, and yet obvious, Christian background.

3 Sedulius Scottus' *Rosae liliique certamen*

The attribution of the *Contest of the Rose and the Lily* to the 9th-century Irish monk Sedulius Scottus is more certain than that of the *Contest of Spring and Winter* to Alcuin. According to Raby's opinion, in this poem "the Irish and the German spirit meet, and the Carolingian pastoral, with its memories of Virgil, of Calpurnius, and of the Nemesian, and northern memories as well, reaches its close" (Raby 1927: 247). As in Alcuin's poem, this text exemplifies the reception of the classical tradition by the peoples of Northern Europe, and it has a distinctive Christian flavor. In theme and tone, the debate is reminiscent of some classical texts such as Aesop's fable (No. 369) of 'The Rose and the Amaranth' (see Perry 1965: 487) and Callimachus's *Iamb* IV.

Although called an "eclogue" by Raby (1927: 195), the poem has fewer bucolic elements than the *Contest of Spring and Winter.* There are no shepherds and there are no bucolic motifs such as the shade of a tree. What we do find is a tri-

25 Latin text from McEnerney 1981, English translation from Godman 1985: 145–149.

partite structure, with a brief prologue and a longer epilogue spoken by the poet (vv. 1–4 and vv. 29–50):

Cyclica quadrifidis currebant tempora metis,
Vernabat vario tellus decorataque peplo.
Lactea cum roseis certabant lilia sertis,
Cum rosa sic croceo sermones prompserat ore:

The cycles of the seasons were running their four-fold course,
the earth was blossoming, arrayed in its many-coloured robe,
and the milk-white lilies vied with the garlands of roses,
when a rose made this declaration with its saffron lips:

Rosae liliique certamen vv. 1–4[26]

Spring, personified both as a girl (called *iuvenis*, "youthful," in v. 29) and as a "father" (vv. 43–44, *Ver genitor*, "the Spring, (their) father"; and *patrio de more*, "as a parent should") is the adjudicator of the debate: it decides to avoid making one of the flowers the winner by declaring a tie. The main characters are the Rose and the Lily, who first present their cases, and then argue in alternating strophes (vv. 5–28). There is in fact a certain *Ringkomposition*, since the initial laconic reference to spring-like weather (v. 2: *vernabat*, "(the earth) was blossoming") finds an echo in the speech of Spring (*Ver*) in the final verses.

The enumeration of the respective advantages and positive qualities of both flowers progresses from purely pagan and mythological reasons (vv. 9–10: *Me... pulcher Apollo / diligit*; "'I am loved by handsome Apollo"; vv. 14–15: *Et me Phebus amat, rutili sum nuncia Phebi; / Lucifer ante meum hilarescit currere vultum*, "and Phoebus loves me; I am the herald of red Phoebus; / the morning star delights to run before my face,"), to subtle but noticeable Christian arguments (v. 23: *Conditor omnicreans*, "the creator and begetter of all things"; and particularly v. 41: *Tu, rosa, martyribus rutilam das stemmate palmam*, "Roses shall provide martyrs with their red sign of victory"). Given this progression, verse 21, *Ut quid deleras verbis, occata vetustas?* (translated Godman 1985: 285 as "Why in the world are you ranting on, you broken down old hag?") is particularly significant. In it, *occata vetustas* could be taken as "ruined Antiquity," and interpreted from a Christian point of view.[27] Indeed, this line comes immediately after Lily

26 Latin text and English translation from Godman 1985: 282–283.
27 Despite its rarity from the point of view of classical Latin, *ut quid* is a frequent subjunction in Medieval Latin (as kindly communicated by Álvaro Cancela), which originates in Biblical Latin, in the Vulgata version of *Matthew* 27, 46: *Deus meus, Deus meus, ut quid dereliquisti me?*

accuses Rose of taking its color from the blood of an eternal wound, referring to a legend according to which Venus injured her foot with the thorns of the rose.[28] Rose then reacts by saying that those are tales of earlier times – literally: "from an antiquity already turned into ruins" (*occata vetustas*). According to Rose, the real explanation of its thorns is that the Christian God, the Creator of all, granted thorns to Rose as a protection to defend its beauty.

The final portion of the piece, once Spring has decreed peace and harmony between both flowers, has a relaxed and playful tone, which brings a kind of closure to the dispute: the two flowers, who are called sisters, kiss each other; by doing so, they also playfully prick each other with their thorns (vv. 45–50):

> *Lilia tunc croceae dant oscula grata sorori,*
> *Illa sed huic ludens spinetis ora momordit.*
> *Lilia vernigenae ludum risere puellae,*
> *Ambroseo bibulum potant et lacte rosetum.*
> *At rosa puniceos calathis fert xenia flores*
> *Ac niveam largo germanam ditat honore.*

> The lily then gave pleasant kisses to her saffron sister,
> but she, playing a trick, nipped the lily's mouth with her thorns.
> The lily laughed at the jest of that maiden born in the spring,
> and gave the thirsty rose a drink of ambrosial milk.
> The rose carried gifts of purple flowers in her basket
> generously to enrich and honour her snow-white sister with them.
> *Rosae liliique certamen* vv. 45–50[29]

In the end, neither is declared the winner.

4 The *Ecloga Theoduli:* Truth Against Falsehood

A further step in the marriage of eclogue, debate, and Christianity is represented by the so-called *Ecloga Theoduli*, a rather mysterious text (Mosetti Casaretto 2013), whose most salient feature is its incorporatation of explicitly Christian themes. The poem is a synthesis of elements from the classical tradition (mainly the works of Vergil and Ovid) and of Christian elements (in particular the Old

28 The myth is narrated, for instance, in a poem attributed to Draconcius (*De origine rosarum*), which is part of the *Anthologia Latina* (no. 874b, translation in Socas Gavilán 2011: 673).
29 Latin text and English translation from Godman 1985: 286–287.

Testament). This combination provided a pioneering model for the later medieval eclogues of religious contents.[30]

The poem is composed of 344 hexameters with leonine rhyme.[31] The problems concerning the text's date of composition are considerable, but it must have been written before the 10th century CE, which is the date of its oldest manuscript (*Etonensis* L.6.5). The identity of the author is also unclear:[32] some believe that Theodulus was a poet of Italian origin versed in Greek, who lived in the 10th century;[33] others think that Theodulus is a pseudonym either of the famous poet Gottschalk of Orbais (10th century),[34] or of an anonymous monk (Mosetti 1995). Still other scholars believe that the name Theodulus refers not to the poet who wrote the eclogue, but to the text's contents: *Ecloga Theoduli* would mean "eclogue of God, Truth and Deceit."[35]

30 Such as Guarnerio of Basel (mid-11th century) in his *Synodicus*, a debate also in bucolic terms between the Old and the New Testament, represented by the characters of Thlepsis and Neocosmo, with Sophia as a judge (Hamilton 1909: 172). Also, in the 12th century, Metellus of Tegernsee in the ten eclogues included his fifth *Quirinalia* (Cristóbal 1996: 47 and Pejenaute Rubio 2002/2003). Another text, entitled *Pistilegus*, is known only from its quotation in the *Registrum multorum auctorum* by Hugo of Trimber in 1280 (Hamilton: 173). The success that the *Ecloga Theoduli* met is reflected in the successive commentaries that it received already at the end of the 11th and beginning of the 12th century, such as Bernard of Utrecht's and, slightly later, Bernardus Silvestris (*Commentum Bernhardi Silvestris super Theodulum*), the latter known only from references in catalogues of certain Medieval libraries (Hamilton 1909: 173). The *Ecloga*'s success can also be seen in the many manuscript copies that were made in the 13th to 15th centuries (Osternacher 1902 collects 121 of them in his edition). The *Ecloga* was used in school and was eventually included, among other compilations, among the *Auctores octo* (together with *Disticha Catonis, Facetus, De contemptu mundi, Floretus, De parabolis* by Alain of Lille, *Aesopus*, and *Tobias*); see Hamilton 1909: 169–185 and Soons 1973.

31 A final doxology of eight verses was added later and appears only in some manuscripts.

32 A discussion of the different proposals can be found in Mosetti Casaretto 1995.

33 This is indicated, for example, in the *Commentum* of Bernard of Utrecht.

34 I.e., "slave of God," the semantic equivalent of the German meaning of his own name, as proposed long ago by von Winterfeld 1905: 70–71 and supported by other scholars.

35 Note the equivalence *Theo* = God and *Dulo* [variant *Dolo*] = Deception. This was proposed by Beck in his edition of 1836. Green 1982: 111–112, observing that the author seems to be on the side of the woman (the young Alithia beats the shepherd Pseustis; and Phronesis, the judge, is also a woman), suggests that the author was a poet interested in proposing a debate between the sexes (Green 1982: 52). Alfonso X of Castile, in his *General Estoria* II 65 b (ed. Solalinde), points out that the poet "ovo nombre Guerrico, et al libro que ende compuso llaman en el latin Theodulo et en el lenguaje de Castiella Teodoreth" (Arcaz Pozo 1989: 377), without further explanation.

The most remarkable feature of the *Ecloga* is the long succession of verses that oppose stories from classical mythology with stories from the Bible, refuting paganism by contrasting the myths of gods and heroes with similar Christian legends. The author believes that pagan religion was epitomized in classical mythology, so the solution he adopts to refute it is simple and effective. The efforts put into finding these parallels is remarkable: in this respect, Manitius has considered this text a "scientific work of no little importance."[36]

In terms of structure, the *Ecloga Theoduli* presents the usual tripartite structure already seen in other poems: a prologue with an initial presentation (vv. 1–36), the debate itself (vv. 37–336) and, finally, the adjudication (vv. 337–344). At the end, the bucolic setting declared in the first lines is resumed, and the day, the debate, and the text itself are declared finished:

Mortales cuncti quod contendunt adipisci
Nec, si perficiant, vitae discrimina curant,
Ex insperato dominus tibi contulit ultro:
Ut cessare velis devictus supplicat hostis.
Treicius vates commovit pectine Manes,
Te moveant lacrimae; iam tollit cornua Phoebe;
Sol petit Oceanum. frigus succedit opacum:
Desine quod restat, ne desperatio laedat.

God has freely conferred upon you that
which all mortals struggle to obtain (divine grace),
and, if they achieve it, they have no care for life's dangers;
your opponent requests that you, now beaten, will wish to yield.
The Thracian poet (Orpheus) moved the shades with his lyre;
may tears move you. Now Phoebe raises her horns;
the sun seeks Ocean, the dark cool follows.
Desist from the remainder, so as not to be injured by despair.

Ecloga Theoduli 337–344[37]

In the prologue and the adjudication we find the poem's clearest links with Vergil's *Eclogues* (Green 1982 and Arcaz Pozo 1989), whereas in the central part of the poem reference is frequently made to Ovid's *Metamorphoses*, the main source for the pagan myths refuted in the text (albeit not the only one).

The pastoral framework that opens the eclogue has all the stereotypical bucolic elements: a reference to the time of day (vv. 1–2: *Aethiopum terras iam feruida torruit aestas, / in cancro solis dum uoluitur aureus axis*, "The torrid summer

36 "Das Gedicht selbst hat keine ganz unbedeutende wissenschaftliche Arbeit zur Vorbedingung" (Manitius 1911/1931: I 572–573).
37 Latin text from Osternacher 1902: 53–54, English translation from Herren 2007: 230.

now scorches Ethiopian lands, while the golden axis of the sun turns in the sign of Cancer"), a presentation of the characters, a description of the landscape with the inevitable tree,[38] an invitation to debate, a mention of the prize (a musical instrument), and an invitation to a third character to arbitrate. The characters are (1) the goatherd Pseustis, a native of Athens, who represents paganism; (2) the young shepherdess Alithia, a descendant of the lineage of David, who represents Christianity; (3) and the shepherdess Phronesis, who arbitrates the debate. The *causa litigandi* is Pseustis' jealousy of Alithia's musical skills, whose melodies affect the surrounding natural landscape:

> *Substiterat fluuius tanta dulcedine captus*
> *auscultando quasi modulantis carmina plectri*
> *ipseque balantum grex obliuiscitur esum*
>
> Overcome by the sweetness of the music,
> the river is transfixed as though harking to the sounds of the modulating plectrum,
> and the bleating flock happily ignores its fodder.
>
> *Ecloga Theoduli* 11–13[39]

Despite these clear references to Vergil, there are also obvious deviations from the model: first, the shepherds' names are not Virgilian (as opposed to Alcuin's text), but of Greek origin. They are speaking names: Alithia is the "truth" and thus embodies Christianity; Pseustis is "falsehood" and hence a representative of paganism; Phronesis is "prudence" and, as such, rules in favor of Alithia. There is another important difference with its classical forerunners: two of the characters (Alithia and Phronesis) are women, an unusual fact in classical bucolic poetry.[40] The gender of the characters does not correspond with their grammatical gender in Greek, since, although *alḗtheia* and *phrónēsis* are feminine nouns, *pseústis* is also feminine and yet it is represented by a man. It rather denotes some sort of symbolism whereby women, as symbols of Mary, overcome the perfidious devil – a man – that wants to destroy them. This symbolism can be found, for instance, in *Revelation* XII 1–9, in which Satan is defeated by the Virgin Mary after the latter gives birth to Jesus Christ.

The debate itself consists of seventy-five stanzas of four lines each, alternately interpreted by Pseustis (the first in speaking) and Alithia. Not all interventions contain Christian and pagan myths; only twenty of them actually oppose stories

38 There is also an *Arbore sub quadam*, not a *fagus* or a *quercus*, but a *tilia amoena*.
39 Latin text from Osternacher 1902: 30, English translation from Herren 2007: 218.
40 Vergilian shepherdesses, like Amaryllis or Galatea, were mute characters and simple objects of the male shepherds' love.

of paganism with their Christian counterparts; the rest are of miscellaneous content, but clearly linked to the underlying theme of the debate (see Herren 2007: 204). The succession of the pagan stories roughly follows the order of Ovid's *Metamorphoses*, perhaps because Pseustis is the first to speak: first the Golden Age of Saturn, then the reign of Jupiter after the Titanomachy, then the impiety of Lycaon, the flood and the salvation of Deucalion, etc. but soon the train of argumentation is lost. Pseustis marks the way to Alithia, who responds with stories that are chronologically parallel: at the beginning, Adam and Eve in Paradise, the expulsion from Eden, the piety of Enoch against the wickedness of men, the flood and Noah's salvation, and so forth. Occasionally, the connection between pagan and Christian myth is thematic: thus, the romantic pretensions of Phaedra towards Hippolytus (vv. 125–128) are opposed to those of Potiphar's wife towards Joseph (vv. 121–132). The debate develops without interruption: the referee, Phronesis, does not appear on stage until the very end of the eclogue. Although victory is eventually awarded to Alithia, Alithia is not the winner of every round: as stated by Herren 2007: 204, Pseustis also wins in some of the partial duels.[41]

In vv. 333–336 Pseustis admits its defeat (v. 336: *Quo tendit cedo nec me cessisse negabo*, "I yield, and will not deny that I yielded"), but the result was a foregone conclusion: in vv. 293–296, Pseustis states that he wishes to finish the debate, since he feels he has been surpassed by the young shepherdess (v. 296: *Cede dies, caelo, quia nescit cedere virgo*, "Yield, O day, to the sky, since the maiden knows not how to yield"). Phronesis can simply proclaim Alithia's victory, since the pagan rival has already admitted her superiority. It is also Phronesis who, going back to Vergilian models, declares the end of the debate by announcing the arrival of the night (v. 342–343: ... *Iam tollit cornua Phoebe, / Sol petit occasum, frigus succedit opacum*, "Now Phoebe raises her horns; the sun seeks Ocean, the dark cool follows").

5 Conclusions

Overall, it appears that the literary *agṓn* was never given an autonomous formulation in Graeco-Roman literature. However, to a greater or lesser extent, it was present in almost all ancient poetic genres: stemming from folkloric motives and

41 See also Bossy 1971: 16: "One senses, to be sure, that the outcome is predetermined. Yet, just as in Milton's *Paradise Regained* or in Chateaubriand's *Martyrs*, the attractions of the pagan world do effectively rival those of the Christian tradition for the duration of the contest."

from the remote oriental tradition, as explicitly formulated in Callimachus's *Fourth Iamb*, the ἀγών first found its way into theater and choral lyric, and then spread to fables and bucolic poetry. Most noticeably, its presence and development in the latter genre, first in Theocritus and then especially in Vergil, provided an appropriate and fertile compositional scheme for the new genre that emerged during the Early Middle Ages. In these news texts, the popular form of the debate is seasoned with Christian motifs, which gradually increase over time in the three poems studied above.

Bibliography

Adrados, Francisco R. 1972. *Fiesta, comedia y tragedia. Sobre los orígenes griegos del teatro.* Barcelona

von Albrecht, Michael. ³2012. *Geschichte der römischen Literatur. Von Andronicus bis Boethius und ihr Fortwirken.* Berlin: De Gruyter.

Arcaz Pozo, Juan Luis. 1989. Tradición bucólica e innovación cristiana en la *Ecloga Theoduli.* Pp. III, 373–379 in *Actas del VII Congreso Español de Estudios Clásicos*, Madrid: Universidad Complutense.

Bossy, Michel-André. 1971. *The Prowess of Debate: A Study of a Literary Mode, 1100–1400.* Yale University: Unpublished PhD dissertation.

Castillo, Carmen. 1973. La composición del "Conflictus veris et hiemis" atribuido a Alcuino. *Cuadernos de Filología Clásica* 5: 53–61.

Cornish, Francis W., Postgate, John P., and Mackail, John W. 1913. *Catullus. Tibullus. Pervigilium Veneris.* Loeb Classical Library 6. Cambridge: Harvard University Press.

Cristóbal, Vicente. 1980. *Virgilio y la temática bucólica en la tradición clásica.* Madrid: Universidad Complutense.

Cristóbal, Vicente. 1994. Ulises y la "Odisea" en la literatura latina. Pp. II, 481–514 in *Actas del VIII Congreso Español de Estudios Clásicos*, Madrid: Ediciones Clásicas.

Cristóbal, Vicente. 1996. *Virgilio: Bucólicas, edición bilingüe.* Madrid: Cátedra.

Duchemin, Jacqueline. 1960. *La houlette et la lyre. Recherche sur les origines pastorales de la poésie. I. Hermes et Apollon.* Paris: Les Belles Lettres.

Froleyks, Walter J. 1973. *Der ἀγὼν λόγων in der antiken Literatur.* Bonn: Rheinische Friedrich-Wilhelms-Universität.

Godman, Peter. 1985. *Poetry of the Carolingian Renaissance.* Norman: University of Oklahoma Press.

Green, Roger P. H. 1979. *Seven Versions of Carolingian Pastoral.* Reading: University of Reading.

Green, Roger P. H. 1982. The Genesis of a Medieval Textbook: The Models and Sources of the *Ecloga Theoduli. Viator* 13: 49–106.

Hamilton, George L. 1909. Theodulus: A Mediaeval Textbook. *Modern Philology* 7/2: 169–185.

Herren, Michael. 2007. Reflections on the Meaning of the *Ecloga Theoduli:* Where is the Authorial Voice? in *Poetry and Exegesis in Premodern Latin Christianity: The Encounter*

Between Classical and Christian Strategies of Interpretation, ed. W. Otten and K. Pollmann. Leiden: Brill.
Hopkinson, Neil. 2015. *Theocritus. Moschus. Bion.* Loeb Classical Library 28. Cambridge: Harvard University Press.
Horowski, Jan. 1973. Le folklore dans les Idylles de Théocrite. *Eos* 61: 187 – 212.
Jiménez, Enrique. 2017. *The Babylonian Disputation Poems. With Editions of the Series of the Poplar, Palm and Vine, the Series of the Spider, and the Story of the Poor, Forlorn Wren.* Culture and History of the Ancient Near East 87. Leiden: Brill.
Ker, William P. 1904. *The Dark Ages.* Periods of European Literature 1. New York: Scribner.
Manitius, Max. 1911/1931. *Geschichte der lateinischen Literatur des Mittelalters.* München: Beck.
McEnerney, John I. 1981. Alcuin, Carmen 58. *Mittellateinisches Jahrbuch* 16: 35 – 42.
Milazzo, Vincenza. 1980. Polisemia e parodia nel 'Iudicium coci et pistoris' di Vespa. *Orpheus* 3: 250 – 274.
Miller, Frank J. 1916. *Ovid, Metamorphoses.* Loeb Classical Library 42/43. Cambridge: Harvard University Press.
Mosetti Casaretto, Francesco. 1995. È 'Teodulo' il poeta dell' 'Ecloga Theoduli'? *Mittellateinisches Jahrbuch* 30: 11 – 38.
Mosetti Casaretto, Francesco. 2013. Il caso controverso dell' *Ecloga Theoduli. Studi Medievali* 54/1: 329 – 364.
Murray, Robert. 1995. Aramaic and Syriac Dispute-poems and their connections. Pp. 157 – 188 in *Studia Aramaica. New Sources and New Approaches*, ed. M. J. Geller, J. C. Greenfield and M. P. Weitzman. Journal of Semitic Studies Suppl 4. Oxford/New York: Oxford University Press.
Osternacher, Johann. 1902. *Theoduli Eclogam.* Ripariae prope Lentiam.
Pejenaute Rubio, Francisco. 2002/2003. Ecos virgilianos y horacianos en Metelo de Tegernsee. *Archivum* 52/53: 351 – 381.
Perry, Ben E. 1965. *Babrius and Phaedrus. Fables.* Loeb Classical Library 436. London: Heinemann.
Petropoulos, Dimitrios A. 1960. *Θεοκρίτου Ειδύλλια υπό λαογραφική̃ν ἄποψιν ερμηνευόμενα.* Athens.
Rabuzzi, M. Cristina. 1991. Imitazione e parodia in *A. L.* 199 R (*Iudicium coci et pistoris di Vespa*). *Sileno* 17: 259 – 279.
Raby, Frederic J. E. 1927. *A History of Christian-Latin Poetry from the beginnings to the close of the Middle Ages.* Oxford: Clarendon Press.
Rostagni, Augusto. 1964. *Storia della letteratura latina.* Torino: Unione tipografico-editrice torinese.
Schäfer, Antje. 2001. *Vergils Eklogen 3 und 7 in der Tradition der lateinischen Streitdichtung. Eine Darstellung anhand ausgewählter Texte der Antike und des Mittelalters.* Frankfurt: Peter Lang.
Showerman, Grant. 1914. *Ovid: Heroides. Amores.* Loeb Classical Library 41. Cambridge: Harvard University Press.
Socas Gavilán, Francisco. 2011. *Antología Latina. Repertorio de poemas extraído de códices y libros impresos.* Biblioteca Clásica Gredos 394. Madrid: Gredos.
Soons, Alan. 1973. The Didactic Quality of Theoduli Ecloga. *Orpheus* 20/1: 149 – 161.

Teijeiro, Manuel G. 1972. Notas sobre poesía bucólica griega. *Cuadernos de Filología Clásica* 4: 403–425.
Trypanis, Constantine A., Gelzer, Thomas, and Whitman, Cedric H. 1973. *Callimachus: Aetia, Iambi, Hecale and Other Fragments. Musaeus: Hero and Leander.* Loeb Classical Library 421. Cambridge: Harvard University Press.
Vanstiphout, Herman L. J. 2004. *Eduba. Hoe men leerde schrijven en lezen in het Oude Babylonië. Een bloemlezing van literaire teksten uit de scholen van Sumer.* Amsterdam: SUN.
Wagner, Ewald. 1963. Die arabische Rangstreitdichtung und ihre Einordnung in die allgemeine Literaturgeschichte. *Abhandlungen der Geistes und Sozialwissenschaftlichen Klasse. Akademie der Wissenschaften und der Literatur* 1962/8: 437–476.
von Winterfeld, Paul. 1905. Hrotsvits literarische Stellung – Der Mimus und die karolingische Ekloge. *Archiv für Neuere Sprache* 14: 70–71.

Thomas Honegger*

19 Owls, Nightingales, Cuckoos and Other Feathered Disputants

The Genre of the Bird Debate in Middle English, with Special Focus on *The Owl and the Nightingale*

1 Introduction

England before as well as after the Norman Conquest participated and also contributed to the European literary production, be this in Latin, Old English, (Norman) French, or Middle (and later Modern) English.[1] Debate poetry is no exception to this rule and we have specimens of the debate genre in Old English, Latin, French and, of course, in Middle English.[2] The existence of sophisticated (debate) poems in the post-Conquest English vernacular as early as ca. 1200 AD is, however, not just a matter of course. On the contrary, with Latin as the default language of scholarship and (Norman) French as the language of administration and the court, we still have no convincing explanation as for why the obviously well-read and well-educated anonymous author[3] of *The Owl and the Nightingale* chose the allegedly low-prestige Middle English for his poem. Clerics or courtiers showcasing their learning and wit in order to attract the attention of a potential patron and to recommend themselves for promotion, did so (with good reason) in Latin or in French.[4] Attempts to identify the author of *The Owl and the Nightingale* have remained inconclusive, mostly because we lack any external evidence concerning the circumstances and even the exact time-frame in which the poem was composed. Nicholas of Guildford, mentioned as "Maister Nichole of Guldeforde" (Cartlidge 2003: 6, line 191) and agreed upon as judge for the debate between the two birds, is, *faute de mieux*, probably the best possible candi-

* Friedrich-Schiller-University Jena.

1 See Wallace (1999) for an overview of medieval literature in England.

2 For a first overview see the entry 'Streitgedicht' in *Lexikon des Mittelalters* (2002, vol. VIII: 235–240). The standard studies for the medieval Latin tradition are Walther (1920) and Cardelle de Hartmann (2007).

3 See Cartlidge (2003: XIII-XVI) for a concise discussion of the question of authorship.

4 As did, for example, Geoffrey of Monmouth with his *Historia Regum Britanniae* (1136).

https://doi.org/10.1515/9781501510274-019

date put forward.[5] Yet even if we could unambiguously ascribe the authorship to one of the historically attested Nicholases, we would still have not much more than a bare name to connect with the poem. The pursuit of the elusive author promises little success and it is therefore advisable to concentrate rather on the literary context of the poem.

2 The Literary Context

The international genre of debate poetry in its various guises and shapes, and the Middle English debate poems in particular, constitute the immediate genre context for our poem. The corpus of Middle English debate poetry comprises more than a score of poems, often with diachronic links to works either of Old English or Latin literature, and synchronic links to more recent French and Latin texts.[6] Most prominent are two groups: the body-vs-soul poems and the bird debate poems. The latter category constitutes a uniquely English subgenre.[7] Next to these two major groups we have a number of other texts, consisting of exchanges between representatives of different estates (e.g. courtier vs. soldier), personifications (e.g. Mercy vs. Righteousness), or animated items (e.g. carpenter's tools).

The wider yet for our purpose equally important context is that of 'animal literature'. The term does not designate a genre proper but is used rather as a label to refer to texts of different provenience that feature animals prominently. These are, for the context of *The Owl and the Nightingale*, the debates between animals (e.g. the 12th century *Versus de pulice et musca*, i.e. *Debate between Flea and Fly*[8] by William of Blois), the beast fables (e.g. in French in the recension of Marie de France, composed in England in the late 12th to early 13th centuries), the shadowy animal folk tales (e.g. as observable in *De ingrato et gydone*)[9],

5 Several possible candidates with that name who lived in the south of England have been identified (see Cartlidge 2003: 101–102 and Stanley 1972: 19–22).

6 See John W. Conlee's study of the tradition and his critical anthology of the Middle English texts and their backgrounds.

7 See Honegger (1996: 103–166) for a discussion of the poems of this tradition.

8 The *Versus de pulice et musca* shows an astonishing similarity to the Chinese debate between the mosquito and the fly (13th century, see Chaney's contribution in the present volume p. 41–42 with n. 28), although a direct connection between the two is very unlikely.

9 This tale is a variant of the grateful animal tale (AT 554) and can be found, for example, in the *Gesta Romanorum* (tale no. 145, in Dick 1890: 86–92).

the *Physiologus*/bestiary tradition (e.g. in form of the illustrated Oxford, Bodleian Library MS Douce 167, first half of the 13th century), and the beast epic (e.g. *Ysengrimus* 1148–1149, or the widely popular *Le roman de Renart* 1170–1250).[10]

Historically speaking, it was probably the animal folk tale that introduced the concept of animals as interacting and (sometimes) talking protagonists. These characteristics are shared and expanded by the fables by means of some limited anthropomorphization. However, the fable's relative brevity does not allow for more than a superficial characterization of the animal protagonists and they are, as a consequence, not rounded characters but rather literary types. The fox, for example, is typically the clever fox, whereas the wolf is greedy and dangerous yet not very bright, and the lamb is the naïve and innocent animal par excellence, etc. The texts of the *Physiologus*/bestiary tradition, on the other hand, use allegedly naturalistic elements from an animal's behavior or physiology, and interpret them allegorically but without anthropomorphizing the animal per se.

The intersection between these animal tales and the debate tradition is represented by those debates that have animals as adversaries, though they are not very common in the late 12th century. Thus, the *Versus de pulice et musca* represents the only debate immediately preceding *The Owl and the Nightingale* that features two animals.[11] It is satirical rather than moralizing in tone and relies for its argument on the real-world characteristics of the flea and the fly. As such it is, in this particular point, comparable to the *Physiologus* and the later bestiary traditions which also take the (allegedly) real-world naturalistic information as the starting point for the allegorical interpretation of the animal. A typical *Physiologus* chapter is headed by a quotation from the Scriptures, which either explicitly mentions the animal (or other subject) or can be linked to it in some other way. It then continues with a description of the subject's natural habits (the 'natura' part), which is followed by the allegorical interpretation of the characteristics mentioned (the 'significatio' part).[12] The fox, for example, is said to pretend to be dead and thus to lure carrion-eating birds such as crows or magpies into its reach. As soon as they are close enough, it will spring up, catch one of them, and kill it. This behaviour is then interpreted allegorically. The fox is the Devil, who wants men to believe that he is dead (i.e. either non-existent or

10 See Jan Ziolkowski's excellent *Talking Animals* (1993) as well as Jill Mann's likewise recommendable *From Aesop to Reynard* (2009) for an overview of medieval animal literature and its sources.

11 See Mann (2009: 164, fn. 63) for a discussion of the poem's possible link to England.

12 See Honegger (1996: 17–43) for a discussion of the *Physiologus* and its links to the tradition of allegorical interpretation.

no longer active), with the effect that they will give in to temptation and sin and abandon all caution for their spiritual welfare. It is at that stage that the Devil will surprise the poor sinner, catch him *in flagranti* and drag him to hell.

This way of interpreting nature in general and animals in particular did not remain limited to the original *Physiologus* genre, but was applied to fables (cf. Robert Henryson's *The Taill of the Cok and the Jasp*, ca. AD 1480) and even to texts that derive from the beast epic (cf. Henryson's *The Trial of the Tod*). It also provided the clerically trained with interpretative patterns that they applied to quite mundane and secular situations, as the following anecdote about Saint Anselm shows.

In the summer of AD 1097 Anselm left the court and rode with his retinue toward his manor at Hayes. When they encountered a hare on the road, the boys of his household chased it with their dogs and the frightened animal sought refuge between the legs of Anselm's horse. His companions laughed at the terrified hare that did not dare to leave the relative safety of the horse's legs. Yet Anselm was moved to tears and rebuked them for making fun of the unhappy beast with the following words:

> You laugh, do you? But there is no laughing, no merry-making, for this unhappy beast. His enemies stand round about him, and in fear of his life he flees to us asking for help. So it is with the soul of man: when it leaves the body, its enemies – the evil spirits which have haunted it along all the crooked ways of vice while it was in the body – stand round without mercy, ready to seize it and hurry it off to everlasting death. Then indeed it looks round everywhere in great alarm, and with inexpressible desire longs for some helping and protecting hand to be held out to it, which might defend it. But the demons on the other hand laugh and rejoice exceedingly if they find that the soul is bereft of every support. (Southern 1962: 89–90)

Note that Anselm's defense of and sympathy with the hare is not primarily due to his love for all creatures, a trait found in many a saint,[13] but it is more specifically based on his allegorical interpretation of the situation. The hare becomes thus the demon-hunted human soul and the dogs the demons chasing it. It is therefore no wonder that this interpretative approach was found with readers of less naturalistic-realistic situations and texts, and it can be argued that the average medieval reader of any bird debate poem would be aware of the potential and implicit allegorical dimensions of the avian disputants. Yet before turning to the discussion of the possible allegorical elements of *The Owl and the*

13 The most prominent example is, of course, Saint Francis of Assisi. For further examples, see Alexander's study *Saints and Animals in the Middle Ages* (2008).

Nightingale, we have to briefly take a look at the fourth and final category of 'animal literature', namely the beast epic.

The beast epic is the most recent member of the animal literature family, and though it comprises elements from the fable (talking animals, typical characteristics that distinguishing each protagonist), it goes beyond the limits of this more ancient genre. Whereas the fable has nameless types of animals as its protagonists, the beast epic elaborates their characters and individualizes them by means of names. We have thus no longer simply the lion, the fox, the wolf and the bear as in the fable tradition, but now Noble the Lion, Renart the Fox, Isengrim the Wolf, and Brun the Bear. These named animals still retain the basic characteristic traits found in their fable counterparts so that, for example, Renart is still the clever fox and Isengrim the greedy wolf, but the extent of the anthropomorphization differs from that of the fable protagonists. The beast epic animals do not only talk, but they also partake in human courtly and clerical interactions and rituals, and their lives acquire a certain historicity by means of the chronological and causal linking of episodes and events into a temporally (more or less) coherent (pseudo-) historical sequence. All of this contrasts to the eternal here and now of the fables and provides a blueprint for how to combine and mix the human and the animal levels in a sophisticated and entertaining way.

This, then, is the literary landscape into which the Middle English bird debates enter.

3 Middle English Bird Debate Poems

The *bird* debate seems to be an English specialty – at least as a medieval (sub-) genre.[14] It fits perfectly into the larger international tradition of debate poetry,[15] with the simple specification that it is birds that argue and debate with each other. The Middle English bird debate tradition is usually considered to comprise the following poems (listed chronologically):

1) *The Owl & the Nightingale* (c. 1200)
2) *The Thrush & the Nightingale* (2nd half of 13th cent.)
3) *The Parlement of Foules* (Geoffrey Chaucer, c. 1381–82)

---

14 The odd occurrences of talking or debating birds in other contexts, be this in a larger poem such as Nigel of Longchamp's *Speculum stultorum* or the twelfth century Persian poem *The Conference of the Birds* by the Sufi poet Farid ud-Din Attar, provide interesting analogues and parallels, but do not constitute a (sub-)genre.

15 See Walther (1920) and Cardelle de Hartmann (2007).

4) *The Cuckoo & the Nightingale* (Thomas Clanvowe, c. 1400)
5) *The Clerk & the Nightingale I & II* (2nd half 15th cent.)[16]
6) *The Merle & the Nightingale* (William Dunbar, late 15th cent.)

And I would argue that we should also include
7) **The Debate on Dreams between the hen Pertelote and the cock Chauntecleer*[17] (Geoffrey Chaucer, c. 1385)

Although this last text is not an independent poem but part of *The Nun's Priest's Tale* in Geoffrey Chaucer's *The Canterbury Tales*, it possesses all the features of a bird debate: two birds, Pertelote the Hen and Chauntecleer the cock, who are debating heatedly and with great learning whether dreams have prophetic qualities (Chauntecleer's point of view) or are due to a disbalance of humors caused by overeating (Pertelote's argument) and thus without any prophetic value. Chaucer uses the traditional pattern found in, for example, *The Cuckoo and the Nightingale*, which assigns one specific position to each bird, yet the result is far from being a simplistic exchange of arguments as in many of the other poems. This is mainly due to Chaucer's integration of the debate into the larger framework of his tale and the concomitant (partial) identification of the cock with the narrator (the Nun's Priest) and the hen with his superior (the Prioress). Needless to say, Chauntecleer's self-declared victory and his pride in his intellectual supremacy makes him disregard the very conclusion reached by his line of reasoning and invalidates the real-life value of the insights established by means of the debate. I think that with Chauntecleer we have an example of what happens when 'personality' clashes with 'point of view': the cock represents one specific point of view during the argument, yet in the end his 'cockishness' interferes and renders void all rhetorical and logical efforts.

Such play with the different levels is rather the exception than the rule and Chaucer's *Debate of the Cock and the Hen* is as little representative of the bird

16 Even though the debate is, strictly speaking, not between two birds, the two texts that make up this poem are often counted among the 'bird debates' (see, for example, Conlee 1991: 266–277, who includes it in the section 'Bird Debates'). This is to some extent justified by the fact that the mechanics of the poem does not rely on the personalities of the protagonists, who are mere mouthpieces and can thus be seen in the tradition of poems such as *The Cuckoo and the Nightingale* or *The Thrush and the Nightingale*.

17 The asterisk indicates, in good philological tradition, the fictional or (re-)constructed nature of the title. Had Chaucer wanted to anthologize this part of his *The Nun's Priest's Tale* for a volume of Middle English debate poetry, I am certain he would have chosen this title.

debate genre as the multi-vocal *Parlement of Foules*. In order to get an idea of the mechanics of the average bird debate, we have to turn to one of the less complex poems of the tradition, and Thomas Clanvowe's *The Cuckoo and Nightingale*[18] may serve the purpose.

The poem opens with a love-sick and sleepless narrator who goes into the woods early in the morning, hoping to hear the nightingale sing – which would promise success in matters of love for the coming year. He arrives in a *locus amoenus* type of place (ll. 60–85) where birds sing and play and where he falls into a half-slumber, "nought al a-slepe, ne fully waking" (l. 87; translation: "neither completely asleep nor fully awake"). The first bird he hears is the "lewde"[19] cuckoo, a bird of ill omen, and only then does the nightingale raise her voice. And at that point we have the shift from bird-song to bird-speech, which the narrator seems now able to understand. As a consequence, we get to know that the nightingale reproaches the cuckoo for its monotonous ("elenge" = "boring") song (l. 115) and asks him to leave. The cuckoo, however, defends himself and, in turn, attacks the nightingale and her song. He is, as it turns out, a cynic who takes a very negative view on both women and erotic love and develops quickly into the mouthpiece of the (clerical) misogynistic tradition.[20] As such, the cuckoo does not take much effort and time to destroy the nightingale's rather feeble arguments that present an idealized view of erotic (courtly) love.

The poem ends with the nightingale in dire straits: she is unable to counter the numerous and authoritative examples and arguments put forward by her opponent ("I can, for tene, nougt sey oo word more" l. 209; translation: "I cannot, because of (my) grief, say one word more") and the nightingale, in her despair, sees no other solution but to invoke the aid of the God of Love ("Nou god of love, thou help me in some wise" l. 214; translation: "You, god of love, now help me somehow"). Ironically, it is not Cupid who comes to the aid of the nightingale, but the enraged narrator figure, who throws a stone at the cuckoo and chases him away but cannot escape the cuckoo's cynical taunts. This is, of course, not the standard way of how to win a debate, and the reader is left with the impression that the cuckoo has outpointed the nightingale with the superiority of his arguments. Once the cuckoo is gone, the nightingale turns to the other birds for help, and it is agreed that a parliament has to be held to hear out the two

---

18 All references to *The Cuckoo and the Nightingale* are given by line(s), using Conlee's edition of the poem (1991: 251–265).

19 "lewde" means both "ignorant, unlearned" as well as "boorish, uncouth."

20 As such he shares many of the arguments with the clerk in *The Clerk & the Nightingale*, which shows that the bird nature of the misogynistic protagonist is secondary.

opponents and to pass judgment – and the poem ends without a proper conclusion.

The Cuckoo and the Nightingale is a typical representative of (Middle English) debate poetry since it concentrates on one line of argument. Furthermore, it exploits both the naturalistic and the symbolic dimensions of the two birds at least partially. Thus, the poem starts out with the naturalistic detail of the respective qualities of each bird's song, contrasting the monotonous call of the cuckoo with the modulated song of the nightingale, yet it also establishes implicitly the symbolism of the cuckoo as the "lewed" i.e. "uncourtly" and "anti-courtly-love" bird versus the "courtly" nightingale. It is this symbolic dimension that takes center stage in the relatively short and inconclusive exchange of arguments that follows.

The non-conclusion of the argument with the deferred judgment illustrates yet another important point for debate poems in general and bird debates in particular: it is the exchange of arguments that is of importance rather than the final judgment, which is often postponed and constitutes no part of the poem. This can be seen most clearly in two of the most sophisticated bird debates, Geoffrey Chaucer's *The Parlement of Foules*, and the anonymous *The Owl and the Nightingale*. It is the latter we are now going to discuss in greater detail.

4 *The Owl and the Nightingale*

The Owl and the Nightingale, dated to the beginning of the 13th century, stands in splendid isolation within its century. It is one of those puzzling texts that, like e.g. the Middle English *Man in the Moon* lyric (MS. Harl. 2253. ff. 114–15), seems to be one of the few survivors of a rich and sophisticated literary tradition in the native vernacular before Chaucer. As a consequence, it cannot be seen as a representative of an early promise that kick-started a new tradition, nor is it the crowning glory of a development that began from humble beginnings and would reach later such dizzying heights of sophistication. Its relationship with the English (and other) debate and animal poems is complicated,[21] and it seems as if a poet of genius had taken inspiration from some of the existing animal and debate poems in whatever language and used these text types for the composition of his masterpiece.

21 The most recent substantial critical study of the poem and its position within medieval literature is by Mann (2009: 149–191); see also Warren (2018: 103–144).

The poem, with its 1794 lines, is by far one of the longest Middle English debate poems.[22] This gives the poet not only the opportunity to construct a debate with an intricate and complex structure that contrasts positively with the more limited, tit-for-tat, one-line-of-argument found in other debates, but it also allows him to develop his avian protagonists into multi-layered and oscillating characters that makes them very much *sui generis* among debate poetry protagonists.

The poem[23] opens like other (later) bird debates such as *The Parlement of Foules* or *The Cuckoo and the Nightingale* with a *proemium* that introduces the narrator, briefly sketches the setting of the ensuing debate (l. 1: "in one sumere dale," i.e. "a valley in springtime") and presents the two avian antagonists. The nightingale, on the one hand, is hidden in an impenetrable hedge where she is perched on a branch with many beautiful blossoms (ll. 14–18). The owl, on the other hand, sits on an old tree-stump, all grown over with ivy (ll. 25–28). This brief and seemingly naturalistic description of the habitat of the two birds already sets the tone for much of what is to come. Thus, the nightingale is later associated with spring, with love, and with (worldly) joy in general. The owl, by contrast, is seen as representing a monastic-ascetic point of view that, in the *contemptus mundi* tradition, highlights the vanity of worldly joys. This is furthermore combined with the folk-tradition of the owl as a bird of ill omen.[24] Yet though the debate will reference and make use of these symbolic dimensions time and again,[25] it begins very 'unsymbolically' with an *ad personam* attack by the nightingale, who calls the owl "Vnwiȝt"[26] (l. 33) and orders him to leave the area since she feels bothered by his mere presence (ll. 33–40). The owl's reply is not much better and consists basically of a thinly veiled threat to use violence against the weaker nightingale – if he gets the chance to do so (ll. 51–54).

22 Compare, for example, with *Mercy and Righteousness* (192 lines), *The Thrush and the Nightingale* (192 lines), *The Cuckoo and the Nightingale* (290 lines), *Winner and Waster* (503 lines), and *The Parliament of the Three Ages* (665 lines), all of which can be found in the anthology edited by Conlee (1991). Even Chaucer's *The Parlement of Foules* is only 699 lines long.

23 All references to *The Owl and the Nightingale* are given by line(s), using Cartlidge's edition (2001) of the poem.

24 See Honegger (1996: 121–128) for a detailed discussion of these aspects.

25 See the tabular overview in Honegger (1996: 123–125).

26 This can be best translated as "nasty creature." Cartlidge (2003: 2) suggests "You mutant!" which strikes me a bit too modern.

The debate proper[27] begins to develop only with the nightingale's next turn in which she takes the owl's superior strength as her starting point for a rather brief yet recognizably naturalistic characterization of her opponent. She lists the following points: smaller birds band together to mob the owl (ll. 65–68); the body of the owl is ill-proportioned and ugly (ll. 71–74); the owl has big, glaring, black eyes (ll. 75–76); it has talons and a sharp beak (ll. 77–80); and it roosts by day and flies by night (l. 89). All these elements are arguably rooted in real-life characteristics of the owl and per se objective and verifiable facts. Yet the nightingale is not after a scientifically correct description of her opponent but uses these elements to underline her overall denigration of the owl as "lodlich & unclene" (l. 91; translation: "hateful and dirty"). The latter term is traditionally linked to a (negative) moral valuation, which has its roots in the allegorical interpretation of the list of unclean animals in the Old Testament. *Leviticus* 11:13–19 mentions a number of unclean birds, among whom we find several types of owls. The Christian (re-)interpretation of this Biblical (originally Jewish) ritualistic 'uncleanliness' transformed it into a moral 'uncleanliness', and it is this moral dimension of (un-) cleanliness to which the nightingale alludes in good *Physiologus* tradition.

Yet the nightingale knows better than to simply accuse the owl of moral deficiency and a medieval audience, who are likely to have expected something more explicitly allegorical, are given instead an elaboration of another 'natural science' fact, namely that the owl's chicks befoul their nest. This means that the nightingale forgoes the option of raising the argument onto a more abstract and spiritual level and returns to the concrete animal level by specifying the quality of 'uncleanlinesse': "bi þine neste ich hit mene, / & ek bi þine fule brode: / Þu fedest on hom a wel ful fode!" (ll. 92–94; translation: "I'm referring to your nest – and also to your filthy brood; it's a pretty nasty family that you're bringing up!"). This is followed first by a proverb that comments on exactly this behaviour: "Dahet habbe þat ilke best / Þat fuleþ his owe nest." (ll. 99–100; translation: "Cursed be the animal that fouls its own nest."), and then by the fable of the falcon who unknowingly brings up an owl's chick among her own young (ll. 101–126).

The construction of the argument with these two text-types develops in a very complex and at times paradoxical manner. Proverbs differ from related

27 The protagonists themselves and, in their wake, most editors (e.g. Holtei 2002) distinguish between an introductory part (up to line 216), the debate proper which starts only after the two birds have agreed on the debate format and a judge (lines 217–1652), and a conclusion (lines 1653–1794). It is clear, however, that the debate starts already in the introductory part and arguments put forward there are taken up and answered in the later part.

text-types such as maxims by means of their symbolic-allegorical dimension which locates their actual meaning on a level different from that of the literal meaning. In the case of "Dahet habbe ..." we have the literal level of "best" and "nest," with the key semantic component of "non-human." However, the proverb becomes only meaningful when it is interpreted and applied to humans (see Mieder 2012: 1–9). Thus "best" becomes any man or woman and "nest" represents any kind of in-group framework. The proverb therefore compares a person who breaks the rules or violates the (unwritten) codex of an in-group to an animal defecating in its nest,[28] and who has to be punished accordingly – best by expulsion from the group. The fable about the owl-chick in the falcon's nest, then, illustrates and repeats the message of the proverb by means of a longer and more elaborate narrative form. Yet the interpretative mechanism remains the same as in the proverb, in spite of the difference in text-type. This can be seen most clearly in the variants of the fable and their respective interpretations,[29] which suggest that medieval audiences were familiar with the allegorical potential of that specific fable and would not read it simply as an amusing anecdote from the animal kingdom. As a consequence, all the signs point towards seeing the owl and the nightingale as stand-in figures for human protagonists or specific social interest groups, and the naturalistic elements as mere stepping stones to an allegorical interpretation.

However, these reasonable expectations are disappointed by the owl's answer later on in the debate (ll. 625–654). The owl correctly points out that horses and cows as well as little children, irrespective of their rank, relieve themselves in a similar way. On the one hand, this *argumentum ad naturam* effectively counters the nightingale's accusation by proving the ubiquity of the phenomenon under discussion. The owl-chicks may relieve themselves in their nest, but so does every other creature. On the other hand, the owl's references to nature and his insistence on reading things literally, sabotages any attempt of breaking down the borders between the worlds of beasts and men and of establishing a permanent allegorical interpretation.

This does not mean that the allegorical or symbolic dimension is completely absent – on the contrary. It is arguably very much present in both the audience's mind as well as in the allusions and references found in the speeches of either

28 German has a word for such a person: "Nestbeschmutzer" (i.e. a nest fouler; a person who metaphorically befouls his own nest).

29 See, for example, the version in Odo of Cheriton (Jacobs 1985: 75) who interprets the nest as the Church, and those who defile it as Devil-inspired sinners. Marie de France's version of the fable, by contrast, remains on a general level (see Spiegel 1987: 212–213).

bird. This is made explicit already in the characterization of Master Nicholas of Guildford who is proposed by the nightingale as judge for their debate because

> *He wot insiȝt in eche songe, / Wo singet wel, wo singet wronge; / & he can schede vrom þe riȝte / Þat woȝe, þat þuster from þe liȝte*
>
> He knows how to examine every song, and how to tell a good singer from a bad one. He can distinguish what's crooked from what's straight, and what's dark from what's light. (ll. 195–198)

The owl agrees because

> *Vor þeȝ he were wile breme / & lof him were niȝtingale, / & oþer wiȝte gente & smale, / Ich wot he is nu suþe acoled. / [...] / He is nu ripe & fastrede; / Ne lust him nu to none unrede. / Nu him ne lust na more pleie: / He wile gon a riȝte weie.*
>
> [E]ven though he used to be a little bit wild at one time and was rather fond of nightingales and other pretty little things, but I know that he's completely cooled down now. [...] Now he's mature and judicious and these days he has no liking for folly. He has no taste for frivolity anymore: he'll take the proper course. (ll. 211–214)

It is clear that Nicholas' former predilection for nightingales and "oþer wiȝte gente & smale" ("and other pretty little things") does not refer to his taste in matters ornithological but is a playful allusion to his youthful enthusiasm for women. Yet even here we can see that the obvious allegorical-symbolical dimension, which makes the nightingale into a symbol for secular love and pleasure, does not completely replace the animal nature of the protagonists and the avian aspects of their dispute. It is tempting to interpret "songe" (l. 195) in this context as "ideology," "ethos," "philosophy of life," or "point of view," yet the word also retains its original meaning as "birdsong" and it should not be ruled out that Master Nicholas would judge the aesthetic and artistic qualities of their respective singing, too.[30] It is therefore important to note that the avian nature of the protagonists is neither completely transformed nor diminished, but rather developed and used consciously as a contrastive counterpoint to the allegorical potential. This allows the narrator to put a check on our desire for too complete an allegorical interpretation that would turn them into mere mouthpieces for two antithetical ideological views.

In this the birds in *The Owl and the Nightingale* are akin to their later cousins (twice removed, so to speak) in Chaucer's *The Nun's Priest's Tale.*[31] Chaucer's

---

30 See Elizabeth Leach's study on the topos of birdsong in medieval music and poetry.
31 All references to the text are to *The Riverside Chaucer*, edited by Larry Benson (1987).

narrator also oscillates between different levels and keeps his audience on their interpretative toes. The following description of the cock Chauntecleer and his hens may serve as an example:

> *This gentil cok hadde in his governaunce / Sevene hennes for to doon al his pleasaunce / Whiche were his sustres and his paramours, / And wonder lyk to hym, as of colours; / Of whiche the fairest hewed on hir throte / Was cleped faire damoysele Pertelote. / Curteys she was, discreet, and debonaire, / And compaignable, and bar hyrself so faire / Syn thilke day that she was seven nyght oold / That trewely she hath the herte in hold / Of Chauntecleer, loken in every lith; / He loved hire so that wel was hym therwith.* (ll. 4055–66)

> This gentle cock had in his governance / Seven hens to do all his pleasure, / Which were his sisters and his concubines, / And wonderfully like him in their colors; / Of which the fairest colored of her throat / Was called fair demoiselle Pertelote. / Courteous she was, discreet, and gracious, / And companionable, and bore herself so fair / Since that same day that she was seven nights old / That truly she has in possession the heart / Of Chauntecleer, locked in every limb (completely). / He loved her so that well was him because of that.[32]

The narrator begins by striking a delicate balance between the animal and the human levels respectively. On the one hand there is the animal level where we have a cock and his hens, and where the fact that they are all from the same hatch poses no obstacle for polygamous propagation. On the other hand, the narrator presents them in terms appropriate for courtiers and invites us to leave the 'barnyard level' behind and see them as lord and ladies. We may have still the image of a hen's red wattles before our (mind's) eyes when he extols the coloring of her throat, but the fulsome praise expressed by means of a virtual barrage of courtly adjectives is likely to exorcise such lingering interferences from the barnyard – if it were not for the reminder that she seems to have started her love-relationship with Chauntecleer at the tender age of seven nights. A similar yet even more radical and therefore shocking return to the fowl nature can be found after the long and learned debate about dreams (ll. 2892–3156) – a sequence of exchanges full of quotes and references to authorities old and new, which is likely to make even the most attentive reader forget that it is two birds and not two scholars who are arguing. The debate concludes with the cock's self-declared victory and his left-handed compliment to Pertelote.[33] Then Chauntecleer flies down into the courtyard, calls all his hens

---

32 Translation taken from https://sites.fas.harvard.edu/~chaucer/teachslf/npt-par.htm (last accessed November 2019).

33 Chauntecleer's "For al so siker as *In principio, / Mulier est hominis confusio* –" (ll. 3163–64; translation: "For as certainly as *In the beginning, woman is the confusion of man*) and his 'mistranslation' as "Womman is mannes joye and al his blis." (l. 3166; translation: "Woman is man's

since he found a grain of corn, and, as the narrator informs us, "He fethered pertelote twenty tyme, / And trad hire eke as ofte, er it was pryme." (ll. 3177–78; translation: "He feathered Pertelote twenty times / and copulated with her as many times before prime (i.e. the first hour after sunrise)"). This reminds the audience forcefully that birds may speak and use logic, but that they are, in the end, still birds and as such not subject to human morals.

The author of *The Owl and the Nightingale* makes the same point though less graphically since he never allows the reader to lose sight of the avian nature of the protagonists. It is actually not so much the anthropomorphic qualities of the owl and the nightingale that are in the focus of the debate but rather the birds' usefulness to humans. This view starts to develop from the discussion of the usefulness and quality of their respective songs (ll. 411 ff) and becomes the mutually acknowledged yardstick against which either bird's qualities are measured. The owl, for example, defends her consumption of mice with the argument that he thus helps to keep the barns and also the Church free of vermin (ll. 605–12). The nightingale, too, repeatedly refers to her usefulness to mankind, though with her it is less practical. She argues, for example, that her song reminds man of the blissful rejoicing in heaven and therefore motivates him to lead a virtuous and God-pleasing life (ll. 707–42).

As a consequence, the debate has a decidedly anthropocentric bias in the debate. Yet at the same time almost all arguments have their origin in the birds' nature, and narrator as well as protagonists insist on linking these elements back to nature and thus make sure that the application of human morals is not overextended.

5 Conclusion

Our brief *tour d'horizon* of the Middle English bird debate tradition with special focus on *The Owl and the Nightingale* has shown that we have a number of poems leaning heavily towards an allegorical-symbolical reading where the avian protagonists almost completely disappear behind their role as spokespersons or mouthpieces of a particular point of view (e.g. in *The Cuckoo and the Nightingale* or *The Clerk and the Nightingale*). On the other side, we have

joy and bliss.") is aimed as much at the hen as it is at the Nun's Priest's superior, the Prioress, who obviously knows no Latin. Yet applied to Chauntecleer, the double truth of woman (i.e. Pertelote) being the cause for man's confusion as well as being his bliss becomes immediately visible since the hen is the source for the cock's (sexual) bliss, which makes him forget the warning message of the dream.

poems like **The Debate on Dreams between the hen Pertelote and the cock Chauntecleer*, a part of Chaucer's *The Nun's Priest's Tale*, where they become representatives of specific views, such as how to interpret dreams, yet without being transformed into mere anthropomorphized mouthpieces or personifications. In order to avoid such a transformation, Chaucer uses the avian reality to juxtapose and contrast the allegorical dimension. The anonymous poet of *The Owl and the Nightingale* takes a third way. On the one hand, he alludes to and plays with the allegorical potential of his avian protagonists. On the other, he keeps them safely within the limits of 'nature' (*pace* their ability to speak) and constructs a link to the human level not so much by personification or anthropomorphization, but by making their usefulness to mankind the moral yardstick against which their characteristics and qualities are measured.

As we can see, approaches among English bird debate poems vary and this uniquely English genre gave rise to some of the arguably most sophisticated texts of the (English) debate tradition. The anonymous poet of *The Owl and the Nightingale*, like Geoffrey Chaucer two centuries later, illustrates the poetic potential of the combination of the debate format and bird-protagonists and how they can, in the hands of a skilled author, overcome the limitations of the genre. This becomes all the more obvious if we compare their avian protagonists to other debaters both natural and allegorical. *The Owl and the Nightingale* is therefore not so much a typical debate poem as an exploration of the genre's possibilities towards a more complex and sophisticated characterization of the bird protagonists. As a consequence, they become as much rounded characters as this is possible within the context of medieval literature. Although *The Owl and the Nightingale* will remain the prime representative of the English bird debate tradition, its protagonists share important characteristics with Chaucer's *The Nun's Priest's Tale* and therefore also make a clear gesture towards the beast epic.

Bibliography

Alexander, Dominic. 2008. *Saints and Animals in the Middle Ages.* Woodbridge: The Boydell Press.

Benson, Larry D. (ed.). 1987. *The Riverside Chaucer.* (Third edition. Based on *The Works of Geoffrey Chaucer*, edited by F.N. Robinson. 1957.) Oxford: Oxford University Press.

Cardelle de Hartmann, Carmen. 2007. *Lateinische Dialoge 1200–1400. Literaturhistorische Studie und Repetitorium.* Leiden/Boston: Brill.

Cartlidge, Neil (ed. and trans.). 2003. *The Owl and the Nightingale. Text and Translation.* Revised and corrected edition. Exeter: University of Exeter Press.

Conlee, John W. (ed.). 1991. *Middle English Debate Poetry: A Critical Anthology.* East Lansing: Colleagues Press.
Dick, Wilhelm (ed.). 1890. *Die Gesta Romanorum. Nach der Innsbrucker Handschrift vom Jahre 1342 und vier Münchener Handschriften.* Erlangen & Leipzig: A. Deichert'sche Verlagsbuchhandlung Nachfahren.
Holtei, Rainer (ed. and trans.). 2002. *The Owl and the Nightingale.* Online edition and translation. user.phil-fak.uni-duesseldorf.de/~holteir/companion/Navigation/Anonymous_Texts/Owl_and_the_Nightingale/SurveyOwl/surveyowl.html (accessed 12 October 2016).
Honegger, Thomas. 1996. *From Phoenix to Chauntecleer. Medieval English Animal Poetry.* Tübingen/Basel: Francke Verlag.
Jacobs, John C. (ed. and trans.). 1985. *The Fables of Odo of Cheriton.* Syracuse, NY: Syracuse University Press.
Leach, Elizabeth E. 2007. *Sung Birds. Music, Nature, and Poetry in the Later Middle Ages.* Ithaca/London: Cornell University Press.
Lexikon des Mittelalters. 2002. Nine volumes. Munich: Deutscher Taschenbuch Verlag.
Mann, Jill. 2009. *From Aesop to Reynard. Beast Literature in Medieval England.* Oxford: Oxford University Press.
Mieder, Wolfgang. 2012. *Proverbs. A Handbook.* New York: Peter Lang Publishers.
Southern, R.W. (ed. and trans.). 1962. *Eadmer: Vita Sancti Anselmi (The Life of St Anselm, Archbishop of Canterbury).* London: Nelson.
Spiegel, Harriet (ed. and trans.). 1987. *Marie de France: Fables.* Toronto: University of Toronto Press.
Stanley, Eric Gerald (ed.). 1972. *The Owl and the Nightingale.* Revised edition. First edition 1960. Manchester: Manchester University Press.
Wallace, David (ed.). 1999. *The Cambridge History of Medieval English Literature.* Cambridge: Cambridge University Press.
Walther, Hans. 1920. *Das Streitgedicht in der lateinischen Literatur des Mittelalters.* Quellen und Untersuchungen zur lateinischen Philologie des Mittelalters 5/2. Munich: Beck.
Warren, Michael J. 2018. *Birds in Medieval English Poetry. Metaphors, Realities, Transformations.* Cambridge: D.S. Brewer.
Ziolkowski, Jan M. 1993. *Talking Animals: Medieval Latin Beast Poetry, 750–1150.* Philadelphia: University of Philadelphia Press.

Laëtitia Tabard*

20 De la dispute des clercs au dialogue des *acteurs*

L'expansion du débat poétique en France à la fin du Moyen Âge

Débats entre partisans de la chasse à courre et de la chasse au vol, débats entre animaux et querelles de préséance, débats entre femmes et sur les femmes, débats sur l'amour ou disputes entre l'amant et la dame se multiplient à la fin du Moyen Âge, notamment au milieu du XVe siècle.[1] Ces textes centrés sur un dialogue conflictuel entre des personnages manifestent le goût du public médiéval pour le spectacle de l'altercation, mais s'inscrivent aussi dans une très longue tradition d'écriture, dont témoignent les études réunies dans ce volume. La saisissante permanence du débat poétique déconsidère pourtant l'abondante production médiévale, qui ne répond pas apparemment au goût moderne pour l'originalité ou l'invention formelle: de nombreux critiques y voient la répétition d'une convention assez plate. Situer les formes de la dispute dans la longue durée conduit pourtant à mettre en valeur avant tout la vitalité des pratiques de l'écriture du conflit et de la polémique, dont l'héritage ne se maintient qu'en se transformant. Il s'agit moins alors d'identifier des sources et des permanences, que de chercher quelles diverses traditions de lecture et d'interprétation président à la réception de ces textes, pour expliquer le succès durable du genre.

C'est d'abord le rôle de l'enseignement rhétorique, dont le débat semble une émanation, qui peut être invoqué pour comprendre la continuité de cette inspiration: le dialogue serait ainsi formaté sur le modèle de la controverse, opposant deux personnages ou deux entités sur un point de divergence théorique. L'inlassable reprise de ce principe, malgré les différences thématiques et registrales au sein des textes, a ainsi conduit à considérer qu'écrire un débat relevait de l'exercice rhétorique neutre, ce que Paul Zumthor appelle un «type-cadre» (Zumthor 2000: 508): ce schéma de développement du discours tiendrait à un automatisme de l'écriture, marque de l'influence savante dans le domaine poétique, et notamment de l'emprise des juristes. C'est là un point que nous voudrions discuter ici, car l'attention est alors centrée plutôt sur les discussions

* Laboratoire 3 L.AM, Le Mans Université.

1 Dans le cadre de cet article, nous présenterons, trop rapidement peut-être, quelques-unes des conclusions de notre thèse (Tabard 2012), à laquelle nous nous permettons de renvoyer pour des précisions sur le corpus des débats et sur l'évolution du genre.

https://doi.org/10.1515/9781501510274-020

entre des allégories et sur la prégnance des modèles latins, alors que le renouvellement des formes et des thèmes des débats, aux XIVe et XVe siècles, nuance considérablement cette image. Si l'on essaie d'envisager l'ensemble des textes français de cette période, il semble en effet que le modèle-type se déplace, en raison de l'importance prise par la dispute amoureuse, issue de la tradition lyrique. C'est à partir de ce premier constat que nous aimerions revenir sur les conditions de production et de réception du genre. Si l'on peut dire en effet que dans le débat poétique de la fin du Moyen Âge convergent la dispute des clercs et celle des poètes, on pourrait aussi se demander laquelle absorbe l'autre. Est-ce nécessairement la poésie qui devient scolaire ? Ne peut-on penser plutôt que la pratique rhétorique se rénove en retrouvant l'énergie vivante de la joute poétique ?

1 Panorama du *debat* poétique français à la fin du Moyen Âge: des traditions parallèles ou un genre littéraire ?

La diversité des sujets de dispute, à laquelle s'ajoute celle des pratiques de la compétition dans lesquelles s'inscrivent éventuellement les textes, laisserait penser qu'il n'existe aucune conception unifiée du débat, mais plutôt une culture de l'échange qui traverse tous les milieux intellectuels de la fin du Moyen Âge (Cayley 2006), sous des formes plurielles, aussi bien dans la littérature courtoise, avec les dialogues entre poètes, la casuistique amoureuse, les échanges de poèmes ou de lettres et les réécritures d'une question en réponse à un auteur, que dans les écrits à vocation politique, comme dans les traités philosophiques et politiques sous forme dialoguée, ou dans le théâtre des *moralités*, ou encore dans les formes fictives du procès et les parodies des exercices scolaires. La thèse consacrée au genre du débat par Toshiki (1974) témoigne de la difficulté, car l'auteur a renoncé à trouver une cohérence dans cet ensemble, considérant qu'il existait en fait des traditions parallèles et concurrentes. De fait, la forme dialoguée est en elle-même un mode d'organisation textuelle très souple qui ne peut définir véritablement un genre. Maingueneau (2006: 42) considère ainsi le dialogue comme un *hypergenre*; il s'agit d'un «type élémentaire d'organisation textuelle dans lequel alternent des tours de parole», mais dont les contraintes assez pauvres autorisent des mises en scène très variées. Il importe de distinguer entre des modèles d'organisation, qui ont chacun une «scénographie» particulière.

On peut repérer en fait parmi les dialogues en français des filiations formelles et thématiques. Badel (1988: 101–102) établit ainsi une partition entre les textes de dispute où le dialogue tient à une opposition, même faible, entre des personnages, et les dialogues didactiques qui mettent face à face un élève et un maître. Ces derniers correspondent à un modèle différent, dit «catéchitique», donnant lieu à une tradition distincte, où le dialogue se présente parfois comme une commodité d'exposition. Pour distinguer nettement les dialogues dramatiques et les débats, qui selon Pierre-Yves Badel ne reposent pas sur une action mais sur la discussion d'une question, la tâche se révèle plus difficile: d'une part, comme l'a montré Thiry (1986), l'action n'est pas une dimension définitoire du théâtre médiéval; d'autre part, la dimension intellectuelle des débats peut s'effacer au profit du conflit personnel et se faire querelle de préséance, si bien qu'il faut plutôt penser les formes dans une continuité.[2] Mais on peut distinguer dans l'ensemble des dialogues oppositionnels un genre prenant plus ou moins modèle sur la scénographie judiciaire, pour examiner un problème.

Le mot *debat* renvoie cependant plus précisément à une *matiere*, à un sujet spécifique pouvant servir à catégoriser les textes; celui-ci ne correspond pas nécessairement à la conception moderne attachée au terme *debat*, dont le sens évolue en moyen français. Les prologues et les épilogues, où s'exprime assez nettement une conscience des genres et des codes, proposent des titres fluctuants, mais permettent d'identifier le motif de l'altercation entre des personnages comme structurant: la discussion progresse en allant vers la querelle, et c'est ce mouvement conflictuel allant de la parole à la violence que le terme *debat* désigne en ancien et en moyen français, et non une discussion réglée et organisée dans le cadre de la procédure. Au XVe siècle, le terme apparaît de manière beaucoup plus nette comme signal générique, pour des poèmes centrés sur le dialogue conflictuel. Cette évolution, retracée ici à grands traits, conduit à relativiser la portée intellectuelle des débats pour définir le genre: nombre de textes intitulés ainsi sont des querelles de préséance qui n'ont que très peu à voir

2 Nous rejoignons ici la perspective proposée par Cardelle de Hartmann (2007) pour l'étude des dialogues latins: tout en distinguant quatre type de dialogues (didactiques, polémiques, philosophiques et introspectifs), elle précise qu'il faut situer les textes dans un *continuum*. C'est notamment le cas pour les procès de Satan, textes peu étudiés auxquels elle a consacré des pages éclairantes (2004; 2007: 233–239; voir également son article à paraître, que nous la remercions très vivement de nous avoir communiqué): les textes appartenant à cette tradition de réflexion sur la question du salut développent dans certains cas un véritable procès, et comprennent de longues parties narratives, mais aussi des dialogues très vifs, ainsi que des éléments de dramatisation, et cette mixité de formes explique leur postérité plurielle dans les langues vernaculaires, aussi bien dans la poésie narrative que dans les genres dramatiques ou didactiques (2007: 238–239).

avec le cadre judiciaire, même quand finalement le public est appelé à trancher entre les personnages: cette possibilité d'interprétation reste à l'arrière-plan de ce qui se présente avant tout comme un conflit.

Cette conception de la dispute poétique la rattache plus directement aux genres lyriques médiévaux qu'aux formes latines du dialogue. La *tenson*, par exemple, repose sur un dialogue contradictoire, strophe à strophe, entre troubadours: ce genre «qui met en valeur les qualités poétiques ou oratoires des intervenants et exige pour cela, du moins en principe, la présence d'un public» (Bec 2000: 21) repose sur une structure musicale rigoureuse qui offre une dynamique à l'improvisation et à l'expression, souvent caractérisée par la verdeur du ton, le goût de l'insulte inventive et la mise en scène d'une rivalité personnelle entre les poètes. Du point de vue formel, les débats n'obéissent pas à la même structure, et présentent des parties narratives, un développement plus libre des répliques, et une versification variée, ce qui les rattache davantage à la logique du *dit*. Cette différence de composition explique la définition négative que donne Pierre Bec du genre, qui se situerait plutôt selon lui dans la tradition des *conflictus* latins (Bec 2000: 22–23) et se développe surtout au XIVe siècle:

> «Il vaut mieux (...) réserver la désignation de débat à des pièces qui n'exigent pas une performance oralo-musicale, où l'alternance strophique n'est pas fonctionnelle, et où la présence d'un public (réel ou supposé) ne s'impose pas (...).» (Bec 2000: 21)

Les *tensons* dites «fictives» représentent pourtant un point de passage puisqu'elles s'écartent du schéma le plus courant de la joute poétique et inscrivent la querelle dans un cadre narratif, en substituant des personnages aux interlocuteurs réels: elles montrent qu'on peut penser un continuum entre les formes lyriques et lyrico-narratives.

Les débats font régulièrement allusion à cette tradition antérieure, en signalant cependant le changement de ton qui s'est opéré. Christine de Pizan écarte ainsi du dialogue les invectives et les paroles virulentes. La «tenson» du *Livre du Debat de deux amans* est «gracïeuse, non mie en contençon» (Altmann 1998: 86 v. 81): «aimable, sans agressivité», cet échange est parfaitement réglé par les conventions de la politesse courtoise, qui veut que l'on laisse parler les dames en premier, ainsi que le rappelle le chevalier (Altmann 1998: 94, v. 407–414), et l'abondance des concessions témoigne de la modération qui guide les discours, même lorsque les interlocuteurs se contredisent fermement. La discussion entre la Noire et la Tannée dans *Le Debat de deux demoiselles* est également dépourvue de «noise ne tençon» (de «querelle et de dispute»), et l'auteur n'y voit que des «plaisirs sans mélange» («que parfaiz esbas», Delsaux 2006: 52 v. 182–183). Dans *Le Livre des quatre dames* d'Alain Chartier, les mots désignant la situation obéissent à une gradation: d'abord simple rivalité, compétition qui passe par la comparaison lorsque les deux premières dames se livrent à un «estrif» («affrontement»), l'opposition devient «debat» («conflit») avec la troisième, puis la quarte «[p]ar doulx moz aux autres tença» (Laidlaw 1974: 274 v. 2534): alors même que la virulence du discours est indiquée par le verbe *tencer*, qui signifie «chercher querelle», elle est désamorcée par l'antithèse avec la douceur.

Les débats amoureux peuvent de fait être rattachés à la forme plus codifiée du jeu-parti, variante de la *tenson* liée davantage au registre courtois. La particularité du genre, né de la poésie occitane mais pratiqué en particulier à Arras au XIIIe siècle (Gally 2004), est de ritualiser l'échange en imposant des règles. Le jeu-parti est ainsi une compétition entre poètes sur une alternative amoureuse. Après la question posée, l'échange de strophes, probablement sur un schéma mélodique simple, aboutit à une demande de jugement. Le grand seigneur désigné est appelé à trancher un problème de casuistique amoureuse, mais surtout entre les participants, dont on apprécie la performance comme compositeurs et comme acteurs. Le débat sur un problème amoureux se présente comme une transposition narrative du jeu-parti, dont il reprend souvent les thèmes (Tabard 2012: 290 – 304); il opère un déplacement en incarnant les cas dans des personnages, car le dialogue ne se déroule plus entre ceux qui discutent d'un cas amoureux abstrait, mais entre les êtres directement pris dans la situation dont on discute. En revanche, le poète intervient pour mettre le dialogue par écrit et le présenter à un dédicataire, afin qu'il soit jugé.

Ce type de débat inspiré de la joute lyrique a une importance déterminante dans l'histoire des formes, car c'est à partir de ce modèle, mis à l'honneur par Guillaume de Machaut, que l'on voit se constituer une tradition d'écriture. Dans le *Jugement dou roi de Behaingne* (Hoepffner 1908: 56 – 135), Machaut reprend la structure des «jugements d'amour» latins,[3] dans lesquels deux personnages féminins, après une dispute sur les mérites amoureux respectifs du clerc et du chevalier, présentent leurs cas au tribunal du dieu Amour. Une question proche de celle des jeux partis se substitue cependant à la comparaison entre les amants: il s'agit de savoir qui est le plus malheureux, une dame dont l'ami bien-aimé est mort ou un homme dont la dame est infidèle. Plusieurs motifs récurrents dans les débats ultérieurs se dessinent dans cette œuvre: la présence continue d'un *je*, qu'on identifie au poète, qui fait figure de chasseur «embuschié» («en embuscade»), observant les amants depuis une cachette, son inter-

3 Pour l'étude de cette tradition, voir Oulmont 1911; Faral 1912 et 1913: 251 – 69; Delbouille 1936; Ruhe 1974: 78 – 81; Walther 1984: 145 – 149; Grossel 1995.

vention dans le dialogue, la présentation des personnages à un juge réel loué pour ses vertus, tous ces éléments instaurent une scénographie pour la réception des débats, posant en principe une écoute et une lecture attentives à juger des subtilités des discours et de la mise en forme. La forme strophique choisie par Machaut pour ce long poème narratif sera ensuite reprise par Christine de Pizan dans ses trois débats amoureux (Altmann 1998), comme par Alain Chartier dans le *Débat de Deux Fortunés d'Amours* ainsi que dans le *Livre des quatre dames* (Laidlaw 1974), avec quelques variations, ce qui constitue, avec la reprise de la question des malheurs en amour, un signe visible d'intertextualité.

Avec Christine de Pizan, le genre se resserre autour du noyau central que constitue la dispute: le poème s'achève sur l'adresse à un juge, et la question posée demeure donc en attente d'un jugement. La poétesse retrouve ainsi la structure des jeux-partis, et accentue nettement l'importance du conflit entre les personnages, au détriment de son règlement par une instance juridique. De même, dans les débats d'Alain Chartier, rien ne vient trancher entre les êtres qui s'opposent; mais Chartier va plus loin encore dans l'effet d'énigme avec *La Belle Dame sans mercy* (Hult et McRae 2003) dans la mesure où la question à trancher n'est pas présentée nettement: le dialogue, plus proche de la forme dramatique en raison de la réduction des parties narratives et de l'alternance de répliques souvent réduites à une strophe, demeure obscur dans ses enjeux, et c'est au public de s'interroger sur les personnages comme sur les intentions de l'auteur, ce qui a donné lieu à des réponses, prolongements et imitations du dialogue initial, qui sont souvent copiés avec les œuvres de Chartier dans les manuscrits (Piaget 1901, 1902, 1904, 1905; Hult et McRae 2003; Cayley 2006: 136–88).

La rupture formelle est ici déterminante, et fonde une écriture du débat qui se distingue de celle des «jugements», même si le prolongement du conflit en procès reste une des possibilités d'interprétation pour les textes: à partir de Christine de Pizan, les débats se terminent très majoritairement par une ouverture finale, que la discussion soit proposée à un dédicataire précisément identifié ou bien que l'auteur s'adresse au public en général. Au contraire, les formes antérieures s'achèvent en général par un jugement. Malgré la diversité des formes et des thèmes, on voit ainsi se mettre au point une structure ouverte, fondée sur l'encadrement du dialogue par la voix narrative, qui appelle à la réflexion du lecteur ou de l'auditeur, structure que l'on retrouve également alors dans les débats sur des sujets politiques, dans le *Livre du Chemin de longue étude* de Christine de Pizan par exemple (Tarnowski 2000).

S'il faut classer les textes selon la «matiere» (le «sujet») que recouvre le mot *debat* au XVe siècle, ce n'est donc pas nécessairement en prenant en compte le thème de la dispute, ni selon les types d'arguments, ni selon les degrés du conflit, ce qui n'est guère possible dans la mesure où le développement du dialogue suit bien souvent une progression dramatique et va en s'envenimant. La logique du genre tient au dévoilement d'un conflit et de ses enjeux masqués, et l'on peut donc les différencier plutôt selon les degrés d'explicitation et de mise en forme des questions: alors que les récits de querelles, les jugements et les procès vont jusqu'au verdict, les débats demandent que l'on tranche une question qui reste en suspens, les dialogues conflictuels qui s'interrompent supposent qu'on s'interroge sur le problème avant de trancher, et, à la limite, dans les dialogues rapportant seulement des discours parallèles, on se demande même s'il y a un enjeu à saisir. Ces textes forment un *continuum*, selon la plus ou moins grande formalisation du problème à résoudre, et donc selon le degré de participation requise du public pour l'éclaircissement du débat. Ils supposent une culture juridique de la part de leur auditoire, mais se présentent avant tout comme des scènes à décrypter. Dès lors qu'on prend en compte l'évolution du genre, qui aboutit à la prédominance de la forme «ouverte» au XVe siècle, on peut voir le *debat* plutôt comme une amplification du jeu-parti des poètes que comme une transposition de la dispute savante.

2 La dispute des clercs

Il nous faut donc revenir sur les sources des débats poétiques pour situer les textes de la fin du Moyen Âge par rapport à la tradition savante à laquelle on les rattache. Il est tentant, tout d'abord, de faire le rapprochement avec la *disputatio* universitaire. Certains thèmes signalent des convergences possibles: ainsi les débats du corps et de l'âme[4] héritent des dialogues latins, en particulier de la *Visio Philiberti*.[5] Mais en fait cette convergence est trompeuse, car outre qu'il est difficile, comme le signale Cardelle de Hartmann (2007: 244), d'établir des liens entre les textes en se fondant sur la récurrence de motifs très largement répandus, la transposition en débat poétique joue surtout dans le sens de la parodie, y compris dans les poèmes latins eux-mêmes, souvent rattachés à la tradition goliardique. La défense de la foi par la raison est par exemple assurée par un moine tentant d'échapper aux assauts d'une nonne amoureuse dans un fragment de poème latin, repris dans la *Priere d'amour d'une nonnain a ung jeune adolescent, en forme de dialogue* au début du XVIe siècle (Montaiglon 1858 VIII: 170–75).

4 Sur les versions de ces débats à la fin du Moyen Âge, voir Tabard 2013b.
5 Sur les poèmes latins, voir Walther 1984: 63–74 et 211–214; Cartlidge 2006.

La poésie, qui joue sur la dynamique du conflit, semble faire la part belle à tout ce que la dispute universitaire tente d'écarter. Comme le montrent les recherches de Weijers (1999: 513) sur les rapports entre la joute dialectique et la dispute scolastique, cette dernière de fait récuse la polémique et «n'est pas un duel entre deux opposants». Elle relève de la *logica moderna*, et non de la tradition plus ancienne de la joute dialectique, qui en revanche a pu influencer les formes du débat, notamment oriental. L'énergie du combat oratoire est de fait certainement réinvestie dans les exercices lorsque la dispute est fictive (les disputes dites *obligationes*), ou bien justement dans les formes poétiques fondées sur l'altercation, mais elle n'en procède pas, et l'on peut reprendre sur ce point la formule de Paul Zumthor, qui évoque une « forme d'expression de tradition ancienne en Orient non moins qu'en Grèce» qui serait seulement «récupér[ée]» par l'enseignement médiéval, «et qui par ailleurs engendra plusieurs genres poétiques: dialogue symbolique du Christ ou d'un saint avec l'un de ses fidèles, mais aussi bien la *tenso* et le *joc-partit* des troubadours ou le *débat* allégorique» (Zumthor 1987: 92).

Les rapprochements que l'on peut faire avec les exercices de rhétorique liés à l'apprentissage judiciaire semblent en revanche plus probants. La pratique du procès fictif, hérité de l'enseignement rhétorique et juridique romain, peut en effet donner lieu à l'écriture de dialogues oppositionnels destinés à être jugés. On a conservé les *Suasoriae* et les *Controversiae* de Sénèque le Père, recueils inspirés d'exercices définis ainsi par Michel (1999: 26): dans les *suasoriae* «l'orateur essayait, par l'imitation et la prosopopée, de se mettre à la place d'un personnage de l'histoire ou de la mythologie»; les *controversiae* sont des «causes fictives qui mettaient en présence des devoirs ou des lois contradictoires: le fils du tyran a tué son père». Certains débats en français relèvent apparemment d'une démarche analogue. Ainsi la *Dispute de Dieu et de sa mère* écrite vers 1417 (Langlois 1885) soulève la question de la distribution inégale des lieux de culte entre Jésus et Marie, mais en la présentant comme un problème de succession: Jésus se plaint que sa mère l'ait spolié de son héritage paternel. La question, censée être présentée devant le Pape à Avignon, semble plutôt faire allusion à l'opposition entre le clergé séculier et les ordres mendiants, représentés par le Fils accusé de vivre dans la pauvreté et de mal gérer les biens, et donc exclu de la propriété.

La notion de parodie ne se révèle pas forcément opératoire pour aborder ces traitements quelque peu déroutants des personnages religieux; le débat semble plutôt mettre en forme un *cas*, c'est-à-dire un exemple singulier qui pose problème, qui défie la norme juridique et qui permet donc la réflexion sur la loi elle-même, pour la nuancer ou la préciser, voire en révéler les limites.[6] Les *Processus Satanae* ne se contentent pas ainsi de calquer la procédure mais portent aussi une interrogation sur le droit: donnant en modèle la figure de Marie, qui défend le genre humain contre les revendications du diable, le procès révèle surtout la supériorité de la logique de la grâce et de l'amour, contre la rhétorique judiciaire que le diable manie à la perfection (Cardelle de Hartmann 2004: 426–27). Plus que d'une réécriture des textes latins, les débats poétiques français pourraient transposer la pratique de mise en «cas» juridique, qui se développe à partir de l'identification d'un problème à éclaircir.

Dans le domaine latin, les formes dialoguées rapportant une querelle, sa formalisation en «cas», et sa transformation en procès, peuvent se comprendre alors dans un mouvement continu d'amplification rhétorique, passant par un dialogue initial pour mener une exploration du sens, et pour révéler ainsi toutes les facettes d'un problème complexe, comme cela se pratique dans les commentaires dialogués.[7] De ce point de vue, la figure du dialogisme accompagne la méditation en prêtant une voix aux personnages d'un texte, donnant ainsi corps à l'exercice interprétatif. On peut comprendre ainsi les développements qui se créent autour d'un élément problématique du texte biblique, par exemple dans les séries de réécritures du débat de la Vierge et de la Croix. Les trois poèmes français[8] ont connu une diffusion minime, mais se rattachent par l'idée qu'ils

---

6 Voir sur le principe du «casus» les analyses de Jolles (1972: 137–157). On peut également citer, comme exemple de cas d'école, le débat latin où Lazare ressuscité revendique ses biens et plaide contre Marie-Madeleine. Après avoir loué le roi qui doit trancher leur différend, les deux parties échangent leurs arguments, et le poème se termine par un verdict du roi en faveur de Marie-Madeleine, corrigé par un second juge qui, tout en reconnaissant le bien-fondé de la sentence, choisit de restituer ses droits à Lazare, par une mesure exceptionnelle. Ce jugement constitue apparemment un cas d'école pour le traitement de cas complexes d'héritage, selon Walther (1984: 126–129), et il a été attribué récemment à Dreux de Hautvilliers, enseignant le droit à Reims (Bachmann 2002).

7 Voir l'exemple des commentaires sur les propos de Jésus au jardin de Gethsemani, étudiés par Tóth (2012); Cardelle de Hartmann (à paraître) met également en avant l'influence des pratiques dévotionnelles, encouragée par la spiritualité franciscaine, sur l'écriture de scènes bibliques, destinées à favoriser la compréhension intime et affective du texte sacré: de cette «exégèse narrative» témoignent la floraison d'écrits autour des plaintes de Marie mais aussi plus généralement les drames liturgiques, les sermons et les méditations incluant des dialogues, et elle n'est pas absente de la tradition des procès de Satan.

8 *Le Débat de la Vierge et de la Croix* (XIIIe s.) (Långfors 1914: 22–27); *Débat de Notre Dame et de la Croix* (XIVe s.), ms. Londres, British Library, Add. 46919 (avant 1333), f° 79–80; *Devote meditacion de la Vierge Marie a la croix en se complaignant d'elle* (XVe s.), ms. Poitiers, Bibl. mun. 95 (XVe s.), f° 87v°-91. Sur ces textes, nous nous permettons de renvoyer à notre article (Tabard 2013). Sur les plaintes de Marie, voir Dronke 1992: 457–89.

abordent à un poème latin assez célèbre de Philippe le Chancelier, qui commence par l'apostrophe «*Crux de te volo conqueri*» (Dreves 1895: 20 – 21). Ce chant, destiné peut-être à la liturgie,[9] se situe dans la continuité d'une longue tradition de méditation sur les souffrances de la Vierge lors de la passion, où l'écriture d'un discours attribué à Marie éclaircit le mystère du texte sacré en comblant un silence («*juxta crucem stabat Maria*»[10]: «près de la croix se tenait Marie») et en explorant l'image par les mots. La forme du dialogue adoptée par Philippe le Chancelier peut apparaître comme une ultime expansion de ce mouvement d'amplification, qui à partir de l'apostrophe à la croix mène au développement d'un conflit, par l'écriture de la prosopopée de la croix.[11] En cela la pratique rhétorique, transposée poétiquement, ne se réduit pas à un exercice de mise en forme, mais forge une nouvelle perception de la scène: la complainte de Marie s'oriente vers la plainte judiciaire, comme l'annonce dès le premier vers du poème de Philippe le Chancelier le double sens de *conqueror*, «déplorer», ou «porter plainte». Cette fiction permet une interrogation sur le mystère que représente la Passion en lui donnant une formulation juridique (c'est la punition injuste d'un innocent), même si c'est pour mieux dépasser cette vision. Le débat poétique incarne cette tension entre une vision humaine, qui se traduit dans le ton juridique presque décalé, et une logique supérieure portée par la poésie et la force des images.

Si l'héritage de l'école est patent dans quelques textes, pour lesquels les dialogues latins ont pu servir de modèles, cela ne signifie donc pas pour autant qu'on puisse établir de filiations directes avec les exercices rhétoriques ni avec les disputes. Peu de débats poétiques des XIVe et XVe siècles ont en fait des antécédents latins identifiables, et quand c'est le cas, comme pour les dialogues entre l'âme et le corps, l'eau et le vin, l'hiver et l'été, ou la Vierge et la Croix, il s'agit de réécritures tardives et relativement peu diffusées de versions françaises

---

9 Le poème appartient au genre des *conduits*, chants originellement destinés à accompagner une procession religieuse, mais dont on ne connaît pas exactement les conditions de performance. Pour une étude de ces compositions de Philippe le Chancelier, voir la thèse de Rillon-Marne (2012).

10 *Évangile selon saint Jean*, XIX, 25.

11 Pour l'analyse de la rhétorique de Philippe le Chancelier et notamment dans ce poème, on se référera à l'article très stimulant de Tilliette (2017), qui situe précisément l'apport de Philippe le Chancelier dans la transposition poétique de la rhétorique judiciaire. La forme du poème, qui oppose l'accusation de Marie à la défense de la croix, tient peut-être à l'influence de la *Poetria nova* de Geoffroy de Vinsauf, qui donne beaucoup d'importance aux figures de l'apostrophe et de la prosopopée, et cherche à «mettre à contribution de façon rigoureuse les instruments langagiers d'une rhétorique judiciaire en vue de la formulation d'une poésie authentiquement chrétienne» (Tilliette 2017: 226).

du XIIIe siècle. Mais les pratiques rhétoriques latines semblent bien à l'arrière-plan du débat français si l'on considère qu'elles ont forgé une conception du dialogue comme amplification d'un texte source, dans laquelle la mise en voix vise la compréhension intime des personnages, et où le mouvement du conflit, qui appelle une mise en forme juridique, est associé à l'effort pour dévoiler une vérité complexe. Cette tradition de pensée et d'écriture est certainement celle sur laquelle s'appuie le genre du débat, dans sa production mais peut-être surtout dans sa réception, puisqu'il requiert finalement du public qu'il sache percevoir les enjeux du cas qu'on propose à sa sagacité.

3 Le débat poétique, un texte à lire, à dire ou à jouer ?

On peut dès lors s'interroger sur la manière dont les débats français ont pu s'actualiser: d'une part ils pourraient sembler destinés à une lecture attentive en raison de leur complexité et parce qu'ils demandent interprétation et jugement; d'autre part, l'écriture du dialogue fait entendre la vérité affective du personnage et use ainsi des ressources sonores de la poésie comme de la dramatisation, ce qui suppose plutôt une oralisation, voire une mise en scène – et ce d'autant plus que la forme ouverte du débat s'impose. Pour nous renseigner sur ces modes de lecture du débat, on dispose des preuves externes que constituent les sources historiques, qui donnent des indications sur les conditions, notamment matérielles, de la réception; le témoignage des manuscrits concernant les commanditaires et les propriétaires renseigne sur la circulation des œuvres, et les textes copiés avec les débats ou même les titres donnés peuvent constituer des indices de la manière dont les textes sont perçus. Enfin on peut s'appuyer sur les allusions internes à l'actualisation, orale et/ou visuelle,[12] voire au caractère ludique du texte, notamment dans les moments stratégiques que constituent les seuils de l'œuvre comme les prologues, conclusions ou explicits, mais aussi dans les interventions et commentaires de l'auteur. Dans le cadre nécessairement limité de cet article, nous nous bornerons à évoquer quelques exemples de recherches menées sur les débats à partir de ces indices.

Les grands personnages auxquels Christine de Pizan rend hommage dans ses poèmes appartiennent tous à l'institution ludique qu'est la « Cour amoureuse » dite de Charles VI, sorte de cour de justice fictive qui offre une distraction à la cour en 1400, dont on ne sait cependant si elle eut une existence réelle. Ce

12 Pour une étude précise et éclairée de ces indices internes de réception, voir Haug 2016.

tribunal amoureux, institué par une *Charte* consignant les noms des participants et les règles du jeu, suppose la lecture publique d'écrits consignant des cas à juger:

> [les] escriptures seront leues ainsy que ordonné sera et aprés seront baillés, toutes seelees, es mains de noz amoureux Presidens ou de l'un d'eulx, pour en déterminer et décider la sentence amoureuse ainsy que le caz requerra a jour de saint Valentin et non a autre jour. (Bozzolo: 41 l. 260–263)

> Les écrits seront lus selon ce qui sera prévu et ensuite seront remis, tous scellés, aux mains de nos Présidents d'Amour ou de l'un d'entre eux, pour qu'ils se prononcent et décident de la sentence amoureuse selon ce que le cas requerra, le jour de saint Valentin et non pas un autre jour.

Que l'on doive lire en se référant à ce qui est «ordonné» peut laisser supposer une mise en scène codifiée ou une improvisation réglée, suivie apparemment d'un examen attentif par celui qui doit «décider la sentence». L'expression de «jeu de rôle» dont use Cerquiglini-Toulet (1993: 53) pour désigner cette pratique ludique rend bien compte de son ambiguïté: entre jeu de société et théâtre, la Cour amoureuse offre ainsi un espace de représentation possible pour des débats amoureux, sous la forme d'une lecture à une ou plusieurs voix. Cependant aucun des textes censés être produits dans ce cadre n'étant conservé, on ne peut qu'imaginer cette mise en scène, et rien ne dit que les écrits concernés avaient une forme dialoguée, ni que les débats que nous possédons étaient vraiment adaptés à ces conditions de lecture. Les œuvres de Christine de Pizan, de même que certains des textes d'Alain Chartier, comprennent des parties narratives développées, et l'on imagine mal dans ce cas comment ils pouvaient être représentés.

On peut s'appuyer cependant sur trois cas où une mise en scène semble attestée pour un débat. En 1454, lors d'une rencontre princière, George Chastelain met en scène *Les Epitaphes d'Hector*, pièce qui consiste en un débat entre Alexandre, qui évoque la gloire d'Achille, et Hector qui récuse cette louange indue; bientôt confronté dans les Enfers à son rival, devant Alexandre promu au rang de juge, il pardonne à son meurtrier. Autour de la question du meilleur des héros, la pièce suggère des rapprochements avec les événements historiques, et met en œuvre ce que Doudet (2005: 65) nomme un «système de masques» pour évoquer le meurtre de Jean sans Peur. Les comptes mentionnent la rémunération de quatre personnes pour le jeu (trois acteurs et l'auteur, Chastelain), ce qui peut signaler que l'auteur avait participé à la mise en scène: «la pièce comporte quatre rôles, puisqu'un acteur monte sur scène au début et à la fin, pour s'adresser au public» (Doudet 2005: 64 n. 6). Le *Debat du Corps et de l'Ame*, qui apparaît dans un recueil de pièces dramatiques, semble également avoir fait l'objet d'une représentation du même ordre, puisqu'on trouve un *Mystère du débat du corps et de l'âme* représenté à Amiens en 1489 (Petit de Julleville: 347). Le prologue et l'épilogue encadrant le dialogue des deux entités, attribués à «l'Acteur», sont pourtant de véritables récits, à la troisième personne.

Le monologue de Coquillart intitulé *Le Debat des armes et des dames* (Freeman 1975: 245–71) constitue un cas un peu différent. Le poème donne la parole à un *acteur*, qui rapporte un dialogue et l'offre finalement au jugement du prince, lui demandant de dire quel «passetemps» il préfère, celui des armes ou celui des dames, ce qui correspond donc bien à la structure du débat. Or cette pièce a fait apparemment l'objet d'une déclamation lors d'une entrée royale.[13] Le *Debat* dans son ensemble se présente comme la partition d'une performance d'acteur, le narrateur devant incarner un personnage et lire les deux rôles, à en croire les derniers vers:

Sire, par vous soit pardonné
Au rude engin et simple sens
Du povre Honneste fortuné,
Qui a leu les deux passetemps. (Freeman 1975: v. 510–513)

Seigneur, veuillez pardonner
L'art grossier et la simplicité d'esprit
Du pauvre Honnête Fortuné,
Qui a lu les deux divertissements.

L'exemple du débat de Guillaume Coquillart tendrait donc à montrer que le genre peut en effet se lire comme un monologue dramatique, destiné à l'élaboration d'un jeu avec le public.

Ces trois œuvres, dont deux sont tardives, constituent peut-être des cas particuliers, mais elles révèlent au moins que le passage sur scène est possible, y compris pour des textes comprenant des parties narratives; elles incitent également à s'interroger sur la diversité des modes de lecture ou de jeu à envisager pour un même texte. Le dialogue polémique entre les deux personnages du *Debat du content et du non content d'amours* de Jean du Prier s'achève ainsi par une tirade de l'Acteur qui semble mentionner plusieurs actualisations possibles:

Pour vous deux mettre en union,
Que plus ne soyés debatans,
Je dy et suis d'oppinion,
S'on lit se livre en passant temps,

13 La date de cette entrée royale est discutée: il peut s'agir de l'entrée de Charles VIII à Reims ou à Paris en 1484, ou de celle de Louis XII en 1498 (Collard 2005; Quéruel 2005).

Que ceulx qui seront acoutant
Estans du lisant viz a viz
Ensamble tous les assistans
En jugent selon leur aviz. (Jean du Prier: f° 13 v°)

Pour vous réconcilier tous deux,
Afin que vous ne vous querelliez plus,
Je déclare, telle est ma décision,
Que, si on lit ce livre en guise de divertissement,
Ceux qui écouteront attentivement,
Étant face à celui qui lit,
Et tous les assistants avec eux,
Devront en juger selon leur avis.

Le débat semble conçu pour une lecture publique divertissante, où un «lisant» fait face à des auditeurs choisis, au milieu d'une assistance, et suggère effectivement une interprétation par une seule personne, mais c'est seulement une possibilité, «s'on lit ce livre en passant temps». Les passages et transpositions sur scène sont peut-être à considérer comme des effets de réception, c'est-à-dire comme des adaptations qui en fait éloignent le genre de son fonctionnement intrinsèque, pour lui permettre de toucher un public plus large, quand les circonstances l'exigent, un peu comme les films tirés d'une œuvre littéraire actuellement. Initialement fait pour la lecture, le débat serait transposable en jeu, sous des formes variables.

L'inverse est cependant tout aussi envisageable: le débat garderait la mémoire d'une performance, serait lui-même une adaptation, pour la lecture, d'un jeu qui aurait eu lieu. Le texte dramatique circule alors avec les autres œuvres de son auteur, ou bien avec les œuvres avec lesquelles il entre en résonance thématique ou générique, même s'il a fait l'objet, par ailleurs, d'une représentation. C'est ce qui arrive par exemple dans le cas des *Epitaphes d'Hector* étudiées par Doudet (2005). Lorsque, comme c'est le cas pour le manuscrit unique du *Debat du Content et du non content d'amour* de Jean du Prier, le texte circule sous la forme d'un livret, qui fait penser aux plaquettes qui accompagnent aujourd'hui encore les représentations théâtrales, on imaginerait volontiers là encore que le manuscrit, offert à un dédicataire, garde en fait sous une forme livresque la mémoire d'une performance. Le manuscrit de Bruxelles du *Livre du debat de deux amans* de Christine de Pizan ne contient ainsi que cette œuvre, dans un format plus petit que les autres manuscrits, et semble le plus ancien témoin de la circulation de cette pièce (Altmann 1998: 37–39). Une des images représente Christine de Pizan dans la posture de la lectrice, avec un «rollet» (un petit rouleau) à la main, désignant du doigt les deux amants du débat au duc Louis d'Orléans.[14] L'auteur semble jouer le rôle de présentateur de la représentation, et peut-être de metteur en scène. Le discours de l'*acteur* qui présente l'objet de la discussion, le décor et les personnages, deviendrait ainsi récit dans le livre: selon les mots de Christine de Pizan, dans la ballade dédicatoire à Charles d'Albret, «le livret le fait vous represente» (Roy 1886, I: 231 v. 29), c'est-à-dire qu'il permet à l'esprit de se faire une image de l'action, mais peut-être aussi la présente de nouveau, une seconde fois, mais sous forme narrative.

Même si le texte se pense comme une œuvre à lire, il appelle de fait une visualisation, et entre en résonance avec les œuvres dramatiques, comme le signale un commentaire du narrateur dans *Le Débat du hérault, du vassault et du villain* d'Alain Chartier:

> *Me sembloit d'eulx ouïr parler*
> *Qu'antr'eux jouassent une farce* (...). (Laidlaw 1974: 435 v. 425–426)

> Il me semblait, à les entendre parler,
> Qu'ils jouaient entre eux une farce (...).

Les adaptations scéniques témoignent de cette lecture du genre. Le *Monologue fort joyeulx auquel sont introduicts deux advocatz et ung Juge devant lequel est plaidoyé le bien et le mal des Dames*[15] forme ainsi un débat en miniature, à partir de la question des biens et des maux en amour, déjà posée entre autres par Christine de Pizan et Alain Chartier:

> *Nous faindrons cy deux Advocatz*
> *Et ung juge premièrement*
> *Par fourme de procédement,*
> *Dont l'ung des Advocatz sera*
> *Mal-Embouché qui playdera*
> *Le mal qu'i scet aux dames estre,*
> *Et l'autre de la partie dextre*
> *Sera nommé Gentil-Couraige,*
> *Deffendeur a leur advantaige,*
> *Qui soustiendra de grantz biens d'elles.*
> *Mais il y a bien des nouvelles,*
> *Car vécy la chaire et refuge*
> *Ou se soirra Monsieur le Juge,*

14 L'image, tirée du manuscrit de Bruxelles, Bibl. Royale, 11034, f° 2, est reproduite dans l'édition de Barbara Altmann (1998: 55).

15 Ce texte est daté plutôt du début du XVIe siècle (Montaiglon XI: 176–191; Petit de Julleville: 261–262).

Lequel premièrement joueray
Et puis après je parferay
Par ordre chascun personnaige,
Mal-Embouché, Gentil Couraige
Comme vous verrés aux pourchatz. (Montaiglon XI: 181–182)

Nous ferons semblant ici d'être deux avocats
Et un juge, en premier,
Selon la procédure;
L'un de ces deux avocats sera
Mal-Embouché, qui plaidera
Qu'il connaît le mal inhérent aux dames,
Et l'autre, du côté droit,
Sera nommé Noble-Cœur,
Défenseur en leur faveur,
Qui soutiendra qu'elles apportent de grands biens.
Mais il y a bien des annonces à faire,
Car voici le siège, à part,
Où s'assiéra Monsieur le Juge,
Que je jouerai en premier;
Et puis après je ferai
Dans l'ordre chaque personnage,
Mal-Embouché, Noble-Cœur,
Comme vous le verrez par la suite.

Cette version actualise en quelque sorte une lecture possible du débat, laissant de côté la question du tort et du droit (le narrateur dit auparavant ne guère savoir «qui a le tort») pour mettre l'accent sur la création des personnages, à partir de quelques éléments de caractérisation et d'un décor minimal. Transposé dans l'univers dramatique, l'homme qui blâme l'amour (le chevalier dans le débat de Christine de Pizan) devient ainsi «Mal-Embouché», nom qui dévoile en même temps un aspect du personnage initial qui pouvait donner lieu à un jeu de scène: pour reprendre les termes dont use l'acteur pour présenter son art, le «cas sortira son effaict» (Montaiglon XI: 180), c'est-à-dire que la situation abstraite du personnage, telle que le débat la présente, trouvera dans le monologue une application pratique, se traduisant dans les postures de l'acteur.

L'adaptation scénique du débat peut donc être envisagée comme une possibilité du genre, non seulement parce que le discours peut donner lieu à un jeu, mais aussi parce que cette traduction en image est appelée par les auteurs pour que le texte produise tout son effet. Ainsi nous on avertit Froissart, dans les premiers vers de *La Plaidoirie de la Rose et de la Violette:*

> *Devant Ymagination,*
> *Ou on doit par droite action*
> *Mettre memores et escrips,*
> *Fu une fois .i. plais empris*
> *Entre rose et la violette.* (Fourrier 1979: 191 v. 1–5)
>
> Devant Imagination,
> Où l'on doit, pour suivre correctement la procédure,
> Placer les mémoires et les écrits,
> Fut un jour entrepris un procès
> Entre la rose et la violette.

Pour une «droite action», une procédure correcte, il faut une transposition de l'écrit dans l'imaginaire, et la lecture doit donner lieu à une représentation, fût-elle seulement mentale. Malgré les incertitudes qui demeurent, on peut donc conclure au moins que le genre du débat repose sur un imaginaire de la performance scénique, que ce soit celle du poète en compétition, celle de l'avocat en cour ou celle de l'acteur en scène. Objet mixte dont la représentation est possible, même s'il est destiné aussi à la lecture individuelle ou collective, il donne lieu à une forme médiévale de ce que Musset a appelé un «spectacle dans un fauteuil».

Les grandes tendances novatrices du genre du débat poétique que nous avons essayé de dégager pour le XVe siècle ne doivent pas masquer les permanences: le débat du corps et de l'âme continue de faire l'objet de réécritures tardives, et il existe bien quelques poèmes directement inspirés de textes latins. Mais il ne faut pas minimiser non plus la prégnance, en cette période, du modèle du débat amoureux tel que l'élaborent Guillaume de Machaut, Christine de Pizan et Alain Chartier, qui semblent avoir mis au point, à partir des disputes lyriques, une forme de dialogue conflictuel orienté vers la dramatisation et le spectacle peut-être autant, voire plus, que vers l'examen de questions à trancher. Il nous semble donc qu'il faut relativiser, dans nos représentations du genre, l'importance du débat allégorique savant et l'influence de l'enseignement rhétorique, ou bien penser différemment ce dernier. Les débats latins dont héritent les versions françaises feraient plutôt figure eux-mêmes d'audacieuses créations, dans lesquelles les prestiges de la rhétorique ou les cas des juristes se trouvent investis de sens – et en même temps subtilement subvertis – en se mettant au service de la méditation sur le texte sacré et sur ses mystères. Mettant en œuvre cette conception rénovée du dialogue, dans laquelle l'amplification rhétorique est un instrument d'exploration du sens caché, les débats français ne nous semblent pas avoir dénaturé l'héritage millénaire de la dispute: ils développent un art d'écrire la voix et de donner l'illusion de la performance, pour mieux inciter à s'interroger sur des personnages saisis dans leur complexité.

Bibliographie

Altmann, Barbara. 1998. *The Love Debate poems of Christine de Pizan*. Gainesville: University Press of Florida.

Anonymus. *Débat de Notre Dame et de la Croix* (XIVe s.), ms. Londres, British Library, Add. 46919 (avant 1333), f° 79 – 80.

Anonymus. *Devote meditacion de la Vierge Marie a la croix en se complaignant d'elle* (XVe s.), ms. Poitiers, Bibl. mun. 95 (XVe s.), f° 87v°-91.

Bachmann, Michael. 2002. *Discussio litis super hereditate Lazari et Marie Magdalene. Ein Streitgedicht des 13. Jahrhunderts*. Berne: Peter Lang.

Badel, Pierre-Yves. 1988. Le Débat. Pp. 95 – 110 dans *La Littérature française aux XIVe et XVe siècles. Grundriss der romanischen Literaturen des Mittelalters* VIII/1, éd. Daniel Poirion. Heidelberg: Winter.

Bec, Pierre. 2000. *La Joute poétique. De la tenson médiévale aux débats chantés traditionnels*. Paris: Les Belles Lettres.

Bozzolo, Carla. 1982. *La Cour amoureuse dite de Charles VI*. Paris: Le Léopard d'or.

Cardelle de Hartmann, Carmen. 2004. Die «Processus Satanae» und die Tradition der Satansprozesse. *Mittellateinisches Jahrbuch* 39: 417 – 430.

Cardelle de Hartmann, Carmen. 2007. *Lateinische Dialoge 1200 – 1400. Literaturhistorische Studie und Repertorium*. Leiden/Boston: Brill.

Cardelle de Hartmann, Carmen. À paraître. Satan's lawsuits and dialogues on salvation in the Late Middle Ages. Dans *Apocryphisation. Debates in Biblical Disguise*, éd. Joannis Papadogiannakis et Peter Tóth. Oxford: Oxford University Press.

Cartlidge, Neil. 2006. In the silence of a midwinter night: a re-evaluation of the Visio Philiberti. *Medium Ævum* 75: 24 – 45.

Cayley, Emma J. 2006. *Debate and Dialogue: Alain Chartier in his Cultural Context*. Oxford: Clarendon press.

Cerquiglini-Toulet, Jacqueline. 1993. *La Couleur de la mélancolie: la fréquentation des livres au XIV^{ème}siècle, 1300 – 1415*. Paris: Hatier.

Collard, Franck. 2005. Un Débat à rouvrir: de quand date le Débat des armes et des dames de Guillaume Coquillart ? Pp. 79 – 93 dans *Les Mondes théâtraux autour de Guillaume Coquillart (XVe siècle)*, éd. Jean-Frédéric Chevalier. Langres: Dominique Guéniot.

Delbouille, Maurice. 1936. *Le «Jugement d'Amour» ou «Florence et Blancheflor»; première version française des Débats du Clerc et du Chevalier*. Paris: Droz.

Delsaux, Olivier. 2006. *Le Débat de la noire et de la tannée: édition critique (2ème version)*. Mémoire de licence, Université Catholique de Louvain, Louvain-la-Neuve.

Doudet, Estelle. 2005. Un dramaturge et son public au XVe siècle: George Chastelain. *European Medieval Drama* 9: 61 – 85.

Doudet, Estelle. 2006. Mettre en jeu, mettre en écrit. Les Grands Rhétoriqueurs bourguignons face aux textes de théâtre. Pp. 83 – 95 dans *L'Écrit et le manuscrit*, éd. Tania Van Hemelryck et Céline Van Hoorebeeck. Turnhout: Brepols.

Dreves, Guido Maria. 1895. *Analecta Hymnica Medii Aevi* XXI. Leipzig: O. R. Reisland.

Dronke, Peter. 1992. *Intellectuals and Poets in Medieval Europe*. Roma: Edizioni di Storia e Letteratura.

Faral, Edmond. 1912. Les *Débats du clerc et du chevalier* dans la littérature des XIIe et XIIIe siècles. *Romania* 41: 473 – 518.

Faral, Edmond. 1913. *Recherches sur les sources latines des contes et romans courtois*. Paris: Champion.

Fourrier, Anthime. 1979. *Jean Froissart: «Dits» et «débats»*. Genève: Droz.

Freeman, Michael J. 1975. *Œuvres de Guillaume Coquillart suivies d'œuvres attribuées à l'auteur*. Genève: Droz.

Haug, Hélène. 2016. La lecture des débats en moyen français: approches d'un jeu courtois. *Le Moyen Âge* 122: 275–302.

Hoepffner, Ernest. 1908. *Œuvres de Guillaume de Machaut, I*. Paris: Firmin Didot.

Gally, Michèle. 2004. *Parler d'amour au puys d'Arras. Lyrique en jeu*. Orléans: Paradigme.

Grossel, Marie-Geneviève. 1995. «Savoir aimer, savoir le dire»: notes sur les *Débats du clerc et du chevalier*. Pp. 279–293 dans *Le Clerc au Moyen Age. Actes du vingtième colloque du Centre universitaire d'études et de recherches médiévales d'Aix* (*Sénéfiance* 37). Aix-en-Provence: CUERMA.

Hult, David F. et McRae, Joan E. 2003. *Le Cycle de la Belle Dame sans merci, une anthologie poétique du XVe siècle (BNF MS FR. 1131)*. Paris: H. Champion.

Jean du Prier, *Le Debat du Content et du Non Content d'Amours*, ms. Paris, BnF, f. fr. 1685.

Jolles, André. 1972. *Formes simples*. Paris: Seuil.

Laidlaw, James. 1974. *The Poetical Works of Alain Chartier*. Cambridge: Cambridge University Press.

Långfors, Arthur. 1914. Notice du manuscrit français 17068 de la Bibliothèque Nationale. *Romania* 43: 18–28.

Langlois, Ernest. 1885. Notice du manuscrit ottobonien 2523. *Mélanges d'archéologie et d'histoire, Publications de l'École de Rome* V: 25–80.

Maingueneau, Dominique. 2006. Le Dialogue comme hypergenre. Pp. 35–46 dans *Le Dialogue ou les enjeux d'un choix d'écriture: pays de langues romanes. Actes du colloque international organisé par l'Équipe d'accueil ERILAR les 17 et 18 octobre 2003 à l'Université Rennes 2*, éd. Philippe Guerin. Rennes: Presses Universitaires de Rennes.

Michel, Alain. 1999. La Rhétorique, sa vocation et ses problèmes: sources antiques et médiévales. Pp. 17–44 dans *Histoire de la rhétorique dans l'Europe moderne (1450–1950)*, éd. Marc Fumaroli. Paris: Presses Universitaires de France.

Montaiglon, Anatole de. 1855–1878. *Recueil de poésies françaises des XVème et XVIème siècles, morales, facétieuses, historiques*, I-XIII. Paris: Jannet.

Oulmont, Charles. 1911. *Les Débats du clerc et du chevalier dans la littérature poétique du Moyen Âge*. Paris: H. Champion.

Petit de Julleville, Louis. 1967. *Répertoire du théâtre comique en France au Moyen Âge* [1886]. Genève: Slatkine Reprints.

Piaget, Arthur. 1901. *La Belle Dame sans merci* et ses imitations. *Romania* 30: 22–48 et 317–351.

Piaget, Arthur. 1902. *La Belle Dame sans merci* et ses imitations. *Romania* 31: 315–349.

Piaget, Arthur. 1904. *La Belle Dame sans merci* et ses imitations. *Romania* 33: 179–208.

Piaget, Arthur. 1905. *La Belle Dame sans merci* et ses imitations. *Romania* 34: 375–428 et 559–597.

Quéruel, Danielle. 2005. Des Entrées royales au monologue dramatique: le Débat des dames et des armes de Guillaume Coquillart. Pp. 61–78 dans *Les Mondes théâtraux autour de Guillaume Coquillart (XVe siècle)*, éd. Jean-Frédéric Chevalier. Langres: Dominique Guéniot.

Rillon-Marne, Anne-Zoé. 2012. *«Homo considera». La pastorale lyrique de Philippe le Chancelier: une étude des conduits monodiques.* Turnhout: Brepols.
Roy, Maurice. 1886–1891. *Œuvres poétiques de Christine de Pisan* I-III. Paris: Firmin Didot.
Ruhe, Doris. 1974. *Le Dieu d'Amours avec son paradis. Untersuchungen zur Mythenbildung um Amor in Spätantike und Mittelalter.* München: Wilhelm Fink Verlag.
Tabard, Laëtitia. 2012. *Bien assailly, Bien deffendu. Le débat dans la littérature française de la fin du Moyen Âge*, thèse de doctorat, Université de Paris IV-Sorbonne, Paris.
Tabard, Laëtitia. 2013a. Le sourire du clerc. Pp. 47–65 dans *Labor Eruditus. Études sur la vie privée de l'érudition*, éd. Pascale Hummel. Paris: éditions Philologicum.
Tabard, Laëtitia. 2013b. Les débats du corps et de l'âme: la scène intérieure. Pp. 83–100 dans *Intus et foris: une catégorie de la pensée médiévale*, éd. Marie-Pascale Halary, Manuel Guay et Patrick Moran. Paris: Presses Universitaires de Paris-Sorbonne.
Tarnowski, Andrea. 2000. *Christine de Pizan. Le Chemin de longue étude.* Paris: L.G.F.
Thiry, Claude. 1986. Débats et moralités dans la littérature française du XVe siècle: intersection et interaction du narratif et du dramatique. *Le Moyen français* 19: 203–244.
Tilliette, Jean-Yves. 2017. Modèles et contre-modèles de la poésie lyrique de Philippe le Chancelier: Adam de Saint-Victor et Gautier de Châtillon. Pp. 209–227 dans *Philippe le Chancelier prédicateur, théologien et poète parisien du début du XIIIe siècle*, éd. Gilbert Dahan et Anne-Zoé Rillon-Marne. Turnhout: Brepols.
Toshiki, Ito. 1974. *Les Débats dans la littérature française du Moyen Âge.* Thèse de doctorat, Université de Paris IV, Paris.
Tóth, Peter. 2012. La vision du Christ dans le jardin de Gethsemani: un dialogue pseudo-apocryphe comme exemplum théologique. Pp. 423–443 dans *Formes dialoguées dans la littérature exemplaire du Moyen Âge*, éd. Marie-Anne Polo de Beaulieu. Paris: H. Champion.
Walther, Hans. 1984. *Das Streitgedicht in des lateinischen Literatur des Mittelalters,* édition de 1920 revue par Paul Gerhard Schmidt. Hildesheim/Zürich/Berlin: Georg Olms Verlag.
Weijers, Olga. 1999. De la joute dialectique à la dispute scolastique. *Académie des inscriptions et belles-lettres. Comptes-rendus des séances* 2: 509–517.
Zumthor, Paul. 1987. *La Lettre et la voix, de la «littérature» médiévale.* Paris: Seuil.
Zumthor, Paul. 2000. *Essai de poétique médiévale* [1972]. Paris: Seuil.

Section IV **Contemporary Disputation Texts**

Alessandro Mengozzi*

21 Neo-Aramaic Dialogue and Dispute Poems

The Various Types

Neo-Aramaic dispute poems are a marginal, exceptional, though very instructive phenomenon in the history of the "intercultural transmission" of the Mesopotamian dispute. Jiménez (2017: 125–26) describes the diffusion of this type of literary text as "a millenary relay race, in which one culture bequeaths an ever-changing baton to the next" and summarizes the structural features of the allegedly intercultural genre as follows:

(1) poetic form,
(2) tripartite structure (introduction, disputation proper, and conclusion),
(3) few or no narrative portions,
(4) usually inanimate disputants,
(5) supremacy or precedence as main matter of debate.

Jiménez (2017: 126–7) maintains that it would be daring to think that such a relatively uncommon text type, defined on the basis of structural features rather than contents, developed independently in various cultures that have been in contact for sometimes long periods of their histories, whereas it is easier to postulate an intercultural transmission. However, "not once is the same disputation poem attested in two different languages" and therefore "the precise ways in which this transmission happened ... cannot be specified."

Neo-Aramaic (henceforth NA) dispute poems are exceptional because some of them are direct translations of Classical Syriac texts and for all of them the ways in which transmission happened are quite easily traceable. On the whole, NA dispute and dialogue poems exemplify a number of constitutive characteristics of Christian Neo-Aramaic literature. Most of the texts derive from classical models and represent a continuation and adaptation of Syriac – especially late East-Syriac – literature in the modern tongue. Arguably, orientalists' choices may have interfered in the selection of genres and texts to be translated into NA and therefore in the formation of the corpus of NA literature. Some texts, including the two dialogue poems that have been preserved only in NA, clearly demonstrate to what extant late East-Syriac and Neo-Aramaic literatures belong to

* University of Turin.

https://doi.org/10.1515/9781501510274-021

the so-called Islamicate world, as literary expressions of cultural minorities. Using Jiménez' terminology, we may say that intercultural transmission happened therefore in two directions, the vertical derivation from Classical Syriac literature, with the possible catalyst of late 19th-century German scholarship, and the horizontal contact with neighboring cultures.

1 Aramaic Dialogue and Dispute Poems

In a number of publications – such as, for instance, Brock (1991), from which I borrowed the title of the present contribution – Sebastian Brock has shown that in Syriac literature dispute poems – i. e. poems that display the formal features of the Mesopotamian dispute as described by Jiménez – represent a specific subgroup within a wider corpus of texts, the vast majority of which are poems and in which dialogue is a more or less salient structural feature. It is sometimes difficult to distinguish between dialogue poems and dispute poems proper.

Similar considerations can be made for the far smaller corpus of NA dialogue and dispute poems. Moreover, besides the NA versions of Classical Syriac dialogue and dispute poems (see, below, the following section), we have NA translations of Classical Syriac texts in which direct speech – dialogue or monologue – plays a prominent role. One of the most frequently copied NA poems is the translations of two hymns *On Joseph the Patriarch*,[1] attributed to Narsai (c. 413–503 CE), that contain quite a number of dialogue sections. Various anonymous NA versions are known of the popular hymns *Tell me, Church!* (Mengozzi and Ricossa 2013) and *When I was in Bethlehem, I heard the voice of Mary* (Mengozzi 2006), that contain monologues in the form of a list of questions to an imaginary interlocutor and Jesus as a baby. The latter monologue hymn, a highly theological lullaby sung by Mary to her child, shares with many Classical Syriac dialogue and dispute poems the opening narrative formula in which the poetic "I" declares that he has actually heard the dialogue he is about to sing, usually presenting it as a miracle, a remarkable and wonderful event. The vertical and horizontal relationships among poems containing various combinations of narrative and direct speech (monologue, list of questions, dialogue, dispute) and therefore their definition as (a) literary genre(s) should be carefully investigated in all literatures.

1 The translations are attributed to Joseph 'Azarya of Telkepe in a manuscript of the London Sachau collection and to Stephen Rayes in other manuscripts (Mengozzi 2011: xx). At least sixteen manuscripts of the Iraqi collections catalogued at the Hill Museum & Manuscript Library (www.hmml.org) contain one or both hymns in NA.

In the case of Classical Syriac literature, following Grelot (1958) and Murray (1995), Brock (1984: 35–36) thinks that the Mesopotamian dispute was adopted early and adapted by major authors like Ephrem (c. 306–373 CE) and Jacob of Serugh (c. 451–521) to their purposes and in various forms: simple allusions to disputes or disputes as substantial parts of *madrashē* (stanzaic hymns) and *mēmrē* (metrical homilies). In a second phase, which includes the largest number of texts, the stanzaic hymn called *soghithā* is the almost exclusive form given to anonymous dialogue and dispute poems. The adoption of the Mesopotamian dispute in a Christian culture, dominated by the Bible, has resulted in a perceptible change of setting and tone. Most Syriac dialogues are not disputations or precedence disputes, but argumentative discussions on specific – biblical or theological – topics. Brock (1983a: 44) suggests that the transition from dispute to argumentative dialogue is an indication of the Christianization of the genre.

Most Syriac dialogue and dispute poems share forms of expression, function as liturgical hymns and history of transmission. The *soghithā* hymn is certainly the commonest genre and metrical form used for disputes, dialogues and, in general, poetry containing direct speech. In a *soghithā* verses usually consist of four seven-syllable lines and an alphabetic acrostic often marks the pairs of verses in which the disputants alternate in direct speech (see Brock in this volume). The term *soghithā* would seem to be a cognate of Jewish Aramaic *sughyā*, which is technically used for a specific type of Talmudic discussion (Brodsky 2014). Most *soghyāthā*, however, do not contain any dispute, discussion or direct speech whatsoever. If the etymological connection with the Jewish *sughyā* is correct, then we may assume that the term originally indicated dispute poems and was then extended to all hymns having this metrical form.

Christian Syriac literature is not the only Aramaic literature that would have preserved, adopted and adapted the genre of the Mesopotamian dispute. Rhythmical compositions, sometimes with alphabetic acrostic, that contain a dialogue or a dispute, are interpolated within the Aramaic translation of various Biblical passages in the Palestinian Targums.[2] Disputants may be Biblical characters

2 A list can be found in Smelik (1995: 414–5). Text and translation of a number of Targumic disputes, with an insightful commentary, can be found in Rodrigues Pereira (1997). Lieber (2018) gives an English translation of Jewish Palestinian Aramaic dialogue and dispute poems (*Moses and the sea*, *Moses and the angels*, *Daniel's friends and Nebuchadnezzar*, *Joseph and Potiphar's wife*, the dispute of the *Trees*, the *Months*, *Body and soul*), as published by Yahalom and Sokoloff (1999).

(e. g., Cain and Abel),[3] inanimate subjects (usually more than two: the months of the year,[4] the trees[5] or five stones)[6] or a combination of members of both groups (Moses and the sea).

Since a very short dispute between the thornbush and the Pomegranate is encapsulated in the proverb section of the Official Aramaic *Story of Aḥiqar the wise man*, preserved in a 5th-century papyrus, it is tempting to hypothesize that Syriac and Jewish Aramaic disputes represent the continuation and blooming of the ancient Mesopotamian genre in the Aramaic literatures of the first millennium CE. The Bible, which preserves a couple of disputes of trees in which the thornbush has a central role,[7] would have served as a bridge between the Aramaic disputes that must have existed in the Achaemenid period – as the *Story of Aḥiqar* would prove – and Christian, i. e. Syriac, and Jewish Aramaic disputes of late antiquity.

3 These interpolated midrashic hymns are often known in different versions. Chilton (1982) speaks of kaleidoscopic variation for the dialogues between Cain and Abel preserved in the Palestinian Targums.

4 Rand (2012) lists six Jewish Palestinian Aramaic disputes of the months and publishes text and translation of a dispute attributed to Sahlan ben Avraham (Jewish Iraqi community of Fustat, 11th century) in the acrostic of the last verse.

5 Various Hebrew and Aramaic versions are known of the dispute of the trees that discuss to decide which will offer its wood to build Haman's gallows (Esther 5:14). In *Esther Rabbah*, all trees gladly volunteer to offer their wood and a Biblical quotation and/or a liturgical function is associated to each of them: like in the famous Jotham's fable of the trees (Judges 9:7–21), the thorn bush eventually wins. On the contrary, in the *Targum Sheni* and other Aramaic versions, the trees refuse to offer themselves and God decides at the end that the cedar is the only tree big enough to hang Haman on it. The text seems to be the parody of a rabbinical discussion, the dispute as a literary genre and *ekphrasis* as a rhetorical exercise. The use of formulae and, in some versions, of the alphabetic acrostic give the text a rhythmical structure, transparent and easy to memorize. Besides the parodic effect, the text may have a pedagogic function, to memorize Biblical quotations and liturgical items that involve the use of trees (Mengozzi 2016).

6 A kind of precedence dispute between the five stones of 1 Samuel 17:40 is inserted in the so-called *Song of the lamb*, a long hymn with alphabetical acrostic added to a Targum of 1 Samuel 17:43. The names of the five patriarchs Abraham, Isaac, Jacob, Moses and Aaron are engraved on the stones that quarrel to decide which one will have the honor to hit Goliath's forehead. Only Abraham's stone speaks, perhaps because the text is an abbreviation of a complete dispute in which all the stones presented their arguments. God eventually grants the victory to Aaron's stone (Aramaic text, Eng. transl. and commentary in Houtman-Sysling 2009: 114–8; Eng. Transl. in Hayward 2013: 84–6).

7 See Jotham's fable of the trees in Judges 9:7–21 and the diplomatic exchange between thistle and the cedar of Lebanon in 2 Kings 14: 9–10. See Piquer Otero in this volume.

However, the comparison of disputes and dialogue poems with the same characters that have been preserved in Syriac and Jewish Aramaic (Cain and Abel, Joseph and Potiphar's wife, the months of the year) reveals the paradox of the relative uniformity of a supposedly inherited genre and the high degree of cultural idiosyncrasy between literary traditions that share more or less the same language as well as the historical and possibly socio-cultural macro-contexts (Münz-Manor 2010). In two literatures that express themselves in varieties of the same Aramaic language group, we find the contradiction observed by Reinink and Vanstiphout (1991: 2) as a general phenomenon in the vertical/diachronic and horizontal/synchronic diffusion of the Mesopotamian dispute:

> one is struck by the apparent contradiction between the diachronic, 'historical' lineage of the formal features ..., and the synchronic location within a 'contemporary' literary framework of each composition which, on the level of the contents, has also much to do with the genre's explicit or implicit function within the prevailing socio-cultural environment, be it school, church, court, or an association of poets.

In the more elaborated Jewish versions (Targums Neophyti and Pseudo-Jonathan), for instance, the dialogue between Cain and Abel is structured in two pairs of stanzas, in which Abel reverses by antithesis Cain's cynical statements about God's injustice and the inexistence of an ultramundane justice. The two versions of the dialogue of Cain and Abel preserved in Syriac have the more elaborated structure of the classical *soghithā*. Abel tries every argument to defend himself from his brother and the theme of God's judgment surfaces only at the end of the poem.

In the *Fragment Targum* the months dispute about which of them will be the month in which Israel will be saved from Egypt and therefore Pesach will be celebrated.[8] The arguments used by the months are various: some refer to Biblical events and Jewish liturgy, others to nature, agriculture and economy. The winner is the spring month Nisan as stated by Moses in Exodus 12:2, where the poem is interpolated. On the other hand, the Syriac *Dispute of the Months* (Brock 1985; see below, no. 1 in the Appendix) is a complete calendar inserted in the framework of an incomplete Mesopotamian precedence dispute. The first verse briefly sketches the narrative context, and the deity who functions as an arbiter in the Mesopotamian dispute is here replaced by the personification of the year, who sits among the months to judge their case. The disputants boast about the won-

---

8 The Jewish *Dispute on Nisan's Primacy* is known in two almost complete, though rather corrupt, versions (Klein 1980: vol. 1, 72–3, vol. 2, 37–9 and Brock 1985: 209–11; Klein 1986 I 186–9 and Rodrigues Pereira 1997: 68–75, 310–12, 393–5) and a very short one (Klein 1986 I 192–3 and Rodrigues Pereira 1997: 66–7, 310, 392–3). See also Rand 2012: 102–3.

ders of nature and the agricultural products linked to each of them. Only one verse, possibly interpolated, has explicit Christian contents. The narrative frame is not closed at the end, since there is no final judgment or proclamation of the winner. Brock (1985) collects a number of Syriac texts, including the *Dispute of Gold and Wheat* (no. 2 in the Appendix), that contain entire or partial calendars and correctly points out that another Syriac poem (*Soghitha II*, Brock 1985: 187, 204–7) has the rhetorical structure of an ekphrastic description rather than a disputation of the months.

Rather than Mesopotamian disputes, the Jewish Aramaic and Syriac *Dispute of the Months* and related texts look like popular calendars in verses or poems referring to this type of calendar, with the pedagogical function of associating the names of the months with nature, agriculture, economy, liturgy and sacred history. The theme of Nisan's precedence may reflect the fact that competing calendars, with new year in the autumn or in the spring (Nisan), were in use in the Near East. This would explain why these disputes were popular "in the literatures of this area, but not in Greek or Latin" (Brock 1985: 186).

2 The Neo-Aramaic Versions of the Cherub and the Thief

NA varieties represent the modern continuation of the language sub-family that we commonly call "Aramaic." Quite faithfully reflecting the geographical distribution of Old Aramaic in the first millennium BC, NA languages form today a "geographically discontinuous dialect continuum" (Kim 2008: 511) which encompasses Western NA (Maʿlula and other villages in the Qalamūn valley of the Anti-lebanon mountains), Central NA (also known by the autoglottonym Ṣurayt or Ṭuroyo, viz. the language of Ṭur ʿAbdīn in south-eastern Turkey), North-Eastern Neo-Aramaic (NENA) varieties, and perhaps Neo-Mandaic too (Khuzestan province of Iran and southern Iraq). NENA dialects are or were spoken by Jews and Christians of various denominations and represent the largest portion of the Neo-Aramaic continuum, today spread across south-eastern Turkey, northern Iraq and north-western Iran. All speakers of Jewish NENA varieties migrated to Israel in the early Fifties and most NENA-speaking Christians have abandoned their unstable and insecure homeland and live in a global diaspora, like the Assyro-Australian author of the dialogue of *A Man and a Flower* presented below in

English translation. Christian NENA varieties are also known as Modern Syriac and Vernacular Syriac or by the autoglottonyms Sureth and Assyrian.[9]

The first written records of Neo-Aramaic date back to the late 16th and early 17th centuries, for both Jewish and Christian communities of northern Iraq. These early documents are religious, usually paraenetic, texts written by relatively learned but poor rabbis and priests, engaged in the adaptation and popularization of traditional contents among their flocks, who were almost certainly illiterate and unable to understand the classical languages, i.e. Hebrew and Babylonian Talmudic Aramaic for the Jews and Classical Syriac for Christians. Before the 19th century, when Western missionaries introduced the printing press to Urmia and Mosul, written NA literary texts were circulated among East Syrians in manuscript form. They were religious poems called *durekyāthā* and were included among Classical Syriac hymns of similar content and form (usually belonging to the liturgical genres of *'onyāthā* or *soghyāthā*) or in separate collections of hymns exclusively in the vernacular, sometimes entitled *kthābē d-durekyāthā*. From a quantitative point of view, Neo-Aramaic texts represent in both cases (isolated vernacular texts in Classical Syriac collections or vernacular collections) a marginal phenomenon in comparison with the massive production of Classical Syriac manuscripts – especially biblical and liturgical ones, but also containing original works – which were copied and written within and around the so-called "School of Alqosh," in northern Iraq, in the 15th to 19th centuries (Murre-van den Berg 2015).

One of the three known NA versions of the *Dispute of the Cherub and the Thief* (text C in Pennacchietti 1993)[10] belongs to this native network of manuscript transmission. The oldest dated copy known so far is added as an NA translation of the homonymous Classical Syriac *soghithā* for Easter attributed to Narsai in the manuscript 421 of the Chaldean Cathedral of Mardin, dated 1737 and recently catalogued by Grigory Kessel.[11] Thanks to this manuscript, the author of the NA translation can be definitively identified as the priest Marawgen son of Hasado, of the village Sharukhya near Dyarbakir, active at the beginning of the 18th century (Wilmshurst 2000: 60). We also have evidence of the use of NA versions of this text in the liturgy as early as in the first half of the 18th century.

Despite the fact that the disputants are animate, the Classical Syriac *Soghithā of the Cherub and the Thief* and its NA versions have most of the features

9 On the term "Assyrian" in Syriac and the adoption of the Assyrian identity among modern (East-) Syriac Christians, see Butts (2017).

10 See no. 5 in the Appendix for more bibliographic information.

11 CCM 00421 in the catalogue of the Hill Museum and Manuscript Library, www.hmml.org.

of the Mesopotamian dispute. It is perhaps the only Syriac dispute poem for which we have substantial, direct and indirect, evidence about the *Sitz im Leben*. The rite is known in the popular abbreviation Gayasa 'the thief' (Harrak 2011: 81) and dozens of video-recordings from all over the world can be retrieved by searching for 'gay(y)as(s)a' or ' كياسا ' on YouTube. The very popular Easter rite associated with this poem may have been instrumental for the introduction of the NA vernacular into East-Syriac liturgy (Mengozzi-Ricossa 2013).

During the Easter vigil, on Easter Sunday or as an expiatory rite for the death during the first week after Easter (Pennacchietti 1993: 5–7, 11, 75), the East Syriac – Assyrian and Chaldean Catholic – liturgy involves a sacred drama of extraordinary efficacy, which is still greatly appreciated. One of the congregation, usually a young layman, plays the role of the first man who was saved, the good thief of Luke 23: 39–43, known as Titus in the Syriac tradition and in apocryphal texts such as the *Arabic Gospel of the Infancy*. He approaches the altar – a space that in the Eastern churches symbolizes Eden and therefore paradise and heaven – where one or more deacons or prelates dressed in liturgical garments play the role of the cherub with the flaming sword that God placed to guard the tree of life after Adam's expulsion from paradise (Mengozzi-Ricossa 2013).

The thief and the cherub quarrel about the right of the man to re-enter paradise and therefore about the supremacy of the New Testament promise made by Jesus on the cross ("Today you shall be with me in paradise," Luke 23:43) over Adam's condemnation in the Old Testament (Genesis 3: 24). In the actual performances of the text that we can see on YouTube, a number of interesting theatrical features, such as scene costumes, interaction between actor and audience, hitting and shoving, laughter and final applause, would seem to turn the *sughithā* from a sacred drama into a comedy. Nevertheless, the dispute preserves its semiotic efficacy and the strength of its theological message. It becomes almost a duel and the dramatic tension reaches its climax when it becomes clear that there is no solution. Then, quite suddenly, the thief puts an end to the dispute by showing the Cross as a sign of reconciliation between heaven and earth, God and mankind. Arguably, this is the characteristic and perhaps the only form of cosmic reconciliation acceptable in a Christian theological perspective and therefore the most typical translation of a common epilogue of the Mesopotamian dispute in a Christian culture.

3 Neo-Aramaic Versions of Classical Syriac Dialogue and Dispute Poems

In the last decades of the 19th century, European travelers and orientalists, such as Eugen Prym (1843–1913), Albert Socin (1844–1899) and Eduard Sachau (1845–1930) collected NA texts and asked local clergy and professional copyists to compile manuscript collections, usually accompanied by Arabic translations.[12] Especially prose texts were translated from Arabic or Classical Syriac into NA, whereas for poetry copyists drew from and combined earlier copies of popular songs and *durekyāthā*. Occasionally they may have produced ad hoc translations in Neo-Aramaic verses of Classical Syriac texts.

The research interests and literary tastes of the orientalists had some influence in the choice of genres and text types. The translation of a specific set of Biblical texts, geographical *mirabilia*, sacred geography and local history as well as *Arabian Nights* stories regularly feature among the prose texts collected by Sachau. Erotic triplets, traditional *durekyāthā* and translations of dialogue and dispute *sughyāthā* are the genres that we most commonly find in the orientalists' collections of NA poetry.

The erotic triplets were appreciated for their popular flavor and living imagery, that somehow recalled the Biblical poetry of the *Song of Songs* (Nöldeke 1882: 679–80). Late 19th-century German orientalists also appreciated dialogue and dispute *sughyāthā* as a poetic genre. Editors and translators of Narsai's metrical homilies and the *sughyāthā* attached to them in East-Syriac manuscripts agreed in preferring the rhythm and vivacity of the latter. According to Martin (1899: 449), the quasi dramatic structure and the compactness of the verses give the *sughithā* a degree of neatness and immediacy that homilies cannot reach. Feldmann (1896: 4) observes that the metrical homilies are lengthy and repetitive, while dialogue *sughyāthā* better respond to modern literary taste. Moreover, the dialogic structure probably appealed to European scholars for linguistic reasons, as a way to access something close to spontaneous conversation, albeit encoded in a rather elaborate literary form.

The NA translations of seven dialogue and dispute poems were included in the manuscript 336 of the Berlin Sachau collection, among other poems and

12 On Prym and Socin's methods in collecting Ṣurayt texts, see Tardieu (2011); on Sachau collections of Neo-Aramaic (both Ṣurayt and Sureth) texts, see Mengozzi (1999 and forthcoming) and Bellino and Mengozzi (2016). The French Dominican missionary Jacques Rhétoré (1841–1921) was also very active in the collection and study of Sureth texts and an author himself of Sureth texts in prose and poetry (Poizat 2013).

prose texts in Kurdish, NA and Classical Syriac.[13] They are: 1. the disputes of *The Months of the Year*, 2. *Gold and Wheat*, 3. *Cup, Jar and Wineskin*, 4. *Simon Peter and Simon Magus*, and 5. *The Cherub and the Thief*; 6. the dialogues of *Satan and the Sinful Woman* and 7. *Christ and Mary* (*Mary and the Gardener*).[14] With the remarkable exception of *The Cherub and the Thief* we do not have evidence of a liturgical use of these NA poems.

The manuscript was written in 1883 in Telkepe, near Mosul, by Francis Miri who was a versatile and creative scribe and a Sureth poet himself. He added, for instance, a colophon-like verse with signature to the hymn *On Shmuni and her Seven Sons* by Israel of Alqosh (early 17th century), in the collection of *durekyāthā* that he copied for Sachau in 1882 (Berlin Syr. 123, Sachau 223): "My name is *Fransi*. I wrote this *durekthā* by myself. May Shmuni be my mother!" (Mengozzi 2002: 69 – 70).

The dialogue and dispute poems to be translated into NA were selected in collections of poems on wine and other subjects attributed in late East-Syriac

---

13 The manuscript Berlin Syriac 134 (Sachau 336; Sachau 1899: vol. 1,437 – 42) is a typical example of Sachau's methods in collecting texts in various languages. It contains:

A. A Kurdish poem, also attested in Berlin Syriac 133 (Sachau 200; on Kurdish Garshuni texts in manuscripts of the Sachau collection, see Dehqan 2016a and 2016b; text editions and a thorough investigation of these materials, interesting from both a literary and linguistic point of view, are still badly needed).
B. NA erotic triplets.
C. The NA *Durekṯā on Mary* (Incipit: *b-shemmā d-bābā u-bronā*), which was composed by the famous Chaldean bard David the Blind, perhaps in cooperation with Father Rhétoré, and has become a kind of national anthem for the Chaldeans of the Mosul plain (Mengozzi 2011: xv; Poizat 2013: 129 – 32).
D. *Story and Proverbs of Aḥiqar* in Classical Syriac.
E. Aesopic fables, in Classical Syriac.
F. NA poems: 1. The Months of the Year, 2. Gold and Wheat, 3. Mamo loved by a bishop of Azerbaidjan, 4. The guests and a stranger (by Khamis bar Qardaḥe, in Classical Syriac), 5. Cup, Jar and Wineskin, 6. Satan and the Sinful Woman, 7. Simon Peter and Simon Magus, 8. Christ and Mary Magdalene?, 9. The Cherub and the Thief.
G. NA prose *Story of a duenna* (qāhrāmānah), *her dragoman and a prince* (published by Lidzbarski 1896: NA text vol. 1, 328 – 43; German transl. vol. 2, 267 – 79; on these NA versions of *Arabian Nights* stories, see Mengozzi, forthcoming).

Jeremiah Shamir, scribe, informant and book dealer who worked for Sachau and other orientalists, copied (Berlin Syr., Sachau 343) and translated Francis' manuscript collection into Arabic (Berlin Syr., Sachau 200). Despite Francis' repetitions and shortcomings in orthography, Lidzbarski (1896, vol. 1, II) preferred to use his manuscript as base text for his edition since Jeremiah Shamir allowed himself too much freedom in changing the text.

14 Editions, translations and unpublished manuscript copies of these texts and the Classical Syriac originals are listed in the Appendix.

manuscripts to Khamis bar Qardaḥe, a poet active in the last decades of the 13th century and very sensitive to the influence of Arabo-Persian poetry (Pritula 2016 and Mengozzi 2015). Brock (1985: 182 and 200, n. 37), for instance, noticed the strange relationship between Berlin Sachau 336 and the East-Syriac hymnary Cambridge Add. 2820, copied by Joseph 'Azarya in 1882 near Telkepe: the NA version of the *Dispute of the Months* corresponds rather faithfully to the Classical Syriac text as preserved in Add. 2820, 98a-98b, whereas the NA version of the *Dispute of Gold and Wheat* derives from a Classical Syriac *Vorlage* quite different from the text as preserved in Add. 2820, 96b–98a. The *Dispute of the Months* is certainly not an original work by Khamis, since it is known from a much earlier West-Syriac liturgical manuscript (British Library Add. 17141, 8th-9th century) and Anton of Tagrit (9th century) quotes the first part in his *Rhetoric* as an example of prosopopoeia (Brock 1985: 181–3). It is also reasonable to assume that the *Dispute of Gold and Wheat* had circulated earlier than in the 13th century.

The translation from Syriac to NA is not complete and the dispute of *Cup, Jar and Wineskin* is preceded in Berlin Sachau 336 by a short dialogue poem in the classical language, in which a new guest asks to be admitted to a company of drinkers. Both texts are probably original works by Khamis and exemplify his successful attempts to express in Syriac and translate into a Christian culture the Arabo-Persian genre of the *ḫamriyyāt* or wine songs.[15] Even if the author is not Khamis, he shares with the 13th-century East-Syriac poet a brilliant use of forms and motifs of the Islamicate literatures of that time. Indeed, the dispute of *Cup, Jar and Wineskin* is particularly intriguing in that it contains all formal features of the Mesopotamian disputation and combines the structure of a *munāẓara* with motifs characteristic of the *ḫamriyyāt.* In the first part of the poem, wine praises itself as the chief of all banquets and boasts about its beautiful colors. Then a quarrel arises as to which container best exalts its qualities. The tavern-keeper is finally awoken, as the judging god at the end of a Mesopotamian dispute, to grant victory to the joyful and generous cup over jar and wineskin, which keep wine hidden.

Since all the poems probably derive from a collection of Classical Syriac texts attributed to Khamis and one text has been left untranslated, we cannot rule out the possibility that one author, perhaps the scribe Francis of Telkepe himself, actually translated the texts or some of them using a collection of poems on wine and other subjects such as Cambridge Add. 2820, that he completed a year earlier in Telkepe.

---

15 See Taylor (2010) on wine songs in Syriac literature.

The NA prose translation of the dialogue poem of *Mary and the Magi* (no. 8 in the Appendix) comes from a later and totally different context. It is written on four pages of a 20th-century notebook and is marked as "sughithā no. 3" in the title and in a short colophon, that contains the name of the translator: Hormez Denḥā Dawīd of Araden, a Chaldean village near Amadiya in northern Iraq. It may belong to a series of NA versions and therefore to a native scholar's project to study and translate East-Syriac *soghyāthā* into the modern language.

4 Two Dialogue Poems Preserved Only in Neo-Aramaic

As we have seen, the Classical Syriac dispute of *Cup, Jar and Waterskin*, translated into NA together with other dispute and dialogue poems attributed to Khamis bar Qardaḥe, shows the impact of influential Arabo-Persian forms and motifs on the literature of the so-called Syriac Renaissance (11th-14th centuries). The outcome of the process of assimilation to the dominant culture that began in the Syriac literature of the Mongol period is clear in two poems preserved only in the modern language and erroneously reported in the literature as disputes: *Two Boys and the Teakettle* and *A Man and a Flower* (nos. 9 and 10 in the Appendix). Like and even more so than Khamis' poetry, they show the belonging of Christian NA literature to the Islamicate world.

Despite the fact that both NA dialogues are described with the Syriac technical term *durāshā* 'dispute, discussion' in the first verse or in the title, they would fail Jiménez' test to recognize the structural features of a Mesopotamian dispute. Neither has a full tripartite structure and what is more important is that in neither text is supremacy or precedence the matter of debate. The two boys urge the teakettle to warm up the water so that they may prepare tea, eat a snack and go back to play. The man engages the flower in a philosophical conversation about the origin and goal of their existence as God's creatures. In both dialogues, human beings converse with inanimate objects, against the more or less strict rules of homogeneity and inanimacy of the disputants in the Mesopotamian dispute.

The *Two Boys and the Teakettle* is an anonymous poem in the Christian NA literary language of Urmia. It was published in 1909 in the Urmi periodical *Kokḇā* and re-published both in Syriac script and Roman transliteration, and with an English translation, by Yaure (1957). In his introduction, Yaure (1957: 76) is perhaps a little too enthusiastic in describing it as "a true and genuine Sughithā," that "favorably compares with the best of this type ever produced by the classical

Syriac poetry." At the same time, he is perhaps pessimistic in defining the language in which it is written as "one of the last decaying branches of the Aramaic language." Unlike most dialogue *soghyāthā*, in which the characters speak two verses each, in this poem the two boys and the teakettle regularly alternate one verse each. There is no alphabetic acrostic and all lines of a quatrain rhyme with each other, as is typical of late *soghyāthā*, influenced by Arabo-Persian poetry. Instead of the more or less canonical seven-syllable lines, each quatrain has four pairs of iambic feet.

The setting, content and function of the poem do not derive from the Syriac tradition and resemble, on the contrary, the late Persian disputes (Massé 1961: 144–47) and the popular disputes collected by Bouriant (1893) and Littman (1951) in Egypt, Holes (1995, 1996, 1998) in various Arabic dialects of the Gulf and Wagner (2005) in Yemeni Arabic. Indeed, in modern times, the *munāẓara* appears to be a vernacular genre cultivated in oral traditions throughout the Middle East and the Arab World. Texts are only occasionally written down or published and they seldom attract scholarly attention (Holes 1996: 302 and Holes in this volume). It would not be surprising to find Kurdish, Azeri or Turkish models for the poem in Urmi NA.

Interestingly, Yaure (1957: 79) suggests a fanciful Persian setting:

> Finally, to facilitate better understanding of the exotic setting and context of the story, we must imagine ourselves in a Persian garden where a jolly company of young people have gathered and are sitting around while attendants are serving dainties. But the company cannot begin with the repast until the customary Persian tea is served which is meanwhile being prepared by boys who are busily engaged with boiling water in the teakettle and seasoning the tea in the teapot. At this point, after an introductory stanza, the dramatic dialogue between the boys and the teakettle begins.

The *Two Boys and the Teakettle* is neither a satirical piece nor a dispute, but it shares certain comical, playful, almost childish tones of Persian and vernacular Arabic debate poems like *Coffee and Tea*, *Bowl and Narghile*, *Water Melon and Date*. Similarly influenced by Persian Islamic models, but with a much more serious content is the dialogue of *A Man and a Flower* by Esh'aya Elisha' Khenno (Sydney, Australia), published in 1984 in the NA section of the Swedish Assyrian periodical *Ḥujådå*.

Dispute with a flower[16]
By Esh'aya Elisha' Khenno (Sydney, Australia)[17]

16 The poem is called by Brock (1991: 109) *The Man and the Rose*. As is well known, there is no

Man: Beautiful flower, I will question you and you shall answer me.
I have nobody who speaks to reveal me the truth except you.
You can tell me in all truth where is your secret
to give form to your substance and grow beautiful. Whom are you waiting for?[18]

Flower: How I have grown and formed my substance I do not know myself.
This hidden secret has been known also by my creator,
but I know that both you and I have received a substance
from the heart of earth through a force hidden in eternity.

Man: Shining flower, I understood all that you mean,
but I need to know more to understand you.
How will you prove that both of us have been begotten from one act,
me as a living being, complete and discerning, whereas you do not have a soul?

Flower: This difference has been explained and does not need to be explained
that we have a human being that is called the eternal Being.
He who created your first father Adam, he created me
and created us from the soil, me without a spirit and you intelligent.

Man: Splendid flower, explain to me yourself something more
so that I may understand your thought and agree with your opinion.
How did you understand that the nature of both of us has a creator?
Where is such a powerful maker hidden?

Flower: My beloved friend, I will answer to your question
so that I may convince you with a pure light, above your expectation.
There is One who puts order among all breathing and non-breathing beings,
He who dwells in the highest dwelling place and is the Owner of nature.

Man: Desirable flower, you are enjoyable in your exposition.
I have perhaps still a thought that hinders me on the way to know you.
Although it is undeniable that your beauty is wonderful and your look attractive,
how did you dare to join Eve's son?

Flower: Wise man endowed with speech, we are both naturally attracted from the seed
each one to the family that gives life and raises the seed.
You exert active force whereas I am passive
or, in other words, I am weak whereas you are discerning.

---

specific name for roses in Middle-Eastern languages. NA *wardā* may indicate roses as well as any other "handsome flower" (Oraham 1943: 137). On the basis of the illustrations surrounding the poem, in which a certain A. Aziz drew various kinds of flowers (daisies, gentianellas, petunias, peach flowers...) but no roses, I prefer to translate *wardā* as "flower" rather than "rose."

17 I did not find much information on the author. From Beth_Mardutho (https://www.librarything.com/work/18058421/132208847, last accessed November 2019) it appears that he is the author of poems in honor of Saint Ephrem, translated (?) by the deacon Giwargis d-Beth Benyamin of Ashita.

18 Lit. "Whom did you wait for?"

Man: All-attractive flower, your answer is truthful.
You filled my mind with marvel so that I may truly accept your decisions,
but tell me what the purpose is of Our Lord the Most High
who built for you a body from greenness and for me a human body.

Flower: You have been created in His image and likeness to remember Him constantly.
To me he gave beauty to cajole you so that you may not forget Him.
He gifted you with knowledge to sow my seed at its time,
but the grain that has come out of it has grown up on its own.

Man: Beloved flower, allow me also to bow here my head
and thank you for your indisputable advice.
Only, let me know why I have a tongue
and wonderful sight, whereas you do not have them and cannot move.

Flower: Yes, you are perfectly right. He gave you these gifts
so that you may see His creatures and lift glory to Him with the word of your lips.
He gave me bright colors and a fragrant smell
so that you may wonder at His deeds and may not forget the powerful Almighty.

Man: Wonderful flower, when sometimes I was exceedingly distressed
you gave me courage and drove away my sadness, though remaining silent,
but you are perfectly right, I cannot oppose the truth of your gifts.
Allow me to honor you with all my heart by writing your story.

Flower: I do not have a tongue to thank you speaking with my lips.
Give to Our Lord this honor that you gave to me!
I am a flower and you are a man, you know it by yourself.
Only the Lord your creator deserves honor and glory.

The heterogeneity of the speakers, a human being and an inanimate flower, is the matter of debate. Although in a couple of passages the man would seem to defend a higher position in creation as a being endowed with speech, the dialogue is built as a series of philosophical questions of the man to which the flower, as a wise and competent counselor, answers. The flower intends to demonstrate that they are both created in a providential plan in which animate and inanimate, "breathing and non-breathing," intelligent and speechless beings are bound to glorify God. In a kind of role reversal, the speechless creature becomes eloquent and explains to a supposedly knowledgeable human what their respective positions in the universe are.

Phraseology of a living conversation occurs throughout the verses: "I see what you mean, but please tell me more...," "You are perfectly right, but then..." However, the poem has not the canonical tripartite structure: there is no narrative prologue and the final reconciliation does not derive from a divine verdict but is the flower's invitation to praise God as in a closing doxology. Much more than a Mesopotamian dispute, the text looks like a chain of *robāʿiyāt* that are structured and linked with each other around the rhetorical skeleton of the Persian *so'āl o javāb* (Bausani 1960: 301 and Chalisova 2009) explicitly evoked in the first line: "I will question you and you shall answer me."

Like in *The two Boys and the Teakettle*, the two participants regularly alternate one verse each. Moreover, quatrains consist of four fifteen-syllable lines, with rhyme pattern AABB, in contrast with seven-syllable lines of the classical *soghithā* and the monorhyme verses of late East-Syriac *soghyāthā*.

5 What Does NA Literature Teach Us About the Intercultural Transmission of the Mesopotamian Dispute?

A survey of the ten known NA dialogue and dispute poems suggests cautiousness in dealing with the possible transmission of the Mesopotamian dispute, more or less strictly defined, through cultures, literatures, languages and ages. They show that a number of methodological and critical issues are at stake in drawing vertical and horizontal lines in a possible stemma of the witnesses and that the direction of the transmission must be carefully checked case by case and text by text, even within the very same literary tradition.

The provisional results of this survey can be summarized as follows:

1. In Classical Syriac and Christian NA literatures dispute poems represent a small sub-group in the corpus of liturgical dialogue poems. Dialogues and disputes proper share form (the *soghithā* hymn), contents (Biblical and hagiographical stories, exegetical motifs) and performance arena (the liturgy) and can be regarded as one, flourishing genre in the Syriac tradition.
2. Even though composed in varieties of the same language group (Late Aramaic), Classical or Modern Syriac and Jewish Aramaic dialogue and dispute poems represent quite divergent genres, as regards forms, contents, transmission and functions of the texts.
3. Most NA dialogue and dispute poems are translations or adaptations of Classical Syriac originals, but the vitality of the genre in the modern tongue is certain only in the case of *The Cherub and the Thief*. Other translations may have been asked or selected by German scholars who were active in the collection of NA texts at the end of the 19th century.
4. From the 19th century until now we have plenty of information on the *Sitz im Leben* only of *The Cherub and the Thief*, in the classical language as well as in various NA vernaculars. The spirit and style of the performance have changed over time, from a solemn liturgical setting to theatrical and almost

comical representations. Tradition needs to be dynamic, innovative indeed, to survive. The dynamic aspect of tradition may explain the high degree of variation in the vertical and horizontal transmissions of the Mesopotamian dispute as well as within the individual literatures in which the genre is attested.

5. The dispute of *Cup, Jar and Wineskin* does not belong to the Classical Syriac tradition. It was probably written when Arabo-Persian models were dominant and appealing among Syriac Christians and looks like a contamination of the Persian and Arabic genre of the *munāẓara* with themes inspired by Islamic wine poetry (*ḫamriyyāt*).
6. Two poems preserved only in NA are usually presented in the literature as disputes: *Two Boys and the Teakettle* and *A Man and a Flower.* As a matter of fact, they are dialogue poems of very different contents and come to NA literature from two quite distinct literary traditions. The anonymous *Two Boys and the Teakettle* is a playful song that recalls subjects and mood of late vernacular *munāẓarāt*, as attested in Farsi and many Arabic dialects. *A Man and a Flower* is an authorial series of quatrains of philosophical and theological contents, chained together in a rigid sequence of questions and answers. Form, rhetorical structure and Aristotelian terminology have a clear Persian-Sufi ring.

Appendix[19]

Table 1: Neo-Aramaic Dialogue and Dispute Poems

		Classical Syriac	Neo-Aramaic		
		Editions and translations	**Editions and translations**	**Manuscripts**	
1.	*The Months of the Year*	Brock (1982, 23 and 1985); Ḥoshabba (2002: 195–6) Other mss.: Baghdad Church of the East 6 (1719), 214–6; Baghdad Church of the East 10 (19th cent.?) 226–32;	Lidzbarski (1896: vol. I, 442–5; NA and Arabic transl.) and (1896: vol. 2, 344–7; German transl.); Mengozzi (2019a)		D

19 In the table I list manuscripts of unpublished texts or manuscripts that were not known when the texts were published (column "Editions and translations"). The letters in the rightmost column indicate that the text is a precedence dispute (D) and that at least the classical version has an alphabetic acrostic (A).

Table 1: Neo-Aramaic Dialogue and Dispute Poems *(Continued)*

		Classical Syriac	Neo-Aramaic		
		Editions and translations	**Editions and translations**	**Manuscripts**	
		Trichur 25 (19th-20th cent.?) ff. 86a-b			
2.	*Gold and Wheat*	Brock (1982, 24 and 1985); Ḥoshabba (2002: 197–8); Other mss.: Borgia Sir 33, 256a-7b (15th century); Trichur 25, 86b-7b (19th or 20th century)	Lidzbarski (1896: vol. 1, 447–51; NA and Arabic transl.) and (1896: vol. 2, 348–51; German transl.);		D
3.	*Cup, Jar and Wineskin*	[*Cup and Wine* in Brock (1991 and 2011)]; Ḥoshabba (2002: 218–9); Volpicelli (2013)	Lidzbarski (1896: vol. I, 453–7 [NA and Arabic transl.] and 1896: vol. 2, 353–6 [German transl.])		A D
4.	*Simon Peter, Simon Magus and the Romans*	unpublished text, attributed to Khamis bar Qardaḥe[20]	Mengozzi (2018)	Berlin Sachau 336 (Telkepe, 1883), 89b-91a	D
5.	*The Cherub and the Thief*	Sachau (1896: 195–208); Qelayta (1926: 142–7); Graffin (1967: 481–90; French transl.); Brock (1982, 13 and 1987: 28–35); Pennacchietti (1993); Glenthøj (1994; Engl. transl.); Benyamin (1996: 158–65); Brock (2002)	Sachau (1896: 208–15); NA A (Pennacchietti 1993, with Italian transl.)		A D
			Alichoran (1957: 241–5); NA B (Pennacchietti 1993, with Italian transl.); Alichoran (1957)		
			NA C (Pennacchietti 1993, with Italian transl.) and Poizat (2005; 8 verses)	CCM 00421 (1737), 47v-52r (www.hmml.org) Ir. Dept. no. 30543 (19th cent.?), 2r and 18v (Harrak 2011: 106)	

20 Mss. (http://syriaca.org/work/1255, where the text is entitled Peter and Paul): Vatican Syr. 188, f. 20v-22v; Vatican Borg. Syr. 33, f. 210v-211v; Cambridge Add. 2820, f. 27–29; Cambridge Add. 2041, f. 13–16; Jerusalem Greek Patr Syr. 31, f. 222v-224; Münster, Coll. Ad. Rücker, "Liederhandschrift", p. 36–40 (Rücker 1920).

Table 1: Neo-Aramaic Dialogue and Dispute Poems *(Continued)*

		Classical Syriac	Neo-Aramaic		
		Editions and translations	**Editions and translations**	**Manuscripts**	
				DFM 00387 (end 19th. cent.), p. 139 (Poizat 2013: 97–9)	
6.	*Satan and the Sinful Woman II*	Brock (1988)	Zetterstéen (1906) Mengozzi (2008)		A
7.	*Mary and the Gardener II*	Brock (1983b); Beshara (1988: 66–7; Engl. transl. by Brock); Brock (2010: 146–7; 2011: 70–5; Engl. transl.)	Mengozzi (2019b)	Berlin Sachau 336 (Telkepe, 1883), 91b-92b	
8.	*Mary and the Magi*	Lamy (1882: I, col. 129–44); Feldman (1896, I); Gwynn (1898: 287–9; Engl. transl. by A.E. Johnston); Mingana (1905, III); Efrem, Christmas Hymns (*Soghitha* IV; Beck 1959); Patriarchal Press (1970: I, 98–104); Brock (1982, 8); Beshara (1988: 85–8; Engl. transl. by Brock); Brock (2006; 2010: 139–45; 2011: 49–68; Engl. transl.);		DFM 00295 (20th cent.), 2 ff	A
9.	*Two Boys and the Teakettle*		*Kokḇā* (Urmia) 24 November 1909 (Yaure 1957, with Engl. transl.)		
10.	*A Man and a Flower*		*Ḥujådå* (Södertälje, Sweden) 7 August 1984, 48–9		

Bibliography

Alichoran. Francis Y. 1957. *Nuhrā d-'almā*. Kirkuk: Maṭba'thā d-Ninwē.

Bausani, Alessandro. 1960. Letteratura neopersiana. Pp. 149–875 in *Storia della letteratura persiana*, ed. Antonino Pagliaro and Alessandro Bausani. Milano: Nuova Accademia.

Beck, Edmund. 1959. *Des heiligen Ephraem des Syrers Hymnen De Nativitate (Epiphania)*. Corpus Scriptorum Christianorum Orientalium 186–87, Scriptores Syri, 82–83. Leuven: Peeters.

Bellino, Francesca, and Alessandro Mengozzi. 2016. Geographical *'Aǧā'ib* in a Neo-Aramaic Manuscript of the London Sachau Collection. *Le Muséon* 129: 423–56.

Benyamin, Daniel d-Beth. 1996. *Kthāvā d-turgāmē d-ṭaksā da-mshamshānē wa-d-Bim 'am soghyāthā*. Chicago.

Beshara, Ronald N. 1988. *Mary, Ship of Treasures*. New York: Diocese of St. Maron, USA.

Bouriant, Urbain. 1893. *Chansons populaires arabes en dialecte du Caire*. Paris: Leroux.

Brock, Sebastian. P. 1982. *Soghyāthā Mgabyāthā*. Losser: Monastery of St. Ephrem.

Brock, Sebastian. P. 1983a. Dialogue Hymns of the Syriac Churches. *Sobornost. Eastern Churches Review* 5: 35–45.

Brock, Sebastian. P. 1983b. Mary and the Gardener: An East Syrian Dialogue Soghitha for the Resurrection. *Parole de l'Orient* 11: 223–34.

Brock, Sebastian. P. 1984. Syriac Dialogue Poems: Marginalia to a Recent Edition. *Le Muséon* 97: 29–58.

Brock, Sebastian. P. 1985. A Dispute of the Months and Some Related Syriac Texts. *Journal of Semitic Studies* 30: 181–211.

Brock, Sebastian. P. 1987. *Sogiatha. Syriac Dialogue Hymns*. The Syriac Churches Series 11. Kottayam: Jyothi Book House.

Brock, Sebastian. P. 1988. The Sinful Woman and Satan: Two Syriac Dialogue Poems. *Oriens Christianus* 72: 21–62.

Brock, Sebastian. P. 1991. Syriac Dispute Poems: The Various Types. Pp. 91–119 in *Dispute Poems and Dialogues in the Ancient and Mediaeval Near East: Forms and Types of Literary Debates in Semitic and Related Literatures*, ed. Gerrit J. Reinink and Herman L. J. Vanstiphout. Leuven: Peeters.

Brock, Sebastian. P. 2002. The Dispute between the Cherub and the Thief. *Hugoye* 5/2: 169–93.

Brock, Sebastian. P. 2006. Mary and the Angel, and other Syriac dialogue poems. *Marianum* 68: 117–30.

Brock, Sebastian. P. 2010. *Bride of Light: Hymns on Mary from the Syriac Churches*. Piscataway, NJ: Gorgias Press.

Brock, Sebastian. P. 2011. *Mary and Joseph, and Other Dialogue Poems on Mary*. Texts from Christian Late Antiquity 8. Piscataway, NJ: Gorgias Press.

Brodsky, David. 2014. From Disagreement to Talmudic Discourse: Progymnasmata and the Evolution of a Rabbinic Genre. Pp. 173–231 in *Rabbinic Traditions between Palestine and Babylonia*, ed. Ronit Nikolsky and Tal Ilan. Leiden: Brill.

Butts, Aaron. M. 2017. Assyrian Christians. Pp. 599–610 in *A Companion to Assyria*, ed. Eckart Frahm. Hoboken, NJ: John Wiley & Sons.

Chalisova, Natalia. 2009. Rhetorical Figures. *Encyclopaedia Iranica* [www.iranicaonline.org/articles/rhetorical-figures; last visit June 2018].

Chilton, Bruce. 1982. A Comparative Study of Synoptic Development: The Dispute between Cain and Abel in the Palestinian Targums and the Beelzebul Controversy in the Gospels. *Journal of Biblical Literature* 101: 553–62.
Dehqan, Mustafa. 2016a. A Kurdish Garshuni Version of Mem û Zîn. *Gerdûn* 11: 5–10.
Dehqan, Mustafa. 2016b. Sachau 204: A Kurdish Garshuni Poem. *Manuscripta Orientalia* 22: 68–70.
Feldmann, Franz. 1896. *Syrische Wechsellieder von Narses*. Leipzig: Harrassowitz.
Glenthøj, Johannes B. 1994. The Cross and Paradise – The Robber and the Cherub in Dialogue. Pp. 60–77 in *In the Last Days: On Jewish and Christian Apocalyptic and its Period*, ed. Knud Jeppesen, Kirsten Nielsen and Bent Rosendal. Aarhus: Aarhus University Press.
Graffin, François. 1967. La soghitha du chérubin et du larron. *L'Orient Syrien* 12: 481–90.
Grelot, Pierre. 1958. Un poème de saint Éphrem: Satan et la Mort. *L'Orient Syrien* 3: 443–52.
Gwynn, John. 1898. *Selections Translated into English from the Hymns and Homilies of Ephraim the Syrian*. A Select Library of Nicene and Post Nicene Fathers II.13. New York: The Christian Literature Company.
Harrak, Amir. 2011. *Catalogue of Syriac and Garshuni Manuscripts. Manuscripts Owned by the Iraqi Department of Antiquities and Heritage*. Corpus Scriptorum Christianorum Orientalium 639, Subsidia 126. Leuven: Peeters.
Hayward, C.T. Robert. 2013. The Aramaic Song of the Lamb (The Dialogue between David and Goliath). Pp. 272–86 in *Old Testament Pseudepigrapha. More Noncanonical Scriptures*, vol. 1, ed. Richard Bauckham, James Davila, Alex Panayotov, and James H. Charlesworth. Grand Rapids, MI: Eerdmans.
Holes, Clive D. 1995. The Rat and the Ship's Captain: a dialogue poem from the Gulf, with some comments on the social and literary-historical background of the genre. Pp. 101–20 in *Dialectologia Arabica: A Collection of Articles in Honour of the Sixtieth Birthday of Professor Heikki Palva*. Studia Orientalia 75. Helsinki: Finnish Oriental Society.
Holes, Clive D. 1996. The Dispute of Coffee and Tea: a debate-poem from the Gulf. Pp. 302–15 in *Tradition and Modernity in Arabic Language and Literature*, ed. J.R. Smart. London: Curzon Press.
Holes, Clive D. 1998. The Debate of Pearl-Diving and Oil Wells: a poetic commentary on socio-economic change in the Gulf of the 1930s. *Arabic and Middle Eastern Literatures* 1: 87–112.
Ḥoshabba, Shleymun Isho'. 2002. *Khamis bar Qardaḥē. Mêmrē w-mushḥāthā*. Dohuk: Prisāthā da-Nṣibin.
Houtman, Alberdina and Harry Sysling. 2009. *Alternative Targum Traditions: The Use of Variant Readings for the Study in Origin and History of Targum Jonathan*. Studies in the Aramaic Interpretation of Scripture 9. Leiden: Brill.
Jiménez, Enrique. 2017. *The Babylonian Disputation Poems. With Editions of the Series of the Poplar, Palm and Vine, the Series of the Spider, and the Story of the Poor, Forlorn Wren*. Culture and History of the Ancient Near East 87. Leiden: Brill.
Kim, Ronald. 2008. Stammbaum or Continuum? The Subgrouping of Modern Aramaic Dialects Reconsidered. *Journal of the American Oriental Society* 128: 505–31.
Klein, Michael L. 1980. *The Fragment-Targums of the Pentateuch: According to their extant sources*. Analecta Biblica 76. Rome: Biblical Institute Press.

Klein, Michael L.1986. *Genizah Manuscripts of Palestinian Targum to the Pentateuch.* Cincinnati: Hebrew Union College.
Lamy, Thomas Joseph. 1882. *Sancti Ephraem Syri Hymni et sermones*, vol. 1. Malines: H. Dessain.
Lidzbarski, Mark. 1896. *Die neu-aramäische Handschriften der Königlichen Bibliothek zu Berlin.* Weimar: Emil Felber.
Lieber, Laura Suzanne. 2018. *Jewish Aramaic Poetry from Late Antiquity. Translations and Commentaries.* Cambridge Genizah Studies Series 8. Leiden: Brill.
Littmann, Enno. 1951. Neuarabische Streitgedichte. Pp. 26–66 in *Festschrift zur Feier des Zweihundertjährigen Bestehens der Akademie der Wissenschaften in Göttingen*, II Philologisch-historische Klasse. Berlin: Springer.
Martin, François. 1899. Homélie de Narsès sur les trois docteurs nestoriens. *Journal Asiatique*, IXe série, 14: 446–92.
Massé, Henri. 1961. Du genre littéraire "Débat" en arabe et en persan. *Cahiers de Civilisation Médiévale* 4: 137–47.
Mengozzi, Alessandro. 1999. The Neo-Aramaic Manuscripts of the British Library: Notes on the Study of the Durıkyātā as a Neo-Syriac Genre. *Le Muséon* 112: 459–94.
Mengozzi, Alessandro. 2002. *A Story in a Truthful Language: Religious Poems in Vernacular Syriac by Israel of Alqosh and Joseph of Telkepe (North Iraq, 17th century).* Corpus Scriptorum Christianorum Orientalium 590, Scriptores Syri 231. Leuven: Peeters.
Mengozzi, Alessandro. 2006. La versione neoaramaica di un inno siriaco per Natale. Pp. 489–98 in *Loquentes linguis. Studi linguistici e orientali in onore di Fabrizio A. Pennacchietti*, ed. Pier Giorgio Borbone, Alessandro Mengozzi and Mauro Tosco. Wiesbaden: Harrassowitz.
Mengozzi, Alessandro. 2008. A Neo-Aramaic Version of the Soghitha of the Sinful Woman and Satan. Pp. 405–19 in *Malphono w-Rabo d-Malphone. Studies in Honor of Sebastian P. Brock*, ed. George Kiraz, 405–19. Piscataway, NJ: Gorgias Press.
Mengozzi, Alessandro. 2011. Religious Poetry in Vernacular Syriac from Northern Iraq. Pp. v-xxiv in *Religious Poetry in Vernacular Syriac from Northern Iraq (17th-20th Centuries). An Anthology*, ed. Alessandro Mengozzi. Corpus Scriptorum Christianorum Orienalium 628, Scriptores Syri 241. Leuven: Peeters.
Mengozzi, Alessandro. 2015. The Book of Khamis bar Qardaḥe: History of the Text, Genres and Research Perspectives. Pp. 415–36 in *Syriac Encounters. Papers from the Sixth North American Syriac Symposium, Duke University, 26–29 June 2011*, ed. Maria Doerfler, Emanuel Fiano, Kyle Smith. Eastern Christian Studies 20. Leuven: Peeters.
Mengozzi, Alessandro. 2016. Foglie di fico, spine di rovo e cedri del Libano. Piante silenti e dialoganti nella Bibbia e dintorni. *Kervan* 20: 63–79.
Mengozzi, Alessandro. 2018. Simon Magus and Simon Peter in Rome. The Sureth Version of a Late East-Syriac Hymn for the Commemoration of Saints Peter and Paul. *Kervan* 22: 65–90.
Mengozzi, Alessandro. 2019a. The Sureth Dispute of the Months and its East-Syriac Vorlage. *Hugoye* 22.2: 319–344.
Mengozzi, Alessandro. 2019b. A Sureth Version of the East-Syriac Dialogue Poem of Mary and the Gardener. *Kervan* 23: 155–74.
Mengozzi, Alessandro. Forthcoming. D'Ahiqar au tapis volant du roi Salomon, des mirabilia géographiques à Sindbad le marin en araméen moderne: adab et recherche orientaliste

à la fin du XIXème siècle. In *Actes du colloque international " L'adab, toujours recommencé: Origines, transmission et métamorphoses " (Paris, IISMM et INALCO, Jeudi 1er -Samedi 3 décembre 2016)*, ed. Francesca Bellino, Catherine Mayeur-Jaouen, and Luca Patrizi.
Mengozzi, Alessandro and Luca Basilio Ricossa. 2013. The Cherub and the Thief on YouTube: An Eastern Christian Liturgical Drama and the Vitality of the Mesopotamian Dispute. *Annali dell'Istituto Orientale di Napoli* 73: 49–65.
Mingana, Alphonse. 1905. *Narsai Doctoris Syri Homiliae et Carmina*, vol. II. Mosul: Typis Fratrum Praedicatorum.
Münz-Manor, Ophir. 2010. Liturgical Poetry in the Late Antique Near East. A Comparative Approach. *Journal of Ancient Judaism* 1: 336–61.
Murray, Robert. 1995. Aramaic and Syriac Dispute-Poems and their Connections. Pp. 157–87 in *Studia Aramaica: New Sources and New Approaches*, ed. J. Greenfield, M. Geller, and M. Weitzman. Oxford: Oxford University Press.
Murre-van den Berg, H.L. 2015. *Scribes and Scriptures. The Church of the East in the Eastern Ottoman Provinces (1500–1850).* Eastern Chrstian Studies 21. Leuven: Peeters.
Nöldeke, Theodor. 1882. Recension über A. Socin, *Die neu-aramäischen Dialekte* ... . *Zeitschrift der deutschen morgenländischen Gesellschaft* 36: 669–82.
Oraham, Lexander Joseph. 1943. *Dictionary of the stabilized and enriched Assyrian language and English.* Chicago: Consolidated Press (Assyrian Press of America).
Patriarchal Press. 1970. *Homilies of Mar Narsai*, 2 voll. San Francisco, CA: Patriarchal Press.
Pennacchietti, Fabrizio A. 1993. *Il ladrone e il cherubino. Dramma liturgico cristiano orientale in siriaco e neoaramaico.* Torino: Silvio Zamorani.
Poizat, Bruno. 2005. Un manuscrit retrouvé du P. Jacques Rhéthoré. Pp. 413–23 in *Studi afroasiatici*, ed. Alessandro Mengozzi. Milano: FrancoAngeli.
Poizat, Bruno. 2013. *Jacques Rhétoré. La versification en soureth (araméen contemporain).* Corpus Scriptorum Christianorum Orientalium 647, Subsidia 131. Leuven: Peeters.
Pritula, Anton. 2016. 'O Ringodove! Where are You Heading For?' A Syriac Dialogue Poem of the late 13th Century. Pp. 351–60 in *Syrische Studien. Beiträge zum 8.Deutschen Syrologie-Symposiumin Salzburg 2014*, edited by Dietmar W. Winkler. Wien: Lit Verlag.
Qelayta, Yawsep d-Beth 1926. *Turgāmē w-ṭaksē da-mshamshānuthā w-soghyāthā.* Mosul.
Rand, Michael. 2012. An Aramaic Dispute between the Months by Sahlan ben Avraham. *Melilah: Manchester Journal of Jewish Studies* 9: 101–13.
Reinink, Gerrit J., and Herman L.J. Vanstiphout (eds.). 1991. *Dispute Poems and Dialogues in the Ancient and Mediaeval Near East.* Orientalia Lovaniensia Analecta 42. Leuven: Peeters.
Rodrigues Pereira, Alphons S. 1997. *Studies in Aramaic Poetry (c. 1000 B.C.E. – c. 600 C.E.).* Studia semitica neerlandica 37. Assen: Van Gorcum.
Rücker, Adolf. 1920. Über einige nestorianische Liederhandschriften, vornehmlich der griech. Patriarchatsbibliothek in Jerusalem. *Oriens christianus* 9: 121–23.
Sachau, Eduard. 1896. Über die Poesie in der Volksprache der Nestorianer. *Sitzungsberichte der königlich-preussischen Ak. der W. zu Berlin* XI.8: 179–215.
Sachau, Eduard.1899. *Verzeichniss der syrischen Handschriften der Koniglichen Bibliothek zur Berlin.* Berlin: A. Asher & Co.
Smelik. Willem F. 1995. *The Targum of Judges.* Old Testament Studies 36. Leiden: Brill.

Tardieu, Michel. 2011. Le collectage de la tradition orale du Tûr ʻAbdîn par Prym et Socin (1869). Pp. 11–28 in *L'orientalisme, les orientalistes et l'Empire ottoman de la fin du XVIIIe siècle à la fin du XXe siècle*, ed. Sophie Basch, Pierre Chuvin, Michel Espagne, Nora Seni, and Jean Leclant. Paris: Académie des Inscriptions et Belles Lettres.

Taylor, David G.K. 2010. "Your sweet saliva is the living wine": Drink, desire, and devotion in the thirteenth-century Syriac wine songs of Khamis bar Qardaḥe. Pp. 31–52 in ed. Herman Teule and Carmen Fotescu Tauwinkl. Eastern Christian Studies 9. Leuven: Peeters.

Volpicelli, Monica. 2013. *Poesie sul vino di Khamis bar Qardahe (XIII secolo): analisi linguistica e filologica.* MA Thesis, University of Turin.

Wagner, Mark. 2005. The Debate Between Coffee and Qāt in Yemeni Literature. *Middle Eastern Literatures* 8: 121–49.

Wilmshurst, David. 2000. *The Ecclesiastical Organisation of the Church of the East. 1318–1913.* Corpus Scriptorum Christianorum Orientalium 582, Subsidia 104. Leuven: Peeters.

Yahalom, Joseph, and Michael Sokoloff. 1999. *Shirat Bne Maʻarava. Aramaic Poems from the Land of Israel in the Byzantine Period* [in Hebrew]. Jerusalem: Israel Academy of Sciences and Humanities.

Yaure, Lazarus. 1957. A Poem in the Neo-Aramaic Dialect of Urmia. *Journal of Near Eastern Studies* 16: 73–87.

Zetterstéen, Karl V. 1906. Ein geistliches Wechsellied in Fellīḥī. Pp. 497–50 in *Orientalische Studien. Theodor Nöldeke zum siebzigsten Geburtstag (2 März 1906) gewidmet von Freunden und Schülern*, vol. 1, ed. Carl Bezold. Gieszen: Töpelmann.

Clive Holes*

22 Modern Vernacular Disputation Poems from Bahrain and the Wider Gulf

Speculations on Their Origin

1 Vernacular Disputation Poems from the Periphery of Arabia

In the first section of this chapter I will outline the structure and topoi of the modern Gulf vernacular disputation poem – the GDP for short – including examples from southern Iraq, which, from the point of view of its Arabic dialects and popular culture, forms part historically of the same area, and also (in passing) from Yemen, with which the Gulf also has ancient demographic and linguistic links. The GDP is composed in an 'artistic' register of local dialectal Arabic, that is, not in everyday Gulf speech and not in Classical Arabic either, but somewhere between the two. But since the language and style of the GDP is not the focus of attention in this section of the chapter, the illustrative poetic extracts quoted below are in my published English translations.[1]

The second and longer section of this chapter discusses the cultural context of this type of poetry, based on what we know about the demographic and cultural history of the Gulf littoral and neighbouring regions. The objective is to show that the poets who composed GDPs come from communities which share three characteristics: (1) they still speak, or must have spoken, Arabic dialects of one specific type; (2) their communities historically led a 'sedentary' life of farming, fishing and cottage industries, not a 'nomadic' one of animal husbandry; and (3) they still observe certain popular religious practices which the evidence suggests are pre-Islamic in origin. None of these characteristics are shared with the Arabs of central Arabia.

In Arabic, the GDP is variously termed *munāẓara*, *mufākhara*, *mubāraza*, *muḥāwara* and *muqārana* in Arabic, all pattern III verbal nouns which have overlapping meanings involving the comparing, disputing, and vaunting of the merits of one thing over another. I have collected around twenty examples over the

* University of Oxford.

1 Interested readers can find the transliterated Arabic texts in the references cited.

https://doi.org/10.1515/9781501510274-022

last 40 years, all composed by poets who live near or on the Eastern Arabian seaboard, from southern Iraq in the north, down through Bahrain, Qatar, the UAE, and the Sultanate of Oman. The tradition is also found in South Yemen in the south-west corner of Arabia. The disputation poem in the form it exists in the Gulf seems to be largely absent from the so-called *nabaṭī* tradition of Bedouin tribal poetry[2] whose epicentre has always been Najd, and which is sharply different in its diction, motifs and societal functions. The GDPs I'll be dealing with here were mainly collected from cheap, locally printed anthologies of popular Arabic literature, bought *in situ* in Bahrain, Qatar, the UAE and Oman, and in a couple of cases directly from the mouths of the poets.

For the modern period, the oldest disputation poems we have from this region date from the late 17th century CE and are attributed to the Yemeni Jewish poet Shalom Shibzi. The ones I'll be referencing in this chapter are more recent, all composed between c. 1930 and the late 1950s. The most recent example I have is from the late 1970s and is by the UAE poet Sulṭān al-Zaʕābi who was born in 1956. This, of course, proves nothing about how old GDPs in vernacular Arabic may be. Before the 1920s, literacy was rare even among the upper echelons of Gulf society, and it took until the mid-1970s for it to become the norm among the general population. In any case, the GDP was originally probably part of an orate culture, not a literate one, and composed in a language register close to ordinary speech; *ipso facto* it was considered inferior to work in the Classical language, and not worth preserving.

The range of poetic combatants in the GDP, and I include here Iraq, is broad. Here are some of the examples I have collected, with their places of composition:

Inanimate
Coffee v Tea (Bahrain; Qatar)
Coffee v Tobacco (Bahrain)
Clay Pipe (= the old-fashioned way of smoking) v the Cigarette (= the new way) (Iraq).
Summer v Winter (Iraq; Bahrain; Oman)
Pearl-Diving v Oil-Wells (Bahrain)
Date-stone (used as animal feed) v Date (human food) (Oman)
Rest v Fatigue (Iraq)
Present v Past (Oman)

Animals
Lion v Ox (Iraq)

2 Examples do exist in the Bedouin tradition, but seem to be few and limited to particular common dyads, such as coffee and tobacco. They may be the product of contact with sedentary populations.

Human
Indian v Briton (UAE)
Pale-Skinned Girl v Brown-Skinned Girl (Iraq)

Mix of human and non-human
Rat v Ship's Captain (Bahrain)
Farmer v Barley (Iraq)
Coat v its Owner (Bahrain)
Poet v Mosquito (Bahrain)
Poet v Congregational Mosque in Ṣūr (Oman)

More than two contestants
The Four Colours (of silk) (Bahrain)

Structurally, the GDP is usually tri-partite. It starts with a scene-setting opening in which the combatants appear before the poet, who is typically lying in bed and unable to sleep. They enter arguing, sometimes one chasing the other, and then turn to the poet, inviting him to adjudicate as to which of them is the most beautiful, the most fruitful, the most useful, the tastiest, or some other relevant parameter. The poet reluctantly accepts the invitation, and declares that he will see fair play and announce the winner at the end. A typical opening is from the *Disputation of Pearl-diving and Oil-wells* (Holes 1998: 95) composed in about 1935:

'Bahrain today has wells of oil, they bubble boil and spout,
The pearl industry has had its day; its fire has quite gone out!
Midnight struck with me awake, and my thoughts wandering far,
When suddenly a doe-eyed maid, fair-skinned, Canopus' star,
Burst in on me, unveiled, revealed, tears pouring down her face,
A lad– no less beside himself – to this young maid gave chase.
"Look here!" said I, "Don't tell me please, whatever fix you're in,
Don't bother me, I'm all confused, my mind is in a spin!
From where've you come? And why to me (I mumbled with a sigh)
I'm feeling quite bewildered and my cares you multiply."'

Part two, the disputation proper, then begins, with boast, insult, charge and counter-charge furiously exchanged by the antagonists, often until things reach the point of a battle (*maˁraka*). Here is an extract from *Conversation between a Rat and a Ship's Captain* (Holes 1995: 114–15) in which the Rat has taken up residence in a trading boat laid up for the winter months on the shore. After the Captain complains to the poet about him, the Rat is summoned to account publicly for his actions:

The Captain:
"What's brought thee 'ere?" the Captain said, "Just pack thy bags and quit!
My store was choc-a-bloc with rice – now every bag thou'st split!
Dost thou not know that t'price these days 'as reached sixteen Rupees?!
Thou'st buggered up our careful plans – bang goes our life of ease!
Me clouts 'ave all got teeth marks in, me jacket's gnawed right through,
Get off me boat, go one, buzz off, find summat else to chew!
Look, why not take a stroll on t'beach? Thou'rt bound to find canoes,
If pleasing me is thy desire, well, test a few, and choose!"

The Rat:
"Why leave a place like this?" said Rat, "My belly I can fill,
Drink water cold, eat t'food in t'hold, and pick t'best bits at will!
Sometimes rice, sometimes tea, sometimes sugar sweet,
P'raps a bit o' pudding too, a really tasty treat!
Were I to leave thy jolly-boat, jump ship upon a whim,
Why all o't'town would know for sure that I was pretty dim!
By heck, they'd not be wrong, 'n' all, if they thought I'd gone nuts,
I'd be a laughing-stock to folk – there'd be no 'ifs' or 'buts'!

And so the disputation proceeds, often with threats of violence and retribution. But, in all the poems, and just in the nick of time, the poet steps in to announce part three of the proceedings, in which he calls a halt to the dispute, outlawing the threatened fisticuffs, and finally delivering his verdict (*ḥukm*) like a judge in a courtroom. In the *Disputation of Pearl-diving and Oil-wells*, the poet rules as follows:

'I said to them, "Be quiet now, and no more clever quips!
If judgement's what you want from me, well listen, read my lips!
No more will I allow you two, if you think you've been wronged,
To answer back – your worth's now clear, your weak points and your strong.
As for pearling, yes it's true, his wealth's no parallel,
We've never seen the like of it in cities where folk dwell.
We've witnessed ragged vagabonds become rich trading men,
But by and by they stumble, fall, and end up poor again.
We hope that these unfortunates can rise up strong once more,
Return the untold wealth they've lost, investors' cash restore.
But oil, today the victory's yours, you've won here fair and square,
You've launched a war on poverty, at which all folk despair.
Your glory days stretch out ahead, with you flows time and tide,
The unemployed queue up to work – select your men with pride!"' (Holes 1998: 104)

A key feature is that the verdict (*ḥukm*) often includes a section, sometimes separately labelled and sometimes not, in which the poet, or some *deus ex machina*, reconciles the combatants, often in amusing and innovative ways. This is called *ṣulḥ* 'truce', or even *ṣulḥ wa zawāǧ* 'truce and marriage'. Thus although Oil-wells is declared the victor at the conclusion of the *Disputation of Pearl-diving and Oil-wells*, as it observably was in the contemporary Gulf economy of the 1930s, the poet tells the two combatants to shake hands and make up, and depicts them in the final verses of the poem happily driving away together in a motor car, the oil-powered futuristic symbol of the world the Gulf States were just beginning to enter. But there are other variations on this theme. In the Bahraini *Disputation of Summer and Winter*, composed, the poet tells us, after the scorching summer of 1950, it is another season, Spring, that pops up unexpectedly at the very end of the poem to strip each contender of his 'weapons' – Summer of his 'heat like red-hot embers' and Winter of his 'freezing snow'– and use each to neutralise the other, declaring himself, Spring, to be 'the ruler of you both' (*šēkhkum*) and the winner of the disputation because of his 'flowers, soft breezes and delicious fruits'. In the Iraqi disputation between the same two combatants, it is Autumn that suddenly appears to perform a similar function.

What of the societal functions of the GDP? Although jocular in tone, with many puns, clever allusions and jokes, it often rehearses a current social or political issue of its time, or sometimes makes a general moral point, what the Arabs call a *ḥikma*. The Bahraini *Disputation of Coffee and Tea* (Holes 1996) for example, is not only about the differing pleasures of tea and coffee as drinks, but about two rival ethnicities. 'Coffee', a black, bitter drink, stands for the dark-skinned, rough mannered but perennially hospitable Arabs of the Gulf; 'Tea', agate-coloured and sweet, with its samovars, imported crockery, and alien social rituals, stands both for the pale-skinned tea-drinking Persians who have for millennia been a highly visible element in the coastal population of the Arab side of the Gulf, as well as the Europeans and Americans who arrived much more recently with the advent of the oil-industry. In this disputation, as in the Summer v Winter one, the poet declines to award either victory but reconciles them by sipping alternate cups of tea and coffee – a practice I witnessed myself in Bahrain in the 1970s when doing field-work with fishermen – ingeniously 'marrying them' on his tongue. This is typical of the genre: the underlying 'message' of the GDP is one of 'live and let live'.

2 'Peripheral Arabia' as a Cultural, Linguistic and Religious Unit

It should be clear from the above that the GDP shares a lot with much older disputations from Mesopotamia both in terms of its structure and (perhaps) the commentary it provides on the society that produced it. The question is, is this similarity merely a coincidence, or does the GDP stand at the end of a direct line of descent from the Sumerian, Akkadian, Aramaic/ Syriac and Arabic forebears which succeeded each other in the neighbouring geographical space of southern Iraq? There is some evidence –linguistic and cultural – that it may be: enough, I think, to make a direct connection with the Mesopotamian disputations plausible. There is certainly no reason to assume that the GDP is just a late development of the Classical Arabic disputation poem. The traditional view that 'everything came from Classical Arabic' has been debunked both by evidence from recent Arabian epigraphy and by the work of Arabic dialectologists. We know that graffiti in Arabic were being carved on rocks at least 700 years before the invention, if I can call it that, by Iraqi grammarians of Classical Arabic, even if we are never likely to know the structure of those ancient dialects in any detail. The first word that we can positively identify as Arabic is much older than even these graffiti, and appears in a monumental cuneiform inscription dating to 853 BCE. It is 'Gindibu' the name of an Arab chieftain defeated by the Assyrians in battle, and an Arabic word still in use today in the form *ǧundub* 'grasshopper'. Bedouin naming practices which use the flora and fauna of the desert, of which this seems to be an obvious example, were still the norm as late as the 1920s when the Czech anthropologist Alois Musil published his celebrated ethnographic study of Rwala Bedouin of the Syrian Desert (Musil 1928). If Arabic as a spoken language is far, far older than the written records we have for it, there is no reason to assume *a priori* anything different in regard to forms of Arabic verbal art.

3 Language

Let's now take a look at the *linguistic* evidence for an ancient Gulf link with Mesopotamia:

The Arabic dialects of eastern, south-eastern and southern Arabia show evidence of a long-standing historical stratification that, much later, took on social significance. Three dialectal layers can be distinguished which date back to different periods, though they are now less distinct in some Gulf locations than in others because of social factors. Chief among these has been the differential impact of population movements over the last 1500 years: pulses of Bedouin migration from central Arabia to the coast occurred periodically, largely for economic reasons, but the geographical impact of these was uneven. The last major movement occurred in the mid-18th century and had a major effect on the demography of Bahrain and Qatar. This incomer population and its dialects have gradually supplanted the oldest dialectal layer. Another factor in dialect change has been intermarriage between the co-religionist groups which formed the other two layers. I will label these dialect layers 'B', 'A1', and 'A2' in descending order of their age, but will focus here on the oldest one, the 'B' layer, still spoken in the communities that produced all the poets who composed the GDPs I have been exemplifying.

These typologically 'B' dialects are spoken by 'sedentary' farming and fishing communities in eastern Saudi Arabia, the Shīˁa villages of Bahrain, the coastal regions of the UAE, the mountainous and riverine areas of Northern Oman and parts of southern Yemen. The ethnic origins of the speakers of the 'B' dialects are diverse: it has been claimed that one major element of the 'B' dialect communities, the so-called Baḥārna, who are found not only in Bahrain but the whole length of the Gulf, are (Serjeant 1968: 488) 'descended from converts from the original population of Christian (Aramaeans?), Jews, and Majūs inhabiting the coastal provinces of eastern Arabia at the time of the Arab conquest'. When I questioned them about this in the 1970s, 'B' dialect speakers themselves claimed a rather more tribally respectable descent from the Azd and ˁAbd al-Qays, Arab tribes of Yemeni origin which migrated to the coast of eastern Arabian by no later than the beginning of the 7th century. Whatever the truth of these claims, what is striking to an Arabic dialectologist is that the 'B' dialects form a broken chain around the periphery of Arabia from southern Iraq to southern Yemen, and, despite the large distances which separate the 'links' in this chain, show an extraordinary degree of structural similarity with one another. This is strongly suggestive of an ancient common origin. It will be remembered that the poetic tradition of which the GDP is an element is found in exactly these (now physically separated but uncannily similar) 'dialect islands'. As a group, these 'B' dialects of Bahrain, eastern Saudi Arabia, the UAE, Oman and Yemen are quite distinct from those spoken by other Gulf communities descended from the more recently arrived (18th century CE) central Arabian Bedouin, what I call the'A2' group, but also from the much older 'A1' group whose forebears have always been based in the coastal regions on both sides of the Gulf, but, unlike the 'B' layer of the population, were mainly engaged in maritime trade within the Gulf and outside it.

The 'B' dialects seem ultimately to be of ancient Yemeni origin, and probably spread eastwards into Oman and up the Gulf coast via migrations which were pre- or early Islamic. But one of the most remarkable things they share linguistically, and which took several years of fruitless searches of the Classical Arabic lexica to make clear, is that a large number of the terms they use for farming and fishing implements and activities, basket types, building materials, crops, and other everyday objects and events are not of Yemeni or even of Arabic origin at all: many of them turned out to have close cognates in Akkadian and/or Aramaic. This might have been expected in Iraqi Arabic dialects, but the distributional profile of these items down the Gulf coastline as far south as Oman came as a surprise. I have listed below around thirty examples (cf. Holes 2016: 12–18), together with their cognates in other Semitic languages, and a note of the Gulf locations where they were in common use when I was doing fieldwork in the mid-1970s.

Table 1: Agriculture–related lexis

Akk.[3]/Aram.	meaning	Arabic	meaning	Attested in
Akk. *ikkaru*[4]	'farmer, ploughman'	*ʕakkār*	'palm-tree cultivator'	Bah, I
Akk. *xaṣṣinnu*, Aram. *xaṣṣīna*	'axe, hatchet; field tool for clearing shrubs, bushes'[5]	(a) *ṣaxxīn* (b) *xaṣīn*	(a) 'hoe/spade for digging and clearing weeds'; (b) 'axe, hatchet'	(a) Bas, Bah, Kuwait, U; (b) U, O
Akk. *gidimmu*	'shovel for digging out irrigation channels'[6]	*gaddūm*	'pick-axe; type of shovel'	K, I, Bah
Akk. *nīru*, Aram. *nîrâ*[7]	'yoke (for ploughing animals)'; 'cross-beam'	*nīr/ nīra*	same meanings (in Bahrain 'cross-beam on a loom')	Bah, I
(a) Akk. *sekēru*; (b) Akk. *sikru*, Aram. *sikərā*	(a) 'to block off, dam up (a water channel); (b) 'dam, barrage'	(a) *sakkar*[8] (b) *skār*	(a) 'to block off a water channel' (b) 'material for blocking channels'	Bah, SY
Akk. *Palgu*, Aram. *plg*?[9]	'ditch, canal (usually for irrigation)'	*falağ/ falay/ falag*	'irrigation channel'	Bah, U, O
Akk. *šuṣû*, Aram. *šīṣā*	'poor quality dates'	*šīṣ*	same meaning	Bah, SI

3 The main reference works consulted were the *Assyrian Dictionary of the University of Chicago*; Black, George and Postgate 2000; and lexicographical studies by Armas Salonen.
4 The Akkadian form is itself a borrowing from Sumerian, *engār*, with the same meaning. See also Kaufman 1974: 85 and Salonen 1950: 405.
5 Salonen 1968: 150. See also Kaufman 1974: 54.
6 Salonen 1968: 132.
7 See Kaufman 1974: 77–78.
8 Landberg 1920–1942: 1956 says on the use of this term in south Yemen that it is 'without doubt an Aramaic borrowing'.
9 See Kaufman 1974: 79.

Table 1: Agriculture–related lexis *(Continued)*

Akk.[3]/Aram.	**meaning**	**Arabic**	**meaning**	**Attested in**
Akk. *angāšu*	'plum'	*ʕangēš/ ʕangāš*	'edible pulp of lotus fruit'	Bah, I[10]
Akk. *xassū*[11], Aram. *xassā*	'lettuce'	*xass/ xast*	same meaning	Bah, I
Akk. *sumundû/ šumuttu* (Sum. *sumun-dar*)[12]	'beetroot'	*šuwandar*	same meaning	Bah, I
Akk. *liptu*, Aram. *lafta*[13]	'turnip'	*lift*	same meaning	Bah, I
Akk. *silqu*, Aram. *silqā*	'mangold'	*silg*	'chard'	Bah, I
Akk. *xurpū*	'early crop'	*harfi*	'fresh, young (meat); early (crop)'	Bah, I
Akk. *gidlu/ gidil*	'plait (of onions), plaited string'	*giḏla/ gidla*	'plait, fringe, forelock'	Bah, SI
Akk. *xēpû*	'to break up clods of earth'	*xaff*	same meaning	Bah

In these tables: Bah = Bahrain; Bas =Basra; I= Iraq; K= Kuwait; O= Oman; SI = Southern Iraq; SY= South Yemen; U = United Arab Emirates; WG = Whole Gulf

Table 2: Sea-faring and fishing-related lexis

Akk. *sikkānu*	'rudder, steering paddle'	*sukkān*	same meaning	WG
Akk. *xinnu*[14]	'ship's cabin'	*xinn*	'ship's hold'	Bah, K, U

10 In the Christian Baghdadi dialect the meaning of *ʕanǧāṣ* is 'plum', as in the Akkadian cognate. See Thompson 1949: 307 and Landsberger 1966: 258 n. 52.

11 See Kogan 2012:253.

12 See Thompson 1949: 50.

13 See Thompson 1949: 51.

14 See Kaufman 1974: 56.

Akk. *ṭebû*[15], Aram. *ṭabaʕ*	'to sink (of a ship)'	*ṭabaʕ*	'to sink, run aground (of a ship)'	WG
Akk. *gigurru*	'reed basket'	*gargūr*[16]	'bee-hive fish-trap' (= a basket made of woven palm sticks, and turned upside down[17])	Bah, U
Akk. *bâru*	'to catch (fish, birds)'	*bāra*	'to collect fish from a fish-trap; hunt, search (the sea-bed for pearls)'	Bah, K, U

Table 3: General lexis

Akk. *šulum šamši*	'sun-set'	*slūm iš-šams*	same meaning	I, Bah, U, O
Akk. *kalakku*[18], Syr, *klkʾ*[19]	'metal box'	*kalak*	'metal bucket; box-shaped metal brazier '	Bah, U
Akk. *quppu*,[20] *qappatu*	'box, basket made of reeds'	*guffa*	'palm-leaf basket or pot'	Bah, SI
Akk. *zabbīlu*, Aram. *zəbīlā*[21]	'basket'	*zabīl/ zan-bīl/ zambīl*	'large oval-shaped palm-leaf basket with handles'	I, WG
Akk. /Aram. *qapīru*[22]	'container for fish/ dates'	*gafīr/ ğifīr*	'palm-leaf basket'	Bah, K, U
Akk. *burû*, Aram. *būriyā*	'reed mat'	*bāri* pl *bawāri*	'reeds (used as a building material)'	Bah, SI
Akk. *manû*	'unit of dry weight'	*mann* pl *amnān*	'unit of dry weight' (cf. Eng. *maund*)	I, WG
Akk. *šurānu*, Aram. *sinnawr*	'(domestic) cat'	*sannūr*	same meaning	I, (parts of) Bah[23]

15 The Semitic pharyngeal consonants disappeared in all positions in Akkadian.
16 *gargūr* < *gigurru* via dissimilation.
17 This was the original method of construction; by the 1970s, wire-mesh was used instead of palm-stick lattice work.
18 This word also means 'raft' in Akkadian, still its normal sense in Iraqi Arabic.
19 See Kaufman 1974: 61.
20 See Kaufman 1974: 86.
21 See Kaufman 1974: 111.
22 See Abraham and Sokoloff 2011: 46.
23 In Bahrain this is a Baḥārna-only word; the ʕArab of Bahrain use *gaṭu* (ultimately < Latin *cattus*).

Akk. *nadānu* Aram. *natan*	'to give'	*naṭa*	same meaning	I, (parts of) Bah[24]
Akk. *dalāxu*	'to muddy, stir up'	*dallax*	'to discolour, render turbid, muddy'	Bah, U
Akk. *abāru*	'to bind tightly (limbs)'	*habbar*	'to bind (broken limbs)'	O
Akk. *rabāšum*	'protest'	*rabša*	'commotion, tumult'	Bah, O

Some of these cognates are very striking, and I will pick out a couple here. First, the phrase *sulūm iš-šams* 'sunset' used by Gulf farmers, fishermen, and other members of traditional Gulf societies to mark the end of the working day. I also recorded the associated verb *silim* in phrases like *lēn silmat iš-šams...* 'when the sun had set...' and the participial form *silmān* as in *iš-šams silmāna* 'the sun is setting'. To my knowledge this verb with this meaning occurs in no other Arabic dialect, and is also absent from Classical Arabic. After years of searching for its origin, I had a eureka moment one day when thumbing through the *Chicago Dictionary of Assyriology.* I discovered that *sulūm iš-šams* 'sunset' has an exact structural and semantic cognate in the Akkadian phrase *šulum šamši.* As far as I know, a cognate phrase does not exist in Old Aramaic, though I would love to be told I am wrong by someone more knowledgeable than me. So, could this phrase have passed directly from Akkadian into the ancient Gulf Arabic dialects, and if so how? Three possibilities suggest themselves: (1) it was an ancient contact-induced borrowing; (2) it was a shared Semitic lexeme, which the mediaeval Arab lexicographers failed to record; (3) it was a linguistic 'left-over'– a substrate element from a time when some variety of Akkadian was still a vernacular language in the Gulf region. Whatever the answer, the elemental nature of what it denotes suggests that this must be an old expression. After this serendipitous discovery, the flood gates opened, and I found the source of many other puzzling words was probably the same. A second example is the verb used by Bahraini farmers for closing off an irrigation channel and redirecting the water flow: *sakkar,* and the thing, usually a clod of earth or a ball of rags, used to do this: *skār.* These words also have direct Mesopotamian cognates: Akkadian *sekēru* with Gulf *sakkar* 'to dam or block a water channel', and Akkadian *sikru* and Aramaic *sikərā*, nouns which mean the same as Gulf *skār*, 'water channel blocker'. By contrast, the root *s-k-r* in Classical Arabic has to do with intoxication, not with irrigation. The only other Arabic dialects I know of in which the

24 Used only in a small number of Baḥārna villages; all the ˤArab and most Baḥārna have *ˤaṭa*.

s-k-r root occurs with its Gulf meaning of 'to close off' are, significantly, those of Lebanon and Syria, where it has long been known that there is an Aramaic/ Syriac substrate.

So my theory is this: the oldest layer of the Gulf coastal population was formed over several centuries from a fusion of the early mixed population of Christians, Jews and Zoroastrians mentioned by Serjeant, with later, but still pre-Islamic, migrants from southern Arabia. In support of this theory, the Arab historians record the disparaging opinion of the early Muslim conquerors on the population of Bahrain, which at that time meant the Gulf seaboard roughly from Basra down to the Qatar peninsula, not just the eponymous archipelago of today. They described the people they found there as *nabīṭ* or *anbāṭ*, a somewhat slighting appellation by which they meant farmers who did not speak Arabic like they did, and who were likely speakers of Aramaic, like the pre-conquest farmers of the Mesopotamian *sawād*, or alluvium, who the conquering Arabs also generically referred to as *nabīṭ*.[25] Christianity had been widely practiced in the Gulf region for about three centuries before the conquest, and we know that the Christian bishops of the two Gulf dioceses, Qatrāya and Mazūnāya, corresponded among themselves and with the Catholicos on the other side of the Gulf in Syriac. What languages the ordinary Gulf population spoke we don't know, but there are a number of old settlements in Bahrain whose names are clearly of Aramaic/Syriac origin: *Dēr*, *Māḥūz* and *Galālī* being examples, and we know from the work of Beaucamp and Robin that in pre-Islamic Bahrain Christianity was widely practiced and its sacraments respected even at the humblest of social levels: the pearl-divers (Beaucamp and Robin 1983). The type and distributional profile of the Gulf's lexical links with Mesopotamia shouldn't come as a surprise, as in antiquity the region was subject to Babylonian political control and cultural influence for many centuries. Could then the modern Gulf disputation poem, like the everyday vocabulary I have just exemplified, have been another vestige of Mesopotamian culture which has continued on into the modern world? And what other Mesopotamian cultural legacies might there be which might also lend credence to this suggestion?

---

25 An intriguing reference to this occurs in the 13th century Arabic dictionary *Lisān al-ˁArab* under the lemma *n-b-ṭ*, in which a saying is attributed to a certain Ayyūb b. Qiriyya: '... the people of Bahrain are Nabateans (*Nabīṭ*) who have been Arabized (*istaˁrabū*)'.

4 Popular (Religious) Rituals

However much they are portrayed locally as having an Islamic origin and meaning, there are a number of Gulf-wide religious practices which clearly do not. Once again, like the vocabulary we have just been talking about, their distributional profile is suggestive, as they occur in all the states of the modern Gulf but not in the Arabian interior. There is only space here to describe one such: termed variously *ḥiyya biyya* (in Bahrain and Qatar), *ḍahiyya* (southern Iraq and Kuwait), and *dōxala* (eastern Saudi Arabia).[26]

This ritual was performed over the first ten days of the pilgrimage month of Dhū al-Ḥijja. Young girls planted seeds or pulses in small pots made of palm fibres (*guffa*), filling them with earth, putting them in a dark place and watering them regularly. The seeds or beans rapidly germinate, and by the time of the ˁĪd there is a rich green growth in the plant pots. On the night before the ˁĪd on the 10th day of Dhū al-Ḥijja, the girls of the neighbourhood would walk in procession, followed by their brothers and other boys, down to the sea-shore, or, if they lived inland, to a well or an irrigation channel. There they would whirl the plant pots, suspended by a length of palm-rope, around their heads, singing a ditty as they did so, and fling them into the sea, well, or water channel as the case might be. A Kuwaiti version of the ditty is:

yā ḥiyyati	'O my *ḥiyya*,
yā biyyati	O my *biyya*,
ḥiyya li ummi	A *ḥiyya* for my mother,
ḥiyya li abūyi	A *ḥiyya* for my father,
sabaˁ ḥiyyāt	Seven *ḥiyyas*'.

A Bahraini version is:

ḥiyya biyya,	'*ḥiyya biyya*
rāḥat ḥiyya wa yāt biyya	A *ḥiyya* has gone, and brought me back
ˁala darb l-iḥnēniyya	On the path of Ḥnēniyya.
ˁaššēnāk u ġaddēnāk	We fed you lunch and fed you dinner,
wa lēlat il-ˁīd lā tiddaˁīn ˁalayya	So on the night before the *ˁĪd*, don't make accusations against me!
ḥallilīna w ibray ḏimmati	Absolve me and exonerate me!
maˁa s-salāma, yā ḥiyyati!	Good-bye, my *ḥiyya*!

26 See Holes (2004) for a more detailed account.

The girls would then return home. The official gloss put on this is that it is a children's version of the Islamic sacrifice ritual which concludes the pilgrimage. But that begs several questions. Why must the plant-pot and its contents be *thrown into water?* Why must the throwers be *girls?* And what does the word *ḥiyya* actually mean? The usual answer to the last question is that it is the local pronunciation of the Classical Arabic word *ḥiǧǧa* 'pilgrimage', as throughout the Gulf etymological *ǧīm* is pronounced as a palatal glide, so *ḥiǧǧa* becomes *ḥiyya*. But the ditty the girls sing has them saying 'a *ḥiyya* for me (*biyya)*' and then 'a *ḥiyya* for my father' and 'a *ḥiyya* for my mother', 'seven *ḥiyya*s'. It is true that the pilgrimage involves a seven-fold circumambulation of the Kaʕba, but *ḥiyya* supposedly means a complete 'pilgrimage' not just a 'circumambulation' (which is *ṭawāf*) and the girls plainly use the word *ḥiyya* to refer to *the plant* they have grown and are sacrificing 'for me', 'for my father' and 'for my mother'. But if we look beyond Classical Arabic, *ḥiǧǧa/ḥiyya* has another entirely separate dialectal meaning, as Landberg pointed out a century ago: '*chose, objet, affaire*' ('thing, object, matter') (Landberg 1920 – 1942: 355). So if that local dialectal meaning is the correct interpretation, what might this ritual signify, and where did it come from?

In Drower (1956: 41) we read:

> 'In the countries bordering the Mediterranean the Adonis-cult inspired the making of 'gardens of Adonis', grain forced into temporary growth in receptacles which were later thrown into the sea or river together with images of the god, at the season when women lamented the 'youth untimely slain', a season which also commemorated his yearly revival. When I was in Sicily many years ago, I saw in the churches during Holy Week beds of sand, sometimes coloured, upon which were set pots of wheat forced into pale growth by being grown in cellars. These were called sepolcri and on Holy Thursday the figure of Christ was lifted from the crucifix and laid upon them.'

Sir James Frazer, in his description of the Adonis ritual, which he states originated in western Asia, claims that it is 'the best proof that Adonis was a deity of vegetation', noting that the sowing of wheat, barley, lettuces, flowers, etc in baskets filled with earth was 'chiefly or exclusively the preserve of women' (Frazer 1995: 337). He interprets the ritual as charms to promote the growth or revival of vegetation by a process of homoeopathic or imitative magic: by mimicking the growth of crops, the women hope to ensure a good harvest, and by throwing the dead 'gardens of Adonis' into water, they hope to secure a supply of fertilising rain.

Coming closer geographically to the Gulf, Lauterbach writes at length on the practice and origins of the Babylonian Jewish custom of Tashlik (lit. 'Thou Shalt

Throw'), describing one version of it as follows, based on Rashi's (11th century) commentary on the Babylonian Talmud:

> 'About two or three weeks before Rosh Hashanah (Jewish New Year) they make baskets from the leaves of the palm-tree and fill them with earth and manure. For every young boy or girl in the house they make such a basket into which they sow Egyptian beans, or other kinds of beans or peas. They call it *farfisa*, "propitio." On the day before New Year's Day each person takes his or her basket, turns it around his or her head seven times, saying: "This is for this (evidently pointing to the basket and to himself or herself), this is to be in exchange for me, this is to be my substitute," and then he or she throws the basket into the river.' (Lauterbach 1951: 370)

These descriptions closely match the modern Gulf practice of ḥiyya biyya, right down to the seven-fold whirling of the plant pots round the thrower's head, and the ditty that is sung with it. It looks as if, down the ages, what started as a fertility cult in ancient Greece and the Levant was later reinterpreted in the popular Judaic practice of southern Iraq as a repentance and atonement ritual in which the devil, who was believed to reside in water, was propitiated with a sacrifice instead of him taking the sinners themselves. This is in fact quite similar to the meaning of the traditional Islamic pilgrimage and sacrifice: it too is kaffāra ʕan iḏ-ḏunūb 'atonement for sins'. But it seems that it is the Babylonian Jewish reinvention of the Adonis cult described in the Talmud, considerably older than the Islamic Pilgrimage, which most closely resembles the Gulf version in the detail of its performance and quite probably (to judge from the words of the ditties) in its meaning. Of course, the Bahraini women who described this custom to me in the 1970s had no idea of its significance; it was simply something every girl of their generation learnt to do. Consonant with the modern tendency to 'Disneyfy' Gulf heritage, the TV stations now dress the little girls up in national costume and get them to swing their ḥiyyas to and fro in time before the cameras as they chant the ditty that 'this ḥiyya is for me, and 'this ḥiyya is for my father' and so on. They would have us believe that what we are watching is an age-old children's version of the Hajj sacrifice. This explanation imposes a cosy and politically convenient Islamic patina on its origin, but it is probably far from the historical truth of how it arose.

In conclusion, I hope I have shown that anthropological 'digging' into the dialectal vocabulary of the Gulf's traditional material culture and into the history of its popular customs can provide suggestive evidence of its links with ancient Mesopotamian societies, languages and cultures. This is what makes me think that modern Gulf disputations like Pearl-Diving v Oil-Wells, and Tea v Coffee may indeed be the descended from ancient Akkadian ones like Tamarisk v Palm-Tree. But of course no-one will ever be able prove it, and the evidence for it will remain circumstantial, not direct. Allahu ˀaˁlam, as the Arabs say – God knows best!

Bibliography

Abraham, Kathleen, and Michael Sokoloff. 2011. Aramaic Loanwords in Akkadian – A Reassessment of the Proposals. *Archiv für Orientforschung* 52, 22–76.

Beaucamp, Joëlle and Christian Robin. 1983. L'évêché nestorien de Masmāhīğ dans l'Archipel d'al-Baḥrayn. Pp. 171–196 in *Dilmun: New Studies in the Archaeology of Bahrain*, ed. Dan Potts. Berlin.

Black, Jeremy, Andrew R. George, and Nicholas Postgate (eds.). 2000. *A Concise Dictionary of Akkadian*. Harrassowitz: Wiesbaden.

Drower, Ethel S. 1956. *Water into Wine: a Study of Ritual Idiom in the Middle East*. London: John Murray.

Frazer, James G. 1995. *The Golden Bough (Abridged Edition)*. Touchstone: London.

Holes, Clive. 1995. The Rat and the Ship's Captain: a dialogue poem (*muḥāwara*) from the Gulf, with some comments on the social and literary-historical background of the genre, *Studia Orientalia* 75: 101–120.

Holes, Clive. 1996. The Dispute of Coffee and Tea: a debate-poem from the Gulf. Pp. 302–15 in *Tradition and Modernity in Arabic Language and Literature*, ed. Jack Smart. Curzon Press: London.

Holes, Clive. 1998. The Debate of Pearl-Diving and Oil Wells: a poetic commentary on socio-economic change in the Gulf of the 1930s, *Arabic and Middle Eastern Literatures* 1/1: 87–112.

Holes, Clive. 2004. Arabian Gulf *ḥiyya biyya*, Jewish Babylonian *farfisa*, Christian Sicilian *sepolcri:* popular customs with a common origin? *Journal of Semitic Studies* 49/2: 275–287.

Holes, Clive. 2016. *Dialect, Culture and Society in Eastern Arabia. Vol III: Phonology, Morphology, Syntax, Style*. Leiden: Brill.

Kaufman, Stephen A. 1974. *The Akkadian Influences on Aramaic*. Chicago: University of Chicago.

Kogan, Leonid. 2012. Les noms de plantes akkadiens dans leur contexte sémitique. Pp. 229–267 in *Language and Nature: Papers Presented to John Huehnergard on the Occasion of His 60th Birthday*, ed. Rebecca Hasselbach and Na'ama Pat-El. Chicago: The Oriental Institute.

Landberg, Le Comte. De. 1920–42. *Glossaire Dathînois*. Leiden: Brill.

Landsberger, Benno. 1964/1966. Einige unerkannt gebliebene oder verkannte Nomina des Akkadischen, *Welt des Orients* 3: 48–79 and 246–268.

Lauterbach, Jacob Z. 1951. *Rabbinic Essays*. Cincinnati: Hebrew Union College Press.

Musil, Alois. 1928. *Manners and Customs of the Rwala Bedouins*. New York: American Geographical Society.

Roth, Martha T. et al (eds.) 1956–2010 *Assyrian Dictionary of the Oriental Institute of the University of Chicago*. Chicago: University of Chicago.

Salonen, Armas. 1950. Akkadian Lexicography, *Orientalia* 19: 404–407.

Salonen, Armas. 1968. *Agricultura Mesopotamica nach Sumerisch-Akkadischen Quellen.* Helsinki: Suomalainen Tiedeakatemia.

Serjeant, Robert B. 1968. Fisher-folk and fish-traps in al-Bahrain, *Bulletin of the School of Oriental and African Studies* 31: 486 – 514.

Thompson, Reginald C. 1949. *A Dictionary of Assyrian Botany.* London: The British Academy.

Section V **Other Traditions of Disputations**

John A. Chaney*

23 Ludic Disputations in the East-Asian Cultural Sphere

An Overview

1 Introduction

In this research, I will mainly focus on ludic disputations, which are totally fictional works, leaving out the political ones, which are reality-based narratives.[1] Starting with the *Disputation of Tea and Alcohol* (*Chajiulun*), I will show that this work is part of an existing Chinese tradition. I will then compare the Chinese examples to what we find in Vietnamese, Korean, and Japanese literature, in order to highlight both the similarities and differences.[2] My research does not claim to be exhaustive, as reading all Chinese, Vietnamese, Korean, and Japanese literature is clearly an impossible task.

2 Previous Research

Ludic disputations have received little attention from scholars. The majority of them have been studied primarily for their content rather than for their structure and form. For example, scholars studying the tea culture in China often make reference to the *Disputation of Tea and Alcohol*, and the *Disputation of Sake and Rice* (*Shuhanron*) is usually used to examine the religious and social context of early 16th century Japan.[3] For Japan, I refer to Ichiko's study (1955: 347–77) which speaks of "tales of disputation" (*ronsō-mono*) but without defining a specific category in his discussion of the stories featuring non-humans (*irui-shōset-*

* ESTAS, UNIGE / IAO, ENS de Lyon. I would like to thank Dr. Emmert Clevenstine and Prof. Zhang Ning, for reading draft versions of this article, and my colleagues for having offered advice.

1 The most famous example of a reality-based political disputation is certainly the *Disputation on Salt and Iron* (*Yantielun*), in which some ministers engage in a violent polemic with a group of Confucian scholars. It is an expanded account of the disputation held at the court in 81 BCE.

2 The Vietnamese, Korean, and Japanese texts could be written with Chinese characters or in indigenous scripts, respectively *chữ nôm*, *han'gŭl*, and *kana*.

3 For example, see Benn 2015: 44–53; Watanabe 2009: 259–78.

https://doi.org/10.1515/9781501510274-023

su). Thompson's dissertation (1999: 460 – 548) is very useful, because she discusses and indexes the tales featuring non-humans (*irui-mono*), with a short summary for each of them. Furukawa (1974: 26 – 43) and Watanabe (1976: 53 – 72) are the first to speak of the lineage of the Japanese disputations. Tokuda (1994: 130 – 31) lists some stories under a section entitled "tales of disputation," but these texts are also classified under other sections in the same article. For China, Zhang (2002: 191 – 221) has been interested in the "pattern of vying for glamor" (*zhengqi xing*) and in trying to reconstitute the lineage of the Chinese disputations, and Pan (2002: 95 – 102) has studied the "Novels vying for glamor" (*Zhengqi xiaoshuo*). For Korea, I refer to the study of Yun (1995: 210 – 40) concerning the stories of the type "Plum and Willow vying for spring" (*Maeyu chaeng-ch'un*) and that of Yun (2014: 545 – 75) which compares the prose-poems of the type "Prose-poem on the Three Capitals" (*Samdobu*). For Vietnam, Zhu (2012: 67 – 92) has studied the disputations written in Chinese characters. Although these scholars have sometimes compared the disputations of the different East-Asian countries, only Kim Moonkyong (2005: 42 – 52; 2014: 19 – 40) has studied the lineage of the disputations in East Asia in general, to a limited extent. But as Brisset (2014: 21 n. 33) pointed out: "Il n'existe à l'heure actuelle aucune étude de fond sur ce 'groupe historique' – pour reprendre l'expression de Jauss – constitué par les disputations parodiques."

3 Chinese Disputations

The most famous Chinese ludic disputation is the *Disputation of Tea and Alcohol* by an otherwise unknown poet, Wang Fu, that was found in seven manuscripts in the Buddhist caves near Dunhuang and composed during the Tang dynasty (618 – 907 CE). It is a popular work written in the form of a prose-poem (*fu*)[4] that features a tripartite structure: introduction, disputation, and adjudication. It begins with a brief preamble setting the scene:

> We venture to note thus:
> "After Shennong[5] had tasted the hundred herbs, the Five Grains were classified.[6] After Xua-

4 *Fu* is a difficult to define literary genre that is partway between verse and prose. Since it has no exact counterpart in Western literature, many translations exist for this term in English: prose-poem, rhyme-prose, exposition, rhapsody, etc.

5 Shennong, the "Divine Farmer," is a legendary ruler who invented the hoe and the plow and developed agriculture.

6 "Five Grains" is a general expression for all kinds of cereals.

> nyuan[7] had made clothes, he handed down the techniques concerned so as to civilize his posterity. After Cangjie[8] had invented writing, Confucius explained and cultivated the causes of his teachings. [All these histories] cannot be related in detail from the very beginning. However, while summing up the most important points of them, let us pause for a moment and ask Tea and Alcohol which one of you two is meritorious and which one of you two ought to be called the inferior or the superior. Today, each of you must establish your own grounds, and it is for the stronger to describe all his grounds first." (Chen 1961: 277; tr. modified)

After this, the disputation begins. Tea is first to present its arguments:

> Thereupon, the Tea came out, saying:
> "All of you! Don't be clamorous and listen to me a little. I am the chief of the hundred herbs and the heart of the ten thousand plants. In order to honor me, people take my stamens, and, to esteem me, they pick my buds. I am called Mingcao and named Cha.[9] (...) Naturally I am the superior and honorable, and what need is there to say anything else in praise of my merits." (Chen 1961: 277–78; tr. modified)

And Alcohol replies:

> Then Alcohol turned up, saying:
> "What a ridiculous speech! From ancient times till now, tea has been disdained while alcohol has been honored. After a goblet of alcohol had been sprinkled in the river, soldiers of the three forces [of Chu] could all become drunk.[10] When Emperors and Kings drink me, they give their courtiers [the right to speak] without fear. When the various courtiers take me, they shout: 'Long live [the Emperor]!' (...) Naturally I ought to be called the superior, and what need is there to compare me with anything else?" (Chen 1961: 278–79; tr. modified)

Tea and Alcohol continue arguing. Finally, after Tea's last speech, Water intervenes. In this third part, Water does not give a verdict in favor of one of them, but demonstrates its own superiority, and calls for a reconciliation between the two parties:

> While Tea and Alcohol were arguing about [the merits of] each other, they did not realize that Water was standing by their side. Water said to Tea and Alcohol:

---

7 Xuanyuan is the personal name of Huangdi, the "Yellow Emperor," a legendary ruler considered to be the common ancestor of the Chinese people.
8 Cangjie is the legendary scribe of the Yellow Emperor who invented Chinese characters.
9 Mingcao means "Tender Herb," and Cha "Tea." Both are names for tea.
10 This refers to an episode where the King of Chu, wanting to share a cup of alcohol with his army, threw it in the river. After having drunk from its water, the soldiers, thus fortified, defeated their enemies.

> "You two! Don't get excited. Who has given you permission to discuss your merits, to defame each other, and to talk recklessly like this? In one's life, there are only four great things: Earth, Water, Fire, and Wind. If tea had no water, what would be its appearance? If alcohol had no water, what would be its complexion? (...) Even so, I do not call myself the capable and the sainted, so what need is there for both of you to argue about your merits? From now on, you two must be friendly and co-operative, so that wine shops will be prosperous, while tea houses will not be poor. Forever you two are brothers, and it must be so from the very beginning till the very end. And, if people read this text, they would never suffer from being mad with alcohol and tea!" (Chen 1961: 283–84; tr. modified)

This text presents a tripartite structure and stages a disputation between personified non-humans, characteristics quite similar to those of the Near Eastern disputations.[11] Since East Syriac documents were discovered in the Dunhuang caves, we must ask whether this disputation is a scion of the Syriac tradition, or if it is a part of a Chinese tradition that originated independently.[12]

The origin of the prose-poem was already being debated in ancient China.[13] This literary genre seemingly had its origin in the literary tradition of Chu, and emerged in its mature form during the Western Han (206 BCE-8 CE).[14] The first epideictic prose-poems were written by the Han poet Mei Sheng (d. 141 BCE). The most important of them, and the most influential, was the *Seven Stimuli* (*Qifa*), written before 154 BCE.[15] More important than its content is the form in which it was written. The poem is constructed around a dialogue between a prince of Chu, who was suffering from an illness, and a guest from Wu, who asserts that he knows how to cure him. Quite unexpectedly, the guest from Wu does not cure him with a medical treatment, but through the persuasive force of "essential words and marvelous doctrines" (Knechtges and Swanson 1970–1971: 99–100). Knechtges and Chang (2010: 319) have pointed out that: "In 'Qi fa,' the guest tries gradually to rouse the prince's interest through the use of the words. This is very much like the way in which some Warring States traveling persuaders gained the confidence of a ruler." Since the *Seven stimuli* greatly influenced the prose-poem tradition, it makes good sense to say that this tradition

---

11 For a general presentation of the different traditions of disputation, see Jimenez 2017: 125–53.
12 The question has been raised by Jimenez 2017: 137–38.
13 For further details, see Knechtges and Chang 2010: 317–18.
14 The tradition of Chu is mainly represented by the *Verses of Chu* (*Chuci*), a collection of late Warring States period and Han dynasty poems associated the southern state of Chu.
15 For a translation, see Knechtges and Swanson 1970–1971: 106–16.

was closely connected to the art of speech during the Warring States period (453–221 BCE).[16]

Thinking, too, that the prose-poems had a close connection to the rhetorical tradition of the Warring States period, Cai (2008: 60) remarks that these are commonly framed around a disputation between three people with significant names. The most famous example is the *Prose-poem of Sir Vacuous/on the Imperial Park* (*Zixu/Shanglinfu*)[17] by the most-distinguished prose-poem writer Sima Xiangru (179–117 BCE). It begins with a brief preamble, setting the scene:

> When Chu sent Sir Vacuous as an envoy to Qi, the king of Qi mobilized all of his chariots and horsemen and went out to hunt with the envoy. When the hunt was finished, Sir Vacuous went over to boast to Master Improbable. Lord No-such was also present. After everyone was seated, Master Improbable asked: "Was today's hunt enjoyable?" Sir Vacuous replied: "Quite enjoyable." "Was your catch large?" He said: "It was small." "If this is so, then what did you enjoy about it?" Sir Vacuous replied: "I enjoyed the King of Qi's attempt to brag about his multitude of chariots and horsemen, while I replied to him with an account of our Yunmeng Preserve." Master Improbable said, "May I be permitted to hear it?" Sir Vacuous said, "You may." (Xiao 1987: 53)

When the disputation begins, Sir Vacuous (Zixu) first presents a lavish description of the King of Chu's Yunmeng preserve:

> (...) The King of Qi said, "Nevertheless, tell me roughly what you have seen and heard." I replied, "Very well, very well. I have heard that Chu has seven marshes, but I have seen only one of them, and I have never seen the others. What I have seen is only the very smallest of them. Its name is Yunmeng. Yunmeng is nine hundred *li* square. At its center are mountains.
>
> The mountains:
> Twisting and twining, tortuously turning,
> Arch aloft, precipitously piled. (Xiao 1987: 55)

Then, Master Improbable (Wuyou Xiansheng) rebuts him and boasts about the King of Qi's seashore revels:

> Master Improbable said, "How mistaken are your words! Your Excellency does not consider a thousand miles too far to travel, but comes to favor the state of Qi with his presence. The King has mobilized all of the soldiers in his realm and provided a multitude of chariots and

16 For further details on the art of persuasion in the Warring States period, see Graziani 2012: 41–78.

17 The prose-poem was divided into two distinct texts in the *Selections of Refined Literature* (*Wenxuan*), a literary anthology of the sixth century.

> horsemen, and has joined the hunt with the envoy. He has expended his entire effort obtaining a good catch to entertain his company. How can you call this bragging? (...)
>
> Moreover, Qi
> On the east borders the great ocean;
> To its south is Langye.
> Our King inspects Mount Cheng,
> Shoots at Zhifu,
> Sails on the Boxie Gulf,
> And roams the Mengzhu marsh. (Xiao 1987: 69)

Finally, Lord No-such (Wushi Gong), an imperial envoy, criticizes them and describes the Imperial Park:

> Lord No-such grinned and laughed, saying: "Chu has lost its case, but neither has Qi gained anything to its credit. Having the vassal lords present tribute is not for the articles and presents themselves, but is a means for them to report on the administration of their offices. (...) Furthermore, how are the affairs of Qi and Chu worth mentioning? Have you not seen what is truly great and beautiful? Have you alone not heard of the Imperial Park of the Son of Heaven?
>
> To its left is Cangwu,
> To its right is Western Limits;
> Zhe Cinnabar River traverses its south,
> The Purple Gulf intersects its north. (Xiao 1987: 73–75)

Overwhelmed by Lord No-Such's arguments, Sir Vacuous and Master Improbable concede defeat. A description of the losers' physical and psychological condition closes the prose-poem:

> Thereupon, the two gentlemen paled, changed expressions, and seemed dispirited and lost in thought. As they retreated and backed away from the mat, they said: "Your humble servants have been stubborn and uncouth, and ignorant of the prohibitions. Now this day we have received your instruction. We respectfully accept your command." (Xiao 1987: 112–13)

All the later prose-poems featuring a disputation, such as the *Prose-poem on the Three Capitals* (*Sandufu*) by the Western Jin poet Zuo Si (ca. 250–305 CE),[18] present the same characteristics and structure as that of Sima Xiangru. The only difference lies in the number of participants. Sometimes, the prose-poem does not

---

18 The prose-poem describes the capitals of the three states during the Three Kingdoms period and ends with the victory of the Wei capital. The Western Jin Dynasty (265–317 CE) succeeded the Wei Dynasty (220–265 CE), which is considered by tradition to be the legitimate successor. For a translation, see Xiao 1982: 336–477.

feature three people, but only two. In this case, there is no third party, and the second part ("disputation") is then combined with the third ("adjudication"); the arguments of the second disputant surpass those of the first one. An example is the *Prose-poem on the Two Capitals* (*Liangdufu*) by the Eastern Han (25–220 CE) poet Ban Gu (32–92 CE): overwhelmed by the speech of the Eastern Capital host, the Western Capital guest loses all expression and admits his inferiority.[19]

It is worth noting that Benn (2015: 44–45) has pointed out that the *Disputation of Tea and Alcohol* "shares many characteristics with a now somewhat obscure genre of medieval writing known as 'hypothetical discourse' (*shelun*)."[20] The hypothetical discourse, sometimes called "responses to questions" (*duiwen*), whose prototype is the *Response to a Guest's Objections* (*Dakenan*) by the witty writer and court jester of the Western Han Dongfang Shuo (ca. 160–93 BCE), is now considered by most modern scholars to be a type of prose-poem (see Knechtges and Chang 2014: 837).[21] It is framed around an imaginary dialogue between the author, clearly identified by his name, and an imaginary person named "guest" or "retainer" who criticizes him for his lack of success in public life (see Declercq 1998: 3–4). The author must then defend himself against this accusation. Declercq (1998: 44–45) links it to the literature and the art of persuasion from the Warring States period: "To state one's case more effectively by casting it in dialogue form is a technique common to much pre-Qin literature." It seems that the structure around which the *Disputation of Tea and Alcohol* is framed fits in with a Chinese tradition of the art of speech and persuasion dating back to the Warring States period.

The use of personification in Chinese literature is a more delicate question that goes beyond the scope of this research. As Zeitlin (2017: 215) has pointed out, it is generally accepted that "personification is a literary device sparsely used in the Chinese tradition." As we have seen in the prose-poem of Sima Xiangru, Chinese texts prefer to use significant names, a tendency that goes back to the *Zhuangzi*.[22] The best explanation for this phenomenon has been offered by Franke (1974: 23–24): "This is particularly true for the abstract ideas which are in China almost never represented as such in an anthropomorphic way,

19 Ban Gu's prose-poem was written as a rebuttal to the people who desired to move the capital back to Chang'an, the old capital of Western Han. For a translation, see Xiao 1982: 92–179.
20 The hypothetical discourse has been carefully studied by Declercq (1998). The last ones date back to the Jin dynasty (265–420 CE).
21 For a detailed discussion on why the hypothetical discourses are not categorized as prose-poems, see Declercq 1998: 87–92.
22 The *Zhuangzi* is one of the two basic Taoist texts traditionally attributed to Zhuang Zhou (4th c. BCE). This text had a great influence on all subsequent fictive literature.

only indirectly by exemplary figures, either legendary or historical ones. On the other hand, the fact that Chinese family and personal names have inevitably a definite and identifiable meaning has produced a tendency to play with names. All Chinese names are what German philologists call 'redende Namen' [significant names]. Here, then, was a possibility to incarnate and personify ideas and non-human realities by giving them a name, the constituents of which expressed or alluded to the characteristic features or events linked up with the particular ideas or reality." Contrary to the Near Eastern tales, which are overflowing with personified animals or inanimate objects, Chinese tales usually stage humans with significant names or talking humans and dumb animals, and only rarely contain a direct address by an inanimate object (see Idema 2015: 248–50).

For the pre-Tang period, apart from some stories of the *Zhuangzi* and the *Han Feizi*,[23] two of the rare occurrences of talking animals are the *Prose-poem on the Divine Bird* (*Shenwufu*)[24] and the *Prose-poem on the Falcon and the Sparrow* (*Yaoquefu*) by the Three Kingdoms (220–265 CE) poet Cao Zhi (192–232 CE). The first text, found in tomb no. 6 at Yinwan and dated to the first century BCE, is usually seen as a popular example of a prose-poem, in contrast to the traditional prose-poems like those of Sima Xiangru or Zuo Si (see Van Ess 2003: 610). It is interesting that these two texts share many similarities with another popular Tang dynasty prose-poem, found in two versions in the same caves as the *Disputation of Tea and Alcohol*, the *Prose-poem on the Swallow* (*Yanzifu*), which features a court case between a swallow and a sparrow.[25]

Concerning the address by an inanimate object, Chennault (2003: 338 n. 12) remarks that "[t]he possibility of direct address by the objects begins only in the fifth century." This feature appears in a literary subgenre of the Southern dynasties (420–589 CE), called "ode on things," (*yongwu shi*) that developed from a type of prose-poem increasingly common during the Eastern Han called "prose-poem on things" (*yongwu fu*).[26] It seems that, during the Southern dynasties, these odes on things were composed and chanted at banquets during which the guests had to guess the thing described, but the majority of them are now found in the collections of individual poets (see Zeitlin 2017: 210). Fortunately, some complete sets have been preserved, for example, *Together We Write*

23 The *Han Feizi* is a work exposing a theory of state power attributed to Han Fei (ca. 280–233 BCE).

24 For a translation, see Van Ess 2003: 611–18.

25 For a translation of the long version, see Waley 1960: 11–24. For a translation of the short one, see Yang and Yang 1986: 153–61.

26 See Zeitlin 2017: 210; Chang and Owen 2010 (vol. 1): 128–29.

Poems, Each on an Object Seen from Our Seats at the Feast (*Tong yong zuoshang suojian wu*). Here is the poem from the Southern dynasties poet Xie Tiao (464–499 CE) describing a mat:

> I was born at a Dawn and Twilight Pond,
> Where the setting sun shone on my uneven array.
> Flat shoals were covered over by pollia,
> On dark islands selinea wrested place.
> Then you gathered me in time by the skirtful,
> Who raise a gold chalice to the Throne of Jade?
> My only wish is to be swept by your silk gown,
> Don't let a pale dust pile up on me. (Chennault 2003: 340)

In the middle of the ninth century, riddle-tales involving personified inanimate objects appeared (see Allen 2014: 180–94), and it was pointed out by Zeitlin (2017: 210) that one of their literary sources was the ode on things. In addition to that, some pseudo-biographies (see Franke 1974: 23–31) and other parodies (*id.* 1971: 237–51) that gave voice and human identity to objects also emerged during the Tang dynasty. Although the device of personification is said to have been rarely used in Chinese literature, it seems that it was not so unusual in popular works, and it became more and more common from the Southern dynasties onward.

The Chinese ludic disputations are not limited to prose-poems like those of the Han dynasty or the *Disputation of Tea and Alcohol*. We find them in different literary genres, especially from the Tang dynasty. The collection of strange tales (*zhiguai*)[27] *Records of Xiao and Xiang* (*Xiao Xiang lu*), compiled by the otherwise unknown scholar Liu Xiang in the ninth century, contains a disputation between a Buddhist and a Taoist that ends with a woodcutter overwhelming them with his arguments. The collection of anecdotes *Forest of Tang Words* (*Tang yulin*), compiled by the Song scholar Wang Dang in the late eleventh century, relates a discussion between the Tang poet Gu Kuang (ca. 725–814 CE) and a friend of his: the former tells the friend that he dreamed once of a disputation between the mouth, the nose, the eyes, and the eyebrows about their respective places, ending with the eyebrows defeating the other disputants. His friend then realizes that Gu Kuang is joking. In *The Drunken Man's Talk* (*Zuiweng tanlu*), a thirteenth century collection of poetry, jokes, anecdotes, etc., compiled by the otherwise unknown author Luo Ye, a disputation between an ant, a fly, and a mosquito,

27 The "strange tale" refers to a short, simple prose anecdote which incorporates strange and supernatural events, appearing from the fall of the Han dynasty. Sometimes, they are affiliated with a particular teaching like Taoism and Buddhism.

that ends with the mosquito defeating both the others, is found precisely in the section "Humorous quips."[28] Collections of jokes from the Ming dynasty (1368–1644 CE) contain many short disputations. A good example is *Tea and Alcohol vying for pre-eminence*, a very short version of the *Disputation of Tea and Alcohol*, found in the *Expanded Treasury of Laughs* (*Guangxiaofu*) by the great figure of vernacular fiction Feng Menglong (1574–1646 CE).

The oldest preserved collection of vernacular stories (*huaben*)[29] with the title *Stories from the Hall of the Clear and Quiet Mountain* (*Qingping shantang huaben*), edited in the sixteenth century by the book-lover Hong Pian, contains a fragmentary text entitled *Plum and Apricot vying for spring* (*Mei Xing zhengchun*) featuring a disputation between two young ladies about their respective virtues. Its peculiarity is that it ends with their master conciliating them. In his collection of folksongs *Mountain Songs* (*Shange*), Feng Menglong included one entitled *Mrs. Kettle and Lady Bamboo insulting each other,* in which two ladies are conciliated by their husband.[30] A poem by a minor Song poet, Lu Meipo, features a disputation ending with a draw ruled by the poet himself:

> The plum and the snow both vying for spring and neither admitted defeat;
> The poet laid down his brush and gave his verdict:
> The plum must yield to the snow, three-tenths whiter,
> But the snow cannot match a wisp of the plum's scent. (Kim 2014: 22)

The Ming journeyman-editor, writer, and compiler Deng Zhimo (ca. 1570–1630 CE) wrote seven very interesting disputations, named "Novels vying for glamor" by modern scholars:[31] *Flowers and Birds vying for glamor* (*Huaniao zhengqi*), *Mountains and Rivers vying for glamor* (*Shanshui zhengqi*), *Wind and Moon vying for glamor* (*Zhengyue zhengqi*), *Catamites and Prostitutes vying for glamor* (*Tongwan zhengqi*), *Vegetables and Fruits vying for glamor* (*Shuguo zhengqi*), *Plum and Snow vying for glamor* (*Meixue zhengqi*), and *Tea and Alcohol vying for glamor* (*Chajiu zhengqi*). All of them, without exception, adhere to the same structure: argument between the two parties, memorial to a ruler who usually orders them to contest their merits by composing literary works, draw declared

28 For a translation, see Luo 2015: 53–54.
29 The "vernacular story" refers to a short story from the Song (960–1279 CE) to the Qing (1644–1911 CE) dynasties, written in colloquial language.
30 The songs are written in Suzhou dialect. Ōki and Santangelo (2011: x) describe the language used as "vulgar and full of crude expressions or salacious double meanings, offensive terms, and allusions to sexual and erotic behavior."
31 See section 2.

by the ruler. The disputation occupies only the first volume of each of these works. The other volumes consist simply of pieces of writing about the two parties (See Kim 2014: 24–25; Pan 2002: 96). It appears that no writer before or after Deng Zhimo has written this type of disputation, but since this kind of popular work is rarely studied by modern scholars, our knowledge is still limited.[32]

The last context in which disputations are found is the theater. Idema (1985: 20) has already pointed out that the *Disputation of Tea and Alcohol* could have been intended for stage performance. It is true that the first speeches of Tea and Alcohol are introduced by the formula "Thereupon Tea/Alcohol comes out and speaks," but, as Idema (1985: 20–21 n. 2) highlights, the problem is that "Water in his concluding remarks specifically refers to the reading of the text." Good examples of theatrical disputations are two Ming farce plays (*yuanben*).[33] The first, the *Great Peace Entertainment* (*Taiping leshi*) by the Ming playwright Chen Duo (ca. 1488–1521 CE), features a series of disputations between various sellers, for example, between a firewood-seller and a charcoal-seller, mediated by the *mo*, a type of character in Chinese theater. The disputation between the alcohol-seller and the tea-seller is particularly interesting, because it takes up the topic of the *Disputation of Tea and Alcohol.* After the sellers have made their arguments, a peddler enters and confronts them one after the other. The peddler defeats his opponents and, at the end, celebrates his victory (see Idema 1984: 66–67). The second example, *A Noontime Dream in a Garden Grove* (*Yuanlin wumeng*) by the Ming writer and playwright Li Kaixian (1502–1568 CE), features a fisherman who, having found little to choose between the heroines of two novels, dreams of both of them and their maidservants disputing with, and insulting each other, endlessly (Idema 1984: 64–65). Here is an extract from the disputation of the two maidservants:

(Hongniang speaks:)
All your life you've worn tattered shoes.
(Qiugui speaks:)
For years you've been dressed in a threadbare jacket.
(...)
(Hongniang speaks:)
You reek of powder and rouge.
(Qiugui speaks:)

32 See Kim 2014: 25. Other Ming works are entitled "vying for glamor," but none features a disputation.

33 During the Yuan (1271–1368) and Ming dynasties, the farce play designates a short farce presented as an independent entertainment or as an item in a variety show.

You stink of oil and salt, sauce and vinegar.
(Hongniang speaks:)
You're the mainstay of the "breeze and moonlight market."
(Qiugui speaks:)
You're the manager of the skin and meat business. (Idema 1984: 73)

4 Vietnamese Disputations

In Vietnamese literature, we find many texts clearly influenced by Chinese disputations. Three examples illustrate very well their variety. The first is the *Judgment on the Deaf and the Blind* (*Lũng cổ phàn tù*), found in the *Posthumous Manuscript of Thánh Tông* (*Thánh Tông di tảo*), that presents a disputation between a deaf and a blind person that ends with the judgment by the 5th emperor of the Later Lê dynasty (1428 – 1788 CE) Lê Thánh Tông (1442 – 1497 CE, r. 1460 – 1497 CE), passed in favor of the deaf. The second is the *Record of the Discussion of the Two Clan* (*Nhị thị ngẫu đàm kí*), found in *Collected Miscellanies* (*Xuyết thập tạp ký*) by the writer and court official of the Nguyễn dynasty (1802 – 1945 CE) Lý Văn Phức (1785 – 1849 CE), that presents a disputation between a member of the Black Robes clan and one of the Mysterious Female clan which ends in a draw declared by a Blue Collar.[34] The third is the *Old Story of the Spider and the Silkworm* (*Thù tàm cổ truyện*), found in the *Unofficial History* (*Dã sử*), that features a disputation between a spider and a silkworm, ending with the latter overcome by the former's arguments and admitting its defeat. Apart from those disputations written in Chinese characters, we find some in *chữ nôm*. The most famous is *The Quarrel of the Six Beasts* (*Lục súc tranh công*) dated to ca. the 18th-19th century.[35]

The major difference with Chinese disputations is how the disputation ends: contrary to the Chinese examples, which end with the third party overcoming the two disputants or, more rarely, with a judge ruling a draw, the Vietnamese disputations usually end with a judge ruling a draw or passing a judgment in favor of one of them. The ones that preserve the classical Chinese ending are those featuring only two people without a third party. Their structure is reminiscent of the *Prose-poem on the Two Capitals* by Ban Gu.

34 The disputants represent respectively Buddhism, Taoism, and Confucianism.
35 For a translation, see Anonymous 1987: 1 – 92. Nowadays, this work remains popular in Vietnam.

5 Korean Disputations

In Korean literature, the oldest example of a ludic disputation is a Korean adaptation of the *Prose-poem on the Three Capitals* by Zuo Si dated to the Koryŏ dynasty (918–1392 CE). The *Prose-poem on the Three Capitals* (*Samdobu*), found in the *Selections of Refined Literature in Korea* (*Tongmunsŏn*), was written by the writer and poet Ch'oe Cha (1188–1260 CE) during the evacuation of the capital at Kanghwa-do at the beginning of the Mongol invasions.[36] During the Chosŏn dynasty (1392–1897 CE), Yi Mok (1471–1498 CE) and Cho Wŏn (1544–1595 CE) both wrote a *Prose-poem on the Three Capitals* in order to praise Hanyang, the new dynastic capital.

There are other Korean ludic disputations influenced by the Chinese ones. The most prominent are those of the "Plum and Willow vying for spring" type, produced during the Chosŏn dynasty. Their title is, perhaps, an allusion to the first verses of a poem written by the Tang poet Li Bai (701–762 CE):

> Green grass already covers the earth,
> And the willow and the plum contest the spring. (Kim 2014: 37)

In these texts, the disputants argue in front of a judge, usually a ruler, and the debate ends with the judge ruling it a draw, or passing a judgment in favor of one of them (see Yun 1995: 215). These disputations share some similarities with the "Novels vying for glamor" by Deng Zhimo.

The *Disputation of a Woman's Seven Companions* (*Kyujung ch'iru chaengnon ki*), written during the Chosŏn dynasty, is particularly interesting. In the first part of the text, while the lady sleeps, seven objects (a yardstick, a pair of scissors, a needle, blue and pink threads, a thimble, a long-handled iron, and a regular iron) debate about which is the worthiest. The disputation ends when the lady is awoken by the noise, saying in anger: "What merits are you talking about? It is my eyes and hands that make you do what you do. How can you wrangle impudently behind my back and indulge in self-praise?" (Lee 2017: 186). The second part consists of a description of the seven objects' complaint about the remarks made by their mistress.

36 The *Selections of Refined Literature in Korea* is a literary anthology from the fifteenth century. The disputants are a man from Sŏdo, viz. Sŏgyŏng, and one from Bukgyŏng, viz. Kaesŏng, two old capitals of the Koryŏ, who are defeated by the argument of a man from Kangdo, the new capital. The move of the capital was seen as the revitalization of the dynasty.

The major difference with Chinese disputations is in how they end: as in Vietnamese disputations, the Korean examples can conclude with a judgment in favor of one of the two parties.

6 Japanese Disputations

The first Japanese text that shows the clear influence of Chinese ludic disputations is *Indications of the Goals of the Three Teachings* (*Sangō shīki*), written during the Heian period (794–1185 CE) by Kūkai (774–835 CE), scholar, poet, calligrapher, and founder of the Shingon school, one of the major Buddhist schools in Japan. This disputation features the same characteristics as can be found in Chinese ludic disputations, as the preface (dated to 797 CE) shows:

> Here in my writing I should like to propose Tokaku (Hare's Horn) as host, with Kimō (Tortoise Hair) as guest speaker for Confucianism, Kyobu (Nothingness) as spokesman for Taoism, and Kamei-kotsuji (Mendicant X) as representative of Buddhism. These speakers will debate over Shitsuga (Leech's Tusk), the nephew, and admonish him. The work will consist of three parts and be called the *Indications of the Goals of the Three Teachings*. (Hakeda 1972: 103)

Compared to the Chinese examples, this disputation differs on two points. The first is that each of the three parts, entitled "Argument[37] of X," introduces a new disputant with a narrative section. Secondly, each part ends with one party admitting the superiority of the other. It can be summarized in this way:

1. "Argument of Kimō": Kimō presents his arguments to Tokaku and Shitsuga, who admit the superiority of Confucianism.
2. "Argument of Kyobu": Kyobu presents his arguments to Kimō, Tokaku, and Shitsuga, who admit the superiority of Taoism.
3. "Argument of Kamei-Kotsuji": Kamei-Kotsuji presents his arguments to Kimō and the others, who admit the superiority of Buddhism and repent.

Apart from that, as in the Korean and Vietnamese literature, we can find some perfect imitations of Chinese ludic disputations until the end of the Edo period (1603–1867 CE). Two examples are sufficient for demonstrating this Chinese influence. The first is the *Disputation of Sake and Rice*,[38] attributed to the Muroma-

37 The character translated by "argument" is the same as that translated by "disputation," but, since there is only one person in the title, we cannot use the latter translation.
38 For a translation, see Leggeri-Bauer, Brisset, and Béranger 2014: 87–109.

chi (1392–1490 CE) scholar and prolific poet Ichijō Kaneyoshi (or Kanera; 1402–1481 CE), in which Sake and Rice are incarnated as Nagamochi, "Lasting-Long," Director of the Sake-Brewing-Office, and the monk Kōhan, "Rice-Lover" and overcome by Nakahara Nakanari.[39] The second is the *Disputation of Sake and Tea* (*Shucharon*), written by the prelate of the Buddhist Rinzai sect, Ranshuku Sōshū (?-1599 CE) in 1576, in which Sake and Tea are personified as Bōyūkun, "Master Forget Sorrow" and Dekihanshi, "Sir Cleanse Troubles." An idle man defeats both of them with his arguments.[40] In addition, we have a Japanese adaptation by an otherwise unknown Edo poet, Sankō Honshō, of the *Prose-poem on the Three Capitals* (*Santofu*) of Zuo Si.[41]

Contrary to the Vietnamese and Korean disputations, the endings of the Japanese examples correspond to those of the Chinese ones: they all end with the third party defeating the other disputants. It is worth remarking that none feature the device of personification. Instead, all the participants have significant names.

We find some influences from Chinese ludic disputations in the warrior tales (*gunki-mono*), a major genre in medieval Japanese literature.[42] Amongst them, there are some parodic warrior tales featuring non-humans (*irui gunki-mono*) that appeared during the Muromachi period and remained popular during the Edo period. Usually, these texts feature a war initiated by a thwarted love story, or waged to avenge an insult, and end either with both leaders taking the tonsure, with the defeat of one of them, or with a reconciliation of both sides.[43] The best examples are *The Tale of the War of the Crows and the Herons* (*Aro kassen monogatari*), ascribed to Ichijō Kaneyoshi, and the *Tale of the Fish and the Vegetarian Food* (*Shōjin gyorui monogatari*), attributed to Ichijō Ka-

---

39 His name contains the characters for "middle" (*naka*) twice.

40 For a detailed comparison between the Chinese work and this disputation, see Zhang and Zhang 2007: 75–77.

41 The disputants are a man from the capital of the Sesshū province, viz. Osaka, and one from the Imperial Capital, viz. Kyoto, who are defeated by the arguments of a person from the Eastern Capital, viz. Edo. Osaka represents the Toyotomi clan, rival of the Tokugawa, that were eliminated by the latter in 1615 CE. Kyoto was the city where the Emperor, the legitimate leader of Japan, resided during the Edo period. Edo was the seat of the Tokugawa shogunate that actually controlled Japan during the Edo period.

42 The warrior tale deals with warfare, especially with the civil wars of 1156–1221 CE. Usually, they include three parts, which describe the causes of the war, the war itself, and its aftermath. One of the best-known warrior tales is the *Tale of Heike* (*Heike monogatari*) that relates the Genpei War (1180–1185 CE) fought between the Genji, or Minamoto clan, and the Heike, or Taira clan.

43 See Thompson 1999: 270.

neyoshi or Nijō Yoshimoto (1320 – 1388 CE), scholar and poet of the Northern and Southern courts (1333 – 1392 CE). Two of these parodies present an interesting peculiarity: they are entitled "disputation," and the war is the result of a debate about each other's merits. The *Disputation of Sake and Tea* (*Shucharon*) and the *Disputation of Sake and Ricecakes* (*Shuheiron*) are thus halfway between a ludic disputation and a war tale. It is worth noting that both texts end with the reconciliation of the two parties.

Closely connected to the ludic disputation is the poetry contest (*uta-awase*), a unique and complex phenomenon,[44] whose practice began to appear at the court of Uda, the 59th emperor of Japan (867 – 931 CE, r. 887 – 897 CE). Two of them deserve to be mentioned: *The Contest of Dialogue Poems Judged by Mitsune* (*Mitsune han mondō uta-awase*)[45] held around 923 CE and *The Empress's Spring and Autumn Poetry Contest* (*Kōgō gū shunjū uta-awase*) organized by Fujiwara no Hiroko (1036 – 1127 CE), empress-consort of the 70th emperor of Japan Go-Reizei (1025 – 1068 CE, r. 1045 – 1068 CE), in 1056 CE. The first consists of a series of disputations about the relative merits of spring and autumn, summer and winter, and longing and love. Each disputation begins with a poem ending with the phrase "... between X and Y, which is the best" (... X *to* Y *to wa idure masareri*), and every poem concludes with "... X/Y is the best" (... X/Y *wa masareri*) (see Bundy 2006: 3). In the second, the assigned topic was a disputation between spring and autumn, and the ladies of the Left and the Right were dressed to respectively represent the spring and the autumn (see Itō 1991: 5). This topic is reminiscent of a poem from the Nara period (710 – 794 CE) found in the *Man'yōshu*[46] and attributed to Princess Nukata (ca. 630 – 690 CE), one of the most famous female poets of the seventh century, in which she passes judgment in favor of autumn.[47]

A scion of this genre appeared in the twelfth century, the poetry contest with oneself (*jika-awase*). In these, only one person has written the poems of the Right and the Left, and a friend or patron supplied the judgments.[48] As Thomp-

---

44 The typical poetry contest consisted of a confrontation between two teams, the Left and the Right, who had to compose poems on assigned topics, and was organized in rounds. During each round, poems on the same topic were paired, and a judge evaluated them to determine win, lose or draw. At the end, the victorious team was the one who had won the most rounds.

45 Bundy (2006: 3) says that all the poems were likely written by Ōshikōchi no Mitsune (active ca. 890 – 925 CE) himself.

46 The *Man'yōshu* is the oldest and the most revered anthology of Japanese poetry. For a translation of the poem, see Vovin 2017: 66 – 68.

47 Disputations concerning the merits of the seasons, especially spring and autumn, were part of the poets' repertoire in Japan. See Ōtani 2008: 17 – 22.

48 See Brower and Miner 1961: 238, 506; Bundy 2006: 3 – 13.

son (1999: 252) pointed out, this type of poetry contest became "one of the literary sources for the purely fictional poetry contests" that began to appear in the Kamakura period (1185–1333 CE). The earlier form of fictional poetry contest is known as the "poetry contest of artisans" (*shokunin uta-awase*) that features different types of persons representing various professions (Thompson 1999: 253–54). The first one is the *Poetry Contest of Artisans at the Tōhokuin* (*Tōhokuin shokunin uta-awase*) dated to Kamakura. During the Northern and Southern Courts, the *Poetry Contest of Ricecakes and Sake* (*Mochisake uta-awase*) attributed to Nijō Yoshimoto, stages a contest in which people compose poems on rice cakes and sake, according to their preference (see Kim 2014: 34; Thompson 1999: 520). Fictional poetry contests featuring non-humans (*irui uta-awase*) began to appear in the Muromachi period and remained popular until the Edo period. The first one is *The Poetry Contest between the Twelve Animals* (*Jūnirui uta-awase*),[49] in which the contest is the cause of a war (see Saitō 2014: 1–8; Thompson 1999: 258). As the *Poetry Contest of the Furniture* (*Chōdo uta-awase*)[50] by the Muromachi scholar and influential courtier Sanjōnishi Sanetaka (1455–1537 CE) shows, the protagonists can also be inanimate objects.

As in China, some disputations are found in the theater. Some good examples are two *kyōgen*.[51] The first, *The Battle of Fruits and Nuts* (*Komi arasoi*), stages a petty quarrel between a chestnut and a tangerine over the viewing of cherry-blossoms, leading to a war. Before a winner emerges, a strong wind blows the armies away. The second is *The Controversy* (*Shūron*) in which two Buddhist monks, one of the Lotus sect and the other of the Pure Land sect, boast about the superiority of their respective sects.[52] Finally, they end up getting so lost in their arguments that each one uses the formula of the other. These plays continue to be performed today.

7 Conclusion

We have observed that in China there is a tradition of ludic disputations whose origin can be traced back to the rhetorical tradition of the Warring States period. In Chinese literature, the ludic disputation never formed a genre in itself, but is found within different literary genres and registers, especially in popular literature. This tradition has been taken up by other East-Asian countries since the

49 For a translation, see Thompson 1999: 37–106.
50 For a partial translation, see Ito 1991: 352–359.
51 The *kyōgen* is the classical comic theater and the oldest dialogue-based drama in Japan.
52 For a translation, see Sieffert 1979, 1: 246–266.

Tang dynasty at the latest. Usually these countries imitated the Chinese models with slight modifications, especially in how the disputation is resolved. In Japan, the Chinese ludic disputations occasionally merged with a Japanese literary genre, the warrior tale. Furthermore, Japanese literature developed another tradition of ludic disputation that is seemingly found only there: the fictional poetry contest.

This research must be refined, because there are certainly many texts to be found in East-Asian literature, especially in the popular works that are neglected by scholars. For example, in Tibet there is a *Disputation of the Tea and Beer Goddess* (*Ja-chang lha-mo'I bstan-bcos*) that is a Tibetanized version of the Chinese *Disputation of Tea and Alcohol*, and the Buyi people have a story entitled *Tea and Alcohol* (*Cha he jiu*).[53] Other texts closely connected to the ludic disputation, and found in all East-Asian literature, are the court cases involving animals and the dialogues in which the protagonists do not seek to establish which is superior.[54] I hope that my work will contribute towards making this particular aspect of East-Asian literature better known and encourage scholars to study it more in depth in order to better understand its mechanisms.

Bibliography

Allen, Sarah M. 2014. *Shifting Stories: History, Gossip, and Lore in Narratives from Tang Dynasty China*. Harvard-Yenching Institute Monograph Series 95. Cambridge: Harvard University Asia Center.

Anonymous. 1945. *Truyên Trê cóc* [Story of the Catfish and the Frog]. Translated by Văn Lang Bùi. Hanoi: Edition Alexandre de Rhodes.

Anonymous. 1987. *The Quarrel of the six beasts* (Lục súc tranh công). Translated by Huỳnh Sanh Thông. Lạc Việt series 4. New Haven: Council on Southeast Asia Studies, Yale Center for International and Area Studies.

Benn, James A. 2015. *Tea in China: A Religious and Cultural History*. Honolulu: University of Hawai'i Press.

Bon-grong-pa. 1993. *The Dispute Between Tea and Chang (Ja-chang lha-mo'l bstan-bcos)*. Translated by Alexander Fedotov and Sangye Tandar Naga. Dharamsala: Library of Tibetan Works and Archives.

53 See Kim 2014: 28–29; Zhang 2002: 209–217. For a translation of the Tibetan work, see Bon-grong-pa 1993.

54 See Anonymous 1945; Nakae 1984; Idema 2015: 245–289; Spring 1993: 45–48. I have not found real court cases involving animals in Japan, but quite a similar story to the Chinese *Court Case of the Mouse and the Cat* is *The Cat's Story* (*Neko no sōshi*) in which a mouse and a cat complain to a venerable Buddhist monk. For a translation, see Skord 1991: 33–43.

Brisset, Claire-Akiko. La Disputation sur le saké et le riz (Shuhanron emaki): une controverse parodique dans le Japon medieval. *L'Atelier du Centre de recherches historiques* 12: 1–24.
Brower, Robert H., and Earl R. Miner. 1961. *Japanese Court Poetry.* Stanford: Stanford University Press.
Bundy, Roselee. 2006. Solo Poetry Contest as Poetic Self-Portrait: The One-Hundred-Round Contest of Lord Teika's Own Poems: Part One. *Monumenta Nipponica* 61, no. 1: 1–58.
Cai, Zong-qi. 2008. *How to Read Chinese Poetry: A Guided Anthology.* New York: Columbia University Press.
Chang, Kang-i Sun, and Stephen Owen (eds). 2010. *The Cambridge History of Chinese Literature.* 2 vols. Cambridge: Cambridge University Press.
Chen, Tsu-lung. 1961. Note on Wang Fu's Ch'a Chiu Lun. *Sinologica* 6: 271–287.
Chennault, Cynthia L. 2003. Odes on Objects and Patronage in the Early Qi. Pp. 331–398 in *Studies in Early Medieval Chinese Literature and Cultural History, in Honor of Donald Holzman and Richard B. Mather*, ed. Paul W. Kroll and David R. Knechtges. Provo: Tang Studies Society.
Declercq, Dominik. 1998. *Writing against the State: Political Rhetorics in Third & Fourth Century China.* Sinica Leidensia 39. Leiden/New York/Köln: Brill.
Franke, Herbert. 1971. A Note on Parody in Chinese Traditional Literature. *Oriens Extremus* 18/2: 237–251.
Franke, Herbert. 1974. Literary Parody in Traditional Chinese Literature: Descriptive Pseudo-Biographies. *Oriens Extremus* 21/1: 23–31.
Furukawa, Mizumasa. 1974. Shucharon no keifu [The Lineage of the *Disputation of the Sake and the Tea*]. *Fūzoku* 12/3: 26–43
Graziani, Romain. 2012. Rhetoric that Kills, Rhetoric that Heals. *Extrême-Orient Extrême-Occident* 34: 41–78.
Hakeda, Yoshito S. 1972. *Kūkai: major works, translated, with an account of his life and a study of his thought.* New York: Columbia University Press.
Ichiko, Teiji. 1955. *Chūsei shōsetsu no kenkyū* [Research on Medieval Stories]. Tokyo: Tokyo daigaku shuppankai.
Idema, Wilt. 1984. *Yüan-pen* as a Minor Form of Dramatic Literature in the Fifteenth and Sixteenth Centuries. *Chinese Literature: Essays, Articles, Reviews* 6/1–2: 53–75.
Idema, Wilt. 1985. *The Dramatic Oeuvre of Chu Yu-tun (1379–1439).* Sinica Leidensia 16. Leiden: E.J. Brill.
Idema, Wilt. 2015. Animals in Court. *Etudes chinoises* 34/2: 245–289.
Ito, Setsuko. 1991. *An Anthology of Traditional Japanese Poetry Competitions: Uta-awase (913–1815).* Bochum: Brockmeyer.
Jiménez, Enrique. 2017. *The Babylonian Disputation Poems: with Editions of the Series of the Poplar, Palm and Vine, the Series of the Spider, and the Story of the Poor, Forlorn Wren.* Culture and History of the Ancient Near East 87. Leiden/Boston: Brill.
Kim, Moonkyong. 2005. Higashi Ajia no irui-ronsō bungaku [The Disputation featuring Non-humans Literature in East-Asia]. *Bungaku* 6/6: 42–52.
Kim, Moonkyong. 2014. The Lineage of Ludic Literature about Comparative Debates in East Asia. *Acta Asiatica* 107: 19–40.
Knechtges, David R., and Jerry Swanson. 1970–1971. Seven Stimuli for the Prince: The Ch'i-Fa of Mei Ch'eng. *Monumenta Serica* 29: 99–116.

Knechtges, David R., and Taiping Chang (eds). 2010. *Ancient and Early Medieval Chinese Literature: A Reference Guide, Part One.* Handbook of Oriental Studies, Section Four: China 25/1. Leiden/Boston: Brill.
Knechtges, David R., and Taiping Chang (eds). 2014. *Ancient and Early Medieval Chinese Literature: A Reference Guide, Part Two.* Handbook of Oriental Studies, Section Four: China 25/2. Leiden, Boston: Brill.
Lee, Peter H. (ed.). 2017. *An Anthology of Traditional Korean Literature.* Honolulu: University of Hawai'i Press.
Legeri-Bauer, Estelle, Claire-Akiko Brisset, and Véronique Béranger (eds). 2014. *Des mérites comparés du saké et du riz: illustré par un rouleau japonais du XVII*[e] *siècle.* Paris: Diane de Selliers, BnF.
Luo, Ye (comp.). 2015. *The Drunken Man's Talk: Tales from Medieval China.* Translated by Alister D. Inglis. Seattle/London: University of Washington Press.
Nakae, Chōmin. 1984. *A Discourse by Three Drunkards on Government.* Translated by Nobuko Tsukui. New York/Tokyo: Weatherhill.
Ōki, Yasushi, and Paolo Santangelo. 2011. *Shan'ge, the "Mountain Songs": Love Songs in Ming China.* Emotions and States of Mind in East Asia 2. Leiden/Boston: Brill.
Ōtani, Masao. 2008. *Uta to shi no aida: wakan hikaku bungaku ronkō* [Poems written in Japanese and Poems written in Chinese: Comparative studies of Japanese and Chinese Literature]. Tokyo: Iwanami shoten.
Pan, Jianguo. 2002. Ming Deng Zhimo "zhengqi xiaoshuo" tanyuan [A Survey of Deng Zhimo's "Novels vying for Glamor" in the Ming Dynasty]. *Shanghai shifan daxue xuebao (Zhexue shehui kexue ban)* 31/2: 95–102.
Saitō, Maori. 2014. *Irui no uta-awase: Muromachi no kichi to gakugei* [Poetry Contests featuring Non-humans: Wit and Arts of the Muromachi period]. Tokyo: Yoshikawa kōbunkan.
Sieffert, René. 1979. *Nô et Kyôgen.* 2 vols. Paris: Publications orientalistes de France.
Skord, Virginia. 1993. *Tales of Tears and Laughter: Short Fiction of Medieval Japan.* Honolulu: of Hawai'i Press.
Spring, Madeline K. 1993. *Animal allegories in T'ang China.* American Oriental Series 76. New Haven: American Oriental Society.
Thompson, Sarah. 1999. "The War of the Twelve Animals (*Jūnirui kassen emaki*): A Medieval Japanese Illustrated Beast Fable." PhD diss., Columbia University. ProQuest (AAT 9956426).
Tokuda, Kazuo (ed.). 1994. 40 Otogi-zōshi jutsugo-shu [40 collected Terms relating to Otogi-zōshi]. *Kokubungaku: kaishaku to kyōzai no kenkyū* 39/1: 112–131.
Van Ess, Hans. 2003. An Interpretation of the Shen-wu fu in Tomb no. 6 of Yinwan. *Monumenta Serica* 51: 605–628.
Vovin, Alexander. 2017. *Man'yōshū (Book 1).* Leiden/Boston: Brill.
Waley, Arthur. 1960. *Ballads and Stories from Tun-huang.* London: George Allen and Unwin.
Watanabe, Morikuni. 1976. Shucharon to sono shūhen [The *Disputation of the Sake and the Tea* and related matters]. *Ōtsuma joshi daigaku bungakubu kiyō* 8: 53–72.
Watanabe, Takeshi. 2009. Wine, Rice, or Both? Overwriting Sectarian Strife in the Tendai Shuhanron Debate. *Japanese Journal of Religious Studies* 36/2: 259–278.

Xiao, Tong. 1982. *Wen Xuan or Selections of Refined Literature, Volume I: Rhapsodies on Metropolises and Capitals*. Translated by David R. Knechtges. Princeton: Princeton University Press.

Xiao, Tong. 1987. *Wen xuan or Selections of Refined Literature. Volume II: Rhapsodies on Sacrifices, Hunting, Travel, Sightseeing, Palaces and Halls, Rivers and Seas*. Translated by David R. Knechtges. Princeton: Princeton University Press.

Yang, Xianyi, and Gladys Yang. 1986. The Swallow and the Sparrow. *Chinese Literature: Fiction, Poetry, Art* Summer 1986: 153–161.

Yun, Chup'il. 1995. "Maeyu chaengch'un" ryu uŏn ŭi yangshik chŏk t'ŭksŏng [Stylistic Characteristics of the Allegories of the Type "Plum and Willow vying for spring"]. *Minchok munhwa* 18: 210–240.

Yun, Hochin. 2014. Un'gang Cho Wŏn ŭi "Samdobu" yŏngu [Study of Un'gang Cho Wŏn's "Prose-poem on the Three Capitals"]. *Yŏlsang kojŏn yŏn'gu* 40: 545–575.

Zeitlin, Judith T. 2017. The Ghosts of Things. Pp. 205–221 in *Fantômes dans l'Extrême-Orient d'hier et d'aujourd'hui*, vol. 1, ed. Marie Laureillard and Vincent Durand-Dastès. Paris: Presses de l'Inalco.

Zhang, Hongxun. 2002. Dunhuang sufu "Chajiulun" yu "Zhengqi xing" gushi yanjiu [Research on the popular prose-poem "Disputation of the Tea and the Alcohol" of Dunhuang and the story following the "pattern of vying for glamor"]. Pp. 191–221 in *Dunhuang suwenxue yanjiu* [Research on the popular literature of Dunhuang]. Lanzhou: Gansu jiaoyu chubanshe.

Zhang, Hongxun, and Zhen Zhang. 2007. Zhigen yu bianyi: Riben "Shucharon" yu Dunhuang "Chajiulun" de bijiao yanjiu [Root and Variations: Comparative studies of the Japanese "Disputation of Sake and Tea" and "Disputation of Tea and Alcohol" of Dunhuang." Pp. 73–89 in *Zhuanxing qi de Dunhuang xue* [Dunhuang Studies in the Transitional Stage], ed. Liu Jinbao and Tokio Takata. Shanghai: Shanghai guji chubanshe.

Zhu, Fengyu. 2012. Cong Yuenan hanwen xiaoshuo kan zhengqi wenxue zai hanzi wenhua quan de fazhan [Examining the Development of the vying for Glamor Literature in the Chinese-character Cultural Circle from Vietnamese Novels written in Chinese]. *Chengda zhongwen xuebao* 38: 67–92.

Index of Contestants

Abel
– vs Cain 164, 170, 172, 394 – 395
Abraham
– vs Isaac 164, 170
Age cf. Parliament of the Three Ages
Air
– vs Water 182
Ajax
– vs Odysseus 338 – 339
Alcohol
– vs Tea 435 – 438, 441 – 442, 444 – 445, 452
Alcohol–seller
– vs Tea–seller (= Great Peace Entertainment) 445
Alexander
– vs Hector (= Epitaphes d'Hector) 380, 382
Alithia
– vs Pseustis (and Phronesis) 347
Almond cf. Fruits vs Fruits
Angel
– vs Mary 165, 172
– vs Zacharias 165,
Animals cf. Twelve Animals
Ant
– vs Flea 221
– vs Fly 336
– vs Fly and Mosquito 443 – 444
Apple cf. Fruits vs Fruits
Apple Wine
– vs Arak 287 – 293
– vs Bersh 287 – 293
– vs Boza 287 – 293
– vs Cherry Liqueur 287 – 293
– vs Coffee 287 – 293
– vs Hashish 287 – 293
– vs Mead 287 – 293
– vs Müselles 287 – 293
– vs Opium 287 – 293
– vs Tobacco 287 – 293
– vs Wine 287 – 293
Apricot
– vs Mulberry 182
– vs Plum 444
– cf. Fruits vs Fruits
Arab
– vs Persian 5, 244 – 247, 262 – 270, 276 – 278
Arak
– vs Apple Wine 287 – 293
– vs Bersh 287 – 293
– vs Boza 287 – 293
– vs Cherry Liqueur 287 – 293
– vs Coffee 287 – 293
– vs Hashish 287 – 293
– vs Mead 287 – 293
– vs Müselles 287 – 293
– vs Opium 287 – 293
– vs Tobacco 287 – 293
– vs Wine 287 – 293
Arms
– vs Ladies (= Armes et Dames) 381
– vs Letters cf. Sword vs Pen
Arrow
– vs Bow 284
Artisan cf. Contest of Artisans
Ash
– vs Poplar 92 – 95, 98, 152
Assyrian Tree cf. Palm vs Goat
Author (of the text)
– vs Blackbird Chick (= Discourse on Wisdom) 313 – 314, 316
Autumn cf. Winter
Ba
– vs Man 124, 130 – 134
Back
– vs Belly 175
Baker
– vs Cook 339
Ball
– vs Polo Stick 303
Barley
– vs Farmer 417
Beast
– vs Man 302 – 303
– cf. Six Beasts

Bee
– vs Bull 302 – 303
– vs Fish 302 – 303
– vs Hawk 302 – 303
– vs Leopard 302 – 303
– vs Parrot 302 – 303
– vs Snake 200 – 303
Beer
– vs Wine (= Vin et Bière) 106, 115, 122 – 123
Beer Goddess
– vs Tea Goddess 452
Believer
– vs Non–believer 221
Belle Dame sans mercy 374
Belly
– vs Back 175
– vs Feet (= Estomac et Pieds) 107, 113 – 114
– vs Head (= Corps et Tête) 105 – 116, 121, 123
– vs Members (= Membres et Estomac) 114
Beloved
– vs Lover 251
Benjamin
– vs Joseph 165, 172
Bersh
– vs Apple Wine 287 – 293
– vs Arak 287 – 293
– vs Boza 287 – 293
– vs Cherry Liqueur 287 – 293
– vs Coffee 287 – 293
– vs Hashish 287 – 293
– vs Mead 287 – 293
– vs Müselles 287 – 293
– vs Opium 287 – 293
– vs Tobacco 287 – 293
– vs Wine 287 – 293
Bicycle
– vs Donkey 182
Bird
– vs Birds 200, 303
– vs Fish 1 – 2, 11 – 12, 14 – 15, 26 – 28
– vs Flowers 444
– cf. Divine Bird
Black Robes Clan
– vs Mysterious Female Clan 446
Black
– vs Whites 175
Blackbird Chick
– vs Author (of the text) (= Discourse on Wisdom) 313 – 314, 316
Blind
– vs Deaf 446
Boat
– vs Train 182
Body
– vs Head 4
– vs Soul 160, 162 – 164, 172+28, 173, 217, 219 – 224, 261, 310 – 311, 316 – 317, 321 – 325, 327, 354, 375, 378, 380, 385
Bow
– vs Arrow 284
– vs Lance 262, 321
Bowl
– vs Narguile 403
Boys
– vs Girls 175
– (Two) Boys vs Teakettle 402 – 403, 406 – 407, 409
Boza
– vs Apple Wine 287 – 293
– vs Arak 287 – 293
– vs Bersh 287 – 293
– vs Cherry Liqueur 287 – 293
– vs Coffee 287 – 293
– vs Hashish 287 – 293
– vs Mead 287 – 293
– vs Müselles 287 – 293
– vs Opium 287 – 293
– vs Tobacco 287 – 293
– vs Wine 287 – 293
Bramble
– vs Pomegranate 151
Briton
– vs Indian 417
Brown–Skinned Girl
– vs Pale–Skinned Girl 417
Buddhist
– vs Buddhist (= The Controversy) 451
– vs Taoist 443
– vs Taoist and Confucian (= Three Teachings) 448

Bull
– vs Bee 302–303
– vs Fish 302–303
– vs Hawk 302–303
– vs Leopard 302–303
– vs Parrot 302–303
– vs Snake 200–303
Bus
– vs Tram 182
Cain
– vs Abel 164, 170, 172, 394–395
Camel
– vs Horse 182
Candelabra
– vs Chandelier 182
Candle
– vs Censer 304
– vs Moth 305
Capital cf. Three Capitals; cf. Two Capitals
Captain cf. Ship's Captain
Carpenter's Tools 354
Catamites
– vs Prostitutes 444
Cedar
– vs Other trees 150–152
– vs Thistle 148, 153
– vs Wine 171
Censer
– vs Candle 304
Chandelier
– vs Candelabra 182
Charcoal–seller
– vs Firewood–seller (= Great Peace Entertainment) 445
Chastity
– vs Marriage 311
– vs Virginity 311
Cheekdown
– vs Hairlocks on the Temple 182
Cheese
– vs Olives 182
Cherry Liqueur
– vs Apple Wine 287–293
– vs Arak 287–293
– vs Bersh 287–293
– vs Boza 287–293
– vs Coffee 287–293
– vs Hashish 287–293
– vs Mead 287–293
– vs Müselles 287–293
– vs Opium 287–293
– vs Tobacco 287–293
– vs Wine 287–293
Cherry cf. Fruits vs Fruits
Cherub
– vs Thief 5, 168, 171–172, 396–398, 400, 406, 408–409
Chestnut
– vs Tangerine (= Fruits and Nuts) 451
– cf. Fruits vs Fruits
Christ
– vs John the Baptism 166, 172
– vs Mary 376, 400
Christianity
– vs Paganism 347
Church
– vs Sion 170
– vs Synagogue 169–170
Cigarette
– vs Clay Pipe 416
Civet
– vs Musk 175–176
Clan cf. Black Robes Clan and Mysterious Female Clan
Clay Pipe
– vs Cigarette 416
Clergyman
– vs Knight cf. Pen vs Sword
Clerk
– vs Nightingale 358, 366
Coat
– vs its Owner 417
Cock
– vs Dog 175
Cock Chauntecleer
– vs Hen Pertelot 358, 364–367
Coffee
– vs Apple Wine 287–293
– vs Arak 287–293
– vs Bersh 287–293
– vs Boza 287–293
– vs Cherry Liqueur 287–293
– vs Hashish 287–293
– vs Mead 287–293

– vs Müselles 287–293
– vs Opium 287–293
– vs Tea 1, 403, 416, 419, 430
– vs Tobacco 287–293, 416
– vs Wine 287–293
Color
– vs Colors 417
Confucian
– vs Taoist and Buddhist (= Three Teachings) 448
Congregational Mosque in Ṣūr
– vs Poet 417
Content
– vs Discontent (Content et non content) 381–382
Contest of Artisans 451
Contest of Furniture 451
Cook
– vs Baker 339
Copper
– vs Silver 11–12, 14
Cornelian Cherry cf. Fruits vs Fruits
Courtier
– vs Soldier 354
Cross
– vs Virgin (Mary) (= Vierge (Marie) et Croix) 377[+8], 378
Crow
– vs Heron 449
– vs Parrot 296–297
– cf. Birds vs Birds
Cuckoo
– vs Nightingale 358–361, 366
Cucumber cf. Fruits vs Fruits
Cup
– vs Jar and Wineskin 400–402, 407–408
– vs Water-Pipe 248
– vs Wine 161
Cyril
– vs Nestorius 169
Date
– vs Date-stone 416
– vs Water Melon 182, 403
– cf. Fruits vs Fruits
Date-stone
– vs Date 416
Day
– vs Night 4, 191–213, 221, 231–232, 262, 304
Deaf
– vs Blind 446
Death
– vs Life 338
– vs Satan 159, 161, 171
Desire
– vs Intellect 221
Dinar
– vs Dirham 182
Dirham
– vs Dinar 182
Discontent
– vs Content (Content et non content) 381–382
Divine Bird 442
Dog
– vs Cock 175
Donkey
– vs Bicycle 182
– vs Other animals (?) 91, 93–95, 98
Dove
– vs Goat (judged by Ibex) 254–255
Dumuzi
– vs Enkimdu 12–14
Earth
– vs Heaven 182, 250, 261–262, 298, 310–311, 316–321, 323–325, 327
Edubba'a D 35[+8], 36, 38, 41, 43[36], 47, 50–51
Elegy
– vs Tragedy 338
Elena
– vs María 217
Eloquent Peasant 124, 126–130, 133–134
Enkiḫeĝal
– vs Enkitalu (= Dialogue 2) 35[+8], 36–38, 41[30], 42–44, 46, 48–50
Enkimanšum
– vs Ĝirinisa (= Dialogue 3) 35[+8, 9], 36–40, 44–47, 50, 58[3],
Enkimdu
– vs Dumuzi 12–14

Enkitalu
– vs Enkiḫeĝal (= Dialogue 2) 35[+8], 36–38, 41[30], 42–44, 46, 48–50
Enmerkara
– vs Ensukukešdana 12–15
Ensukukešdana
– vs Enmerkara 12–15
Evil
– vs Good (= Bien et mal des dames) 383–384
Ewe
– vs Ezinam 11–12, 14, 16–26, 28, 77–79, 239, 243, 253
Eye
– vs Heart 261
– vs Mouth, Nose, Eyebrows 444
Eyebrows
– vs Eye, Mouth, Nose 444
Ezinam
– vs Ewe 11–12, 14, 16–26, 28, 77–79, 239, 243, 253
Faith
– vs Philosophy 232
Falcon
– vs Sparrow 442
Falsehood
– vs Truth 122–124, 182, 344–348
Farmer
– vs Barley 417
– cf. Dumuzi and Enkimdu
– cf. Eloquent Peasant
Fatigue
– vs Rest 416
Feet
– vs Belly (= Estomac et Pieds) 107, 113–114
Fig
– vs Grape 182
– cf. Fruits vs Fruits
Fig Tree
– vs Other trees (= Fable of Jotham) 143–156
– vs Sycamore (= Dispute between Trees) 108, 122–123
Firewood-seller
– vs Charcoal-seller (= Great Peace Entertainment) 445
Fish
– vs Bee 302–303
– vs Bird 1–2, 11–12, 14–15, 26–28
– vs Bull 302–303
– vs Hawk 302–303
– vs Leopard 302–303
– vs Parrot 302–303
– vs Snake 200–303
– vs Vegetarian Food 449
Flea
– vs Fly (= Versus de pulice et musca) 354–355
– vs Mosquito 221
Flower
– vs Birds 444
– vs Flowers 200
– vs Man 396–397, 402–407, 409
Fly
– vs Ant 336
– vs Ant and Mosquito 443–444
– vs Flea (= Versus de pulice et musca) 354–355
Fowl cf. Parlement of Foules
Fox
– vs other animals (Series of the Fox) 91–93, 98
Fruits
– vs Fruits 299–302
– vs Nuts 451
– vs Vegetables 444
Furniture cf. Contest of Furniture
Gardener
– vs Mary 168–169, 171, 400, 409
Generosity
– vs Miserliness 182, 221
Ĝirinisa
– vs Enkimanšum (= Dialogue 3) 35[+8, 9], 36–40, 44–47, 50, 58[3],
Girls
– vs Boys 175
Glass
– vs Gold 182
Goat
– vs Dove (judged by Ibex) 254–255
– vs Palm 4, 195, 238–239, 242–243, 246, 249, 253–254, 261, 326

Goatherd
– vs Shepherd 347
Going Abroad
– vs Staying At Home 182
Gold
– vs Glass 182
– vs Wheat 161, 394–395, 400–401, 408
Good
– vs Evil (= Bien et mal des dames) 383–384
Grace
– vs Justice 161
Grain
– vs Palm 95
– vs Sheep cf. Ezinam (Goddess of Grain) and Ewe
– vs Wheat 92–93
– cf. Gold and Wheat
Grape
– vs Fig 182
– vs Wine and Philosopher 314–316
– cf. Fruits vs Fruits
Greed cf. Miserliness
Guest from Wu
– vs Prince of Chu (= Seven Stimuli) 438–439
Hairlocks on the Temple
– vs Cheekdown 182
Hashish
– vs Apple Wine 287–293
– vs Arak 287–293
– vs Bersh 287–293
– vs Boza 287–293
– vs Cherry Liqueur 287–293
– vs Coffee 287–293
– vs Mead 287–293
– vs Müselles 287–293
– vs Opium 287–293
– vs Tobacco 287–293
– vs Wine 2, 284, 287–293
Hawk
– vs Bee 302–303
– vs Bull 302–303
– vs Fish 302–303
– vs Leopard 302–303
– vs Parrot 302–303
– vs Snake 200–303
Hazel Nut cf. Fruits vs Fruits
Head
– vs Belly (= Corps et Tête) 105–116, 121, 123
– vs Body 4
Heart
– vs Eye 261
Heaven
– vs Earth 182, 250, 261–262, 298, 310–311, 316–321, 323–325, 327
Hector
– vs Alexander (= Epitaphes d'Hector) 380, 382
Hecuba
– vs Helena 335
Helena
– vs Hecuba 335
– vs Jews 170
Hen Pertelot
– vs Cock Chauntecleer 358, 364–367
Herald
– vs Soldier and Villain (= Héraut, Vassault et Villain) 383
Herons
– vs Crows 449
Hoe
– vs Plough 11–12, 14, 181
Homosexual
– vs Womanizer 299
Honey
– vs Sugar 304
– vs Syrup 304
Hoopoe cf. Birds vs Birds
Horse
– vs Camel 182
– vs Ox 91–94, 98
Horus
– vs Seth 115, 122–124
Ibex
– arbiter of Dove vs Goat 254–255
Ignorance
– vs Knowledge 181
Indian
– vs Briton 417
Insects
– vs Spider 92–94, 98

Intellect
– vs Desire 221
Ipuwer
– vs Lord of All 124, 128–130, 133–134
Iranian cf. Persian
Iron
– vs Needle, Scissors, Thimble, Thread, Yard-stick (= Women's Seven Companions) 447
– vs Salt 4351
Isaac
– vs Abraham 164, 170
Jar
– vs Cup and Wineskin 400–402, 407–408
Jesus cf. Christ (= Dieu et sa mère)
Jews
– vs Helena 170
Job
– vs Wife 165
John the Baptism
– vs Christ 166, 172
Jordan
– vs Pishon 166
Joseph
– vs Benjamin 165, 172
– vs Mary 165–167
– vs Potiphar's Wife 165, 172
Jotham, Fable of cf. Olive, Fig, Vine, Thorn–Bush
Jugement dou roi de Behaingne 373
Just Argument
– vs Unjust Argument 335
Justice
– vs Grace 161
Knight
– vs Clergyman cf. Sword vs Pen
– vs Lady (= Deux amans) 372, 382
Knowledge
– vs Ignorance 181
Labourer
– vs Rich 261
Ladder
– vs Staircase 239
Ladies
– vs Arms (= Armes et Dames) 381
Lady Bamboo
– vs Mrs. Kettle 444
Lady
– vs Knight (= Deux amans) 372, 382
– cf. Belle Dame sans mercy
– cf. Jugement dou roi de Behaingne
– cf. Livre des quatre dames
– cf. Noire et Tannée
Lance
– vs Bow 262, 321
– vs Sword 182
Land
– vs Sea 182, 221
Laurel
– vs Olive 337
Lemon cf. Fruits vs Fruits
Leopard
– vs Bee 302–303
– vs Bull 302–303
– vs Fish 302–303
– vs Hawk 302–303
– vs Parrot 302–303
– vs Snake 200–303
Letters
– vs Arms cf. Pen vs Sword
– vs Letters 218
Life
– vs Death 338
Lily
– vs Rose 342–344
Lion
– vs Ox 416
Livre des quatre dames 372–374
Longing
– vs Love (= Contest of Dialogue Poems) 450
Lord cf. Enmerkara and Ensukukešdana
Lord of All
– vs Ipuwer 124, 128–130, 133–134
Love
– vs Longing (= Contest of Dialogue Poems) 450
– vs Reason 261
Lover
– vs Beloved 251
Lute
– vs Trumpet 261

Lyre
– vs Syrinx 339
Magi
– vs Mary 165, 172, 402, 409
Maidenhood
– vs Marriage 336
Man
– vs Ba 124, 130–134
– vs Beast 302–303
– vs Flower 396–397, 402–407, 409
– vs Woman 221
María
– vs Elena 217
Marriage
– vs Chastity 311
– vs Maidenhood 336
Mary
– vs Angel 165, 172
– vs Gardener 168–169, 171, 400, 409
– vs Jesus (= Dieu et sa mère) 376
– vs Joseph 165–167
– vs Magi 165, 172, 402, 409
– vs Satan (= Processus Satanae) 377
Master Improbable
– vs Sir Vacuous 439–440
Mead
– vs Apple Wine 287–293
– vs Arak 287–293
– vs Bersh 287–293
– vs Boza 287–293
– vs Cherry Liqueur 287–293
– vs Coffee 287–293
– vs Hashish 287–293
– vs Müselles 287–293
– vs Opium 287–293
– vs Tobacco 287–293
– vs Wine 287–293
Meat
– vs Olive Oil 178, 182
Melon cf. Fruits vs Fruits
Members
– vs Belly (= Membres et Estomac) 114
– vs Members 224
Mercy
– vs Righteousness 354, 361[22],
Merle
– vs Nightingale 358
Miserliness
– vs Generosity 182
Month
– vs Months (= Dispute of the Months) 160–161, 171–172, 177, 221, 394–395, 400–401, 407–408
Moon
– vs Sun 182, 261
– vs Wind 444
Mosque cf. Congregational Mosque in Ṣūr
Mosquito
– vs Fly and Ant 443–444
– vs Poet 417
Moth
– vs Candle 305
Mountains
– vs Mountains 218
– vs Rivers 444
Mouth
– vs Eye, Eyebrows, Nose 444
Mrs. Kettle
– vs Lady Bamboo 444
Mulberry
– vs Apricot 182
– cf. Fruits vs Fruits
Müselles
– vs Apple Wine 287–293
– vs Arak 287–293
– vs Bersh 287–293
– vs Boza 287–293
– vs Cherry Liqueur 287–293
– vs Coffee 287–293
– vs Hashish 287–293
– vs Mead 287–293
– vs Opium 287–293
– vs Tobacco 287–293
– vs Wine 287–293
Musical Instruments 284
Musk
– vs Civet 175–176
Muslim
– vs Zoroastrian 246, 262–264, 270–276
Mysterious Female Clan
– vs Black Robes Clan 446
Narcissus
– vs Rose 178, 182

Narguile
– vs Bowl 403
Needle
– vs Thread 261
– vs Iron, Scissors, Thimble, Thread, Yard-stick (= Women's Seven Companions) 447
Nestorius
– vs Cyril 169
New Testament
– vs Old Testament 345
Night
– vs Day 4, 191–213, 221, 231–232, 262, 304
Nightingale
– vs Clerk 358, 366
– vs Cuckoo 358–361, 366
– vs Merle 358
– vs Owl 353–357, 360–364, 366–367
– vs Thrush 357, 361[22]
– cf. Birds vs Birds
Noire
– vs Tannée (= Deux demoiselles) 372
Non–believer
– vs Believer 221
Nose
– vs Eye, Eyebrows, Mouth 444
Nuts
– vs Fruits 451
Odysseus
– vs Ajax 338–339
Oil Wells
– vs Pearl-Diving 1, 5, 416–419, 430
Old Man
– vs Young Man 232
Old Testament
– vs New Testament 345
Olive
– vs Laurel 337
– vs Other trees (= Fable of Jotham) 143–156
Olive Oil
– vs Meat 178, 182
Olives
– vs Cheese 182
Opium
– vs Apple Wine 287–293
– vs Arak 287–293
– vs Bersh 287–293
– vs Boza 287–293
– vs Cherry Liqueur 287–293
– vs Coffee 287–293
– vs Hashish 287–293
– vs Mead 287–293
– vs Müselles 287–293
– vs Tobacco 287–293
– vs Wine 287–293
Orange cf. Fruits vs Fruits
Owl
– vs Nightingale 353–357, 360–364, 366–367
– cf. Birds vs Birds
Owner, Its
– vs Coat 417
Ox
– vs Horse 91–94, 98
– vs Lion 416
Paganism
– vs Christianity 347
Pale-Skinned Girl
– vs Brown-Skinned Girl 417
Palm
– vs Goat 4, 195, 238–239, 242–243, 246, 249, 253–254, 261, 326
– vs Grain 95
– vs Other trees 153, 155
– vs Tamarisk 3, 75–89, 91–93, 95, 98, 152, 430
– vs Vine 92–94, 152, 182
Parlement of Foules 357, 359–361
Parliament of the Three Ages 361[22]
Parrot
– vs Bee 302–303
– vs Bull 302–303
– vs Crow 296–297
– vs Fish 302–303
– vs Hawk 302–303
– vs Leopard 302–303
– vs Snake 200–303
– cf. Birds vs Birds
Partridge cf. Birds vs Birds
Past
– vs Present 416
Peach cf. Fruits vs Fruits

Peacock cf. Birds vs Birds
Pear cf. Fruits vs Fruits
Pearl-Diving
– vs Oil Wells 1, 5, 416–419, 430
Pederasts
– vs Womanizers 299
Pen
– vs Scissors 229–230
– vs Sword 181–182, 185, 200, 217, 221, 225–230, 239–242, 285, 294–296, 338–339
Penis
– vs Vagina 261
Perfumes 182
Persian
– vs Arab 5, 244–247, 262–270, 276–278
Philosopher
– vs Grape and Wine 314–316
Philosophy
– vs Faith 232
Phronesis cf. Alithia vs Pseustis
Pishon
– vs Jordan 166
Pistachio cf. Fruits vs Fruits
Plough
– vs Hoe 11–12, 14, 181
Plum
– vs Apricot 444
– vs Snow 444
– vs Willow 436, 447
– cf. Fruits vs Fruits
Poet
– vs Congregational Mosque in Ṣūr 417
Poetry
– vs Prose 231
– vs Mosquito 417
Polo Stick
– vs Ball 303
Pomegranate
– vs Bramble 151
– cf. Fruits vs Fruits
Pomegranate Seeds
– vs Rice 182
Poplar
– vs Ash 92–95, 98, 152
Potiphar's Wife
– vs Joseph 165, 172
Precious Stones 182, 200
Present
– vs Past 416
Prince of Chu
– vs Guest from Wu (= Seven Stimuli) 438–439
Prose
– vs Poetry 231
Prostitutes
– vs Catamites 444
Pseustis
– vs Alithia (and Phronesis) 347
Quince cf. Fruits vs Fruits
Rat
– vs Ship's Captain 417–418
Reason
– vs Love 261
Red Date cf. Fruits vs Fruits
Reed
– vs Tree 11–12, 14, 152
Rest
– vs Fatigue 416
Rice
– vs Pomegranate Seeds 182
– vs Sake 435, 448–449
Ricecakes
– vs Sake 450–451
Righteousness
– vs Mercy 354, 361[22],
Rivers
– vs Mountains 444
Romans
– vs Simon Peter and Simon Magus 400, 408
Rose
– vs Lily 342–344
– vs Narcissus 178, 182
– vs Violet 384–385
Sake
– vs Rice 435, 448–449
– vs Ricecakes 450–451
– vs Tea 449–450
Salt
– vs Iron 435[1]
– vs Sugar 304
Satan
– vs Death 159, 161, 171

– vs Mary (= Processus Satanae) 377
– vs Sinful Woman 166, 171, 400, 409
– vs St Marina 170
Scissors
– vs Iron, Needle, Thimble, Thread, Yardstick (= Women's Seven Companions) 447
– vs Pen 229 – 230
Scribe cf. Edubba'a D; cf. Two Scribes
Sea
– vs Land 182, 221
Seth
– vs Horus 115, 122 – 124
Sheep
– vs Grain cf. Ewe vs Ezinam (Goddess of Grain)
Shepherd
– vs Goatherd 347
– cf. Dumuzi vs Enkimdu
Ship's Captain
– vs Rat 417 – 418
Silkworm
– vs Spider 446
Silver
– vs Copper 11 – 12, 14
Silverberry cf. Fruits vs Fruits
Simon Magus
– vs Simon Peter and the Romans 400, 408
Simon Peter
– vs Simon Magus and the Romans 400, 408
Sinful Woman
– vs Satan 166, 171, 400, 409
Sion
– vs Church 170
Sir Vacuous
– vs Master Improbable 439 – 440
Six Beasts 446
Sky cf. Heaven
Sleep
– vs Wakefulness 200
Snake
– vs Bee 302 – 303
– vs Bull 302 – 303
– vs Fish 302 – 303
– vs Hawk 302 – 303
– vs Leopard 302 – 303
– vs Parrot 200 – 303
Snow
– vs Plum 444
Soldier
– vs Courtier 354
– vs Herald and Villain (= Héraut, Vassault et Villain) 383
Soul
– vs Body 160, 162 – 164, 172^{+28}, 173, 217, 219 – 224, 261, 310 – 311, 316 – 317, 321 – 325, 327, 354, 375, 378, 380, 385
– cf. Man and Ba
Sour Cherry cf. Fruits vs Fruits
Sparrow
– vs Falcon 442
– vs Swallow 442
Spider
– vs Insects 92 – 94, 98
– vs Silkworm 446
Spring cf. Summer
St Marina
– vs Satan 170
Staircase
– vs Ladder 239
Staying At Home
– vs Going Abroad 182
Stones
– vs Stones (Five Stones) 394
– cf. Precious Stones
Stork cf. Birds vs Birds
Student cf. Enkiḫeĝal and Enkitalu; cf. Enki-manšum and Ĝirinisa
Sugar
– vs Honey 304
– vs Salt 304
– vs Syrup 304
Summer (and Spring)
– vs Winter 4, 11 – 12, 14 – 15, 175 – 189, 231, 261, 284, 297 – 298, 336, 340 – 342, 378, 416, 450
Sun
– vs Moon 182, 261
Ṣūr cf. Congregational Mosque in Ṣūr
Swallow
– vs Sparrow 442
– cf. Birds vs Birds
Sword
– vs Lance 182

– vs Pen 181–182, 185, 200, 217, 221, 225–230, 239–242, 285, 294–296, 338–339
Sycamore
– vs Fig Tree (= Dispute between Trees) 108, 122–123
Synagogue
– vs Church 169–170
Syrinx
– vs Lyre 339
Syrup
– vs Honey 304
– vs Sugar 304
Tamarisk
– vs Palm 3, 75–89, 91–93, 95, 98, 152, 430
Tangerine
– vs Chestnut (= Fruits and Nuts) 451
Tannée
– vs Noire (= Deux demoiselles) 372
Taoist
– vs Buddhist 443
– vs Buddhist (= The Controversy) 451
– vs Buddhist and Confucian (= Three Teachings) 448
Tea
– vs Alcohol 435–438, 441–442, 444–445, 452
– vs Coffee 1, 403, 416, 419, 430
– vs Sake 449–450
Tea Goddess
– vs Beer Goddess 452
Teakettle
– vs Two Boys 402–403, 406–407, 409
Tea-seller
– vs Alcohol-seller (= Great Peace Entertainment) 445
Telegraph
– vs Telephone 182
Telephone
– vs Telegraph 182
Thief
– vs Cherub 5, 168, 171–172, 396–398, 400, 406, 408–409
– cf. Two Thieves
Thimble
– vs Iron, Needle, Scissors, Thread, Yardstick (= Women's Seven Companions) 447
Thistle
– vs Cedar 148
Thorn–Bush
– vs Other trees (= Fable of Jotham) 143–156, 394
Thread
– vs Needle 261
– vs Iron, Needle, Pair of scissors, Thimble, Yardstick (= Women's Seven Companions) 447
Three Capitals 436, 440, 447, 449
Thrush
– vs Nightingale 357, 361[22]
Tobacco
– vs Apple Wine 287–293
– vs Arak 287–293
– vs Bersh 287–293
– vs Boza 287–293
– vs Cherry Liqueur 287–293
– vs Coffee 287–293, 416
– vs Hashish 287–293
– vs Mead 287–293
– vs Müselles 287–293
– vs Opium 287–293
– vs Wine 287–293
Tool cf. Carpenter's Tools
Tragedy
– vs Elegy 338
Train
– vs Boat 182
Tram
– vs Bus 182
Tree
– vs Other Trees 394
– vs Reed 11–12, 14, 152
– cf. Palm vs Goat (= Assyrian Tree)
Trumpet
– vs Lute 261
Truth 204
– vs Falsehood 122–124, 182, 344–348
Twelve Animals 451
Two Boys cf. Boys
Two Capitals 441, 446

Two Scribes (= Dialogue 1) 35[+8], 36–37, 40–41, 47, 49–51, 58[3],
Two Thieves 160–161, 167, 171
Two Women A 35[7, 8], 58[3], 66[22], 71
Two Women B 35[7, 8], 50–51, 57–73
Unjust Argument
– vs Just Argument 335
Vagina
– vs Penis 261
Vegetables
– vs Fruits 444
Vices
– vs Virtues 339–340
Villain
– vs Herald and Soldier (= Héraut, Vassault et Villain) 383
Vine
– vs Other trees (= Fable of Jotham) 143–156
– vs Palm 92–94, 152, 182
Violet
– vs Rose 384–385
Virgin (Mary)
– vs Cross (= Vierge (Marie) et Croix) 377[+8], 378
Virginity
– vs Chastity 311
Virtues
– vs Vices 339–340
Vulture cf. Birds vs Birds
Wakefulness
– vs Sleep 200
Walnut cf. Fruits vs Fruits
Water
– vs Air 182
– vs Wine 217–218, 231, 378
Water Melon
– vs Date 182, 403
– cf. Fruits vs Fruits
Water–Pipe
– vs Cup 248
Wax Candle
– vs Wine 182
Wealth
– vs Wisdom 231
Wheat
– vs Gold 161, 394–395, 400–401, 408
– vs Grain (Nissaba) 92–93
Whites
– vs Black 175
Wife
– vs Job 165
Willow
– vs Plum 436, 447
Wind
– vs Moon 444
Wine
– vs Apple Wine 287–293
– vs Arak 287–293
– vs Beer 106, 115, 122–123
– vs Bersh 287–293
– vs Boza 287–293
– vs Cedar 171
– vs Cherry Liqueur 287–293
– vs Coffee 287–293
– vs Cup 161
– vs Grape and Philosopher 314–316
– vs Hashish 287–293
– vs Hashish 4, 284
– vs Mead 287–293
– vs Müselles 287–293
– vs Opium 287–293
– vs Rose 264
– vs Tobacco 287–293
– vs Water 217–218, 231, 378
– vs Wax Candle 182
Wineskin
– vs Cup and Jar 400–402, 407–408
Winner
– vs Waster 361[22]
Winter (and Autumn)
– vs Summer 4, 11–12, 14–15, 175–189, 231, 261, 284, 297–298, 336, 340–342, 378, 416, 450
Wisdom
– vs Wealth 231
Woman
– vs Man 221
– cf. Two Women A
– cf. Two Women B
– cf. Satan and the Sinful Woman
Womanizer
– vs Homosexual 299
– vs Pederasts 299

Wren 153
Yardstick
– vs Iron, Needle, Scissors, Thimble, Thread (= Women's Seven Companions) 447
Young Man
– vs Old Man 232
Zacharias
– vs Angel 165
Zoroastrian
– vs Muslim 246, 262–264, 270–276

www.ingramcontent.com/pod-product-compliance
Lightning Source LLC
Chambersburg PA
CBHW052040220426
43663CB00012B/2391
* 9 7 8 1 5 0 1 5 2 7 2 5 8 *